DOMESDAY NOW

DOMESDAY NOW

New Approaches to the Inquest and the Book

Edited by David Roffe and K. S. B. Keats-Rohan

THE BOYDELL PRESS

© Contributors 2016

All Rights Reserved. Except as permitted under current legislation
no part of this work may be photocopied, stored in a retrieval system,
published, performed in public, adapted, broadcast,
transmitted, recorded or reproduced in any form or by any means,
without the prior permission of the copyright owner

First published 2016
The Boydell Press, Woodbridge
Paperback edition 2018

ISBN 978 1 78327 088 0 hardback
ISBN 978 1 78327 300 3 paperback

The Boydell Press is an imprint of Boydell & Brewer Ltd
PO Box 9, Woodbridge, Suffolk IP12 3DF, UK
and of Boydell & Brewer Inc.
668 Mt Hope Avenue, Rochester, NY 14620–2731, USA
website: www.boydellandbrewer.com

The publisher has no responsibility for the continued existence or accuracy
of URLs for external or third-party internet websites referred to in this book,
and does not guarantee that any content on such websites is,
or will remain, accurate or appropriate

A CIP catalogue record for this book is available
from the British Library

Contents

List of Illustrations	vii
Abbreviations	x
Preface and Acknowledgements	xiv

	Introduction *David Roffe*	1
1.	Domesday Now: a View from the Stage *David Roffe*	7
2.	A Digital Latin Domesday *J. J. N. Palmer*	61
3.	McLuhan Meets the Master: Scribal Devices in Great Domesday Book *David Roffe*	81
4.	*Non Pascua sed Pastura*: the Changing Choice of Terms in Domesday *Frank Thorn*	109
5.	Domesday Books? Little Domesday Book Reconsidered *Ian Taylor*	137
6.	Hunting the Snark and Finding the Boojum: the Tenurial Revolution Revisited *Ann Williams*	155
7.	A Question of Identity: Domesday Prosopography and the Formation of the Honour of Richmond *K. S. B. Keats-Rohan*	169
8.	The Episcopal Returns in Domesday *Pamela Taylor*	197
9.	Geospatial Technologies and the Geography of Domesday England in the Twenty-First Century *Andrew Lowerre*	219

10.	Condensing and Abbreviating the Data: Evesham C, Evesham M, and the Breviate *Howard B. Clarke*	247
11.	'A Deed without a Name' *Sally Harvey*	277
12.	Talking to Others and Talking to Itself: Government and the Changing Role of the Records of the Domesday Inquest *David Roffe*	289
	Caroline Thorn: an Appreciation *Frank Thorn*	305
Index		311

Illustrations

FIGURES

David Roffe: *McLuhan Meets the Master: Scribal Devices in Great Domesday Book*

Figure 1: GDB, 209, the opening folio of the account of Bedfordshire, reproduced with the permission of Alecto Historical Editions   83

Figure 2: GDB, 281v (detail), the manor of Arnold and its sokeland, reproduced with the permission of Alecto Historical Editions   84

Figure 3: GDB, 195, part of Count Alan's fee in Cambridgeshire, reproduced with the permission of Alecto Historical Editions   87

Figure 4: GDB, 172v (detail), the Wick Episcopi entry, reproduced with the permission of Alecto Historical Editions   94

Figure 5: GDB, 66v (detail), the church of Glastonbury's estates of Langley and Langford, reproduced with the permission of Alecto Historical Editions   95

Figure 6: GDB, 264v, part of the earl of Chester's fee in Cheshire, reproduced with the permission of Alecto Historical Editions   97

Figure 7: GDB, 181v, the lands of the canons of Hereford, reproduced with the permission of Alecto Historical Editions   98

Figure 8: GDB, 154, the account of Oxford, reproduced with the permission of Alecto Historical Editions   101

Figure 9: a. GDB, 57 (detail), the manor of Lower Basildon in Berkshire; b. GDB, 38v (detail), Nether Wallop in Hampshire, reproduced with the permission of Alecto Historical Editions   102

Figure 10: GDB, 337v–338 (details), the various parts of the soke of Grantham in Lincolnshire, reproduced with the permission of Alecto Historical Editions   105

Ann Williams: *Hunting the Snark and finding the Boojum: the Tenurial Revolution Revisited*

Figure 1: Armingford hundred, Cambridgeshire. 156

Andrew Lowerre: *Geospatial Technologies and the Geography of Domesday England in the Twenty-first Century*

Figure 1: Lands of Wulfmær of Eaton and Eskil of Ware and their men, created using downloadable PASE Domesday dataset in GIS. County boundaries provided by the Historic County Borders Project (http://www.county-borders.co.uk/hcbp_4.htm) 230

Figure 2: Domesday places in the four-county pilot study area shown as points and polygons, along with hundred and county boundaries 233

Figure 3: Density per square kilometre of non-servile population recorded in Domesday Book 234

Figure 4: Variation from the average amount (standard deviation) of woodland per vill using the four main woodland measures, combined with miscellaneous references to woodland, underwood, scrubland, ash groves and spinney 235

Figure 5: Proportions per vill of: (A) ploughlands held by King William; (B) ploughlands held by religious houses; (C) ploughlands held by all other tenants-in-chief; (D) total simplified TRW value held in demesne 236–237

Figure 6: Distribution of the eight most commonly recorded forms of tenure for TRE landholders 238

Figure 7: Distribution of different methods of recording TRW values in whole pounds 239

Figure 8: Scatterplot comparing ploughland values to vill areas in Bedfordshire. The dotted line shows the linear trend in the data 241

Figure 9: Standard deviations of OLS regression analysis residuals for each vill polygon 244

TABLES

John Palmer: *A Digital Latin Domesday*

Table 1: *SI* and *si* 64

Table 2: *geldo* and *geldum* by circuits 65

Table 3: *geldo* and *geldum* by counties 65

Table 4: Unique graphic forms in Suffolk fief 14	71
Table 5: Forms of *sunt* by circuit	73
Table 6: Forms of *pastura*	73
Table 7: Forms of *leuo* or *leu1*	74
Table 8: A database record for words	77
Table 9: A database record for names	77

David Roffe: *McLuhan Meets the Master: Scribal Devices in Great Domesday Book*

Table 1: Interlocking patterns of estates in Armingford hundred, Cambridgeshire	89
Table 2: Interlocking patterns of estates in Papworth hundred, Cambridgeshire	89
Table 3: The manors of the bishop of Worcester in Oswaldslow hundred, Worcestershire	93
Table 4: Blank lines in the chapters of Walter d'Aincourt and Peterborough abbey	103
Table 5: The representation of the soke of Grantham, Lincolnshire	104

Ann Williams: *Hunting the Snark and finding the Boojum: the tenurial revolution revisited*

Table 1: Abington Pigotts, 5 hides TRE (ICC, 60)	158
Table 2: Guilden Morden, 5 hides (ICC, 53–4)	160
Table 3: Steeple Morden, 10 hides (ICC, 51–2)	162
Table 4: Shingay, 5 hides (ICC, 54, 59, 60)	163
Table 5: Litlington, 5 hides (ICC, 53, 59, 60)	165

Andrew Lowerre: *Geospatial Technologies and the Geography of Domesday England in the Twenty-first Century*

Table 1: Results of Ordinary Least Squares regression analysis comparing Bedfordshire ploughlands, woodland (in pigs) and meadow (in ploughteams) with vill polygon area	242

Abbreviations

Abingdon A	D. C. Douglas, 'Some Early Surveys from the Abbey of Abingdon', *EHR* 44, 1929, 623.
Abingdon B	D. C. Douglas, 'Some Early Surveys from the Abbey of Abingdon', *EHR* 44, 1929, 623–25.
ANS	*Anglo-Norman Studies.*
ASC	*The Anglo-Saxon Chronicle: A Revised Translation*, ed. D. Whitelock, D. C. Douglas, S. I. Tucker, 2nd ed., London 1965.
Attenborough	*The Laws of the Earliest English Kings*, ed. F. L. Attenborough, Cambridge 1922.
Bath A	*Two Chartularies of the Priory of St Peter at Bath*, ed. W. Hunt, Somerset Record Society 7, 1893, 67–8.
Bath B	*Two Chartularies of the Priory of St Peter at Bath*, ed. W. Hunt, Somerset Record Society 7, 1893, 35–6.
BL	The British Library, London.
CL	Classical Latin.
DB	*Domesday Book*, ed. J. Morris and others, 34 vols, Phillimore, London 1974–86, followed by abbreviated county. Unless otherwise stated, reference is to the revised online version, *The Electronic Edition of Domesday Book: Translation, Databases and Scholarly Commentary, 1086*, 2nd. ed., at https://hydra.hull.ac.uk/resources/hull:domesdayTranslation or http://discover.ukdataservice.ac.uk/catalogue?sn=5694, accessed 03/10/2015.
DM A	*The Domesday Monachorum of Christ Church Canterbury*, ed. D. C. Douglas, London 1944, 80–1.
DM B	*The Domesday Monachorum of Christ Church Canterbury*, ed. D. C. Douglas, London 1944, 81–98.
DM D	*The Domesday Monachorum of Christ Church Canterbury*, ed. D. C. Douglas, London 1944, 98–9.
DM E	*The Domesday Monachorum of Christ Church Canterbury*, ed. D. C. Douglas, London 1944, 99–104.
DMLBS	R. E. Latham, D. R. Howlett, and others, *A Dictionary of Medieval Latin from British Sources*, Oxford 1975–2013.
EcHR	*Economic History Review.*

EHD, I	*English Historical Documents, c. 500–1042*, ed. D. Whitelock, 2nd ed., London 1979.
EHD, II	*English Historical Documents, 1042–1189*, ed. D. C. Douglas and G. W. Greenaway, London 1953.
EHR	*English Historical Review*.
Ely A	*Inquisitio Comitatus Cantabrigiensis*, ed. N. E. S. A. Hamilton, London 1876, 168–73.
Ely B	*Inquisitio Comitatus Cantabrigiensis*, ed. N. E. S. A. Hamilton, London 1876, 174–5.
Ely C	*Inquisitio Comitatus Cantabrigiensis*, ed. N. E. S. A. Hamilton, London 1876, 175–83.
Ely D	*Inquisitio Comitatus Cantabrigiensis*, ed. N. E. S. A. Hamilton, London 1876, 184–89.
Evesham A	P. H. Sawyer, 'Evesham A, a Domesday Text', *Miscellany 1*, Worcestershire Historical Society, 1960, 22–36.
Evesham C	Below, p.263–8.
Evesham F	BL, Cotton MS Vespasian B xxiv, f. 11r.
Evesham K	BL, Cotton MS Vespasian B xxiv, f. 57r–62r.
Evesham M	Below, p.269–75.
Evesham P	BL, Harleian MS 3763, f. 71v.
Evesham Q	BL, Harleian MS 3763, f. 82r.
Excerpta	*An Eleventh-Century Inquisition of St Augustine's, Canterbury*, ed. A. Ballard, Records of the Social and Economic History of England 4, London 1920, 1–33.
EYC	*Early Yorkshire Charters*, ed. W. Farrer and C. T. Clay, Edinburgh and Yorkshire Archaeological Society, Record Series, Extra Series, 10 vols, 1914–55.
Exon	*Libri Censualis, vocati Domesday Book, Additamenta ex Codic. Antiquiss. Exon Domesday; Inquisitio Eliensis; Liber Winton; Boldon Book*, ed. H. Ellis, London 1816.
GDB	Great Domesday Book, followed by folio number (unqualified signifies recto number and v signifies verso), cited from *Domesday Book, seu Liber Censualis Willelmi Primi*, 2 vols, London 1783, I, or from *Great Domesday Book: Library Edition*, ed. A. Williams and R. W. H. Erskine, London 1986–92; followed by *DB*, the abbreviated county name, and entry number.
ICC	*Inquisitio Comitatus Cantabrigiensis*, ed. N. E. S. A. Hamilton, London 1876, 1–96.
IE	*Inquisitio Comitatus Cantabrigiensis*, ed. N. E. S. A. Hamilton, London 1876, 97–167.
John of Worcester	*The Chronicle of John of Worcester*, ed. R. R. Darlington and P. McGurk. II-III, Oxford 1995–8.
Kentish Assessment List	R. S. Hoyt, 'A Pre-Domesday Kentish Assessment List', *A Medieval Miscellany for Doris Mary Stenton*, ed. P. M. Barnes and C. F. Slade, Pipe Roll Society ns 36, 1960, 199–202.

LDB	Little Domesday Book, followed by folio number, unqualified signifies recto, number and v signifies verso), cited from *Domesday Book, seu Liber Censualis Willelmi Primi*, 2 vols, London 1783, II, or from *Little Domesday Book: Library Edition*, ed. A. Williams and G. H. Martin, London 2000; followed by *DB*, the abbreviated county name, and entry number.
Malmesbury, *Gesta Regum*	*William of Malmesbury, Gesta Regum Anglorum: the History of the English Kings*, ed. and trans. R. A. B. Mynors, R. M. Thomson, and M. Winterbottom, 2 vols, Oxford 1998–9.
Mon. Ang.	*Monasticon Anglicanum*, ed. J. Caley, H. Ellis, and B. Bandinel, 6 vols in 8, London 1817–30.
ML	Medieval Latin.
OLD	*Oxford Latin Dictionary*, ed. P. G. W. Glare, Oxford 1968.
Orderic	*The Ecclesiastical History of Orderic Vitalis*, ed. and trans. M. Chibnall, 6 vols, Oxford 1969–80.
Poitiers	*The Gesta Guillelmi of William of Poitiers*, ed. and trans. R. H. C. Davis and M. Chibnall, Oxford 1998.
Regesta, Bates	*Regesta Regum Anglo-Normannorum: the Acta of William I (1066–1087)*, ed. D. Bates, Oxford 1998.
Robertson	*The Laws of the Kings of England from Edmund to Henry I*, ed. A. J. Robertson, Cambridge 1925.
RS	Rolls Series (Chronicles and Memorials of Great Britain and Ireland during the Middle Ages, Published under the Direction of the Master of the Rolls).
S	P. H. Sawyer, *Anglo-Saxon Charters: an Annotated List and Bibliography*, Royal Historical Society Guides and Handbooks 8, 1968; *The Electronic Sawyer, http://www.esawyer.org.uk/searchfiles/index.html*.
TNA	The National Archives, Kew, London.
TRE	*Tempore Regis Eadwardi* ('in King Edward's time'), i.e. 1066.
TRHS	*Transactions of the Royal Historical Society*.
TRW	*Tempore Regis Willelmi* ('in King William's time'), i.e. 1086.
VCH	*Victoria History of the Counties of England*.
Worcester A	*Hemingi Chartularium Ecclesiae Wigornensis*, ed. T. Hearne. Oxford 1723, 83–4.
Worcester B	*Hemingi Chartularium Ecclesiae Wigornensis*, ed. T. Hearne, Oxford 1723, 298–313.

This volume is dedicated to the memory of Caroline Thorn, Latinist, palaeographer, and historian, to whom Domesday scholars will ever be indebted.

Preface and Acknowledgements

The present volume emanates from a conference entitled 'Domesday Now' held at The National Archives on 17 September 2011. After a decade of vigorous debate on the purpose of the Domesday enterprise, it was gratifying to bring together almost all the specialist scholars in the field to take stock of what had been achieved and what had yet to be done. There was no sudden outbreak of agreement. At the end of the day the fault lines that had characterized differing understandings of the Domesday inquest and Domesday Book remained as visible as ever. However, a consensus had emerged on the way forward. It became clear that there was no prospect of resolving the issues raised without a new edition of the Domesday texts. The papers presented here provide the intellectual underpinning for such a project. Six of the seven read on the day have been revised for this publication; the rest have been especially commissioned to complement them. Together they cover almost all the major areas of disagreement. Sadly the late Nicholas Brooks was unable to complete his chapter on the Domesday Monachorum before his death in 2014.

We thank Elizabeth Hallam-Smith, a former keeper of Domesday Book, for chairing the conference and for her unstinting enthusiasm and continuing support for a new edition of Domesday Book. We are also grateful to Jess Nelson and the staff of The National Archives for the smooth running of the conference. The authors in their turn express their thanks to an anonymous reader for several incisive comments. The images from Domesday Book are reproduced with the kind permission of Alecto Historical Editions. Finally, we are indebted to Caroline Palmer of Boydell and Brewer for commissioning the book and Nick Bingham for seeing it through the press.

DR, KKR, January 2015

Introduction

David Roffe

ACCORDING TO RICHARD fitzNigel, writing in the Dialogue of the Exchequer around about the year 1179, Domesday was accorded its name by the native English. Eight hundred and fifty or so years later the Book has a higher profile in the popular mind than it has ever had. A Google Alert with the search terms 'Domesday Book' regularly unearths tens of new pages on the internet each week; as fact, icon or myth, Domesday crops up in a bewildering number of contexts in England as around the world. Much of this is more of sociological or psychological interest than historical. Nevertheless, in parallel, if largely invisibly to a wider world, Domesday Book has also been the subject of intense academic study. In 1985 David Bates listed 1847 publications in *A Bibliography of Domesday Book*. There has been no up-date since, but a new edition would add perhaps thousands more to that total. The last thirty years has seen an exponential growth in Domesday studies. It comes as some surprise, then, to the informed outsider that there still remains no consensus on the purpose of the text, much less the inquest on which it was based. Major new studies have challenged the received wisdom of over 200 years of academic study. Compilation, date, data, purpose and even the very centrality of Domesday Book itself have now been brought into question.

Domesday studies are in turmoil. To take stock, a conference entitled *Domesday Now* was convened at The National Archives in Kew, UK, by the editors of this volume in September 2011. Leading scholars in the field were invited to assess developments since the last conference on Domesday in the year 2000 and suggest new ways forward. The papers here presented are the result. David Roffe opens with an overview of Domesday studies outlining the main themes that have emerged in the last few years. Much of the work has been of technical import. A notable achievement has been a general recognition of the importance of 'diplomatic', that is, the changing forms of the text. This approach has, for example, led to a broad agreement on the order of writing of Great Domesday Book (GDB), which has in its turn afforded a glimpse of the scribe's developing programme as he wrote, and a better understanding of the various forms of lordship. Differences on fundamentals remain. The inquest as an investigative and consultative process has informed much of the new thinking in Domesday studies, leading to not only a novel characterization of the Domesday enterprise but also of Anglo-Norman governance and society. For others, however, the inquest is still an entirely executive instrument of government and existing narratives have been forcibly restated.

These are views that are fundamentally irreconcilable. If impasse there be, a way forward is promised by the new categories of evidence that are explored in the papers in this volume. In 'A Digital Latin Domesday' John Palmer examines a dataset that has not previously been identified, much less exploited, as part of a project to make the complex text of Domesday Book machine searchable. In an eloquent analysis of the different forms of contraction and suspension marks, he finds a pattern that suggests that the GDB scribe was less a compiler than a copyist. Equally importantly, these diacritics cast light on his understanding of the data before him. It becomes clear, for example, that the scribe intended the geld figures to relate to both 1066 and 1086 unless otherwise stated. The data hold out considerable potential for elucidating many long-standing problems of meaning and import. Most immediately, though, Palmer's analysis contributes to the debate on the nature of the Domesday returns, the first formulation of the findings of the inquest for presentation to central government.

So too does David Roffe's paper 'McLuhan Meets the Master', albeit from a somewhat different direction and perspective. It has long been recognized that square and rustic initial letter forms were used to signal the status of land in the folios of Circuit VI, the first to be compiled by the scribe. What has not been appreciated hitherto is that he continued to use the devices with purpose throughout the remainder of the volume. Thus, there emerges evidence for extended soke structures in Cambridgeshire not previously identified and tight manorial structures in counties as diverse as Worcestershire, Middlesex and Wiltshire which are not otherwise explicit. Later in the course of writing the scribe used the distinctive letter forms for other purposes and it becomes clear that they must ultimately be derived from the sources that he employed. Again, here is a largely unrecognized dataset that radically modifies the reading of many entries. More generally, it shows that the Domesday scribe compiled from a much greater range of sources than is often supposed. If circuit returns were produced for every area of England (and that is still debated), then he also had before him the documents from which they were culled.

Frank Thorn addresses the ways in which the Domesday commissioners, and more specifically the GDB scribe, grappled with these diverse sources to develop a standardized account. The terms of the inquiry and its vocabulary, partly preserved in the preface to the *Inquisitio Eliensis* (IE), were determined at an early stage, possibly even at the Gloucester meeting when the inquest was first mooted in 1085. Because of the thoroughness and the particular slant of the survey, new terms were invented and categories created. The description of people, for example, amounts to a new classification of the population. So much for planning. In the course of the inquiry people and resources were encountered which did not fit into the established categories, leading to a slackening and obfuscation of the initial prescription as spellings were changed and terms amended (albeit new forms were not always consistently applied thereafter). In this way the changing usage of the scribe throws light on the priorities of William's advisers and their perceptions as the 'Domesday style' evolved, providing yet another rich new perspective on the Domesday text.

In 'Domesday Books? Little Domesday reconsidered', Ian Taylor takes issue with the notion of LDB as a circuit return. Much has hitherto been made of its similarities to Exon and it has therefore been interpreted, in one way or another, as a precursor of GDB. In reality, however, LDB is *sui generis*. That it was consciously used as a formal model by the GDB scribe is now abundantly clear. But it too, like the more accomplished volume, was an abbreviation: the ploughland data were systematically stripped out of the account. It is, then, in its own terms a Domesday Book. Its production is here related to the special circumstances that obtained in East Anglia in the crisis of 1085/6 that precipitated the Domesday inquest. East Anglia seems to have been considered more vulnerable to invasion by King Cnut of Denmark than the rest of the country – it had attracted, if not welcomed, Danish armies before on several occasions in the reign of William the Conqueror – and special measures were taken to secure it. It is suggested that LDB was compiled to aid the process in a region in which the Norman settlement had been late and incomplete and, as such, it stands as a separate enterprise in the Domesday process.

The mechanisms of that settlement in Cambridgeshire and beyond are the subject of Ann Williams's paper 'Hunting the Snark and Finding the Boojum: the Tenurial Revolution Revisited'. Much of the literature on the transfer of land from English to Norman has signally failed to distinguish between personal and tenurial status, that is between commendation and soke. Domesday tells us repeatedly that commendation did not confer land and yet many analyses have been founded upon it with the result that no patterns of transfer have been identified. Abington Pigotts in Armingford hundred in Cambridgeshire has been held up as a typical example of the disintegration of Anglo-Saxon patterns of tenure and lordship after the Conquest in these terms. Here, however, the abundant evidence for underlying soke is uncovered to show that in 1086 there was a neat succession to pre-Conquest dues that perpetuated a pre-existing tenurial structure. Similar processes are found throughout the country when the often difficult data are decoded.

This study shows the importance of looking beyond the family relationships that are the usual subject of prosopographical research to status. In 'A Question of Identity: Domesday Prosopography and the Formation of the Honour of Richmond', Katharine Keats-Rohan argues that prosopography misses the point if it confines itself to genealogy. Kinship groups and marriage alliances figure large in most studies, but they tell only half the tale and that can be misleading. Rights in land were many and various. An understanding of the diverse forms of lordship that were the necessary backdrop to the transfer of land from English to Norman reveals a rationale to the formation of the honour of Richmond that is not otherwise comprehensible in terms of simple identity. It was predominantly pre-Conquest tenures that determined the shape of the fee, even when, as in Yorkshire, a geographical area was granted to Count Alan. Based upon notions of inheritance from a predecessor, the Norman settlement was a predominantly ordered process. Prosopography, then, only realizes its true potential when it recognizes the dynamics of the society which it aims to reconstruct.

If antecessorial succession was more important than is sometimes apparent and usually allowed, there can be no doubt that tenants-in-chief subsequently pressed their perceived rights as far as they were able in the Domesday inquest. In her discussion of episcopal returns in Domesday Pamela Taylor examines the extent to which English bishops were able to influence what was recorded in the Domesday inquest and what found its way into Domesday Book. The bishops held estates in every Domesday county except Rutland and some of their endowments, unlike the recent assemblages of the bishops of Norman sees, provide examples of associated private hundreds. Otherwise routinely involved in local government, they were therefore well placed to negotiate the whole inquest process with maximum efficiency. Two examples of effectively unaltered returns, those of Bishop Wulfstan of Worcester for Oswaldslow and Abbot Baldwin of Bury within Suffolk, include some tendentious claims, but it is unhelpful to conflate two distinct issues, embedded returns and so called 'manipulation'. Taylor's examination of other exceptional episcopal returns and their local administrative context shows that there were very few unaltered returns and no necessary relationship between any that exist and manipulation. Beneficiaries routinely produced documents which were regularly tested by oath of the community. There is little evidence, then, of a concerted effort to 'cook the Book'. If bishops were well placed to influence the documentation of the inquest and could not, it seems likely that the Domesday process was less open to influence than has often been assumed.

By and large, the king and his commissioners probably got what information they demanded. To what use they put it is still a matter of debate. It may be that they were interested only in the salient details of the resources of the tenants-in-chief: the summaries preserved in Exon, IE, and GDB itself record simple totals by county for each honour. Fortunately, Domesday Book preserves the data from which they were calculated. How we can best represent them to reconstruct the local economy and society is the subject of Andrew Lowerre's paper, 'Geospatial Technologies and the Geography of Domesday England in the Twenty-First Century'. Scholars have made maps based on the information for more than a century, H.C. Darby's *Domesday Geography* series being the most famous and most comprehensive body of Domesday maps to date. It is now, however, more than thirty years since the publication of the final volume in Darby's series. The decades since have seen dramatic changes in the understanding of Domesday Book and how it was made, as well as in the capabilities and ubiquity of computers and digital map-making software. Three different systems allowing geographical interrogation and mapping of Domesday materials via the Internet appeared in 2010 alone. Lowerre examines how various geospatial technologies and digital datasets based on Domesday Book now available make it possible to map, analyse and interpret Domesday material in new ways. Where even that consummate master, the GDB scribe, could not fully standardize his text, modern techniques of statistical analysis and mapping technologies can smooth out the data. For the first time, for example, it becomes possible to map woodland even though it is recorded in a bewildering number of incommensurate units. Above all, strategies can be developed to test the scope and integrity of the data. Here the proposition that the Domesday inquest concerned itself only with land assessed to the geld is tested.

The range of information in Domesday Book is enormous, but it is not exhaustive. If LDB is itself an abbreviation with its omission of ploughlands, GDB redacts even more of the data that the commissioners had so carefully collected: livestock, and no doubt other items of information, was probably excised because it was felt to be of only ephemeral interest in a permanent record. Domesday Book was subsequently to be further abbreviated. Copies of a breviate exist from the thirteenth century, but Howard Clarke suggests that their exemplar is much earlier. Two surveys from Evesham abbey in Worcestershire provide hints that abstracts were already being produced from GDB in the late eleventh century and, if so early, thus indicate that Domesday Book too was compiled very soon after the inquest in 1086. If the Worcester surveys are indeed derived from GDB, then they make an important contribution to the debate on the purpose of the Domesday inquest and the documents that it produced.

Sally Harvey agrees on the early date of Domesday Book and takes issue with the notion that it was the product of consensus and communal action. The name 'Domesday' first makes its appearance in the records in the late twelfth century and is there glossed in Latin as 'the Book of Judgements'. The idea of judgement, nevertheless, is a theme that recurs in earlier references to the Book. Early on it is called a *descriptio*, a 'writing down', with connotations of assessment to taxation, and later variously as 'the king's book', 'the book of Winchester', 'the king's charters', and the like. Harvey argues that examination of the record itself shows how the processes of the inquest intimidated the jurors, notably by introducing the ordeal to elicit truth. The paper concludes that the full majesty of the king was used to confirm the new Norman order in what was an exercise of royal prerogative.

By way of contrast, David Roffe argues that the later perceptions of Domesday Book and its use by government in the later Middle Ages are a misleading guide to the business of the Domesday inquest. In 'Talking to Others and Talking to Itself', he examines the subtly changing ways in which royal government related to its records. Verdicts themselves were of central importance to the immediate business in hand, whether it be those of 1086 or of the great inquests of the twelfth and thirteenth centuries. Thereafter it was their data that were of interest and the change in focus impinged on government's understanding of their purpose. Abbreviation transformed a basis for negotiation into hard political fact and the data were used accordingly. It is not surprising, then, that the first notices of Domesday Book emphasize its authority. In particular it served as a useful precedent in the context of the development of a common law in the later twelfth century. Richard fitzNigel's reference to the connotations of the name Domesday for the English is more than convenient. To take it seriously as an indication of the original purpose of the Domesday inquest is to fail to understand the dynamics of record taking and record keeping.

With these last two studies we come full circle: there remains an irreconcilable divide in the understanding of the Domesday process. Nevertheless, there is a way forward. Where there is agreement it is on the need for a modern critical edition of Domesday Book, and the equally important records of the Domesday inquest, that will represent the new categories of evidence presented here as well as a more conventional scribal history. This volume provides the intellectual underpinning for this ambitious undertaking, and the new analyses that it will facilitate. In this way it points to the future of Domesday studies. With such a text, it may well be possible to determine once and for all the character of an inquest and a book that undoubtedly shaped medieval England and arguably informed the modern state of its roots.

I

Domesday Now: a View from the Stage[1]

David Roffe

LIKE THE 'NOW' of the Domesday text itself, the title of this book presupposes a 'then'. In February 2000 the Public Record Office, since re-branded as The National Archives or TNA for short, hosted a conference at its new headquarters in Kew entitled 'Domesday Book: New Perspectives'. The aim of that conference was in large measure to take stock of developments in Domesday studies since the novocentenary of the Domesday inquest in 1986. There was much to celebrate. In the intervening fourteen years, the Alecto facsimile of the text had been published and a new standardized translation was produced by a team of scholars. New technologies were beginning to be brought to bear on the data with startling new perspectives and there had been many significant analyses of 'the Making of Domesday Book'. It looked as if Domesday Book, for so long a hoary old mystery, was beginning to yield up its secrets. Despite the modification of detail and the odd rumbling from the wings,[2] there was then generally consensus on the events of 1086. Domesday as geld book had been demolished by V. H. Galbraith in 1942 and more comprehensively so in 1961,[3] and it was generally accepted that its production was the aim of the Domesday inquest. The purpose of the book remained contentious, but its centrality was undisputed. As the late Henry Loyn succinctly put it in 1986, if

---

[1] I am grateful to Katharine Keats-Rohan, John Palmer, Pamela Taylor, and Ann Williams for commenting on earlier versions of this paper. All errors of fact, interpretation, and taste remain my very own.
[2] W. E. Kapelle, 'Domesday Book: F. W. Maitland and his Successors', *Speculum* 64, 1989, 620–40; D. R. Roffe, 'The Making of Domesday Book Reconsidered', *The Haskins Society Journal* 6, 1994, 153–66; J. O. Prestwich, 'Mistranslations and Misinterpretations in Medieval English History', *Peritia* 10, 1996, 322–40.
[3] V. H. Galbraith, 'The Making of Domesday Book', *EHR* 57, 1942, 161–77; V. H. Galbraith, *The Making of Domesday Book*, London 1961.

perhaps a little presumptuously: 'We are all Galbraithians now.'[4] The unlocking of Domesday was in sight.

Consensus is no more and its dissolution can be conveniently dated to Domesday Book: New Perspectives. At that conference Frank and Caroline Thorn produced an account of the writing of Great Domesday Book (GDB) that laid bare the methods of the scribes and their various campaigns of correction in unprecedented detail. Their analysis convinced them of the fixed points in Galbraith's understanding of the Domesday process – the cohesion of the Domesday inquest and the centrality of Domesday Book – but they made important modifications to the model that streamlined the process and made it more credible. Stephen Baxter also developed the model. He analysed 'the language of lordship' and argued for the hard-headed manipulation of the process by tenants-in-chief who contrived 'to cook the Book'. He thereby underlined the notion that the production of Domesday Book was not only the expression of royal will, but also an exercise in predatory Norman lordship.

The present author, by contrast, outlined a new analysis of the Domesday process. I argued that the Domesday inquest and the production of Domesday Book were two completely different enterprises. The inquest was directly related to a political crisis of the first order. In 1085 England was under threat of invasion from Denmark and a large number of mercenaries had been brought to the country to defend the realm. By Christmas the threat had not gone away but had somewhat eased, and William the Conqueror ordered the 'survey of the whole of England' to raise cash to offset the expenses incurred and, equally importantly, to reform service in order to meet a renewal of the threat and future emergencies. The outcome was a survey of royal regalia, an extension of the geld, and a re-negotiation of knight service. The book, by contrast, was compiled from the returns of the inquest somewhat later, possibly after the revolt against William Rufus in 1088 but conceivably any time up to the early years of Henry I's reign, as a purely administrative aid within the Exchequer.

Much of the subsequent debate in Domesday studies has revolved around the issues that were thereby raised. The 'then' implied by 'Domesday Now' is thus the year 2000. The years since have seen some solid progress. The standard translations

---

[4] Thus in a lecture he delivered at Sutton Bonington in Nottinghamshire, one in a series he gave throughout the country in that novocentenary year. For his espousal of Galbraith's thesis, see H. R. Loyn, 'A General Introduction to Domesday Book', in *Domesday Book Studies*, ed. A. Williams and R. W. H. Erskine, London 1987, 1–21. D. C. Douglas, it seems, did not see fit to modify his view of 1937 that the Book was compiled no earlier than the reign of Henry I in his re-print of the article in 1977 ('The Domesday Survey', *History*, ns 21, 1936, 249–57; *Time and the Hour: Some Collected Papers of David C. Douglas*, London 1977, 223–33; R. H. C. Davis, 'David Charles Douglas, 1898–1982', *Proceedings of the British Academy* 69, 1983, 521–42). The term 'Galbraithian' is hereafter used as shorthand for anyone who sees the production of Domesday Book as an integral part of the Domesday process initiated in late 1085.

have become machine searchable, datasets have been made available, and considerable advances have been made in the codicology of the text. In parallel, there has been much basic analysis of the forms of Domesday Book with the aim of elucidating the order in which it was written and the nature of the lands and tenures to which it refers. Otherwise, the new paradigm has led to a questioning of almost all items of Domesday data. The results have been uneven. On the one side economic and social historians have by and large chosen to ignore new insights into the referents of the text, while on the other there has emerged a new characterization of the Domesday economy and society.

This review, by one in the thick of many of the debates, thus aims to chart trends in Domesday studies since the year 2000[5] and, further, to identify areas of fruitful research for the future. By necessities of space and time, not all studies in which Domesday evidence is invoked can be covered. As the fundamental source for the early history of England, Domesday is cited in just about every work on the period. Here the emphasis is on those studies that directly impinged on the interpretation of the source and the wider implications for an understanding of English and Anglo-Norman society in the eleventh century. The review begins with the texts, examining the new resources that are available in print and electronic media. The two volumes of Domesday Book do not stand alone as a testimony to the event of 1086. For the West County there survives the *Liber Exoniensis* (Exon), an extensive account of the lands of tenants-in-chief produced earlier in the Domesday process, while for Cambridgeshire there is the geographically arranged and equally early *Inquisitio Comitatus Cantabrigiensis* (ICC) along witih the related *Inquisitio Eliensis* (IE). There are in addition some thirty or so less substantial texts that in one way or another emanate from the Domesday inquest. Recent work on all these sources is reviewed before current ideas on the purpose of the Domesday enterprise are examined. A discussion of changing interpretations of content then follows in roughly the same order that the data are presented in Domesday Book itself.

Texts and databases

The full text of Domesday Book was made available in a facsimile which supersedes the photozincographic edition of the 1860s with the publication of Little Domesday (LDB) in 2000 to accompany GDB which appeared in 1986.[6] Translations are now also widely available in print. The Phillimore edition, set in parallel with the Farley Record Type transcript, was completed in 1986. Due to various factors, it does not provide a standardized text and its translation of technical terms in modern English

---

[5] For the best general guide to Domesday studies, see the web version of the *Domesday Explorer* Help file which can be downloaded from http://www.domesdaybook.net/, accessed 17/01/2013.
[6] *Domesday Book*, ed. R. W. H. Erskine, A. Williams, and G. H. Martin, London 1986–2000.

equivalents is unfortunate. These deficiencies, however, have in large part been mitigated by a systematic revision undertaken in recent years by John Palmer at the University of Hull. The revised translation has now been published online with an extensive commentary.[7] The Alecto edition and translation, formerly available only in the expensive County Edition but now published in paperback, provides a more traditional rendering of the Latin.[8]

Both editions have been digitized and published on CDROM.[9] Phillimore goes under the name of *Domesday Explorer* and is confined to GDB.[10] It provides the whole of the printed edition of the translation, with the photozincographic facsimile, in a fully searchable form. It is, nevertheless, much more than an electronic index. All the data are tagged in a wide variety of ways, enabling sophisticated multi-variate searches. However, tabulation and statistical analysis were not supported in this early version, but full datasets, both GDB and LDB, in Access format were put online by John Palmer in 2009.[11]

Domesday Explorer and the statistical datasets are powerful tools which have not yet been fully exploited. They are, however, often difficult to use.[12] *The Digital Domesday*, incorporating the whole of the Alecto edition, with the exception of the discussions of hundreds and wapentakes county by county, is more modest in its aims and has been designed for ease of access.[13] It incorporates the Alecto facsimile, the Farley transcript, translation, county introductions, glossary, and bibliography up to 2004 in a package that allows simple searching of words and phrases in the translation and apparatus. Tagging is kept to a minimum, but the search engine supports Boolean operators and proximity delimiters, enabling simple isolation of information. The first edition was marred by a number of typos in the translation, notably the frequent elision of place-names with the following word, but most of these have been corrected in *Digital Domesday 1.1*. The standard edition has low resolution images of the text and is serviceable for normal use. The high resolution version allows more expert examinations of the manuscript.

---

[7] *Electronic Edition of Domesday Book: Translation, Databases and Scholarly Commentary, 1086*, http://www.data-archive.ac.uk/findingdata/snDescription.asp?sn=5694, accessed 24/09/2014.
[8] *Domesday Book: a Complete Translation*, ed. A. Williams and G. H. Martin, London 2002.
[9] For a general review, see R. Fleming and A. Lowerre, 'Review Article: MacDomesday Book', *Past & Present* 184, 2004, 209–32.
[10] *Domesday Explorer*, CDROM, J. J. N. Palmer, M. Palmer, and G. Slater, Chichester 2000.
[11] http://www.data-archive.ac.uk/findingdata/snDescription.asp?sn=5694, accessed 24/09/2014.
[12] For *Domesday Explorer*, see D. R. Roffe, https://scholarworks.iu.edu/dspace/handle/2022/5414, accessed 24/09/2014. As of December 2014 version 1.1 is promised which will be available as a free download from the Domesday Explorer website at http://www.domesdaybook.net/. It provides on-board search terms to facilitate the interrogation of the text.
[13] *The Digital Domesday*, CDROM, Alecto Historical Editions, London 2002.

The Alecto edition also forms the basis of the two online versions. Both Getmapping, via Domesday Extracts,[14] and The National Archives,[15] provide databases that can be searched by postcode or place-name, returning basic information on the place and/or the folio on which it occurs. An image from the Alecto facsimile and a translation can be downloaded for a fee. Both sites are heritage orientated and are not suitable for serious academic use. John Palmer and Anna Powell-Smith's open source translation, as reported below (pp.224–9), promises to be a more valuable resource. It is based on the datasets developed at Hull linked to the Ordnance Survey facsimile and presents a broader range of data for each place or person with a graphical interface. The same datasets and facsimile are also accessed by an iPad app developed by Daniel Jarvis.[16]

The new technologies have facilitated access to GDB and LDB. However, in the process of developing high-profile electronic resources, usually with media fanfares, more basic priorities have gone by the board. Although a transcription of the two volumes of Domesday Book in Record Type was produced for Parliament by Abraham Farley in 1783,[17] there are extended Latin texts for only fifteen out of the thirty-three Domesday counties, dating from the 1870s, and they are of varying degrees of accuracy.[18] For the rest of the Domesday corpus, the state of scholarship is even worse. There are still no critical editions of major sources like Exon, ICC, and IE – our texts are Record Type transcripts[19] – let alone machine searchable versions. Apart from Evesham A,[20] few of the other so-called 'satellite' texts[21] have been subject to modern editing and publication.

A major outcome of the Domesday Now conference has been the determination on the part of the scholars in the field to rectify the omission. A project is now under way to produce machine-readable Latin texts for the whole of the Domesday corpus under the auspices of the newly convened Domesday Texts Committee. For Domesday Book itself, the new edition will be based on John Palmer's invaluable 'Digital Farley' (below, pp.61–3), but will not be confined to a simple expansion of

[14] http://www.domesdayextracts.co.uk/, accessed 24/09/2014.
[15] http://www.nationalarchives.gov.uk/domesday/, accessed 24/09/2014.
[16] http://itunes.apple.com/us/app/domesday/id492843995?mt=8, accessed 16/01/2012.
[17] *Domesday Book; seu Liber Censualis Vocati Domesday Book*, ed. A. Farley, London 1783.
[18] Bedfordshire, Cambridgeshire, Cheshire, Derbyshire, Devon, Hampshire, Kent, Leicestershire, Middlesex, Northamptonshire, Rutland, Shropshire, Suffolk, Surrey, Sussex, Wiltshire, Worcestershire. For references, see D. Bates, *A Bibliography of Domesday Book*, Woodbridge 1985, nos. 1004, 1306, 1406, 1704, 1603, 2208, 2610, 2803, 3004, 3205, 3501, 3606, 3902, 4003, 4110, 4406, 4503.
[19] ICC and IE: *Inquisitio Comitatus Cantabrigiensis...Subjicitur Inquisitio Eliensis*, ed. N. E. S. A. Hamilton, London 1876.
[20] P. H. Sawyer, 'Evesham A, a Domesday Text', in *Miscellany 1*, Worcestershire Historical Society, 1960, 22–36. Howard Clarke has edited the remaining Evesham surveys including Evesham C and Evesham M below, pp.263–8 and 269–75.
[21] 'Satellite texts' is prejudicial; 'inquest records' is to be preferred.

the text. It will incorporate a full scribal history – the contribution of the various hands, the additions, deletions, marginalia, and the like – as well as the forms of the manuscript. As I report in a paper on scribal practices in this volume (pp.81–108), the scribes laid out their texts with purpose and the forms that they employed can be elegant testimony to the sources they employed and the purposes to which they put them. The datasets will be searchable in terms of both content and form. Three counties will shortly be available online which are linked to a new translation by Frank Thorn.

Codicology and scribal history of Domesday Book

The first systematic examination of the materials and make-up of the Domesday MSS was undertaken in 1952 on the occasion of its rebinding. There the analysis was confined to visual examination and its conclusions were largely confirmed in 1983 when the volumes were again disbound for the production of the Alecto facsimile. Both volumes were found to be generally in a good condition and it was determined that the folios of GDB were all sheepskin, while calfskin was used for some quires in LDB. In 2008 a more scientific examination was undertaken by TNA in partnership with teams from Wales, Denmark, and France to ascertain the state of preservation of the MSS. Five small fibres were taken for x-ray diffraction analysis and all the folios were subject to microscopic examination.[22] The headline result was alarming: despite the apparent good condition of the parchment, the collagen of which it is composed has dissolved, suggesting that the MSS are far more fragile than they appear. The finding has led to a new preservation regime that further restricts access to the MSS. On the plus side, however, the examination of the folios enabled a mapping of the calfskin and it was found that it was also used in GDB, notably in Cambridgeshire and Hertfordshire.[23] This study remains unpublished and so its implications are as yet to be explored.

The writing of the MSS is now somewhat better understood. It seems that there were five GDB scribes but the contribution of four is miniscule: GDB is overwhelmingly the work of one man. It has been claimed that characteristics of his hand suggest that he was associated with the Durham scriptorium.[24] However,

---

[22] Nancy Bell and David McPhail, 'Managing Change: Preserving History', *Materials Today* 10, 2007, 50–6.

[23] I am indebted to Nancy Bell for providing me with a copy of the paper she read on the subject at the Domesday Now conference at TNA in September 2011.

[24] P. Chaplais, 'William of Saint-Calais and the Domesday Survey', in *Domesday Studies: Novocentenary Conference, Royal Historical Society and Institute of Geographers, Winchester 1986*, ed. J. C. Holt, Woodbridge 1987, 65–78. Caroline Thorn expressed reservations about the Durham connection since the evidence comes from the 1090s, which she considered too late for Domesday Book, and not specific enough (Frank Thorn and Caroline Thorn, 'The Writing of Great Domesday Book', in *Domesday*, ed. Elizabeth Hallam and David Bates,

a full scribal history is still wanting and many of the conclusions that have been drawn must therefore be treated as provisional.[25] Some themes, nevertheless, have become evident. In broad outline an order of writing has now been established. The original binding of the MS was probably somewhat later than compilation; the rubbing of the outer folios of the quires which make it up suggests that they were initially used as separate pamphlets.[26] The preparation of the parchment and vellum and the forms of the text provide evidence for an original order. The experimental diplomatic of the Yorkshire folios is compelling evidence that they were the first to be written.[27] Ruling patterns and developing formulas indicate that the scribe continued with the other counties of the northern circuit, then went on to the east Midlands and the south-east. A second well-established sequence commences with Gloucestershire and takes in the Welsh marches and then goes into the central Midlands, ending with Leicestershire. The only disagreement is over the position of the five south-western counties. Within this group there is a neat development of diplomatic from Wiltshire through to Cornwall, but there are no unambiguous diagnostic links with other areas. Its place within the work is debated. On the one hand, it has been suggested that its forms are closer to those of the south-east and west Midlands and the change from a ruling pattern with horizontal lines, as in the Yorkshire sequence, to one without, as found from Gloucestershire onwards, half way through the south-western shire most likely places it between the two well-attested sequences.[28] On the other, however, it has been urged that compression of the text more likely places the south-western folios at the very end of the process of writing,[29] a contention strengthened by a rare hidage formula in Oxfordshire which is common in Wiltshire.[30] To this can be added the evidence of a post-rubrication campaign of addition and correction in the Derbyshire and Nottinghamshire folios.

Stroud 2001, 37–73 at 71). Nevertheless, 'Caroline admitted that the slight indications point to Durham and its bishop rather than to anywhere else and that Chaplais' wider arguments have considerable weight' (pers comm., Frank Thorn).

[25] Caroline Thorn's study, with Michael Gullick, will appear in due course (pers. comm., Frank Thorn).

[26] A. R. Rumble, 'The Palaeography of the Domesday Manuscripts', in *Domesday Book: a Reassessment*, ed. P. H. Sawyer, London 1985, 28–49 at 29–32.

[27] D. R. Roffe, 'Domesday Book and Northern Society: a Reassessment', *EHR* 105, 1990, 310–36; D. R. Roffe, *Domesday: the Inquest and the Book*, Oxford 2000, 191–211. Sally Harvey, *Domesday: Book of Judgement*, Oxford 2014, 100–1, doubts that the Yorkshire folios were the first to be written on the ground that they did not become the model for the rest of Domesday. The argument here is that it is the *developing* formulas, along with rulings, that provide the evidence for an order of writing, an analysis with which Harvey does not engage.

[28] Roffe, *Domesday: the Inquest and the Book*, 207.

[29] Thorn and Thorn, 'The Writing of Great Domesday Book', 42–6.

[30] C. Flight, *The Survey of the Whole of England: Studies of the Documentation Resulting from the Survey Conducted in 1086*, British Archaeological Reports, British Series 405, Oxford 2006, 20–4.

There the scribes uses the *olim* formula of the value clause which only otherwise occurs in the West Country folios, suggesting that the scribe still had this formula in mind when revision commenced. However, other explanations for the phenomenon remain possible. More minute analysis of the diplomatic may resolve the matter in the future.

The working methods of the GDB scribes have been comprehensively explored by Frank and Caroline Thorn.[31] They have shown how the main scribe revised his own work and, at some point after rubrication of his text, was associated with a second scribe in further checking, correction, and emendation. For such a complex text, errors are remarkably few and the Thorns have concluded that the whole of the text must have been abbreviated from more or less fully compiled exemplars, what they categorize as 'circuit returns'. John Palmer, in this volume, concurs (pp.64–5). In an elegant analysis of the diverse words forms of the text, he shows that their distribution is predominantly by circuit. He concludes that the main Domesday scribe was less a draftsman, compiling and abbreviating at will, than a copyist of the work of others. Exon, indubitably the main source of the GDB account of the south-western shires, is held to exemplify the type of source that he employed.

Exon is clearly an important source, but doubt has nevertheless been expressed as to whether it was a circuit return, on the one hand, and whether it was typical of the sources used by the GDB scribe on the other. I have argued that Exon emanated from a process of 'inbreviation', the first writing down of the returns of the tenants-in-chief, and was pressed into service in the writing of Domesday Book for want of anything better. The more usual source of GDB was geographically-arranged documents like ICC, some of which otherwise incongruously survive in the folios of Domesday Book itself, compiled somewhat later in the course of the Domesday inquest from Exon-like sources.[32] In this volume I adduce further evidence from the layout of the text, specifically the form of initial letters, that the GDB scribe had access to a number of different types of schedule which he used to compile and order his text (pp.96–101). 'Conversion tables', such as the Yorkshire Summary and Evesham K, would have facilitated the re-arrangement of ICC-like sources to the GDB format and minimized errors in the process.

For Galbraith LDB was a fair copy of an Exon-like source that was never incorporated into GDB; more recently Sir James Holt has argued that it was directly comparable.[33] It remains a relatively under-studied source. Knowledge of the scribes

---

[31] Thorn and Thorn, 'Writing of Great Domesday Book'.
[32] Roffe, *Domesday: Inquest and Book*, 172–80; Roffe, *Decoding Domesday*, Woodbridge 2007, 87–97.
[33] Galbraith, *Making of Domesday Book*, 30–2; J. C. Holt, 'Domesday Studies 2000', in *Domesday Book*, ed. Hallam and Bates, 19–24 at 23, on the basis of Frank and Caroline Thorn's arguments for Exon being the source of the GDB entries for the south west. The Thorns themselves were more equivocal, confining their views to Exon ('Writing of Great

of LDB is still dependent on the pioneering work of A. R. Rumble in 1985.[34] Rumble identified seven scribes, six of whom contributed substantial portions of the text. Unfortunately, space did not permit him to go much beyond a palaeographical analysis and he has not followed up the work since. Michael Gullick subsequently identified two of the scribes as English, the remaining five being of Continental origin, and I myself have briefly examined the peculiarities of each in the Alecto edition of the Norfolk folios, suggesting that one who exhibits a higher degree of flexibility in expression may have supervised the others.[35] Pamela Taylor has also examined the diverse sources of the account of Colchester in the Essex folios. She too identifies various schedules that were available to the scribe who compiled the account.[36] Otherwise, the most substantial contribution to the scribal history of LDB in the last ten years has been Lucy Marten's tentative association of the MS with the Bury St Edmunds scriptorium. None of the hands, however, is obviously of Bury provenance.[37] There still remains much to be done. The interchange of scribes has made it difficult to ascertain an order of writing – the contributions of the six main scribes do not appear to follow any meaningful pattern – but more detailed analysis of the formulas of the text may open up wider vistas.

It is now clear that the ultimate source of LDB was also documents arranged by hundred. The forms of entries and the position of communal information such as the dimensions of vills and arrangements for the payment of the geld echo those of Cambridgeshire and indicate that the text was derived from ICC-like accounts.[38] Within chapters the hundred, as opposed to the manor, remains the fundamental division of the text. To my mind, these characteristics distinguish it as a different type of document from Exon.[39] The text is more carefully drafted and, above all, unlike Exon, it is an abbreviation: ploughland data are systematically omitted. Its affinities are rather with GDB, notwithstanding its record of livestock. Thus, LDB realized its forms – the division into counties, separate accounts of boroughs, the articulation of estates – for the first time in the Domesday corpus and clearly provided the GDB scribe with his model. He took the running heads of LDB, which identify fees as opposed to shires, over into the first folios of the account of Yorkshire, along with the dimensions of vills, the inclusion of disputes, and

---

Domesday Book', 65–9), while Flight recognizes LDB as a different stage in the process (*Survey of the Whole of England*, 25–37).

[34] Rumble, 'Palaeography of the Domesday Manuscripts', 28–49.

[35] M. Gullick, 'The Great and Little Domesday Manuscripts', in *Domesday Book: Studies*, ed. A. Williams and R. W. H. Erskine, London 1987, 93–112; D. R. Roffe, 'Introduction', in *Little Domesday: Norfolk*, ed. A. Williams and G. H. Martin, London 2000, 9–43 at 11–12.

[36] P. Taylor, 'Introduction', in *Little Domesday: Essex*, ed. A. Williams and G. H. Martin, London 2000, 7–32 at 13–14.

[37] L. Marten, 'The Impact of Rebellion on Little Domesday', *ANS* 27, 2005, 132–50 at 149.

[38] Roffe, 'Introduction', in *Little Domesday: Norfolk*, 19–21.

[39] Roffe, *Domesday: Inquest and Book*, 220–3; Roffe, *Decoding Domesday*, 98–9.

probably even the grouping of manorial appurtenances with the manorial centre. As Round divined in the 1890s on purely empirical grounds,[40] volume II of Domesday Book was in origin volume I.

Domesday Book, then, I would argue, is not the ill-matched marriage of necessity that it has often been portrayed. It had never been intended to incorporate the account of the LDB counties into GDB. It is true that it was almost certainly not conceived as one work. Ian Taylor (below, pp.137–53) argues that LDB was compiled specifically with the special circumstances of East Anglia in mind: the Norman settlement there was late and it remained a particularly unstable area of the realm which demanded immediate attention in 1086. Nevertheless, LDB and GDB became a single work. The programme that produced it was an evolving one. If the forms of LDB have yet to be studied in detail, those of GDB are becoming clearer. Much of the variation in the content and expression of its data is a direct function of the main scribe's sources. This, which has been termed the vertical element in the diplomatic of the text,[41] has long been used to identify the seven circuits of the inquest. The identification of a horizontal layer, the variations in expression that have enabled a sequencing of the text, has provided novel insights into a developing schema. LDB provided the scribe with a general format, but from the outset he decided to enrol boroughs at the head of each county, a departure from previous practice not only in LDB but in the inquest records as a whole (below, pp.30-3), to dispense with the details of livestock and to enter ploughlands. So much for intentions. In practice, the scribe's taxonomy was challenged by the realities of the North.[42] What constituted a manor was far from clear and his definition changed with time. Likewise, by the time he got to Circuit III he began to realize that it was not always possible to represent manorial structure and thereafter he took less and less interest in the manor. Even the enrolment of the borough as a community often went by the board as his work progressed. The account became leaner, with even ploughlands jettisoned in the West Midlands, and by the end had become honed down to an economical read.

In parallel with changes in content, there was also a refinement of expression. Frank Thorn explores the vocabulary of Domesday Book below (pp.109–36). Comparing the terms used in the so-called 'articles of inquiry' preserved in the *Inquisitio Eliensis*, he argues that the Domesday scribe gradually whittled down the multiplicity of terms that he found in his sources with the aim of producing a standardized text. He never succeeded in eliminating all variation, but he gradually evolved a terminology, approximating as closely as possible to Classical Latin forms, which was concise and to the point. Domesday Book was a work in progress.

---

[40] J. H. Round, *Feudal England*, London 1895, 119.
[41] Roffe, *Decoding Domesday*, 52.
[42] Roffe, *Domesday Inquest and Book*, 211–20; Roffe, *Decoding Domesday*, 98–108.

Other Domesday texts

It is inevitable that most attention has been paid to Domesday Book itself as the major source. Nevertheless, there have been significant studies of other texts in the Domesday corpus. Colin Flight has re-examined Exon and identified twenty scribes who contributed substantial sections of text.[43] It was two, however, as divined by Welldon Finn before him,[44] who carried out the bulk of the work. Flight's detailed mapping of these scribes to the Exon text is the most detailed to date and a considerable advance on previous analyses. Hitherto, commentators have been confused by the apparently haphazard interrelationship of all these scribes: their stints often commence in the middle of sections, even at times half way through sentences, and there seems to be no underlying rationale such as the structure of hundreds. Nevertheless, Flight has essayed an explanation based on the assumption that ICC-like sources lay behind the whole of the text. Hypothesizing that the sources were divided into a number of pamphlets to speed up copying and that the scribes copied from them as they became free, he has produced an algorithm to account for changes in hands.[45] The solution is ingenious, but ultimately unconvincing: the algorithm should produce a more regular hundredal sequence in Exon and the corresponding parts of GDB than has as yet been demonstrated.[46] For the time being Tessa Webber's explanation may be preferred. She has identified three of the Exon hands with those of the Salisbury scriptorium and points out that this method of copying was common at that centre.[47]

Caroline and Frank Thorn's work on Exon is fundamental to an understanding of the source. They have collated its entries with those of GDB and provided an extensive commentary in the Phillimore edition of the five south-western shires of Domesday Book. There remains, however, much work to be done on the composition of the text and its own sources. The absence of hundred rubrics is mysterious. For Galbraith, the characteristic was proof that the commissioners were intent on producing an account of fees from the very start of the enterprise. However, the likely sources of the data would suggest that the hundred must have participated in the process. If Exon finds its origins in inbreviations, then it might be expected that skeletal lists of hundreds and vills gave each presentment its form. *A fortiori*, a geographical stratum should be present if it was compiled from a full account of

---

[43] Flight, *Description of the Whole of England*, 49–59.
[44] R. Welldon Finn, 'The Exeter Domesday and its Construction', *Bulletin of the John Rylands Library* 41, 1958–9, 360–87.
[45] Flight, *Description of the Whole of England*, 38–48.
[46] Roffe, *Decoding Domesday*, 38 n.
[47] T. Webber, 'Salisbury and the Exon Domesday: Some Observations Concerning the Origins of Exeter Cathedral MS 3500', in *English Manuscript Studies 1100–1700*, I, ed. P. Beal and J. Griffiths, Oxford 1989, 1–18.

vills.⁴⁸ A new edition and analysis is now under way, with further investigation of, *inter alia*, the order of entries promising to cast light on the origins of the source.⁴⁹

With the recognition of Exon as an important text, interest in other inquest texts suffered an eclipse and none more so that ICC. While not exactly characterized as aberrant, ICC came to be seen by Galbraith as a local peculiarity. Despite his anathema, the text has, nevertheless, recently come to the fore as a significant source. Its rehabilitation began with John Palmer's perceptive analysis of the representation of manors in Cambridgeshire and how they are articulated in Domesday Book.⁵⁰ He drew attention to the fact that the different entry forms of GDB were directly related to their enrolment in ICC. Where manors were coterminous with vills, the statement of geld liability of the whole vill in the latter was transferred directly to the former. In divided vills, the same formula was used for the first manor, then *In x* for subsequent ones. Palmer's analysis at once opens up the possibility that ICC was the direct source of the former. Such intertextual analysis has subsequently been used, as in LDB, to suggest that at least twenty-three counties are derived from similar sources.⁵¹.

It is now generally agreed that the production of a geographically arranged recension of the data in most, if not all, counties was a significant objective in the Domesday enterprise. IE is closely related to such sources. Its date of composition remains contentious. Round maintained that it was drawn up shortly after the Domesday inquest, citing a writ addressed to Archbishop Lanfranc which references Bishop Geoffrey of Coutances and Bishop Walkelin of Winchester as commissioners in a survey of the lands of Ely abbey.⁵² The survey in question was subsequently identified by Edward Miller as that in Kentford in 1080.⁵³ That dating in its turn was queried by Galbraith.⁵⁴ Focusing on the summaries, he argued that the record of increased value in the time of Abbot Symeon indicates that the compilation of IE must postdate his death in 1096. However, I have argued that this provides no point of reference since the diplomatic of the IE summaries is identical with those of Exon which, by definition, date from the time of the inquest.⁵⁵ Colin Flight has

---

⁴⁸ It should be noted, though, that the absence of the 'In *X y* hides…' entry type in both Exon and GDB militates against an ICC-type progenitor.

⁴⁹ The project is led by Professor Julia Crick at King's College, London. See http://www.exeter-cathedral.org.uk/content/news/exon-domesday-book-unlocked-for-future-generations.ashx, accessed 10/01/2015.

⁵⁰ J. J. N. Palmer, 'The Domesday Manor', in *Domesday Studies*, ed. Holt, 139–54.

⁵¹ Roffe, *Decoding Domesday*, 87–97.

⁵² Round, *Feudal England*, 133–4.

⁵³ E. Miller, 'The Ely Land Pleas of the Reign of William I', *EHR* 62, 1947, 438–56. For a dissenting voice, see *Regesta Regum Anglo-Normanorum: the Acta of William I 1066–1087*, ed. D. Bates, Oxford 1998, no. 127.

⁵⁴ Galbraith, *Making of Domesday Book*, 135–45.

⁵⁵ Roffe, *Decoding Domesday*, 95 n.

subsequently tried to square the circle by arguing that IE was re-worked sometime after the Domesday inquest.[56]

The matter remains undetermined. All, however, are agreed that IE contains material that pre-dates Domesday Book. The so-called 'articles' which open the text have been widely accepted as the terms of reference of the inquiry. Frank Thorn restates the case below (pp.110–13), but the assumption has been questioned by myself.[57] I recognize, of course, that there must have been articles of inquiry of some kind and they would have included questions like those recorded in IE. As they stand, though, the IE *capitula* cannot have informed the inquest for there are no questions relating to livestock. The subject matter and the order in which the articles are recorded conform more closely to those of Domesday Book than of inquest records and the fact suggests to me that, if not a twelfth-century confection from earlier records, then the articles as recorded here were most likely compiled as a guide to the abbreviation of LDB and/or GDB.

The list of jurors, approximating to those recorded in ICC, has not been questioned as products of the inquest. The most detailed study has been undertaken by Christopher Lewis who found that the jurors were generally from a landholding class that is not systematically named in either the inquest records or Domesday Book.[58] He identified them as undertenants and this characterization has had a considerable influence in the way in which the Domesday juries have been understood. It is now widely assumed that they were in the pockets of powerful lords and, in consequence, were often suborned (see below, pp.24–6).[59]

While the account of the lands of Ely is now recognized to pre-date Domesday Book, debate has turned on the form of the sources behind it. There has been general agreement from the time of Round that the Cambridgeshire entries were copied from the ICC exemplar or a very similar source, albeit with some possible re-working. Likewise, it is assumed that the Hertfordshire and Huntingdonshire sections are derived from the same type of document. Essex, Norfolk, and Suffolk have caused more problems. P. H. Sawyer showed in 1955 that at least the Essex

---

[56] *Survey of the Whole of England*, 98.
[57] Roffe, *Domesday: Inquest and Book*, 114–17.
[58] C. P. Lewis, 'Domesday Jurors', *The Haskins Society Journal* 5, 1993, 17–44; C. P. Lewis, 'The Domesday Jurors', in *Studies on the Personal Name in Later Medieval England and Wales*, ed. D. Postles and J. T. Rosenthal, Studies in Medieval Culture 44, Kalamazoo 2006, 307–39.
[59] See, for example, S. Baxter, 'The Representation of Lordship and Land Tenure in Domesday Book', in *Domesday Book*, ed. Hallam and Bates, 73–102; A. Cooper, 'Protestations of Ignorance in Domesday Book', in *The Experience of Power in Medieval Europe, 950–1350*, ed. R. Berkhofer, A. Cooper, and A. Kosto, Aldershot 2005, 169–82; R. Fleming, 'Oral Testimony and the Domesday Inquest', *ANS* 17, 1994, 101–22; R. Fleming, *Domesday Book and the Law: Society and Legal Custom in Early Medieval England*, Cambridge 1998; P. Taylor, 'Domesday Mortlake', *ANS* 32, 2009, 203–29.

section must have been derived from a geographically-arranged document since it retains the order of vills within a different sequence of hundreds from the LDB account.[60] Galbraith did not reference the study, presumably dismissing the hundredal structure as a function of procedure. Rather he focused on the use of the term *breve* which he interpreted as a seigneurially-arranged return.[61] For him, the account of the lands of Ely abbey was proof positive of the organization of the data by fief from the outset of the Domesday process.

Where Galbraith dated the summaries to the vacancy of 1096–9, Welldon Finn saw them as handy epitomes of the resources of each tenant-in-chief produced in the course of the inquest.[62] He hitched them firmly to the Galbraithian schema for the making of Domesday Book. I myself have recognized that the summaries attest an interest in the estates of each lord in the shire, but have since tied them to different referents.[63] What is remarkable about the IE summaries is that they conform so closely in form and diplomatic to those in Exon and GDB. All of them highlight the number of ploughlands in the fee, the number of manors held, and the increase in value in a common language that indicates that these were primary items of data for the Domesday commissioners. The summaries provide the closest that we have, I would maintain, to the articles of the inquest and eloquently reveal its concern with tax capacity and service.

The schedules at the end of IE have proved the most difficult parts to interpret due to their extreme terseness. Round, Galbraith, and Welldon Finn distinguished three separate sources which they called the Breviate, the Nomina Villarum, and the Claims.[64] By contrast, I distinguish four, dividing the Claims into two, and renaming them all Ely A, Ely B, Ely C, and Ely D. The first two have generally been thought not to have been a product of the Domesday inquest but to have been especially drawn up when IE was compiled from its disparate sources.[65] I tentatively suggest, though, an origin in the early stages of the inquest when lords drew up skeleton lists of estates and their resources. In either case, the lists have provided insights into the scope of the inquest. The account of the Huntingdonshire manors, for example, indicates that data on slaves were edited out at an early stage in the compilation of the returns for Circuit VI. As for the Claims, I have identified the first part, Ely C, as lands that had been sworn to the abbey in earlier pleas and

---

[60] P. H. Sawyer, 'The "Original Returns" and Domesday Book', *EHR* 70, 1955, 189. Flight has revisited the data and comes to broadly similar conclusions (*Survey of All England*, 99–103).

[61] Galbraith, *Making of Domesday Book*, 135–45.

[62] R. Welldon Finn, 'The Inquisitio Eliensis Reconsidered', *EHR* 75, 1960, 385–409 at 394–7.

[63] Roffe, *Domesday: Inquest and Book*, 180–3; Galbraith, *Making of Domesday Book*, 146–55.

[64] Round, *Feudal England*, 129; Galbraith, *Making of Domesday Book*, 135–45; Welldon Finn, 'Inquisitio Eliensis Reconsidered', 397–8.

[65] Round, *Feudal England*, 129; Welldon Finn, 'Inquisitio Eliensis Reconsidered', 397–8.

had continued to render dues through into 1086. How it relates to the Domesday process remains mysterious.

The numerous Kentish sources have also been the subject of significant studies, being variously identified as pre-Domesday texts, on the one hand, and post-Domesday abstracts on the other. Texts of this kind are notoriously difficult to interpret since they are not amenable to analysis in terms of stemmas and dead dating.[66] By definition, inquest records draw on a number of sources and often contain information of completely different provenance. Diplomatic indicates relationship but can rarely provide a chronology. It is rather re-arrangements of material that provide the best clues. The Domesday Monachorum documents present particularly difficult problems in this respect. The initial list of manors (DM A) does not exhibit the same order as the corresponding entries in Domesday Book, apart from those belonging to the bishop of Rochester, and therefore ought to be independent or very early in the Domesday process. I, like Galbraith before, opted for the latter on the ground that it dictated the order of the more extensive description of the same manors that follows (DM B) which exhibits much, but by no means all, of the content and diplomatic of the Domesday text.[67] I have tentatively concluded that A was a preliminary list of manors presented by Christ Church before the early sessions of the inquest, the *inquisitio geldi*, where B is an annotated version produced thereafter.[68]

Flight has a similar analysis.[69] He does not discuss the initial list (DM A), but interprets B (his C1 á2 text) as the answers to a preliminary questionnaire sent out by the commissioners. However, he distinguishes between early and later versions. The same text is found in Canterbury Cathedral, Register K (C4 á1) and he sees that version as Christ Church's initial reply. The somewhat fuller B text, by contrast, represents the same document as annotated by the commissioners after formal inquest sessions in open court. Flight does not venture an opinion as to which stage a further copy, R1 á3, a copy of the Rochester section alone, belongs.

Neither analysis entirely comes to grips with the difference in organization of the text compared with the Domesday account. If DM B, in whatever version, incorporates the verdicts of jurors (but see Pamela Taylor, below, pp.210–12), it might be expected that it followed the order thereof, unless, of course, it does not represent the official version. And yet the text contains the same range of data as the hundredally-arranged Excerpta of St Augustine's, Canterbury, which more closely follows the sequence of hundreds and lathes.[70] Flight claims this latter source as an

---

[66] Roffe, *Decoding Domesday*, 54–61.
[67] Roffe, *Domesday: Inquest and Book*, 110; Roffe, *Decoding Domesday*, 31.
[68] Roffe, *Domesday: Inquest and Book*, 136–7.
[69] Flight, *Survey of the Whole of England*, 111–13; C. Flight, *The Survey of Kent: Documents Relating to the Survey of the County Conducted in 1086*, British Archaeological Reports, British Series 505, 2010, 33–65.
[70] *An Eleventh-Century Inquisition of St Augustine's, Canterbury*, ed. A. Ballard, Records of the Social and Economic History of England 4, London 1920, 1–33.

extract of an ICC-like document,[71] but there is no intrinsic reason why it should not be a shortened version of a source akin to DM B which he accepts as a discrete document. The Excerpta, perhaps, has the best claim to be a record of the inquest sessions which, as Galbraith hypothesized, was later supplemented by seigneurial returns.[72]

Finally, DM E, the Kentish Assessment List, has also been re-assessed. Whereas Douglas considered the document an abstract of GDB, Hoyt identified it as a pre-Domesday assessment list, and Harvey has since argued that it was pressed into service in the Domesday inquest.[73] Flight, in the latest analysis, has reverted to Douglas's original interpretation.[74] Dismissing Hoyt's and Harvey's dating evidence as illusory, he accepts that the exemplar of the list contains data that cannot have been derived from GDB, but asserts that the fact merely indicates that the original scribe had access to additional sources, probably the circuit return. An abstract of all the fees in Kent, saving those of Canterbury, St Augustine's, and Rochester, its main source was clearly GDB, for the scribe scanned the account of the lands of the bishop of Bayeux a number of times in order to bring the lands of each of his tenants together. He concludes that the document was an official breviate produced in Winchester in the late eleventh century, as attested by the hand of the scribe, probably for use in local administration by the sheriff of Kent.

Detailing the lands and assessments of the king and each tenant-in-chief with summary totals supplied, DM E is directly comparable to Evesham C and M which are analysed in this volume by Howard Clarke (pp.247–62). Relating to Domesday fees in Worcestershire and Gloucestershire, these latter two documents substantially reproduce the order of entries as found in the corresponding passages in GDB and their content. A close relationship is clearly indicated, with additional detail supplied primarily from local knowledge. Clarke concludes that Evesham C and M were most likely abbreviated from GDB, probably from before 1095, again for use in local government.

The production of breviates by central government and their distribution to the localities could account for the light use of Domesday, the folios of which exhibit relatively little rubbing and wear. That such documents were generally in circulation is perhaps attested by their enrolment in early cartularies in preference to extracts from Domesday Book itself. Nevertheless, abstraction from GDB is not the only possible provenance for such texts. Both Flight and Clarke admit of

---

[71] Flight, *Survey of Kent*, 72–88.
[72] Galbraith, *Making of Domesday Book*, 135–45.
[73] Douglas, 'The Domesday Survey', 254; R. S. Hoyt, 'A Pre-Domesday Kentish Assessment List', in *A Medieval Miscellany for Doris Mary Stenton*, ed. P. M. Barnes and C. F. Slade, Pipe Roll Society, ns 36, 1962 for 1960, 189–202; S. P. J. Harvey, 'Domesday Book and its Predecessors', *EHR* 86, 1971, 753–73.
[74] Flight, *Survey of Kent*, 201–13.

a possible input from the sources of Domesday Book and assume that these must have been seigneurially-arranged circuit returns. The Rochester section of DM B, however, indicates that lists of a similar type were produced at a much earlier stage in the inquest. That text apparently precedes the full seigneurial returns and yet still has an order of entries that found its way into GDB. It would also seem that that sort of document could be subject to the rescanning that appears to associate E so clearly with GDB. Section 1 of B, the lands of the archbishop of Canterbury, was subsequently re-arranged to distinguish the demesne from the enfeoffed estates some time before GDB was compiled. The grouping of the manors of each tenant in Odo of Bayeux's fee could have been contemplated at any time in the course of the inquest – as Douglas noted, it was relevant any time after Odo's forfeiture in 1083[75] – although here the format did not find its way into GDB.

The context, procedure, and purpose of the inquest

These and the other texts associated with the Domesday process are extremely slippery. Their study is not for the faint-hearted. Nevertheless, for many they continue to hold the key to the Domesday riddle. As befits our times, the most complete taxonomy has been characterized as neo-Galbraithian. Colin Flight has rejected Galbraith's later analysis of the Domesday process and has developed the ideas put forward in his 1942 article.[76] There Galbraith retained a place for the ICC-like source, which he was subsequently to dismiss not quite as an aberration but as a local peculiarity, while maintaining that the feudal form of Domesday Book was intended from the very start of the Domesday enterprise. For Flight this remains a central insight. He argues that the whole business of the inquest is to be sought in the production of accounts of land vill by vill within the shire. Drafts were drawn up by local officials and these were then checked and corrected by commissioners who were sent out into a number of shires. The result, his 'B' texts sworn to by the jurors of the hundred, was the production of ICC-like accounts for the whole of the country. It was these texts, as Round before had hypothesized,[77] that were returned to Winchester and it was there that the process of producing a feudal account commenced. Initially, it was organized on a regional basis. Here the type text is Exon in which the lands of each tenant-in-chief in a string of counties are entered in a continuous account. Almost immediately these 'C' texts were copied to produce what for him was the permanent record of the inquest, an extended account county by county like LDB, the only surviving example of his 'D' texts. 'DB', standing for 'D text breviate' in Flight's notation, that is GDB, was then compiled as a handy, albeit incomplete, summary.

---

[75] *DM*, 27–33.
[76] Flight, *Survey of the Whole of England*, 1–99 and passim.
[77] Round, *Feudal England*, 6–27.

In common with Peter Sawyer and Alan Thacker,[78] Flight finds no convincing evidence for circuits. For most Domesday scholars, however, the differences in expression in Domesday Book itself and various references to the shires assigned to individual commissioners are compelling reasons to allow a regional forum for data collection and compilation.[79] The general consensus view among 'Galbraithians', restated most recently by Frank and Caroline Thorn,[80] remains that feudal accounts were drawn up in the localities to inform the production of Domesday Book. The scribes of Domesday Book, wherever it was composed, already had feudally arranged accounts of land to draw on. There is agreement, however, that returns in that form were the aim of the whole Domesday enterprise. For Flight, that aim was realized in the production of his D texts, of which LDB alone survives, for others in GDB itself.

In this reconstruction, the whole business of the Domesday inquest is seen as an entirely executive process, a direct product of the king's fiat. Its purpose has been variously interpreted.[81] Domesday Book is a record of the Norman settlement, a feodary, an administrative aid, a tax book, a quartermaster's inventory, and much else. However, whatever use was intended for it, it is conceived as an expression of power. George Garnett, followed by Stephen Baxter and echoed by Sally Harvey, has most fully articulated the idea, seeing in Domesday Book a deep political purpose.[82] In appealing to the 'time of King Edward', it is ostensibly restoring the legitimacy of the Old English state after, according to the Norman propaganda, the usurpation of Harold Godwineson. In reality, it is argued, the survey effects and documents a radical change in English society. Domesday Book confirms the dispossession of the English and asserts a novel theory that the Normans who succeeded them held from the king

This understanding of the Domesday process draws heavily on the Whig idea of 'the Norman Yoke'. It is not without medieval authority. Contemporary sources assert that there was much discontent at the levying of new taxes in 1086 and the idea of discipline and oppression was a leitmotif of later sources. Thus, in the late twelfth century Richard fitzNigel asserted that the inquest was designed to bring the English under the rule of written law, while in the mid thirteenth Matthew Paris opined that with the compilation of Domesday Book 'here began the manifest oppression of the

---

[78] A. Thacker and P. H. Sawyer, 'Domesday Survey', *VCH Cheshire*, I, 293–341 at 293–7.
[79] For a summary of the evidence, see Roffe, *Decoding Domesday*, 71–4.
[80] 'The Writing of Great Domesday Book'.
[81] For a summary, see Roffe, *Decoding Domesday*, 6–16.
[82] G. Garnett, *The Norman Conquest: a Very Short Introduction*, Oxford 2009; G. Garnett, *Conquered England: Kingship, Succession, and Tenure, 1066–1166*, Oxford 2007, 1–44; G. Garnett, 'What the Norman Conquest Can Teach Us about "Regime Change"', http://www.historyextra.com/oup/what-norman-conquest-can-teach-us-about-regime-change, accessed 08/07/2012; S. Baxter, *Domesday*, DVD, BBC, 2010; Harvey, *Domesday: Book of Judgement*, chapter 1 and passim.

English'.[83] Sally Harvey, in this volume (pp.278–80), argues that this is a perception that is inherent in the name 'Domesday' itself. She cites Richard fitzNigel's assertion in c.1179 that the word was understood by the English as 'the book of judgements' and argues that this was the reality of the inquest in 1086. Successive jurors of the vill, hundred, and shire were forced to recognize their own dispossession and that of their kinsmen, often by the humiliating process of the ordeal.

The jurors, then, according to this view of the Domesday inquest, were pawns at the mercy of predatory Norman kingship and lordship. They were unwilling participants in a process of legitimization of Norman interests. Alan Cooper has observed that their best defence was to know nothing.[84] Even then, though, they could not always resist the demands of their new lords; as Robin Fleming argued in the 1990s,[85] they had to represent their interests regardless of the merits of their right. For their part, tenants-in-chief are characterized as playing the system for all it was worth. In an analysis of the church of Worcester's chapter in the Worcestershire folios, Stephen Baxter has argued that they were not above subverting the Domesday process.[86] There the account begins with a partial statement of the liberties of the church and continues with a description of its manors that is clearly drawn from estate management records. The whole was evidently drafted by the church, as opposed to the commissioners, to the end of maximizing its interests.

The notion of 'cooking the Book' is an attractive one, not the least because of the resonance of the phrase, and has found favour widely.[87] It is, however, open to criticism, as Pamela Taylor points out in an examination of episcopal returns in this volume (p.197–217). There is little indication of systemic distortion. It has long been recognized that much of the Domesday data must have been presented by the tenants-in-chief themselves.[88] Local juries cannot have been au fait with the minutiae of estate structure and management and therefore by necessity they had to be provided by the lord. References to the process are found in both GDB and LDB, most commonly where 'no one answered' for the manor in question, and indeed variations in content and expression from chapter to chapter are apparent throughout. Self-assessment was an integral part of the process. It might be expected, then, that lords would present their interests in the best possible light. There were,

---

[83] *Dialogus de Scaccario, the Course of the Exchequer, and Constitutio Domus Regis, the King's Household*, ed. C. Johnson, London 1950, 62–3; *Matthei Parisiensis, Monachi Sancti Albani, Historia Anglorum*, ed. F. Madden, 3 vols, RS 44, 1866–8, III, 172.
[84] Cooper, 'Protestations of Ignorance', 169–82.
[85] R. Fleming, 'Oral Testimony and the Domesday Inquest', *ANS* 17, 1994, 101–22; Fleming, *Domesday Book and the Law*.
[86] Baxter, 'Representation of Lordship in Domesday Book'.
[87] Marten, 'The Impact of Rebellion on Little Domesday', 149; Taylor, 'Domesday Mortlake', 203–29; Palmer, below, pp.70–2; D. Pratt, 'Demesne Exemption from Royal Taxation in Anglo-Saxon and Anglo-Norman England', *EHR* 128, 2013, 1–34 at 17–18.
[88] Galbraith, *Making of Domesday Book*, 82, 119–20.

however, checks and balances, as Baxter himself is careful to note. The most important manorial statistics – geld assessment and possibly values – were a matter of record and were already available to the commissioners.[89] Above all, tenants-in-chief were not scoring off the English. Jurors of hundred and vill, French and English, as recorded in ICC and IE, were of a different social class and were therefore not in competition with their lords. Disputes, whether over land or dues, were predominantly between tenants-in-chief. Thus one lord's gain was another lord's loss and so in consequence subversion of the process must have been very difficult precisely because lords had a vested interest in a more or less equitable procedure. Tension between jurors and lords, beyond the usual anxieties of communal life, has probably been exaggerated. Indeed, tenants-in-chief must themselves have been jurors in the shire courts to which they were suitors: the verdicts of the shire that are intermittently found throughout the text are theirs.[90]

Sally Harvey does not recognize the participation of landholders in this way. She has, nevertheless, made a case for accountability.[91] The survey of boroughs in Domesday Book is very different in form and content from that of royal and seigneurial estates – in particular, there is much criticism of royal officials – and she sees the anomaly as evidence of an 'inquest of sheriffs' which she associates with a process of checking recorded by Robert of Hereford in a contemporary note.[92] A purge of local government in the initial stages of the inquest has been suggested before,[93] but Harvey sees it as a late initiative, probably after the Oath of Salisbury in early August 1086. For her one of the main outcomes of the survey was the documentation of the extent to which *curiales* in particular had encroached on the lands of English free men. In the face of a claim to the kingdom every bit as valid as his own, William the Conqueror saw in this a threat to the stability of his realm. Motivated by both conscience and expediency, he therefore determined to bring officials to book with the aim of legitimizing his regime in the eyes of the English.

There are later medieval precedents for such a procedure, but it may be doubted that reform of local government was a priority in the crisis of 1085/6 and its aftermath, much less attacks of conscience. The so-called 'satellite' texts that contain data on towns clearly shows that there was no special survey of boroughs (below pp. 30–3) and it is more likely that the complaints were the *querele* that all inquests generated.[94] There is a considerable body of evidence to suggest that the lands of

---

[89] Baxter, 'Representation of Lordship in Domesday Book', 81–2; Roffe, *Decoding Domesday*, 190–7, 240–50.
[90] Roffe, *Decoding Domesday*, 271–3.
[91] Harvey, *Domesday: Book of Judgement*, chapter 9.
[92] W. H. Stevenson, 'A Contemporary Description of the Domesday Survey', *EHR* 22, 1907, 72–84.
[93] Roffe, *Decoding Domesday*, 68–9.
[94] For a review and summary, see David Roffe, 'Inquests in Medieval England', *The Haskins Society Journal Japan* 4, 2011, 18–24.

the king and his regalia were the subject of a separate procedure: the Anglo-Saxon Chronicle implies a two-stage survey, Exon refers to an *inquisitio geldi*, the *terra regis* is absent from ICC, and the diplomatic and organization of the king's land in Domesday Book depart from the usual forms of the rest of the text. That this survey was earlier is indicated by the fact that the documentation that it produced, such as the Yorkshire Summary, ordered the data subsequently collected. It is in this initial survey that complaints against sheriffs were most likely recorded, although their misdeeds were not necessarily a primary concern.[95]

All this is consonant with the nature of the inquest. Its workings, both before Domesday as far as it can be perceived and after, was the starting point of my own reassessment of the Domesday process.[96] Twelfth-century and later experience suggests that abbreviations of inquest records were post hoc enterprises that were peripheral to the main concerns of the inquests. Domesday Book, both GDB and LDB, shows every sign of being no different. It omits the names of the sworn jurors, an essential prerequisite for admitting inquest records in court proceedings, and there are indications that GDB at least was written sometime after the death of William the Conqueror. I have argued that its compilation was probably undertaken in the reign of William Rufus, possibly c.1090 in the aftermath of the revolt of 1088 but conceivably anytime up to the early years of the reign of Henry I, for purely administrative purposes. The production of Domesday Book is unlikely to have been the aim of the Domesday inquest (below, pp.285–304).

The Domesday inquest finds its rationale in itself. Its concerns were manifold. First of all, there was the audit of regalia, the usual precursor of all the major inquests in the later Middle Ages, which was overseen by the sheriff and suitors of the communities of the shire in the shire court. Drawing on its records, the survey of seigneurial lands followed which was entrusted to commissioners appointed for the purpose in regional centres. For Galbraithians, the jurors' pronouncements are self-evidently judgements. However, determination of title and the like was not a central concern: where it figured at all large, it was a matter that was postponed for later consideration. The inquest interested itself in the simpler issue of tenure.[97] In common with both earlier and later inquests, the jurors' verdicts provided more or less agreed fact to inform subsequent decisions. The concerns of 1086 are neatly summarized by the little-regarded summaries of IE, Exon, and GDB itself. These documents, produced late in the Domesday process, total the number of manors

---

[95] David Roffe, 'A Profession of Ignorance: an Insight into Domesday Procedure in an Early Reference to the Inquest', in *Rulership and Rebellion in the Anglo-Norman World, c.1066–c.1216: Essays in Honour of Professor Edmund King*, ed. Paul Dalton and David Luscombe, Farnham 2015, 45–60.

[96] Roffe, *Domesday: the Inquest and the Book*. For summaries of the argument, see Roffe, 'Domesday: the Inquest and the Book'; D. R. Roffe, 'Domesday Now', *ANS* 28, 2006, 168–87.

[97] Roffe, 'A Profession of Ignorance', 45–60.

held by each tenant-in-chief, the assessment to the geld, increase in value since 1066, and the number of ploughlands county by county. They suggest that tax capacity and service were the main concerns of the king after the threat of invasion in the previous year.

For me, the Domesday enterprise was above all a communal enterprise. The crisis of 1085 had shown that the resources of the realm were not equal to the threats that confronted it. William had had to hire mercenaries to defend England and billet them on his barons and their men. Cash was needed to meet the expenditure, but above all measures were necessary to obviate such expedients in future. A meeting was held at Christmas in 1085 to agree on a plan of action. The Domesday inquest drew up an account of national resources and negotiations ensued at Salisbury in early August 1086. The result was agreement on the extension of the geld to seigneurial demesnes and a re-definition of knight service. The crisis of 1085 was a threat to the common weal and its organization and communal action was needed to meet it. The outcome was effectively a new social contract which was to define relations between the king and his subjects for the next hundred years or so.

In this I have been taken to task for downplaying the evidence of the contemporary narrative sources.[98] Yes, they clearly show that there was resentment at the levying of new imposts – when were taxes ever paid joyfully? – but that does not preclude a recognition of necessity and a process of consultation. Some historians, it seems, just prefer their medieval kings red in tooth and claw. The debate on the detail of my analysis, though, has largely centred on the date of Domesday Book. In 1996 Christopher Lewis discovered two entries in the Huntingdonshire and Surrey folios of GDB in which William de Warenne was styled earl.[99] Since William was not belted until sometime between late 1087 and mid 1088, it is clear that writing was still in progress at that time. The subsequent sequencing of GDB further suggests that much of the text must have been written after the death of William the Conqueror since the Huntingdonshire reference is just some 100 folios into the work. Galbraithians, however, have dismissed both passages as simple mistakes by the GDB scribe: they argue that he was anticipating later references to different earls.[100] Above all, they assert that, had Domesday Book been written much after 1086, it would have been updated and cite such additions as there are, notably the correction of the assessment of Pyrford in Surrey following its reduction by a charter of 1086, as evidence of a contemporary date.[101] It should be noted, though, that the

---

[98] A. Cooper, review of *Decoding Domesday*, *Speculum* 84, 2009, 491–2; Cooper, 'Professions of Ignorance', 170–1.

[99] C. P. Lewis, 'The Earldom of Surrey and the Date of Domesday Book', *Historical Research* 63, 1990, 327–36.

[100] Holt, 'Domesday Studies 2000', 23–4; Thorn and Thorn, 'The Writing of Great Domesday Book', 71.

[101] The arguments are most recently rehearsed in Harvey, *Domesday: Book of Judgement*, 96–100.

early breviates of the late eleventh and early twelfth centuries, as reported here by Howard Clarke (pp.247–75), were not revised in any way to reflect contemporary tenure. The Herefordshire Domesday of 1160–1170 was annotated with current information,[102] but generally throughout the medieval period abstracts of inquest records, Domesday or otherwise, were simple redacted copies. Even less do additions date the texts to which they are appended: the Pyrford charter, for example, logically provides a *terminus post quem* for the addition of the new assessment, but can hardly afford a *terminus ante quem* for the Domesday text into which it is inserted.[103]

If the date of Domesday Book has dominated debate, the issue of taxation has not been ignored. In the 1980s Sally Harvey argued from variations in the record of the geld that a re-assessment was under way in 1086.[104] David Pratt has most recently developed the argument.[105] He points out that the reduction apparent in many counties between 1066 and 1086 closely approximates to the extent of the land held in demesne by tenants-in-chief and argues therefrom that demesne exemption most likely has its origins in a royal grant dating from *c*.1085. Pratt relates the concession to 'the introduction of knight service', but fails to explain why it came so late in the reign of William the Conqueror. As Pratt himself admits, exemption was short-lived and a more likely scenario is that demesne exemption, if indeed so late, was simply a temporary *quid pro quo* in return for the billeting of mercenaries in 1085.

Knight service itself is still a concern that dares not speak its name; it has been studiously ignored.[106] However, in 2007 John Maddicott independently endorsed the notion of consensus and communal action – a king working with his subjects rather than in spite of them.[107] Placing the Domesday inquest firmly within the context of the events of 1085, he drew attention to a passage in William of Malmesbury's Life of St Wulfstan, previously noticed only by J. O. Prestwich,[108] that refers to a Council meeting called by William the Conqueror immediately after his return from Normandy in September 1085 to decide how to meet the emergency. It was on that occasion that, at the instigation of Lanfranc, it was decided to distribute the

---

[102] *The Herefordshire Domesday*, ed. V. H. Galbraith and J. Tait, Pipe Roll Society, ns 25, 1950.

[103] Roffe, *Decoding Domesday*, 56–7. As I have noted before, a (postscriptal) reference to the Pyrford charter here does not date the body of the article above to 1086.

[104] S. P. J. Harvey, 'Taxation and the Economy', in *Domesday Studies*, ed. Holt, 249–64. The case is re-stated in *Domesday: Book of Judgement*, 210–38.

[105] Pratt, 'Demesne Exemption', 1–34.

[106] C. P. Lewis, 'Recent Trends in the Historiography of Medieval Britain', *The Haskins Society Journal Japan* 5, 2013, 33–50 at 43. But see now Judith A. Green, review of Sally Harvey, *Domesday: Book of Judgement*, Oxford: OUP, 2015, *EHR* 130. 2015, 694-5.

[107] J. R. Maddicott, 'Responses to the Threat of Invasion, 1085', *EHR* 122, 2007, 986–97. Maddicott seems to have been unaware of similar arguments advanced in *Domesday: Inquest and Book*.

[108] J. O. Prestwich, *The Place of War in English History, 1066–1214* , ed. M. Prestwich, Woodbridge 2004, 114.

mercenaries among the households of the tenants-in-chief. Maddicott further analysed the actions that William took thereafter to secure his realm. Foremost among these was the replacement of ineffective clerics in East Anglia with men on whom he could rely. Here Ian Taylor (pp.147–53) explores this theme, arguing that the area was vulnerable to attack less because of ethnic solidarity with the invading Danes than because of a late Norman settlement that had failed to forge a new nexus of patronage.

The boroughs

Historiographically, the Domesday borough has always stood apart from the rest of Domesday studies. It has done so seemingly with good reason. Domesday Book is largely arranged by fee; settlements as such do not get much of a look-in. The borough, by contrast, is apparently described as a community and its seemingly special status is often signalled by its enrolment at the head of the county folios before the lands of the king. To all appearances it is indeed different in kind from the vill. It was usually constituted as a hundred in its own right and, although royal, many of its tenements were held by ecclesiastical and lay lords as appurtenances of rural, so-called 'contributory', manors. Maitland was the first to think critically about these characteristics.[109] He argued that the borough was predominantly a ninth- or tenth-century institution and its tenurial heterogeneity was a function of the provisions made for its defence by the men of the territory attached to it. By the eleventh century, trade had become the predominant activity and the burgesses belonging to the countryside were little more than a source of quitrents. Nevertheless, the borough remained a distinctive institution that demanded separate treatment in the Domesday inquest.

Maitland's 'garrison theory' of the origins of the borough has not met with general agreement.[110] The connections between borough and countryside are now more usually interpreted as a function of the need of rural lords to access urban markets.[111] A house in town was a useful asset and such links might come into being at any time: Domesday Book records their creation as late as 1066. However, that is not to say that some contributory manors may not attest earlier administrative and/or military arrangements. A recent examination of the connections between

---

[109] F. W. Maitland, *Domesday Book and Beyond*, Cambridge 1997, 213–63; F. W. Maitland, *Township and Borough*, Cambridge 1898.

[110] James Tait's unfavourable review of *Domesday Book and Beyond*, EHR 12, 1897, 768–77, has rarely been challenged, even though he was not quite so trenchant in his views in *The Medieval English Borough*, Manchester 1936. His mature attitude, it seems, was less that the phenomenon of contributory manors could not attest a concern with defence than that it did so invariably.

[111] Of recent studies, see, for example, S. Bassett, 'Anglo-Saxon Warwick', *Midland History* 34, 2009, 123–55.

Wallingford and its hinterland has suggested that the best interpretation of the twenty-six tenements in the borough that belonged to manors in Oxfordshire east of the river Thame is that the borough's early tenth-century territory extended across the Thames.[112] There is no intrinsic reason why rural manors might not as well forge links with the borough for military and administrative reasons. Richard Holt's analysis of Worcester has suggested that *hagae* in the city had always been the primary estate nuclei of resident lords to which rural manors were appurtenant.[113] Defence was the essence of the relationship.

Outside of the Danelaw archaeologists have singularly failed to find evidence of the early urbanization that many of Maitland's critics have presupposed. Many, and archaeologists in particular, are thus now more willing to accept a wider interpretation of the phenomenon of contributory manors.[114] Dogmatic analysis of distributions should, nevertheless, be avoided. There is a tendency to treat all tenements of the kind as equal. They were not. Domesday makes the distinction between customary and non-customary and the assumption is often made that contributory manors were always of the latter kind. The reality was more complex. The customs that were reserved varied from town to town and tenement to tenement and some that rendered 'all' might equally be attached to rural manors.[115] Even those at the other end of the scale were not uniform. Some properties were urban liberties – sokes – with their own urban courts that merely shared a lord with a rural manor, while others were simple tenements that owed suit to a rural manorial court. The contrasting types of tenement are often differently represented on the ground, the one being compact, often with a proprietary church, and the other dispersed, and look like phenomena with very different origins.[116] In either case, those origins might as easily be early as late.

The garrison theory has proved contentious. Otherwise, Maitland's explanation for the special treatment of the Domesday borough has, until recently, been accepted.[117] It has been held that it was surveyed as a community and enrolled

---

[112] D. R. Roffe, 'Wallingford in Domesday Book and Beyond', in *The Origins of the Borough of Wallingford: Archaeological and Historical Perspectives*, ed. K. S. B. Keats-Rohan and D. R. Roffe, British Archaeological Reports, British Series 494, 2009, 27–51.

[113] R. Holt, 'The Urban Transformation in England, 900–1100', *ANS* 32, 2009, 57–78.

[114] Jeremy Haslam, *Urban-Rural Connections in Domesday Book and Late Anglo-Saxon Royal Administration*, British Archaeological Reports, British Series 571, Oxford 2012, sees every eleventh-century link to a rural manor as evidence for at least late ninth-century military arrangements.

[115] Roffe, *Decoding Domesday*, 120–7.

[116] See, for example, Winchester (*Winchester in the Early Middle Ages: an Edition and Discussion of the Winton Domesday*, ed. M. Biddle, Winchester Studies, I, Oxford 1976) and Canterbury (W. Urry, *Canterbury under the Angevin Kings*, London 1967).

[117] G. H. Martin, 'Domesday Book and the Boroughs', in *Domesday Book: a Reassessment*, ed. Sawyer, 143–63; S. Reynolds, 'Towns in Domesday', in *Domesday Studies*, ed. Holt, 295–310. See also, Harvey, *Domesday: Book of Judgement*, chapter 9.

as a community because of its special characteristics. His paradigm has now been challenged. I have endeavoured to show that in reality the institution was not treated in any uniform way in Domesday Book.[118] Far from being the norm, the composite entry is only sporadically found: in some counties the whole borough is enrolled 'above the line' in Maitland's phrase, but in the majority, forty-eight out of sixty-one settlements characterized by tenurial heterogeneity, a greater or lesser number of entries appear in the body of the text in the chapter of the lord who held the tenement in question. Moreover, examination of the text and its forms reveals that even the composite entries are derived from a variety of sources. Non-customary tenements, the lands of tenants-in-chief, are normally distinguished from customary, the king's lands, by paragraphoi (gallows marks), usually an indicator of exceptional material derived from a separate source, and schedules of land are often appended at some point subsequent to initial drafting. Such characteristics do not suggest a single, communal survey, and indeed the surviving inquest records – Exon, ICC, IE, DM – indicate that the various items of data were collected in much the same way as their rural equivalents, that is, from both communal presentments and seigneurial returns. I conclude that there was no special procedure for the Domesday borough.

For the Domesday commissioners, then, there was no especial burghal community. As represented in Domesday Book, the borough was largely a creation of the GDB scribe.[119] The composite account first appears in the Norfolk folios (there in the king's chapter), but it was the GDB scribe who enthusiastically took up the form and cobbled together descriptions where his sources allowed him. He had no particular interest in the institution, though, *per se*. There were other categories of data which he enrolled at the head of the county folios. In Cheshire the laws of Chester were entered there, in Kent the lands of St Martin of Dover, and in Gloucestershire and Herefordshire lands in Wales. Above all, there are various summary accounts of the income of the king from the shire as a whole in a dozen or so counties. What is common to all of these data is that the sheriff was directly responsible for the issues of each. The scribe was clearly ordering his materials to compile a work of reference for administration of the shire.[120] His programme is most fully realized in the preliminaries to the Worcestershire folios.[121] First the borough is described and then comes a statement of the value of the city, the demesne manors in the shire, the shire farm and pleas. There follow comments on the yield of hundreds, the king's peace, and finally a statement of military customs. The Domesday borough is evidently a scribal artefact.

---

[118] Roffe, *Decoding Domesday*, 113–19.
[119] V. H. Galbraith, *Domesday Book: Its Place in Administrative History*, Oxford 1974, 152–3.
[120] Roffe, *Decoding Domesday*, 127–32. Cf. J. C. Holt, '1086', in *Domesday Studies*, ed. Holt, 41–64 at 50–2.
[121] GDB, 172: WOR B.

This analysis has informed the examination of several borough entries anew. Understood as accounts of communities, many have been confusing or positively misleading. They make more sense as collections of disparate sources, as Julian Munby has confirmed.[122] The account of Wallingford, for example, has been shown to consist of five distinct elements, at least two of which probably duplicate material. The estimated size of the borough has been readjusted downwards accordingly.[123] The apparent absence of London and Winchester also makes somewhat more sense. For both cities, tenements belonging to manors are described in the body of the text, in much the same way as for other boroughs in which there is no composite account. What is missing is an account of the tenements that paid their dues to the king, presumably little more than a total number of messuages. Had the scribe compiled composite accounts, it is unlikely that we would have had much more than we have already.[124]

Although it is almost de rigueur to bemoan the inadequacy of the Domesday account of boroughs, the text has allowed some remarkably detailed reconstructions of urban space in the eleventh century when interpreted in the light of later sources and archaeological and topographical evidence. In the last few years there have been significant studies of, *inter alia*, Droitwich, Gloucester, Grantham, Norwich, Oxford, Stafford, Wallingford, Warwick, and Worcester.[125] All in one way or another reveal the different types of tenement that are to be found in the Domesday borough and how they relate to rural estates.

Lords and land

The publication of Katharine Keats-Rohan's Continental Origins of English Landholders (COEL) database on CDROM in 2002 brought together all the then

---

[122] J. Munby, 'The Domesday Boroughs Revisited', *ANS* 33, 2011, 127–49.
[123] Roffe, 'Wallingford in Domesday'.
[124] Roffe, *Decoding Domesday*, 119; J. Munby, 'Winchester in Domesday Book', in *Intersections: The Archaeology and History of Christianity in England, 400–1200: Papers in Honour of Martin Biddle and Birthe Kjølbye-Biddle*, ed. M. Henig and N. Ramsay, British Archaeological Reports, British Series 505, 213–18.
[125] S. Bassett, 'Sitting above the Salt: the Origins of the Borough of Droitwich', in *A Commodity of Good Names: Essays in Honour of Margaret Gelling*, ed. O. J. Padel and D. N. Parsons, Donington 2008, 3–27; N. Baker and R. Holt, *Urban Growth and the Medieval Church: Gloucester and Worcester*, Aldershot 2004; D. R. Roffe, 'The Early History of Grantham', in *The Making of Grantham: the Medieval Town*, ed. D. Start and D. Stocker, Heritage Lincolnshire, Heckington 2011, 21–38; B. Ayers, 'The Growth of an Urban Landscape: Recent Research in Early Medieval Norwich', *Early Medieval Europe* 19, 2011, 62–90; J. Haslam, 'The Two Anglo-Saxon Burhs of Oxford', *Oxoniensia* 75, 2010, 15–34; M. Carver, *The Birth of a Borough: an Archaeological Study of Anglo-Saxon Stafford*, Woodbridge 2010; Roffe, 'Wallingford in Domesday'; S. Bassett, 'Anglo-Saxon Fortifications in Western Mercia', *Midland History* 36, 2011, 1–23; Bassett, 'Anglo-Saxon Warwick'.

readily available primary and secondary sources for landholders in 1086 and their successors up to 1166 along with a mass of new research.[126] The Domesday dataset extracts the salient details of each holder – tenant, predecessor, place, hundred, assessment, and value – and the data are linked to contemporary continental sources and the subsequent history of the individuals and their families as evidenced in charters and surveys, which are transcribed *in extenso*, and the Pipe Rolls. Regularly updated and soon to be re-engineered for online access, COEL provides the most comprehensive prosopography of Anglo-Norman England to date. The character of the Norman settlement is now clearer than ever before. Keats-Rohan has demonstrated that there were little more than 1900 individuals of continental origin who held land in 1086 according to Domesday Book. Not all, of course, were Normans, but the most important among them were in the inner ducal circle or had close connections with it. By and large, this class remained endogamous in England. Among those who accompanied them and settled on their lands were the men, lower in the social hierarchy but of key importance none the less, who specialized in local administration. These were the ones who intermarried with the English – more frequently from the second generation onward – and began the slow process of integration.[127]

England's was a tightly stratified society in 1086. Writing in 1926 Corbett classified tenants-in-chief by wealth and concluded that the top-ranking tenants-in-chief were distinguished from the vast majority by their great wealth. There was an elite within the elite.[128] Corbett's analysis, however, has recently been criticized by John Palmer.[129] Much of the land that barons held was enfeoffed and therefore its value, as recorded in Domesday Book, was not available to them. With such adjustments made, an analysis of disposable income indicates that there was a much greater continuity of wealth between the richest tenants-in-chief, other barons, and their tenants. Palmer concludes that William the Conqueror ensured that wealth was more evenly distributed than previously suspected and that a gentry of honorial barons and tenants already existed in 1086.

In highlighting the importance of enfeoffed land, Palmer provides an important

---

[126] K. S. B. Keats-Rohan, *The Continental Origins of English Landholders 1066–1166 Database and the COEL Database System on CDROM*, Coel Enterprises Ltd, 2002. The Domesday names are also available in print as K. S. B. Keats-Rohan, *Domesday People: a Prosopography of Persons Occurring in English Documents, 1066–1166: I. Domesday Book*, Woodbridge 1998.

[127] K. S. B. Keats-Rohan, 'Portrait of a People: Norman Barons Revisited', in *Domesday*, ed. Hallam and Bates, 121–40; K. S. B. Keats-Rohan, 'Domesday People Revisited', in *Foundations: Newsletter of the Foundation for Medieval Genealogy* 4, 2012, 3–20; K. S. B. Keats-Rohan, 'The Impact of the Norman Conquest on Naming in England', in *Anthroponymie et déplacements dans la Chrétienté médiévale*, ed. Monique Bourin and Pascual Martínez Sopena, Collection de la Casa de Velázquez 115, Madrid 2010, 213–28.

[128] W. J. Corbett, 'The Development of the Duchy of Normandy and the Norman Conquest of England', in *Cambridge Medieval History* 5, Cambridge 1926, 481–520.

[129] J. J. N. Palmer, 'The Wealth of the Secular Aristocracy in 1086', *ANS* 22, 2000, 279–91.

corrective to earlier views. Nevertheless, his analysis makes certain assumptions about the nature of tenure in 1086 that may be questioned. First, it is clear that enfeoffees were not a homogeneous group. The record is far from even and it seems likely that in many fees, probably most, only the honorial baronage was recorded. Below them were probably subtenants who are generally omitted from the text.[130] This might suggest that the distribution of wealth was even flatter than Palmer indicates. Crucially, however, it is not clear what sort of share they had in the lands. It is unlikely that either class had unequivocal hereditary right in 1086 and their lords may have retained interests in the issues of the estates that they held. Thus, in some instances manorial values were sums that went into the pocket of the tenant-in-chief rather than those of his men. The nature of Domesday values is discussed below (pp.50–2).

In addition to the newcomers there were probably as many again of English origin who held land after the Conquest. Only a handful were of baronial status, the majority being entered as *taini regis* of one kind or another. As holders of small amounts of land, they have proved difficult to identify as individuals, not the least since their successors are hard to trace. Ann Williams showed in 1994 that they were predominantly *ministri* who had been essential to estate administration in the early years of the Norman settlement.[131] Hugh Thomas has subsequently argued that with the passage of time they proved less useful and they were then systematically disseized of their estates. He concludes that there were few English lords of manors by 1100.[132] By contrast, I have produced evidence to show that in Lincolnshire and elsewhere English families held sokages of manorial proportions in much greater numbers than is immediately apparent from the feudal documentation of the twelfth and thirteenth centuries. Although they did not hold by knight service, and are thus invisible in the sources, they were every bit as much a part of county society as their Norman counterparts.[133]

The pre-Conquest names present more difficult problems of identification. Unlike their post-Conquest counterparts, they are largely undifferentiated in the text and the identity and status of their referents have to be inferred. Various techniques have been developed by Ann Williams and formulated by Christopher Lewis.[134] Titles and by-names are used where they are found, but assumptions have

---

[130] Keats-Rohan, *Domesday People*, 24–6.
[131] A. Williams, *The English and the Norman Conquest*, Woodbridge 1994.
[132] H. M. Thomas, 'The Significance and Fate of the Native English Landholders of 1086', *EHR* 118, 2003, 303–33 at 306–7
[133] D. R. Roffe, 'Hidden Lives: English Lords in post-Conquest Lincolnshire and Beyond', in *The English and Their Legacy, 900–1200: Essays in Honour of Ann Williams*, ed. D. R. Roffe, Woodbridge 2012, 205–28.
[134] C. P. Lewis, 'Joining the Dots: a Methodology for Identifying the English in Domesday Book', in *Family Trees and the Roots of Politics: the Prosopography of Britain and France from the Tenth to the Twelfth Century*, ed. K. S. B. Keats-Rohan, Woodbridge 1997, 69–87.

otherwise to be made. Individuals whose lands passed to a single post-Conquest lord are likely to be the same person, as are people of the same name who held lands in close proximity. Family relationships are sometimes explicit, but are only otherwise suggested by multiple manor entries.

By means of such clues, John Palmer has identified some 2000 persons in the most comprehensive study of the data to date.[135] By necessity, many of the identifications are tentative – sometimes the only evidence is proximity, the least robust indicator of identity – and toponymics are supplied, often seemingly arbitrarily. Imponderables there are many. Nevertheless, all the available evidence is drawn together, including the relatively few references in contemporary sources other than Domesday Book, to provide the best guide to pre-Conquest holders of land. The 'Doomed Elite Project', the results of which will be incorporated into the Prosopography of Anglo-Saxon England (PASE) database, is ploughing the same furrow.[136] It is specifically designed as a search engine for individuals and returns the names of estates, assessment to the geld, and value in 1066 and 1086, reporting in both graphical and tabular forms. In future it promises a more systematic coverage of the data and a new statistical analysis of distribution to introduce rigour into the assessment of proximity. At the present moment, however, detailed analyses have yet to be published and the available system is little more than an onomasticon.

The identification of individuals and families is a preliminary to a study of the dynamics of power in the localities, but neither project has as yet essayed such a prosopography of pre-Conquest England. Ann Williams has shown the potential in numerous local and regional studies of individual families.[137] Her work has revealed how local elites maintained relations with the crown on the one hand and their subordinates in the localities on the other. Amongst others, Stephen Baxter, Lucy Marten, and Andrew Wareham have also produced some first-rate local and regional studies of individuals and families.[138] Key to such studies is the status of pre-Conquest holders of land. In a study of Engelric and the foundation of St Martin le Grand in London, Pamela Taylor has cast doubt on the integrity of the data since lands that are known to have belonged to Engelric are ascribed to

---

[135] http://discover.ukdataservice.ac.uk/catalogue?sn=5694, Ids information, accessed 03/10/2015. The dataset can be downloaded directly from https://hydra.hull.ac.uk/resources/hull:/domesdayTranslation. For Domesday entries in PASE, see http://domesday.pase.ac.uk/, accessed 03/10/2015.

[136] http://www.kcl.ac.uk/artshums/depts/history/research/proj/profile.aspx, accessed 14/07/2012.

[137] See A. Williams, *The World before Domesday: the English Aristocracy 900–1066*, London 2008, for a recent overview.

[138] S. Baxter, *The Earls of Mercia: Lordship and Power in Late Anglo-Saxon England*, Oxford 2007; L. Marten, 'Meet the Swarts', in *The English and Their Legacy*, ed. Roffe, 17–32; A. Wareham, *Lords and Communities in Early Medieval East Anglia*, Woodbridge 2005.

others in Domesday Book.[139] It is now clear that this apparent conundrum lies at the heart of the matter: there was a hierarchy of tenure. Although there have been throw-backs to earlier views,[140] it is now generally agreed that free men who 'could go with their land' did not hold their estates untrammelled by obligations to others. Lordship and land, and the jurisdiction over it, were not unitary concepts. Based on a study of the articulation of *soca*, *commendatio*, and *terra* in the transfer of land from English to Norman holders, I have argued that there were two basic types of lordship over free men and, beyond a demesne, neither devolved upon land *qua* real estate.[141] Soke represented the right to food rents that the king enjoyed from all land. It might be granted to a king's thegn and was held by him as bookland in return for personal service to the king. The lord himself might then grant it outright to a third party or loan it to one of his men, a median thegn, as *laenland*, that is loan-land. Commendation, by contrast, created a personal bond between a lord and his man. It was indissoluble except by death and warranted the law-worthiness of a free man in return for service to the lord. Beyond a demesne, neither relationship was identified with land unless the tenants were unfree. Land itself, although burdened with dues that were owed from it, was generally vested in the free man.

This picture, derived from Domesday evidence, is consistent with the law codes which distinguish the *landhlaford* or *landrica*, the soke lord, from the *hlaford*, the commendation lord. Soke, and the right to *consuetudines*, 'customs', that it conferred, was a fundamental bond between men and the king, as the careful record of its holders in some Domesday counties reveals.[142] Nicholas Brooks has most recently shown just how precisely it articulated military service, a fundamental correlate of bookland, owed by the archbishop of Canterbury to the crown before the Conquest.[143] Nevertheless, Stephen Baxter has doubted that all land was in some sense 'sokeland'.[144] He emphasizes, rightly, that commendation was a significant social and political bond, but does not assign an equally significant role to *soca*. In consequence he has atomized the various relationships. Bookland for him is land, in the modern sense, granted by charter and a separate entity from sokeland or

---

[139] P. Taylor, 'Ingelric, Count Eustace and the Foundation of St Martin-le-Grand', *ANS* 24, 2001, 215–37.

[140] S. Reynolds, 'Bookland, Folkland and Fiefs', *ANS* 14, 1992, 211–27; S. Oosthuizen, 'Sokemen and Freemen: Tenure, Status, and Landscape Conservatism in Eleventh-Century Cambridgeshire', in *Anglo-Saxons: Studies Presented to Cyril Roy Hart*, ed. S. Keynes and A. P. Smyth, Dublin 2005, 186–207; K. A. Bailey, 'Vendere potuit : "He could sell", to Coin a Domesday Phrase', *Records of Buckinghamshire* 40, 2000, 73–88.

[141] D. R. Roffe, 'From Thegnage to Barony: Sake and Soke, Title, and Tenants-in-Chief', *ANS* 12, 1989, 157–76; Roffe, *Decoding Domesday*, 147–63.

[142] Roffe, *Decoding Domesday*, 144–82; Williams, *The World before Domesday*, 75–84.

[143] N. Brooks, 'The Archbishopric of Canterbury and the So-called Introduction of Knight Service into England', *ANS* 34, 2011, 41–62 at 53–4.

[144] Baxter, *Earls of Mercia*, 204–69.

whatever and, on the basis of four ninth- and tenth-century references introduces the further category of folkland to describe comital estates.[145]

It might be noted that, although comital land was not heritable in the same way as bookland, it was similarly held with all customs. Soke was evidently not an archaic survival in the late eleventh century as has been claimed. However the categories of tenure were articulated, it is nevertheless clear that any one individual might hold land in various capacities.[146] The techniques for identifying the different types have been summarized by myself.[147] Commendation is only explicit in Circuits III and VII and, as a personal bond, it is difficult to spot elsewhere. Sokeright is somewhat more easily identifiable. In Derbyshire, Nottinghamshire, Lincolnshire, Yorkshire, and Kent there are lists of holders of sake and soke which identify king's thegns and there are references intermittently throughout the text. I have argued that the simple *X tenuit* formula is also an indicator, albeit not necessarily an intentional one. Those who enjoyed soke and soke are almost invariably said to hold their land without qualification, while those who held in the soke or lordship of others are said to 'hold freely', be able 'to go with their land', or to hold with some other qualification. Accidental omission of such riders is, of course, always a possibility, but on the whole the simple *tenuit* formula seems accurately to identify land that was in one way or another quit. This includes comital land, loanland, and land held in free alms. But tenures of this kind can generally be easily detected from other characteristics of the entries in which they are described, leaving lists of king's thegns who are not otherwise identifiable.[148] These provide a resource for prosopographical analysis independent of family history that has not yet been exploited.

In the light of this more sophisticated understanding of pre-Conquest lordship, Robin Fleming's computer-aided analysis of the tenurial revolution that informed so much thinking on the Norman Conquest in the late twentieth century is no longer tenable.[149] Largely based upon the incidence of commendation in Circuits III and VII, it pointed to aggressive free enterprise as the main motor of the Norman settlement. However, Domesday Book itself repeatedly asserts that commendation was independent of land tenure – *plus ça change* – and Fleming failed to notice underlying soke structures that were not. The *clamores* of Circuit VI reveal that the

---

[145] S. Baxter and J. Blair, 'Land Tenure and Royal Patronage in the Early English Kingdom: a Model and a Case Study', *ANS* 28, 2005, 19–46.

[146] For a diagrammatic representation, see Baxter, *Earls of Mercia*, 212, and Baxter, 'Lordship and Justice in Late Anglo-Saxon England: the Judicial Functions of Soke and Commendation Revisited', in *Early Medieval Studies in Memory of Patrick Wormald*, ed. S. Baxter, C. Karkov, J. L. Nelson, and D. Pelteret, Farnham 2009, 383–420 at 391.

[147] Roffe, *Decoding Domesday*, 287–91.

[148] Baxter's objection to this analysis seems to amount to the fact that the formula is not 100 per cent predictive; see *Earls of Mercia*, 238–40.

[149] R. Fleming, *Kings and Lords in Conquest England*, Cambridge 1991.

right to sake and soke trumped all other claims to land in the northern Danelaw, short of direct grant by the king or some other transaction directly sanctioned by him.[150] In this volume (pp.155–68) Ann Williams shows how soke also determined the transfer of land from *antecessor* to tenant-in-chief between 1066 and 1086 in Cambridgeshire. The apparent free-for-all of the county folios, held up by Fleming as a prime example of Norman lawlessness, is an illusion, as is George Garnett's characterization of Domesday continuity as largely Norman propaganda.[151] With the ready identification of king's thegns, it can now be seen that this mechanism was widespread.[152] There were, of course, instances where lordships and castleries were created by the grant of a whole area. The counties of Kent, Cornwall and Cheshire, the rapes of Sussex and the marcher lordships on the Welsh borders are obvious cases; others might be suggested. Even in such circumstances, though, there may often be pre-Conquest antecedents. Katharine Keats-Rohan shows that the castlery of Richmond was founded in Anglo-Saxon tenures (below, pp.190–3). A consensus is emerging that antecession, the grant of the sokeright of one or more king's thegns, to a single tenant-in-chief, with all the lands of median thegns that that entailed, was the normal method of land transfer in the early stages of the Norman settlement, be it on a regional or local basis. It also remained a significant mechanism subsequently.[153]

It seems that it was English law and English tenures that informed the Norman settlement. This realization has resurrected older debates about the origins of knight service. Sokeright, of course, presupposed attendance on the king with a detachment of armed men and so it is not inherently unlikely that the honour inherited the obligation as it did the right. Indeed, in twelfth-century legal tracts tenure by barony is defined in terms of sake and soke.[154] Nicholas Brooks has argued from charter evidence as well as Domesday Book that there was direct continuity in the lands of the archbishop of Canterbury.[155]

Such continuity makes sense of the Domesday inquest's (if not Domesday Book's) pre-occupation with the manor. Maitland famously hypothesized that a manor was 'a house against which geld was charged', but despite an attempt to

---

[150] Roffe, *Domesday: Inquest and Book*, 28–46.
[151] Garnett, *Conquered England*, 24–33.
[152] Roffe, *Decoding Domesday*, 163–75; A. Williams, 'Meet the *Antecessores*: Lordship and Land in Eleventh-Century Suffolk', in *Anglo-Saxons: Studies Presented to Cyril Roy Hart*, ed. Keynes and Smyth, 275–84. For Williams's reservations, see Roffe, *Decoding Domesday*, 174 n.
[153] J. A. Green, *The Aristocracy of Norman England*, Cambridge 1997, 48–99.
[154] R. R. Reid, 'Barony and Thanage', *EHR* 35, 1920, 161–99; Roffe, 'Thegnage to Barony'.
[155] N. P. Brooks, 'Archbishopric of Canterbury', 41–62. Pratt, 'Demesne Exemption', 9 n.53, criticizes the paper on the ground that the relationship only entailed soke, but this misses the import of the term.

resurrect the concept in the 1980s, the idea has not met with general acceptance.[156] The predominant view has been that the manor probably had no technical meaning and there is a tendency to see it as a Norman innovation. Domesday Book provides abundant evidence of apparent 'manorialization' between 1066 and 1086 in the appropriation of the lands of free men and the like.[157] Christopher Lewis has added substance to the argument by pointing out that the term *manerium* was itself a neologism in 1086.[158] He accepts that the GDB scribe made various attempts to define an institution, as outlined above (p.16), but maintains that this official usage was offset by a private one, indicating that the term was coined to represent the new rights that lords had acquired in the lands that they held after the Conquest.

Against this, however, there are numerous characteristics, notably the apparent incorporation of free men into manors before 1066, that point to an institution with a pre-Conquest identity. In the North it is clear that sokemen, the Circuit VI equivalent of free men, owed dues to their lords TRE. The same must have been true of the free men and sokemen of Circuits III and VII, for they too have a 1066 value and, significantly, the GDB scribe enrolled them in much the same terms (below, pp.85–92).[159] Elsewhere it can often be shown that *liberi homines* owed soke dues of one kind or another to their lord's hall. Above all, the *manerium* is invariably accorded a value for the same time. What evidence there is suggests that *heall*, 'hall', or possibly *heafod botl*, 'head house', was the name that the English used.[160] David Pratt suggests that *manerium* was adopted to reflect the new exemption of demesne in 1086.[161]

This was the starting point for a re-assessment of the manor by myself.[162] I have defined it as 'a point of interception of soke dues'. Manor as soke nexus, TRE as well as TRW, is clearest in the North where it organizes the Domesday text. There are indications, however, that there were similar structures throughout the country (see below, pp.92–6). The Domesday commissioners took an especial interest in them. Intermittently land is said to be held for so many manors, with a careful note being made of what had been added or taken away, and it is often clear that a set number

---

[156] Maitland, *Domesday Book and Beyond*, 140–63; Palmer, 'Domesday Manor'.
[157] The case has been recently restated by Stephen Baxter, 'Lordship and Labour', in *A Social History of England, 900–1200*, ed. J. Crick and E. van Houts, Cambridge 2011, 98–114 at 105–7.
[158] C. P. Lewis, 'The Invention of the Manor in Norman England', *ANS* 34, 2012, 123–50.
[159] *Pace* Oosthuizen, 'Sokemen and Freemen'.
[160] F. M. Stenton, *Anglo-Saxon England*, 3rd edn, Oxford 1971, 480–1. It is tempting, though, to equate this term with the *capitale manerium* of Domesday Book (GDB, 11, 18, 26, 41v, 58, 104, 163, 164, 166, 173, 173v, 181, 223, 367v, 377: KEN 5,192; SSX. 9,4; 12,6. HAM 3,9; BRK 1,46; DEV 6,13; GLS 1,24. 52.19,1; WOR 2,41;55; HEF 1,61; NTH 18,8. LIN 57,14. CK 27).
[161] Pratt, 'Demesne Exemption', 14–15.
[162] Roffe, *Domesday: Inquest and Book*, 239–41; *Decoding Domesday*, 176–82.

had been given to a tenant-in-chief. The totals recorded in the summaries indicate that such sums were a key statistic. I would suggest that the Domesday commissioners were interested in the manor because, as a measure of what were ultimately regalian rights, it was a proxy for service.

In these terms the Norman settlement saw more of an evolution in tenure rather than the revolution that has informed many discourses on the period. George Garnett has made much of the supposedly novel claim by William the Conqueror that all land was held by the crown.[163] In reality, there was a pre-Conquest precedent. King's thegns forfeited their lands to the king if they failed to render the service they owed; bookland itself was thus a dependent tenure.[164] For me, what does seem to mark a significant departure is the Oath of Salisbury of August 1086. In contrast to J. C. Holt who saw it as 'the final seal on the Norman occupation',[165] I have argued that the agreements, and the homage that was sworn to formalize them, created a new tenurial nexus.[166] The king demanded allegiance from 'all those who held land in England' and in so doing effectively forged links with tenants-in-chief and undertenants alike that created, in Old English terms, bookland. Hereditability became a reality, if not in the short term, then in the course of the next twenty or so years. The result was a new relationship between lordship and land. By the early twelfth century lordship had become territorialized and all the incidents that characterized Domesday society – soke, commendation and the like – had largely disappeared.

Settlements, land, and taxation

Like the post-Conquest personal names, place-names were one of the first targets of antiquarian and later academic study of the Domesday texts. Less than 700 names, out of a total of some 29,000, remain to be identified and that number gets smaller every year. The Domesday corpus of names remains a fundamental source for place-name scholars and they continue to be studied as a source for development of orthographies and the like. Colin Flight, for example, has argued that the Latinizing programme of the GDB scribe influenced the forms of place-names in official English documents for the next hundred years.[167] He also draws attention to

---

[163] Garnett, *Conquered England*.
[164] Roffe, *Decoding Domesday*, 152–3. This must, in part, account for the resumption of royal lands noted by R. Lavelle, 'Royal Control and the Distribution of Estates in Tenth-Century England: Reflections on the Charters of King Eadwig (955–959)', *The Haskins Society Journal* 23, 2011, 23–49 at 34–41.
[165] Holt, '1086', 56.
[166] Roffe, *Decoding Domesday*, 179–82.
[167] Flight, *Survey of Kent*, 27–32.

use of the text for vernacular French of the period, a theme that has been taken up by Keith Briggs in two articles on place-names.[168]

The referents of these names continue to provoke discussion. It is now, of course, widely recognized that Domesday place-names do not always point exclusively to discrete nucleated settlements. Some are clearly estate names and as such embrace a number of settlements. In the south and west ancient ecclesiastical estates might embrace vast tracks of land. The role of the vill, in its various local manifestations, in identifying names has proved more problematic. It seems uncontroversial in Cambridgeshire, and yet Caroline Thorn has argued that, by contrast, the twelve-carucate hundred of the northern shires was not used to identify entries: she interprets the *hundredum* of entries such as 'In Gelston hundred…' as parenthetical, connoting that the estate name Gelston was also a hundred name.[169] This reading, however, would seem to be unsustainable in those many cases were the actual location of the estate was different from the settlement that named the hundred. There remains abundant evidence, not considered by Thorn, that it was the hundred that determined entry formation.[170] Conversely, there are instances in which settlement names are explicitly used by the Domesday scribe. It seems safest to conclude that there was no uniform pattern, but that estate, vill, and settlement names were all used, often in the same contexts, depending on the documentation available and the underlying pattern of lordship.[171]

Domesday Book is emphatically not a gazetteer of eleventh-century settlement. Settlement structure must be inferred from other Domesday data. In 1994 Nicholas Higham argued that the phenomenon of overstocking, the excess of working ploughs over ploughlands, was indicative of dispersed settlement.[172] However, there seems to be no great correlation of the data with areas that are known or suspected to have been so characterized in the eleventh century. Mark Bailey has used manorial history to suggest that some free holdings in Suffolk are represented by isolated farms and Mary Hesse has used the insight to investigate the distribution of dispersed and nucleated settlement throughout the county, albeit with equivocal results.[173] Archaeology has provided further clues. The development of settlement archaeology is beyond the

---

[168] K. Briggs, 'The Domesday Book Castle LVVRE', *Journal of the English Place-Name Society* 40, 2008, 113–18; K. Briggs, 'Clare, Clere, and Clères', *Journal of the English Place-Name Society* 41, 2009, 7–25.

[169] J. J. N. Palmer, *Electronic Edition of Domesday Book: Translation, Databases and Scholarly Commentary, 1086*, 2nd edn, 2010, Economic and Social Data Service, Study Number 5694, http://discover.ukdataservice.ac.uk/catalogue?sn=5694, accessed 03/10/2015, LIN, Introduction: small hundreds.

[170] Ibid., NTT, Introduction: small hundreds.

[171] Roffe, *Decoding Domesday*, 184–90.

[172] N. Higham, 'The Domesday Survey: Context and Purpose', *History* 78, 1993, 7–21.

[173] M. Bailey, 'Introduction', in *Little Domesday Book, Suffolk*, 9–30 at 21; M. Hesse, 'Domesday Settlement in Suffolk', *Landscape History* 25, 2003, 45–57.

scope of this survey. Suffice it to say that considerable advances have been made in the understanding of processes of nucleation and its chronology in the last ten years with numerous multi-disciplinary projects targeted on the problem. What has emerged with direct relevance to Domesday studies is that settlement elements in the landscape often correlate with Domesday entries. David Stocker and Paul Everson, for example, have used village plan analysis to show that each manor often had its own space within the landscape of the village with its dependent tofts clustered around it.[174] It cannot always be demonstrated whether this pattern was contemporary with the Domesday inquest, later nucleation always being a possibility. Nevertheless, the pattern goes to show that Domesday Book is not entirely divorced from settlement types as some discussions of Domesday place-names have tended to suggest.

If Domesday Book's record of settlement is equivocal, it has usually been seen as a comprehensive account of land. It is, of course, axiomatic that there were omissions. The precincts of ancient religious houses, for example, are regularly absent from the text. Such omissions, if remarked at all, are usually ascribed to procedural glitches or simple carelessness on the part of the compilers. But where estates are described – and above all Domesday Book is, it is asserted, about estates – it is assumed that all of their lands, be they exempt demesnes or assessed tenancies, are represented in one way or another in their geld assessment. Where Domesday describes estates, it does so in full. Thus it is that the hide, carucate, or sulung becomes, if not exactly a precise measure of land,[175] then an accurate index of landed wealth.

This is a view that was implicitly questioned by Rosamond Faith and has been directly challenged by myself.[176] Both of us have pointed out that the omissions from Domesday Book are not simply accidental. Ecclesiastical precincts like Glastonbury, Athelney, Crowland, and Ramsey were all unassessed to the geld and as such were not subject to the dues and services with which the inquest was concerned. They were omitted from Domesday Book because they were beyond the remit of the survey. They were not alone. Incidental references to *inland* in the Huntingdonshire, Northamptonshire, Oxfordshire, and Warwickshire folios and accounts of the same in twelfth-century surveys reveal that the type was more widespread. Nor was it confined to seigneurial demesne: sokelands might be equally quit and thereby fail to appear in the text.[177] I conclude that, outside the *terra*

---

[174] D. A. Stocker and P. Everson, *Summoning St Michael: Early Romanesque Towers in Lincolnshire*, Oxford 2006.
[175] For a very eccentric view to the contrary, see A. Wright, *Hoax! The Domesday Hide*, Kibworth Beauchamp 2009.
[176] R. Faith, *The English Peasantry and the Growth of Lordship*, London 1997, 48–453; Roffe, *Decoding Domesday*, 198–203.
[177] *Pace* W. E. Kapelle, *The Norman Conquest of the North*, London 1979, 153–77. For sokeland as inland on the Ramsey estates, see E. Day, 'Sokeman and Freemen in Late

regis,[178] Domesday Book describes only what was known in English as *warland*, that is land, including the fiscal demesne, assessed to the geld.

It might be supposed that unassessed land of this type would have been a tempting target for William in the Domesday inquest and the ploughland figures could conceivably be his weapon of choice. The data have been the subject of much debate. Two schools of thought have emerged. Realists, notably John Moore and Nicholas Higham, have argued that the ploughland is a measure of total arable.[179] Nominalists, by contrast, represented by Sally Harvey, have countered that it is a fiscal unit, a tax assessment.[180] Neither has succeeded in convincing a wider audience. The realist case has foundered on the fact that working ploughs often exceed the land said to be available for them and the nominalist on any sign of a new assessment after Domesday. A. R. Bridbury has attempted to cut the Gordian knot by asserting that the ploughland is a measure of service capacity.[181] This formulation, however, hardly come to terms with the word: the ploughland is as much about land as service.

For my part, in the latest review of the evidence I have come down on the side of the realist interpretation but harness it to a concern for a reassessment of taxation.[182] Although it has frequently been asserted that the ploughland disappears after Domesday, there is abundant evidence that it was the standard means of measuring unassessed land in the early twelfth century. It seems likely, then, that it did so in 1086. However, if, as I argue, the Domesday inquest was an information gathering exercise to inform future action, the data were not and could not be assessments in themselves. They were simply the baseline for subsequent negotiation and in the event the outcome seems to have been the lifting of the exemption on the manorial demesne rather than a full re-assessment. The ploughland statistics, then, attest an early stage, that of information gathering, in a *process* of assessment. The important point here remains that the referent was the fiscal hide. Intermittently throughout GDB and consistently in Exon it is said that there were so many hides that such a number of ploughs could plough. The ploughland was a measure of the tax capacity of the *warland*.

Inland was evidently completely above and beyond the concerns of the Domesday

---

Anglo-Saxon East Anglia in Comparative Context', unpublished PhD thesis, University of Cambridge, 2011, 138.

[178] Royal estates, of course, were subject to a separate inquiry with different aims from the survey of non-royal lands.

[179] J. S. Moore, 'The Domesday Teamland: a Reconsideration', *TRHS*, 5th series 14, 1964, 109–30; N. Higham, 'Settlement, Land Use and Domesday Ploughlands', *Landscape History* 12, 1990, 33–44.

[180] S. P. J. Harvey, 'Taxation and the Ploughland in Domesday Book', in *Domesday Book: a Reassessment*, ed. Sawyer, 86–103; Harvey, 'Taxation and the Economy', 249–64.

[181] A. R. Bridbury, 'Domesday Book: a Re-interpretation', *EHR* 105, 1990, 284–309.

[182] Roffe, *Domesday: Inquest and Book*, 149–65; Roffe, *Decoding Domesday*, 203–9.

inquest. It nevertheless goes some way to explain a number of discrepancies in Domesday data. Foremost among these is the nature of hidation. Round's arguments for top-down assessment are as cogent now, notwithstanding recent statistical analysis, as they were in the late nineteenth century when he formulated them. Varying quotas were clearly imposed on different areas.[183] It still remains implausible, however, that taxation and the hide that distributed it was essentially arbitrary as is thereby implied. A hidden reservoir of unassessed land could well resolve this apparent paradox. The hide remained more or less constant, as its correlation with various manorial statistics might suggest,[184] but the extent of unassessed land varied. This certainly seems to be the explanation of the otherwise anomalous assessment of, for example, Nottinghamshire. Compared with neighbouring Leicestershire and Lincolnshire, the county is very lightly assessed, but the great number of recorded ploughs which greatly exceed the carucates to the geld and even the estimated ploughlands, points to a reserve of land that is not recorded in the Domesday text. The mystery of 'overstocking', the excess of ploughs over the land apparently available for them, therefore becomes readily explicable. I conclude that the phenomenon is the best indicator that the text affords of the phantom resource of inland.

Andrew Lowerre outlines a methodology for testing this proposition below (pp.240–3). David Pratt, by contrast, maintains that the whole problem is illusory.[185] He has urged that the exemption of inland was a post-Conquest development, probably dating from as late as 1085 (above p.29). It follows that inland had always been part of the land assessed to the geld and the term *warland*, with which it is contrasted, was a recent coining to articulate a novel distinction. Inland, as used in Circuit IV, was used of 'manorial demesne', that part of the inland that was directly exploited by the lord as opposed to that which was tenanted.[186] Pratt, however, does not consider the implications of the ploughland data nor the post-Domesday evidence for land beyond the cadastre. Patterns of hidation, in Huntingdonshire for example,[187] suggest that inland had never been assessed.

Inland remains a problem; the key to it is the record of working ploughs. Why

---

[183] Round, *Feudal England*, 35–103. For records of quotas, see Roffe, *Decoding Domesday*, 192–3.
[184] For a recent review of the evidence and a critique of method, see A. Wareham and X. Wei, 'Taxation and the Economy in Late Eleventh-Century England: Reviving the Domesday Regression Debate', *ANS* 29, 2007, 214–27. However, a recognition of a relationship between the hide and physical area hardly warrants reductive arguments (Wright, *Hoax! The Domesday Hide*). For a nuanced argument, see G. Barlow, 'The Landscape of Domesday Suffolk', *Landscape History* 32, 2011, 19–36.
[185] Pratt, 'Demesne Exemption', 1–34.
[186] I am grateful to David Pratt for clarification on this point (pers. comm.).
[187] C. Hart, 'The Hidation of Huntingdonshire', *Proceedings of the Cambridge Antiquarian Society* 61, 1968, 55–66. The Domesday hidation accords with that of the early eleventh-century County Hidage.

they should be recorded for all the land rather than just the *warland* is unexplained. The information was available, for, if it is correctly interpreted, the ploughland was usually computed by simply counting the number of ploughs on the geldable land or making a fair estimate. It is possible that the surplus was also recorded simply because they owed ploughing service to the fiscal demesne, but in that case it might be expected that the fact made the land geldable. More mysterious still is why King William apparently did not target the untapped resources of inland. The condition of exemption from geld assessed on *warland* was personal service and the same may have applied to unassessed land.[188] That would seem unlikely, however, to account for the large number of sokemen who were quit. Social structure may suggest an alternative explanation. The highest incidence of overstocking is found in the East Midlands. Intermediate levels are also found in the south-east in Kent, Sussex, and Surrey, while an above average incidence has been inferred for East Anglia.[189] These are all areas with a high degree of freedom and the high proportion of unassessed land may merely be a function of the fact. The phenomenon of inland requires further investigation.

The economy and society

The most significant development in the study of Domesday data has been the publication online of John Palmer's datasets for both GDB and LDB.[190] Domesday statistics have always been a problem. In the past many were worked out by hand on the back of envelopes, or might as well have been, for they have rarely been made available for scrutiny. Differences in interpretation, and more often simply error, have meant that totals for any category, whether locally or nationally, vary widely from study to study. By necessity, it has therefore been customary to cite the range of estimates rather than absolute values. A solid foundation is now available. Any statistics abstracted from a text will inevitably embody ambiguities and deficiencies (see Lowerre below, pp.223–32), but Palmer's arrays set a new standard in transparency. Freely available and well documented, they will provide a firm basis for statistical analysis of Domesday data in the future.[191] It is to be

---

[188] Roffe, *Decoding Domesday*, 183.
[189] Hesse, 'Domesday Settlement in Suffolk', 48–9. The fiscal carucate has been used as a proxy here and the correlation may merely indicate that free men suffered under a greater burden of taxation.
[190] http://www.data-archive.ac.uk/findingdata/snDescription.asp?sn=5694, accessed 24/09/2014.
[191] For a mash up of Domesday mills, for example, see http://www.windmillworld.com/watermills/domesday.htm, accessed 24/09/2014. Female names have also been extracted at http://www.nancy.cc/2012/04/06/female-names-in-the-domesday-book/, accessed 24/09/2014.

hoped that a front-end will be developed to facilitate the interrogation of this most important resource.

Reliable statistics are an indispensable prerequisite of analysis; they are also dangerous. Divorced from their context, neat rows of figures can take on a meaning of their own: as quantities that are amenable to mathematical analysis, they may appear to validate themselves. In the 1980s, John MacDonald and Graeme Snooks demonstrated high correlations between manorial resources and value and they have reiterated their conclusions in a number of papers since.[192] Andrew Wareham and X. Wei revisited their conclusions in 2007 and took them to task for basing their analysis on the manor, thus ignoring intermanorial exchange, and their failure to allow for multicolinearity in the data.[193] They opted for the landholding as their unit of analysis and use various statistical tools to account for the inter-relatedness of the data. They found that in their study area of East Anglia there is a close relationship between tax assessment and the resources available to pay. In contrast to MacDonald and Snooks, though, they detected no indication of a regressive tendency. A further analysis over time showed an inverse relationship between changes in assessment and rental value, that is, taxes fell as income increased, reflecting the findings of Sally Harvey in the late twentieth century. Nevertheless, despite disagreement over statistical method, Wareham accepts the basic integrity of the data as an index of economic activity.

The figures may indeed appear to speak for themselves: the cohesiveness of the data must be a function of a real economy. The reality is that, like any other data, they do no such thing. Statistics do not generate hypotheses – 'data dredging' is an unacceptable methodology – they can only test them and heretofore econometric analysis has been firmly founded in a tacit acceptance of a Galbraithian perspective. As we have seen, economic units are inherent to this analysis. In a process designed to record land holdings for posterity, it is self-evident that the figures relate to estates. Domesday Book, then, records what belonged to the lord or contributed to the income of his demesne. It was an inventory survey and must by definition

---

[192] J. McDonald, *Production Efficiency in Domesday England, 1086*, London and New York 1998; J. McDonald, 'Tax Fairness in Eleventh-Century England', *The Accounting Historians Journal* 29, 2002, 173–94; J. McDonald, 'Using William the Conqueror's Accounting Record to Assess Manorial Efficiency', *Accounting History* 10, 2005, 125–45; J. McDonald, 'The Relative Efficiency of King's, Ecclesiastical, and Lay Estates in Domesday Essex, 1086', *Australian Economic History Review* 52, 2012, 250–69; G. D. Snooks, 'The Dynamic Role of the Market in the Anglo-Norman Economy and Beyond, 1086–1300', in *The Commercialisation of English Society, 1000–1300*, ed. R. H. Britnell and B. M. S. Campbell, Manchester 1993, 27–54; G. D. Snooks, 'A Note on the Calculation of GDP and GDP per capita in 1086 and 1300', in *A Commercialising Society*, ed. Britnell and Campbell, appendix 1.
[193] Wareham and Wei, 'Taxation and the Economy', 214–27.

provide an index of seigneurial wealth in its own terms.[194] Indeed, in some quarters it has even been seen as a sophisticated accountancy system.[195]

A very different view of Domesday data emerges where the Domesday inquest is perceived as a survey of geld and service.[196] The phenomenon of inland is testimony enough that Domesday Book is not primarily about estates. Recent studies of classes of Domesday population underline the 'deficiencies' of the source in this respect.[197] Land and manorial resources, it is argued, cannot have been included because they contributed to the profits of the lord's demesne; many valuable resources were simply omitted. Rather it was liability to render geld and service, generically bundled under the catch-all of *soca*, 'soke', or *consuetudines*, 'customs', that was the criterion of enrolment. Outside the royal demesne where there were different principles of survey, Domesday Book is largely an account of *warland* only. The lands of the lord and the inhabitants of the vill were recorded only so far as they were burdened with public duties. The Domesday economy is a tributary one.

Such divergent views of the Domesday enterprise inevitably produce very different views of the Domesday statistics and, by extension, of Domesday England. For the real economy camp, the lord's demesne effectively embraces the whole of the resources of the vill in both manpower and infrastructure. Villeins were not unfree in the same way that their twelfth-century successors were to be, but they were nevertheless closely tied to the lord's demesne. So too had the free men and sokemen become by 1086. Where their liberty is explicit, they were typically free to go with their lands before the Conquest, but thereafter their enrolment within the manor clearly indicates that they had been subjected to the Norman yoke.[198] Above all, the resources of the manor in woodland, meadow and pasture, mills, fisheries, and churches, were the property of the lord.

That this was the reality of some estates, especially those of the church in Wessex, cannot be doubted. The Danish invasions of the ninth and tenth centuries had

---

[194] A. Wareham, 'The "Feudal Revolution" in Eleventh-Century East Anglia', *ANS* 22, 2000, 293–322 at 296. The notion of accountability has been further developed, albeit from a royal perspective, by A. Godfrey and K. Hooper, 'Accountability and Decision-Making in Feudal England: Domesday Book Revisited', *Accounting History* 1, 1996, 35–54.

[195] Godfrey and Hooper, 'Accountability and Decision-Making in Feudal England', 35–54; J. McDonald, 'Using William the Conqueror's Accounting Record to Assess Manorial Efficiency', *Accounting History* 10, 2005, 125–45; M. Jones, 'Domesday Book as an Example of Embryonic Weberian Administration in a Patrimonial State', Sixth Asia-Pacific Interdisciplinary Research in Accounting Conference, 2010, http://apira2010.econ.usyd.edu.au/conference_proceedings/APIRA-2010-159-Jones-Weberian-administration.pdf, accessed 28/07/2012.

[196] Roffe, *Decoding Domesday*, 210–56.

[197] Day, 'Sokeman and Freemen', 115–38; D. A. Hinton, 'Demography: from Domesday and Beyond', *Journal of Medieval History* 39, 2013, 146–78.

[198] For a forceful re-statement of this view, see Harvey, *Domesday: Book of Judgement*, especially chapter 7.

seen a militarization of society and lords had in consequence extended their power over land. But the pattern was not universal and, in Kent, eastern Mercia, and the Danelaw, perhaps not usual.[199] Villeins paid the geld in 1086 and were therefore personally free. They might not have been free to go with their land, but that did not necessarily mean that it did not belong to them. I have argued that the *recedere* and similar clauses that defined freedom were primarily related to the right of a free man to commend himself to a lord of his choosing.[200] By contrast, the villein, a *tunesman* in English (and many a sokeman where he is contrasted with the *liber homo*), was warranted in the vill itself by the community. *Ipso facto* he might well be of lower status than the free man, but his land was no less free. By the same token, the free man's liberty did not preclude him from rendering service to a lord. His right to free commendation was recorded to indicate that the Norman successor of his lord had no right to his land.[201] His soke nevertheless remained reserved and brought him into a manor in both 1066 and 1086. The traces in the Domesday text are examined below, pp.82–96. As Richard Abels first showed in Bedfordshire and Hertfordshire and Ann Williams has confirmed in Suffolk, the free man strove to ensure that soke and commendation were vested in different lords in order to maximize his independence.[202] There can be no doubt that the dues demanded were increased after the Conquest – Sally Harvey has argued that squeezing the free man was inherently more lucrative than intensive demesne exploitation[203] – and there are high profile examples of lords, notably sheriffs, appropriating men. But the point here is that dues had always been rendered in one direction or another. Wholesale manorialization, and the consequent depression in status, is a myth.

Likewise, the lord did not have unequivocal right to the infrastructure of the manor. Although manorial assets are often categorized as 'stock', the reality was more complex. Mills are a case in point. In his comprehensive study, Richard Holt assumed that all were seigneurial and had to account for ownership of a large number by peasants from the twelfth century onwards in terms of a decline in

---

[199] D. R. Roffe, 'The Danes and the Making of the Kingdom of the English', *Nations in Medieval Britain*, ed. H. Tsurushima, Donington 2010, 32–44.

[200] Roffe, *Decoding Domesday*, 219–33.

[201] Pace Baxter, *The Earls of Mercia*, 219–25, why otherwise the frequent comment that a lord 'only' had commendation?

[202] R. Abels, 'An Introduction to the Bedfordshire Domesday', in *The Bedfordshire Domesday*, ed. A. Williams and R. W. H. Erskine, London 1991, 1–53 at 38–40; R. Abels, 'An Introduction to the Hertfordshire Domesday', in *The Hertfordshire Domesday*, ed. A. Williams and R. W. H. Erskine, London 1991, 1–36 at 30–2; A. Williams, 'Little Domesday and the English: the Hundred of Colneis in Suffolk', in *Domesday Book*, ed. Hallam and Bates, 103–20.

[203] Harvey, *Domesday: Book of Judgement*, chapter 7. There it is assumed that making the pips squeak was Norman policy from early on. However, some, probably many, increases in dues must have been related to the crisis of 1085.

demesne farming.[204] By contrast, I have argued that there was probably no significant change in the pattern of ownership after 1086. There is an implied distinction in Domesday Book between mills that are not given a value, some 47% of a total of just over 6000, and those that are. Where information is given, unvalued mills are said 'to serve the hall' and the like and it would seem that those that were valued merely rendered dues and must therefore have belonged to the peasantry as they were to do subsequently.[205] By implication other separately-valued assets like fisheries rendered dues rather than served the lord directly. The manor was a nexus of tribute rather than property rights.

Such values are considerable, on occasion somewhat greater than the apparent issues of the manor, and bring the nature of the Domesday values in general into question. The *valet* and *valuit* figures of the Domesday account have long been thought of as something very close to rental values. It is held that they represent either what the lord received from his farmer or, where the manor was in demesne, what he might receive if it were leased.[206] Recent debate has centred on whether the sums represent gross or net values. Graeme Snooks has argued that the statistical fit with recorded resources is so precise that they must include the resources needed for the subsistence of the peasantry which worked the land. Nicholas Mayhew has disagreed and has in consequence come up with a higher figure for GDP of £300,000 to £400,000 against Snooks' £137,000.[207] In the most recent contribution to the debate, James Walker has used a Box and Cox analysis to substantiate Mayhew's premise and produce a third figure of £360,281.[208]

With a contribution of about a third by non-demesnal resources, this last total is consistent with the service of two to three days per week that was owed by the dependent peasantry from the twelfth century onwards. It would thus add some substance to Bridbury's view that plough service capacity was part of the Domesday equation.[209] Value to whom remains a problem. In his analysis of the wealth of tenants-in-chief and their men in 1086, Palmer assumed that the sitting tenant

---

[204] R. A. Holt, *The Mills of Medieval England*, Oxford 1988; R. A. Holt, 'Whose Were the Profits of Milling? An Aspect of the Changing Relationship between the Abbots of Glastonbury and their Tenants, 1066–1350', *Past & Present* 116, 1987, 3–25 at 6–8, 11–12; J. Landon, 'Watermills and Windmills in the West Midlands, 1986–1500', *EcHR* 44, 1991, 424–44.

[205] Roffe, *Decoding Domesday*, 235–40.

[206] R. Lennard, *Rural England 1086–1135: a Study of Social and Agrarian Conditions*, Oxford 1959, 105–41.

[207] N. Mayhew, 'Modelling Medieval Monetisation', in *The Commercialisation of English Society, 1000–1300*, ed. Britnell and Campbell, 55–77 at 60–2; N. Mayhew, 'Appendix 2: The Calculation of GDB from Domesday Book', ibid., 195–8 at 195–6; Snooks, 'The Dynamic Role of the Market in the Anglo-Norman Economy', 27–54.

[208] J. T. Walker, 'National Income in Domesday England', http://www.henley.reading.ac.uk/nmsruntime/saveasdialog.asp?lID=35211&sID=119847, accessed 28/06/2012.

[209] Bridbury, 'Domesday Book: a Re-interpretation', 284–309.

was the beneficiary.²¹⁰ There are numerous entries that would indeed suggest such a reading. Equally, however, there are other references that quite clearly show that values were sums that went out of the manor. On that basis, Andrew Wareham opted for the overlord as the recipient.²¹¹ The difference in perception has as much of a bearing on the wealth of tenants-in-chief and their tenants in 1086 (see above, pp.34–5) as of lords in 1066.²¹²

The issue remains undetermined. For some, indeed, the problem is otherwise. In the eleventh and twelfth centuries, as thereafter throughout the Middle Ages, estate surveys did not concern themselves with calculating either gross or net income; they confined their attention to simple issues, recording what a lord received in his hand, be it in cash or kind. I have argued that it is intrinsically unlikely that the Domesday inquest was any different in this respect.²¹³ The connotations of *valet* and *valuit* are not explicit in the Domesday corpus, but the Anglo-Saxon Chronicle account of the survey is more helpful. It states that the commissioners had to determine 'how much money it was worth (*hu mycel feos hit wære wurð*)'.²¹⁴ Values were evidently about the transfer of coin. Bishop Robert of Hereford's contemporary account of the inquest confirms the reading. He states that the survey demanded, *inter alia*, an account of 'the services and payments due from all men in the whole land (*in servitio et censu totius terrae omnium*)'.²¹⁵ This is a formulation which is much closer to the medieval norm.

Analysis of the figures bears out its accuracy. In 1992 Bridbury noticed that Domesday values were very close in magnitude to what were essentially quitrents in twelfth-century surveys of church lands.²¹⁶ Subsequently, I showed that the values of sokemen and free men in LDB represent payments in respect of conventional soke dues, while in the North they were equally conventional tributes of one kind or another. It follows from this that Domesday values were less valuations in the modern sense than records of issues in coin. As such, they should be seen as complementing the various other renders for fisheries, mills, and the like, rather than being a gross or net value, and should be set beside the other issues of the estate in labour and kind. Sally Harvey, in the latest examination of Domesday

---

²¹⁰ Palmer, 'The Wealth of the Secular Aristocracy', 279–91.
²¹¹ Wareham and Wei, 'Taxation and the Economy'.
²¹² J. L. Grassi, 'The Lands and Revenues of Edward the Confessor', *EHR* 117, 2002, 252–83.
²¹³ Roffe, *Decoding Domesday*, 240–50.
²¹⁴ *The Peterborough Chronicle 1070–1154*, ed. C. Clark, 2nd edn, Oxford 1970, 9.
²¹⁵ Stevenson, 'Contemporary Description of the Domesday Survey', 72–84. *Contra* Frank Thorn (pers.comm.) comments that Robert of Hereford 'is trying to write Classical Latin' and in this case is probably using census in the sense 'property in general, wealth, substance, one's fortune'.
²¹⁶ A. R. Bridbury, *The English Economy from Bede to the Reformation*, Woodbridge 1992, 111–32.

values, has largely concurred.²¹⁷ She rejects the notion that all values were soke related,²¹⁸ but accepts the impossibility of valuing non-monetary renders. For her there remains the possibility that some values were estimates of what might be rendered. Either way Domesday values represent only part of manorial output, namely that in coin.

Domesday values may, then, provide an index of monetarization, notional or otherwise, but they are no more a measure of an economy than the renders of later medieval surveys. They will not sustain the burden of interpretation put on them by social and economic historians.²¹⁹ In their own terms, however, they may provide an insight into Domesday England. Again, twelfth-century surveys provide a lead here. In the Burton estates, for example, renders in cash were inversely proportional to the incidence of labour dues.²²⁰ Likewise in LDB increases in value are correlated with a decrease in stock. Where the lord did not exploit his demesne directly, he commuted the services of his peasants to payments in coin. In these terms, values may be the best indicator of the intensity of demesne exploitation in 1086 with increased values suggesting demesne leasing and decreases direct working. With the extraction of coin easier than the improvement of agriculture, Harvey has argued that they thus provide a measure of the increased exploitation of the free peasantry after the Conquest.²²¹ Other uses of the data remain to be explored.

Not surprisingly, lack of value is associated with the phenomenon of waste. There is an extensive historiography that has viewed wasting solely in terms of the economic impact of conquest and settlement.²²² In the south and the Midlands it has been linked with falls in value to plot the footprints of the Norman army in 1066, with a resulting proliferation of otherwise unrecorded sorties and skirmishes. In the North the analysis has been somewhat more sophisticated. There it has been related to the Harrying of the North in 1067–8, but its distribution has been explained in terms of the estate management strategies of lords in its aftermath. All of this was demolished by John Palmer in a pair of incisive articles which systematically tested the hypotheses underlying these analyses and found them wanting.²²³ That the

---

²¹⁷ Harvey, *Domesday: Book of Judgement*, chapter 7.
²¹⁸ She asserts that soke is a regional characteristic. It should be noted, however, that soke was not confined to the Danelaw but, in its various manifestations, was a universal characteristic of English society, articulating all sorts of different relationships. See above, p.37.
²¹⁹ The point is well made by John Grassi in his analysis of the income from his estates of Edward the Confessor ('Lands and Revenues of Edward the Confessor', 281).
²²⁰ 'The Burton Abbey Twelfth Century Surveys', ed. C. G. O. Bridgeman, in *Collections for the History of Staffordshire*, William Salt Archaeological Society, 1916, 209–47; Roffe, *Decoding Domesday*, 249–50.
²²¹ Harvey, *Domesday: Book of Judgement*, chapter 7.
²²² For a review, see Roffe, *Decoding Domesday*, 250–6.
²²³ J. J. N. Palmer, 'War and Domesday Waste', in *Armies, Chivalry and Warfare in Medieval Britain and France*, ed. M. Strickland, Stamford 1998, 256–75; J. J. N. Palmer,

primary referent of waste was taxation was first adumbrated by Christopher Lewis in his analysis of the Herefordshire Domesday.[224] There he noticed that the record is specifically linked to geld payment. This association is in fact widespread.[225] There is considerable evidence that official schedules of waste were drawn up in the course of the Domesday inquest with the aim of recording loss of geld and service.

The reasons for writing down loss on this way are often difficult to assess. There is sufficient data in some cases, however, to determine what measures lords subsequently took to rehabilitate their estates. Stephen Matthews has undertaken one of the best studies to date in his examination of the Cheshire data.[226] In the north-west much of the waste is specifically ascribed to an intermediate period between 1066 and 1086, 'when found' in the terms of the Domesday inquest. With both TRE and TRW values recorded, it is possible to compare the stocking and value of estates by lord and over time and thereby assess recovery strategies in some considerable detail. Lucy Marten has undertaken a similar study in East Anglia to gauge the impact of rebellion on estates in 1075 and their subsequent development.[227] Elsewhere intermediate values are an untapped resource for estate management. They deserve more attention than they have hitherto enjoyed.

The referents of Domesday data remain difficult and contentious. Mapping may not resolve all of the problems, but it can provide a completely different perspective on the data. Andrew Lowerre examines the possibilities below (pp.219–46). Different units of account are a constant problem that has hitherto precluded successful graphical representation of many items of information. Woodland, for example, is measured by area in some counties, while in others there is no data on the resource *per se* apart from the number of pigs that it rendered to the lord in pannage. Lowerre neatly obviates the problem by mapping the various quantities in terms of standard deviations from the mean for whatever unit is employed. With certain assumptions made about the nature of parish boundaries, he is also able to formulate special models for testing the referents of data such as the ploughland. George Barlow has also taken up the challenge in a study of Suffolk.[228] Sensitive

---

'The Conqueror's Footprints in Domesday Book', in *The Medieval Military Revolution: State, Society and Military Change in Medieval and Early Modern Europe*, ed. A. C. Ayton and J. L. Price, London and New York 1995, 23–44.
[224] C. P. Lewis, 'An Introduction to the Herefordshire Domesday', in *The Herefordshire Domesday*, ed. A. Williams and R. H. W. Erskine, London 1988, 1–22.
[225] Roffe, *Decoding Domesday*, 250–6.
[226] S. Matthews, 'William the Conqueror's Campaign in Cheshire in 1069–70: Ravaging and Resistance in the North-West', *Northern History* 40, 2003, 53–70. See also, R. Studd, 'Recorded "Waste" in the Staffordshire Domesday Entry', *Staffordshire Studies* 12, 2000, 121–33.
[227] Marten, 'The Impact of Rebellion on Little Domesday', 132–50.
[228] Barlow, 'The Landscape of Domesday Suffolk'.

mapping of this kind will in the future have much to offer in the analysis of all types of Domesday data.[229]

Communities, estates, and landscapes of lordship

Domesday stands at the beginning of the recorded history of the vast majority of English settlements. It is not surprising, then, that the source figures large in regional and local studies. Notwithstanding Maitland's demonstration of its potential in the late nineteenth century, not so very long ago it was still commonly considered no more than the roots of a medieval future.[230] All that has changed. Nowadays Domesday is as likely to be used for a reconstruction of an unrecorded Anglo-Saxon past. No local history with any claim to competence now fails to take account of the broader context of the evidence. The vill and the hundred, tenurial links and place-names, intercommoning practices and parish boundaries are all brought into play to interpret Domesday entries. The last few years have seen a considerable body of new work.

For a seigneurially arranged source, Domesday Book contains a remarkable amount of information about the communities of the vill and hundred. Much of the evidence for the thirty counties of GDB was collected and analysed in the light of later and better evidenced structures by Frank Thorn in the 1980s and 1990s for the Alecto edition. His measured commentary and careful mapping, regrettably neither of which was included in *The Digital Domesday*, remain fundamental to any understanding of eleventh-century administration in the localities. There is no parallel for the three counties of LDB. There hundred rubrication is largely comprehensive and boundaries were mapped without any discussion. Characteristics of the system were, however, examined by individual county editors. I, for example, addressed the problem of the leets of Norfolk and argued that they were less a peculiar system of geld assessment than of payment. Indeed, there is evidence to show that they functioned in much the same way as the twelve-carucate hundreds of the adjacent Lincolnshire and the Northern Danelaw.[231]

If the workings of vills and hundreds are now well known, the detail remains sketchy. Some data are likely to remain mysterious. The figures that are routinely given for the dimensions of vills in East Anglia and sporadically throughout Domesday Book are evidently of importance, but there seems little chance of finding a way forward in their interpretation.[232] Patterns of assessment, by contrast, may offer up more amenable evidence for the structure of vills. Recent research in the

---

[229] Fleming and Lowerre, 'Review Article: MacDomesday Book'.
[230] Maitland, *Domesday Book and Beyond*.
[231] Roffe, 'Introduction', in *Little Domesday, Norfolk*, 22–4.
[232] C. R. Hart, *The Danelaw*, London 1992, 97–103, and M. Hesse, 'Domesday Land Measures in Suffolk', *Landscape History* 22, 2002, 21–36, suggest that they are an East

Northern Danelaw has suggested that the *terra regis* stood outside the cadastre.[233] Elsewhere the same was true of those estates that rendered the farm of one night, but whether the principle applied more widely has yet to be determined.[234] The possibility suggests a new approach to patterns of hidation that have not always make immediate sense. In the same terms, the assessment of hundreds may also made better sense. Hidation and carucation, much pored over in the nineteenth century, are subjects that may repay reconsideration.

It is still commonplace to assume that vills and hundreds perpetuate ancient estates. They may very well do so in some cases – Cam's concept of the *manerium cum hundredo* is one possible mechanism[235] – but it is clearly a mistake to assume that the administrative landscape of Anglo-Saxon England was characterized by stasis. Pauline Stafford, echoed by Ryan Lavelle, has shown that the organization of royal farm as portrayed in Domesday Book was itself a recent origin in 1086.[236] James Campbell has stressed the importance of administrative innovation in the Northern Danelaw and East Anglia, while Pamela Taylor has charted the complex evolution of hundreds in and around Middlesex and Surrey.[237] Despite arguments for the early date of hundred boundaries in various parts of the country, it is as well to recognize that there is no evidence for the unit *qua* institution in anything like its Domesday form before the Hundred Ordinance of the mid tenth century.

What is true of the Domesday hundred is probably equally so of the Domesday shire. That those of the East Midlands emerged out of the organization known as the Five Boroughs in the early eleventh century has been known for a long while.[238] More recently, Lucy Marten has demonstrated a similar development and

---

Anglian analogue of the ploughland. This view is not easily reconcilable with the record of ploughlands in the usual terms in IE.

[233] D. R. Roffe, 'The Origins of Derbyshire', *Derbyshire Archaeological Journal* 106, 1986, 102–22; D. R. Roffe, 'Hundreds and Wapentakes', in *The Lincolnshire Domesday*, ed. A. Williams and G. H. Martin, London 1992, 32–42 at 33–9.

[234] The placing of Sewell and Biscot in royal manors in Bedfordshire after 1066 apparently took them out of the hundred (GDB, 209v: BDF 1,4;5).

[235] H. M. Cam, '*Manerium cum Hundredo*: the Hundred and the Hundred Manor', *EHR* 47, 1932, 355–76.

[236] P. A. Stafford, 'The "Farm of One Night" and the Organisation of King Edward's Estates in Domesday', *EcHR*, 2nd series 33, 1980, 491–502; R. Lavelle, 'The "Farm of One Night" and the Organization of Estates in Late Anglo-Saxon Wessex', *The Haskins Society Journal* 14, 2005 for 2003, 54–82.

[237] J. Campbell, 'Hundreds and Leets: a Survey with Suggestions', in *Medieval East Anglia*, ed. C. Harper-Bill, Woodbridge 2005, 153–67; P. Taylor, 'Boundaries and Margins: Barnet, Finchley, and Totteridge', in *Medieval Ecclesiastical Studies in Honour of Dorothy M. Owen*, ed. M. J. Franklin and C. Harper-Bill, Woodbridge 1995, 259–79; Taylor, 'Domesday Mortlake', 203–29; P. Taylor, '*Eadulfingtun*, Edmonton, and their Contexts', in *The English and Their Legacy*, ed. Roffe, 95–114. See also, Roffe, 'Introduction', in *Lincolnshire Domesday*.

[238] Roffe, 'Hundreds and Wapentakes', in *Lincolnshire Domesday*, 39–42.

chronology for the East Anglian shires.²³⁹ Elsewhere a precise time frame is not always apparent, but it is nevertheless clear that the century and a half between the Burghal Hidage and Domesday Book saw considerable changes in some areas. Keith Bailey and others, for example, have shown that Berkshire, Buckinghamshire, and Oxfordshire were secondary formations which superseded earlier burghal territories that crossed the Thames.²⁴⁰ In the most recent review of the evidence George Molyneaux has opted for a late tenth-century date for shiring.²⁴¹

Change is equally evident in the structure of estates. Unbridled enthusiasm for the multiple estate model has been tempered by the growing realization that Domesday provides a snapshot of a moment in time in an evolving tenurial landscape. Before the Conquest dues were as much a medium of patronage as land and in consequence parcels of sokeland and the like were frequently transferred from one tenurial context to another. Tewkesbury provides a well-documented example. Extensive Domesday estates were not necessarily ancient in 1086. The introduction of other evidence, usually of much later date, to prove otherwise often merely begs the question; parochial structure, place-names, intercommoning, and the like all have their own peculiar problems of interpretation.²⁴²

A broader perspective, however, can sometimes strengthen an analysis based on these pillars of landscape history. Patterns of tenure that hold true across a number of fees in the same area transcend contingency and must often point to more ancient structures. In the absence for evidence of minster *parochiae*, for example, twelfth- and thirteenth-century records of advowsons can hint at the reservation of ecclesiastical dues to a central church. Waltham in Lincolnshire provides an example.²⁴³ There is not much to suggest a minster church there. Significantly, however, by the thirteenth century when the evidence becomes available the right of presentation to almost all the churches in the area belonged to the lord of Waltham or his men despite the division of the land of each vill between a large number of tenants-in-chief. The pattern strongly suggests that tithes were formerly paid to a single church, probably that in Waltham itself.

If such patterns are testimony to lost ecclesiastical structures, interlocking patterns of tenure may indicate their estate counterparts. Again, where several fees exhibit the same estate structures, it is difficult to escape the conclusion that they

---

²³⁹ L. Marten, 'The Shiring of East Anglia: an Alternative Hypothesis', *Historical Research* 81, 2008, 1–27.

²⁴⁰ A. H. J. Baines, 'The Danish Wars and the Establishment of the Borough and County of Buckingham', *Records of Buckinghamshire* 26, 1984, 11–27; K. A. Bailey, 'The Hidation of Buckinghamshire: Part 2 Before Domesday', *Records of Buckinghamshire* 34, 1992, 87–96 at 89; Roffe, 'Wallingford in Domesday and Beyond', 42–5.

²⁴¹ G. Molyneaux, 'Why Were Some Tenth-Century English Kings Presented as Rulers of Britain?', *TRHS*, 6th series 21, 2011, 59–91.

²⁴² Roffe, *Decoding Domesday*, 280–305.

²⁴³ G. F. Bryant, *Domesday Book: How to Read it and What Its Text Means*, Waltham 1985.

have come into being by the ordered division of a greater whole. I have recently analysed the siltland communities of Cambridgeshire, Lincolnshire, and Norfolk in these terms and have argued that the entities that emerged from the analysis probably date back to at least the middle Saxon period.[244] They incidentally throw light on a marked difference between silt fen and peat fen communities. Techniques of this kind have a great potential for illuminating the beyond of Domesday, especially in areas in which villages were divided.

Continuities in the landscape are seductive, but their pursuit should not blind historians to the equally significant discontinuities. The Humber estuary provides a case in point.[245] The waterway marks a well-defined tenurial boundary in 1086 with few tenants-in-chief holding in both Lincolnshire and Yorkshire. As peripheral as the area may seem, the river was nevertheless far from marginal. All the great lords of both shires, TRE as well as TRW, held important bookland estates on or adjacent to the shore with few signs of earlier structures. A pattern of extensive estates, readily apparent to both north and south, seems, if it ever existed, to have been obliterated by intense activity. The construction of the church of St Peter, Barton on Humber, in the early eleventh century within the divided estate of Barrow on Humber, provides a *terminus post quem* date and suggests that the estate structure of the area reflects concern for the security of the estuary at the same time. Here the absence of discernible antecedents seems to point to the fortification of a march at a time of crisis.

How this pattern emerged is unknown. It is not impossible, however, indeed probably likely, that the process was directed. In an exemplary study of the double hundred of Bampton in Oxfordshire based on Domesday Book and charter evidence, Stephen Baxter and John Blair have shown that the tenurial landscape might be carefully planned.[246] A central demesne fronting onto the Thames was kept in the hands of the king, but land around it was zoned. To the east estates were granted out by book, to the north they were assigned to ministers, and to the west to the earl. This pattern of patronage is far from unique. There were similar complexes of estates, sometimes of equal size, clustered around most boroughs and in many hundreds.[247]

---

[244] D. R. Roffe, 'The Historical Context', in *Anglo-Saxon Settlement on the Siltland of Eastern England*, ed. A. Crowson, T. Lane, K. Penn, and D. Trimble, Lincolnshire Archaeology and Heritage Reports Series 7, 2005, 264–88.

[245] D. R. Roffe, 'Barton: the Early History', in *St Peter's, Barton-upon-Humber, Lincolnshire: a Parish Church and its Community*, ed. W. Rodwell and C. Atkins, 2 vols, Oxford 2011, I, 35–45.

[246] Baxter and Blair, 'Land Tenure and Royal Patronage in the Early English Kingdom'.

[247] Roffe, *Decoding Domesday*, 125–7, for a review of the evidence. For Derby and Huntingdon, see D. R. Roffe, 'Introduction', in *The Huntingdonshire Domesday*, ed. A. Williams and R. H. W. Erskine, London 1989, 1–23 at 21–2; D. R. Roffe, 'Introduction', in *The Derbyshire Domesday*, ed. A Williams and R. H. W. Erskine, London 1989, 1–27 at 19–24; Lavelle, 'Royal Control and the Distribution of Estates in Tenth-Century England', 29–34.

The forest was equally a landscape of lordship. Subject to embryonic forest law,[248] it stood outside the administration of the shire and in consequence is not comprehensively described in Domesday Book. It is clear, however, that it was something more than just a royal hunting ground. The New Forest is a case in point. Karin Mew has argued that the identity of the *Nova Foresta* of the Hampshire folios was derived from its earlier tenure by Earl William fitzOsbern as a military lordship or *quasi* rape along with Southampton and the Isle of Wight and it continued to have military significance at the time of the survey.[249] The pervasive influence of royal authority that might assert itself in such landscapes thereafter throughout the medieval period is illustrated by a perceptive study of Whittlewood Forest by Robert Jones and Mark Page.[250]

Such patterns of lordship are clearly not an exclusively Norman phenomenon and recent historiography has striven to place post-Conquest developments in a wider cultural setting. Perceptions of the castle exemplify the trend. In the past the castle has been understood as the military infrastructure of conquest, an intrusion into English society. Following Charles Coulson's reconstruction of the institution, however, it is now understood as much in terms of display as conquest.[251] With its concomitants of deer park and religious house, it was a marker of status. As such the castle fits neatly into earlier English notions of lordship. The motte was probably a Norman innovation, but every other characteristic of the castle – defended enclosures, towers, churches, and, indeed, probably deer parks[252] – can be found before the Conquest. The Normans were undoubtedly an energetic people, but they did not recast English society anew. Just as they bent English law to the needs of the Norman settlement (above, pp.38–9), so they adapted the physical and cultural landscape to their needs. The continuity of tenure that Domesday Book supposes is written in the landscape of England.

Conclusion

In his review of Domesday studies in 1989 W. E. Kapelle observed that Galbraith's demolition of Round's geld thesis had met with general agreement. However, he

---

[248] D. Jorgensen, 'The Roots of the English Royal Forest', *ANS* 32, 2010, 114–28.
[249] K. Mew, 'The Dynamics of Lordship and Landscape as Revealed in a Domesday Study of the *Nova Foresta*', *ANS* 23, 2000, 155–66.
[250] R. Jones and M. Page, *Medieval Villages in an English Landscape*, Macclesfield 2006.
[251] C. Coulson, 'Cultural Realities and Reappraisals in English Castle Study', *Journal of Medieval History* 22, 1996, 171–208; C. Coulson, 'Peaceable Power in English Castles', *ANS* 23, 2000, 69–95; C. Coulson, *Castles in Medieval Society: Fortresses in England, France, and Ireland in the Central Middle Ages*, Oxford 2003. Recent years has seen an explosion in castle studies; for a review, see O. Creighton, *Early European Castles: Aristocracy and Authority, AD800–1200*, London 2012.
[252] R. Liddiard, 'The Deer Parks of Domesday Book', *Landscapes* 4, 2003, 4–23.

noted that a concomitant stasis had descended on the subject in the face of issues that remained to be addressed.[253] With the dissolution of consensus in the last few years, that stasis is no more. The challenges to received notions have resulted in lively debate and, if answers have not always been forthcoming to the satisfaction of all, the interpretative possibilities of the Domesday corpus have been accordingly extended. There are still many who believe that the production of Domesday Book was an integral part of the Domesday enterprise, but most are now open to the possibility that its compilation came later than previously thought. Above all, there is a greater willingness to allow a plurality of concerns in 1086. The result has been a liberation from the reductive arguments of the past. If the inquest was a dynamic process that responded to events as they unfolded and used the data that it collected to inform the decision made in the face of them, then historians are freed from the tyranny of either/or that has characterized earlier debates. It is hoped that the outcome will be a better understanding of hoary old problems like the nature of taxation and service, of the ploughland and values, and of much more.

Out of debate come new vistas of understanding. What, then, are the priorities for future research? As already noted, a project to produce an extended Latin text is already under way. When complete it will be an invaluable resource for a fuller understanding of the texts and the concepts, aims, and sources that underlie them. For GDB much has already been achieved; much still remains to be done. For LDB and Exon, by contrast, the work has hardly begun. In the categorization of these sources as circuit returns, they have for far too long been branded as satellites to the GDB star, a mere means to an end. If we are to have a greater understanding of the Domesday process, they must be studied as sources in their own right. What was the relationship of Exon to ICC-like sources and how does LDB, perhaps the greatest mystery of the Domesday corpus, relate to the other texts? These are fundamental questions that must be answered before we can claim to fully comprehend the events of 1086. Unburdened of the assumptions of the past, the other inquest texts may also repay a fresh examination in similar terms. They too have the potential to hint at preoccupations that antedate the writing of LDB and GDB.

It seems common sense to derive the purpose of Domesday Book from its content and the assumption may well be warranted. It does not follow, however, that the data are equally a sure guide to the purpose of the inquest. As Ian Taylor shows below (p.152), now as then government inquiries commonly collect information that is tangential to their central purpose. The information collected will not necessarily address their concerns directly. Service, for example, may be an issue without being explicitly noticed in the texts. What, then, were the referents of the various items of information? What is omitted? What can be reconstructed of eleventh-century society from their evidence? Where Domesday is used to reconstruct

---

[253] Kapelle, 'Domesday Book: F. W. Maitland and his Successors', 620–4.

the economy and society of the period, inland clearly becomes a crucial issue in this respect. If the Domesday economy was a tributary one, then there must be a re-thinking of the questions that can be meaningfully asked of the data.

The same applies to the personnel of Domesday Book. The profile of holders of land in 1086 is now better understood. TRE lords have not been so well served. Identification of individuals is clearly important, but it is only a preliminary to a prosopography of elites in 1066. It is how power and influence were wielded that gives us insights into the workings of society in the eleventh century. With the nature of the data limiting the potential for conventional family history, there is a need to widen the evidential base of the enquiry. Tenurial relations, whether explicit or recovered from the diplomatic of the text, are clearly an under-exploited resource. It has been demonstrated in several counties that individuals cluster around prominent predecessors. The patterns of tenure that are thereby suggested are every bit as eloquent of local and regional power structures as the studies based on identity alone. Any prosopography of the English elites of Domesday must examine such patterns systematically.

As the Latin texts become more freely available, other priorities will no doubt come to the fore. The Domesday texts may not always be able to answer the questions that historians wish to ask of them, but they provide a comprehensive account of Domesday England in their own terms. If we ask the right questions, we now have the technology to interrogate them in ways that have been impossible before. We also have the tools for validating our analyses. These are indeed exciting times for Domesday studies.

2

A Digital Latin Domesday

J. J. N. Palmer

IN THE PAST two decades databases and digital translations of Domesday Book have provided powerful tools for searching the text and analysing its content,[1] but these tools do not yet include what might appear to be the most useful one for scholarly purposes, a searchable Latin text. This paper describes a project to create one, outlining the workforce and facilities employed, the problems involved, the characteristics of the edition, progress to date, and results from a preliminary analysis of this first digital text of the Latin Domesday.

A digital Farley

The first stage in the project was to transcribe the Latin text edited by Abraham Farley.[2] This was part of a larger scheme to produce digital versions of the Ordnance Survey facsimile, the Latin text, the Phillimore translation, databases of names, places and statistics, and notes on the identification of Domesday landowners, with the ultimate objective of linking these elements and mapping the data in

---

[1] K. S. B. Keats-Rohan, *Coel: Continental Origins of English Landowners, 1066–1086*, CDROM, Coel Enterprises Ltd 1995; J. J. N. Palmer, Matthew Palmer, and George Slater, *Domesday Explorer*, Chichester 2000; *The Digital Domesday Book*, CDROM, Alecto Historical Editions, London 2002; J. J. N. Palmer, *Electronic Edition of Domesday Book: Translation, Databases and Scholarly Commentary, 1086*, 2nd edn, 2010, Economic and Social Data Service, Study Number 5694, http://discover.ukdataservice.ac.uk/catalogue?sn=5694, accessed 03/10/2015, also available at https://hydra.hull.ac.uk/; Anna Powell-Smith, *Open Domesday*: http://www.domesdaymap.co.uk/ 2011, accessed 04/03/2012; 'Searchable Index of Landowners in 1066 and 1086', *Prosopography of Anglo-Saxon England* http://domesday.pase.ac.uk/, accessed 04/03/2012. Individual folio images, retrieved by name and place searches, can be purchased from the National Archives at http://www.nationalarchives.gov.uk/domesday/, accessed 04/03/2012, and other commercial sites.

[2] *Domesday Book; seu Liber Censualis Willelmi Primi Regis Angliae inter Archivos Regni in Domo Capitulari Westmonasterii Asservatus*, ed. Abraham Farley, 2 vols, London 1783.

them. The Latin text and translation were produced at the University of Hull at the beginning of the 1980s by a team of apprentice typists working on one of the many schemes devised by the Thatcher government to reduce the unemployment it had created.[3] The trainees knew no Latin, worked from poor quality Xeroxes of the Farley edition, had no previous computer training, and had to cope with mainframe software which was extremely user-unfriendly. There were no resources to have their work systematically proof-read. In short, the transcript invites caution. That said, random checks on all parts of the text suggest that the trainees acquitted themselves astonishingly well. Apart from a small number of rogue passages since corrected, the overall error-rate appears to be low, even by professional standards. The research described below tends to confirm this judgement. As an aid to further checking, the text and the Ordnance Survey facsimile are linked on an entry-by-entry basis.

Characteristics of the digital Farley

With one exception discussed towards the end of this paper, the main characteristics of the digital Farley are a product of the period when it was created, the computing facilities then available,[4] and the nature of the workforce employed. Given those constraints, instructions for the trainees were kept to a minimum. In essence, they were asked to reproduce the Farley text except where directed otherwise by annotation on the Xeroxes, this being confined to elementary coding and mark-up (see Appendix). Scribal abbreviations were catered for by representing each by an Arabic numeral between 0 and 9, a list which was short enough to be memorized. Monitoring of the early stages of transcription showed that the trainees coped well, only codes 5 and 6 causing problems. The mark-up defined deletions, gaps for missing information, interlineations, misplaced text, folio references, and continuation lines. By modern standards, this is sparse; but anything more ambitious would have been unrealistic with the resources available at the time.

A secondary function of the mark-up was to define entries and words. For the most part, entries in Great Domesday Book (GDB) are clearly defined by the scribe; but occasionally in that record, and more often in Little Domesday Book

---

[3] The funding body was the Manpower Services Commission. Later funding (1986–2003) was supplied by The British Academy, the ESRC (Economic and Social Research Council), the Arts and Humanities Research Council, and a generous grant from the University of Hull itself.

[4] The hardware was an ICL 1900 series mainframe computer, tended by men in white coats in an air-conditioned room, running the George 3 operating system: 'GEORGE (operating system)', *Wikipedia, The Free Encyclopedia*, 17/01/2012, 14:07 UTC, https://en.wikipedia.org/wiki/GEORGE_(operating_system), accessed 03/10/2015; text was typed and edited on a line editor: 'Line editor', *Wikipedia, The Free Encyclopedia*, 23/02/2012, 11:02 UTC, https://en.wikipedia.org/wiki/Line_editor, accessed 03/10/2015

(LDB), the boundaries between entries would not have been obvious to the trainees. Definition of the entries – using the Phillimore system – was essential to the project since its various elements – Latin text, English translation, facsimile, databases, mapping – would ultimately be linked at this level, allowing more precise retrieval and analysis of the data than folio references provided. Words, of course, normally required no mark-up; but the scribes did create many spurious words by inserting spaces within them, or by omitting spaces between them. In LDB, for instance, they frequently omitted a space between 'In' and the following place-name, and constructions such as *substigando* are not rare. The scribe of GDB was less prone to this habit, though he normally wrote *idest* (sometimes corrected by Farley to *id est*) for *id est*, and occasionally *Ulfenisc* for the English magnate *Ulf Fenisc*.

No attempt was made to correct most other scribal errors or inconsistencies. The scribes, for instance, were sometimes casual about the correct placement of suspension signs, omitted them altogether, or inserted them where they were redundant. In these and other circumstances the trainees reproduced abbreviation signs where they occurred, not where the sense of the Latin required. This makes for a more accurate representation of the manuscript, though it has drawbacks in a searchable text. A Latinist would have been prone – inadvertently or not – to correct such errors.

Preliminary research results

These characteristics complicate searches on the text. Searching an inflected language is itself problematic, and the proliferation of graphic forms of any one word in the digital Farley make it a daunting task, a problem examined below pp.77ff. This characteristic does, however, have one positive aspect. Although many of the variant forms may be no more than symptoms of scribal boredom, exuberance or indiscipline,[5] others appear to be survivals from the layers of documentation behind Domesday Book, and hence clues to their respective contributions to its 'making' and perhaps to its purpose.[6]

A simple example is provided by the distribution of the graphic form *Si*, which occurs 174 times as a separate word (Table 1).[7]

The patterns are evidently not random. Only two circuits employ *Si*, though the words it represents are found throughout Domesday Book. There are also slight traces of the return of a tenant-in-chief for fief 14 in Suffolk, all seven *Si*s as an

---

[5] Compare the verdict of J. H. Round, *Feudal England*, London 1895, 26, that the scribes 'appear to have revelled in the use of synonym and paraphrase'.
[6] Sally Harvey, 'Domesday Book and its Predecessors', *EHR* 86, 1971, 753–73 at 753: 'If we knew how Domesday Book was made, we should then know why it was made'.
[7] *Si* in such institutional names as *abboi de Si edmundo* are not included in this figure. Of 194 such names, one is in Kent, three in Lincolnshire, and the remainder in LDB. All but one (LDB, 371v: SFK 14,163) use the capitalized form.

Table 1: *S1* and *s1*

S1			s1		
County	Count	Headword	County	Count	Headword
LIN	7	*Soca*	DBY	2	*solidus*
NTT	1	*Soca*	LIN	19	*solidus*
YKS	2	*Soca*	NTT	4	*solidus*
SUF	7	*Sanctus*	YKS	127	*solidus*
NFK	1	*seruus*	NFK	2	*seruus*
			NFK	1	*solidus*
			NFK	1	*sum*

Soca: the marginal abbreviation

abbreviation for *Sanctus* appearing on that one fief (more on this later). Although it is not apparent from these tables, the Yorkshire data provides clearer evidence of an individual *breve*, the 127 *s1*s and both *S1*s occurring on the royal fiefs 1 and 29, as also do three of the four in Nottinghamshire and one of the two in Derbyshire. The distribution of *S1* is therefore suggestive of texts compiled at the level of circuit, county and fief.

Analysis of the vocabulary of the geld provides more extensive evidence. Words for the assessment for taxation and other public burdens are among the most common in Domesday Book, particularly *geldo* or *geldum*. Between them, the verb and noun appear almost 10,000 times, in seventy-two graphic forms. Discounting variations due to inflection leaves more than sixty forms, or more than fifty if capitalization is also ignored. Table 2, which lists the distribution of the eight forms which occur more than 100 times each, underlines the role played by circuits. Six of these eight are virtually confined to a single circuit; and for the other two – *geldo* and *geldau1* – the preponderance in one circuit is very marked.

Distribution among counties is also far from random. In GDB it is broadly comparable to the number of entries in the counties of each circuit in most cases. Without exception, all share a graphic form which is scarcely to be found at all in a county outside their circuit; and in the case of circuit VI, all counties except tiny Rutland share a second abbreviation (*gld*) which appears nowhere else in Domesday Book.[8] The distribution in LDB also has a pronounced pattern, Essex standing out as exceptional in this as in many other respects (Table 3).

These distributions appear to point to only one possible conclusion: the master scribe – 'consummate craftsman' and 'administrative genius' though he was[9] – often acted simply as a copyist, transcribing the precise graphic form of the abbreviated

---

[8] Those parts of Rutland recorded under other counties – notably under Northamptonshire – share the forms used in those counties.

[9] David Roffe, *Decoding Domesday*, Woodbridge 2007, 45.

Table 2: *geldo* and *geldum* by circuits

	I	II	II	IV	V	VI	VII	Totals
gldo	0	0	0	0	6	3457	0	3463
geldbo	6	2858	0	1	11	0	0	2876
geldo	180	80	0	8	1116	2	0	1386
gld	0	0	0	0	0	599	0	599
gelto	0	0	0	0	0	0	496	496
gelt1	0	0	0	0	0	0	145	145
g1	0	0	0	0	0	1	143	144
geldau1	104	24	0	1	5	0	0	134
Totals	290	2962	0	10	1138	4059	784	9243

Table 3: *geldo* and *geldum* by counties

geldbo		geldo		gldo		gld			gelto	gelt1	gelt	g1
WIL	399	GLS	117	HUN	142	3		ESS	0	0	1	0
DOR	421	WOR	68	DBY	264	16		NFK	331	6	44	88
SOM	665	HEF	256	NTT	450	74		SUF	165	139	20	55
DEV	1104	SHR	344	RUT	18	0						
CON	269	CHS	331	YKS	1193	396						
				LIN	1390	110						
Totals	2858		1116		3457	599	Totals		496	145	65	143

word in front of him, using one form in a particular circuit and a variant in another with great consistency. This in turn implies that he worked directly from sources compiled at the circuit level, these circuit returns themselves perhaps retaining some forms they found in their sources. How else could circuits be so emphatically distinguished from each other while preserving traces peculiar to individual counties and fiefs? How else could such a high degree of consistency be achieved at such a low level in the data?

Though it appears inescapable, there is a major problem with this conclusion. Of the six circuit returns whose existence it assumes, the only one to have survived – the *Liber Exoniensis* (Exon), for circuit II – does not reproduce the Domesday geld formula. Where Domesday has *geldbo*, Exon more often has *reddidit gildum*, or an abbreviation thereof. There are similar contrasts between Exon and Domesday for all the major formulae: for tenure, ploughlands, plough teams, valuations and – most conspicuously – for Domesday's *T.R.E.*, commonly rendered as *ea die q̃ rex E. f. u. et m.*[10] Numbers apart, very little of consequence was copied exactly from Exon into GDB.

---

[10] *Ea die qua rex Eduuardus fuit uiuus et mortuus*, 'on the day on which King Edward was alive and dead'.

A generation ago this would not have been seen as a problem. The scholarly consensus then was that the Domesday scribe worked from a 'fair copy' of Exon, which may not have shared its 'provincialisms'.[11] But this is now a minority view,[12] the prevailing opinion being that the Domesday scribe worked directly from Exon itself, though evidently not by copying its major formulae.[13] If the 'fair copy' thesis is rejected, where then did the formulae in circuit II originate? The answer is probably provided by three entries in Exon made by the scribe of GDB himself, 'perhaps inserted ... when he was editing and abbreviating the contents of Exon for GDB'.[14] Whatever the reason for their inclusion in Exon, these entries are effectively templates[15] for the Domesday account of circuit II, since all three reproduce the major formulae which the scribe would employ in writing up that circuit, including *geldbo*.[16] Whichever view is taken on the 'fair copy' debate, therefore, the distinctive geld formula of circuit II can be traced to a source compiled at the circuit level.

The other three circuits of GDB also have distinctive forms for recording geld liability. Circuit IV is distinguished by its near-avoidance of the word geld, all forms in that circuit totalling just nineteen cases. The scribe here normally employed the formula *x holds y hides* or the non-committal *here [ibi] x hides*. By contrast, the predominant formula in circuits I and III is *se defendere*.[17] Depending on the translation consulted, manors are said 'to defend' themselves, 'to answer for', or to 'be

---

[11] R. Welldon Finn, 'The Immediate Sources of the Exchequer Domesday', *Bulletin of the John Rylands Library* 40, 1957, 47–78; V. H. Galbraith, *The Making of Domesday Book*, Oxford 1961, 105–13.

[12] Pierre Chaplais, 'William of Saint-Calais and the Domesday Survey', in *Domesday Studies: Papers Read at the Novocentenary Conference of the Royal Historical Society and the Institute of British Geographers, Winchester 1986*, ed. J. C. Holt, Woodbridge 1987, 65–78 at 69, 73, 75–6: 'Perhaps after all he [the Domesday scribe] compiled GDB not directly from Exon, but from an intermediary text, as Galbraith thought'.

[13] Frank Thorn and Caroline Thorn, 'The Writing of Great Domesday Book', in *Domesday Book*, ed. Elizabeth Hallam and David Bates, Stroud 2001, 37–72, 200–3 at 67–9, 203; Roffe, *Decoding Domesday*, 57.

[14] Notes to the Phillimore edition, SOM 4: https://hydra.hull.ac.uk/resources/hull:domesdayTranslation, accessed 03/10/2015; http://discover.ukdataservice.ac.uk/catalogue?sn=5694, accessed 03/10/2015.

[15] The entries are written on two otherwise blank folios (153, 436) and so easily referenced.

[16] GDB, 87v, 97: SOM 4,1.33,1–2. See R. Welldon Finn, 'The Evolution of Successive Versions of Domesday Book', *EHR* 66, 1951, 561–4; Alexander R. Rumble, 'The Palaeography of the Domesday Manuscripts', in *Domesday Book: a Reassessment*, ed. P. H. Sawyer, London 1985, 28–49 at 46–8; both reproduce the relevant entries from Exon and Domesday. As if to emphasis the contrast in styles, an Exon scribe wrote a second version of GDB, 87v: SOM 4,1 using the characteristic Exon formulae (*ibid.* 562). The three entries in Domesday Book itself are not exact copies of those in Exon, though the differences are relatively minor.

[17] There are 1355 occurrences in circuit I; 374 in circuit III; and 20 between the remaining five circuits, half of these in circuit II. Where the scribe of GDB used the *se defendere*

assessed for' so many tax units. Like the verb and noun for geld, *se defendere* appears in a variety of graphic forms; but the interest of *se defendere* is not so much their number – there are nineteen – as what they appear to imply about the meaning of the formula in which they are embedded. One form (*defdo*) is overwhelmingly predominant, and its tense is ambiguous.[18]

Defdo is most naturally expanded as *defendit*, the form favoured by editors, who almost always translate it in the present tense unless the context demands otherwise, though *defendit* is also the past perfect. The nineteen graphic forms contain only two which are unambiguously in the present tense – both occurring once each – whereas more than a third of the forms are unambiguously in the past and between them occur more than fifty times.[19] Should the past tense, perhaps, be the default translation? And, if so, does it matter to anyone other than translators?

There is a surprising amount of evidence suggesting that the answer to both questions is an emphatic 'yes'. The so-called 'satellite' texts from both circuits provide some comparative data. In circuit I, the satellite from St Augustine's, Canterbury, has twenty entries where the *defdo* of the Domesday text is specifically stated to refer to 1066.[20] The corresponding Domesday formula[21] drops the explicit reference to 1066 and associates the ambiguous *defdo* with the tenurial formula for the landholder in 1086, thereby implying – wrongly – that the geld figure applies just to that date.[22]

Another Kentish satellite, the Domesday Monachorum (DM B), is often more revealing.[23] At Darenth, the first rural manor on the archiepiscopal fief, for instance, Domesday Book again associates an ambiguous *defdo* statement with the 1086 tenurial formula[24] while DM B states that Darenth defended itself for two sulungs TRE and 'now similarly'.[25] So Domesday drops the reference both to a specific date and to the fact that the assessment had not changed in two decades. There are

---

formulae for rural manors, Exon did so too (GDB, 99, 100, 100v: DEV 1,4–5, 28; SOM 47,15), though not for the boroughs, described in a separate section (GDB, 75: DOR B1–4).

[18] *Se defdo*, which occurs 1667 times. Only four other forms occur more than five times each: *se defdbo* (20), *se defdobo* (18), *se defendo* (9) and *se defendebo* (6).

[19] *Defendunt* (GDB, 189: CAM B9) and *defendui* (LDB, 305v: SFK 6,18: *defendum*). The context of the six cases of *defdot* requires the present tense: GDB, 31v, 32v, 56v, 58v, 197, 254v: SUR 5,19.8,8; BRK 1,7. 7,10; CAM 22,6; SHR 4,3,15. A large proportion of the remaining 1742 cases are left ambiguous by their context.

[20] The normal formula is *tempore regis Edwardi se defendit pro x solin*. There is a recent edition of the text in Colin Flight, *The Survey of Kent: Documents Relating to the Survey of Kent Conducted in 1086*, British Archaeological Reports, British series 506, Oxford 2010, 78–85.

[21] 'x holds y' *quod se defdo pro ... solin*.

[22] Flight, *Survey of Kent*, 78.

[23] Flight, *Survey of Kent*, 47–64; facsimile in *DM*, plates 1–16 (folios 1–8).

[24] *tenet in domino TARENT. Pro II solins se defdo*: GDB, 3: KEN 2,3.

[25] *Survey of Kent*, 50; DM B, 88. *Derente ... defendebat se in tempore E regis, et nunc similiter*. DM B normally uses the imperfect tense. The satellites for Kent and Cambridgeshire are all

dozens of such entries in the DM B, only occasionally matched by a similar formula in the Domesday text. More usually, the satellite references to assessments for both 1066 and 1086 are replaced in Domesday Book by a single figure whose ambiguous formulation appears to refer only to 1086, and is usually understood in that sense, though wrongly so.

Evidence from the satellite texts from circuit III is even more compelling. The *Inquisitio Comitatus Cantabrigiensis* (ICC) includes several hundred manors in the Cambridgeshire Domesday, and for almost every one of them it supplies assessment figures for both 1066 and 1086.[26] In the majority of cases, the assessment was the same at both dates. Domesday Book does not reveal this fact, merely recording what appears to be the current hidage for 1086. Even more striking is the contrast between Domesday Book and the ICC in the case of the six Cambridgeshire hundreds which had obtained tax reductions since 1066. In a minority of these cases – normally those where the entire vill was in the hands of one tenant-in-chief – Domesday does give geld figures for both dates; but, more frequently, it ignores the reduction and presents the 1066 assessment as though it were current, despite the fact that it had been reduced for 1086.[27] Here the figures are not just misleading but simply wrong. A tax collector attempting to use them would have invited serious trouble.

A similar state of affairs is revealed by the *Inquisitio Eliensis* (IE).[28] The IE also states that the hidages of the three manors which constituted the fief of the abbey of Ely in Hertfordshire were unchanged between 1066 and 1086, a statement ignored by Domesday, which simply records that the manors *se defd*o for so many hides.[29] One should perhaps add Northamptonshire to this list of counties for which Domesday's presentation of the geld figures is deceptive, as its geld figures – once again given in relation to the 1086 landholder – are almost certainly those of 1066 also, since it was on the basis of the Domesday figures that Northamptonshire was assessed in the twelfth century,[30] after the reductions of 1086 had been abandoned nationally and the 1066 assessments largely reinstated as the basis for taxation.[31] In

---

later copies, of course, so *defendebat* may expand an abbreviated form in the original; but it is improbable that other details in the four satellites on dating were altered or added.

[26] ICC, 1–96.

[27] C. Hart, *The Hidation of Cambridgeshire*, Leicester University, Department of History Occasional Papers, 2nd series 6, Leicester 1974, 26–30, 46–67.

[28] ICC, 101–4, 107–9, 113–16, 118–20.

[29] Ibid., 124–5; GDB, 135: HRT 8,1–3.

[30] As evidenced by Pipe Roll receipts: F. W. Maitland, *Domesday Book and Beyond*, London 1897, 400.

[31] Judith Green, 'The Last Century of Danegeld', *EHR* 96, 1981, 241–58 at 243–4; *The Government of England under Henry I*, Cambridge 1986, 69–71. In the twelfth century, Northamptonshire's geld liability (in round terms) was £120, equivalent to 2 shillings on 1,200 hides. The Domesday hidage has been variously calculated at between 1244 and 1365 hides; the pre-Domesday documents known as the County Hidage and the Northamptonshire Geld Roll allocate the county 3200 and 2664 hides respectively: Maitland, *Domesday Book*

eleven other counties, Domesday Book normally supplies the geld figure in the past tense, without ambiguity; and of the twenty occurrences of the formula *se defendere* outside circuits I and III, all but one are unambiguously in the past tense, the exception (*se defdo*) being a Northamptonshire entry.[32] In all these cases, the 1066 assessment was evidently current in 1086: the silence of the record cannot imply the absence of an assessment.

It seems reasonable to conclude from all this that tax assessments in Domesday Book apply to both dates unless stated otherwise. This was so apparent that the Domesday scribe often felt no need to record it explicitly. In this sense, most of Domesday's geld figures are 'Edwardian' and were unchanged for two decades. This has implications for a number of long-running debates as to what Domesday Book can reveal about English government in the later eleventh century: the scale of literacy and record-keeping,[33] the contribution of Anglo-Saxon sources to the inquest proceedings,[34] and even the Conqueror's alleged plans to revise the geld system.[35] In this last context, it is worth noting that the 'Edwardian' geld liability contrasts sharply with the adjacent statistic for ploughlands, almost invariably given unambiguously in the present tense (*Terra est* ...).

A final example of a graphic form illuminating the word it represents must suffice: *recepo*, in the valuation formula *quando recepo*.[36] The phrase is normally translated 'when received' in the Alecto edition and 'when acquired' in that by Phillimore, being understood to mean 'when the manor was' acquired or received, translating *quando recepta* [*est*]. There is, however, not a single graphic form (among almost 1200) of *recepta*, nor one that demands to be expanded as such. By contrast, *recepit* is written in full more than three dozen times and is the only form found in all seven circuits. There are also, of course, scores of entries where 'he', 'she', 'they' or 'it' are explicitly named as receiving the revenues concerned, constructions which occur in all circuits and almost all counties. This is also the predominant format

---

and Beyond, 456–8; C. Hart, *The Hidation of Northamptonshire*, Leicester University, Department of History Occasional Papers, 2nd series 3, 1970, 38.

[32] GDB, 229: NTH 56,64. See note 17. Phillimore and Alecto translate the Northamptonshire *se defdo* in the present tense.

[33] M. T. Clanchy, *From Memory to Written Record: England, 1066–1307*, 2nd edn, Oxford 1993, 26–32; James Campbell, 'Some Agents and Agencies of the Late Anglo-Saxon State', in *Domesday Studies*, ed. Holt, 214–18; reprinted in James Campbell, *The Anglo-Saxon State*, London 2000, 219–25.

[34] Sally Harvey, 'Domesday Book and its Predecessors', *EHR* 86, 1971, 753–73, especially 768.

[35] Sally Harvey, 'Taxation and the Ploughland in Domesday Book', in *Domesday Book: a Reassessment*, 86–103 at 91–3; Maitland, *Domesday Book and Beyond*, 4; David Pratt, 'Demesne Exemption from Royal Taxation in Anglo-Saxon and Anglo-Norman England', *EHR* 128, 2013, 1–34, especially 13–14, 31–32.

[36] *Recepo* is the most common form (1183). Only four other forms occur more than five times: *reci* (79), *recepi* (60), *recepit* (37) and *reco* (28).

in Exon,[37] while *recepit* is often written in full in the ICC even where no owner is named in the valuation formula. In view of all this, 'when he received it' would seem preferable as the default translation.[38]

If circuits and counties are distinguished by the graphic forms they employ, what of fiefs? Can they also be detected in the record, as hinted above in the analysis of *S1*? They are undoubtedly harder to find, but it does appear likely that the Domesday account of fief 14 in Suffolk was directly influenced by a written return from the abbey of Bury St Edmunds, as suggested by Stephen Baxter at the Domesday conference at The National Archives in 2000. In his paper, Baxter described an elaborate methodology for detecting tenants-in-chief who had contrived to 'cook the books' by controlling the form and content of the Domesday account of their possessions. He identified Bishop Wulfstan of Worcester as one such successful lobbyist and indicated that Abbot Baldwin of Bury St Edmunds might be another.[39] The graphic forms on Baldwin's Suffolk fief appear to support this suggestion, being exceptionally distinctive, with a tally of almost 200 forms unique to the fief. As the following table of the most common of them reveals, some represent words which occur frequently elsewhere in Domesday Book, though in different graphic forms (Table 4). Other abbreviated forms of *dare*, for instance, appear roughly 1000 times; of *hominum*, more than 300; and of *terram*, over 1500.[40]

In addition to unique forms, a number of others are found predominantly on this fief. All but one of the fifty-seven occurrences of *scoo* (*sancto*) in LDB appear there, as do fifty-two of the fifty-eight forms of *uendo* (*uendere*) in Domesday Book. Fief 14 also records the only two appearances of the Old English *Litla*, in the place-names of Little Livermere and Little Fakenham.[41] The fief is distinctive in other ways. It is particularly well laid-out, almost every entry being separated from that preceding and following it by spacing, emphasized by the gallows sign and a large initial capital. The great majority of entries begin on a new line, the few continuation lines being clearly defined, with only the very longest entries normally spilling

---

[37] Domesday rarely uses *quando recepo* in circuit II, preferring the ambiguous 'the value is and was' phrasing.

[38] The Phillimore volumes edited by Frank and Caroline Thorn between 1982 and 1986 use this translation, as do the East Anglian volumes.

[39] An 'especially promising target for further research': 'The Representation of Lordship and Land Tenure in Domesday Book', in *Domesday Book*, ed. Hallam and Bates, 73–93, 203–8 at 93.

[40] Names, places, institutions and Roman numerals are excluded from these counts. Curiously, the remainder of the honour adds nothing significant to these figures.

[41] LDB, 366v, 367v: SUF 14,87;97. The 'Feudal Book' of Abbot Baldwin also uses English forms in these two cases: *Feudal Documents from the Abbey of Bury St Edmunds*, ed. D. C. Douglas, British Academy Records of the Social and Economic History of England and Wales 8, London 1932, 20, 24.

Table 4: Unique graphic forms in Suffolk fief 14

	expanded form	count
darı	*dare*	60
remı	*remansit*	15
licı	*licentia*	14
hoıuo	*hominum*	13
remano	*remansit*	13
torı	*terram*	13
hoouı	*hominum*	9
scos	*sanctus*	9
ooe	*omnem*	8
seruitı	*seruitium*	8
uenderı	*uendere*	7
elemosinı	*elemosina*	6
sinı	*sine*	6
tnı	*tamen*	6
Ecloa	*Ecclesia*	5
hooiuı	*hominum*	5

over on to another folio. The combination of these characteristics is found for few other fiefs in LDB so emphatically.

It is tempting to conclude from this that the scribe had the written return from the abbey in front of him from which he simply copied much of the Domesday entry. Some caution is needed, however. This fief was part of a large section of LDB written by the man identified as scribe 5,[42] whose contributions include well over 700 unique graphic forms. Despite this, the obvious conclusion may be the correct one. Unlike the unique forms on fief 14, the remainder by this scribe are scattered across two counties and many fiefs, and only a small number of them do not appear on fief 14 itself.[43] Rather than scribe 5 influencing the graphic forms in fief 14, the graphic forms in fief 14 may have influenced scribe 5. Or perhaps he had a relationship with the abbey or with Abbot Baldwin. Whatever the explanation, it appears probable that the description of the fief in LDB was directly affected by a written return from the tenant-in-chief.

All tenants-in-chief had a vested interest in influencing the form and content of the record of their possessions in Domesday Book, of course; it seems improbable that only two contrived to do so, though it may not be a straightforward task to identify others. The Worcestershire fief of Bishop Wulfstan, for instance, would not

---

[42] Alexander R. Rumble: 'The Domesday Manuscripts: Scribes and Scriptoria', in *Domesday Book*, ed. Holt, 79–100 at 90–1, 99.
[43] The four most common such forms – *comos* and *Comos* (*comes*), *carıṛ* (*caruca*) and *caluopniatur* (*calumpniatur*) – are between them distributed among 35 fiefs.

confidently – if at all – be identified by an analysis of its graphic forms, nor that of Abbot Baldwin of Bury St Edmunds by the techniques outlined by Dr Baxter.

Few of the graphic forms examined so far contain allographs, for the very good reason that this data is unreliable.[44] Although he was meticulous in most respects,[45] Farley did not always faithfully represent the allographs in the Domesday manuscript, sometimes 'correcting' them in accordance with the conventions of his age. He was not entirely consistent in this practice, and neither were the scribes in theirs. All Farley's forms were dutifully transcribed by my trainees, resulting in a dog's breakfast of allographs. Leaving them in this state was not a reasonable option and revising them in accordance with the manuscript was not viable at the time; doing so now would be of doubtful utility and would stall the project. It is normal practice to transcribe the long 's' as a normal 's' (as here); but there is no consensus among Latinists about the correct treatment of 'j' and 'v'; in the digital Farley they have been rendered as 'i' and 'u', apart from the Roman numeral V.

This has inevitably resulted in the loss of graphic information, though the loss does not appear to be serious.[46] The most common of the forms involving a long 's' – *solidus*, *sunt*, *pastura* and *silua* – appear between them almost 34,000 times but produce few significant distributions. Forms of *solidus* are overwhelmingly the most numerous, accounting for roughly two-thirds of the total, yet they show no striking patterns. *folo* (16,999) occurs in large numbers in all circuits, evenly spread among their constituent counties, the only disproportionate figure being that for Staffordshire – enigmatic as ever – its total of 85 representing a little more than 5% of cases in the circuit. Even so, its distribution within the county is fairly even. *folido* (6900) is only a little more interesting, appearing in all circuits and in all but two of the thirty-four counties – Rutland and Essex are the exceptions – but thinly spread in circuits III and VII, and within circuit VI fairly common only in Lincolnshire. A more detailed analysis of the forms of *folidus* would no doubt produce more nuanced results, but it seems unlikely they would be particularly significant. Forms of *silua* appear equally unlikely to yield much of interest. Abbreviations with the long 's' are slightly more than a third of all forms and are found in every county except Rutland, though the proportion of those with long and short 's' varies from county to county.

The distribution of the two most frequent forms of *sunt* is more interesting. As can be seen from the following table (Table 5), all but four of the 230 appearances

---

[44] The long 's' – graphically difficult to distinguish from an 'f' (here used to represent it) – 'j', and 'v'. 'W' has not been converted to 'uu' (see below). Some forms of *si* use a long 's': six in circuit 6, nine in East Anglia.

[45] It is difficult to assess his usage from the printed text alone since he almost always transcribed words ending in both the long and short 's' as a short 's'.

[46] The data was analysed before the allographs were replaced by the characters they represent. There are over 100,000 allographs, roughly 90,000 involving the long 's', the remainder 'j' and 'v'. If it were thought worthwhile to restore them, the link between the digital Farley and the Ordnance Survey facsimile would ease the task.

Table 5: Forms of *sunt* by circuit

	I	II	II	IV	V	VI	VII
funt	1024	9	698	689	876	417	27
fto	3	226	0	0	0	1	0

Table 6: Forms of *pastura*

Circuit	*pastur**	*pastɪ*	*past3**		*past3**
I	57	0	0	MDX	56
II	2266	1	18	HRT	62
III	134	1	217	BUK	2
IV	118	1	2	CAM	96
V	7	0	0	BDF	1
VI	3	43	0		
VII	41	70	0		
Totals	2626	116	237	Total	217

of *fto* are in the single county of Wiltshire, distributed fairly evenly throughout the county, on every fief with more than one or two manors, an exceptionally clear example of survivals from a document compiled at the county level feeding through to Domesday Book.

Similarly, the bulk of the form *paft3** for *pastura* occurs in one circuit, for the most part in three of its five counties; while less evenly distributed than *fto*, it is not confined to a handful of fiefs (Table 6).

Sampling of the manuscript indicates that Farley accurately represents forms of these words, so the results are probably meaningful. It is, however, a modest haul from considerably more than 30,000 examples of the long 's'. Forms with modest counts may no doubt produce other examples. The graphic *fuopfit* (*sumpsit*), for instance, appears just nine times, eight of them in Hertfordshire.[47] But there is little reason to believe that such cases would seriously modify the conclusion suggested above, always subject to the qualification made earlier about Farley's representation of the long 's'.

The lower-case graphic 'v' produces only one significant pattern, but it is an emphatic one, 919 of 921 instances of the forms *lev'* (for league) being in circuit VI. Within that circuit, *levo* appears in Lincolnshire (6) and Yorkshire (50), *levɪ* in all six counties, though disproportionately in Yorkshire (558). Even tiny Rutland (14) uses this form, as does Huntingdonshire (34), which is often distinctive within the circuit in other respects. Sampling of the manuscript forms indicates that Farley

---

[47] But forms of *sumo* are uncommon (16); with one exception (GDB, iv: KEN M13), they are confined to circuit III, where they occur in four of the five counties.

Table 7: Forms of *leuo* or *leuɪ*

Circuit	*leu**		*Leu**		*leu**		*leu**
I	0	CON	129	LEC	30	DBY	1
II	976	DEV	263	NTH	23	HUN	0
III	0	DOR	175	OXF	55	LIN	6
IV	129	SOM	202	STS	8	NTT	3
V	1	WIL	207	WAR	13	RUT	0
VI	154					YKS	144
VII	167						
Totals	1427	Totals	976	Totals	129	Totals	154

almost always distinguished 'v' or 'u' in this context. By contrast, the distribution of the 'u' form (*leu*) produces quite different patterns which, while not without interest, are nothing like as striking; all circuit VII forms are in East Anglia (Table 7).

Other words in lower-case 'v' are fewer and less revealing. Graphic 'v' occurs more than ten times in only four other words, forms of *ualeo*, *uillanus*, *uirga/uirgata*, and *uilla*. Space precludes a detailed analysis, which in any case would repeat to a considerable extent observations made above. Forms of *uillanus* and *uilla* in 'v' are rare, representing less than 1% and 2% of the respective totals for the 'u' and 'v' forms combined, only Middlesex showing much use of the two 'u' forms. By contrast, there is a marked preponderance of 'v' over 'u' – ranging from 79% to 99% – in the forms of *uirga/uirgata* in circuits I, II, IV and V, while the 'u' form dominates circuits III, VI and VII, accounting for 99% or more of all occurrences, though the word itself does not appear all that often in the latter two circuits. *Ualeo*, the most common of the four words, has an irregular distribution which might repay further investigation though significant findings seem unlikely.

A similar analysis of forms containing the graphic 'j' would almost certainly not be worthwhile since in this case eighteenth-century typographical conventions led Farley to replace the manuscript 'i' with 'j' on numerous occasions. In Kent, for instance, 'j' appears more than 200 times in Farley but only half-a-dozen times in the manuscript.[48] Since the text for Kent includes every word containing 'j' in the Farley edition which occurs more than 100 times,[49] and all but six of those which occur ten times or more,[50] analysis of these forms would evidently be wasted effort. As noted above, 'w' has not been converted to a double 'u'; but for the sake of completeness, it can be noted that it produces only one significant distribution, the forms *lewɪ*

---

[48] Twice in *iugum* (GDB, 1, 14v: KEN D24.13,1), twice in *in* (GDB, 9v, 11: KEN 5,131,191), once in *infra* (GDB, 13v: KEN 9,35) and once for the place name *Iaonei* (GDB, 13v: KEN 9,39).

[49] *Huius*, *eius*, *iaceo* and *alius*.

[50] These figures do not include personal names.

(52) and *lewa* (4) for *leuga*. Fifty-five of these fifty-six forms are in Worcestershire, while the one exception – the royal manor of Forthampton[51] – is almost entirely surrounded by Worcestershire, though lying officially in Gloucestershire until transferred by Earl William fitzOsbern to Herefordshire for tax purposes.[52]

To summarize: some graphic forms clearly preserve traces left by scribes responsible for earlier drafts of the data. Analysis of their 'fingerprints' therefore offers an additional technique for detecting sources compiled at the level of county, circuit and fief, and hence a new approach to the perennial question of 'the making of Domesday Book'. In some cases, the graphic forms also help to clarify aspects of the vocabulary and formulae of the text.

Further developments

Whatever its merits in these respects, the digital Farley is ill-suited to searching, normally the principal strength and purpose of an electronic text. The reasons are clear: the language is inflected, the shorthand conventions inconsistent, and the many and various written sources upon which Domesday Book drew are affected by the demotic speech of both natives and their conquerors and subject to the transmission hazards cogently described by Professor Dodgson as 'mishearing, mispronouncing, misreading and miscopying … along the interfaces between different languages and different scripts', and much else besides.[53] Despite the editorial expertise of the master scribe of GDB, the end result is a text which is guaranteed to fail to achieve anything like 100% retrieval rates for any search other than for specific graphic forms. LDB is even more challenging. To mitigate these problems, the project includes two additional elements: an expanded Latin text of Domesday Book and a Domesday Latin dictionary. Both elements will be linked to each other and to the digital Farley on a word-for-word basis, and all three to the facsimile on an entry-by-entry basis.

An expanded text will allow more effective search and retrieval. Anna Powell-Smith has begun exploratory talks with the Wikimedia Foundation with a view to crowd-sourcing further texts and a pilot project has established that it is feasible to match such expanded texts with the graphic forms in the digital Farley under program control.[54] This may offer the best chance of completing the project

---

[51] GDB, 180v: HEF 1,43.

[52] GDB, 163v: GLS 1,35. The distribution of other common forms – variants of *wasta*, *wapentac*, and *berewic* – are largely determined by the distribution of the words themselves. Between them, the four words total almost 90% of forms containing a graphic 'w', personal and place-names excluded; only 1% of forms of *wasta* and *wapentac* begin with 'uu', a reflection of the fact that few names, places or words have an initial 'uu'.

[53] J. McN. Dodgson, 'Domesday Book: Place-names and Personal Names', in *Domesday Studies*, ed. Holt, 121–37 at 123.

[54] Written by Matthew Palmer, who also wrote the software to analyse the digital Farley and to build the dictionaries discussed below.

within a reasonable time-scale.[55] Funding would probably be a problem for other approaches. It has been suggested that Optical Character Recognition (OCR) scanning of the 'Literal expansions' of the Latin texts produced for a dozen or so counties in the nineteenth century could achieve rapid results for those counties, though in my own experience a modestly-competent two-finger typist would not be significantly slower, and would be better able to cope with the inconsistencies between the various 'expansions'. If the Domesday scribe could write GDB in a year or so, a skilled Latinist with good typing abilities and no other commitments could presumably expand the text in a similar period, if such a self-sacrificing paragon were to come forward. Failing that, crowd-sourcing seems the most promising strategy. Despite the 'sniffy caveats'[56] of some professionals, crowd-sourcing has achieved academic respectability when such institutions as Oxford University and UCL enlist the power of crowds for their projects, as indeed does The National Archives for verifying its Domesday data among other projects.[57]

Although an expanded text will be easier to search, it will still be subject to the limitations imposed by an inflected language and erratic spelling. A suitably structured Domesday dictionary will go some way to compensating for these limitations. Some progress has been made in compiling this dictionary, which contains rather more than a million records divided between five principal components: words, names, place-names, institutional names and Roman numerals. All components are initially built by software from the digital Farley, to which the expanded form of the Farley abbreviation and other relevant material is added. A typical record for a word looks like Table 8, and for names in Table 9, with records for places and institutions having similar layouts.

A dictionary of words in this format cannot be completed until expanded texts for all counties are available. While some abbreviations can be expanded without examining every graphic form, many more require each occurrence to be viewed in context. Expanding *tıra* (13462), *p^{a}ti* (11105), *cuo* (10816), *dnoio* (9733), or *p8* (9029) is unproblematic; but *carı* (27258) and *caro* (15628) – which can each represent two words and a number of inflected forms – are more typical of the vocabulary of the digital Farley. A finalized dictionary of words will therefore have to await the completion of expanded texts for all counties, when software can match their words with their graphic forms by their position in the text. A list of all Domesday graphic forms under their dictionary headwords could be produced more readily. Personal

---

[55] An alternative approach may be to employ macros to produce a text from the Electronic Farley. Initial experimentation by David Roffe for the Domesday Texts Project has suggested that it is possible to expand 90%–95% of the text in this way.
[56] *The Observer*, 18 March 2012, 36.
[57] See http://www.papyrology.ox.ac.uk/Ancient_Lives/ (ancient Greek papyri), accessed 03/10/2015; http://www.ucl.ac.uk/Bentham-Project/transcribe_bentham, accessed 03/10/2015. For Domesday, see for instance http://discovery.nationalarchives.gov.uk/SearchUI/Details?uri=D7310047 (Glust, Cheshire), accessed 03/10/2015.

Table 8: A database record for words

ID	3657
Graphic form	Teigno4
County	KEN
Phillimore	2,4
Expanded form	Teignorum
Normalized form	teignus
Headword	tainus
English form	thane
Category	noun
Circuit	1
Folio	3a
Graphic form Hex[1]	546569676E6F34

[1] The Hex field ensures capitalization is retained when sorting or querying the data.

Table 9: A database record for names

ID	1049281
Graphic form	comiteo_Alanuo
County	SUF
Phillimore	26,15
Expanded form	comitem Alanum
Normalized form	comes Alanus
Title/Byname	Alanus comes
English form	Count Alan
Category	name
Circuit	7
Folio	400a–400b
Graphic form Hex	636F6D697465305F416C616E7530

and place-names present fewer problems and can be compiled independently of expanded texts.

As it exists only in skeletal form at the moment, it is premature to speculate as to the potential of this data, though a dictionary of all the words in Domesday Book and their variant forms will have value in itself, many of those words having yet to find their way into any medieval Latin dictionary.[58] In the absence of wordlists – either English or Latin – the vocabulary of Domesday Book remains to be explored, the distribution of individual words – like *incressandum*[59] – promising

[58] J. J. N. Palmer, 'Great Domesday on CD-ROM', in *Domesday Book*, ed. Hallam and Bates, 141–50, 213–15 at 141–2, 213.
[59] Which occurs only in Shropshire (85), where 'for fattening pigs' is the normal formula for

further clues to the sources behind Domesday Book. A complete list of Domesday words and their various forms should also be an asset to linguists investigating the contribution of the native and foreign languages to the Domesday text. It has been claimed, for instance, that the French words and phrases 'embedded in the Latin text of Domesday Book form the largest single contemporary record of the eleventh-century language'.[60] Lists of names and places have been published by Dr Keats-Rohan,[61] but searchable and referenced lists, cross-referenced to all forms of a particular name or place, will have additional utility. A list of place-names and their forms will be an asset to place-name scholars, and such a list could easily be adapted to other projects – an etymology, for instance – by anyone with an elementary knowledge of databases. So, too, for personal names. There are no doubt other possible applications; and as the data is new and the methodology novel, there may be finds to be made which are as unexpected as those reported above.

Appendix

Coded Farley text for GDB, 128: MDX 4,1
.IIII. TERRA SCoI PETRI WESTMON1 IN OSULUESTANE HDo.
M2 In Uilla ubi sedet aeccloa So PETRI. tenet abbo ei9deo
loci .XIII. hid1 7 dim1. T1ra .eo ad XI. car1. Ad dnoium
p2tin1 .IX. hidae 7 I. uirg1. 7 ibi sunt .IIII. car1. Uilloi hnot .VI.
car1. 7 I. car1 plus pot1 fieri. Ibi .IX. uilloi q(i)sq6 de .I. uirg1.
7 I. uillos de .I. hida. 7 IX. uilloi q(i)sq6 de dim1 uirg1. 7 I. cot1
de .V. ac1. 7 XL.I. cot1 q(i) reddot p2 anno .XL. solo p8 ortis suis.
P(a)tuo .XI. car1. Past3a ad pecun1 uillae. Silua .C porc1.
7 XXV. dom9 militu0 abbois 7 alio4 hooum. qui reddot
VIII. solo p2 annuo. In totis ualent1 ualo .X. libo. Q2do
recepo. similit1. T. R. E: XII. libo. Hoc M2 fuit 7 est
in dnoio aeccloae So PETRI. Westmonasterii.

---

woodland, found on the majority of fiefs. Oddly, it only has the one graphic form, *incrassando*, invariably written as *incraffando* in Farley and the manuscript.
[60] *The Survey of Kent*, 29.
[61] *Domesday Names: an Index of Latin Personal and Place Names in Domesday Book*, ed. K. S. B. Keats-Rohan and David E. Thornton, Woodbridge 1997, is constructed on different principles from the Farley database, being essentially the names of landowners and their manors. It does not, therefore, include the names of manorial centres, personal names unattached to landholdings, or repeated names of tenants-in-chief within their fiefs; but it does record *ibidem* and *idem* as the names they stand for; and names, places, hundreds and wapentakes where they are implied in the text but not explicitly named there. It also includes anonymous landowners. The Farley database, by contrast, records all names and places in the text but only where they are explicitly named.

Facsimile

Numeric codes[62]

Codes in the digital Farley

0	~	suspension sign (above letter or through ascender)
1	⸍	suspension sign (follows letter)
2	⸍	above B, M, S; through stem of p, q, Q
3	ꝯ	-ur (above letter)
4	⁊	-rum (above letter)
5	ꝫ	-us, -et (on the line)
6	ꝫ	-ue (below the line)
7	⁊	et Tironian *nota*)
8	ꝑ	pro
9	ꝫ	-us (follows letter)
:	⸵	*punctus elevatus*
( )		superscript letters

Other coding conventions

- | || encloses text moved from another part of the manuscript.
- /   following text is indicated by the scribe – usually by a 'gallows' symbol – to be part of a line though not on it.
- ^ \^ delimits words above the line.
- ( )   delimits letters above words, usually abbreviations: *p(a)i* for *prati*.

---

[62] See Alexander R. Rumble, 'Methods of Textual Abbreviation in Great Domesday Book', in *Domesday Book: Studies*, ed. Ann Williams and R. W. H. Erskine, Alecto Editions, London 1987, 162–3, for a more graphically accurate reproduction of abbreviation signs.

- ? \? marginalia (fief numbers, etc.).
- { } text marked by the scribe for deletion.
- [...] gaps left for missing information (e.g., *Terra est* [...]).
- [ ] enclose editorial corrections.
- < > enclose folio references.

McLuhan Meets the Master: Scribal Devices in Great Domesday Book

David Roffe

THE LAST THIRTY years or so have seen the publication of a remarkable series of eleventh- and twelfth-century sources. Exemplary editions of chronicles, charters, laws, saints lives, literary works, and much more have provided extraordinary new vistas into Anglo-Norman England.[1] Careful analysis has shown that these often intractable sources can yield up insights into the political, social, economic, and spiritual life that were not just invisible to earlier generations but irrecoverable from the then available editions. The finely honed disciplines of codicology, palaeography, diplomatic, and textual criticism that underpin these insights have unlocked a new world. It is the more regrettable, then, that they have not been employed to produce a modern edition of Domesday Book. More than arguably any other source, Domesday exhibits a close interplay between presentation and expression, on the one hand, and our understanding of the society that it represents on the other. This is no more so than in Great Domesday Book (GDB). We now know that the scribe of the work was no mere abbreviator. He conceived of its format, in so far as it differed from what went before it, and had to struggle with his data to realize the programme that he had set for himself.[2] Close attention to the layout and changing forms of his text reveals previously unidentified data on the status of land and individuals and uncovers many of the sources on which he drew.

---

[1] For a critical overview, see C. P. Lewis, 'Recent Trends in the Historiography of Medieval Britain', *The Haskins Society Journal Japan* 5, 2013, 33–50.

[2] For the most recent survey and discussion, see D. R. Roffe, *Decoding Domesday*, Woodbridge 2007, 29–61. The so-called 'correcting' scribe, or scribe B, contributed less than a hundred lines of substantive text, along with some more extensive emendation of detail, following the drafting of GDB and probably its rubrication. There is no evidence that he had a supervisory role in the enterprise, much less that he was the master mind behind it. See F. R. Thorn and C. Thorn, 'The Writing of Great Domesday Book', in *Domesday Book*, ed. E. Hallam and D. Bates, Stroud 2001, 37–73 at 49–55.

Any new edition of the text, it is here argued, must apply all the tools of modern textual scholarship to represent not only the text itself but also the ways in which it is presented.

Some thirty years ago both Henry Loyn and Sir James Holt drew attention to the utility of the manuscript in terms of its layout.[3] GDB, arguably unlike its sources,[4] was written for reference; it was designed as a database. As such it had state of the art finding devices and data retrieval systems, that is, it was sensibly set out. In the first place, it was divided into handy county divisions, reflecting the structure of local government, and an index was provided at the beginning of each to provide a guide to landholders. A two-column format was adopted at the outset. The primary purpose was no doubt efficient use of the parchment, but the visibility of the data was probably also a consideration. Several devices were used to draw the eye to the important information. Chapters were numbered and the headings were written in red ink in large rustic capitals, while the names of individual manors were entered in similar capitals in black and highlighted in red. It was, and remains, a simple matter to find out what any particular lord held in a shire or check up on the details of any particular estate that he held (Figure 1).

This format is more or less consistently maintained throughout GDB. Its utility was such that an attempt was retrospectively made to mark up Little Domesday Book (LDB) in the same way, as far as it proved possible, by rubricating the smaller volume to bring it more or less into line with GDB.[5] However, this was not the full extent of the formatting that the scribe imposed. Early on in the drafting of the Yorkshire folios, the first in GDB to be compiled, he decided to annotate his text to indicate the tenurial status of lands. Initially, he affixed a marginal MNR, for *manerium*, 'manor', and then simple M to manorial entries.[6] Soon, he began to mark berewicks with marginal B, and intermittently sokeland with marginal S, and then he distinguished the place-names of subordinate entries by writing them in lower-case letters, leaving them unrubricated like the body of the text. These conventions

---

[3] H. R. Loyn, 'A General Introduction to Domesday Book', *Domesday Book Studies*, ed. A. Williams and R. W. H. Erskine, London 1987, 1–21 at 7–14; J. C. Holt, '1086', in *Domesday Studies*, ed. J. C. Holt, Woodbridge 1987, 41–64 at 50–2, revised in J. C. Holt, *Colonial England, 1066–1215*, London 1997, 31–57 at 40–2.

[4] For the debate on the relationship between the Domesday inquest and Domesday Book, see above, pp.23–30.

[5] A. R. Rumble, 'The Domesday Manuscripts: Scribes and *Scriptoria*', in *Domesday Studies*, ed. J. C. Holt, Woodbridge 1987, 79–99 at 80–1.

[6] The annotations were initially written against any entry that might be considered manorial. Subsequently, however, digits were added throughout, possibly by scribe B, to indicate the number of manors, usually, although by no means always, corresponding with the number of TRE landholders. The gradual evolution of the system indicates that it was the work of the Domesday scribe himself rather than a form that he found in his sources as argued by V. H. Galbraith (*The Making of Domesday Book*, Oxford 1961, 175).

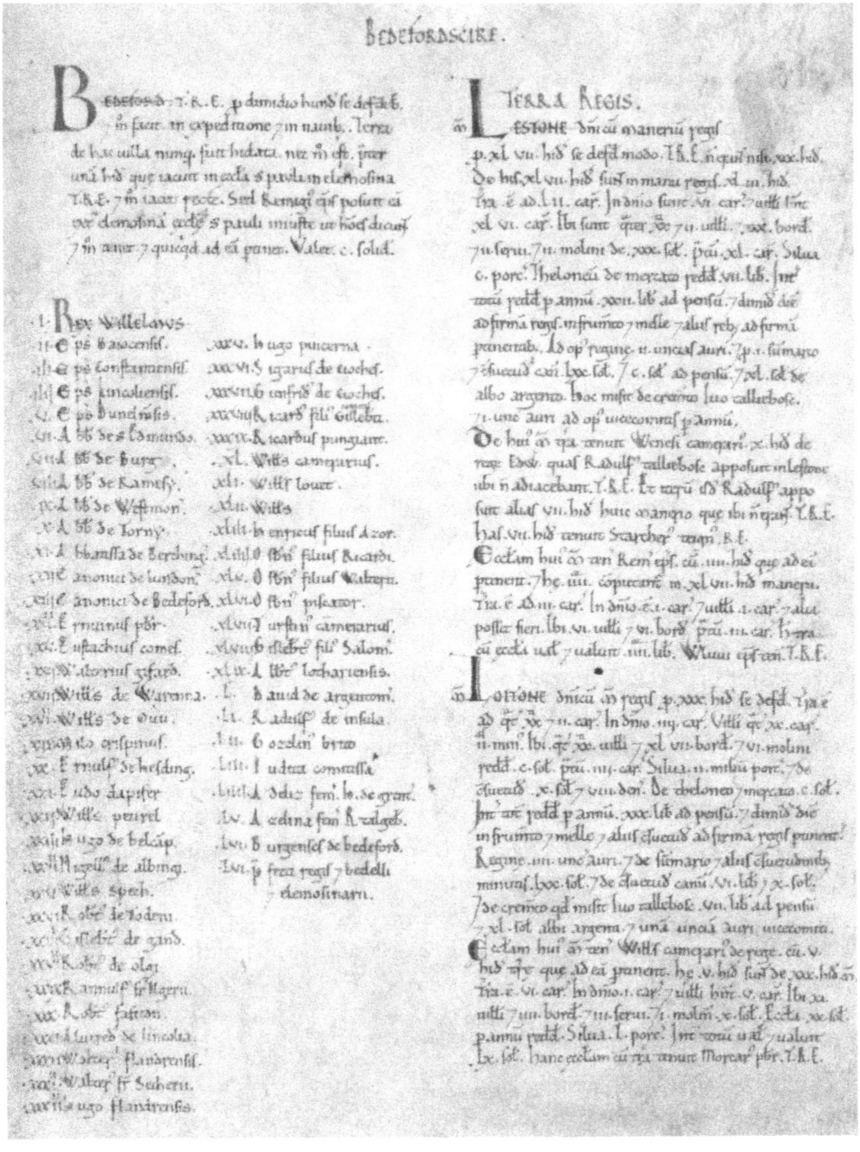

Figure 1: GDB, 209, the opening folio of the account of Bedfordshire, reproduced with the permission of Alecto Historical Editions

crystallized into a schema in the course of writing the Lincolnshire folios, the second county to be compiled, and they were subsequently applied consistently throughout the remaining counties of Circuit VI, that is in Nottinghamshire, Derbyshire, and Huntingdonshire. All that is obvious from a cursory inspection of the manuscript.

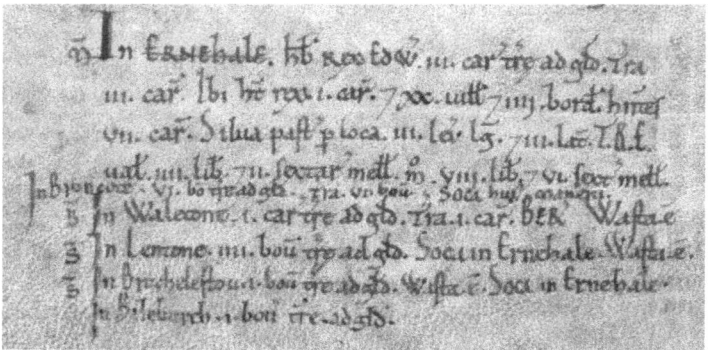

Figure 2: GDB, 281v (detail), the manor of Arnold and its sokeland, reproduced with the permission of Alecto Historical Editions

What is less appreciated is that from fol. 330 or so onwards the scribe also began to distinguish manorial entries from the rest by using a square initial capital letter as opposed to a rustic equivalent for subordinate entries. In the Nottinghamshire folios, for example, the *caput* of the king's manor of Arnold in Arnold itself is signalled by the one form and a berewick and sokelands in Bramcote, Wollaton, Lenton, Broxtow, and Bilborough by the other (Figure 2).[7] The usage is quite deliberate, for on a number of occasions the scribe changed one form to another.[8]

This convention highlights the importance of manorial centres in 1086. The generic term *manerium* was a neologism at the time and at first the GDB scribe appears to have struggled with the concept.[9] Nevertheless, it is clear that he was attempting to represent what was an essentially English institution. On occasion he references it synecdochically as *halla*, a latinization of the English word *hall*, 'hall', or the Latin translation of the same, *aula*.[10] But above all he casts the account of each in the past tense, what Domesday refers to as *Tempore Regis Edwardi*, 'in the time of King Edward the Confessor'. Thus, 'Manor. In Arnold King Edward *had* 3 carucates of land to the geld (*Manerium. In Ernehale habuit Rex Edwardus .iii. carucatas terrae ad geldum*)…'. Subordinate berewicks and sokeland, by contrast, are always described in the present, as far as can be determined,[11] but there are numerous explicit references to both types of land belonging to the lord of the manor TRE. Sokeland in Haconby and Stainfield in Lincolnshire, for example, is said to

---

[7] GDB, 281v: NTT 1,45–50.
[8] GDB, 370v: LIN 67,12.68,4;8; GDB, 274v: 275v: DBY 6,48;70; GDB, 206: HUN 19,13. Changes both ways are represented.
[9] C. P. Lewis, 'The Invention of the Manor in Norman England', *ANS* 34, 2011, 123–50; Roffe, *Decoding Domesday*, 176–82.
[10] For *halla*, see, for example, GDB, 298v, 299: YKS C31–3.1Y1. *Aula* is the more usual elsewhere *passim* in GDB; both terms are found *passim* in LDB.
[11] A verb occurs only occasionally but is almost invariably in the present where found.

have pertained to Ulf Fenman's manor of Edenham in 1066.[12] There are many such entries in the *clamores* sections of the Domesday account of the North. More than anything, though, the record of value underlines the antiquity of the relationship. Unless a parcel of sokeland had a separate identity of one kind or another, the TRE value of the inland and sokeland was included in that of the pre-Conquest manorial centre.

It is thus not surprising that it is an English word, *soca*, 'soke', which expresses relationships within the manor. The term embraced all manner of dues, but in this context it entailed a money render, as represented in the Domesday value, various services of one kind and another, and the profits of justice.[13] These rights were sometimes shared between different lords: one might enjoy the renders, often glossed as simply *terra*, 'land', for example, and another the profits of justice. More typically all were vested in the same individual and went under the catch-all of *saca et soca*, 'sake and soke'.[14] Although formerly thought to be essentially Danish, these dues are now known to be more generally characteristic of early English societies, ultimately being derived from the food rents and services that were owed to the king or earl in the tenth century and before.[15] A grant of land in Hickling and Kinoulton in Nottinghamshire to Ramsey abbey dating from 1000 or so specifies a heavy render in kind where sokemen rendered only a payment in cash to their lord Hemming in 1066 and to his successor Walter d'Aincourt in 1086.[16] Interlocking patterns of tenure suggest that many Domesday manors had come into being through the fragmentation of larger multiple estates.[17] The manor of the North in the eleventh century was less the economic unit of the later Middle Ages than a tributary nexus.

So much for Circuit VI: its peculiarities are well known. Such structures are not regularly represented in the remainder of Domesday Book and historians have tended to see a fundamentally different society elsewhere. The extensive historiography on free men and sokemen in the southern Danelaw has predominantly argued for post-Conquest manorialization and then on an *ad hoc* basis.[18] The grounds for

---

[12] GDB, 364v, 377: LIN 43,14.CK44.
[13] For soke, see D. R. Roffe, *Domesday: the Inquest and the Book*, Oxford 2000, 28–46. *Soca* is often translated as 'jurisdiction', but it is clear that lords did not normally have their own courts.
[14] The Phillimore edition of Domesday Book misleadingly translates this as 'full jurisdiction'.
[15] F. M. Stenton, *Types of Manorial Structure in the Northern Danelaw*, Oxford 1910; *The Kalendar of Abbot Samson of Bury St Edmund's and Related Documents*, ed. R. H. C. Davis, Camden Society, 3rd series 84, 1954, xxxii–l; D. M. Hadley, *The Northern Danelaw: its Social Structure, c.800–1100*, London and New York 2000, 24–5, 107–59. For the survival of archaic forms in the Danelaw, see D. R. Roffe, 'The Danes and the Making of the Kingdom of the English', *Nations in Medieval Britain*, ed. H. Tsurushima, Donington 2010, 32–44.
[16] S. 1493; GDB, 289: NTT 11,30–1.
[17] Roffe, *Decoding Domesday*, 291–304.
[18] F. M. Stenton, *Anglo-Saxon England*, 3rd edn, Oxford 1971, 515–19, summarizes the conventional view. For more nuanced accounts, see C. R. Hart, 'Land Tenure in Cambridgeshire

such a view have always appeared strong. In entry after entry we are told that in 1066 free men and sokemen 'could go with their lands' and the like, but by 1086 their lands were held by Normans. And yet a number of largely overlooked entries in Circuit III – Cambridgeshire, Hertfordshire, Buckinghamshire, Bedfordshire, and Middlesex – the second area to be enrolled, indicate that in certain circumstances free sokemen might be encompassed within the manor before the Conquest. Those in Wain, Ley Green, and Flexmore in Hertfordshire are explicitly said to have always belonged to Hitchin: they, and probably others, rendered £40 in 1066.[19] Other references are more oblique. In Bedfordshire Eskil of Ware held the 10-hide manor of Willington in 1066 and the account adds that 'there were 8 sokemen who could withdraw with their land where they wished. Of this land they had 7 hides.'[20] Here the scribe clearly understood that the sokemen's lands were part of what constituted Eskil's manor in 1066. Again, Aki held the manor of Colmworth in the same county and 'there were 8 sokemen, who could give and sell their land to whom they wished'.[21] There are a further hundred or so entries of a similar kind in the folios of Circuit III. In all but a tiny proportion the sokemen concerned had been free to go with their lands in 1066.

The Domesday scribe was clearly aware that it was not impossible for sokemen to have always owed dues to manorial demesnes. It is, therefore, the more interesting that he continued implicitly to classify lands according to the schema he had developed in Circuit VI. Probably beginning with Cambridgeshire, he jettisoned marginal B and S from the start, but retained marginal M and, significantly, the encoding of initial letters and place-names. Thus, for example, of the thirteen manors in Count Alan's Cambridgeshire fee,[22] held in succession to Eadgifu the Fair or her men, twelve commence with a large square letter,[23] either I for *In* or *Ipse* or the first letter of the capitalized place-name. All the remaining entries, identified simply as *terra*, commence with a rustic I and place-names are in lowercase letters.

on the Eve of the Norman Conquest', *Proceedings of the Cambridge Antiquarian Society* 84, 1996 for 1995, 59–90; S. Oosthuizen, 'Sokemen and Freemen: Tenure, Status, and Landscape Conservatism in Eleventh-Century Cambridgeshire', in *Anglo-Saxons: Studies Presented to Cyril Roy Hart*, ed. S. Keynes and A. P. Smyth, Dublin 2005, 186–207; E. Day, 'Sokeman and Freemen in Late Anglo-Saxon East Anglia in Comparative Context', unpublished PhD thesis, University of Cambridge, 2011. Hart, at 64, reconstructs sokes which he claims to be comparable to those in the Northern Danelaw. However, he equates *soca* with commendation and maps the latter, for which, see below.

[19] GDB, 133: HRT 1,13–15;19.
[20] GDB, 213: BDF 23,11.
[21] GDB, 213v: BDF 23,38. See also 23,22;27.
[22] GDB, 193v–195v: CAM 14.
[23] The exception, Landbeach, probably attests an uncharacteristic lapse in concentration on the scribe's part. He appears to have thought that the holding was simply land, for he omitted marginal M and wrote the name in lower case letters, only subsequently to discover that Landbeach was a manor.

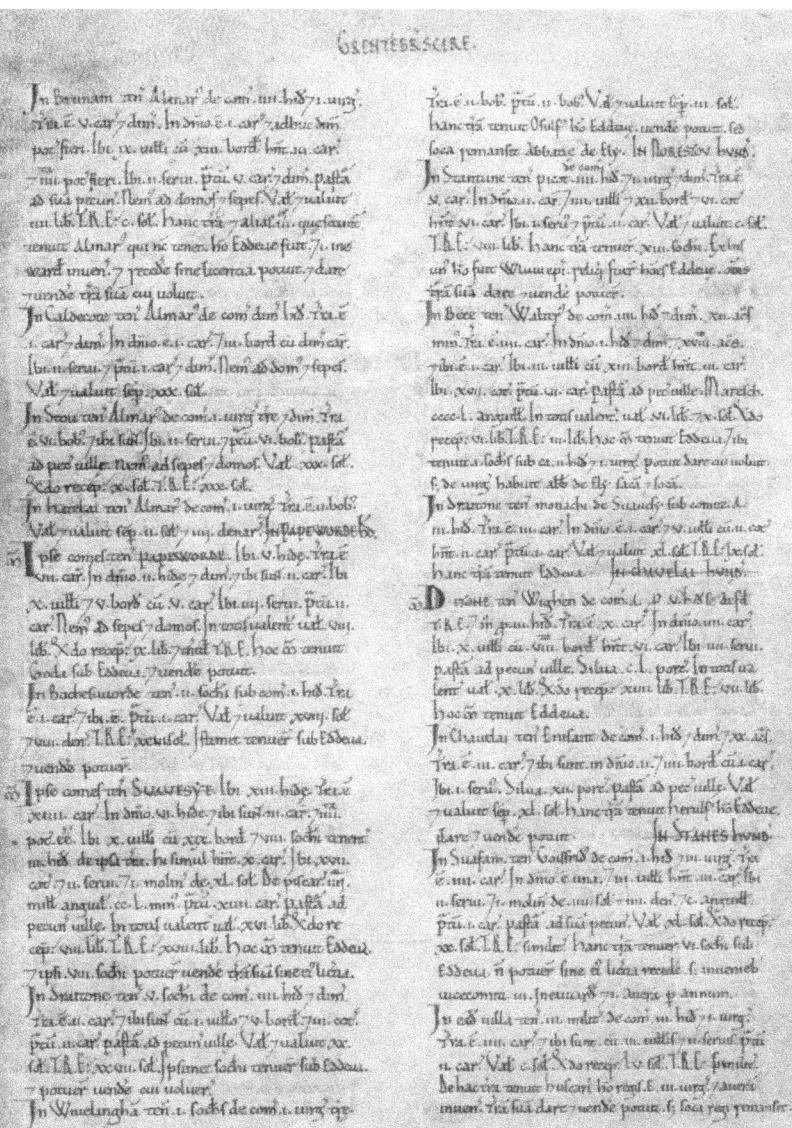

Figure 3: GDB, 195, part of Count Alan's fee in Cambridgeshire, reproduced with the permission of Alecto Historical Editions

Of these, the majority, fifty-six out of sixty-nine, relate to lands held in 1066 by thegns or sokemen of one kind or another who were in all but two cases men of Eadgifu the Fair. Interspersed with their holdings are a further thirteen parcels of land held by Eadgifu herself as detached demesne (Figure 3).

It is difficult to escape the conclusion that the scribe perceived of dependent berewicks and sokeland in Count Alan's fee too. Only two parcels of land are specifically said to have been attached to a manor: Toft and Haslingfield, both berewicks, belonged to Swavesey.[24] But the distribution of the various tenements suggests other connections. The clustering of land around the manor of Burrough Green in Radfield hundred is particularly striking.[25] That all the sokemen in question could not depart with their lands must surely imply a single nexus of dues and services in Burrough itself. Equally, the free sokelands in the north and west of Armingford hundred look as if they constitute a soke centred on Bassingbourn, while Boxworth appears to have belonged to the manor of Papworth.

The correlation of the letter forms with the different modes of tenure in 1066 suggests in itself that these structures were of pre-Conquest origin. That they were even older is demonstrated by the mirroring of the same structures in the surrounding fees. Thus, the distribution of lands belonging to Eadgifu in Armingford hundred is echoed in the holdings of Earl Ælfgar, Ely abbey, Goda, and vestigially others (Table 1).[26] Even the multiple entries for Croydon find their counterparts in other fees. Similar interlocking patterns are also apparent in Papworth hundred (Table 2). There the inlands and sokelands of Eadgifu's manors of Papworth and Swavesey interlock with those of the manor of Fen Stanton which had been held by Ulf Fenman in 1066, lands associated with King Edward's manor of Caxton and vestigially in the estates of Robert Gernon.[27] These distributions are evidently not the result of the *ad hoc* commendations of independent sokemen nor of freelance appropriation after the Conquest. They must attest the ordered division of larger units sometime before 1066 of the kind that is well attested in the North, that is, an existing estate had been split up by its lord to create smaller ones. The sokelands of Count Alan's fee were clearly associated with manorial centres before the Conquest.

They do not stand alone. Throughout the county manorial entries are regularly marked by square initial letters, the odd exception indicating the purposefulness of the device. Whittlesford, for example, was initially entered as dependent land but the scribe subsequently discovered that he was mistaken and added 'Earl Gyrth held

---

[24] GDB, 194v: CAM 14,37;48.
[25] GDB, 195v: CAM 14,75–82.
[26] Eadgifu: GDB, 194–194v: CAM 14,23–33; Earl Ælfgar: GDB, 190, 193–193v: CAM 1,18–20.13,1–7; Earl Gyrth: GDB, 197v: CAM 25,4–6; Earl Ælfgar/Ely: GDB, 198–198v: CAM 26,19–31.
[27] Eadgifu: GDB, 195: CAM 14,53–7; Ulf Fenisc: GDB, 197–197v, 207: CAM 23,1–6. HUN 21,1; King Edward: GDB, 199: CAM 26,43, 44–8; Earl Waltheof: GDB, 197: CAM 21,7–9. The soke of Earl Waltheof's land in Conington is said to belong to *Stantone*. Both the Phillimore and Alecto editions identify the soke centre as Longstanton. However, none of the Longstanton entries was a manor. The interlocking pattern here identified suggests that the manor of Fen Stanton in Huntingdonshire is the more likely referent.

Table 1: Interlocking patterns of estates in Armingford hundred, Cambridgeshire

	Eadgifu the Fair	Earl Ælfgar	Ely	Goda/Ælfgar	Earl Gyrth	E. Ælfgar/Ely
Clopton				I		
Steeple Morden				F		S
Guilden Morden				I		I
Hatley	F				F	
Croydon	FF			F	I	FSF
Wendy	S					F
Shingay				M		
Litlington		M				
Abington Piggots		IS		SF		S
Bassingbourn	M					S
Whaddon		FFSIS	S			SSF
Meldreth	S		SIIS	F		FI
Melbourn	S		I	F		F

M=manor entry, I=inland, F=free to go with land, S=sokeland

Table 2: Interlocking patterns of estates in Papworth hundred, Cambridgeshire

	Edeva	Ulf Fensic	King Edward	Earl Waltheof
Caxton			M	
Fen Stanton		M		
Papworth	M	I	S	
Elsworth		S	S	
Conington		S	S	S
Boxworth	S	S	S	F
Swavesey	M	I		F
Fen Drayton	S	IS		
Willingham	F			
Over			S	

M=manor entry, I=inland, F=free to go with land, S=sokeland

this manor' to the end of the entry and a marginal M at the beginning.[28] Here the initial rustic I was not changed, but it was in the account of the manor of Gamlingay once the scribe realized he was dealing with a manor.[29] Beyond Cambridgeshire similar conventions can be observed. In Middlesex the larger manors are enrolled as a whole since they were constituted as discrete estates. The bishop of London's manor

[28] GDB, 202: CAM, 41,7.
[29] GDB 197v: CAM 25,9.

of Stepney, for example, is described in eleven consecutive entries.[30] Nevertheless, the *caput* is distinguished from the dependent members in the usual way. Sigeræd was free to go with the 2½ hides that he held TRE, although the remaining holders were not. Pre-Conquest sokemen are not commonly recorded in the county, but it is likely that those in Geoffrey de Mandeville's chapter belonged to his predecessor Harold son of Earl Ralph's manor of Ebury, although here, it should be noted, the place-names of the entries are capitalized.[31] The Bedfordshire folios preserve perhaps a more compelling example. Hugh de Beauchamp held all but one of the demesne estates of Eskil of Ware in the county in his own hands.[32] The seven manors are indicated by marginal M, square initial letters and capitalized place-names, while interspersed with them are sokelands entered in the usual form. Two are said to belong to one of the manors, but it seems likely that all were attached in one way or another to others, not the least since the whole section exhibits its own sequence of hundreds, indicating a separate source for the account of these demesne manors.

Contrary to appearances, none of this is inconsistent with the freedom of thegns, free men, and sokemen to go with their lands. As is now widely recognized (above, pp.36–8), there was no simple equation of lordship and land in eleventh-century England. Sokemen in Lincolnshire were every bit as free to dispose of their lands without the lord's consent, as numerous twelfth-century charters attest,[33] but the fact did not preclude them from regularly belonging to one manor or another both before and after the Conquest. Nor, by the same token, is freedom of alienation of *terra*, 'land', incompatible with similar structures in eastern England. As Domesday reminds us time and again, commendation was a personal bond. Norman lords might want to see it otherwise in 1086, but the principle was accepted that it did not confer sound title to land. Soke, the essence of the manor in the North, did. Often articulated as sake and soke (*saca et soca*), it was the single most important determinant of title in 1086, short of a direct grant of land by the king. Ann Williams (pp.155–68) has shown that it also underlies the Norman settlement of Cambridgeshire. The complex tenurial geography of Armingford hundred is entirely explicable in terms of pre-Conquest rights inherent in the manor. The term *terra* of the text, then, may well have much the same connotations as it does in the North. It was less the tenure of land itself than a right to dues from it, whether it be before the Conquest or after. No sokeman, and almost certainly no free man, in Domesday Book had sake and soke over their land, let alone soke over themselves.[34]

[30] GDB, 127–127v: MDX 3,1–11.
[31] GDB, 129v: MDX 9,1–6. For the possible significance of the fact, see below.
[32] GDB, 212v–213: BDF 23,1–12. The status of entries 13–15 is ambiguous.
[33] F. M. Stenton, *The Free Peasantry of the Northern Danelaw*, Oxford 1969.
[34] *Pace* Oosthuizen, 'Sokemen and Freemen', 188. There are no entries in Domesday Book in which sokemen are said to have held with either soke or sake and soke (in both Strumpshaw, *pace* the Alecto translation, and Hemblington in Norfolk it is clear that it was Ralph the staller who was so enfranchised: LDB, 123, 199: NFK 1,98.10,66). Further, of all

The phenomenon was a regional one. The lands of free men and sokemen in Norfolk and Suffolk, enrolled in LDB, owed the same sorts of dues.[35] In the estates of Bury St Edmunds abbey they subsequently went under the catch-all monetary render of *hidagium*, 'hidage', which closely approximates to the Domesday value.[36] In 1086 *consuetudines*, 'customs', was the normal term. Manorial structures, it seems, were every bit as much a part of the tenurial landscape of the southern Danelaw as of the North and were equally important in the distribution of the tenements of sokelands after the Conquest.[37] The failure to represent them in Circuit III almost certainly attests a change of policy in the compilation of GDB rather than any great difference in social and tenurial structure. Evidence for an original programme probably comes from the *Inquisitio Eliensis*. There is preserved a list of questions that has long been taken to be the *capitula*, the terms of inquiry, of the Domesday inquest.[38] The conclusion is perhaps unwarranted, for there is a mismatch between the data apparently demanded and what was collected – most notable is any reference to livestock; it seems impossible that the list, as it stands, can have informed the collection of data.[39] However, it may well have been the blueprint, as it were, for the compilation of GDB or very close to it. The range of data, along with the order in which they are listed, approximates to that in the early folios of the work. It is thus significant that the scribe who originally composed it understood that the basic unit of the inquiry was not the village but the *mansio*, 'manor', and among the details of the institution that were to be collected were the number of free men and sokemen and the extent of the land they held. The treatment of the manor in Circuit VI conforms closely to this model. Thereafter, the GDB scribe appears to have considered

---

those landholders who were free to go with their lands, only one is said to hold with similar liberties: two hides in Trysull in Staffordshire were held by Thorgot with sake and soke and 'he was a free man' (GDB, 250: STS 12,15).

[35] The record of both free men and sokemen in East Anglia has caused much confusion, but the distinction clearly comes down to surety. The *liber homo*, like the thegn, was vouched to warranty by a lord whose name is duly noted in the text. The *sochemannus*, by contrast, was apparently not and it seems probable that, with the villein, he was a member of a tithing. The distinction is not made in the rest of the Danelaw, although it is clear that sokemen were not a homogeneous class: some are said to hold manors in Domesday Book and had men under them, while others held small amounts of land that cannot have distinguished them from the run of villeins and bordars. For a discussion, see D. R. Roffe, 'Introduction', in *The Norfolk Domesday*, London 2000, 9–42 at 35–7, and Roffe, *Decoding Domesday*, 221–4.

[36] Roffe, 'Introduction', *Norfolk Domesday*, 31–4, 38–41; Roffe, *Decoding Domesday*, 245–6.

[37] For a full discussion of this point, see D. R. Roffe, 'The Historical Context', in *Anglo-Saxon Settlement on the Siltland of Eastern England*, Lincolnshire Archaeology and Heritage Reports Series 7, 2005, 264–88 at 268–70.

[38] IE, 97.

[39] Roffe, *Domesday: Inquest and Book*, 114–17. Frank Thorn dissents (pp.111–2), but the point remains in the present context.

it superfluous, even abandoning marginal M in the Hertfordshire folios. It was no longer central to his purpose.

In the rest of GDB the manor plays a secondary role. The scribe's programme came into sharper focus as his work progressed and he decided that its structure was no part of it.[40] From Circuit I – Kent, Sussex, Surrey, Berkshire, and Hampshire – onwards place-names ceased to be coded on a regular basis as the uppercase rustic and rubricated form became the norm for all entries. However, in certain circumstances the distinctive initial letter forms that he had developed continued to signal the manor and its various elements. The account of the bishop of Worcester's hundred of Oswaldslow in Worcestershire, written some midway in the compilation of GDB, is a prime example.[41] The chapter has of late excited much interest since it appears to have been largely drafted by the church of Worcester itself.[42] Much hay has been made from the observation, but it must be doubted that this was an attempt 'to cook the Book', not the least since GDB was, if at all, nothing more than a bureaucratic aspiration when the return was first written.[43] The chapter is, however, fine evidence of a seigneurial return, that is, an account of his lands produced by a tenant-in-chief at an early stage in the Domesday inquest.[44] Normally such accounts were checked against the verdicts of the hundred jurors and, in the process, they were re-arranged. Here, however, it was incorporated, more or less wholesale, into the Domesday text, probably because Oswaldslow was a private hundred. It is thus that the chapter is, exceptionally in Worcestershire, arranged by manor (Table 3).[45] Nine out of twelve are introduced by the distinctive formula 'In the same hundred the bishop/church holds', and subordinate lands throughout are said to be held 'from the same manor'.[46] That is just as one would expect of a report compiled by the lord. Nevertheless, the Domesday scribe imposed his own formatting. The first manor to be described is Kempsey. Since it is at the beginning of the account, the scribe used an ornate drop capital to introduce it. Thereafter, with the apparent exception of Hallow,[47] the *caput* of each manor is signalled by a

---

[40] Roffe, *Domesday: Inquest and Book*, 211–20.
[41] GDB, 172v–4: WOR 2,1–80.
[42] S. Baxter, 'The Representation of Lordship and Land Tenure in Domesday Book', in *Domesday Book*, ed. E. Hallam and D. Bates, Stroud 2001, 73–102 at 82–9.
[43] For a discussion, see above, pp.25–30.
[44] Roffe, *Domesday: Inquest and Book*, 142–3.
[45] I am grateful for Vanessa King's guidance in reconstructing these manors. As in the North, sake and soke seems to have been the essential bond between *caput* and members. See *Regesta*, Bates, no. 349.
[46] The relationship is explicit in only the first entry where a tenant held more than one vill from a manor, but the same is clearly to be understood.
[47] Ten houses in Droitwich are said to 'belong to this manor' (GDB, 173v: WOR 2,68) and the referent is apparently to Hallow itself rather than Sedgeberrow, the next entry above with a square initial.

Table 3: The manors of the bishop of Worcester in Oswaldslow hundred, Worcestershire

Ref	Manor	Members
2,2–5	Kempsey	Mucknell, Stoulton, and Wolverton; Wolverton; Whittington
2,6–14	Wick Episcopi	Holt; Whitley; Kenswick; Clopton; Laugherne; Greenhill; Laugherne; Cotheridge
2,15–21	Fladbury	Inkberrow; Ab Lench; Rous Lench; Wyre Piddle, Moor, and Hill; Bradley Green; Bishampton
2,22–30	Bredon	Teddington; Cutsdean; Redmarley; Pendock; Little Washbourne; Westmancote; Bredons Norton; Bushley
2,31–7	Ripple	Upton on Severn; Croome; Hill Croome; Holdfast; Queenhill; Barley
2,38–44	Blockley	Ditchford; Church Icomb; Daylesford; Evenlode
2,45–7	Tredington	Tidmington; Blackwell; Longdon
2,48–61	Northwick	Tibberton; Worcester; Droitwich; Worcester; Hindlip and Offerton; Warndon and White Ladies Aston; Cudley; White Ladies Aston; Oddingley; Huddington; Whittington and Radley; Churchill; Bredicot; Perry
2,62	Overbury	Pendock
2,63–7	Sedgeberrow	Shipston; Harvington; Grimley; Knightwick
2,68–71	Hallow	Broadwas; Droitwich; Eastbury; Himbleton and Spetchley; Lyppard
2,72–5	Cropthorne	Netherton; Hampton; Bengeworth;

square I, while subordinate entries are distinguished by rustic capitals. Where he had nodded, as in the Wick Episcopi and Overbury entries, the scribe changed a rustic I to a square one (Figure 4).[48]

The same forms are also found in the account of the *terra regis* in the Staffordshire folios. Penkridge, for example, was a smallish manor in the south west of the county which consisted of the *caput* itself in Penkridge and a further six 'members', probably berewicks, in Wolgarston, Drayton, Congreve, Dunston, Cowley, and Beffcote.[49] The initial letter of the Penkridge entry, here an R for 'Rex', is square in form, while those of the appurtenances are rustic. The same convention is used in the account of each manor throughout the chapter.[50] The Leicestershire folios, probably the last to be written (or at least written towards the end of the project), provide an example from a baronial context. Geoffrey de la Guerche held the manor of Melton Mowbray with nine members in Freeby, Wyfordby, Burton, Kettleby, Kirby, Sysonby, Eastwell, Goadby, and Welby in the surrounding area.[51] Again, the *caput* is marked by a square capital and the dependents by rustic ones.

[48] GDB, 172v, 173v: WOR 2,6;62.
[49] GDB, 246: STS 1,7.
[50] Bloxwich, a member of Wednesbury, is an apparent exception (GDB, 246: STS 1,6).
[51] GDB, 235v: LEC 29,3–4.

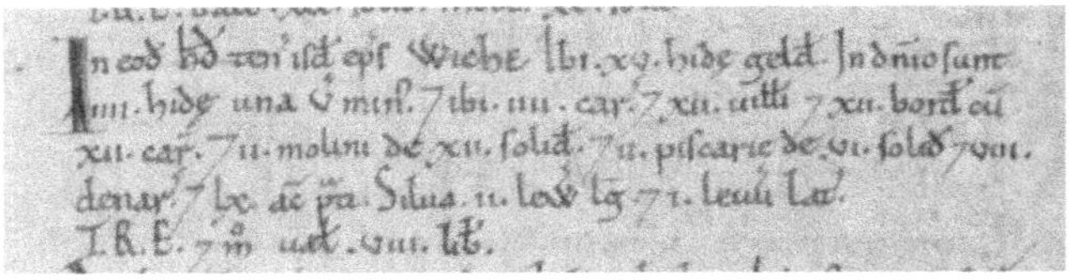

Figure 4: GDB, 172v (detail), the Wick Episcopi entry

Such encoding continued to be used where there were extensive manors and is therefore common in the lands of the king and the church throughout GDB. It can be a useful indicator of tenurial ties where they are not otherwise explicit. An initial rustic I of the account of a hide in Little Fawley in Berkshire, for example, must surely indicate that this parcel of land was a berewick of the preceding manor of Lambourn.[52] There are many such instances throughout GDB. Encoding of this kind is also used to denote groups of manors or holdings within larger units. In the Wiltshire chapter of the church of Glastonbury initial letters are used to distinguish the manors of the church from its loanlands.[53] So, Kington Langley was a demesne manor and is so marked with a square initial I. Thegnland in the same place held by Urse, Roger, and Ralph is described in a sub-entry signalled by an enlarged rustic D of the opening phrase *De eadem terra*, while what looks like a manor in Langford held by Edward in 1086 and two unnamed thegns in 1066 is enrolled in a separate entry introduced with a rustic I.[54] The visual effect is one of a discrete tenurial group – a demesne manor in Idmiston marked in the usual way, which follows, signals the start of a second – and is apparently every bit as deliberate as the layout of manors in the folios of Circuit VI (Figure 5). Again, the same device distinguishes a subordinate manor within the estate of Oakham in Rutland which was held by a Leofnoth who was in all likelihood Queen Edith's reeve TRE.[55]

This particular usage is of especial interest, for it highlights a phenomenon which is only otherwise widely attested by the so-called 'multiple manor entry'.[56] Two or more interdependent manors are frequently described together throughout Domesday Book, but the form is usually confined to dependent tenements in the same place. Wider groups are occasionally noted, as, for example, in Taunton in

---

[52] GDB, 57v: BRK 1,29–30. Otherwise, there is a complex of estates belonging to royal *ministri* around Lambourn in what appears to be a 'landscape of lordship' (above, pp.57–8).
[53] GDB, 66v: WIL 7,1–16,
[54] Appended to the entry is a note indicating that 'in the same vill Edward holds 1 hide of the king, which by right belongs to the thegnland of the abbey'. This thegnland was presumably in apposition to the main entry.
[55] GDB, 293v: RUT R17–18. Leofnoth can be added to the list of the queen's tenants and servants in P. Stafford, *Queen Emma and Queen Edith: Queenship and Women's Power in Eleventh-Century England*, Oxford 1997, 306–23.
[56] Roffe, *Decoding Domesday*, 83, 150 n.32, 159 n, 85, 160, 252, 289 n.41, 290.

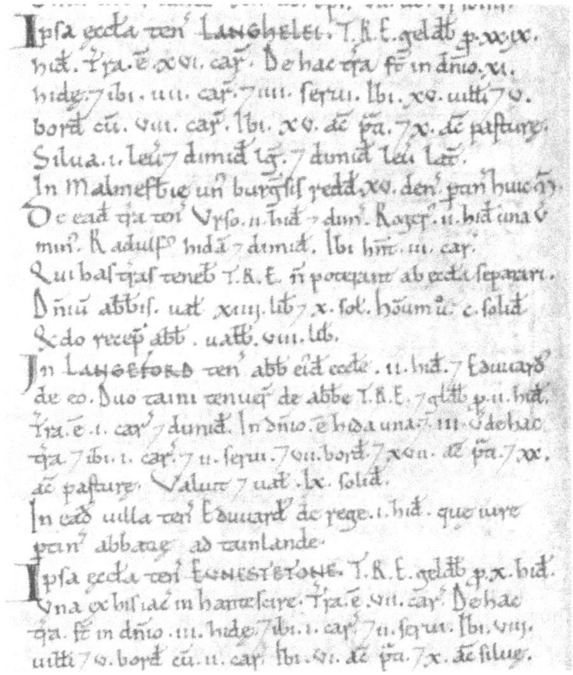

Figure 5: GDB, 66v (detail), the church of Glastonbury's estates of Langley and Langford, reproduced with the permission of Alecto Historical Editions

Somerset, Tewkesbury in Gloucestershire, and West Derby in Lancashire.[57] In this context it is clear that the thegns who were free to go with their lands might, like their counterparts in Circuit III and sokemen, also owe soke to a manor, although here it was what GDB calls a *capitale manerium*, a head manor. But such relationships are rarely explicit.[58] The use of distinctive letter forms can thus indicate a hierarchy of tenure where it is not otherwise apparent. It can by extension be an important indicator of the status of individuals in 1066.

The tributary manor, held together by soke, was clearly more widespread than is immediately apparent from the GDB text and it is the more interesting in that we perceive it almost at the end of its life. Within a generation soke had all but disappeared as a tenurial nexus. The Oath of Salisbury, which brought the Domesday process to its conclusion in early August 1086, created a new relationship between the king, his barons, and their men, and the result was the territorialization of lordship in the following century.[59] The GDB scribe's letter forms hint at a society that

---

[57] GDB, 163–163v: GLS 1,24–39; GDB, 87v: SOM 2,9.
[58] For groups of manors, see Roffe, *Decoding Domesday*, 169, 171–3, 287–91.
[59] Roffe. *Decoding Domesday*, 179–82.

was soon to change for ever. It is unlikely, however, that the device was primarily designed to reveal its structure. The manor was not the only referent of the convention in much of GDB. The point is most graphically illustrated in the Cheshire folios.[60] With the exception of the lands of the bishop of Chester and the church of St Werburgh, the whole of the county was in the hands of Hugh, earl of Chester. The Domesday account begins with his demesne estates and then goes on to those of his honorial barons. The start of each section is signalled by a large square initial for the first letter of the name of the holder but all the entries which follow are distinguished by a rustic I (Figure 6). Here it is the holding rather than the manor which is highlighted.

In this context the use of distinctive letters splits up the long stretches of text of Earl Hugh's chapter into more readily accessible sections. It does much the same in Roger of Montgomery's marcher lordship of Shropshire.[61] It is unlikely, however, that it is just a simple formatting device. Holdings within smaller fees are similarly defined throughout the remainder of Circuit V – Gloucestershire, Worcestershire, and Herefordshire – and Circuit IV – Staffordshire, Leicestershire, Warwickshire, Oxfordshire, and Northamptonshire – which followed it. The focus would appear to be on the tenant himself. This is significant. The record of landholding below the tenant-in-chief is often apparently erratic.[62] Here, though, we appear to have evidence for lists of the lands of the honorial barony, the principal tenants of the honour. This, though, is not the only type of source that the forms might reference. The account of the *terra regis* of Gloucestershire proceeds, with but one exception, hundred by hundred and a square I signals the start of each.[63] The anomalous diplomatic of the text – notably the use of the *x habuit* clause, only otherwise widely found in Circuit VI – indicates a different procedure for royal land in Gloucestershire. Most immediately, though, the distinctive forms of the text probably point to a document arranged by hundred on which the account was based.

That the sources employed might indeed dictate the forms of initial letters in this way is most clearly demonstrated where the scribe ostensibly followed a discrete schedule. The account of the lands of the bishop of Hereford in Herefordshire provides an example.[64] The chapter commences with two parcels of land held by the bishop himself in a form that approximates to that of the rest of the text (Figure 7). A rubric then announces that the lands that follow were held by the canons of Hereford. The first entry in this section is of the otherwise anomalous form 'In Lulham there are 8 hides to the geld…' and is marked with a square initial I; the succeeding entries are in the same form but commence with a rustic capital. Here the

---

[60] GDB, 263–268: CHS.
[61] GDB, 253–259v: SHR 4.
[62] Roffe, *Decoding Domesday*, 163.
[63] GDB, 162v–164: GLS 1.
[64] GDB, 181v–182v: HEF 2.

Figure 6: GDB, 264v, part of the earl of Chester's fee in Cheshire, reproduced with the permission of Alecto Historical Editions

account is explicitly different from what went before and the initial letters signal the change. The list probably reflects a subdivision of the bishop's return or an entirely separate one by the canons.[65] Multiple returns from religious houses of this kind are

[65] For a different interpretation of this section, see Pamela Taylor, below, p.206; the differences in diplomatic remain. For comparanda, see the lands of the monks of Sherborne in

Figure 7: GDB, 181v, the lands of the canons of Hereford, reproduced with the permission of Alecto Historical Editions

well attested elsewhere in Domesday Book. Again, at the end of the king's chapter in Staffordshire is a cursory postscriptal account of some thirty-three parcels of land, all of which commence with a rustic letter.[66] As a note at the end indicates, these

Dorset, and the lands of the church of Tewkesbury in Gloucestershire (GDB, 77: DOR 3, 1–9; GDB, 163v: GLS 1, 26–33).

[66] GDB, 246v: STS 1,33–64. The whole section was written with a different pen and ink after the initial drafting of the chapter, but before rubrication.

estates were waste; ploughland figures were subsequently supplied for the first fifteen entries and integrally for the remainder, but otherwise only the assessment and the TRE lord of each are noted. The section is apparently based on two schedules relating to the hundreds of Pirehill and Totmonslow.[67] Wasted lands are recorded in much the same form in the Yorkshire *terra regis* and the account of the hundred of West Derby in Lancashire exhibits similar characteristics.[68] It seems clear that the survey of the royal demesne included a specific article on waste in certain areas. Both lists are evidently drawn from separate schedules and the scribe marks the beginning of the new source and its constituent entries with distinctive letter forms.

To what extent this was a conscious mental process is impossible to determine. Either way, it suggests an overarching context for the use of distinctive letter forms to differentiate modes of tenure in Circuits VI and III. In the North, as in Cambridgeshire, the inquest data were initially arranged by vill and hundred: GDB incorporates three of the accounts – Rutland, the Isle of Axholme and the vills that belonged to York[69] – directly into the text. These in their turn were probably compiled from seigneurial surveys which were also arranged by vill and hundred. The *Descriptio Terrarum* of Peterborough abbey is probably an example.[70] The make-up of manors, fully articulated in GDB, was evidently derived from separate schedules, elements of which survive in the account of large sokes in the Yorkshire Summary.[71] That the scribe employed these lists to order his text is indicated by the odd mistake. In the Lincolnshire folios, for example, his source told him that Haythby was in the soke of Peterborough abbey's manor of Walcot on Trent but he mistakenly attached it to the account of Walcot by Threekingham 50 miles to the south.[72] It is not unlikely that the distinctive letter forms were related to these schedules. It was less the fact of manorial structure than the source of the information that dictated the scribe's encoding of his work in Circuits VI and III.

The minutiae of scribal practice, then, probably lead us most immediately to the sources of the GDB text. This finding is of considerable interest. Much of recent Domesday historiography has been at pains to demonstrate that GDB was abbreviated from fully compiled circuit returns (above, p.14). Exon and LDB are cited as examples. It is, of course, formally possible that the peculiarities of the text that we have identified were already to be found in such returns and the scribe slavishly copied them. However, the development of the various conventions in the course of writing GDB indicates that this is extremely unlikely. The present analysis suggests

---

[67] In the first *una* is spelt out and in the second it is written as a numeral.
[68] GDB, 301v–302: YKS 1L; GDB, 269v: CHS R1.
[69] GDB, 293v–294, 298v–299, 369–369v: RUT R; YKS C22–35; LIN 63,5–26.
[70] D. R. Roffe, 'The *Descriptio Terrarum* of Peterborough Abbey: an Unidentified Domesday Satellite in the Collection of the Society of Antiquaries', *Historical Research* 65, 1992, 1–16.
[71] GDB, 379–382: YKS SN.SE.SW. See, D. R. Roffe, 'The Yorkshire Summary: a Domesday Satellite', *Northern History* 27, 1991, 242–60.
[72] GDB, 345v: LIN 8,10.

that the scribe had access to far more diverse sources than fully compiled circuit returns; it hints, furthermore, that he may have often composed his text directly from them. The Domesday process was evidently far less monolithic than it has sometimes been supposed.

The conclusion prompts us to look anew at peculiarities of the text that may point to the use of other types of source and, by extension, concern. A multiplicity is most obvious in the account of boroughs. Composite accounts, and their enrolment at the beginning of each county 'above the line', have fostered the notion that towns were surveyed as communities by the Domesday commissioners. Differences in form and content of various sections, however, indicate that the accounts are usually compiled from diverse sources (above, pp.30–3). The paragraphos, or marginal gallows sign, is the most important indicator. In general it is used to draw attention to exceptional or perhaps unexpected material. As such, it may merely be a reminder for the scribe to check the information in question. In the borough, though, it more usually flags the tenements that did not pay customs to the king and its sources are apparently schedules drawn from the usual processes of the inquest. Where the fact is not otherwise explicit, the sign is therefore the most important clue to the status of the various urban tenements described. Without it, it would not be possible to show that some of the mural houses in Oxford, for example, were customary, that is they did not belong to rural manors but were entirely urban and owed their dues to the king (Figure 8).[73] If mural houses were related to repair of the walls, as they seem to have been, then we can conclude that borough work was as much a duty of the townspeople as the thegns of the countryside.[74]

Patterns of rubrication can be equally eloquent. We have drawn attention to its use in distinguishing different types of entry, but as a general phenomenon it has been little studied. Much of the time the highlighting of letters, words, and names is apparently mechanical; it has usually figured in discussions of the text only where it is absent, providing as it does a fixed point in the chronology of compilation and checking.[75] Nevertheless, some interesting patterns are sometimes discernible. Sub-sections of an entry are frequently signalled by a rubricated initial letter at the beginning of a new line and these can provide important insights into the processes of the Domesday inquest. In Berkshire and Hampshire in Circuit I, for example, the account of royal churches is appended to entries in this way. In much of GDB churches are not surveyed in any systematic way. Here, however, considerable detail is given of each foundation in a more or less formal way (Figure 9a). It would

---

[73] GDB, 154: OXF B.
[74] For a different view, see J. Haslam, *Urban-Rural Connections in Domesday Book and Late Anglo-Saxon Royal Administration*, British Archaeological Reports, British Series 571, Oxford 2012, 1–8, 82–95.
[75] Thorn and Thorn, 'Writing of Great Domesday Book', 49–52.

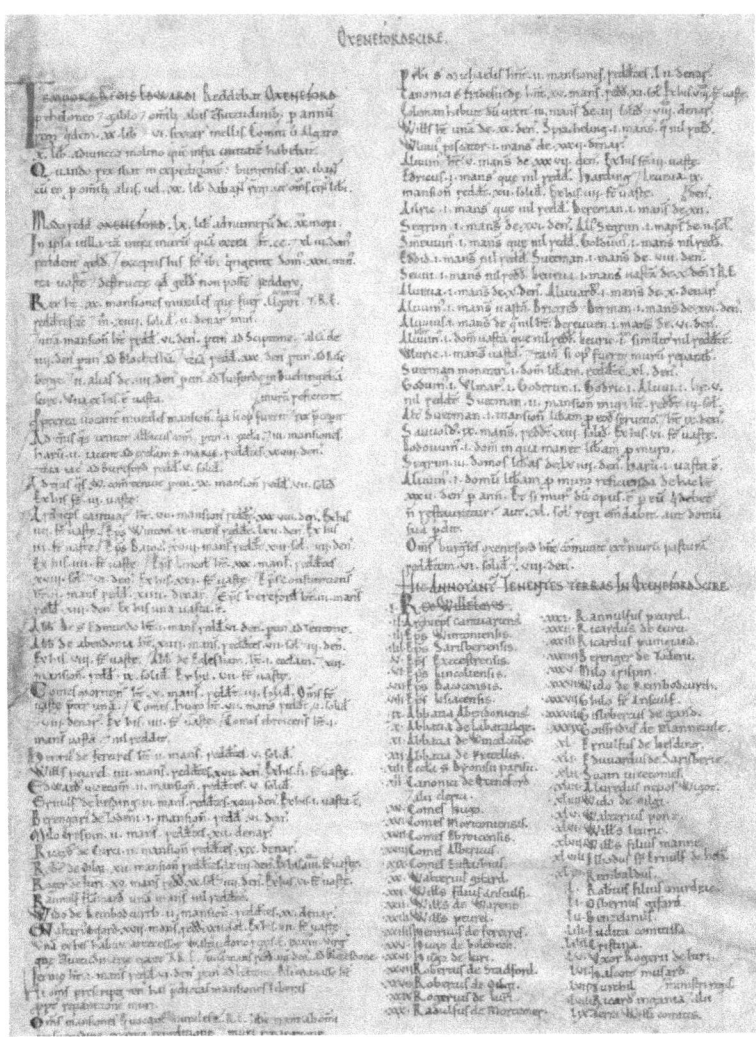

Figure 8: GDB, 154, the account of Oxford, reproduced with the permission of Alecto Historical Editions

seem that, as elsewhere, there had been a survey of royal churches and it had been recorded in a separate schedule.[76]

More enigmatic is the focus on values in the *terra regis* in Circuits I and II and sporadically in other chapters in the same. Typically, the *valuit* and *valet* clause is entered on a new line at the very end of the entry. In the account of Nether Wallop

---

[76] Roffe, *Decoding Domesday*, 76–8.

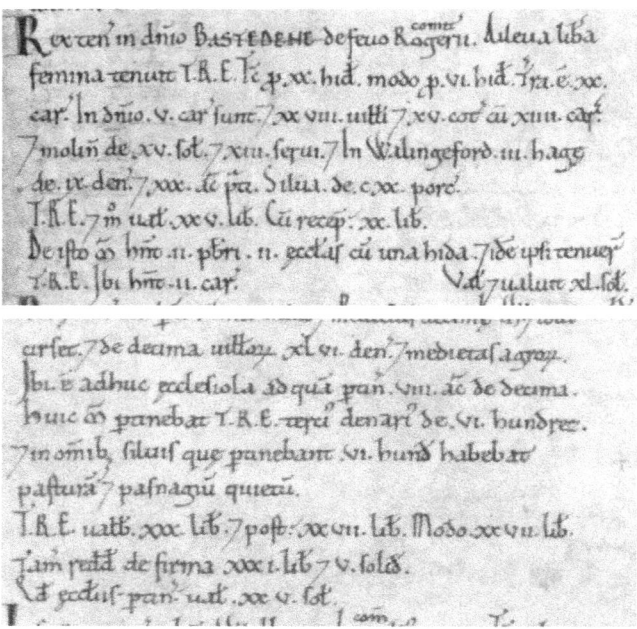

Figure 9: *a*. GDB, 57 (detail), the manor of Lower Basildon in Berkshire; *b*. GDB, 38v (detail), Nether Wallop in Hampshire, reproduced with the permission of Alecto Historical Editions

in Hampshire, for example, the scribe left half a line after the record of the manorial appurtenances before noting the value of the estate (Figure 9b).[77] This layout may signify nothing more than a desire to highlight important information. The value of the manor was after all one of the key metrics of the survey.[78] But the scribe did not routinely accord the data so much prominence. Normally he was at pains to use the parchment as efficiently as possible and so the value clause usually follows on without any formality. So, were the data in Wessex drawn from lists of farms held by the sheriff?

Blank lines are more comprehensible as delimiters of discrete groups of lands. The device is commonly used in Circuits VI and III, although postscriptal additions often fill the spaces. In Lincolnshire, for example, wapentake heads were added to existing spaces in the text on a regular basis in chapters 3, 12, 24, and 31.[79] Subsequently, blank lines are less common as the scribe progressively compressed his work, but remain a significant feature of the text. In the *terra regis* in Kent, for

---

[77] GDB, 38v: HAM 1,19.
[78] Roffe, *Decoding Domesday*, 95–7.
[79] Hundred heads are also inserted interlineally and marginally, indicating that the lines were not left for the purpose.

Table 4: Blank lines in the chapters of Walter d'Aincourt and Peterborough abbey

Lord 1086	Lord and tenant 1066	Division & wapentake
Walter d'Aincourt	1. Thorir,* Siward,† Alwig	K30,24,21/
	2. Arnketil, Hemming,* Godric	K21,26,23/
	3. Healfdene,* his two brothers	K23
Peterborough abbey	1. Peterborough abbey*	LWR14/,K20/,21/,28,H31,K24
	2. Alnoth, Rolf, Hereweard, Alnoth, Eskil	LWR14,17,19,K20,21,20 (?add)

*=holder of sake and soke, LWR=Lindsey West Riding, K=Kesteven, H=Holland. Obliques indicate spaces in the text and the numbers refer to wapentakes by their position in the common Lincolnshire sequence.

example, lines appear to indicate the transition of the account from one leet or hundred to another, again suggesting, perhaps, that the scribe drew on a source arranged by hundreds.[80] Other types of schedule are also indicated. In the abbot of Peterborough's Lincolnshire chapter the device separates demesne from enfeoffed lands, while the three divisions of Walter d'Aincourt's appear to be related to his three predecessors (Table 4).[81]

In both of these cases each of the groups of estates has its own sequence of hundreds, albeit inverted in Walter d'Aincourt's chapter. We have already noticed a similar discrete sequence in the account of Eskil of Ware's demesnes in Bedfordshire and it is common, especially in the *terra regis*, throughout Domesday Book. The phenomenon has been widely related to the recall of juries to provide further information. This interpretation, however, draws on an improbable model of inquest procedure: it is exceedingly unlikely that juries stood by waiting for the clerks while they compiled and checked.[82] In reality the presentments of local juries seem to have been confined to the salient details of each estate – its lord, assessment, and probably value – and it was against the records of these sessions that the other inquest materials were checked. Separate hundredal sequences are therefore more likely to attest the processes of compilation and, by implication, the sources employed. Thus, for example, it is apparent from this type of data that the demesne estates of the crown were surveyed separately from those of the king's immediate tenants.[83]

---

[80] GDB, 2v: KEN 1.
[81] GDB, 345–6v, 361: LIN 8;31. The division of the Peterborough chapter incidentally also reflects title: all the enfeoffed estates were acquired round about the time of the Conquest. It should be noted, however, that there is a similar division of the abbot's chapter in other counties (Roffe, *Decoding Domesday*, 212–13).
[82] Roffe, *Decoding Domesday*, 290.
[83] The same point is made by ICC: none of the demesne estates are described therein. The royal fisc was apparently the subject of a preliminary survey (Roffe, *Decoding Domesday*, 64–74).

Table 5: The representation of the soke of Grantham, Lincolnshire

Manor	Soke 1	Soke 2	Soke 3
M In GRANTHAM	S&B In GONERBY	*In* Somerby	*In* Skillington
	S&B *In* HARLAXTON	*In* Sapperton	
	S In South Stoke	*In* Braceby	
	S In Nongtone	*In* Welton	
	M&S In PONTON	*In* Belton	
		In Harrowby	
		In Dunsthorpe	
		In Londonthorpe	
		In Barkston	
		In Denton	

M=manor, B=berewick, S=sokeland, In=square initial letter, *In*=rustic initial letter, uppercase letters=rubricated rustic capitals

Scribal conventions and forms, then, hint at a number of sources and concerns that are not always explicit in the extant texts. Interpretation is often difficult, not the least since it cannot be assumed that the scribe was always consistent or, indeed, error free. It is unlikely that the handful of corrections of one letter form to another, for example, represents the sum total of his deviations from the norm. Nevertheless, despite limitations and uncertainties the data can afford remarkable insights into the history of individual estates and fees. Grantham in Lincolnshire illustrates their interpretative possibilities and potential for a deeper understanding of the society of late eleventh-century England.

The town nestles in a valley at the confluence of the River Witham and the Mowbeck in the Kesteven division of Lincolnshire. In 1086 it was held by William the Conqueror in succession to Queen Edith.[84] There were 111 burgesses there, but the estate was constituted as a large manor with an extensive soke extending into no less than eighteen of the surrounding villages. The church of St Wulfram was held of the king by Bishop Osmund of Salisbury and was a rich foundation with a parish that was coterminous with the soke, almost the whole of the two wapentakes of Winnibriggs and Threo.[85] Grantham has all the characteristics of a type of estate dating from the earliest period of Saxon settlement if not before: it has been widely held to be a typical ancient multiple estate.[86]

A detailed examination of the Domesday account of the manor indicates that it was anything but. Letter forms provide the decisive clues (Table 5). What is

---

[84] GDB, 337v–338: LIN 1,9–25.
[85] GDB, 343v, 377: LIN 5; CK24.
[86] D. M. Owen, *Church and Society in Medieval Lincolnshire*, History of Lincolnshire Committee, Lincoln 1971, 1–2; D. R. Roffe, 'The Church of St Oswald of Rand', http://www.domesdaynow.co.uk/rand.htm, accessed 26/03/2014.

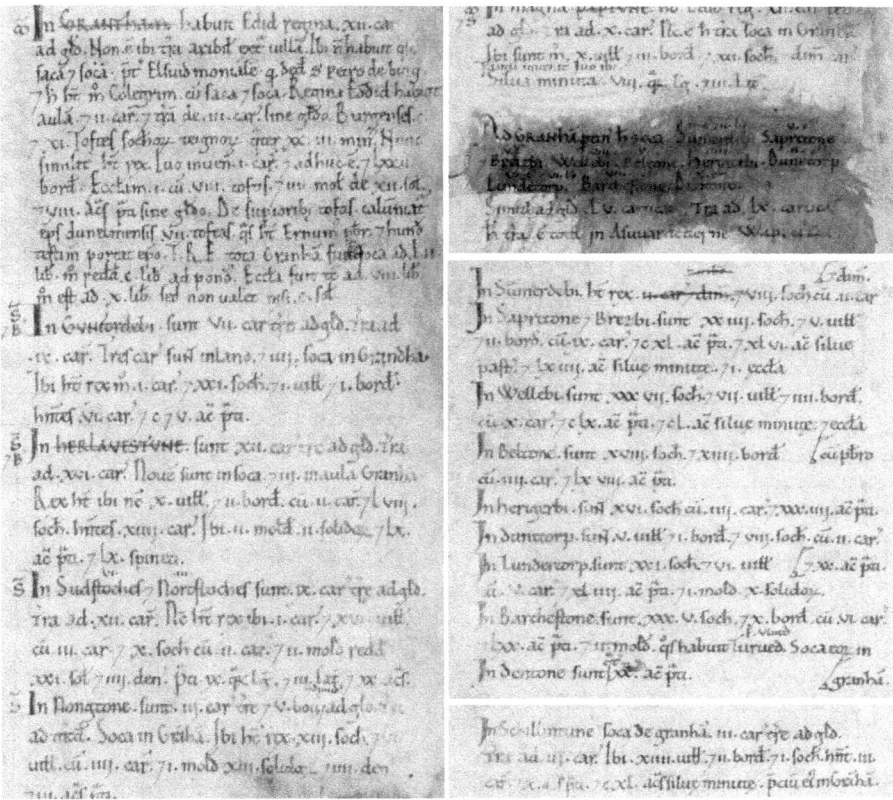

Figure 10: GDB, 337v-338 (details), the various parts of the soke of Grantham in Lincolnshire, reproduced with the permission of Alecto Historical Editions

immediately apparent is that the scribe experienced considerable difficulties in writing the account (Figure 10). He seems to have found his first attempt at describing Grantham itself unsatisfactory, for he deleted the entry and only subsequently entered the present text, in the process ignoring the rulings, after he had written up the rest of the account. Unlike in his normal practice, he entered the soke in three distinct sequences each separated by a blank line. The five entries of the first section are explicitly said to be soke of Grantham. Nevertheless, they all exhibit characteristics of manorial entries. Whereas in the normal course of events, one would expect rustic initials and undifferentiated place-names, all but one of the initial letters are square in form, all the place-names are rubricated and three are written in rustic capitals. Finally, the last, Great Ponton, is marked with a marginal M and S, a TRE lord is recorded as is the norm for a manorial entry, and it is stated that 'This land is now soke of Grantham'.

Great Ponton had clearly been a manor in its own right in 1066: its lord had been Queen Edith. The peculiarities of the account of Grantham begin to make sense. The soke of this former manor can be identified as the second section of the sokeland belonging to Grantham in 1086 which immediately follows the Ponton entry. Beginning with a rubric that acts as a summary, the account is self-evidently derived from a separate schedule and, unlike the land in the first section, its forms are entirely consistent with dependent lands. In all ten entries, the initial letters are rustic in form and the place-names are not distinguished from the rest of the text. The third section, consisting of a single parcel of land in Skillington, is identical in form, but its tenurial context in 1066 is unclear.

The manor and soke of Grantham, as represented in Domesday Book, were patently post-Conquest creations. In 1066 the estate would seem to have had been confined to Grantham itself and four further parcels of sokeland. The forms of these entries, however, suggest that they too were or had formerly been akin to manors. No TRE lords or tenants are recorded, but the text does provide clues that they were held by thegns who owed service to Grantham. The first piece of evidence comes from an entry in the Lincolnshire *clamores*. There it is recorded that 'Northmann son of Merewine had 7 gardens in Grantham of which the soke belongs to the same place, but the gardens themselves belong to Gonerby'.[87] Northmann son of Merewine was the brother of Abbot Wulfketel of Crowland and his land in Gonerby was one of the four sokelands of Grantham in 1066. No other tenants can be positively identified in this way, but the account of Grantham itself hints at their existence. It records that there were there '80 tofts, less 3, of the sokemen of the thegns'. Significantly, there was a high degree of tenurial heterogeneity in Grantham, evidenced from the twelfth century onwards, with at least five lords holding land there which belonged to their rural manors.[88] A tenurial profile of this kind is not typical of the rural soke and it would thus seem that the sokemen of Grantham were men of thegns who held manors in the surrounding countryside.

It is clear from all this that sometime before the Conquest Grantham was not a manor with a seigneurial borough attached, but something more akin to a county borough. The context in which it came into being, and its subsequent transformation into a soke, is beyond the scope of this paper.[89] Suffice it to say that Grantham was a young settlement in 1086: as Domesday Book indicates, it had no fields of its own and what territory it had was squeezed into the corner of the territory of the minor settlement of Houghton. Like Rutland to the south, it was, presumably, a dower

---

[87] GDB, 377: LIN CK21.
[88] D. R. Roffe, 'The Early History of Grantham', in *The Making of Grantham: the Medieval Town*, ed. D. Start and D. Stocker, Heritage Lincolnshire, Heckington 2011, 21–38 at 29.
[89] For a full discussion of the origins of Grantham, see Roffe, 'Early History of Grantham', 29–36.

estate, but the queen was not the sole power in the town nor did she dominate the area. The earl of Mercia was the predominant presence in the surrounding countryside and he was represented in Grantham itself by the manor held by Kolgrimr, the queen's reeve and a man of Earl Morcar. The borough looks like a joint enterprise and can probably be dated to the early 1050s when Earl Leofwine began to establish a network of service in Lincolnshire independent of the power centres of Lincoln and Stamford. Siward of Northumbria, the local earl, was in all likelihood its target and it thus became redundant after Earl Tostig became earl in 1055.

The anomalous forms and formatting of the account of the soke of Grantham alert us to a complex history to which the Domesday scribe was apparently privy. What sources were at his disposal is unclear: the level of detail goes beyond that of the immediate concerns of the Domesday inquest as the expansive description of Grantham itself illustrates. The fact goes to show, nevertheless, that the survey of the royal demesne was very different from that of the tenants-in-chief that followed it. Distinctive letter forms may often hint at processes that cannot be recovered. What is clear is that they have meaning and need to be noticed and taken seriously, the more so when they do not conform to what might be expected.

With Marshall McLuhan,[90] we can conclude that the medium is the message, or at least an important part of it. Our editions and translations of GDB are all deficient in failing to recognize the fact. Farley, in the *editio princeps*, came closest in trying to represent the forms of GDB. But even with the resources of Record Type, he could not, or chose not to, differentiate square letters from rustic. The reprint of his text in the Phillimore edition of Domesday Book has done even more violence to the manuscript by suppressing blank lines to save space. The Alecto translation recognized the importance of the general layout, preserving blank lines and folios alike, but again does not represent differences in initial letters. A new, critical, edition of Domesday Book is urgently required. Amazingly for such a major source, only a limited part is available in a fully extended Latin text,[91] and that of indifferent quality, and a complete scribal history has never been published.[92] The newly constituted Domesday Texts Project aims to remedy the omission. It will produce an electronic edition of Domesday Book, along with all the other texts of the Domesday corpus, that will record all variations in the hands, such as additions, deletions, and interlineations, along with variant letter forms, rubrication, marginal marks, and the like. The resulting text will represent both content and form in a searchable format.

---

[90] M. McLuhan, *Understanding Media: the Extensions of Man*, London 1964.
[91] Cambridgeshire, Cheshire, Derbyshire, Devon, Hampshire, Kent, Leicestershire, Middlesex, Northamptonshire, Rutland, Shropshire, Suffolk, Surrey, Sussex, Wiltshire, Worcestershire (for references, see D. Bates, *A Bibliography of Domesday Book*, Woodbridge 1985, nos. 1004, 1306, 1406, 1704, 1603, 2208, 2610, 2803, 3004, 3205, 3501, 3606, 3902, 4003, 4110, 4406, 4503).
[92] Caroline Thorn was working on an analysis at the time of her death. Frank, her husband, aims to complete the work.

The resource, it is hoped, will do justice to a consummate scribe who too, in his own way, coded his work to organize it and load it with meaning. The Domesday text is a masterpiece of genius. We do not need to apologize for engaging with its minutiae. Indeed, we must most positively do so.

4

Non Pascua sed Pastura: the Changing Choice of Terms in Domesday[1]

Frank Thorn

At first glance the manuscript of Great Domesday (GDB)[2] looks like a work of art, a presentation volume fit for a king. It is essentially laid out in ruled double columns, the work of a single scribe with a neat and legible hand, and furnished with red running heads and rubricated initial capitals, place-names and hundred or wapentake heads.[3] The material seems presented in a standard way, and it is not difficult to find the information one seeks. One needs only to glance at the folios of Exeter Domesday Book (henceforth Exon), to see how superior are the presentation and accessibility of GDB. There is a palpable sense of clear vision and an almost breathless purpose, the presence of a guiding mind producing a work of beauty and utility.

To have been able to attain this degree of finish, clarity, and compression for the wealth of material that had accumulated during the Domesday inquiry suggests that GDB was the end of a long sequence of information-gathering, sorting, trialling and refinement. It is here argued that the language used, in particular the vocabulary,

---

[1] This article opens up a neglected topic and does not make a definitive statement. It is based on an old-fashioned 'read' of the Domesday corpus including 'satellite' texts. A full study must await the arrival of electronic texts. The first draft of this paper was composed in 2009–10 and intended to be read at the 2011 'Domesday Now' conference, although the illness and death of my wife Caroline Thorn prevented this. I am grateful to David Roffe for his encouragement and for finding space for it in this volume.

[2] Domesday Book (DB) is here used as a collective term for GDB and LDB.

[3] See [D. Gifford], *Domesday Rebound*, PRO, London 1954; M. Gullick, 'The Great and Little Domesday Manuscripts', in *Domesday Book Studies*, ed. A. Williams and R. W. H. Erskine, London 1987, 93–112; Frank and Caroline Thorn, 'The Writing of Great Domesday Book' in *Domesday Book*, ed. Elizabeth Hallam and David Bates, Stroud 2001, 37–72, 200–3.

was subject to as intense a scrutiny as other elements and that the style of GDB, notable for its rapidity, its clarity, its attempted consistency, and its occupation of the middle ground between the vernacular and local on the one hand and the grand and embellished on the other is the result of conscious decisions and the application of stylistic norms.

A style is fundamentally the result of a whole series of conscious or unconscious choices: of words, of phrases, of the length and content of clauses and of the structure of sentences. When these choices all tend in a particular direction, say, towards brevity or force or beauty or linguistic purity or grandiosity or euphemism or euphuism, one can talk about a particular style.

Even an article with so narrow a focus involves taking a stance on three of Domesday's big and still controversial questions, yet there is not the space to engage in discussion of them. Firstly, it is taken as read that the 'Domesday Process' had something like seven phases, beginning with the decision to survey made at Gloucester in 1086 and that, by 1 August 1086 at Salisbury, King William had available to him documents which had achieved his objectives; probably in the form of 'circuit volumes' such as Exon.[4] He and his advisers may never have envisaged the final written format at the outset of the process, and it is possible that they were horrified by the bulk of the material, the plurality of scribal hands as well as by the smaller formats and the absence of a clear layout without highlighting in red. This lack of searchability or easy reference in the thousands of folios was the unforeseen outcome of their 'bright idea' at Gloucester a few months before. It may have been that they were forced to rethink their priorities and that clarity, simplicity, and user-friendliness took precedence over bulk and detail in a more clearly navigable abbreviation, which became known as GDB. Material was jettisoned, and a house-style and 'design concept' adopted.[5]

Secondly, there is also not the space to defend the genuineness of that report of the format of the Domesday inquiry conducted in the shire-court as described in the introduction to the *Inquisitio Eliensis* (IE).[6] Despite the criticisms of David Roffe,[7]

---

[4] See H. R. Loyn, *The Norman Conquest*, London 1965, 144–8 and the table at 145; H. B. Clarke, 'The Domesday Satellites', in *Domesday Book: a Reassessment*, ed. P. H. Sawyer, London 1985, 50–70; H. R. Loyn, *General Introduction to Domesday Book*, in *Domesday Book Studies*, ed. Williams and Erskine, 1–21. Anything asserted here, but not corroborated, will be explained at greater length in C. Thorn, F. Thorn and M. Gullick, 'The Scribal History of Great Domesday Book' (in progress).

[5] This does not mean that I at all agree with David Roffe's notion (D. Roffe, *Domesday: The Inquest and the Book*, Oxford 2000, 242–8) that the compilation of GDB is quite separate and dates from the reign of William Rufus; for the present, enough has been said in Thorn and Thorn, 'The Writing of Great Domesday Book', 70–2.

[6] ICC, 96.

[7] See D. Roffe, 'Domesday Now', *ANS* 28, 2005, 168–87 at 170 especially note 9. His objections are elaborated in Roffe, *Domesday, the Inquest and the Book*, 114–17.

the report both of the oath-taking and of the questions posed is here regarded as authentic.[8]

Thirdly, for this study comparative material has to be drawn from documents unhelpfully known as 'satellites'. This is not the place to allocate each to an exact place in the lineage of Domesday Book, especially as there is a need for thoroughly researched editions of each, before we can be certain of the relationship of one to another. However, there are grounds for believing that each of the following was part of the Domesday process, foreshadowed it or was derived from it.[9]

> Preceding the Domesday inquiry:
>   The Exon Geld Accounts
> Associated with the hearing in the shire court:
>   ICC, IE, Evesham A, Bath A
> Circuit volumes and associated texts:
>   Exon, LDB, Evesham C, K, M, and Q. Excerpta, DM B, and E
> The first abbreviation:
>   GDB

Also, there is here one fundamental, but unprovable assumption: that the words and their forms which appear in those satellite documents which are later copies,[10] are exact representations of the original and not errors or scribal preferences. It is also necessary to assume that, where a word, which, on grounds of style, might seem inappropriate for use in GDB, is only found in LDB, the main scribe of GDB would have eliminated it, had he ever abbreviated those folios.

Framing the survey's questions

The famous entry in the Anglo-Saxon Chronicle[11] is rhetorical, partial and partisan. There is a grand vagueness when the chronicler says: 'After this, the king had much thought and very deep discussion with his council about this country: how it was occupied and with what sort of people', which presumably comprehends in a verbal gesture more detailed questions about estate-patterns, tenure, classes of people and their occupations. Even the more detailed mentions that follow concerning 'hundreds', 'royal dues', and the 'land and cattle' held by the king and 'his bishops and his abbots and his earls' and 'how much money it was worth' are insufficiently precise to frame an inquiry. However, it seems that some or all of the detailed questions that were put in the shire court are given in the introduction to the IE:

---

[8] See J. H. Round, *Feudal England*, London 1895, 114. There is a valuable discussion in *Regesta*, Bates, no. 127.
[9] For the details of these satellites, see Clarke, 'Domesday Satellites'.
[10] The only authentic originals are GDB, LDB and Exon.
[11] ASC, 161.

Hic subscribitur Inquisitio Terrarum quomodo barones regis inquirunt: uidelicet per sacramentum uicecomitis scire et omnium baronum et eorum francigenarum et tocius centuriatus presbiteri prepositi vi. uillani[12] *uniuscuiusque uille. Deinde quomodo uocatur mansio. quis tenuit eam tempore regis eduardi. quis modo tenet. quot hide, quot ca(r)ruce in dominio, quot hominum. quot uillani, quot cot[arii] (cothcetli), quot serui quot liberi homines quot sochemani. quantum siluae. quantum prati, quot pascuorum quot mo[lini] (molendine) quot piscine. quantum est additum uel ablatum. quantum ualebat totum simul et quantum modo. quantum ibi quisque liber homo uel sochemanus habuit uel habet. Hoc totum tripliciter scilicet tempore regis Aeduardi et quando Rex Willelmus dedit et quomodo sit modo et si potest plus haberi quam habeatur.*[13]

Written here below is the Land Inquiry as the king's barons made the inquiry, that is, by the oath of the sheriff of the shire and of all the barons and their Frenchmen and of the whole hundred, the priest, the reeve and 6 villagers of each and every vill. Then, [1] What is the manor called? [2] Who held it in King Edward's time? [3] Who holds it now? [4] How many hides? [5] How many ploughs in lordship; how many belong to the men? [6] How many villagers, how many cottagers, how many slaves? [7] How many free men, how many sokemen? [8] How much woodland, how much meadow, how many grazing lands, how many mills, how many fisheries? [9] How much has been added or taken away? [10] How much was it worth altogether and how much now? [11] How much each free man or sokeman had or has there? [12] All this in triplicate; that is, in the time of King Edward, when King William gave it and as it may be now; and [13] if more can be reckoned there than may [currently] be reckoned.

The last question [13] is often poorly translated without appreciation of an idiomatic sense of the Latin verb *habere* ('to have') especially when used in the passive.[14] Be that as it may, what astonishes here is that King William and his advisers believed

---

[12] The grammar requires *uillanorum*; see Round, *Feudal England*, 133–4; R. Lennard, *Rural England: 1086–1135*, Oxford 1959, 213.

[13] The significant variations between MSS are (1) *carruce* (MSS A and B), *caruce* (MS C); (2) *cot'*, presumably for *cotarii* (MSS A and B), *cothcetli* (MS C); (3) *mol'* presumably for *molini* (MSS A and B), *molendine* (MS C). The abbreviation of *cothcetli* would probably be *coth'* not *cot'* (as *soch'* in Domesday for *sochemanus* etc.); the abbreviation of *molendine* would probably be *molend'* not *mol'*. The significance of these variants is discussed below.

[14] The final question is usually translated as 'if more can be had than is had'. However the passive of *habeo* routinely means 'to be said', 'considered', 'reckoned', 'judged', 'estimated', 'assessed', 'rated'. This usage is found eleven times in Exon fols. 530–1 (*in his habentur*: 'in these there are said to be') and in Exon 72a (*isti sunt illi hundreti qui habentur in Cornugallia*): 'these are those hundreds that are said to be in Cornwall'. See GDB, 154v, 185: OXF 1,13; HEF 10,72.

that the population could be specified in five categories and rural resources similarly. Clearly Domesday Book is about tenure, the integrity of manors and the legitimate transfer of land, but it is also about valuation and money, and there were in the English countryside other types of people and resources which could be monetized but which were not mentioned.

Perhaps this is not so surprising bearing in mind the elevation and foreign nature of most of William's council, and the 'broad-picture' level at which they operated.[15] William's own writs in no way prepare us for the proliferation of rural detail revealed by the Domesday inquiry.[16] This is precisely what is clear from the first part of Robert of Losinga's description of the making of the Domesday survey:[17]

> *Hic est annus xxmus Uuillelmi regis Anglorum quo iubente hoc anno totius Angliae facta est descriptio in agris singularum prouinciarum in possessionibus singulorum procerum in agris eorum in mansionibus in hominibus tam seruis quam liberis tam in tuguria tantum habitantibus quam in domos et agros possidentibus in carrucis in equis et caeteris animalibus in seruitio et censu totius terrae omnium...*

This is the 20th year of William, king of the English, on whose orders a written survey was made of the whole of England in that year, concerning the fields in individual counties, concerning the possessions of individual barons in terms of their fields, manors, men, not only slaves but also free men not only in terms of those only living in huts, but in terms of those possessing houses and fields in terms of ploughs and horses and the other animals in terms of the service and dues from the entire land of everyone...

If this reflects the grand and simplifying discussion at the Gloucester court, it explains why the categories of population as recorded in Domesday, despite their sharply differentiated names, overlap when judged by their status and possessions and why the listing of resources is so random. What has not been observed is that Robert dignifies the whole process by writing as far as possible in Classical Latin (CL), and with the balanced structure of a true periodic sentence. He avoids virtually all the specialized vocabulary of the Domesday survey, either by using CL

---

[15] Some idea of the composition of William's 'council' can be gained from two writs issued at Gloucester at the time of the Domesday decision and one from Lacock (Wilts), soon afterwards, probably when the court was on its way to Winchester for Easter: *Regesta*, Bates, nos. 9, 156, 146.

[16] There is an index of Latin words used in the writs in *Regesta*, Bates, at 1009–41.

[17] This derives from a tract of Robert Losinga concerning chronology and the paragraph about Domesday is a digression prompted by the fact that he has mentioned the year 1086 in his chronological calculations. For text and discussion, see W. H. Stevenson, 'A Contemporary Description of the Domesday Survey', *EHR* 22, 1907, 72–84; see also *EHD*, II, no. 198.

words as substitute (*agri* for *hundredi* and then for *hidae*; *prouinciae* for *comitatus*; *proceres* for *barones*; *census* for *geldum*) or by using periphrasis (*in tuguria tantum habitantibus* for *cotariis*; *domos et agros possidentibus* for *uillanis*). In particular his use of *prouincia* has misled.[18] Even the word *carruca* has a presence in the classical world, although in DB, like *mansio, seruitium* and possibly *descriptio*, it is used in a non-classical sense.[19] Here *mansio* stands for the more technical *manerium* and *seruitium* for *consuetudo*: the classical senses of this last might obstruct its use here.[20] The use of *equis* ('horses') is strange because, of equine beasts, only *runcini* ('cob-horses', 'pack-horses') were routinely surveyed as part of the manorial stock. However, the linking of *equi* with *caeteris animalibus* might suggest that Robert cannot let his elevated prose descend to the mention of mere sheep, goats, cows, and pigs. This is only an extreme example of that search for classical purity which to a lesser degree characterizes Domesday Book

It is not certain whether William and his advisers wished to reclassify the English population because the obligations and taxable income of five groups would be far easier to ascertain and exploit than those of fifty, or whether they were unprepared for rural reality. Certainly no direct relationship can be established between the four central categories which appear in the eleventh-century *Rectitudines Singularum Personarum* and other documents[21] (the *geneat*, the *gebur*, the *ceorl* and the *cotsetla*) and the *liberi homines, sochemani, uillani* and *cothcetli/cotarii* of Domesday Book. It may be that whereas the Anglo-Saxon description of classes was based on a mixture of legal, economic, and social status, the Norman replacements were more related to wealth and value which could be used in the valuation and a possible eventual

---

[18] See Henry of Huntingdon, *Historia Anglorum: The History of the English People*, ed. and tr. D. Greenway, Oxford Medieval Texts, Oxford 1996, 400–1: *Misit autem dehinc rex potentissimus justitiarios suos per unamquamque scyram, id est prouinciam Angliae* ... ('Now, next this extraordinarily powerful king sent his justices throughout each and every shire, that is, an English *prouincia*...'). The classicizing Hemming in his mention of Domesday circuits (*Hemingi Chartularium Ecclesiae Wigorniensis*, ed. Thomas Hearne, 2 vols, Oxford 1723, I, 288) uses *prouincia* presumably because he cannot bear the barbaric *scira*.

[19] *Car(r)uca* is a Gallic loan-word in CL. According to the *Oxford Latin Dictionary*, ed. P. G. W. Glare, Oxford 1968 (*OLD*), it there means 'a travelling-carriage' or 'a type of waggon'. It is possible, at least initially in ML, that a *carruca* was a different sort of plough, a 'wheeled plough'.

[20] In CL *seruitium* can mean 'slavery' or 'bondage', 'servitude', 'servility', and is also a collective term for 'slaves'. In CL *consuetudo* can mean 'habit', 'normal practice', 'custom', 'convention', 'habitual use', 'intimacy', 'intercourse'. There seem to be no examples of this word meaning 'customary due' in England before 1066; see R. E. Latham, D. R. Howlett and others, *A Dictionary of Medieval Latin from British Sources*, Oxford 1975–2013, henceforth *DMLBS*.

[21] Translated with similar documents in *EHD*, II, 875–80. For a useful discussion, see H. R. Loyn, *Anglo-Saxon England and the Norman Conquest*, London 1962, 189–95.

new taxation of the whole estate; or the new classification may simply be ignorant and peremptory.[22]

By contrast, on the ground and in the shires, those who assembled the Domesday material will have been faced with people whom they felt they could not enrol in the five key groups. The result was that something like thirty-five other types of 'men' are mentioned in the Domesday folios, some in considerable numbers.[23] Of course, these are not all necessarily further categories, and some are named by their predominant job rather than from their status.

With resources, it may be that various customs, services, taxes, and renders (*consuetudo, scotum, redditus*, including specifics such as *herbagium*), which occasionally appear separately, are usually silently included in the valuation of the estate. In other cases, the difference is probably between the specific and the generic. The alder-grove (*alnetum*), the willow-bed (*salictum*) and the spinney (*spinetum*) might, in other counties, be listed under woodland. Similarly, the dams (*exclusae*) and the weirs (*gort, gurges*) probably belong with the fisheries (*piscinae, piscariae*). But in other cases, additional resources not assimilable to the main five force their way onto the page. Thus the following appear sporadically and insufficiently: hawks' eyries or nests (*aeria* etc., *nidus*); vineyard (*uinea*); lake (*lacus*); mere (*mara*); marsh (*mariscus* etc.); water-meadow (*brocus, broca*); heathland (*bruaria*); ploughable land (*terra arabilis*); moor or fen (*mora*); orchards (*uirgultum, pomerium*) and small-holdings ((*h*)*ortus, gardinum*); assarts (*essarz, exsartum*); quarries (*quadraria*), including a millstone quarry (*molaria*) and one qualified as a stone-pit (*fossa lapidum*); mines (*minieria*); lead-mines (*plumbaria*); a lead-works (*fabrica plumbi*); smithies or forges or places where iron was worked (*ferraria, forgia*); potteries (*ollaria, potaria*); dairies or dairy-farms (*hardwica, wica, uaccaria*); bee-hives (*rusca, uas*); markets (*forum, mercatum*), and saltworks (*salinae*).[24]

The choice of terms in the questions

The above shows how restricted were the terms on which the survey was based. These are: *mansio, hida, car(r)uca, dominium, homo, uillanus, cothcetlus* or *cot*[*arius*], *seruus, liber homo, sochemanus, silua, pratum, pascuum, molinum* or *molendinum, piscina*.

---

[22] See F. W. Maitland, *Domesday Book and Beyond*, Cambridge 1897, 37–60, 328–9; Loyn, *Anglo-Saxon England*, 189–95, 343–53; H. C. Darby, *Domesday England*, Cambridge 1977, 61–83; R. Welldon Finn, *An Introduction to Domesday Book*, London 1963, 116–50; Lennard, *Rural England*, 339–67.
[23] The figures are from Darby, *Domesday England*, 338–45, with some additions.
[24] References to categories of population or to resources can be found in the magnificent *Index of Subjects* provided by Jim Foy for the Phillimore edition (*Domesday Book: Index Part Three: Subjects*, Chichester 1992); there is much detail in Darby, *Domesday England, passim*.

We can leave aside *homo* ('man', 'person' of either sex) which is used in the questions only in a collective sense. Among the others, different principles have probably determined the choice of words. For certain unique features of rural life, the Normans will have needed to keep the Old English (OE) term, though sometimes Latinized: such is the case with *hida*, *sochemanus*, and *cothcetlus*. In other cases, terms were available in Latin, the majority of them CL and were already used to describe the same resource in England and in Normandy (*car(r)uca*, *silua*, *pratum*, *pascuum*, *mol[end]inum*, *piscina*). In the case of *liber homo*, a term may have been made up to describe this class, which overlapped with, or may in fact have been initially regarded as the same as, the *sochemani*. A final group is represented by *uillanus* and *dominium*. The latter in the sense of 'demesne-land', 'land for the lord's own use' seems to have been brought from Normandy. In the same category may be *mansio* (a word with a long history and a considerable range of meanings) in the technical sense of 'manor'. Governing all choice appears to be the desire to choose Latin words of respectable ancestry wherever possible, or, by re-forming them to pretend that a word is Latin, tendencies which can be illustrated by examples from the wider vocabulary of Domesday.

As one follows these individual terms from this first formulation through the various stages represented by several satellites to the final choices made in GDB, there seem to be six conflicting strands.

Continuity

DOMINIUM. The notion of 'feudal lordship' and of 'land reserved for the lord's own use' is overwhelmingly conveyed by this, a CL word, although it is there used more generally as 'rule', 'dominion', 'ownership' There are isolated examples of words from the same root (CL *domus*: 'house'), such as *dominicatus* and *dominicum*,[25] both originating in Medieval Latin (ML) and perhaps spurned by the authors of the terminology and by the main scribe of GDB on that ground alone.[26] It is possible that *dominicatus* is sometimes used in Exon and in the Exon Geld Accounts in the more general sense of 'the sum of the lordship', an individual's 'total demesne'. However, it is not certain that *dominium* was used in the sense of 'demesne land' in England before the Conquest and it is likely that it was introduced by the Normans.[27] It may be that the concept of 'lordship', with its associated obligations

---

[25] The earliest appearance of *dominicatus* in England is in a charter ostensibly of *c.* 1030; see *DMLBS*. It appears in the Exon geld accounts (11a, 17a, 18b etc.) and in Exon proper (67a, 72b etc.). For *dominicum*, see Evesham C 4 and the Excerpta. Stephen Baxter has much on this topic in an important recent paper: S. Baxter, 'The Making of Domesday Book and the Language of Lordship in Conquered England', in *Conceptualizing Multilingualism in Medieval England, c.800–c.1250*, ed. E. M. Tyler, Turnhout 2012, 271–308.

[26] King William's writs appear to have only *dominium* and *dominicum*.

[27] The history of Latin words and their occurrence at different periods can be studied from

and privileges, was more important to the Normans, as it had implications for what they could expect from the holders and their estates.

PRATUM. No alternative to this CL word appears.

VILLANI. The word is from CL *uilla*. It is used before 1066 on the continent and in England, but only in the sense of 'inhabitant of a vill', or (in England) a 'commoner' a *ceorl* in contrast to thanes and earls or ealdormen.[28] It can be so used in Domesday to distinguish what the rest of the men hold apart from the lord, and is thus a synonym for *homines*;[29] but also has a more precise usage, though difficult to define with exactitude, as the upper class of the manorially dependent. This appears to be a post-Conquest usage, As it has no obvious synonym in this sense, it proves remarkably stable through the trail of documents; one has noticed only one occurrence of *uilani*[30] and of *uillici*.[31] This consistency suggests that this is a crucial term recently imposed from above rather than a choice from a proliferation evolved from below.

Spellings

CARUCA or *CARRUCA* is the form given for 'plough' in the IE questions, depending on the MS, whereas *caruca* is the form normally used in GDB. Exon and LDB hesitate between the two.[32] In documents associated with Domesday the derived *carucata* and *carrucata* both appear. It is interesting that the main scribe of GDB uses the CL *arare* ('to plough') but not its derivative *aratrum* ('plough'). *Carruca* was perhaps too firmly entrenched. *arabilis* ('ploughable') occurs quite frequently while *aratura* ('arable land') occurs once in LDB.[33]

---

the *OLD* and *DMLBS*; also A. Souter, *Glossary of Later Latin to 600 A.D.*, Oxford 1949; Du Cange, *Glossarium Mediae et Infimae Latinitatis*, ed. G. A. L. Henschel, Niort and London 1884–1887; J. F. Niermeyer, *Mediae Latinitatis Lexicon Minus*, Leiden, New York, and Cologne 1997; F. Blatt, *Novum Glossarium Mediae Latinitatis*, Hafniae 1957 and in progress; O. Prinz and J. Schneider, *Mittellateinisches Wörterbuch*, Munich 1967–. These works are the source of most of the linguistic observations in the article and are not routinely mentioned.

[28] Thus in the Latin versions of the Laws of Alfred (§39) and III Athelstan (prologue); see F. Liebermann, *Die Gesetze der Angelsachsen*, 3 vols, Halle 1903–16, I, 19, 170. A new edition of Alfred's *Domboc* is being prepared for Early English Laws by Lisi Oliver and Stefan Jurasinski; see www.earlyenglishlaws.ac.uk, accessed 11/06/2015.

[29] See, for example, GDB, 127: MDX 3,3; Exon, 235b3. The routine formula in Exon is, 'The lord has in demesne ... and the villans have ...', even though 'villans', more exactly defined, do not subsequently appear in the detailed list of manorial population.

[30] Exon, 95b.

[31] Evesham A 31–32. In the context it clearly means 'villans', but there may be an ignorant confusion with CL *uil(l)icus* ('farm-manager', 'agent').

[32] King William's writs have *caruca*, *carruca* and *carruga*.

[33] LDB, 2: ESS 1,3.

Variations in words derived from English

Cottars, sokemen and hides are the only terms Latinized from OE. The first two appear to define population groups which the Normans could not initially assimilate to their own and for which there was no appropriate Latin word of any provenance. Probably as a result of their being native terms, there are considerable variations in individual documents, as if the native spellings sometimes asserted themselves via individual English scribes or clerks. Sometimes the forms are English and not declinable as Latin, or have been hastily Latinized. It will be shown below that this is generally true of native terms adopted from English and French.

COTHCETLI or *COT[ARII]*. These are the forms used in the IE questions depending on the MS source. Both are Latinized, but the former is manifestly an OE word whereas the latter is OE *cot* + Latin *-arius*, and would pass as a Latin word for anyone who had a good eye for the forms of words, but without a knowledge of their history. It is possible that *cothcetli* was the initial choice and that *cot[arius]* was substituted in one of the MS of the IE from the scribe's knowledge of its use in IE proper, as in ICC, Exon and GDB: those framing the questions will scarcely have offered a choice of terms. If this is so, the decision to abandon the ugly *cothcetli* was presumably made on stylistic grounds.

Cotarius is the predominant form in GDB; *cottarii* are found in IE.[34] The Exon *quotarii*[35] is merely an example of *qu-* for *c-* and with the assimilation of these sounds, one might have expected *kotarii*. *coteri*[36] might be a bad form of *cotarii*, while Exon *coceti*,[37] *cotsetus*[38] and GDB *cotman(n)i*[39] are attempts at Latinizing the OE for *cot-saeta* or *cotman(n)*.[40] *Cozet*, plural *cozets* (for *cotset*, *cotsets*)[41] and *coscet* plural *coscez* (= *coscets*), as well as *cozez* (presumably for *coscez* or *cotscets*)[42] are not declinable as Latin but are heavily influenced by French spellings of their sounds [*-z* = *-ts*].[43] The difficulty for the student of Domesday as for its surveyors and compilers is to know whether there is more than one class here. Certainly *cotarii* and *cozets*

---

[34] IE, 101. These become *bordarii* in GDB, 199v: CAM 28,2.
[35] Exon, 83a2.
[36] GDB, 316v: YKS 9W64.
[37] Exon, 31b3.
[38] Exon, 39a1.
[39] GDB, 177–177v: WOR 20,6.23,2.26,3;6.
[40] It is conceivable that *cothcetli* contains OE *cot* and *setl* ('seat', 'resting-place'), the origin of 'settler'.
[41] See, for example, GDB, 64–65v, 252, 260v: WIL 1,1;2;4–7,10–11;13–14; SHR 2,2.7,4,6. In some cases, for example GDB, 260v: SHR 7,4, *cozet* is indeclinable.
[42] GDB, 72v: WIL 42,1.
[43] See the electronic Phillimore SHR 2,2 cottager note. The e-Phillimore is available from the Hull University website (http://edocs.hull.ac.uk) or from UK Data Service (SN 5694: Electronic Edition of Domesday Book: Translation, Databases and Scholarly Commentary, 1086, 2nd edn).

appear in the same entry in Wiltshire,[44] and Darby included them in different columns in his magnificent table of population.[45] However, it is not clear whether even a single entry in DB is the product of a single individual or whether information had been fed into it from different sources and not rationalized. It is tempting to see all these 'cottage-people' as a single, but loose class for which the Domesday planners at first settled on a single name, until *bordarii* made their appearance (see below). The same is true of 'radmen' (below).

SOCHEMANI. In contrast to the *cotarii*, there seems to be no doubt that this is a single class of persons.[46] The word is often sharply abbreviated to *sok'* or *sokm'* in LDB or to *sochem'*, but there are enough fuller forms to suggest that the range there is *sokeman(n)i* or *socheman(n)i*. GDB has these variants but also some indeclinable forms, for example *sochemans*.[47] The word from which the first element is derived, OE *soc*, is normally *soca* in GDB, and almost always so in LDB, though there are isolated examples of *soka* and *socha*.[48] This comparative degree of control by all the scribes involved contrasts with the forms that appear in King William's writs, six for sokeman and eleven for soke.

HIDA. By contrast, a hide is always *HIDA*, and one would not pause to think that there were any other possibilities, if it were not for the range of tempting forms, some with the beautiful Greek-derived -*y*- found in King William's writs: *hida, hidda, hidra, hidria; hisdra, hyda, hydda, hyde, hydra, hydria. hyda* also occurs in Exon.

Hesitation between etymologically related words

MANSIO/MANERIUM. *Mansio* is a CL word but not there used in this technical sense. It is derived from the supine or past participle of *maneo manere, mansi, mansus* meaning 'to stay, remain, dwell'. In England before the Conquest it is used as a measure of land, like *hida, cas(s)atus, mansus* and *manens*. All of these are in origin to do with families, dwellings and houses.[49] In GDB the word is found in borough entries, apparently as an alternative for *ma(n)sura* ('messuage' or 'tenement').

---

[44] GDB, 64v: WIL 1,5.
[45] Darby, *Domesday England*, 337–9.
[46] See Maitland, *Domesday Book and Beyond*, 66–79; Darby, *Domesday England*, 61–4; R. Lennard, 'The Economic Position of the Domesday Sokemen', *The Economic Journal* 57, 1947, 179–95; R. Welldon Finn, *Domesday Studies: The Eastern Counties*, London 1967, 198–9.
[47] GDB, 219, 299: NTH 1,1; YKS 1Y2.
[48] For *soka*, see LDB, 118v: NFK 1,70; for *socha*, see LDB, 197: NFK 10,48; for *socha et sacha*, see LDB, 235v: NFK 22,6. King William's writs show the forms *soc, soca, socca, soccha, socha, sochna, sochne, socna, socne, socum, sokne*.
[49] *Hida* is Old English *hīd*, connected with words for family, marriage, and household. *cas(s)atus* is connected with CL *casa* ('hut', 'cottage', 'dwelling').

The notion of the manor seems to have been important to those who planned the inquiry.[50] GDB began by meticulously recording whether a place was a manor or some sort of dependency, although as time and brevity pressed, it tended rather to say when a piece of land was not a manor. The Normans recognized that the thing they wished to define existed before 1066 since one of DB's preoccupations is the status of the TRE holding and many of the *Terrae Occupatae* for the south-western counties, bound up with Exon, concern themselves with the combining or splitting of manors. The matter has provoked much discussion, because it is not entirely clear what the Anglo-Saxons called such a unit, or even if they looked at it in the same way as the Normans. One cannot rule out the possibility that the Normans wished to make the *manerium* central to their concerns about geld, service, and accountability in a way that the same 'estate' had not been TRE. Certainly one is hard pressed to find a comparable word, as Stenton's struggle shows.[51] He cites the use of *heafod botl* for 'head house', but that is rarely found, and what we would call an estate or even a manor is often described in Anglo-Saxon documents as *land* or *bohtei* or *botl* or *hid* and in Latin as *pars* or *particula terrae/telluris/ruris*. If the estate is large, old, and important enough, it is a *uilla*.

Since *mansio* has a long history, it also has a potentially misleading range of meanings. In CL it originates as an abstract noun and can mean 'remaining', 'staying'; 'a continual state'; then 'a dwelling-place'; 'a (night) stopover on a journey', 'an inn', 'an hotel for travelling officials'. To these ML adds 'a resting-place' or 'tomb', 'a lair', 'a monastic house', 'a prison cell', 'a land measure', 'a messuage', 'a manor'. The word *mansio* is occasionally used in this last sense in King William's writs but pre-Conquest English examples are hard to find. One looks in vain for an example where *mansio* became a collective term for a group of hides (not '5 *mansiones*', but 'a *mansio* of 5 hides'). However, examples of *mansio* (and of *mansus*) in something like this sense are cited from earlier times on the continent, but no examples of *manerium* have been found.[52] The use of *mansio* is the norm in Exon,[53] and *manerium* is the norm in LDB.[54] The most probable explanation for the replacement of *mansio* by *manerium* is that *mansio* had too many other meanings and that the Normans already had in their French vocabulary and had or could create in Latin a word which could be used to describe the English thing as they saw it, the sort of

---

[50] This section of the paper was written before Chris Lewis delivered and published his important paper on the manor: C. P. Lewis, 'The Invention of the Manor in England', *ANS* 34, 2011, 123–50. Essentially we have reached the same conclusion, and I have only retained here the skeleton of my argument and some additional details.
[51] F. M. Stenton, *Anglo-Saxon England*, 3rd edn, Oxford 1971, 480–1.
[52] There are seventh-century examples of *mansio* in Niermeyer, *Lexicon Minus* and an eighth-century example of *mansus* in Blatt, *Novum Glossarium*.
[53] But see Exon, 66b2: *in uuincileia manerio regis*.
[54] But see LDB, 25, 415v: ESS 18,36; SUF 33,10. There may be a particular meaning intended in its use in LDB, 93, 96v, 99: ESS 60,1.71,4.90,1.

unequivocal term that the minds behind Domesday were looking for and therefore part of their conscious choice of vocabulary.

As to the etymology of the word, the great dearth of documents means that the precise development of many ML words is difficult to determine. A word may pass into Old French (OFr), acquire a derivative in that language, then both may be re-Latinized, with or without their French spellings that indicate changes in pronunciation. Theoretically, *manerium* could simply be derived by Latin users by a normal process of word formation directly from *manere* either by adding *-ium* or *-erium*; thus *man/erium* from the root of *maneo* as *nauig/erium* from the root of *nauigo*, or *maner/ium* from the infinitive as probably *biber/ium* from *bibere*. However the evolution could be Latin *manere* (infinitive) > OFr *maner* (infinitive) > OFr *maner* (noun) > ML *manerium*. The Latin infinitive *manere* is also used on the continent as a noun, and the OFr noun *maner* is derived from it. This originates in the not uncommon use of the Latin infinitive as an indeclinable neuter noun. However, lack of declension is awkward, so it is possible that *manerium* was derived directly from this in substitution, while the French substantive *maner* came directly from *manere*; it then developed, giving *maneir* and then *manoir* whence English 'manor'.[55]

Some examples of the rural *mansio* remain in GDB instead of *manerium*. Anyone who has systematically tried to substitute one word for another before the arrival of electronic 'find and replace' will know the impossibility of locating and changing all.[56]

MOLINUM or *MOLENDINUM*. Both these forms are used in the IE questions, depending on the manuscript. It is the shorter form that is predominant in GDB, assuming that the common abbreviation *mol'* stands for it. The word is created in ML but consists of *mol-* derived from the root of the CL verb *molo molere* ('to grind', 'to mill') and the noun *mola* ('a grind stone', 'a millstone'), with the common termination *-inus*. In form it parallels *pistrinum*, the CL word for a mill (itself connected with *pistor*: 'baker'). The Normans would have been familiar with the OFr word *molin* (Modern French *moulin*), from *molinus/-um*. An alternative medieval word for the same machinery is *molendinum*, presumably from the Late Latin verb *molendo* which is itself built on the present participle of *molo* (*molens*) or on the gerund (*molendum*) derived from it. This occurs in several of the satellites (it is the norm in Exon) and (together with *molinum*) in LDB. In the latter, as in GDB,

---

[55] For the word *manere* as a noun, see Niermeyer, *Lexicon Minus*, under *manere*. He cites an example from before 1040 from the Vendôme Cartulary.
[56] See GDB, 100cv: DEV 1,21: *hae tres mansion[es]*, which occurs shortly before a summarizing *haec xix maneria*. See also GDB, 69v, 252: WIL 25,1; SHR C10. The word *tenementum* ('holding') appears in Evesham C 3–5, where *manerium* might be expected. Evesham C also has the latter (see, for example Evesham C 7).

mol' or *molin'* predominates; a close study might reveal some significant patterns, by holder, hundred or circuit.

PASCUA. The form in the IE questions is *pascua* (*quot pascuorum*), implying the plural of the CL second declension noun *pascuum* ('pasture', 'grazing land'). A few occurrences in GDB suggest that it was there mistaken for a first declension noun (*pascua, pascuae*), a fate common to such CL neuter plurals. However, both in ICC and in IE, *pascua* has been replaced by *pastura*, which is the only form found in LDB, whereas Exon retains *pascua*. Similarly, although *silua pascualis* is found in GDB, the predominant form there is *silua pastilis*, which, although not derived directly from *pastura* looks more like it. The origin of both *pascua* and *pastura* is the CL deponent verb *pascor*. While *pastura* is a Late Latin not a CL word, it would probably be familiar to the Norman-French speakers from OFr *pasture* (Mod French *pâture* and *pâturage*).[57] It is possible that this familiarity dictated the change just as the varying declension of *pascuum/pascua* would have resulted in uncertainty about the number of pastures.

There are a number of instances of *pascuum/pascua* in GDB where *pastura* might be expected. They amount to about twenty-five, a very small total compared with the figure for *pastura*. This poses something of a dilemma for the translator, even if it seems probable that these instances are all a failure to convert one term to another, rather than being a subtly differentiated resource or render.[58]

PISCINA. The IE questions have this form, whereas, at the other end of the process, Domesday predominantly has *piscaria*. In between one notes *piscina* predominantly in ICC and IE, *piscatio* as well as *piscina* and *piscaria* in LDB, whereas in addition to *piscaria* and *piscatio*, Exon has *piscatia, pescaria, piscatoria* and *piscuarium*. The root of all these words is CL *piscis* ('a fish'). From this was derived in the Classical period *piscina* ('fish-pond', 'fishery', but also 'swimming pool' and 'plunge-bath'), consisting of *pisc+ina*. The basic noun (*piscis*), the derived verb (*piscor*) and the agent noun (*piscator*, 'a fisherman') are also found in Domesday. The forms *piscaria* and *piscuarium* are ML usages, the first being *pisc-* with the CL termination *-aria*;[59] the second has the same root, but has the ML termination *-uarius*, arising by misdivision.[60] Both Domesday's *piscarius* and *piscuarius* are adjectives in origin ('involving fish', 'fish-related', 'fishy'). The noun *piscatio* is strictly 'an act of fishing', 'a fishing expedition', rather than 'a fishery', whereas *piscatoria* is derived from an adjective meaning 'concerning/involving a fisherman'. The sheer variety of these

---

[57] The word *pasture* is only found in Old French texts from the twelfth century, but its arrival in the language may date from considerably earlier.

[58] In the Phillimore edition, *pascua* and *pastura* are both normally translated as 'pasture', but see GDB, 42v: HAM 6,17, where 'pasturage' occurs.

[59] *Piscarius-a-um* is used only as an adjective in CL.

[60] Of such words as *actuarius, antiquarius, aquarius, Februarius, sumptuarius* where the *-u-* is in fact part of the stem (*actu-arius*, not *act-uarius*).

words shows how simple it is to create a word for a 'fish thing' as needed, any more exact meaning being only discernible from the context.

It is easy to guess why *piscina* was largely rejected: with too many meanings, the sense needed in Domesday was unclear. It may be that some of those who answered the Domesday questions used their own particular 'fish-thing' word and that ultimately *piscaria*, which had the necessary meaning and none other and looked like a good Latin word, almost won the day. The implication of this for understanding the text of Domesday is that these diverse words have the same meaning (a 'fish-place', 'a place where fish are had'), and that any conclusion, say, that *piscina* is a fish-pond or pool and *piscaria* a riverine or coastal fishery is mistaken.[61]

Describing woodland

The IE questions make reference only to *silua* and that is the overwhelming choice of the GDB scribe.[62] CL had few words for 'wood' or 'woodland'. Apart from *silua*, it had the vague but evocative *saltus* ('wooded mountains', 'wild wood', 'woodland glades'), and *lucus* and *nemus*, both of which could mean 'grove', 'sacred wood', with ritual and numinous associations. The overwhelming choice of Exon is *nemus*, with its diminutive *nemusculus* converted into GDB's *silua minuta* ('underwood'). *nemus* does not occur at all in LDB, but is found quite frequently in GDB in the phrase *nemus ad sepes* ('a wood/woodland for fences') and variants. It might be argued that *nemus* designates a separate and isolated wood reserved for this purpose, but it is improbable, as *silua ad sepes* is also found.[63] It is likely that *nemus* proved too resistant to change in this frequently occurring phrase.[64] The word *lucus* is found once,[65] but nothing in the context suggests that it is other than a *silua*, and the same is probably true of *graua*.[66]

---

[61] There is a *piscina et passagium aquae* ('a fishery and a ferry/river-crossing') in GDB, 273: DBY 1,37 at Weston-on-Trent and a *piscina et passagium* at Southwell in GDB, 283: NTT 5,1. Since both ferries are clearly on the River Trent, it is likely that the fisheries are preserves within that river.

[62] He is not even tempted by *sylua*, which appears in King William's writs and in Exon, alongside *silua*, but never in LDB or GDB.

[63] *Rispalia ad sepes* ('brushwood for fences') occurs at GDB, 140v: HRT 35,2.

[64] GDB, 34v: SUR 19,12 seems to prove the point: *silua v. porc[orum]; aliud nemus sibi retinuit Ricardus* ('a wood producing 5 pigs; Richard has kept another wood for himself'). In translation these could nonetheless be differentiated as 'woodland' and 'wood'.

[65] GDB, 64v: WIL 1,2.

[66] The word is OE *graf, grafa* ('a grove'). It appears not to have been used as a Latin word before DB in England or on the continent. In GDB there are examples in HAM, OXF and WAR. The Phillimore translation has 'copse' but *graua* does not imply a coppiced wood. Moreover, although some *grauae* are small (5 acres in GDB, 155v: OXF 6,13), some are larger (1 league long, 2 furlongs wide in GDB, 157v: OXF 24,50) which suggests that these are *siluae* by another name.

The Normans, would, however, have been familiar with *boscus*, a word of Germanic origin which is found as *bosc* or *bois* in many French place-names. It is found in satellites, where the corresponding GDB entries have *silua*,[67] and it is tempting to assume that it had some presence in the Domesday material but was eliminated on stylistic grounds.[68] It also occurs in personal names.[69]

Major substitutions

COTARII/BORDARII. For the dependent manorial population, the IE questions mention only *uillani, cothcetli* or *cot[arii]* and *serui*. GDB lists 109,230 *uillani*, 6,947 *cotarii* and their variants, 28,235 slaves and 81,849 *bordarii*.[70] On the face of it, the questions have been revised and this last category added. While *bordarii* are listed in every county, *cotarii* and their variants are missing from 17 counties. It might be thought that this population group was peculiar to some counties of England, as were sokemen. However, in some counties, *cotarii* appear exclusively in some hundreds and *bordarii* in others, as if the choice of term were made by the hundredal jurors or their clerks and scribes.[71] Moreover, what occur as *cotarii* in some satellites have been converted to *bordarii* when the same estate is found in others or in GDB.[72] The word *bordarius* (Modern French *bordier*) was apparently introduced by the Normans and is derived from OFr *borde* ('plank', 'planked hut') referring presumably to those who lived in such;[73] they were thus similar to those who lived in 'cots', and it is not clear why *bordarius* was not chosen to describe them from the

---

[67] Evesham A 166 has *boscum*, where GDB, 172: WOR 1,1c has *siluam*; Evesham M 43 has *inter boscum et planum* where GDB, 165v: GLS 10,11 has *inter siluam et planum. de bosco et pastura* is found in IE, 125, but *de consuetudinibus siluae et pasturae* in the corresponding entry in GDB, 135: HRT 8,1. See also GDB, 2, 135v, 138v: KEN P5; HRT 10,9. 28,4.

[68] Exon, 27a has *boscus de hauocumba*, perhaps of a particular wood; repeated in GDB, 75: DOR 1,2.

[69] A significant alternative for Hugh of Boscherbert is Hugo *de nemore Herberti* (Exon Geld Accounts, 17b). One notes also that apparently the same man occurs as William *de silua* in LDB, 342v: SUF 7,115 and as William *de nemore* in LDB, 344: SUF 7,134 and probably LDB, 373: SUF 16,3 and as William *de nomore* (a misspelling) in LDB, 424, 425: SUF 39,5;11.

[70] Darby, *Domesday England*, 337–8.

[71] F. H. Baring, *Domesday Tables for the Counties of Surrey, Berkshire, Middlesex, Hertford, Buckingham, Bedford and for the New Forest with an Appendix on the Battle of Hastings*, London 1909, 1, 9–10, 40, 43.

[72] For example in ICC and Bath A. For the latter see *Domesday Book*, ed. J. Morris, 8: *Somerset*, ed. C. Thorn and F. Thorn, Chichester 1980, Appendix III.

[73] There are two similar words in French, *le bord* ('edge', 'rim', 'side of a ship') and *la borde* ('board', 'plank'), both derived from separate Germanic words. For the unlikely notion that *bordarius* comes from *le bord* and thus the man lives on the margins of the cultivated area, see S. P. J. Harvey, 'Evidence for Settlement Study: Domesday Book', in *Medieval Settlement: Continuity and Change*, ed. P. H. Sawyer, London 1976, 195–9.

outset unless there was at first perceived to be a difference of status or obligations between the English and French peasants, which finally, in view of the broadness of the categories, was thought to be of no importance.[74] Although *cotarii* certainly appear on Glastonbury land in Exon and in GDB, the summaries of the fief in Exon only have villans, bordars, freedmen and fishermen,[75] as if the *cotarii* had been subsumed into the *bordarii*. It may be that it was intended to replace all occurrences of the word *cotarii* by *bordarii*, but that it as imperfectly carried through.

The wider picture

It would be impossible in any reasonable space to examine all the other terms used in Domesday, but the evolution of a few may adumbrate the larger picture. Overall it seems that the main scribe of GDB, and to a lesser extent the scribes of LDB and Exon, were aiming at a simplicity, purity and consistency of style, which they did not wholly achieve, partly because of the number of matters that simultaneously demanded their attention as they wrote, and partly because aims were at odds with one another: for example, an indispensable technical term might be a barbarism. While the main scribe of GDB tried to impose uniformity, he was to some extent a victim of the diverse expressions and quality of his material. It would have been superhuman to have eliminated every differing formula and turn-of-phrase which the circuit volumes presented, for they themselves, despite attempts to impose consistency, will have reflected the form and content of the information from hundreds of individuals with their own idiosyncratic verbal preferences and these had already been re-organized and re-expressed by layers of officials representing important individuals, as well as vills, hundreds and the county and by different clerks and scribes. The main scribe, in abbreviating and standardizing, will have had difficulty in deciding whether the expressions before him described different realities, not always envisaged by those who framed the survey, or were simply different expressions of the same reality. Nevertheless, he seems to have applied the following general principles.

Avoidance of the grandiose

There is a certain pompous, bombastic, hyperventilating style which throughout the Middle Ages was felt appropriate for weighty subjects. One aspect of this is the direct importation from the terms used in Ancient Rome to designate officials. It

---

[74] See Finn, *Introduction to Domesday Book*, 122–6; Darby, *Domesday England*, 69–72; Maitland, *Domesday Book and Beyond*, 23–5, 38–40; F. Seebohm, *The English Village Community*, 4th edn, Cambridge 1926, 95–7; P. Vinogradoff, *English Society in the Eleventh Century*, Oxford 1908, 456–61.
[75] Exon, 173a2, 528a1–3.

is a common style in the charters of some periods, where it contrasts with others that are plain and direct. Elements of this style are found in the writs of William I and it is interesting to see how few are used in Domesday. Their absence defines the Domesday style as occupying the central ground. Thus there is no sign of the excessive *antistes*, *pontifex*, *prelatus* and *presul* (for 'bishop' or 'abbot') where Domesday uses *episcopus* or *abbas*.[76] Neither is there *archipresbiter* nor *archipresul* ('archbishop') for *archiepiscopus*, nor *basileus* ('king') for *rex* nor *basilica* ('church/monastery') for *ecclesia/monasterium*. The Latin *dux* ('leader', 'ruler', 'duke'), *princeps* ('leading man', 'noble', 'baron'), *rector* ('ruler (of Normandy)', 'head of'),[77] *pretor* ('official')[78] and *genetrix/genitrix* ('mother') or *genitor* ('father') are absent, as are *nobiles* and *optimates* (originally '(Roman) nobles', so 'barons'). In Domesday a countryman or peasant is, appropriately, a *rusticus* and not a verbally self-regarding *solicolus* or *ruricola*.[79] On the other hand LDB uses *consul* (originally 'a (Roman) consul') for *comes*,[80] as does ICC[81] and William's writs, where it refers either to a ruler of Normandy or to an earl or count. LDB also uses the derived *consulatus* (originally 'the (Roman) consulship'),[82] here the office of earl or count, the earldom or *comté*; earls and counts are thus assimilated to the pre-eminent officials of the glorious Roman republic. There are no examples in GDB and one assumes that the main scribe of Domesday would have had nothing to do with such words. Moreover, *sacerdotes* ('holy men', 'priests') – a CL word – appears in LDB[83] and in Exon.[84] The main scribe uses *clerici* or *presbiteri* presumably wishing to have nothing to do with the high priests of pagan cults.

Avoidance of the local and colloquial

On the other side of the middle way lie words which, although they are Latin, do not date from Classical antiquity but are Latinized from the language of the Celts or the various Germanic colonizers of France or from Anglo-Saxon, or are re-Latinized from the debased forms of Latin that became Romance, the mother of the Romance languages and dialects. The main scribe of Domesday and certainly his master, whoever he was, would have been schooled in a careful choice of the pagan classics

---

[76] IE, 194 has *presul* in a section unrelated to Domesday.
[77] *Rector navis* ('captain', 'steersman') occurring in LDB, 200: NFK 10,76 shows an uninflated use of the word.
[78] A Roman republican position below that of consul.
[79] *Regesta*, Bates, nos. 286 and 324; the latter is a forgery but shows the style.
[80] LDB, 20v, 118: ESS 12,1; NFK 1,70.
[81] ICC, 83. In Exon, 312b1 and 313a3 *uiceconsul* appears for *uicecomes* referring to Baldwin the sheriff.
[82] LDB, 91, 118: ESS 52,2; NFK 1,70.
[83] LDB, 389b: SUF 25,10.
[84] Exon, 86b1, 194b3 = GDB, 100v, 104v: DEV 1,18.13a,1; in the second instance *presbiteri* are on the same page of Exon (194b1–2).

of Rome and on the elegant and elevated Latinity of the Christian fathers. He will have been well aware that French was the result of the evolution or the degeneration of the CL *sermo uulgaris*, the language of ordinary people, and that the Latin of his day was a mongrel language among whose words a careful choice had to be made if one had any pretensions to style and taste. Words that were manifestly not of Latin origin, or whose provenance was suspect, the main scribe and some of the scribes who preceded him would have been inclined to abhor, if there was a term of purer blood available.

Thus *rusca* for a bee-hive (from a Gallic word that passed into Late Latin; OFr *rusche*, Modern French *ruche*) is found in LDB, alongside the respectable *uas*; neither occurs in GDB.[85] Neither *grangia* nor *horreum* (ML and CL words respectively for 'granary') appear in GDB, though both are found in King William's writs. The word *grangia* occurs in LDB: it is a French mangling of ML *granaria*,[86] on its way to becoming French *la grange*.[87] Its absence from GDB could be because no granaries are listed, though one suspects that the main scribe might have chosen a better word.[88]

The word *forgia* ('forge', 'smithy') is from OFr.[89] There is a solitary appearance in the Customs of Hereford,[90] notable for other unusual uses;[91] otherwise, GDB uses the classical, or classical-looking, *ferraria*[92] or *fabrica ferri*,[93] although the exact sort of 'iron-thing' is sometimes unclear.[94]

In Domesday three adjectives *albus*, *blancus* and *candidus* are used to describe coinage. A linguist is likely to regard these as meaning 'white', 'white' and 'white', drawing attention to the different shades of white in the CL *albus* and *candidus*, respectively ordinary or gentle white as in the dawn[95] or brilliant white as in white-hot (from the root of the verb *candeo*) or in the especially whitened toga of a 'candidate' for Roman office. On the other hand, *blancus* is distinguished from these by being not of Latin origin, but a Germanic word occurring in Romance, whence Italian *bianco*, French *blanc* etc. Some Domesday commentators have been inclined

---

[85] For *rusca*, see, for example, LDB, 385, 443v: SFK 21,45.67,28. GDB, 180v: HEF 1,47 has the diminutive *uasculus*; see GDB, 259v: SHR 4,27,21, where it is used of corn.
[86] From CL *grana*.
[87] LDB, 290, 294v: SUF 1,122b. 3,55.
[88] GDB, 74v: WIL 68,29 has *granetarius*, for a 'granary-keeper'.
[89] OFr *forge* <Romance *faurga* <CL *fabrica*. For the purer *fabrica ferri*, see note 93.
[90] GDB, 179: HEF C8.
[91] The customs of Hereford are based on those of Breteuil in Normandy; see M. Bateson, 'The Laws of Breteuil', *EHR* 15, 1900, 73–8, 302–18, 496–523, 754–7; ibid. 16, 1901, 92–110, 332–45; J. Tait, *The Medieval English Borough*, Manchester 1936, 350–2.
[92] GDB, 22v, 45v, 70v, 344: SSX 10,102; HAM 23,38; WIL 26,14; LIN 7,1.
[93] GDB, 360v: LIN 30,29;31.
[94] *Ferraria* is from the CL adjective *ferrarius* (from *ferrum* ('iron')), used as a noun.
[95] Latin (*lux*) *alba* ('white light') gives Old French *albe* or *aube*, Modern French *l'aube* ('dawn').

to take *blancus* as having a different and technical meaning ('blanched'), although *blancus* has no verbal force. However, all the occurrences of the word, apart from one, are in LDB[96] and this suggests that there is no difference in the meaning of the three terms, but that the main scribe of GDB was trying to eliminate *blancus*. By contrast, there appears to be only one occurrence of *albus* in LDB,[97] and only two of *candidus*.[98] It is noteworthy that in a group of Essex entries *blancus* is used in the same context as *candidus*.[99]

Finally, the satellite Evesham C has *cainas* where the corresponding Domesday entry has *quercus*. These are 'oak trees', the first derived from a Gallic word which ultimately gives French *le chêne*, the latter a CL word.[100] It looks as if one of the precursor of Evesham C, possibly the lost circuit volume for the West Midlands,[101] had the rebarbative *cainas* and the main scribe made it Classical.

Retaining CL spelling

The concept of *Latinitas* meant that there should be one form of Latin throughout the Roman empire, and this included the stable tradition of spelling which had become established in the early imperial period. In the chaos that followed the collapse of the empire, and in particular the cessation of most formal education and the growth of vernaculars, there was a notable loosening of orthography, syntax, accidence, and lexis. Moreover new words for which there was no standard CL form came into Latin, often in several forms and genders.

As regards the spelling of CL words, the main scribe of Domesday, as well as the various scribes of some satellites, made an effort to enforce standard spellings and eliminate barbarisms. Thus poor forms such as *cumputatur* for *computatur* are avoided.[102] Similarly with *sagena* ('fishing-net', 'drag-net'), a Greek-derived CL word, the main scribe of GDB eschews the rustic *sargina* of ICC.[103]

The word *burgus* (of Germanic origin) occurs in CL in inscriptions and it would

---

[96] GDB, 39v: HAM 1W4: *tamen reddit xii libras blancas de viginti in ora* ('however, it pays 12 white pounds at 20 [pence] to the *ora*'). This is essentially identical to GDB, 164: GLS 1,58: *modo redd[unt] xl lib[ras] alborum num[m]orum de xx in ora* ('now, they pay 40 pounds of white money at 20 [pence] to the *ora*'), but with *blancas* instead of *albas*.

[97] LDB, 121: NFK 1,82.

[98] LDB, 29v, 30v: ESS 20,36;45.

[99] For *blancus*, see LDB, 30, 30v: ESS 20,37,43; for *candidus*, see LDB, 29v, 30v: ESS 20,36;45.

[100] Evesham C 13 = GDB, 172v: WOR 2,13. The Gallic *cassanus* gives Old French *chasne*, the change to *chesne, chêne* being due to the influence of CL *fraxinus*> Old French *fraisne/ fresne*> Modern French *le frêne* ('ash-tree').

[101] Cf. Howard Clarke, below, pp.248–52.

[102] Exon, 109b2.

[103] ICC, 7.

be expected that its ML derivatives would retain the -*u*-. Thus *borgenses*[104] and *bergenses*[105] for *burgenses* are avoided. The form *bergensis*, along with the nicely formed *burgarius*, occurs in King William's writs. Domesday uses the CL *pecunia* (as 'livestock'), and avoids irregular spellings such as *peccunia* (in King William's writs).[106]

There was an important florescence of words in ML built on the root *camb-* from a Gallic word meaning 'exchange'. It is represented marginally in CL by the verb *cambio, cambire*, which had been supplemented by the fourth century with the easier to conjugate *cambio, cambiare*. The noun *cambium* occurs in ML as well as numerous other derivatives and compounds. *excambium* (noun) and *excambiare* (verb) are the origin of the modern French *échange* and *échanger* via Medieval French *eschange* and *eschanger/eschangier*. In LDB, the basic verb *cambio* appears occasionally.[107] Otherwise, LDB exhibits the very French *escangium*[108] which the main scribe of GDB probably abhorred and preferred to use the verb *excambio*[109] and the derived noun in the form *excambium*.[110] The occurrence of *in escangio*[111] in the Yorkshire Claims (a subsidiary document to the main GDB account) suggests a momentary lapse of concentration, probably when he was trying to shorten and make sense of these 'shouts' and 'screams' (*clamores*). A derived noun, *excambitio*, of abstract formation, occurs once.[112]

The word chosen for the sub-division of the Kentish *sulung* (see below) was *jugum*, a CL word meaning 'yoke', and which is normally so translated in Domesday. The scribe is not tempted by the form *iocum* found in DM B.[113]

Spelling of terms Latinized from English and French

Among a proliferation of spellings both original and Latinized, the main scribe of GDB tends to settle on a single respectable form: thus *geldum* (and the derived

---

[104] Exon, 91a5; *borg'* occurs in LDB, 286v: SUF 1,97.
[105] Exon, 105a1.
[106] The tendency to double up consonants in this way is a characteristic of Old French, as a means to indicate a short vowel; see M. K. Pope, *From Latin to Modern French*, Manchester 1952, sections §§ 729, 1217. The alternative *pecus, pecoris*, is found in IE, 101, 106. That form of *pecus* is also found in King William's writs, along with the allied *pecus, pecudis*. There is an example of *arrare* (for *arare*) in Exon (25a2).
[107] For example, LDB, 211v: NFK 14,32.
[108] For example, LDB, 6, 15, 16v, 37v, 38, 69, 160, 165v, 331, 409: ESS 1,27.6,11.8,9. 22,13;21;23.33,3; NFK 8,18;64; SUF 7,4.31,50–1.
[109] For example, GDB, 148v, 149v, 214v: BKM 17,2.19,1; BDF 25,1.
[110] For example, GDB, 100v, 101v, 114v, 145v, 210, 212v, 213, 213v, 214, 214v: DEV 1,24.2,10.34,54; BKM 5,10; BDF 3,10.23,7;16;41;43;55.25,1.
[111] GDB, 376v, 377: LIN CK13,19.
[112] GDB, 176: WOR 11,1.
[113] DM B, 94. As formed, the word is the Latin for 'joke'. Douglas' edition also contains the satellite text DM E.

geldare) for OE *geld* or *gield* ('geld'), where the satellites and LDB offer ten or so alternatives and there are three more in King William's writs. For OE *denn* ('pig-pasture'), GDB uses the Latinized *dena*, hypercorrectly simplifying the authentic double consonant found, for example, in the Excerpta.[114] For OE *þeg(e)n* ('thane') it overwhelmingly uses *teignus*, although there are isolated examples of *taigni*, *tegnus* and *tanus*, with *teinus* occurring about thirty times.[115] This contrasts with five other forms found in LDB and the satellites and the eighteen forms in King William's writs.

Adoption of native terms

Here 'native' means terms that were familiar to the English or 'French' in their own languages. This a category of words that bear specific ('technical') meanings and which are not easily replaced by words drawn from ML or CL. Many of these words could easily have been given a Latin termination and placed in a declension, and are found thus Latinized in other documents of the period, but the scribe of GDB in particular did not do so. This habit is so common that it almost looks like a policy to let these native technical terms stand out as such.

In the case of marsh, OFr *maresc*, Modern French *marais*,[116] both LDB and GDB have indeclinable *maresc* or *maresch* which contrasts with Latinized forms (*mariscus* etc.) in satellites and King William's writs.

Likewise, assart, in origin a French word meaning 'clearance of woodland', occurs three times in Herefordshire, twice in the form *essarz* and once in the Latin form *exsartum*.[117] The phrase *agros et exserta* occurs in the Exon Geld Accounts,[118] while King William's writs show a preponderance of Latinized forms: *assartum*, *essartum*, *sartum* contrasting with *essart*.

Many other terms are often left untouched in GDB, occasionally given a Latin ending; thus *arpent*, plural *arpenz* (a land-measure, usually of vineyards), is sometimes Latinized and always so in King William's writs. The English (*ge*)*bur* is sometimes

---

[114] Excerpta, 2.
[115] The differentiated vowel -*ei*- is adopted from French to provide an equivalent of this English diphthongal sound.
[116] *mariscus* is said to be an ML word derived from a West German (Frankish) **marisk*. OE *mersh*, *merisc* comes from the same Germanic root. However, *marisca* in CL means a 'rush' or 'reed'. DB seems to represent the first appearance of *maresc*(*h*) in England.
[117] GDB, 179v, 180, 184v: HEF 1,7;10a.10,48–9). The word is OFr *essart*, Anglo-Norman (AN) *assart*. It derives from ML *exsarta* or *exsartum*, which gives the verb *exsartare* ('to clear woodland'). Ultimately, these words are from CL *sar(r)io* ('to hoe', 'to weed'). *sartum sarti*, a neuter noun, also exists in ML as 'cleared land'. Neither *sartum* nor *exsartum* is found in England before the Conquest.
[118] Exon, 20a.

given an (English) plural as *bures*, sometimes Latinized as *buri*.[119] In the case of OE *feorþing* ('ferling' or 'ferding', that is, 'a quarter'), OE *sulung* the Kentish measure equivalent of the hide),[120] OE *hundred* (the 'hundred' as an administrative unit) and OE *radman* and *radcniht* ('road man' and 'road knight' often translated as 'radman' and 'radknight'), the words are more often left in the vernacular than Latinized.

When it comes to what must have seemed outlandish English terms, the clear tendency is to leave them untouched. Thus *burgherist* ('borough-right'), *gribrige* ('breach of the peace'), *heinfara* ('house-breaking'), *herdigelt* ('hearth-tax'), *legrewita*, ('adultery'), *thol et theim* ('toll and team' or 'market-rights').[121]

Overall, one detects some difference between the practice of the scribes of LDB and the main scribe of GDB, The former are inclined to Latinize more than the latter, though the latter has a greater concern for good Latinity. There is a parallel case in that both in LDB and in Exon there is a tendency to give Latin terminations to the names of persons and places, whereas the main scribe of GDB is inclined to treat the names as indeclinable, as well as choosing, guessing or restoring more English forms of them.[122]

Eliminating alternatives

By the eleventh century, thanks to the ease of forming words in Latin, there was a proliferation of words meaning the same thing: the various words for 'fishery', for 'lordship' and for 'exchange', considered above, have illustrated this. In some cases, the Domesday scribes seem to have tried to settle for a single 'Domesday word' from alternatives. Thus *antecessor* is invariably used for 'tenurial predecessor', leaving aside the more than acceptable *predecessor* of the Exon Geld Accounts.[123] The word *herbagium* is always used in GDB for 'grass render', 'rent from grazing', thus leaving aside the *herbacio* (= *herbatio*) of IE[124] and the *herbatia* of ICC.[125] The writs of William I offer a further form in *herbatura*.[126] The fighting-men or knights (*milites*) who are often assigned particular portions of manors are described only by that word

---

[119] For the apparent equivalence of *coliberti* and *bures, buri*, see GDB, 38, 38v, 174v: HAM 1,10;23;WOR 8,10).
[120] OE *sulh* (dative *sylg, sylh*) 'plough' and *lang* ('long'); see J. Bosworth and T. Northcote Toller, *An Anglo-Saxon Dictionary*, Oxford 1882, Supplement by Toller, 1921, Revised and Enlarged Addenda by A. Campbell, 1972, under *sulh*.
[121] For *herdigelt, fumagium* ('smoke-due') is found in GDB, 181: HEF 1,49 and for *legrewita, adulterium* in GDB, 1, 26, 56v: KEN D19; SSX 12,1; BRK B7.
[122] See P. H. Sawyer, 'The Place-Names of the Domesday Manuscripts', *Bulletin of the John Rylands Library* 38, 1955–6, 483–506.
[123] Exon, 1b.
[124] IE, 101.
[125] ICC, 10–11, 29.
[126] *Regesta*, Bates, no. 281. The charter is suspect.

in GDB, though DM B has *equitem* ('horseman', 'knight').[127] It has always been surprising that Domesday uses *milites* when the Latin *eques* was available for what are assumed to be mounted soldiers, cavalry or knights.[128] The Latin word *uestura* appears in the Excerpta,[129] but is converted to the 'Domesday word' *uestitus* in DM B, as in GDB.[130]

The word *acra* (from OE *æcer*) seems unavoidable, both as a subdivision of the hide (so, in effect, a 'fiscal acre') and as a measure of pasture or woodland (etc.) where it is an actual areal measure, though probably an estimate in many cases and perhaps varying by locality. It is overwhelmingly the choice of LDB and GDB and is found in the Exon Tax Returns,[131] in DM E[132] and in ICC.[133] In DM B there occurs the more English form (*æceres*).[134] Nonetheless, this choice may have been made as the Domesday inquiry proceeded, since Exon normally has *ager*, the CL for a field, which is, in origin, neither a fiscal nor areal measure.[135] It is possible that whoever supervised the composition of that circuit volume preferred a classical word, here as in other instances. As with *pascua* and *mansio*, a few cases seem to have missed the process of conversion.[136] In the choice of *acra* over *ager*, we see two principles in conflict: the desire to write a pure and timeless Latin and the need to use precise terminology.

Ignoring alternatives

It would have been impossible for the main scribe to have eliminated all variations and while he was concentrating on the main tasks, some of these minor matters seem to have passed him by. A few examples will suffice.

CL presented him with *aula* and *curia* which came to be used for 'hall', 'court (of the manor)', to which was added OE *hall*, *heall* ('hall') Latinized as *halla*, or

---

[127] DM B, 87.
[128] However, in GDB, 280: NTT B9–10, *equites* simply appear to be 'horsemen', 'men with horses', so, in effect, the word had already been allocated for something else.
[129] See Excerpta, 20.
[130] DM B, 89 = GDB, 3: KEN 2,2; it is also *uestitus* in Excerpta, 23.
[131] For example, Exon, 7b, 9a, 15b. It is sometimes masculine (*acros*), as if this were the Latin *agros*, with the *g* unvoiced.
[132] DM E, 99–100.
[133] For Example, ICC, 6.
[134] DM B, 88.
[135] Both OE *æcer* and Latin *ager* are from a hypothetical Indo-European *agros although they came to England by different routes and with differentiated meanings.
[136] For example, GDB, 64v, 86v, 122: WIL B5; SOM 1,9; CON 5,2,7–8;22. It does not appear in LDB, and once in GDB, 38v: HAM 1,19 in the phrase *medietas agrorum* 'a half-share of the fields', it probably has its normal sense.

sometimes, as if *aula* and *halla* were the same word, as *haula*.[137] LDB does not have *haula*, but both LDB and GDB have the others.

For 'market', the ML *mercatum*, (from CL *mercatus*) was the obvious choice; it is the ultimate origin both of English market and French *marché*, but the scribe of GDB, or someone else, was tempted by the classical *forum*[138] which has a misleadingly wider range of meanings.

For 'hunting', the obvious and regular choice is *uenatio*, the 'act of' noun from the past participle of the deponent verb *uenor* ('to hunt').[139] The Hereford customs, unusual in other ways, have *quando rex uenatui instabat* ('when the king was intent on hunting'),[140] using the fourth declension noun from the same part of the same verb.

There is no stalling of game in the woods in LDB and not much in GDB. Latin *stabilitio* characterizes the process as *ad stabilitione[m] u[er]o mittebat uicecomes xxxvi homines pedites* ('The sheriff sent 36 men on foot for [game-]stalling').[141] An apparent synonym *stabilitura* may refer to a contrivance rather than stalling by a group of men.[142]

For 'corn', *frumentum* ('corn' or 'wheat', 'cereal crop') and *annona* ('annual crop of corn/wheat', 'cereals') seem interchangeable in GDB. However, there existed also the French word *blatum* (OFr *blet*, Modern French *blé* from a West Germanic (Frankish) or Gallic word which tempted an LDB scribe once)[143] and *bled annonae* appears in that unusual section *Redditus Edwardi Sarisber[iensis]* ('renders of Edward of Salisbury') in Wiltshire[144] where *annonae* might, in fact, be an incorporated gloss on the word.

For 'castle', GDB normally uses *castellum* (Old French *castel*, *chastel*, Modern French *château*), but occasionally *castrum*. Theoretically, there should be a difference, *castellum* being a diminutive, but this is not evident in particular cases, and not entirely clear even in CL usage.[145] King William's writs have both. For 'castlery',

---

[137] See GDB, 72: BRK 36,4, contrasting with *hallae* GDB, 72: BRK 36,6.
[138] See GDB, 163, 163v, 173v, 219v, 356: GLS 1,15;47; WOR 2,51; NTH 1,8; LIN 24, 91.
[139] See GDB, 56v, 165v, 173, 179v, 186, 252: BRK B11; GLS 10,11; WOR 2,15;22;31; HEF 1,3.24,5; SHR C3.
[140] GDB, 179: HEF C3.
[141] GDB, 252: SHR C3; see also GDB, 56v, 179: BRK B11; HEF C3.
[142] GDB, 269v: CHS R1,40a: *in silua haias et stabilituras*; the parallel with *haias* ('hedged enclosures', 'game traps') suggests some sort of structure.
[143] LDB, 274: NFK 66,5: *iiii carrucatas de blato*.
[144] GDB, 69: WIL 24p. The 'of' means 'to' or 'enjoyed by'.
[145] In terms of strategic position, there appears to be no difference in meaning among those facing Wales: most are *castella* but Montgomery in GDB, 253v, 254: SHR 4,1,15;35) is both a *castellum* and a *castrum*.

that is, land, or the sum total of land dependent on a castle, the preferred term is *castellaria*, although *castellatus* is found twice, once in the same entry as *castellaria*.[146]

For 'reeve', which is a technical term, the English *gerefa* offered a word which, though not Latin-looking, already appeared to have a Latin termination. However, it is nowhere used in the DB corpus. Instead two CL words, *prefectus* and *prepositus*, widely used in the Middle Ages, are pressed into service. The Introduction to the IE questions uses *prepositus*, but GDB has both.

The word 'homage' is infrequent in the 'feudal' Domesday Book: it appears as *homagium* in LDB,[147] but once as *hominatio* (a better form) in GDB.[148]

'Heriot', that is, 'relief' or 'death-duty', is sometimes represented by a form of the English word in Domesday (*heriet, heriete* in GDB, *herigete* in LDB)[149] and, like other words in this category, it is not declined as Latin. In GDB efforts are made to replace it with Latin words based ultimately on the verb *leuo* ('to lift', 'raise', 'lighten', 'remove'), but there is no settled form: *releuamen*,[150] *releuamentum*,[151] and *releuatio* are found.[152]

Roads make an occasional appearance in GDB, usually in reference to a royal highway or where some royal right has been infringed, although once the partition of one virgate of land is made clear 'as the road divides it'.[153] In the Kentish *Excerpta* the word *callis* appears. This is a CL word for a 'rough track' or 'path', found in Modern Spanish as *calle*. Although, in theory, it means 'path', 'track', or 'street', and is therefore not a synonym for *uia* ('road', 'highway'), the scribe of GDB replaces an occurrence of *callis regis* in the Excerpta with *publica uia regis*.[154] However, examples of *callis* survive into GDB for Kent.[155]

For 'to be an outlaw', LDB uses the monstrous verb *utlago*, sometimes reflexively and once in the form *utllagauit*;[156] for 'outlawry', it has *utlagaria*.[157] These imply the existence of the noun *utlagus* ('an exiled man', 'an exile'), although it does not

---

[146] For *castellatus* see GDB, 332: YKS 30W3. Both words appear in GDB, 381: YKS SN,CtA4.

[147] LDB, 116v, 172: NFK 1,61. 8,134. The word is OFr/AN *homage*, from hypothetical ML *hominaticum*, based on CL *homo* ('human being').

[148] GDB, 225v: NTH 35,1j. This is the only citation in *DMLBS*.

[149] GDB, 336v, 376, LDB, 119: LIN S4–5; LIN CW9;11; NFK 1,70. The word is OE *heregeatwa* from *here* ('army') and *geatwa* ('equipment').

[150] GDB, 1: KEN D7; probably also GDB, 30v: SUR 1,8: *releuam'*.

[151] GDB, 179, 252: HEF C9; SHR C7.

[152] GDB, 1: KEN D7; see also GDB, 298v: YKS C40.

[153] GDB, 249: STS 11,38.

[154] See Excerpta, 31 = GDB, 1: KEN D12.

[155] GDB, 2: KEN C6 has *de rectis callibus*, but *uias* in the same entry. *in uiis* occurs in GDB 2: KEN C7. *Callis* appears also in GDB, 1, 2: KEN D14; 23. C2.

[156] LDB, 48, 49v, 274, 342v: ESS 24,66.25,5; NFK 66,5; SUF 7,114 twice. LDB, 24: ESS 18,23 has *udlagau'*.

[157] LDB, 59: ESS 30,16. These words are derived from late OE *utlaga* ('an outlaw').

appear; instead, LDB has one example of *exlex*, a thoroughly Latin 'outside the law'.¹⁵⁸ The main scribe of GDB attempts to start from the CL *ex(s)ul* ('an exiled man'), which gave the noun *ex(s)ilium* ('exile') and the verb *exulo exulare* ('to be an exile', 'to go into exile').¹⁵⁹ In the case of Kent he has converted the *huthlagus* of the Excerpta to *exul*.¹⁶⁰ Elsewhere he nearly succeeded, but the borough entry for Chester has *utlagh* ('an exiled man') twice.¹⁶¹

At first sight the co-existence of *equi* and *caballi* in GDB is a further case of the failure of the main scribe of GDB to eliminate duplicates. *Caballus* (a Gallic word adopted into CL) is found there as a 'riding-horse' or 'pack-horse', but it also gives 'cavalry', 'cavalier' and 'chivalry', having acquired some prestige as time passed. There are no examples of *caballus* in LDB, but plenty of *equus*; however, in GDB, although there may be overlap in the middle ground, *equus* and *caballus* can appear to be different beasts. Thus, it is an *equus* which is provided for the king's service, or for Ralph *paynel* when he goes on an 'expedition' and it is *equi* who accompany the king from Leicester to London.¹⁶² On the other hand, many *caballi* in GDB are pack animals. Salt is mentioned in the terms of a *summa caballi* ('a packhorse's load') and there is a provision in the same entry against anyone *qui caballum ita onerabat ut dorsum frangeret* ('who so loaded a [pack-]horse that he broke its back').¹⁶³ In terms of borough customs, in Lewes it is *qui in burgo uendit equum* ('a man who sells a horse in the borough'),¹⁶⁴ and the customs of Hereford distinguish between 'he who had a horse and he who did not' (*qui equum habebat/non habebat*), whereas there is also a reference in the same customs to *burgensis cum caballo* also *ad locandos caballos*¹⁶⁵ and in Shrewsbury to *burgenses caballos habentes*.¹⁶⁶ Moreover, the escort of the king from Shrewsbury to the first *mansio* in Staffordshire is thus described: *Cum rex abiret de ciuitate mittebat ei xxiiii caballos uicecomes Lenteurde* ('When the king was leaving the city, the sheriff sent 24 horses for him [from] Leintwardine').¹⁶⁷ The interchangeability of the terms, at least in some cases, is shown by *Burgensis cum caballo seruiens cum moriebatur, habebat rex equum et arma ejus* ('when a burgess who did service with his horse (*caballus*) died, the king had his horse (*equus*) and his

---

¹⁵⁸ LDB, 200: NFK 10,77.
¹⁵⁹ For example, see GDB, 1, 154v, 186, 252v, 280v, 336v: KEN D21; OXF 1,13; HEF 19,3; SHR 3d7; NTT S2; LIN C33. In GDB, 1: KEN D9 *i. utlage* is written above *cujusdam exulis*.
¹⁶⁰ See Excerpta, 32 = GDB, 1: KEN D21.
¹⁶¹ GDB, 262v: CHS C4.
¹⁶² GDB, 197, 230, 377v: CAM 22,6; LEC C2; LIN CK53.
¹⁶³ GDB, 268: CHS S2.
¹⁶⁴ GDB, 26: SSX 12,1.
¹⁶⁵ GDB, 179: HEF C3;5; see also GDB,181: HEF 1,49.
¹⁶⁶ GDB, 252: SHR C3.
¹⁶⁷ GDB, 252: SHR C10.

weapons').[168] The *pro equo transfretando* ('for carrying an *equus* across the Channel') of the Excerpta becomes *the pro caballo transducendo* ('for taking a *caballus* across') of GDB.[169]

Tailpiece

One of the recurrent themes of this article is that different words do not necessarily mean different things. However true this may be, it poses a problem in translation, if one follows the logic of the argument and gives a single translation for what are different words. This makes the decision for the reader. It has been common for translations of Domesday Book to treat the same Latin word differently and to render different Latin words by the same term. There is an argument for leaving technical terms in the Latin ('a *boscus*, 2 leagues by 3 furlongs') because 'to translate is to betray',[170] but the friendlier alternative is to render each Latin word in one way only and to distinguish that word in translation from others which may or might have the same meaning.[171]

The intention of this article has been to open up a large topic. Not only can examples of the words listed above be increased, but there are many other words and the interpretations may well change in the light of further evidence. It might be possible, in due course, to tie particular verbal choices to individual scribes of LDB or Exon or to particular landholders, hundreds or circuits and to see if and how the choice of terms by the main scribe of GDB changed during his writing, since the approximate order of composition of groups of counties can be deduced from other evidence.[172] Further, the choice of words is only one aspect of the 'Domesday Style' as phrases, clauses, tenses, moods and the main scribe's techniques of abbreviation and clarification would repay detailed study.

---

[168] GDB, 179: HEF C3.
[169] See Excerpta, 24 = GDB, 1: KEN D3.
[170] Thus the French '*traduire, c'est trahir*'; compare the Italian '*traduttore, traditore*' ('translator: betrayer').
[171] The present author is currently (in 2014) working on new translations of GDB, LDB and Exon following such principles.
[172] See Thorn and Thorn, 'The Writing of Great Domesday Book', 43; David Roffe, *Domesday, the Inquest and the Book*, Oxford 2000, 186–223.

5

Domesday Books?
Little Domesday Reconsidered[1]

Ian Taylor

IN THE NOVOCENTENARY of Domesday, in 1986, it would have been considered eccentric to claim that, in broad outline, any great mysteries hung over the relationship between the documents that made up the Domesday corpus. Although a revolution in Domesday studies had taken place some twenty years before, a new consensus had emerged. It was understood that the production of Great Domesday Book (GDB) had been the aim of the Domesday process from the very start and that all the documentation which came out of the process could be fitted into a tight schedule to that end. Any questions that remained were simply matters of detail, the overarching structure of the process was not affected. Today there is no such confidence and consensus is no more. A radical reassessment of the Domesday inquest, the documents that were produced from it and the relationship of the two, has argued that the inquest and the book were two entirely different enterprises.[2] The result has been a recognition of the possibility, on the one hand, that inquest records do not necessarily speak of the concerns that initiated the inquiry in the first place, and, on the other, that subsequent abbreviations of the same records may have been produced for entirely different purposes. All the certainties of Domesday studies dissolve.

Debate continues on the purpose of the Domesday inquest and its relationship to Domesday Book. However, there is a growing recognition that all the Domesday texts do not have to be shoe-horned into a coherent taxonomy. This prompts a

---

[1] The germ of this paper, that the writing of LDB was related to the special circumstances of the military crisis of 1085/6 in East Anglia, is to be found in my undergraduate thesis, 'Domesday Book as a Quartermaster's Manual: Context and Compilation', University of Glasgow 2008. I am grateful to David Roffe for transforming an inchoate idea into a coherent argument; the extent of his contribution is apparent from the radical change in the title.
[2] David Roffe, *Domesday: The Inquest and the Book*, Oxford 2000.

re-examination of the documents of the Domesday corpus. With GDB understood as the aim of the inquest, everything else became 'satellites'; they were merely means to an end. In consequence, they have been studied largely in terms of how they pre-figured GDB. This is no more so than with Little Domesday (LDB), which is perhaps the least studied document to come out of the Domesday process and in many ways the most mysterious. Its forms are here examined anew in their own terms.

LDB, volume II of what is now called Domesday Book, contains an expansive description of the eastern counties of Essex, Norfolk and Suffolk hastily written by a team of six scribes. Volume I, GDB, covers the remaining counties of England south of the Tees in a much more accomplished style and is predominantly the work of one man. Apparently unlike its companion volume, it is a digest of the survey findings, that is an abbreviation that omits extraneous material, notably the ephemeral livestock statistics, and imposes an overall schema. The contrast between the two parts of Domesday Book is marked. In 1895 J. H. Round wrote: 'I have never seen any attempt at a real explanation of the great difference both in scope and excellence between the two volumes, or indeed any reason given why the Eastern counties should have had a volume to themselves.'[3] These are questions that have still not been satisfactorily answered.

For his part Round reasoned, on purely empirical grounds, that LDB was the first attempt at the writing of Domesday Book and that the entries for the remaining counties of GDB were more radically abbreviated in order to prevent the work from becoming too lengthy for effective use.[4] This, however, was an explanation that did not stand the test of time. For Round it was axiomatic that both GDB and LDB were compiled from geographically-arranged sources, what he termed 'the original returns', of which the *Inquisitio Comitatus Cantabrigiensis* (ICC) is an example.[5] To him, therefore, any seigneurially arranged text must by definition have been a precursor of Domesday Book. In 1942, and more fully in 1961, V. H. Galbraith put forward a radically different analysis. A central perception for him was that the production of GDB was the aim of the Domesday survey from its inception and that the accounts of land were arranged by lordship at an early stage. Galbraith argued that the *Liber Exoniensis* (Exon), a pre-GDB account of the south-western counties arranged by lordship, represented the original return of the commissioners assigned to that area, and he hypothesized that LDB was a fair copy of a similar circuit return which was produced in eastern England.[6] LDB, then, became, in Galbraith's terms, a satellite text: it represented a stage in the production of Domesday Book rather than an end in itself. Whereas the data in Exon were ultimately abbreviated and

---

[3] J. H. Round, *Feudal England*, London 1895, 140–1.
[4] R. Welldon Finn, *Domesday Studies: the Eastern Counties*, London 1967, 64.
[5] Round, *Feudal England*, 7–8.
[6] V. H. Galbraith, *The Making of Domesday*, Oxford 1961, 1–11.

entered in GDB, LDB never was and Galbraith suggested that it was probably the death of William the Conqueror in 1087 that arrested the work prematurely.[7]

The concept of the circuit return and the fair copy, and the characterization of Exon and LDB as respective examples, has proved to be an influential hypothesis. With the recognition that the compilation process may have extended into 1088,[8] other reasons for the omission of the eastern counties from GDB have subsequently been put forward, notably that the complexities of tenure defied abbreviation. Otherwise, the broad outline of Galbraith's argument has been widely accepted. The analysis has been forcefully restated by Colin Flight.[9] He has reverted to Galbraith's earlier understanding of a process that saw successive re-drafting of the Domesday data until it attained its final form, for Galbraith in GDB, for Flight in the circuit return fair copies represented by LDB. Others, by contrast, have sought to modify 'radical recensionism'[10] of this kind. In a seminal paper on the writing of GDB, Frank and Caroline Thorn demonstrated that Exon was the direct source of the GDB account of the south-western counties and suggested that similar sources lie behind the accounts of other areas.[11] Sir James Holt summed up the conclusion that naturally follows: 'The layer of fair copies of the local summaries, which Galbraith brought into play to explain the function of Little Domesday, is unnecessary. Great Domesday is based directly on the local summary as we have it in Exon.' While Galbraith was half way there, his problem was that 'he could not abandon his notion that Little Domesday was something other than a working copy'.[12] At once the making of Domesday Book could be fitted into a manageable schedule. Exon and LDB were essentially the same type of document.

Neat as all of this is, doubts nevertheless persist. Conceptually the argument is coherent, but it begins to falter in the face of even the most cursory examination of the manuscripts. It is difficult not to concur with Welldon Finn's judgement:

> Consideration of the text makes it obvious that 'Little Domesday' is a fair copy, and the validity of this judgement is enhanced when it is compared with the earliest surviving circuit draft, the Liber Exoniensis. Though the text of the

---

[7] ibid., 8.
[8] C. P. Lewis, 'The Earldom of Surrey and the Date of Domesday Book', *Historical Research* 63, 1990, 327–36; David Roffe, *Domesday: The Inquest and the Book*, Oxford 2000, 221; Caroline Thorn and Frank Thorn, 'The Writing of Great Domesday Book', in *Domesday Book*, ed. Elizabeth Hallam and David Bates, Stroud 2001, 37–72 at 72.
[9] Colin Flight, *The Survey of the Whole of England*, British Archaeological Reports, British Series 405, Oxford 2006.
[10] A term coined by David Roffe (*Decoding Domesday*, Woodbridge 2007, 82).
[11] Thorn and Thorn, 'Writing of Great Domesday Book', 48; P. Chaplais, 'William of Saint-Calais and the Domesday Survey', in *Domesday Studies*, ed. J. C. Holt, Woodbridge 1987, 65–78 at 66.
[12] J. C. Holt, 'Domesday Studies 2000', in *Domesday Book*, ed. Hallam and Bates, 19–24 at 23.

eastern circuit is by no means adequately arranged, and its errors are numerous, it is a distinct improvement on what we know as the Exeter Domesday. The proportion of marginalia is very much higher in the latter than the former, strongly suggesting that it belongs to a time earlier in the work of the Inquest than that of volume ii.[13]

Exon is organized by fee within groups of shires – lands in Wiltshire and Dorset are enrolled together without distinction as are those in Somerset, Devon and Cornwall – and there is little internal structure. It is, in effect, a series of notes and as such has been characterized as no more than 'an office file'.[14] This stands in stark contrast to LDB, which is carefully compiled, county by county and fee by fee, within a rigid geographical structure. The affinities of LDB in this respect are with GDB rather than with Exon.

David Roffe has shown just how close those affinities are. The seriation of GDB, the order of writing as reconstructed by him,[15] describes a neat geographical sequence that starts in the north and then proceeds to the east, the south, and west, before finishing up in the Midlands. If the scribe had intended enrolling East Anglia, he would have most likely written it up after the east Midland counties of Circuit III, probably following Cambridgeshire.[16] He did not do so. The developing forms of the text indicate why. LDB is characterized, *inter alia*, by running heads that indicate the fee, the association of dependent land with a manorial centre, the record of the dimensions of villages, the enrolment of *invasiones*, that is disputes, and the account of boroughs by settlement as opposed to fee.[17] All of these features are found in the Yorkshire folios where the GDB scribe started his work, but were variously dropped as he proceeded. It is difficult to escape the conclusion that LDB was the initial model for GDB.

More than this, as a class of document it was of the same type. Its extensive record of demesne livestock and of assessment and value 'when acquired' would seem to associate it with ICC and Exon, which record the same information. Unsurprisingly, many have found it difficult to resist the conclusion that all three must come from the same stage in the Domesday process. But these characteristics are misleading. The data, it is true, are found only intermittently in GDB and LDB is undoubtedly earlier. But, unlike Exon and ICC, both are abbreviations. The redaction of GDB

---

[13] Welldon Finn, *Domesday Studies: The Eastern Counties*, 65.

[14] Roffe, *Decoding Domesday*, 59.

[15] Subsequent analyses by Frank and Caroline Thorn and Colin Flight have differed in their placement of the Circuit II shires. See above, pp.13–14, for a discussion.

[16] Roffe, *Domesday: Inquest and Book*, 191–211; Roffe, *Decoding Domesday*, 103. See also Thorn and Thorn, 'Writing of Great Domesday Book', 43; Flight, *Survey of the Whole of England*, 10–24, esp. 16 n.15.

[17] ibid., 117–18. See also R. Welldon Finn, *An Introduction to Domesday Book*, London 1963, 56–9.

is obvious, the jettisoning of livestock was accompanied by a programme of standardization of expression. With LDB it is less apparent but nevertheless significant. It seems clear that the articles of enquiry required that a record of ploughlands be made throughout the country.[18] The statistics are duly found in earlier records of the survey as well as most of GDB. The data were undoubtedly collected in East Anglia too – the figures are preserved in the summaries of the *Inquisitio Eliensis*[19] – but they were systematically omitted from LDB.

LDB was thus an abbreviation and therefore cannot have been a circuit return in the sense in which the term is usually understood. It was not a complete record of the inquest as Galbraith had assumed.[20] Was, then, Round's intuition right? Was LDB the first attempt at an epitome of the Domesday survey into a final record and hence the GDB scribe never intended incorporating it into his work? It may well have been. It is often forgotten that its forms, namely the division into counties, separate accounts of boroughs and the articulation of estates, pre-figures the forms of GDB for the first time in the Domesday corpus. The possibility, though, raises the further questions of why East Anglia and when? Roffe has argued that GDB was compiled somewhat later than usually thought, possibly *c.*1090 after the rebellion against Rufus, but conceivably at any time up to the early years of the reign of Henry I.[21] But, while rejecting the concept of the circuit return, he could suggest no context for the compilation of LDB apart from it being earlier than GDB. An examination of the context and purpose of the inquest may point to an answer.

Over the years Domesday Book has been interpreted as a geld book, a feodary, the final settlement of the Norman occupation, and much else of a high political nature.[22] In the process, the immediate context of the survey has often been forgotten. Contemporary sources attest that this was a time of crisis. In 1085 England was threatened with invasion by a formidable alliance of King Cnut of Denmark and Robert, count of Flanders. Cnut's claim to the English throne was as good as William the Conqueror's and Robert had been a long-time supporter of William's enemies.[23] The alliance's threat to their common enemy had been made at an auspicious time as England was in turmoil. William's son and presumptive heir Robert had left court and, if not in revolt, had known sympathies with his uncle Count

---

[18] *EHD*, II, 851.
[19] Roffe, *Domesday: Inquest and Book*, 163–5.
[20] Galbraith, *Making of Domesday Book*, 5.
[21] Roffe, *Domesday: Inquest and Book*, 191–211. The dating has been challenged: see Holt, 'Domesday Studies 2000', 23–4.
[22] For a review of the historiography, see Roffe, *Decoding Domesday*, chapter 1.
[23] Eljas Oksanen, *Flanders and the Anglo-Norman World, 1066–1216*, Cambridge 2012; N. Higham, 'The Domesday Survey: Context and Purpose', *History* 78, 1993, 7–21; R. Nip, 'The Political Relations between England and Flanders (1066–1128)', *ANS* 21, 1998, 145–67 at 155.

Robert.²⁴ William had lost his wife Matilda and his powerful lieutenant Odo, bishop of Bayeux and earl of Kent, had been imprisoned. William's regime was weaker than it had been at any time since 1066.²⁵

Characteristically, William acted decisively. The Anglo-Saxon Chronicle records that 'When William, king of England, who was then in Normandy ... found out about this [the threatened invasion], he went to England with a larger force of mounted men and infantry from France and Brittany than had ever come to this country, so that people wondered how this country could maintain all that army.'²⁶ This was apparently no exaggeration.²⁷ The Chronicle goes on to say that these troops were billeted on his vassals, 'each in proportion to his lands'. Tense months must have passed, but in the event Cnut was unable to launch the invasion armada from its moorings in the Limfjord before the onset of winter and by the end of the year William stood down some of the mercenaries, while maintaining a more limited garrison over winter into the following year.

The invasion was never to materialize and Domesday scholars have all too often tended to examine the survey from that perspective. However, it is anachronistic to attribute this knowledge to William and his administration in the Christmas court of 1085 when the Domesday inquest was planned. Why Cnut failed to launch his invasion remains obscure.²⁸ He apparently remained a powerful force in Denmark during the winter. William of Malmesbury asserts that Cnut levied fines from a number of the nobles whom he believed to oppose him and he put his brother Olaf, the future king of Denmark, in chains and sent him to Robert of Flanders for safe keeping.²⁹ It should not be discounted, then, that the delay in attack was a deliberate attrition strategy on Cnut's part directed at the Anglo-Norman defenders, a

---

[24] William M. Aird, *Robert 'Curthose', Duke of Normandy (c. 1050–1134)*, Woodbridge 2011, 83.

[25] Higham, 'Domesday Survey', 11–12, 'William the Conqueror had good reason to take seriously this threat to England'. See also David Bates, *William the Conqueror*, Stroud 2001, 196.

[26] ASC (E), 161.

[27] The obvious comparison is the invasion force brought to England by William the Conqueror in 1066, modern estimates for which average out at about 6,000–8,000 men. See Higham, 'Domesday Survey', 14; R. A. Brown, 'The Battle of Hastings', in *Anglo-Norman Warfare: Studies in Late Anglo-Saxon and Anglo-Norman Military Organisation and Warfare*, ed. M. J. Strickland, Woodbridge 1992, 161–81 at 170; Stenton, *Anglo-Saxon England*, 293; Bernard S. Bachrach, *Warfare and Military Organisation in Pre-Crusade Europe*, Aldershot 2002, XIV, 2–5. There is no reason to presume that the chronicler was excluding the army of 1066 from his comparison, especially if the extravagant recruiting recounted by William of Malmesbury is to be believed, which described the hiring of men from every province this side of the Alps and even the French king's brother Hugh the Great. See Malmesbury, *Gesta Regum*, III. 283.

[28] S. Oakley, *The Story of Denmark*, London 1972, 45.

[29] Malmesbury, *Gesta Regum*, III, 262.3.

ploy that the Conqueror himself had employed at Dives-sur-Mer in 1066.[30] Cnut's attention was drawn elsewhere with the outbreak of a revolt in northern Jutland in spring 1086[31] and the threat of invasion was only removed with the king's death in the following July.[32] Even then, there must have been a delay in the news reaching England. William cannot have been satisfied that the threat had been removed much before late 1086.

William was indeed embattled when he had his deep speech with his counsellors at Gloucester on Christmas day 1085. The implications of this for an understanding of the Domesday inquest were succinctly summarized long ago by F. M. Stenton:

> there are signs in the text of the Survey of haste and urgency which cannot easily be reconciled with the carrying out of long-term financial or judicial purpose. In the background of the inquest, the king's officers had been faced with the operation of distributing a large force of fighting men among the king's barons in proportion to the productivity of their demesnes. In searching for the purpose of the Survey, it seems pointless to go beyond the fact that the recent threat of an invasion had impressed on the king and his council the inadequacy of their knowledge of the economic resources at their immediate command in an emergency.[33]

In such a time of continuing crisis, it seems highly unlikely that long-term legal and fiscal objectives were a high priority. The immediate concerns of the Domesday inquest must be related to the military crisis.

This was the starting point for Nicholas Higham's analysis of the process. He has argued that Domesday Book was compiled as an aid to the equitable distribution of mercenaries among the tenants-in-chief.[34] Up-to-date information must certainly have been at a premium in 1085. According to William of Malmesbury, it was Lanfranc who suggested that mercenaries be billeted in the courts of the magnates, and it is likely that it was they who had to pay their wages.[35] Clearly, any distribution of the burden to 'each in proportion to his lands' required data and in Higham's analysis Domesday was an update of this existing data.[36] As Roffe

---

[30] *Poitiers*, xxiv; Bachrach, *Warfare and Military Organisation*, XIV, 8–9; J. Gillingham, 'William the Bastard at War', in *Anglo-Norman Warfare: Studies in Late Anglo-Saxon and Anglo-Norman Military Organisation and Warfare*, ed. Strickland, 143–60 at 158–9.
[31] Oakley, *Denmark*, 45.
[32] John of Worcester, III, 45.
[33] Stenton, *Anglo-Saxon England*, 657. The point has often been forgotten. See Roffe, below, pp.289–303.
[34] Higham, 'Domesday Survey', 7–19.
[35] J. R. Maddicott, 'Responses to the Threat of Invasion, 1085', *EHR* 122, 2007, 986–97 at 987–9.
[36] In this way the Domesday process could be compared to the 1296 grain ordinance laid down by Edward I, in which a royal clerk and the sheriff consulted records of assessment

has observed, 'What is striking about the Domesday inquest is that it is precisely a record of all the resources of tenants-in-chief of which the billeting of 1085 could have availed itself.'[37]

However, as Roffe goes on to assert, neither the inquest records nor Domesday Book can have provided a 'quartermaster's manual' in the way in which Higham argues. Though the threat of invasion remained, by early 1086 billeting was largely over and done with, if the chronology of the 1085 annal is to be believed. The record of tenure that the inquest initially produced could have been used in the resolution of disputes and grievances over past billeting – the bishop of Worcester would have certainly aired the problems that he was experiencing[38] – but by necessity its application would have had to have been mainly retrospective. Domesday Book itself is even less suited to such a purpose. Data there were that were relevant to future billeting, but much is irrelevant. The details of TRE tenure, for example, serve no useful purpose in such a context. Conversely, there is much that might have been of use that was omitted. Higham himself had no explanation for the failure to record livestock in GDB given the pressing need to provision mercenaries.[39] If billeting were still an issue in 1086, and there is little in the texts to suggest it was, it would seem that it was contingent to the main business of the Domesday inquest.

Roffe has made a more compelling case for that business being the collection of evidence to inform a renegotiation of geld liability and, most importantly, military service.[40] That there was a review of the geld is clear from the Anglo-Saxon Chronicle's account of the inquest: it notes that the king wished to know 'how many hides there were in the shire ... and what dues he ought to have in twelve months'. There are references to an *inquisitio geldi* found in Exon along with summary geld accounts.[41] Service is more elusive in the sources, but Roffe has argued that the manor stands in as a proxy for it.[42] In documents known as 'summaries', which were compiled late on in the process of data collection, the number of manors held by each tenant-in-chief is indexed against assessment to the geld, total value, and ploughlands to provide a convenient guide to his resources.[43] Roffe has concluded that they probably informed negotiations on service that preceded the

---

to determine an indenture between the sheriff and the assessor as to what level of prise was appropriate to each landholder. See M. Prestwich, *War, Politics and Finance under Edward I*, London 1972, 128.

[37] Roffe, *Domesday: the Inquest and the Book*, 70.
[38] Emma Mason, *St Wulfstan of Worcester c.1008–1095*, Oxford 1990, 140.
[39] Higham, 'Domesday Survey', 9.
[40] Roffe, *Domesday: the Inquest and the Book*, 240–1.
[41] R. Welldon Finn, *Domesday Studies; the Liber Exoniensis*, London 1964, 97.
[42] Roffe, *Decoding Domesday*, 177–9, 311.
[43] Welldon Finn, *Domesday Studies: Liber Exoniensis*, 124–5.

taking of an oath of fealty 'by all those who held land in England' at Salisbury in August 1086.[44]

Contemporary evidence of all this is wanting: the sources of the time are eloquent on the when and the how of the inquest but are silent as to the why. However, something very like this reconstruction of events appears to have been the understanding of Orderic Vitalis. Writing in the early twelfth century in what is, it is often forgotten, the earliest recorded explanation of the purpose of the Domesday inquest, he links the process with the assessment of knight service.[45] In the context of the invasion crisis, it should not surprise that such matters were upper-most in William's mind. The hiring of so many mercenaries cannot have been anything but financially draining, both for the king and his tenants-in-chief, and billeting was disruptive. The imposition of a duty of 'defence of the realm' on the tenant-in-chief must have seemed an attractive alternative. What arrangements existed before are unknown, but, despite Sir James Holt's doubts,[46] military service was certainly owed and its level had probably been determined by personal agreement between the king and his magnates.[47] A more formal system would demand the distribution of the burden more equitably in accordance with the resources available. A late medieval tradition, as preserved in the Crowland Chronicle, maintained that exempt monastic demesnes were a particular concern.[48] If this was the deal, then the quid pro quo for the determination of *servitia debita* was the confirmation of land holders in their fees.

If the linked matters of taxation and service characterize the Domesday inquest, then neither is the overwhelming preoccupation of GDB. Assessment to the geld is found in every entry, although arguably it was not a matter of central importance; as Galbraith pointed out, the arrangement of GDB was not conducive to the collection of a tax that was based on the hundred.[49] Service certainly does not play a prominent part in the record. The account of the counties of Circuit VI, the first to be compiled after LDB, does exhibit a concern with its proxy, the manor. In Yorkshire the scribe went to great lengths to define the institution and to represent it satisfactorily. Initially, he simply stated what was a manor and attempted to enrol all of its dependent lands with it. In the course of time, however, he introduced

---

[44] The process is echoed in the *Carte Baronum* of 1166 where a statement of military service is linked to an oath of allegiance (W. L. Warren, *Henry II*, London 2000, 278).
[45] Orderic, IV, 53.
[46] Holt, 'Domesday Studies 2000', 24.
[47] Stenton, *Anglo-Saxon England*, 625–34; See also, N. Brooks, 'The Archbishopric of Canterbury and the So-called Introduction of Knight-Service into England', *ANS* 34, 2011, 41–62 at 60; J. Green, *The Aristocracy of Norman England*, Cambridge 1997, 226–9.
[48] *Ingulph's Chronicle of Croyland: with the Continuations by Peter of Blois and Anonymous Writers*, ed. H. T. Riley, London 1854, 159.
[49] Galbraith, *Making of Domesday Book*, 26.

marginal annotations to indicate status, M for manor, S for soke, and B for berewick.⁵⁰ By the time he got to the Lincolnshire folios, the second county to be compiled, he generally arranged his text entirely by estates and so he continued through the Nottinghamshire, Derbyshire, and Huntingdonshire folios. Upon reaching Circuit III he began to lose interest in such technicalities, progressively abandoning marginal annotations and making less effort to represent estates. Thereafter, notice of the manor is almost entirely incidental. The scribe developed his programme in the course of writing GDB and the manor was ultimately no part of it.

All of this is in contrast with the focus of LDB. The Norfolk and Suffolk folios exhibit a special concern with the geld. Attached to certain entries is a record of the proportion of the tax that the estate owed when the leet of which it was a part paid one pound. This formula has usually been interpreted as a system of tax assessment peculiar to East Anglia. However, it is paralleled by something very similar in twelfth-century Lincolnshire and it would seem that it is less a record of assessment than a record of payment. The diplomatic of the text indicates that the information was taken by a source similar to ICC from which LDB was ultimately compiled. Comparable data, notably the total assessment of the vill, at least for Cambridgeshire, were generally not copied into GDB.⁵¹ Above all, LDB is preoccupied with the manor. Each is not so well articulated as was to be its counterpart in Lincolnshire. However, demesne in LDB is consistently associated with manorial centres⁵² and other dependent lands are often enrolled with the same even if the practice violated the underlying geographical structure of the account of each fee. More than this, time after time land is said to be held for so many manors or to be 'of the number' of the lord's fee,⁵³ while what was added or taken away is carefully recorded.⁵⁴

It is from this concern, it would appear, that the scribe of GDB took his lead in attempting to articulate the manor in Yorkshire, soon to realize that it was no part of his purpose. While equally an abbreviation, LDB had a different programme. Livestock and all, it was much closer to the business of the inquest. The colophon at the end has often been taken to indicate when it was compiled:

> This survey (*descriptio*) was made in the year one thousand and eighty six from the incarnation of the lord and the twentieth of the reign of William, not only throughout these three counties but also throughout the others.

---

⁵⁰ Roffe, *Decoding Domesday*, 177–8.
⁵¹ David Roffe, 'Introduction', in *Little Domesday, Norfolk*, ed. A. Williams and G. H. Martin, London 2000, 9–43 at 22–4.
⁵² Welldon Finn, *Domesday Studies: Eastern Counties*, 49.
⁵³ See, for example, LDB, 265: ESS 20,4–5 where Count Eustace's manors of Orsett and Gravesend are said not to have belonged to his 100 manors.
⁵⁴ See, for example, Exon, 48v, where three manors are claimed as two.

The term *descriptio*, however, is the usual word for the inquest itself rather than the records that came out of it.[55] Nevertheless, it cannot be doubted that, in contrast to GDB, LDB was compiled when the concerns of taxation and service were still current. It was not the first attempt at Domesday Book but a separate enterprise.

Why, then, did East Anglia and Essex come to merit a separate Domesday Book? It may not be coincidental that the area appears to have been of especial concern to William in 1085. In his life of St Cnut of Denmark, Ailnoth of Canterbury asserts that 'castles were strengthened, town walls repaired and guarded and men deputed to keep the coasts, and so large was the mercenary army that its soldiers filled the houses in English towns, hardly leaving room for their inhabitants'.[56] Preparations for defences clearly extended beyond the distribution of mercenaries. At the outset, however, a decision was apparently made not to defend the whole of the eastern and southern seaboards. King Harold had attempted to do just that in 1066 and the outcome was his defeat. William did not make the same mistake. The Anglo-Saxon Chronicle records that in 1085 he 'had the land near the sea laid waste, so that if his enemies landed, they should have nothing to seize on so quickly'.[57] Domesday Book does not record any great concentrations of waste in either the coastal areas of Lincolnshire or eastern England. Nor are there any great drops in value TRW that might hint at extensive destruction.[58] It is only in Yorkshire, notably in the North Riding, that there is significant waste and it may be that the policy was confined to that area.[59] Indeed, the apparently well-informed Crowland chronicler states that the campaign of wasting in 1085 was in Northumbria.[60] The North had a long history of Danish sympathies, at least in so far as they suited the separatist aspirations of local elites, and Norman control was probably still precarious. A scorched-earth policy had put down rebels in 1069; it now served to deny an enemy of sustenance if they were to invade.

A proactive defence strategy was probably confined to England south of the Humber. Troops were billeted in the west, as at Worcester, from where they were probably intended to counter an attack from the Bristol Channel. Due to their proximity to the Continent, it was the south and the east that were the most vulnerable to seaborne attack. Kent and the English Channel coast were already well defended since Dover was a royal stronghold and the king held the estates of the imprisoned

---

[55] R. H. C. Davis, 'Domesday Book: Continental Parallels', in *Domesday Studies,* ed. Holt, 15–39 at 15.
[56] Maddicott, 'Responses to the Threat of Invasion', 986.
[57] ASC (E), 161.
[58] Pamela Taylor, 'Introduction', in *Little Domesday: Essex,* ed. A. Williams and G. H. Martin, London 2000, 9–32.
[59] H. C. Darby and I. S. Maxwell, *The Domesday Geography of Northern England,* Cambridge 1962, 139–50; J. J. N. Palmer, 'War and Domesday Waste' in *Armies, Chivalry and Warfare in Medieval Britain and France,* ed. Matthew Strickland, Stamford 1998, 256–75 at 262.
[60] *Ingulph's Chronicle of Croyland,* 159.

earl of Kent, Bishop Odo of Bayeux. William could also depend on the support of the castleries of Sussex. This line of defence was strengthened by his alliance with Eustace II of Boulogne.[61] With the parallel Norman coast under his control and the Cinque Ports fleet at his command, William must have been confident that he could counter an attack from the Channel.[62]

Faced with an attack from Flanders, East Anglia and Essex were much more problematic. There is no record of specifically military preparations in this region, but there were significant appointments to key churches that speak of equally important preparations in the area. In the synod that followed the Christmas council in 1085 Maurice was elected bishop of London and William bishop of Thetford. Both were royal clerks and their election then may have been coincidental. Thetford in particular had been vacant for two years. John Maddicott, however, has argued that the replacement of Wulfketel at Crowland and Folcard of St Bertin at Thorney by Ingulf and Gunter of Le Mans at the same time suggests a closer concern for the security of the area.[63] East Anglia was part of what was to become known as the Danelaw, Danes had settled there in the late ninth century and an Anglo-Scandinavian society had developed in the area. It experienced successive raids in the late tenth and early eleventh centuries and remained an attractive target for Danish incursions after the Conquest. An army had invaded in 1068 and 1069 and again in 1070, when it allied itself with the English rebels in the fenland. As late as 1075 Ralph of Gael, earl of East Anglia, had appealed to the Danes for support in his rebellion against William the Conqueror.[64]

It has been tempting to interpret all of this in purely ethnic terms. Indeed, it has often been asserted that East Anglia was susceptible to Danish raids precisely because of the Anglo-Scandinavian sensibilities of the local population and was thus a potential Trojan horse in 1085.[65] The reality was more complex. There can be no doubt that Danish allies had from time to time been welcomed in East Anglia, but, as in the North,[66] the motivation was almost certainly less ethnic solidarity than pursuit of local interests. So it was after the Conquest.[67] The revolt of 1070–1 was

---

[61] H. Tanner, 'The Expansion of the Power and Influence of the Counts of Boulogne', *ANS* 14, 1991, 251–86 at 276–7
[62] C. W. Hollister, *Anglo-Saxon Military Institutions on the Eve of the Norman Conquest*, Oxford 1965, 103–4.
[63] Maddicott, 'Responses to the Threat of Invasion', 991–5.
[64] Orderic, II, 227, 317.
[65] Green, *Aristocracy of Norman England*, 229.
[66] For a recent discussion of the historiography, see W. M. Aird, 'Northumbria and the Making of the Kingdom of the English', in *Nations in Medieval Britain*, ed. H. Tsurushima, Donington 2010, 45–60, and D. R. Roffe, 'The Danes and the Making of the Kingdom of the English', ibid., 32–44.
[67] B. Golding, *Conquest and Colonisation: The Normans in Britain, 1066–1100*, Basingstoke 2013, 43.

clearly an English affair, the rebellion of a dispossessed English aristocracy against Norman rule and the Danes were certainly useful allies in their struggle. Even then, though, the enemy's enemy was not necessarily an unalloyed friend: the sacking of Peterborough abbey by the mercenary force seems to have appalled locals as much as foreigners.[68] Danes were welcome only so long as they served the ends of local interests.

The fall of Ely put an end to the revolt and the settlement of Cambridgeshire and the East Midlands swiftly followed.[69] By contrast, the pre-Conquest aristocracy of East Anglia remained largely in place. In 1066 Archbishop Stigand of Canterbury was the pre-eminent power within the region with extensive estates in Norfolk and Suffolk.[70] He was deposed in 1070, but almost equally powerful were pre-Conquest Breton and Norman settlers who remained. How Ralph the staller came to prominence is unclear. His father was Breton and his mother English and he had been born in Norfolk. Equally obscure are the antecedents of William Malet and Robert fitzWymarc.[71] However, it cannot be doubted that they and their men had become fully integrated into local society. LDB records the large number of Englishmen who had been commended to them in 1066.[72]

As a group they had submitted to William soon after the Conquest and in consequence had retained their lands. The Norman settlement of East Anglia followed only after the revolt of Ralph the staller's son, Ralph of Gael, in alliance with Roger of Hereford, against William in 1075. Archbishop Lanfranc characterized Ralph of Gael as 'Breton dung',[73] but the ethnic labelling was only for political effect.[74] Prior to his revolt, Ralph, like his father, was known as Ralph *Anglicus*, Ralph 'the Englishman',[75] to his continental peers and, moreover, it is clear that he was supported by at least one prominent member of the English aristocracy. Earl Waltheof's role in the rebellion was ambiguous at the time and remains unclear now. It is possible that it was nothing more than gamesmanship, an attempt to win a reward for capitulation as he had in 1070–2.[76] If so, he miscalculated: he

---

[68] ASC, (E), 151–3.
[69] See Keats-Rohan, below pp.174–81.
[70] M. F. Smith, 'Archbishop Stigand and the Eye of the Needle', ANS 16, 1993, 199–219 at 199.
[71] ASC, (D and E), 156–8; K. S. B. Keats-Rohan, 'Domesday Book and the Malets', *Nottingham Medieval Studies* 41, 1997, 13–53 at 22–31.
[72] See, Keats-Rohan, below pp.181–90.
[73] *The Letters of Lanfranc Archbishop of Canterbury*, ed. H. Clover and M. Gibson, Oxford 1979, 124–7.
[74] Lucy Marten, 'Lordship and Land: Suffolk in the Tenth and Eleventh Centuries', unpublished PhD thesis University of East Anglia 2005, 230–2, suggests that Lanfranc's designation of Ralph as Breton was probably designed to counteract his perceived Englishness.
[75] Hubert Guillotel, *Actes des ducs de Bretagne (944–1148)*, Rennes 2014, no. 99.
[76] Golding, *Conquest and Colonisation*, 44–5.

had clearly given support to the rebels. Lucy Marten has shown that other English landholders, probably Ralph's men, also followed him into revolt.[77] The motivation behind the uprising is unexplained in the contemporary sources. Ralph's journey to Denmark in search of support might suggest that a restoration of a Danish dynasty was contemplated.[78] Writing in the 1090s, the anonymous author of a Life of Cnut IV claims that Cnut's aim in invading England in 1075 was 'to alleviate by military force the heavy yoke of unworthy slavery experienced by the English'.[79] Orderic also hints that the legitimacy of William's rule was at issue.[80] One way or another, the matter resonated with wider political interests. Nevertheless, the revolt of Ralph in East Anglia should be seen as, in effect, the last of the English rebellions against Norman rule. In its aftermath, William distributed the lands of the rebels, especially those of the earl, to men of his choosing for the first time.[81]

Within this context, the preoccupation with ecclesiastical appointments in East Anglia in 1085 becomes more comprehensible. The bishop of London held extensive estates in Essex which guarded the eastern approaches to London.[82] Equally, the bishop of Thetford commanded a considerable endowment in East Anglia. The appointment of royal clerks to the sees ensured that these lands were administered in the king's interest. By comparison, the endowments of Crowland and Thorney were of much more limited consequence; neither was of the first order of English monasteries. They do, however, seem to have been important centres of local loyalties. The *Liber Vitae* of Thorney abbey shows that this monastery articulated a complex web of relationships in and around the fenland in Cambridgeshire, Huntingdonshire, Lincolnshire, and Norfolk.[83] Crowland probably occupied an even more important

[77] Marten, 'Lordship and Land', 246–9.
[78] Orderic, II, 317.
[79] *Vitae Sanctorum Danorum*, ed. M. Cl. Gertz, Copenhagen 1908, 67; E. van Houts, 'The Norman Conquest through European Eyes', *EHR* 110, 1995, 837 n.3.
[80] Orderic, IV, 120–1.
[81] Welldon Finn, *Domesday Studies: Eastern Counties*, 23–4; Stenton, *Anglo-Saxon England*, 612.
[82] A writ conferred on the new bishop of London the strategically important castle of Stortford, lying as it does on the western border of Essex where Stane Street crosses the river Stort. The absence of a similar writ for Maurice's predecessor Hugh d'Orivalle suggests that William had been, during the intervening decade, keeping the castle out of the London see (P. Taylor, 'The Endowment and Military Obligations of the See of London: a Reassessment of Three Sources', *ANS* 14, 1991, 287–312 at 309). By bestowing the castle upon the new bishop of London, William seems to have demonstrated his concern to defend the approach to London from Essex in 1085. Douglas believed the two writs referring to the grant of Bishop's Stortford to Maurice were 'doubtless' issued during the meeting at Salisbury in 1086. If so, then strategic considerations for Essex were still prominent at the Salisbury meeting (D. C. Douglas, *William the Conqueror: The Norman Impact upon England*, Norwich 1964, 356–7. See also, *Early Charters of the Cathedral Church of St. Paul, London*, ed. M. Gibbs, London 1939, 11–12, 14–15).
[83] K. S. B. Keats-Rohan, 'Domesday People Revisited', *Foundations* 4, 2012, 3–20 at 17–19;

place in the local consciousness. Before the Conquest its saints, notably Guthlac and Etheldritha, expressed a strong local identity and this was to become even more explicit in 1076 when Abbot Wulfketel accepted the body of Earl Waltheof for burial at Crowland. Perceived as a martyr, Waltheof became a potent symbol of Englishness in the face of the reality of a Norman conquest as a cult rapidly developed at his shrine.[84]

Wulfketel's deposition in 1085 was therefore a sensible precaution. Ingulf, his successor, was apparently tasked with countering the localism that he had promoted. Although an Englishman himself, he had spent many years as a monk and then prior at the Norman monastery of Saint-Wandrille. Hence he could be relied upon to represent the king.[85] The methods that he employed were typical of Norman placemen in the English ecclesiastical hierarchy. The Crowland Chronicle, from which almost all of his actions have to be gleaned, emphasizes the central place that St Wulfram, one of the founding saints of Saint-Wandrille, played in his decision to take up the abbacy of Crowland. He took relics of the saint with him to England and, apparently, promoted a cult in opposition to local saints.[86] How successful he was is largely unrecorded. It is clear, though, that the attempt was made: Wulfram was introduced into the liturgy at Crowland and his cult supplanted Guthlac and Etheldritha at Grantham in Lincolnshire, a pre-Conquest cell of the abbey.[87]

These measures reveal just how precarious the Norman hold on East Anglian sensibilities was in 1085. There are hints that similar measures were taken elsewhere in the region. After the Conquest St Edmund, king and martyr, was promoted as a specifically regional saint at Bury St Edmunds; subsequently he was identified

---

eadem, *The Thorney* Liber Vitae; *London, British Library, Additional MS 40,000, fols1-12r*, ed. Lynda Rollason, Woodbridge 2015, 211–68.

[84] Emma Mason, 'Invoking Earl Waltheof', in *The English and their Legacy, 900–1200: Essays in Honour of Ann Williams*, ed. David Roffe, Woodbridge 2011, 185–204; Joanna Huntington, 'The Taming of the Laity: Writing Waltheof and Rebellion in the Twelfth Century', *ANS* 32, 2009, 79–95; Paul A. Hayward, 'Translation-Narratives in post-Conquest Hagiography and English Resistance to the Norman Conquest', *ANS* 21, 67–93 at 92–3; John Hudson, 'The Fate of Earl Waltheof and the Idea of Personal Law after 1066', in *Normandy and Its Neighbours, 900–1250*, ed. D. Crouch and K. Thompson, Turnhout 2011, 223–35.

[85] Henry Loyn, 'Abbots of English Monasteries in the Period Following the Norman Conquest', in *England and Normandy in the Middle Ages*, ed. David Bates and Anne Curry, London 1994, 95–103 at 100–1.

[86] *Ingulph's Chronicle of Croyland*, 150–3. The cult of Waltheof was revived only after the fire of 1091 and the rebuilding of the church (Mason, 'Invoking Earl Waltheof', 187-8). It was Wulfram, however, who had predicted the conflagration.

[87] David Roffe, 'The Early History of Grantham', in *The Making of Grantham: The Medieval Town*, ed. David Start and David Stocker, Heritage Lincolnshire, Heckington 2011, 21–38. Roffe argues for the introduction of the cult of St Wulfram before 1086 since the dedication is noted in the Lincolnshire folios of Domesday Book. However, he now thinks that this may merely reflect a later date for the compilation of GDB (pers. comm.).

with England and then by the 1090s suppressed.[88] A Norman settlement had been effected in the region, albeit belatedly, but hearts and minds remained to be won. East Anglia was open to the allure of Danish intervention less because of ethnic affinities than because local communities had yet to embrace a Norman identity. East Anglia, ten years on from the rebellion of its own earl, was still unfinished business and the prospect of invasion must have underlined the threat it posed to the stability of the Norman regime. This scenario provides a possible context for the writing of LDB.

Paradoxically, the records of an inquest are often a poor guide to its purpose. The process was one of collecting more or less agreed fact as a precursor to negotiation and then action. As we have seen, there are good reasons for believing that taxation and service were the core business of the Domesday inquest and yet the matters are, at best, peripheral to the tenor of the surviving inquest sources. Were LDB a circuit return, it would be difficult, if not impossible, to determine its purpose without context. Fortunately, it would appear that it was not. As an abbreviation, its purpose is more transparent since the act of abbreviation suggests how it was intended to be interrogated. Digests of inquest records were regularly made in the Middle Ages to preserve data that were considered of more than temporary interest to routine administration.[89] They therefore point at their intended use. With its clear statement of the dues of the borough and county at the head of each section and the arrangement of the rest of the text by landholder, GDB is perhaps best interpreted in these terms as a handy reference guide to the issues that the king could expect from the shire.[90] The aftermath of the rebellion of 1088 remains a possible context, although an equally plausible context could be the levying of 10,000 marks by Rufus in 1096, apparently along feudal lines, in order to secure Normandy from Robert Curthose.[91] LDB too is arranged by landholder but lacks this interest in the issues of local government. Its focus on the manor suggests that service was the prime concern. We are left with the possibility that LDB was compiled shortly after the inquest as a register to inform a re-assessment of service with the ultimate aim of stabilizing East Anglia.

---

[88] Tom Licence, 'The Cult of St Edmund', in *Bury St Edmunds and the Norman Conquest*, ed. Tom Licence, Woodbridge 2014, 104–30.
[89] Davis, 'Continental Parallels', 24–5.
[90] Welldon Finn, *Introduction to Domesday Book*, 266–78.
[91] J. O. Prestwich, *The Place of War in English History 1066–1214*, Woodbridge 2004, 51–2, first highlighted the reference by a Worcester chronicler to a geld in 1096 that was levied on the tenant-in-chief instead of the vills and hundreds. The language of the Worcester chronicler is indeed exceptional and suggests an unusual outrage, one that could represent the net doubling of the rateable assessment which Sally Harvey discovered the 'ploughlands' unit in GDB would achieve (S. Harvey, 'Domesday Book and Anglo-Norman Governance', *TRHS*, 5th series 25, 1975, 175–93 at 188).

Though less likely, a later date is not impossible. The rebellion of Roger Bigod, sheriff of Norfolk and Suffolk, in 1088, along with 'the most powerful Frenchmen who were in the country', was probably as disruptive as of that of Ralph of Gael in 1075. The course of events in East Anglia is largely unknown, there is no sequel to the Domesday inquest to illustrate its consequences, but contemporary sources report that the rebels invaded the lands of the king and those few Normans who had remained loyal to him.[92] It is likely that the aftermath saw much tenurial upheaval in East Anglia. Something like LDB would have been invaluable in establishing pre-existing rights, especially those of the king, in whatever settlement that followed. It is very unlikely, however, that service would have been a priority if that were the primary aim of compiling LDB.

The argument, then, comes full circle. The most likely date for the compilation of LDB was indeed 1086–7, but this analysis suggests that it was neither a circuit return nor the first attempt at the compilation of Domesday Book. Rather it was a separate enterprise prompted by the special circumstances that obtained in East Anglia and Essex in the reign of William the Conqueror. This is a formulation that begins to explain why the GDB scribe took it as his model. His programme, he slowly came to realize, was different from that of the mastermind behind LDB, but he understood that it was the same type of document: it was a register and that was precisely what he wanted to compile for the rest of England. Divorced, no doubt, from the immediate business of the Domesday inquest, for him it was already a 'Domesday Book'. If its rubrication followed that of GDB, then this was no more than a recognition of the similarity.[93] What was good enough for him, should be good enough for us. LDB deserves to be treated as the end in itself that it was. Perhaps then it will receive the critical attention that, as a mere 'satellite', it has hitherto been denied.

---

[92] ASC, (E), 166–8.
[93] A. R. Rumble, 'The Domesday Manuscripts: Scribes and *Scriptoria*', in *Domesday Studies*, ed. Holt, 79–100 at 99–100.

6

Hunting the Snark and Finding the Boojum: the Tenurial Revolution Revisited

Ann Williams

DOMESDAY BOOK IS not only a record of those who held land in England in King William's day but also of those who occupied the same estates before the Conquest. Various strategies have been developed to identify these pre-Conquest holders, who constitute (collectively) the Snark of this paper's title.[1] One aspect which has not, perhaps, received the attention it deserves, is status – the Boojum. Indications of status are not rare in Domesday Book, but they are rarely unambiguous. The distinction between personal and tenurial dependency is not always clear, and even when tenurial dependency is plain, it is not always obvious what kind of dependency is intended. Yet status is not only important in helping to attach names to individuals, it also tells us something about the wider society to which those individuals belong. This in turn not only illuminates the structure of English landed society in the reign of Edward the Confessor, but also the process of social and tenurial change after the Norman conquest and settlement.

I shall discuss the problem of status, personal and tenurial, with reference to a particular vill, namely Abington Pigotts, in the hundred of Armingford, in southwest Cambridgeshire. It is not a random selection, for Abington Pigotts has been used as an example of 'the disintegration of pre-Conquest patterns' of tenure and lordship in which 'every component of this Cambridgeshire vill was either broken down after the Conquest or used to form a new composite lordship'.[2] This paper will propose a rather different conclusion.

---

[1] Christopher Lewis, 'Joining the Dots: a Methodology for identifying the English in Domesday Book', in *Family Trees and the Roots of Politics*, ed. K. S. B. Keats-Rohan, Woodbridge 1997, 68–87.
[2] Robin Fleming, *Kings and Lords in Conquest England*, Cambridge 1991, 120–2 and figure

Figure 1: Armingford hundred, Cambridgeshire.

The format of Domesday Book does little to encourage the study of English vills. Within each shire, the account of non-royal and non-burghal land is arranged by the fiefs of those who held directly of the king, and within each fief, by the individual tenements of those lords and their subordinates, albeit organized either explicitly or implicitly by the hundred within which the tenement lay. Given an index,

4.2, 117. There are some disparities between Professor Fleming's table and mine (Table 1), which I have been unable to reconcile.

it is a simple, if laborious, task to reconstruct the vills, but for Cambridgeshire, the work has already been done, in the *Inquisitio Comitatus Cantabrigiensis*, the Cambridgeshire Inquest, known to Domesday scholars as the ICC. Though preserved only in a twelfth-century copy, it is earlier than Domesday Book, and bears witness to the survey of 1086 on which Domesday Book is based. Unlike Domesday Book, the information in the ICC is organized not fief by fief but hundred by hundred, and within each hundred, vill by vill; only the borough and the lands of the king are omitted.[3]

The ICC records that Abington Pigotts was assessed at 5 hides in King Edward's day, reduced to 4 at the time of the 1086 survey (see Table 1).[4] Before the Conquest, in the time of King Edward (TRE), this hidage was divided between six tenements. Only one of these, a holding of 2½ hides and half a virgate, is described as a manor, 'which belongs and belonged to the church of St Peter, Winchester' (*iacet et iacuit in ecclesia sancti petri Wintonie*). Of this manor, half a virgate had been held by a sokeman under (*sub*) Stigand, archbishop of Canterbury, who before the Conquest held the bishopric of Winchester in plurality; this sokeman could 'withdraw and sell to whom he wished without his leave' (*potuit recedere et vendere cui voluit absque eius licentia*).

A second tenement consisting of half a hide and held by the king lay in Litlington, and was valued there (*iacet in litlintona ... est appreciata cum litlintona*). The third tenement consisted of a hide and 1½ virgates, of which a hide and half a virgate had been held by two sokemen, the men of Earl Ælfgar, who could 'give and sell to whom they would', while the remaining virgate had been held by a third sokeman who was a man of the king. The fourth tenement (*terra*), assessed at a virgate which lay in Shingay, had been in the hands of Goda, man (*homo*) of Earl Ælfgar. A tenement of half a virgate which 'lies and always lay in Morden' had been held by Osgot of (*de*) Archbishop Stigand, and the last tenement, also of half a virgate, by Alwine *hamelecoc*, the king's beadle, who 'could not give nor sell it outside Litlington' (*non potuit dare nec vendere extra Litlintonam*).

By 1086, the manor in Abington Pigotts, including the half-virgate held by Stigand's sokeman, was held by Stigand's successor as bishop of Winchester, Walkelin. The rest of the vill was divided between the king, Hardwin de Scales, Earl Roger of Montgomery and Picot, sheriff of Cambridgeshire. It has been argued that the division of Earl Ælfgar's men between Hardwin de Scales and Earl Roger, and of Archbishop Stigand's men between the bishop of Winchester and Picot the sheriff shows how 'the lands ... were reorganized along completely new lines'.[5] Let us test this conclusion by examining the personal and tenurial relationships in Abington Pigotts before and after the Conquest.

---

[3] At the moment the only edition of ICC is that of N. E. S. A. Hamilton, London 1876.
[4] ICC, 60.
[5] Fleming, *Kings and Lords*, 121.

Table 1: Abington Pigotts, 5 hides TRE (ICC, 60)

Hidage	1066	How held	Lord	Soke	1086	tenant
2h 2½v [½v]	Winchester sokeman	Manor could withdraw and sell without leave	*sub* Abp Stigand		bishop of Winchester	Hugh *pincerna*
½h in Litlington				valued with Litlington	King	
1h 1½v [1v]	2 sokemen 1 sokeman	could give and sell	*de* Earl Ælfgar king	[?Litlington]	Hardwin [de Scales]	Ralph and Robert
1v in Shingay	Goda		*homo* of Earl Ælfgar	in Shingay	Earl Roger [of Montgomery]	
½v	Osgot		*de* Abp Stigand	lies and lay in Morden	Picot *vicecomes*	
½v	Alwine *humelcoc, de rege*	could not give nor sell	king's beadle	Litlington	King	*Istemet* Alwine

A glance at the table (Table 1) which summarizes the ICC's account of the vill will make it clear that the descent of the land in Abington Pigotts cannot be understood without reference to the neighbouring vills of Litlington, Shingay, and Morden.[6] First, however, it is necessary to clarify some of the terminology. To take a single example, when Goda is described as the man (*homo*) of Earl Ælfgar, the meaning is that Goda was commended to the earl. Personal commendation, however, does not in itself imply tenurial dependency, and says nothing *per se* about the status of any land which the *commendatus* might hold. It is probably significant, however, that whereas ICC calls Goda *homo comitis algari*, the equivalent entry in Domesday Book says that Goda held under (*sub*) the earl, which perhaps implies that Goda's land was *lænland*, that is to say leased (or more precisely lent) to him by Earl Ælfgar for a fixed term; the land is the earl's, but Goda has been granted the temporary use of it.[7] Tenurial as opposed to personal dependency is also implied in statements to the effect that a holder 'could give or sell' his land, or 'withdraw' from it, but in this case the land (*terra*) is free, that is, it belongs to the individual holder and his family, whereas the dues from it (Domesday Book calls them *consuetudines*) belong to the lord of another manor whose centre might lie elsewhere; this is the essence of sokeland. Thus to understand why the land of Archbishop Stigand's sokeman went to the bishop of Winchester while that of Stigand's man Osgot went elsewhere, and why Earl Roger received the land of Goda, while that of two sokemen also commended to Earl Ælfgar went to Hardwin de Scales, we must follow the tenurial links indicated, explicitly or implicitly, in the texts of ICC and Domesday Book. The differing destinations of lands held by men commended to Archbishop Stigand depend on those of their parent manors. The half-virgate held by the archbishop's sokeman passed, with the manor of Abington Pigotts to which it was appurtenant, to Stigand's successor as bishop of Winchester. The half-virgate held by Osgot of (*de*) the archbishop was not part of this manor, but 'lies and always lay in Morden', identified in the two most recent translations of Domesday Book as Guilden Morden.[8]

Osgot did indeed hold land in Guilden Morden (see Table 2); it was assessed at 1½ hides, from which he could withdraw, though (as at Abington Pigotts), 'the soke remained in Morden'.[9] Since, however, no tenement of manorial status is described in the account of Guilden Morden, it is more likely that both Osgot's tenements were appurtenant to the manor in the neighbouring vill of Steeple Morden

---

[6] The five vills, Abington Pigotts, Litlington, Shingay, and Temple and Guilden Morden lie adjacent in the south-eastern corner of Armingford hundred.
[7] GDB, 193: CAM 13,3; David Roffe, *Decoding Domesday*, Woodbridge 2007, 162 and n. 98.
[8] GDB, 200v: CAM 32,13.
[9] ICC, 52; the equivalent entry in Domesday Book (GDB, 200v: CAM 32,8) lumps Osgot's tenement with those of two other *homines* of the archbishop, Godwine and William.

Table 2: Guilden Morden, 5 hides (ICC, 53–4)

Tenement	1066	How held	Lord	Soke	1086	Tenant
3½h	8 sokemen:				Picot the sheriff	
[1½h]	Osgot	could give and sell				
[3v]	Gotman and Alwine	could withdraw	*homo* of Abp Stigand	soke in Morden		
[½v]	Almar	could withdraw	*homines* of Earl Ælfgar	the earl		
[1v]	Godwine and William		*homo* Eadgifu *pulchra*			
[3v]	Ælnod and Alward		*homines* of Abp Stigand sokemen of King Edward			
2½v	Goda		*homo* of Earl Ælfgar	Shingay	Earl Roger	
[4 acres]					Hardwin de Scales	Alvred *occupavit super* Earl Roger
3v	Godwine wambestrang	could give and sell	Esger the staller		Geoffrey de Mandeville	Richard
½v	Winterled	could not give/sell	Earl Ælfgar	Litlington	Hardwin de Scales	Alvred

(Table 3).¹⁰ This vill, assessed at 10 hides, contained three holdings, the largest of which was a manor of 8 hides, held in 1086 by the bishop of Winchester, which 'lies and always lay in the church of St Peter, Winchester'; a second tenement of 3¾ virgates was held by six sokemen who could withdraw, but whose soke remained in Steeple Morden. By 1086 the manor of Steeple Morden had passed to the bishop of Winchester, but the six who held in Steeple Morden itself now held of Hardwin de Scales, while both Osgot's tenements, in Abington Pigotts and in Guilden Morden, were in the hands of Picot the sheriff of Cambridgeshire. Why this should be so is unclear; it could be that Hardwin and Picot had been given the bishop's dependent land or had illegally seized it, but they could just as well be holding in succession to the pre-Conquest tenants; the fact that Osgot's only recorded lands in the shire were the dependencies in Abington Pigotts and Guilden Morden, and that both passed to Picot, might suggest the latter. Whether the bishop was able to claim his *consuetudines* from the sheriff of Cambridgeshire is another matter, but there are numerous instances in Domesday Book where land (*terra*) was held by one tenant-in-chief and soke by another.

The third tenement in Steeple Morden was held by Earl Ælfgar's man Goda, and had passed to Earl Roger of Montgomery. The earl also held Goda's land in Abington Pigotts, as an appurtenance of Shingay; another dependency of Shingay, also held by the earl in succession to Goda lay in Guilden Morden.¹¹ The ICC describes Shingay as a vill of 5 hides (Table 4), consisting of a single holding (*terram*), held in 1086 by Earl Roger in succession to Goda, man (*homo*) of Earl Ælfgar.¹² It was in this way that Goda's tenement in Abington Pigotts passed to Earl Roger 'as part of his own manor' (*in proprio suo manerio*) of Shingay.¹³ In fact Earl Roger seems to have received nearly all Goda's Cambridgeshire holdings, not only at Steeple Morden, Shingay, Guilden Morden and Abington Pigotts, but also at Meldreth and Melbourn (all in Armingford hundred).¹⁴ The only glitch was that

¹⁰ ICC, 50–1. In ICC the description of Steeple Morden (in which Picot held no land) opens the account of Armingford hundred, whereas that of Guilden Morden follows later, after Tadlow, and itself followed by Clopton, Hatley, and Croydon, with Abington Piggots later in the sequence; the same order is followed in the account of Picot's fief in Domesday Book (ICC, 51–7; GDB, 200–200v: CAM 32,7–13).
¹¹ ICC, 53–4.
¹² ICC, 59.
¹³ ICC, 61.
¹⁴ GDB, 193–193v: CAM 13, 12;4–7. The only other Cambridgeshire land entered in Goda's name is five hides at Papworth in Papworth hundred (GDB, 195: CAM 14,53), held *sub Edeva* (Eadgifu the fair). The names Goda (masc.) and Gode (fem.) are often confused by the Domesday scribe and in the Phillimore edition Earl Ælfgar's *homo* is treated as female and Eadgifu's man as male. All the Cambs references may, however, relate to the same (female) Gode, who has been further identified with Golde (*sic*), who with her son Wulfric held the manor of Woolley (Hunts) both before the Conquest and in 1086 (GDB, 206, 207v: HUN 19,21.29,5) and Gode who with her son held Welwyn (Herts) from (*de*)

Table 3: Steeple Morden, 10 hides (ICC, 51–2)

Tenement	1066	How held	Lord	Soke	1086	Tenant
Steeple Morden (ICC, 51-2)						
8 hides	Winchester	Manor			bishop	
1h ¼v	Goda	Could sell	de Earl Ælfgar		Earl Roger	
3¾v	6 sokemen	Could withdraw		soke in Morden	Hardwin de Scales	Same sokemen
Lands in Morden: Guilden Morden (ICC, 53)						
1½h	Osgot	Could withdraw	Abp Stigand	soke in Morden	Picot the sheriff	
Lands in Morden: Abington Pigotts (ICC, 60)						
½v	Osgot		Abp Stigand	soke in Morden	Picot the sheriff	

Table 4: Shingay, 5 hides (ICC, 54, 59, 60)

Tenement	1066	How held	Lord	Soke	1086	tenant
Shingay, 5 hides (ICC, 59)						
5h	Goda		Earl Ælfgar		Earl Roger	
Lands in Shingay: Guilden Morden (ICC, 54)						
2½v					Earl Roger	
[4 acres]	Goda		Earl Ælfgar	Shingay	Hardwin de Scales	
Lands in Shingay: Abington Pigotts (ICC, 60)						
1v	Goda		Earl Ælfgar	Shingay	Earl Roger	Alvred *super* Earl Roger

4 acres of the tenement at Guilden Morden had been squatted upon (*occupavit*) by Alvred, the man of Hardwin de Scales, in Earl Roger's despite (*super comitem Rogerium*).[15]

It was the same Hardwin who held the land of three sokemen, two commended to Earl Ælfgar and the third to the king, in Abington Pigotts. To understand how this might have come about, we need to look at the manor of Litlington, of which two holdings in Abington Pigotts were part (see Table 1). Litlington was a royal manor and the omission of the *terra regis* from the ICC perhaps explains why no details are provided for the first of these tenements, half a hide held by the king which belonged to and was valued in Litlington. More detail is given for the second tenement, half a virgate which Alwine *hamelecoc* the king's beadle held *de rege* and which he could neither give nor sell out of Litlington (*non potui dare nec vendere extra Litlintonam*). Another dependency of Litlington lay in Guilden Morden (see Table 2), namely half a virgate held by Winterled of (*de*) Earl Ælfgar; like Alwine, he could neither give nor sell his land, which belonged to Litlington.[16]

Litlington itself (see Table 5) was a vill assessed at 5 hides, which contained two tenements. The larger, assessed at 4 hides and 2½ virgates, was a manor belonging to Earl Ælfgar, and it was presumably to this that the tenements in Abington Pigotts and Guilden Morden were attached.[17] By 1086, it was held at farm of the king by two royal officials, William the chamberlain and Otto the goldsmith, and appears in Domesday Book as part of the *terra regis*.[18] The king also held the dependent half-hide of land at Abington Pigotts, and Alwine *hamelecoc* continued to hold his half-virgate *de rege*, just as he had in King Edward's day. The tenement at Guilden Morden, held by Earl Ælfgar's man Winterled, had, however, passed to Alvred, man of Hardwin de Scales, presumably the same Alvred who had illegally occupied 4 acres of the tenement in the same vill held by the earl's man Goda (see Table 2).

It was another of Hardwin's men, Adelulf, who held the second tenement in Litlington, consisting of 2½ virgates, 2 virgates of which had been held by Algar, the man (*homo*) of Archbishop Stigand, who could withdraw, and half a virgate by Alwi, man of Earl Ælfgar, who could neither give nor sell it out of Litlington. It might be assumed that these were two separate holdings, amalgamated after the Conquest into a new 'composite lordship', but the simple fact of their separate enumeration

---

Queen Edith in King Edward's day (GDB, 140: HRT 34,4); this Gode had other estates in Herts, one of which (GDB, 137v: HRT 18,1) had passed to Earl Roger of Montgomery. See John Palmer, 'Great Domesday on CD-ROM', in *Domesday Book*, ed. Elizabeth Hallam and David Bates, Stroud 2001, 141–50 at 147–9, 215 n.65, n.68.

[15] ICC, 54.
[16] ICC, 55.
[17] ICC, 59–60.
[18] GDB, 190: CAM 1,18. The king's half-hide in Abington Piggots and Alwine *hamelecoc*'s half-virgate also appear as *terra regis*.

Table 5: Litlington, 5 hides (ICC, 53, 59, 60)

Tenement	1066	How held	Lord	Soke	1086	Tenant
Litlington (ICC, 59)						
4h 2½v	Earl Ælfgar	Manor			King	William chamberlain, Otto goldsmith, *ad firmam*
	Algar (2v)	could withdraw	*homo* Ap Stigand			
2½ v	Alwi (½v)	could not give/sell	*homo* E. Ælfgar	soke in Litlington	Hardwin de Scales	Adelulf *ad firmam*
Land belonging to Litlington: Abington Pigotts (ICC, 60)						
2v				Valued with Litlington	King	
½v	Alwine *hamelcoc*	could not give/sell	king's beadle	Litlington	King	same Alwine
Land perhaps belonging to Litlington: Abington Pigotts (ICC, 60)						
1h 1½v	sokemen (1h ½v) sokeman (1v)	could give and sell	*de* Earl Ælfgar king		Hardwin de Scales	Ralph and Robert
Land belonging to Litlington: Guilden Morden (ICC, 53)						
½v	Winterled	Could not withdraw	*homo* of Earl Ælfgar	Litlington	Hardwin de Scales	Alvred

does not mean that they did not form a single unit in King Edward's day.[19] It was not uncommon for the holders of an estate to hold discrete portions of it, nor was it unusual for joint holders (even when members of the same family) to be commended to different lords.[20] Whatever the case, the structure of Litlington and its dependencies in 1086 suggests that King William had created a separate holding for Hardwin out of the royal manor, giving him both a portion of the chief vill and the dependency of Guilden Morden; it had long been the custom for composite estates to be divided element by element, with lands in the dependencies being distributed between the original centre and the new holding.[21] Indeed the relationship between Litlington and Shingay, both of which had dependencies in Guilden Morden and Abington Pigotts (see Tables 4 and 5), might suggest that Shingay too had once been part of Litlington, and had been hived off by Earl Ælfgar for his man Goda. It was perhaps in this way that Hardwin received the tenement in Abington Pigotts held by his men Ralph and Robert, previously in the hands of three sokemen, two commended to Earl Ælfgar and one to the king. The holding was clearly a dependency, for the earl's men could give and sell their land, and though the parent manor is not named, it seems at least possible that this tenement too was a dependency of Litlington.

It seems that, far from being dismembered and re-constituted, the lands in Abington Pigotts passed to their new owners in an orderly fashion which respected pre-Conquest tenures. The bishop of Winchester had retained his church's manor in Abington Pigotts, including the half-virgate held by Archbishop Stigand's sokeman, while Earl Roger received his land in the vill by antecessorial descent from Goda, Earl Ælfgar's man, as part of the latter's manor of Shingay. The tenement held by Alwine *hamelecoc* had likewise passed to the king, along with its parent manor of Litlington, as had the half hide of royal land which also lay in that manor. If Hardwin de Scales's tenement in Abington Pigotts was also a dependency of Litlington, then his tenure might be the result of a division of Litlington and its lands in accordance with pre-Conquest custom. The only sour note is Picot the sheriff's tenure of Osgot's land. It is true that Picot had an evil reputation at Ely as

---

[19] The language of the entry (ICC, 59–60) is consistent with the proposal that this was always a single holding: *de his v hidis tenet adelulfus de hardeuuino de scales dimidiam hidam et dimidiam uirgam ad firmam ... Hanc dimidiam hidam tenuit algar homo archiepiscopi stigandi potuit recedere tre. Et Aluui tenuit dimidiam uirgam homo algari comitis. Non potuit dare nec uendere extra manerium Litlingetona.*

[20] Ann Williams, 'Little Domesday and the English', in *Domesday Book*, ed. Hallam and Bates, 103–20.

[21] David Roffe, 'The *Descriptio Terrarum* of Peterborough Abbey', *Historical Research* 65, 1992, fig.2; Roffe, *Decoding Domesday*, 291–304. See also the division of the manor of Deerhurst, Gloucs, between the abbeys of Westminster and Saint-Denis, Paris, and the division of Pershore abbey's land between Pershore and Westminster (GDB, 166, 174v–175v: GLO 19,1–2.20,1; WOR 8.9).

a despoiler of church property, but it may be significant that Osgot's tenements in Abington Pigotts and Guilden Morden constitute the only land entered under his name in the Cambridgeshire folios.[22] There is no reason not to suppose that Picot simply succeeded Osgot as holder of the lands (*terrae*) while continuing to render soke and *consuetudines* to the episcopal manor of Steeple Morden.

I have concentrated on one small vill in south-east Cambridgeshire, but neither Abington Pigotts nor Cambridgeshire are unique, save that the sources are comparatively loquacious on the subject of status. Yet such exercises might be repeated in most English shires, even though the sources may be less immediately informative. The shires of Circuit IV, for instance, have little to say about pre-Conquest tenure in comparison with those of Circuits V and VII, but the example of Esbern, who held eight tenements in Leicestershire, is directly analogous to that of Goda in Cambridgeshire. Seven of his holdings, at Oadby, Peatling, Cosby, Frolesworth, Sharnford, Willoughby Waterless, and Heather, had passed by 1086 to Countess Judith, but the eighth, at Swepstone, was held by Henry de Ferrers.[23] The explanation appears in the text: Oadby and its dependencies had been held by Judith's husband, Earl Waltheof and Esbern, described as a free man (*hanc terram totam Wallef comes tenuit et Sbern I liber homo*), while Swepstone had been divided between Esbern, who held 2 carucates and 'could go where he would' (*quo voluit ire potuit*), while Leofric held (*tenuit*) the rest of the land (8 carucates).[24] Though the relationships are not as explicit as in Cambridgeshire, it seems reasonable to conclude that Esbern's land at Swepstone owed *consuetudines* to Leofric, while Oadby and its dependencies owed their dues to Earl Waltheof.

In conclusion, it should be said that the post-Conquest incomers knew well how to exploit the complexities of personal commendation and tenurial dependency, but in doing so they were utilizing rather than overriding pre-Conquest custom. The whole purpose of recording the situation in King Edward's day was to establish that just as King William was King Edward's legal heir, his men (and their men) held their lands with the same rights and, more importantly, the same obligations as their

---

[22] Compare the relationship between the bishop of Worcester and Urse d'Abitot, sheriff of Worcestershire, at the same date: Ann Williams, 'The Spoliation of Worcester', *ANS* 19, 1997, 383–408 at 397–9. Urse, like Picot, had a bad name as a despoiler of church property, but Urse was able to put his side of the case to the 1086 commissioners. No source remains to exonerate or excuse Picot, but it would be a mistake to believe that right lay exclusively on the ecclesiastical side; bishops and abbots were just as capable of spinning the facts as any lay official.

[23] It might be questioned whether the man who held at Oadby and the rest was also the holder at Swepstone, but Heather, one of the dependencies of Oadby, lay adjacent to Swepstone, and the name Esbern does not appear elsewhere in Leicestershire. I am grateful to Chris Lewis and Duncan Probert, of the 'Profile of a Doomed Elite' project at King's College, London, for this information.

[24] GDB, 233v, 236: LEI 14,23.40,1–7.

pre-Conquest predecessors. Just as the laws of King Edward were never repealed, though they might be amplified, interpreted and added to, so post-Conquest tenurial structures were built upon those of the Old English past.[25] It is only by identifying these structures of lordship and dependency that individual landholders and their relationships can be identified; for the Snark is a Boojum, you see.

[25] David Roffe, 'From Thegnage to Barony: Sake and Soke, Title, and Tenants-in-Chief', *ANS* 12, 1990, 157–76.

7

A Question of Identity: Domesday Prosopography and the Formation of the Honour of Richmond

K. S. B. Keats-Rohan

PROSOPOGRAPHY IS ABOUT identity and about context. Domesday Book offers a peculiarly satisfying challenge for those who enjoy the jigsaw puzzles of the method. Some 45,000 personal names occur in the text, and 29,000 place-names.[1] The textual context of a name is an obvious primary clue when seeking to resolve these many thousands of name-records into names of individual persons and places, but these necessary onomastic exercises are merely to find the corner pieces. Those stalwarts of prosopographical analysis, genealogical links, provide the straight pieces that form the frame of the puzzle. If we wish to see the full picture, however, we should be aware that over-reliance on family relationships, and the ostensible inheritance gains of marriage alliances, may steer us away from, rather than towards, the full potential offered by a prosopographical approach to Domesday Book. That potential is nothing less than a full understanding of how society changed between 1066 and 1086, because it will establish just how title to land passed from the English to the Normans and their allies, and reveal the varied links that formed the bonds of society. Various mechanisms of land transfer have been proposed. The most visible was antecession, that is, the sokeright of one or more named thegns was given to a newcomer and made the basis of the latter's tenancy-in-chief or honour. The lands of the *antecessor*'s median thegns also became the newcomer's to distribute to his own mesne tenants. Whilst the principle of antecession seems predominantly to govern the legal transfer of land from one person to another throughout the

---

[1] Statistics from various databases, including my own COEL database give roughly similar pictures.

period 1066 to 1086, there are exceptions based on a direct grant by writ of the king. Then there are the so-called hundredal grants, geographically defined estates that are more artificially created for strategic purposes, such as the rapes of Sussex and the marcher county of Cheshire. Also alleged as mechanisms are usurpation and marriage alliances.

In order to achieve both the identification of individuals and to say something useful about them, we need to approach the task within the framework of a set of questions suggested by a layered approach to the overall context of Domesday Book. The basic context is the aftermath of the Conquest of 1066, which saw the top tier of English society, the earls and many king's thegns, swept away in a maelstrom of death in battle or subsequent forfeiture. That much we know from chronicle evidence. It is one of the very few things that all commentators can agree upon. The lands of the fallen were re-distributed over the next twenty years almost exclusively to the victorious Normans and their allies from elsewhere in northern France. Who were these people? Where did they come from, and what does that tell us about the conquest? How are they distinguished in the text? The second context is the inquest of 1085–6 that generated the wealth of information subsequently abbreviated in Domesday Book. In return for providing full details of their lands, with their associated revenues and tax dues, and an oath of homage, the tenants-in-chief established after 1066 were granted full title to them, meaning that they could pass them on to their heirs. What can we learn about the structure and function of the new honours by studying the clues in the Domesday text about the status of the English tenures on which they were based and their geographical distribution? On what basis, and by what means, had the English tenures been re-distributed to the newcomers? Was there continuity or disjuncture ('tenurial revolution'), and to what extent? Can the details be used to construct a prosopography of the English? The third context is chronology. The inquest concerned itself with two main dates: who had the land on the day Edward the Confessor was alive and dead in 1066, and who held when the commissioners asked the question? There is a fair amount of extra detail about the interstices, especially in areas where revolts had produced great upheaval, most notably in East Anglia and the North, between 1069 and 1075, when further forfeitures and re-grants occurred. Also possible were references to former tenants-in-chief who no longer held, whether through death (Queen Matilda, Earl William), forfeiture (Earl Ralph II), imprisonment (Odo of Bayeux), or surrender of land (Count Aubrey). What can we learn about the process of settlement from these chronologies? Is antecession more likely as a basis for land redistribution earlier in the process, and hundredal grant more likely later, as has been suggested by Robin Fleming? How was the settlement process affected by post-Conquest revolts and re-distributions of forfeitures? Fundamentally, we are seeking the legal basis for the creation of the post-Conquest honours and baronies from a mass of detail about who had what from whom and how in 1066. Such estates were the cornerstone of local, regional and national administration and social organization so there is no more important question to answer. The final context, then, is the text itself. Close attention to the formulae employed to describe the nature and composition of tenure, and to the stratigraphic clues as to how estates were organized, as abundantly demonstrated by David Roffe and Ann Williams in this book and elsewhere, will help to tease out otherwise irrecoverable information of prime importance for the goal of a complete prosopography of Domesday Book.

Self-evidently, none of these lines of enquiry can be divorced from the others if a complete prosopography is to be the end result. But, despite the extraordinary and unparalleled richness of the Domesday data, the challenges are huge. So far, only the continental origins of the incomers has been treated in depth as a specific inquiry covering the whole of Domesday, Little and Great. This work was undertaken by myself and published in 1999 as *Domesday People* and the COEL database. Further research continues to inform the question, and, together with Ann Williams's masterly *The English and the Norman Conquest* (1995), it has encouraged new initiatives in attempting the more challenging prosopography of the English class of '66. It has also fed into a burgeoning interest into the formation of an English national identity, and more nuanced explorations of the experience of living in a post-Conquest world with a complex of different regional identities and languages. *Domesday People* has been of fundamental importance in outlining the basic composition of the continental elite that replaced the Old English one.[2] The research showed that the number of persons mentioned in the text was very much smaller than the number of persons who would have held one form or other of tenement in 1086. Around 2500 persons were identified from the 29,000-odd name-records, including around 600 Englishmen and women. It is evident from this number alone that not all those who held land can have been mentioned in the text, and there is plenty of external evidence from jurors lists and contemporary charters that this was the case.[3] John Palmer has estimated that around 8,000 newcomers had settled by 1086.[4] Domesday only notes the tenures of the tenants-in-chief and their tenants (the mesne-tenants, or honorial barony), not infrequently omitting the latter. It does not, by and large, note the tenures of those who held from the tenants (sub-tenants). Where they have been identified they are usually found to have been the English, who have not therefore disappeared, but either remained where they were or had lost status and slipped down the tenurial ladder.[5] Another

---

[2] *Domesday People*, Woodbridge 1999. A new edition of the work, revising, expanding, and correcting the first edition, as well as addressing the many inconveniences caused by the first edition's origins in a computer database, is in preparation.
[3] See, for example, C. P. Lewis, 'The Domesday Jurors', *Haskins Society Journal* 5, 1993, 17–43.
[4] John Palmer, 'The Wealth of the Secular Aristocracy in 1086', *ANS* 22, 1999, 279–91 at 286–7.
[5] Keats-Rohan, *Domesday People*, 28–9; Ann Williams, *The English and the Norman Conquest*, Woodbridge 1995.

15,000-odd name records relating to English tenures in 1066 were included in the COEL database for purposes of analysis, but were not treated separately in the prosopography.[6] The status of these people and their land determined those of the holder or holders in 1086, however the land was acquired, as shown by David Roffe and Ann Williams both in this book and elsewhere. On the basis of identification alone, though, it is clear that the tenants-in-chief of 1086 represented a new elite that had all but completely replaced the Old English elite who had held in 1066. At this topmost level the tenurial revolution was real.

This elitism is to some extent reflected in the marriage strategies of the newcomers.[7] Intermarriage at a high social level was confined to just two instances, of which the most high profile was that between the king's niece Judith and Earl Waltheof, which ended disastrously with Waltheof's revolt in 1075 and subsequent execution. Otherwise it occurs rarely among tenants-in-chief, and then normally among the lower-ranking Normans, or the non-Normans. Such as there were probably occurred early, as was certainly the case in the marriage between Robert d'Oilly and Ealdgyth, daughter of Wigod of Wallingford, and probably that between the Breton Geoffrey de la Guerche and Ælfgifu, daughter of Leofwine and sister and heir of Leofric *cilt* in Leicestershire, Nottinghamshire, Lincolnshire, Warwickshire, and Yorkshire.[8] The only other example of intermarriage at a high social level is the marriage between the Breton Count Alan and Gunhilda, daughter of King Harold and Eadgifu Swanneshals or *Pulchra*, according to a study by Richard Sharpe who has argued convincingly that their daughter Matilda, later wife of Walter d'Aincourt,

---

[6] In the belief that the English would be studied by others. Unfortunately, no comprehensive study of the English has yet been done, though there are a number of important contributions available, notably a number of studies by Ann Williams, and Chris Lewis's methodological paper, 'Joining the Dots: a Methodology for Identifying the English in Domesday Book', in *Family Trees and the Roots of Politics: the Prosopography of Britain and France from the Tenth to the Twelfth Century*, ed. K. S. B. Keats-Rohan, Woodbridge 1997, 69–87. The contribution by the PASE database at KCL to date has proved disappointing: it is not a true prosopography and is at present of limited practical use (http://www.pase.ac.uk/, accessed 30/12/2014). For now the most useful tool is John Palmer's Ids database (http://discover.ukdataservice.ac.uk/catalogue?sn=5694, ids information, accessed 03/10/2015; the dataset can be downloaded directly from https://hydra.hull.ac.uk/resources/hull:domesday Translation).

[7] Keats-Rohan, *Domesday People*, 27–9; Elisabeth van Houts, 'Intermarriage in Eleventh-Century England', in *Normandy and its Neighbours, 900–1250: Essays for David Bates*, ed. D. Crouch and K. Thompson, Turnhout 2011, 237–70.

[8] On Wallingford, K. S. B. Keats-Rohan, 'The Genesis of the Honour of Wallingford', in *The Origins of the Borough of Wallingford*, ed. K. S. B. Keats-Rohan and D. R. Roffe, Oxford 2009. The form *Leduinus* (Leodwine) occurs in Lincolnshire, where another of Geoffrey's predecessors was Leofric *cilt*. On balance it seems more likely that *Leduin* refers to Leofwine father of Leofric *cilt* as elsewhere, as suggested also by G. Fellows-Jensen, 'On the Identification of Domesday Tenants in Lincolnshire', *Nomina* 9, 1985, 31–40 at 33–4; see Palmer, Ids dataset, under 'Leofwine [father of Leofric]'.

was born *c.* 1073.⁹ The scale and importance of Count Alan's vast honour of Richmond and its relatively abundant documentation from Domesday onward have made it the subject of a number of publications, including two volumes of the inestimable *Early Yorkshire Charters*. As Sharpe has pointed out, however, the stages by which Alan built up his huge estates are not known, and no detailed study of his tenurial *antecessores* has been made. Such a study is the primary focus of this paper. It will add to a body of work showing that a decoding of Domesday formulae points to antecession as overwhelmingly the predominant mechanism of the transfer of title to land, and will add weight to cautions about over-interpreting marriage alliances. It is an inquiry that will address each of the four contexts outlined above and follow the Domesday text through the vicissitudes of settlement throughout the reign of William I.

Analysis of the Domesday tenants-in-chief and their men showed that, as expected, the majority were Normans, who formed over 83% of all newcomers. Overall, the Norman personnel clearly reflect the influential groups around William in his duchy, men who had been with him throughout the troubled years of his minority and gradual emergence as a leader of considerable energy, talent, and ruthlessness. The remaining 17% of newcomers fall broadly into two groups, of which it is the Bretons who are of interest to us here. The undoubted figurehead of this group until the latter part of 1069 was King William's second cousin Count Brien and was thereafter Brien's brother Alan Rufus. Count Alan left by far the greater mark on Domesday Book, which shows that he profited handsomely from the redistribution of lands in the east and north of the country following the revolts of 1069 to 1075. Chronicle and charter evidence shows the importance of the Bretons during the initial stages of the conquest, from the invasion onward.¹⁰ The size and significance of the Breton contingent among post-Conquest landholders left its mark in the records of the time, and nowhere more so than in Domesday Book. Count Brien is last heard of in the *Anglo-Saxon Chronicle* repelling the second attack from an Irish base made by the sons of the fallen king Harold Godwinson in mid 1069. He probably left England later in the same year or soon after, only reappearing once, in Brittany, in 1084.¹¹ Anything Brien had held was dwarfed by the holdings of his brother Alan

---

⁹ R. Sharpe, 'King Harold's Daughter', *Haskins Society Journal* 19, 2008, 1–27.
¹⁰ *Poitiers*, 120–1; Orderic, II, 174–5; *The* Carmen de Hastingae Proelio *of Guy, Bishop of Amiens*, ed. F. Barlow, Oxford 1999, 24–5.
¹¹ ASC D; Orderic, II, 23–4, 227–8; Keats-Rohan, *Domesday People*, 48; A. Wilmart, 'Alain le roux et Alain le noir, comtes de Bretagne', *Annales de Bretagne* 38, 1929, 576–95 at 583 n.8. LDB, 291–2: SFK 2. Brien had held a modest fee in Suffolk, held in 1086 by Robert of Mortain, where his predecessor was Wulfnoth. Wulfnoth's principal holding was in Stow hundred, where he held in laenage of King Edward (*tenuit Ulnoth liber homo sub rege*) at Combs, with fifty men commended to him; it was valued at £10 in 1066, but struggled to pay its dues of £16 in 1086. He held 2 carucates at Creeting St Olave as a manor, and a further carucate in Creeting St Peter: LDB, 291: SFK 2,9–10. He may have been the Wulfnoth

in 1086, at which date Alan was by any measure one of the most richly endowed men in England.[12] How did this come about, and what can it tell us about the pre and post-Conquest society in the period 1066–1086?

Based primarily on the evidence of the Domesday text and the four contexts outlined above, the following analysis of the creation of the honour of Richmond will attempt to establish the means by which the constituent parts of the honour were created (antecession, hundredal grant etc.) and the most likely time-frame in each case. It will concentrate on three primary groupings in the honour: first, the estate of Eadgifu, centred in Cambridgeshire with outliers in neighbouring counties, which will show that with very few exceptions, her lands passed to Alan by antecession; secondly, estates acquired primarily in East Anglia as a result of the forfeitures of the period 1070–1075, and the estate in Lincolnshire formerly held by Ralph I of East Anglia, likewise acquired by antecession but raising also questions relating to the revolt of his son Ralph II in 1075 and the redistribution of the latter's estates; thirdly, the castelry of Richmondshire in North Yorkshire, created sometime between 1072 and *c*. 1080. This too, despite apparently fitting the profile of a 'hundredal grant', was acquired through antecession.[13]

The lands of Eadgifu *Pulchra*

There is no known deed of William I which was attested by both Count Brien and Count Alan.[14] The earliest of many acts of the king witnessed by Count Alan – the

who had held 40 acres as a manor in Benhall, in Plomesgate hundred, under the patronage of Robert Malet's predecessor; the same Wulfnoth was one of seven free men under the patronage of the king's thegn Algar in Saxmundham: LDB, 338v, 389, 344: SFK 7,71;140. Another *antecessor* was Anand, a free man who had held the manor of Helmingham: LDB, 291v: SFK 2,12; a man of the same name also held from Count Alan: LDB 293v, 294: SFK 3,32–3;46–7. Robert of Mortain's small holding in Norfolk, where Wulfnoth preceded him in Roughton, and Earl Harold in *Clareia*, may also first have been Brien's: LDB, 144: NFK 3,1–2. The formula *In Rustuna tenuit Vlnoth* identifies him as a king's thegn.

[12] For the best assessment of relative wealth, see Palmer, 'The Wealth of the Secular Aristocracy'.

[13] This conclusion was reached by both Paul Dalton, *Conquest, Anarchy and Lordship: Yorkshire 1066–1154*, Cambridge 1994 (see note 101 below), and Judith A. Green, *The Aristocracy of Norman England*, Cambridge 1997, 48–99, esp. 48–54, 165–6, who pointed out that detailed studies of post-Conquest honours and the relationships between the new tenants-in-chief and their English *antecessores* and tenants are still very few in number. Although she does not analyse the Domesday concept of soke, Green says (p.48): 'The speed and completeness of the changes in the elite tend to confirm … that where possible the transfer was intended to be both orderly and controlled. The aim at least was that the newcomers stepped into the shoes of one or more predecessors or, as Domesday Book describes them, antecessors (*antecessores*).'

[14] Count Brien attested *Regesta*, Bates, nos. 138 and 254, both 1069, probably around Easter, the second given at Winchester.

only means we have of assessing his nighness to the king at a practical level – was probably either a charter for Saint-Ouen de Rouen of 1066x77 or one for St Paul's London of 1070x78.[15] In marrying the daughter of Eadgifu and Harold he had marked his arrival on the scene with some éclat. His first grant of land was probably the estates of his mother-in-law in Cambridgeshire where more than seventy of his eighty-two holdings had been held by Eadgifu *Pulchra* in 1066 (discussed in detail by Roffe above). Jeulin estimated that about 26% of the value of Alan's honour lay in there.[16] His was the dominant holding in the southern hundreds and he held manors in much of the rest of the county. Only a 13½-hide manor at Exning formerly held by Eadgifu failed to pass to him, being held by the king in 1086; twelve further parcels of land that had been held by men commended to her were in various hands.[17] In all cases where Eadgifu *Pulchra* had had full jurisdiction, as indicated by the formula *hoc manerium/hanc terram tenuit Eddeua*, or *tenuit Eddeua*, the holder in 1086 was Count Alan.

Eadgifu is likely to have forfeited most or all of her land soon after the battle of Hastings, and certainly after the raids in the south-west by her sons in 1068 and 1069. Her manors at Exning and Great Sampford were both comital holdings that she had acquired through her association with Earl Harold, as is evident from the fact that they both pertained to the earldom held by Ralph de Gael who forfeited his holdings after his rebellion in 1075. A valuable indicator to the lands Ralph had held as earl is that after his fall they were administered on the king's behalf by his former steward Godric. In Suffolk these included a number of places on the Suffolk/Cambridgeshire border where Eadgifu had had the soke and commendation of thirty-six free men, all of them added to the king's manor of Norton in the time of Earl Ralph II (1069/70x75).[18] Before 1066 the manor belonged to the abbey of Bury St Edmunds from which Eadgifu held in laenage for her lifetime. All this suggests that Eadgifu did indeed forfeit her lands, that some of them, particularly in Suffolk and Essex, derived from Harold's one-time tenure of the earldom of East Anglia, and that they were accordingly redistributed.

Even so, it appears that the bulk of Eadgifu's holdings in Cambridgeshire, Buckinghamshire, and Hertfordshire was her own, a sizeable estate that had made her a suitable wife for an ambitious earl.[19] The valuable manor of Fulbourn, Cambs,

---

[15] *Regesta*, Bates, nos. 244, 185.
[16] P. Jeulin, 'Aperçus sur le comté de Richemont', *Annales de Bretagne* 42, 1935, 265–302 at 271.
[17] Count Alan's holdings, GDB, 193v–195v: CAM 14; Exning, GDB, 188, 189v: CAM 1,12, then held by Godric for the king showing that it had been held until 1075 by Earl Ralph II; commendations, GDB, 193v: CAM 13, 8–10; GDB, 196v: CAM 19,4; GDB, 198, 198v: CAM 26,16;38;40; GDB, 199v: CAM 29,10; GDB, 200: CAM 31,3;7; GDB, 200, 201–v: CAM 32,8;31–2;44; GDB, 201v: CAM 35,1.
[18] LDB, 284v, 286: SFK 1,61;63;88.
[19] I. W. Walker, *Harold: The Last Anglo-Saxon King*, Stroud 1997, 61, 72, 127–31.

which opens the account of Alan's lands, had been held by Godwin *cild*, a man of Eadgifu, who could not withdraw; he had two further tenements from her on the same terms.[20] Many other entries show the same pattern of dependence between Eadgifu and her men. Others show a freer tenurial relationship, such as that of Merwin who held from Eadgifu 12 acres in Haslingfield which he could sell. Eight free men had held land in the valuable demesne manor of Bassingbourn which they could sell, though the soke remained with her; similarly, a further eight free men held with the right to sell in Eadgifu's manor of Swavesey, held in demesne by Count Alan in 1086; here the relationship was more akin to sokage tenure in which the soke was reserved to Eadgifu.[21] Others held from her in laenage, such as Goda who had held under (*sub*) Eadgifu at another demesne manor, Papworth, or Thorbern at Orwell.[22] Some of those named as her men were still holding from Alan in 1086, including Colswein and his son Almaer of Bourn. Both were jurors in Armingford hundred.[23] Their tenures were mixed. Almaer held land in Bourn, Caldecote, and Longstowe from Alan which he had held from Eadgifu with the right to sell and to withdraw without permission. Colswein held half a hide from Alan in Whaddon which he had held from Eadgifu with the right to sell; elsewhere, he held from Alan in Meldreth what he held *sub* Eadgifu, which probably indicates that this was loan land supplementing the family land he held from her.[24] There is little sign of any suppression of the status of the surviving English in this fief.

A similar picture emerges from the lands of Eadgifu peripheral to the Cambridgeshire heartland. A Godwin who had been a man of Eadgifu held from Alan at Watton in Broadwater hundred, Hertfordshire, in 1086; an Alward holding in 1086 in Reed, also in Hertfordshire, succeeded Turbern a man of Eadgifu, while Leviet succeeded her man Osgot in one virgate in Clothall.[25] Turbern and Osgot had both held with the right to sell. Godwin, however, had held on loan from St Peter's, Westminster, with reversion due on his death, but his wife had instead 'turned with force' to Eadgifu with the land, which she held in 1066. Sixteen acres had been removed since then and were held under the archbishop by Ansquetil de Rots, but Count Alan paid the tax. This is the only case of blatant misappropriation of land in this honour – and it was perpetrated before 1066 by an Englishwoman.

---

[20] GDB, 193v: CAM 14,1;6;80.18,3.35,1.41,13–14. in Weston Colville, under William de Warenne, two free men who were men of Godwin *cild* had owed cartage and escort duty in 1066.
[21] GDB, 194: CAM 14,27;36;38;41;55.
[22] GDB, 194v: CAM 14,41;53.
[23] Williams, *The English*, 88–9, suggests the two jurors were Alan's tenants; this is demonstrated by *EYC*, V, 12, a fee list of the honour of Richmond names Warin son of Ralph son of Ailmer son of Colswein and Stephen de Turre who then owed one knight's service for castle-guard at Richmond.
[24] GDB, 194v, 195–v: CAM 14,28;32–3;47;49–52;81–2.
[25] GDB, 136v, 137: HRT 16,1,3;6.

Continuity can also be discerned in the lands bordering Suffolk and Cambridgeshire. Count Alan's fee in Suffolk falls into two unequal parts. The first eighty-five entries appear to have originated either in comital lands that had been held at some stage by Earl Ralph the staller or his son Ralph II, or the sokeland of Eadgifu; the last twenty entries lay within the soke of St Etheldreda.[26] Eadgifu's sokeland lay primarily if not exclusively in the huge royal and comital manor of East Bergholt in Samford hundred and its berewicks, held successively by earls Harold and Gyrth and augmented by Ralph I.[27] It seems to have formed a separate but interlocking estate, quite probably originating in her marriage to Harold.[28] Some of her men still held from Alan in 1086. Wulfstan, a free man of Eadgifu, held 50 acres as a manor from the count at Boynton in the soke of East Bergholt; a Thurstan had held in the soke and commendation of Eadgifu in five manors, all of which were held by the king's thegn Ælfric the priest from Alan in 1086. In 1066 Ælfric the priest had held the valuable manor of Parham, held by Haimo de Valeines in 1086; he may have been the free man Ælfric who held 16 acres and free men of the count in the manor of Thurleston.[29] Godwin, who had held 30 acres in Brantham as a manor in the soke of East Bergholt, still held in 1086; he was probably the

---

[26] LDB, 292v–296, 296–7: SFK 3,1–85;86–105. The former included manors in Bramfield, Wissett, Earl Soham, East Bergholt, and Ipswich, the latter in Wantisden and Great Glemham. Some of the former include manors that had been given to Earl Ralph as forfeitures, such as Manni Swart's holdings in Cowlinge and Brantham, SFK 3, 1–2.

[27] Wulfstan, LDB, 296: SFK 3,81. Ælfric, LDB, 287–v, 289v, 295–6: SFK 1,100–5;119.3,67–86, apart from 3,79, the land in Hintlesham of Siward a free man of Stigand. Even where not explicit, all these holdings appear to relate to Eagifu's sokeland in East Bergholt and its berewicks.

[28] Probably including *Beria* in Claydon hundred which she had held herself; unnamed others held there in her soke: LDB, 295: SFK 3,69.

[29] LDB, 295–v, 296: SFK 3,64;74–8;81. The king's holdings in East Bergholt were under the administration of Ælfric Wanz; LDB, 287–v: SFK 1,100–5. Another part of Thurleston was held by Ælfric son of Rolf burgess of Ipswich as a vavassour; LDB, 446: SFK 74,8. Parham, LDB, 296: SFK 3,88, then held by Haimo [de Valeines]; probably the same man was one of two named as under the patronage of Robert Malet's predecessor [Eadric of Laxfield] in Carlton, also held by Haimo, the whole in the jurisdiction of the abbot of Ely; LDB, 296v: SFK 3,94. Ælfric was possibly the father of Osward de Turston to whom Abbot Leofstan of Bury gave the land and church of Thurston (*Feudal Documents from the Abbey of Bury St Edmunds*, ed. D. C. Douglas, Records of the Social and Economic History of England and Wales 8, British Academy, 1932, 98). He occurs in Cambridgeshire where he had held one virgate in Papworth from the abbot of Ely, appropriated by Richard fitzGilbert before 1086; Papworth was a demesne manor of Count Alan, which had been held by Goda under Eadgifu, and she could sell: GDB, 195, 196v: CAM 14,53.19,1. For Goda's identity, see Ann Williams above, p.161 n.14. Haimo's descendants held the Valeines (*not* Valognes) fee from the honour of Richmond, owing seven knights' service and castle-guard in December and January in the time of Henry I, including half a fee in Rookwith, Yorks: *EYC*, V, 11, 234–7. It is probable that Domesday's *Hamo de Valenis* was the *Haimo de Doll'* who attested the foundation charter of Swavesey: *EYC*, V, 2.

Godwin son of Ailsi, thegn of Queen Edith, who had had another manor there, with the soke, held in 1086 by Hubert [de Montcanisy] from Robert Malet.[30] In the same hundred, in Dodnash and Brantham, an Edwin had held land as a manor in Eadgifu's soke; Goding held it from Count Alan in 1086.[31] He also had 60 acres as a manor in Stutton in the soke of East Bergholt, and a 30-acre manor in Wantisden, in the soke of Ely.[32]

If Count Alan was clearly the primary successor to Eadgifu the Fair, there were a few exceptions, principally in areas other than the main blocks in Cambridgeshire and Suffolk. Alan held Eadgifu's manors in Hertfordshire, with the sole exception of Bishop's Stortford, which had been purchased by the bishop of London; in Essex, except for Great Sampford, then in the king's hands administered by Godric the steward as a holding of Earl Ralph until his forfeiture in 1075.[33] Eadgifu's only manor in Buckinghamshire, the substantial 18-hide manor of Mentmore, went to Earl Hugh, from whom the land was held by Robert of Rhuddlan, a man who had served King Edward the Confessor as a squire in his youth and been knighted by him before returning to Normandy.[34] Jocelyn Brito held what Eadgifu's man Alwine had held with the right to sell at Soulbury and Yardley.[35] The manors of Harkstead and Gusford in Suffolk formerly held by Eadgifu *Pulchra* were in 1086 held by the king's half-sister, the countess of Aumale. The countess's modest Suffolk fee is one of the few that appear to have been formed from disparate elements, rather than one or two *antecessores*. Apart from Eadgifu, she derived title also from Wulfric a thegn of King Edward, Ælfric of Wenhou, and Burgric a man of Ralph the staller, while in Debach were three free men commended to Eadric Grim, all in only twelve entries in the text.[36]

Count Alan, then, succeeded to all the lands of Eadgifu to which she had more or less full rights, a clear case of antecessorial succession. There is good reason to believe that these lands formed the first grant made to Alan, and there are some strong clues as to the date of the grant. His establishment of two priories in Cambridgeshire hint

---

[30] LDB, 296, 306: SFK 3,82.6,27.

[31] LDB, 295, 295v: SFK 3,68–9;72–3.

[32] LDB, 296: SFK 3,83;86. This Edwin was a predecessor of Godric the steward in Godric's own modest tenancy-in-chief in Suffolk and Norfolk, where he occurs as a thegn who had held Great Melton, and, in laenage, Little Melton, from St Benet of Holme. Little Melton later passed from Godric and his wife Ingreda to their son Ralph, who held on the same terms (*Mon. Ang.*, III, 87). Edwin's family is known from a series of surviving wills, which show that he was uncle to a Godric who might well be the steward (LDB, 355v, 356: SFK 13. Williams, *The English*, 108–9).

[33] GDB, 134: HRT 4,22; LDB, 7: ESS 1,30.

[34] Orderic, IV, 136–8; GDB, 146v: BUC 13,1.

[35] GDB, 146v, 148v, 152: BUC 13,1.17,9.44,2;5.

[36] LDB, 430v, 431: SFK 46,1–12; cf. LDB, 91v; ESS 54. The countess's fee looks a bit like an afterthought.

that his early endowment was there. The first was probably Swavesey priory, where a monastery was recorded in Domesday Book. The substantial 13-hide manor had been held by Eadgifu in 1066.[37] This was given to the great Angevin abbey of Saints Serge and Bacchus, a favourite with some Bretons and certainly of Alan's family. The act of foundation survives only as a later transcript. It makes no reference to a nuclear family, but it does refer to Queen Matilda's influence in the grant of an honour in England to him.[38] This would date that grant after 11 May 1068 and well before he was granted forfeitures by Stigand and others from April 1070 onward by the king. The second foundation was Linton priory, originally located in Isleham but soon removed to Alan's demesne at Linton. This was placed under the Breton monastery of Saint-Jacut.[39] Subsequently, the foundation was praised by Alan's father Count Eudo, who stopped at Saint-Jacut on his way home from Normandy. The date is unknown, but Eudo died in January 1079. Very probably, both were ventures belonging to the earliest stages of Alan's implantation. The later transcript of the foundation charter shows that the main household officers, Wihomarc the steward and Odo the chamberlain, and the count's (half-) brothers Bodin, Ribald, and Bardulf, were witnesses. Swavesey was a large administrative estate, the *caput* of the honour in Cambridgeshire, and it was there that a castle was established in the late eleventh century.[40] An additional witness to the Linton charters, also later documents, was Enisan Musard, ancestor of the later constables of Richmond.[41]

Additional estates based on forfeiture *c.* 1069–76

Alan's modest holdings in Hampshire may also be early, but are not connected with Eadgifu. His three holdings there were originally acquired as one manor; Wulfweard could go with his land in Crofton, but not in Funtley; the count's manor of Crofton

---

[37] The endowment was for all his tithes in Swavesey and its berewicks in Papworth, Toft, Wimpole, Landbeach, and whatever he had in demesne in Dry Drayton: *EYC*, IV, 1–2; GDB, 194v, 195-v: CAM 14,44;47;53;55;59;60 (*in Draitone tenent monachi de Suauesy sub comite*).

[38] *Hanc autem elemosinam dedit ipse comes pro anima sua et pro anima domini sui regis Anglorum Willelmi et pro anima Mathildis regine, cujus auxilio honorem adquisivit* (*EYC*, IV, 1–2).

[39] J. A. Everard, 'The Foundation of an Alien Priory at Linton, Cambridgeshire', *Proceedings of the Cambridge Antiquarian Society* 86, 1997, 169–74. The endowment was in his demesne at Linton and West Wickham, held by Eadgifu TRE, and at Barham, where his tenant was Ansquetil (de Furnellis), and Isleham, where the tenant was Geoffrey [de Burgh], both held TRE by Eadgifu. At Linton there had been a free man who had found cartage for the sheriff: GDB, 193v, 194, 195v: CAM 14,7–9;72.

[40] A. Lowerre, *Placing Castles in the Conquest: Landscape, Lordship and Local Politics in the South-Eastern Midlands, 1066–1100*, British Archaeological Reports, British Series 385, 2005, 233–4.

[41] GDB, 195: CAM 14,62

had been held by the brothers Ansgot and Almaer from the king.[42] Wulfweard was probably the thegn Wulfweard White, who had been a minister of Queen Edith (d.1075). He was dead in 1086 when his widow still held land in Keynsham, Somerset.[43] Some of Alan's holdings in Suffolk and Norfolk were also probably acquired at the same time as Eadgifu's land, but there he had more than one *antecessor* and some of the land will have come to him later. The primary reason for this seems to be the tenurial disruption caused by outlawry or forfeiture of TRE holders, unrelated to the Earls' Revolt of 1075 of which Alan was a major beneficiary. One of them was Manni Swart, father of king's thegn and housecarl Ulf, another of the count's *antecessores*, his Suffolk fief being divided between Count Alan and Robert de Tosny, with the lion's share going to Alan, including the demesne manors of Cowlinge and Bramfield, and Bruisyard, held in 1086 by Haimo de Valeines.[44] Ulf was Alan's predecessor in the Norfolk manor of Hethersett. The once-considerable estates of these men and their family in East Anglia and elsewhere had ended up in the hands of Earl Ralph II, whose lands were divided primarily between the king and Alan in 1076. Manni and Ulf must have forfeited them some time between 1066 and 1075. As a result, the tenurial and territorial integrity of their family holdings, here and in several other counties, were badly mangled; they have recently been skilfully reconstructed by Lucy Marten.[45]

Another of Alan's holdings may have come to him by a circuitous route following the Ely revolt of 1069/70 and the later Earl's Revolt of 1075. This was the land held by Eadric Grim in Suffolk. His principal personal holding was the valuable manor of Kettleburgh, in Loes hundred, Suffolk, and its constituents and all this was granted to Count Alan. Eadric had held it partly under the commendation of Eadric of Laxfield, *antecessor* of Robert Malet and partly under that of Ely.[46] Some of the men commended to Eadric Grim were in the hands of a number of other tenants-in-chief, including Roger of Poitou and Hugh de Montfort by 1086. All his other land was held under Eadric of Laxfield and appears in the *breve* of Robert Malet. Eadric had become a man of King Edward when Eadric of Laxfield was outlawed, but had subsequently been permitted to return to Eadric of Laxfield's allegiance after the latter's pardon. Eadric Grim did not have a sympathetic hearing from the

---

[42] GDB, 44: HAM 19,1–3.
[43] Williams, *The English*, 99–10; GDB, 87: SOM 1,28.
[44] LDB, 292v, 298: SFK 3,1;3;101.
[45] Lucy Marten, 'Meet the Swarts', in *The Legacy of the English: Essays in Honour of Ann Williams*, ed. David Roffe, Woodbridge 2012, 17–32.
[46] LDB, 293v–294: SFK 3,34–52. Two thirds of his demesne tithes in Kettleburgh were later given by Alan's youngest brother and successor Count Stephen to Rumburgh, a cell of St Benet of Holme, attested by Osbert of *Wiechesham* (Witchingham) and Algar de *Chetelburgia* (Kettleburgh): *EYC*, V, 12. Malet's land there was assessed in Eadric of Laxfield's manor of Dennington; Ely's land had been held by its free man Wulfmaer and had passed to Roger of Poitou by 1086: LDB, 325, 347v: SFK 6,261;269.8,21.

Domesday jurors, following the outlawing of Eadric of Laxfield after the Ely revolt 1070/71, and was a ruined man in 1086, when he held land at South Cove from Robert Malet worth just 3 shillings.[47] Much of his land and the men commended to him were then held from Count Alan by Haimo de Valeines.[48] He may also have held land directly from Count Alan, since he is often distinguished in the text as *homo Alani*.[49]

None of Count Alan's holdings in Norfolk are directly connected with Eadgifu, though he held both manors and men formerly held by Earl Harold.[50] He also held the huge manor of Costessey and its berewicks, a former manor of Earl Gyrth clearly focused on the guard of the Norfolk coastline.[51] In fact, all of the Norfolk manors appear to have been granted to Alan as a direct result of a string of forfeitures starting in 1070, with the fall of Stigand and his brother Bishop Æthelmaer. In many cases the fact is stated explicitly: 'now the Count holds because Earl Ralph held'. The significance of the former lands of Earls Ralph I and II for the composition of the honour of Richmond is already apparent. It is to these men and the revolt of 1075 that our attention now turns.

The lands of Ralph the staller in Lincolnshire

Domesday Book does not always distinguish Ralph the staller, subsequently earl of East Anglia, from his son Earl Ralph de Gael or Wader. However, they are normally readily identifiable from the timeframe. Any reference using the descriptor staller, constable or *vetus* refers to the father and to 1066 and before, while the son is indicated by reference to his forfeiture in 1075. In the Lincolnshire folios Domesday

---

[47] Discussed fully in Palmer, Ids dataset, under Edric [Grim]: LDB, 293–4, 296: SFK 3,21–3;28;34–42;50–2;89;94–5. The details of problems with the jurors are related under Fordley, LDB, 310v–311: SFK 6,79. See also Lucy Marten, 'Lordship and Land: Suffolk in the Tenth and Eleventh Centuries', unpublished PhD thesis, University of East Anglia 2005, 139–42.

[48] LDB, 298: SFK 3,102 is an unusual reference to the complexity of sub-tenures: *In Gliemham ii liberi homines. Wacra sub commendatus antecessori Malet et Vlueua commendata antecessori Malet ... hoc totum tenet Haimo de comite. Soca abbatis [Sancti Edmundi]*.

[49] One example occurs in Happisburgh in Happing hundred in Norfolk, where there were 100 acres of land before 1066. Sixty acres had been in the soke of Happisburgh when Earl Ralph forfeited, but they had been annexed by Eadric, who testified to that effect. He had also annexed free men and land in Ludham and Palling in the time of Earl Ralph and held when division of the land was made between the king and the count. Eadric and Godwin men of Eadric of Laxfield and Laxfield himself had all held the lands in Happing divided between king and count: LDB, 138v–39, 148v–50: NFK 1,197–9.4,38–42;51.

[50] Norfolk has the least number of English tenants of any part of Alan's honour. They were Alestan, who held in 1066 and 1086, Godric, a Turstin who succeeded a free man, Ketelbern, and Modgifu, a free woman of Ælfgar, whom the text elsewhere identifies as a man of Earl Harold: LDB, 129v–30, 146, 147, 149v, 150: NFK 1,169–71.4,21;31;46;50.

[51] LDB, 145–v, 150v: NFK 4,9–15;54–6.

lists both 'Ralph the staller' and 'Earl Ralph' among those who had held with sake and soke in 1066,[52] but close examination of the text, including the *Clamores*, shows that in all cases Ralph the staller is meant, even though he only acquired the title of earl after October 1066.[53]

Ralph the staller was a Breton nobleman who acquired the soubriquet *Anglicus* because he had been born in England, quite probably to an English mother, as suggested by the name of his brother Godwin; he appears with that designation in Breton charters dated 1024x32.[54] His otherwise unknown father is most likely to have come to England in the service of Queen Emma, sister of Richard II of Normandy, at the time of her first marriage *c.* 1002 to Æthelred II, remaining in her service thereafter during her second marriage to Cnut (1016–35), when she exercised vice-regal powers in East Anglia.[55] By 1050 Ralph *Anglicus* had become a curial minister under Emma's son Edward the Confessor who had, late in his reign, appointed him staller, an important office between that of sheriff and earl. Like all the stallers in late 1066, he submitted early to the new king, though he alone achieved the status of earl under William I, presumably in recognition of his support following the Conquest. William followed his predecessor's policy of using locally powerful men as ministers in order to facilitate and legitimize the transfer of sovereignty. Ralph appears in early documents of the new reign overseeing the redemption of their lands by the English. A number of Bury writs attest the grant of his earldom of Norfolk and Suffolk early in the reign.[56] This was formerly known as the earldom of East Anglia, where his predecessors included the late King Harold, Earl Ælfgar and Harold's brother Earl Gyrth, who was also killed at Hastings. There is nothing in the Domesday text to indicate that Ralph, unlike Alan, had held land or authority in Essex, but the Norfolk fee of Count Alan indicates that he was earl in Norfolk, in succession to Earl Gyrth, as is clear from the accounts of Swaffham, a royal manor given to Ralph by King Edward, and the valuable complex manor of Costessey held by Earl Gryth and his men.[57]

---

[52] GDB, 337: LIN T5.

[53] The most telling examples relate to Drayton and Gosberton: GDB, 348: LIN 12,60;76. CK66,68. He is once referred to as Earl Ralph the staller in LDB, 287: SFK 1,101, where he is noted as adding an outlier to Earl Gyrth's manor of Bentley.

[54] *Actes des ducs de Bretagne (944–1148)*, ed. Hubert Guillotel, Rennes 2014, no. 22, p. 211, no. 28, p. 232; his son occurs in an act of 1089 as *Radulfus Anglicus, comes*; ibid., no. 99, p. 387.

[55] Keats-Rohan, 'Le rôle des bretons dans la politique de la colonisation de l'Angleterre', *Mémoires de la Société d'histoire et d'archéologie de Bretagne* 73, 1996, 181–215, followed by Marten, 'Lordship and Land', 231–2. On Emma and the eight and a half Suffolk hundreds, later Bury's liberty of Wicklaw, Marten, 'Lordship and Land', 94–6; R. Sharpe, 'The Use of Writs in the Eleventh Century: a Hypothesis based upon the Archive of Bury St Edmunds', *Anglo-Saxon England* 32, 2004, 247–91.

[56] *Regesta*, Bates, 35–8; *Feudal Documents*, nos. 1, 3–5.

[57] LDB, 144, 145: NFK 4,1,9.

All of Ralph's land in Lincolnshire was given to Count Alan, under whose name it appears in 1086, accounting for 21% of the value of his honour.[58] It includes the manors of Waltham and Drayton with their extensive sokes, as well as the five manors of Hough-on-the-Hill, Brant Broughton, Fulbeck, Leadenham and Long Bennington and their associated hundreds, all in Loveden wapentake in Kesteven, which were required to provide horse feed (*ad victum equorum*).[59] Otherwise unique in Domesday, this imposition probably relates to the earl's administration.[60] David Roffe has demonstrated the link between these manors and Washingborough as holdings of Earl Siward of Northumbria, who had given land in the estate to his third wife Goda. As the *breve* of the king makes clear, Earl Siward had been succeeded there by Ralph the staller.[61] The Domesday text shows that Ralph the staller was Count Alan's *antecessor* in the bulk of his Lincolnshire fee, and that Ralph held during the reign of Edward the Confessor. His original tenure was therefore as staller, and only from late 1066/early 1067 could it have been as part of his earldom. Probably therefore his Lincolnshire lands were held under an earl, or as caretaker after the death of Earl Ælfgar *c.* 1062/3.

Earls and other officials certainly figure among Alan's predecessors in Lincolnshire. In the berewick of Holbeach and Whaplode, in Elloe wapentake, Earl Ælfgar of Mercia had held one carucate as an outlier of Fleet. The king's officers claimed this from Count Alan for the king's use in 1086. In the same place Earl Ælfgar had held land in the soke of Gedney. Count Alan had 5 carucates of this land, held of him by Landric. The text states that it was adjudged for the king's use. Corresponding entries are found under the king's lands.[62] Landric's descendants, the Welton family, retained their holding under the honour of Richmond. Lincolnshire had been assigned to the earldom of Northumbria in the 1050s and other parts of Alan's fee had links with Earl Siward of Northumbria (d. 1055). Siward's manor of Coleby was held by the king in 1086, but Ralph the staller had held sokeland there, assessed in Washingborough.[63] A Siward was Alan's predecessor in the manor of

---

[58] GDB, 347–348v, 377, 377v: LIN 12,21–39;43–49;60–76;91.CK23,51;66;68; Jeulin, 'Aperçus', 271.

[59] Hough-on-the-Hill was quite possibly the site of an English thegnal *burh*, since the surviving outlines of a motte and bailey castle, situated on a natural mound (Castle Hill), and bounded by a stream, enclose a Saxon church; http://www.pastscape.org/hob.aspx-?hob_id=325849, accessed 04/12/2014. P. Cope-Faulkner and G. Taylor, 'Archaeological Watching Brief of Maintenance Work on the Churchyard Wall at All Saints Church, Hough-on-the-Hill, Lincolnshire', http://archaeologydataservice.ac.uk/archives/view/grey-lit/details.cfm?id=15118, accessed 04/12/2014.

[60] C. Hart, *The Danelaw*, London 1992, 193, favoured the ministry of staller; D. Roffe, 'Lady Godiva, Washingborough and the Book', *Lincolnshire Past and Present* 12, 1993, 9–10.

[61] GDB, 337v: LIN 1,7.

[62] GDB, 338–v, 348, 377v: LIN 1,32–4.12,83–4.CK 71.

[63] Roffe, 'Washingborough'; GDB, 336v, 337: LIN 1,7–8.

North Hykeham in Graffoe wapentake; Kolgrimr held it of Count Alan in 1086, when he also held of the count in the nearby manor of South Stoke, held by the staller in 1066; in 1086 the king had land there pertaining to Grantham. Kolgrimr had another holding in South and North Stoke from Drogo de la Beuvrière. As Roffe has shown elsewhere, Kolgrimr was probably a reeve of Queen Edith in Grantham, from which he was named in a charter for Ramsay abbey. He had sake and soke in a manor in Grantham which had formerly belonged to Peterborough; it was probably held as loanland since it was subsequently returned to the abbey.[64] He survived the Conquest as progenitor of the Ingoldsby family, named from the *caput* of his tenancy-in-chief. All these holdings were subsequently absorbed into the Wensley fee of the honour of Richmond. In the time of Henry I Kolgrimr's son Osbert owed the service of four knights as castle-guard at Richmond castle in February and March.[65] This is a rare documented example of an English family of ministerial status that survived with its status intact well into the post-Conquest period. The text shows no signs of interrupted tenure between Ralph the staller and Count Alan. In all probability Ralph's sub-comital authority in Lincolnshire – where no earl was appointed after 1066 – was acquired by Alan soon after Ralph's death in 1069/70, after he had been granted Eadgifu's lands and before he received the Yorkshire lands of Ælfgar's son Earl Edwin of Mercia, sometime after the latter's death in 1071.

The lands of Ralph de Gael in Norfolk and Suffolk

In Lincolnshire Alan clearly succeeded Ralph the staller by taking over the lands held by sake and soke, i.e. antecession. The forfeiture of Ralph II, his son, was a different kettle of fish, but nonetheless led to a reassignment of his lands on the basis of his right at the moment of his forfeiture. Much of the account of Norfolk and Suffolk in Little Domesday reads like a game of musical chairs. The status quo when the music stopped – i.e. when Ralph was declared forfeit – determined the assignment of landed right thereafter. The so-called Earls' Revolt of 1075 which led to Ralph's forfeiture is key to understanding the composition of much of Alan's holdings in East Anglia and Essex.[66]

Ralph I appears to have died after Easter 1069, and before the deposition of Bishop Æthelmaer on 11 April 1070 and thereafter Ralph II was made earl of Norfolk and Suffolk, apparently because of his English ancestry.[67] There has been

---

[64] D. Roffe, 'Hidden Lives: English Lords in post-Conquest Lincolnshire and Beyond', in *The English and Their Legacy 900–1200*, ed. Roffe, 205–28; GDB, 337v, 347v, 348v, 370, 370v; LIN 1,7.12,48;52;55;91–2.67.
[65] *EYC*, V, 11, 255–8.
[66] As it probably is to understanding LDB itself: see the arguments by Ian Taylor, this volume, and Lucy Marten, 'Lordship and Land'.
[67] ASC D 1075; Marten, 'Lordship and Land', 236.

an assumption that the holdings of the two Ralphs passed from father to son, and in many instances in Norfolk and Suffolk there is direct evidence that this was so.[68] For family property this would be expected, but it was not necessarily the case where tenure related to the exercise of an office such as staller or earl.[69] Examining the Domesday text for clues about the status of the tenures attributed to these earls and their successors is the only means we have of distinguishing family from ministerial lands. Much of it was bookland, which often makes a distinction very difficult for offices of middling rank. For comital lands, though, the clues are usually clearer; the statement that Sporle and Swaffham, held by Ralph the staller in 1066, had belonged to the royal demesne indicates that these are likely to have been grants *ex officio* by King Edward.[70] The holdings of other members of the family, Ralph the staller's brother Godwin and nephew Alsi, and his younger son Hardwin, might represent heritable bookland, but in Suffolk, where men of these common names are specifically identified, the holdings are either commendations or usurpations.[71]

Closely related, Godwin *avunculus Radulfi comitis* and *Alsi nepotis Radulfi comitis* were not necessarily father and son, and there is no certain case of a direct succession from one to the other. In Norfolk Godwin held a carucate in Brundall under the patronage of Earl Gyrth; after King William came it was held by Earl Ralph (I); Alsi had held 2 carucates in Thelveton of the king; both were held by Gilbert Arbalaster in 1086.[72] Robert de Verly succeeded to Godwin's holdings at Burnham Thorpe and Field Dalling after 1075; in Burnham Godwin had been succeeded by Ralph II sometime before 1075.[73] Godwin survived the Conquest by at least three years since that was when he usurped Godric the steward's holding at Quidenham under the abbey of Bury St Edmunds, held by Godric for the king in 1086.[74] A Godwin the thegn had also held manors at Sall, Saxthorpe, Mannington, Lessingham, and Palling, all of them the king's manors in Godric's keeping in 1086.[75] Godwin was also a predecessor of Isaac, a man of Ralph II who survived his lord's fall and held a modest tenancy-in-chief in Suffolk in 1086.[76] Alsi had free men commended to

---

[68] Unambiguous examples are very few: LDB, 409v: SFK 31,53.
[69] Stephen Baxter and John Blair, 'Land Tenure and Royal Patronage in the Early English Kingdom', *ANS* 28, 2005, 19–46.
[70] LDB, 119v, 144: NFK 1,71.4,1.
[71] LDB, 131v: NFK 1,185 (Sall). The probable estates of Ralph II's cousin Alsi and his uncle Godwin have been reconstructed by Ann Williams and John Palmer: Williams, *The English*, 61–2; Palmer, Ids dataset, Alsi [nephew of Earl Ralph]. Both seem to favour the view that Alsi was a son of Godwin, which I rather doubt.
[72] LDB, 269: NFK 52,3–4.
[73] LDB, 262: NFK 38,2–3; *In Bruneham Torp tenuit Goduinus tempore regis Edwardi et postea Radulfus quando se foris fecit 1 carucatam terre.*
[74] LDB, 127v: NFK 1,144.
[75] LDB, 132v, 133v, 134: NFK 1,193–4;198;200.
[76] LDB, 264: NFK 47,3;5–6. Isaac's lands were subsequently held for a serjeanty as king's jester (Keats-Rohan, *Domesday People*, 281; Marten, 'Lordship and Land', 251).

him in Old Newton and Gislingham; he was probably the Alsi who with his wife held Gislingham in laenage from the abbot of St Edmunds, as well as the commendation of eight men.[77] The agreement in respect of Gislingham was that after their deaths the manor, with another of the couple's manors, at Euston, should revert to the abbey. In 1086 Gislingham was held by Gilbert Arbalaster but Euston was held by Adelund from the abbey.[78] Under the land in Norfolk formerly held by Ralph II and administered by Godric on behalf of the king in 1086 is the manor of Cantley, which an Alsi had held from Ralph II; Alsi a thegn of King Edward had held Fersfield.[79] Sixteen free men of Alsi held in Limpenhoe under Earl Ralph I, and Godwin uncle of Earl Ralph II held Sall before 1066; the soke of nine and a half sokemen there was in the king's manor of Foulsham.[80] These entries and those connecting them in the text all show succession from Ralph I to Ralph II and therefore relate to comital land. Probably the same Alsi held the manor of Market Weston which also passed to Robert de Verly.[81] Another member of the family was the younger Ralph's brother Hardwin, whose holdings in Norfolk passed to William de Ecouis, consisting mainly in Witchingham and commendations in Repps, Limpenhoe, Plumstead, and Stokesby, where he is shown as active before 1066.[82] William also acquired Hardwin's holdings in Suffolk at Blakenham, Weston, and Cookley, where his primary *antecessor* was the thegn Ælfric.[83] Two other manors probably associated with the same Hardwin were acquired by Ralph de Limesy at Didlington, and at Brundon in Essex, on the Suffolk border.[84] None of the occurrences of Hardwin shows that his tenements were held or acquired before 1066, possibly because he was a younger son of Ralph I and not old enough to hold earlier.[85] If there ever had been a core family estate behind all this, it was comprehensively broken up by Ralph's forfeiture in 1075 and its consequences, which swept this briefly influential family completely from view.

Where was Count Alan in 1075? One of the oddities of the 1075 revolt is that disquiet or disobedience or some such had been trailed before the main event, since the regent Archbishop Lanfranc was well aware of it, and indeed had reported it to the king, then on the continent, assuring him that there was no need to return home. Some sources allege that the problem began when Earl Ralph wanted to marry the sister of the young Earl Roger of Hereford and was refused permission by the king.

---

[77] LDB, 350v, 321, 324, 374: SFK 8,50.6,216;233.16,12.
[78] LDB, 367v, 444v: SFK 14,98.68,5.
[79] LDB, 130v, 276, 279v: NFK 1,174–181.66,61;102.
[80] LDB, 122v, 123, 131, 131v: NFK 1,94–5; 185 (Alsi), 96 (Hassingham, refers to Ralph I becoming earl after 1066).
[81] LDB, 437: SFK, 60,1; Williams, *The English*, 62 n.
[82] LDB, 223v, 224v, 224: NFK 19,32; LDB, 223v, 224v, 235: NFK 19,20;27–8;32;36.
[83] LDB, 353: SFK 9,1–3.
[84] LDB, 245: NFK 28,2: *Dudelingatuna tenuit Hardwinus*. LDB, 90v: ESS 49,1.
[85] As suggested by Ann Williams in *The English*, 62–3 and n.78.

The marriage took place anyway in the manor of Exning, in Cambridgeshire, on the Suffolk border, according to John of Worcester.[86] No doubt it was originally a royal manor that Eadgifu owed to a grant by Harold. The count's steward Wihomarc held a second tenement there of the count in 1086; Ailsi a man of Eadgifu had held the land in 1066 and could withdraw. If this was indeed the venue for the wedding one can see that a statement of some sort was being made. The Anglo-Saxon Chronicle puts the wedding at Norwich, which is where the final act in the drama was played out, but the chronicler states unequivocally that the king had given permission for the wedding. Chris Lewis has suggested that dissatisfaction with their honours may have been the basis for the discontent evidenced by the earls.[87] Roger of Hereford had been restricted to a reduced portion of the English lands his father Earl William had held, and none of the Norman lands. Earl Ralph, who probably profited handsomely from the fall of Stigand and his family in East Anglia, had seen his father's lands in Lincolnshire go straight to Count Alan, who also dominated Cambridgeshire. Earl Waltheof had done rather better than he might have expected, given the fate of all other English earls; he held the counties of Huntingdonshire and Northamptonshire, with Bamburgh, a part of Northumbria, and he had married the king's niece despite having fought against the Normans in York in 1069, but he held less than had his ancestors the earls of Northumbria. His honour recognizably survived his execution in the hands of his wife Judith. He was named as her *antecessor* in estates in Leicestershire, Northamptonshire, Rutland, Essex, and Middlesex, and the names of his men occur regularly in her *breves*.[88] For all this, though, the scale and value of Waltheof and Judith's fief in Cambridgeshire was dwarfed by that of Count Alan and his *antecessor* Eadgifu *Pulchra*. Could it be that the dominance of Count Alan in Cambridgeshire, as well as his acquisition of formerly comital manors in Lincolnshire and Suffolk, were part of the itch that the revolt was designed to scratch?[89]

---

[86] See Williams, *The English*, 66–7; Lucy Marten, 'The Rebellion of 1075 and its Impact in East Anglia', in *Medieval East Anglia*, ed. C. Harper-Bill, Woodbridge 2005, 168–82.

[87] Christopher Lewis, 'The Early Earls of Norman England', *ANS* 13, 1990, 207–23.

[88] Godwin *scild* (whom we have already met as Godwin *cild*, a man of Eadgifu), Tuffa, Wulfric, Sbern, a free man, Stric, and Almaer: GDB, 236: LEI 40,1–7; LDB, 92: ESS 55,1 (the single but valuable manor of Walthamstow); GDB, 228–v: NTH 56,1–6;20;22;39; GDB, 293v: RUT 2,7;11;12; GDB, 130v: MDX 24,1. For Godwin, see Palmer, Ids dataset, Godwin [the Noble]. On Judith and her mother Adelaide of Aumale in relation to the conquest settlement, K. S. B. Keats-Rohan, 'Portrait of a People', in *Domesday Book*, ed. Hallam and Bates, 137–40.

[89] In Norfolk the comital manors were Costessey, a manor of Earl Gyrth, LDB, 144v, 145–v: NFK 4,9–15; Swaffham, given to Ralph the staller, LDB, 144: NFK 4,1; Bylaugh, held by the staller before 1066, LDB, 147: SFK 4,30, but it seems likely that these manors came to Alan as part of the division between him and the king after Ralph II's fall. Demesne tithes in Costessey and Swaffham were granted by Count Stephen to Rumburgh c. 1135 (*EYC*, V, 12–13); note 46 above.

It is easy to sympathize with Lanfranc's 'stupid boy' view of Roger, who certainly seems more of a bit player in view of the more serious threat posed by the disaffection of Ralph and Waltheof, with their Danish allies off the eastern coast. The later execution of Waltheof and his unofficial veneration as a local saint make understanding his motives all but impossible. Two later chroniclers both chose to explain events through the lens of a well-known biblical story. The author of the mid twelfth-century Warenne (Hyde) Chronicle based his account on the story of Absalom, the ungrateful son of King David, alleging that Waltheof, who had been fully engaged against the Normans in the Revolt of the North in 1069, never lost his burning rage against them, in spite of the grant of lands and a royal bride by William.[90] A similar strategy was employed by Orderic Vitalis, this time using the story of Ahitophel, the evil counsellor of Absalom. Here the villain is Ahitophel, played by Earl Ralph. This is more interesting still because it is a thinly veiled attack on the legitimacy of William's rule. It takes the more usual view of the chroniclers that Waltheof was an innocent, even saintly victim of events, rather than a serial offender who patently could not be trusted. On the other hand Hyde abbey had suffered badly after Harold's death, perhaps because its abbot had been his relative and it had sent a contingent to the battle of Hastings. Isolated though it may be in its view of Waltheof, it is probably more realistic. The Anglo-Saxon Chronicle suggests that there was increasing irritation with a king who spent too much time – and English blood – fighting his wars on the continent, most recently settling unrest in the county of Maine, where he would have to return in the 1080s.[91] Englishmen such as Waltheof and Ralph II might well have expected their king to focus his primary attention on his kingdom. It may be that the idea of a three-fold division of the kingdom, harking back to the great earldoms of old, was their solution to the problem of governance in a kingdom of which the king was often absent. If so, it was unconvincing, and perhaps as perplexing to contemporaries as it is to us. Certainly, the revolt was short-lived and soon crushed because there was limited support and the main allies on the west and east coasts were prevented from meeting. Ralph was routed at Fawdon in Whaddon, Cambridgeshire – probably the part that Saevia had held under Eadgifu and that had been held by Earl Ralph on the day he rebelled.[92] In 1086 it was held by Richard fitzGilbert of Clare, whose aid in suppressing the revolt earned him his wide holdings in East Anglia.[93]

---

[90] *Liber Monasterii de Hyda*, ed. E. Edwards, RS 45, 1866, 294, recently re-edited as *The Warenne (Hyde) Chronicle*, ed. and trans. Elisabeth M. C. van Houts and Rosalind C. Love, Oxford, 2013, 24–5. Van Houts has shown that this chronicle was composed in response to Henry II's action in depriving King Stephen's son William and his wife Isabella de Warenne of part of the former king's estates awarded to them in the treaty of 1153; Elisabeth van Houts, 'The Warenne View of the Past 1066–1203', ANS 26, 2004, 103–22.
[91] Marten, 'Lordship and Land', 216–28.
[92] Williams, *The English*, 63; GDB, 196v: CAM 19,4.
[93] Marten, 'Lordship and Land', 253–4.

The revolt, as Lucy Marten has pointed out, is usually discussed in ethnic terms.[94] Contemporaries themselves bandied ethnonyms about. At the climax of his fury Lanfranc wrote to William that the kingdom had been purged of 'Breton dung' when Earl Ralph was forced to take flight after his failure, leaving his wife to face a three-month siege of Norwich castle before she was allowed to leave unharmed and follow him into exile. Marten has claimed that this is the only example of outright 'ethnic hostility' shown by one group to another.[95] But is it really? Both versions of the Anglo-Saxon Chronicle most unusually detailed a genealogy for Ralph, declaring him the son of an Englishman from Norfolk and a Breton woman. The point here is surely to emphasize his Englishness: 'Earl Ralph and Earl Roger were principals in this foolish plan, and they seduced the Bretons to them.' Hardly ethnic hostility. The Bretons were in fact the most loyal of the Norman kings' subjects, maybe partly because they had much to lose. Even Count Alan was not well endowed in Brittany – his father had at least five legitimate sons – and most of the others came from very small lordships. The most significant among them was in fact Ralph II, whose seigneurie of Gaël first comes into full view on his return in 1075, shortly before he is found fighting against William at the siege of Dol (an event otherwise unrelated to those in England). Contemporaries were aware of ethnicity, as was hardly surprising in an England that had suffered two foreign conquests within fifty years. But ethnicity has always been a very flexible concept: what it might be used to define or memorialize one day could soon after be forgotten or completely reinvented.[96] Where borders were particularly porous, or emigration particularly common, such as north-eastern Brittany, south-western Normandy, and Maine, ethnonyms are common, though transient. They were usually soon dropped, leaving what I have termed 'ancestral origins' to be evidenced only through repeated onomastic patterns, such as the names in the family of Judhael of Totnes.[97] In the case of the earls of Norfolk, we might never have known of their origin had Ralph not rebelled: the first 'Breton' name evidenced in his family was that of his son Alan, who accompanied his parents on the First Crusade in 1097. Some of the men who fell with him had more distinctively Breton names, such as Eudo son of Clamarhoc and Wihenoc.[98] What is significant, surely, is that Ralph II had a view of himself as an Englishman with acquired rights in England and English government, and also

---

[94] Marten, 'Lordship and Land', 231.
[95] Marten, 'Lordship and Land', 228; her supporting page reference to Hugh Thomas, *The English and the Normans, Ethnic Hostility, Assimilation and Identity 1066–c. 1220*, Oxford 2003, should be to p. 40.
[96] As my study of the prosopography of the Thorney abbey *Liber Vitae* shows (forthcoming).
[97] Keats-Rohan, *Domesday People*, 41–3, 285–6. A particularly striking example, he was son and father of an Alfred, a favoured Breton name, and father also of Aanor, a distinctive Breton form of Eleanor. Wherever he started from in 1066, he certainly had Breton ancestors.
[98] Discussed in Keats-Rohan, 'Le rôle des Bretons', 182–5, 209–10.

as a Breton. In neither role was he likely to take kindly to being upstaged by his contemporary Count Alan, his social superior in Brittany and the king's kinsman.

If jealousy or resentment of Alan's implantation in the east had played any part in the actions of Ralph II and Waltheof, it proved a costly miscalculation. Alan was further enriched by Ralph's fall in 1075, and his status was fully recognized by the division of Earl Ralph's lands between himself and the king. He was, and had long been, the most senior Breton in England, and was evidently the figurehead of the group, as his attestation of the Monmouth priory charters shows.[99] It seems unlikely that he was in England in 1075, rather than with William on the continent. Lanfranc's language about 'Breton dung' was intemperate in view of the importance of Alan and his relationship to the king. It is more than likely, though, that Alan would have agreed with him about Ralph. Alan's loyalty, like that of his brothers and successors in the reign of William II, proved unshakeable, and his rewards were well deserved.

Richmondshire

William came back to England in the autumn of 1075 and it was possibly then that Alan received the grant of Richmondshire in Yorkshire, though it could have been acquired as early as 1072 or as late as 1080. In 1086 it formed over 35% of the landed extent of his honour, and about 16% of its value.[100] What is clear from the Domesday account of his Yorkshire fee is that Alan must at some time have invested a good deal of personal time and effort in overseeing the organization of his fee there. Not for him the absenteeism and alienation to others most markedly shown in the fees of Count Robert of Mortain and Earl Hugh of Chester. Apart from that, the process of implantation in Richmondshire both shared the main characteristics of other Yorkshire tenancies-in-chief and differed from all of them in certain marked ways, as has been deftly demonstrated by Paul Dalton.[101] This very compact lordship comprising lands previously held by fifty-four thegns as clients of the earls of Northumbria, constituted a castelry of 199 manors, with 40 additional manors, in 1086. It was based around two large and complex manors in particular, those of Gilling and Catterick, both of them former holdings of Earl Edwin and probable administrative centres of the wapentakes of Gilling, Hang, and Hallikeld. There is evidence for four earthwork castles in the castelry, at Catterick, Killerby (in Catterick), Kirkby Fleetham, and Ravensworth. It is unlikely that building of the great castle at Richmond had begun, though perhaps a stone circuit replacing the earl's hall at Gilling had been built at the future Richmond in order to secure the

---

[99] *Regesta*, Bates, nos. 268 and 270.
[100] Jeulin, 'Aperçus', 270.
[101] Dalton, *Conquest, Anarchy and Lordship*, 39–40, 42–7, 66–7, 71, 73–4, 90, 99, 114–17, 144.

Swale crossing.¹⁰² The place was still called *Hindrelaghe* in Domesday Book; when constructed the castle seems to have been part of a designed castle borough.

The tenurial as well as geographical coherence of this vast complex strongly suggests its origin in a pre-Conquest estate, in the same way as Alan's holdings in Lincolnshire and the various holdings of Eadgifu, most notably in Cambridgeshire. The impression is reinforced by the way that the Gilling and Catterick estates interlocked with Earl Edwin's third great manor of Northallerton, held in 1086 by the king. In Yorkshire as in Alan's lands elsewhere, the principle of antecession is clear.¹⁰³ Equally clear is that whilst a newcomer might be given the estate of one or more *antecessores* in order to create a new honour, often with a distinct strategic purpose in mind, as was certainly true of Richmondshire, where Gilling and Catterick formed the core of the pre- and post-Conquest 'castelry' of Richmondshire, the lands of those *antecessores* could themselves represent both ancient estates and entities that had also been created with strategic purpose in more recent times, as again is true of Richmond. In Alan's Yorkshire holdings he had multiple *antecessores* and the principle can even be demonstrated among the honorial barony. Enisan, whose fifteen knights' fees were later known as the Constable's fee, was given the lands of Thorr, whilst Bodin held the lands of Thorfinnr; both these king's thegns are named among those few who had held with sake and soke in Yorkshire in 1066.¹⁰⁴ Bodin also had the land of Ulfketill at Broughton and in Newsham, where Ulfketill had had a hall; in the latter Sprottr had also held a hall, which went to Count Alan.¹⁰⁵ The count also took the land of Gospatric in Dalton, leaving Thorfinnr's land there to Bodin; Gospatric still held another manor there as he had in 1066.¹⁰⁶ Bodin's land afterwards formed the Bedale fee, divided sometime after his withdrawal into religion into the Bedale and Ravensworth fees.¹⁰⁷ Enisan's lands were also later divided, because he apparently left two daughters at his death, one of whom married Roald fitzHarscoit and was ancestor of a line of constables of Richmond stretching well into the thirteenth century. Enisan was probably responsible for the ringwork castle at Pickhill.¹⁰⁸ Gospatric was the son of Arnketill, a rebel in 1068 who had

---

¹⁰² GDB, 309v, 310v: YKS 6N26,31;52;56; C. Constable, 'Aspects of the Archaeology of the Castle in the North of England c. 1066–1216', unpublished PhD thesis, Durham University 2003; L. Butler, 'The Origins of the Honour of Richmond and its Castles', *Château-Gaillard* 16, 1955, 353–98, reprinted in *Anglo-Norman Castles*, ed. R. Liddiard, Woodbridge 2003, 91–104.
¹⁰³ GDB, 299: YKS 1Y2; Dalton, *Conquest, Anarchy and Lordship*, 73.
¹⁰⁴ Enisan, GDB, 309–313: YKS 6N6–8;12–16;18–25;64;66;68;104;109;122;136 (unnamed); 145–6; Bodin, GDB, 309–11: YKS 6N7;11;18;38–44;47;50–1;67;73;75;78; 80;86;91;135.
¹⁰⁵ GDB, 310: YKS 6N45–6.
¹⁰⁶ GDB, 310: YKS 6N47–8.
¹⁰⁷ Of five and three fees respectively: *EYC*, V, 196–200.
¹⁰⁸ Butler, 'The Honour of Richmond', 102.

given his son as a hostage to King William. He was the only thegn who held land as a tenant-in-chief in Yorkshire in 1086, as well as nineteen other tenements held of the count. Subsequently most of his land was held as mesne tenancies in the steward's fee of the honour of Richmond, but he was ancestor of a number of local families, including the Hebden, Thoresby, Staveley, and Mohaut families.[109] The steward's fee was one of the great fees of the honour, but most of it lay in Cambridgeshire, indicating that it was one of the earliest. In Yorkshire, Wihomarc had just three tenements, two of them, at Aske Hall and Harmby, previously held by the thegn Thorr.[110]

Another tenant, Picot of Lascelles, succeeded Gillepatric and Halldorr, who had each had a hall in Solberge; Picot and Count Alan had half the land each.[111] The count's half-brother Ribald also took a number of Gillepatric's manors, which later formed the Middleham fee.[112] Ribald probably built the earliest castle there, a ringwork at William's Hill.[113] The patterns are so regular that the names can be supplied of the three knights who held of the count in Patrick Brompton in succession to Gille[patric] and Thorfinrr, who had halls, i.e. Ribald and Bodin, and Gospatric in succession to Arnketil who had not had a hall there.[114] Of the three unnamed knights with tenures in Hesselton formerly held by Orm and Thorfinnr, one was Enisan, and one of the others will have been Bodin.[115] Thorfinnr has been described by Chris Lewis as an important thegn, the most important landowner in western Yorkshire, his lands dominating the tops of all the Yorkshire dales. Moreover, he had lands in the north-west in Amounderness, mostly waste in 1086, which passed to the king, and in Craven which were given to Roger of Poitou. The creation of this assemblage was down to Earl Tostig (1055–65), who thus made Thorfinnr responsible for oversight of a section of the Pennines that had been used by Viking, Scots, and Cumbrian raiders for centuries. He was 'guardian of the Vale of York'.[116] Torfinnr and Thorr still held their land, and presumably its strategic function, in 1066 and indeed to the point where it was given to Count Alan. The exact date cannot be determined, but the coherence of the tenancies already created by Alan in the parts of the honour settled earlier meant that he had men ready to be slotted

---

[109] GDB, 310v–313: YKS 6N61–2;65;67;70;72;79;89;112;113;116–18;135;149–50.
[110] GDB, 310v, 311v: YKS 6N57;100;101.
[111] GDB, 309v: YKS 6N28–9.
[112] GDB, 311: YKS 6N90;94;99;102.
[113] Butler, 'The Honour of Richmond', 101.
[114] GDB, 312v: YKS 6N137.
[115] GDB, 312: YKS 6N136; cf. *EYC*, V, 83, 298.
[116] C. Lewis, 'Introduction to Domesday Lancashire', in *The Lancashire Domesday*, ed. A. Williams and G. H. Martin, London 1991, 1–41 at 33–4. His precise identity is unknown, though Lewis notes the possibility that he may the Thorfinnr son of Thore granted rights by either Gospatric I or II of Northumbria in the mid eleventh century (*Anglo-Saxon Writs*, ed. F. E. Harmer, Manchester 1952, 419–24).

in to these more testing holdings. Maintaining good relations with the English tenantry was presumably key to his success.

Alan could have received his Yorkshire fee soon after the death of Earl Edwin in 1071. In his blitzkrieg of 1072 William had marched into Scotland and taken homage from King Malcolm. The issue was that Edgar Ætheling and his sisters had taken refuge at Malcolm's court. They embodied the last of the Old English royal line. Malcolm would marry one of them, Margaret, the mother of the future queen Edith-Matilda of England, wife of Henry I. William then bustled off back to the Continent. Starting the process of mastering the North before he went abroad would have been a shrewd move. The origins of the compact post-Conquest castelries of Yorkshire may well date to this time. The honour of Richmond was created in order to secure the northern borders from its dominating position in Swaledale, developing, in conjunction with Roger of Poitou's holdings in Craven, a beefed-up version of the role assigned previously to their *antecessor* Torfinnr. To maintain it fit for purpose required the dedication of some time and thought. Alan's strategy involved the family firm of his three half-brothers (Ribald, Bodin and Bardulf) and a brother-in-law, Enisan, who shaped the key military (constable's) fees of the combined honour of Richmond, the 'household' fees of the chamberlain and steward having been created earlier, based on the lands of Eadgifu. There was, of course, a practical estate management aspect as well, most notably in the development of the estates in the fertile lowland eastern part of the shire, leaving the rugged uplands of the west, probably also ravaged during the Harrying of the North in 1070, largely as waste. It is often said that the higher incidence of English and Anglo-Scandinavian tenants surviving in the North is an indication of the relative lateness of Norman implantation in a notoriously restive area, meaning that infeudations proceeded more slowly. Perhaps, but not necessarily so. In such rural and unpopulous areas a reliance on the native English was a necessity. Several Yorkshire lordships, including Richmond, tended to concentrate enfeoffment nearer their chief manors and their castles, leaving the rugged and potentially treacherous outliers as waste. Alan's demesne manors were all close to York; his tenanted manors all lay within the manors of the castelry, within a 10-mile radius of the probable castle sites mentioned above.[117]

Continuities and conclusions

In the case of the honour of Richmond, the English had tenures from the beginning, often either continuing from 1066 or in succession to the holder in 1066; in many cases they were able to pass them on to their own heirs. More unusually still, they not only acquired household offices, like Ralph son of Meldred of Middleton,

---

[117] Dalton, *Conquest, Anarchy and Lordship*, 74, 116.

a chamberlain of Earl Conan c. 1160, but they also travelled with the counts to Brittany.[118] Alan himself put the seal on his English undertaking by being buried at Bury St Edmunds in Suffolk, an abbey with which he had numerous tenurial connections through his *antecessor* Eadgifu.[119] In due course, though, the monks of St Mary's, York, would reclaim the count's remains as their own. In a departure from the principle of antecession, whether of all or part of an individual's sokeright, Alan had been given the church of St Olave in York and the manor of Clifton once held by Earl Morcar by a writ of the king c.1074x85.[120] Before 1086, towards the end of his life, he used this grant as the core foundation of St Mary's. After his death in 1093 the abbey was re-founded and substantially endowed by William II, who claimed Alan as 'after me and my father the beginner and founder of this abbey'.[121]

There have been many suggestions that marriage between the incomers and the English was used to legitimize the new tenures. This proves hard to document. Even in the cases where such marriages occurred, the point can hardly have been legitimization *per se*. William claimed to be the legitimate ruler of the country, and his disinheritance of those who had supported his predecessor was in that circumstance right and proper. Repeated studies of Domesday fees have tended to confirm overwhelmingly the principle of antecession, even where new estates were being created for strategic purposes, such as the Sussex Rapes and the marcher lordships. The Domesday inquest established exactly who had what and through whom. Only after that could a principle of heritability be established. Marriages created personal alliances and extended personal influence. In the higher echelons of society they could be a diplomatic minefield. Waltheof alone of the revolting earls lost his head because he had betrayed his lord after having married into his family. His widow retained his lands because it suited the king to use his daughters to transfer them to more reliable men. Where the results of marriages were inconvenient, such as a single daughter for one of the most powerful and important men in the turbulent North, Count Alan, she could simply be passed over for a competent male successor, having been allowed to make a token grant of her family's land to St Mary's, York. 'Peaceweaving' marriages such as that between Wigod of Wallingford's daughter and Robert d'Oilly may have created fond illusions among the families involved, but the king was not bound by them, and we should not exaggerate their significance. In this respect the language of antecession, referring as it does to inheritance (*inhaeredo*), has confused the issue. Much more important for the uncovering of a wide range of relationships, whether biological, tenurial or ties of personal dependency,

---

[118] *EYC*, IV, 168.
[119] Sharpe, 'King Harold', 8 n.33.
[120] *Regesta*, Bates, no. 8.
[121] Dalton, *Conquest, Anarchy and Lordship*, 137. We await the new edition of Abbot Stephen's account of the foundation of the abbey by Richard Sharpe, forthcoming in the Surtees Society collections.

is detailed attention to the language of lordship in Domesday Book, whether at the micro level of individual estates, as demonstrated here by David Roffe and Ann Williams, or at the macro level of whole honours such as Richmond. This is where the full power of antecession as the primary legal basis of the post-Conquest settlement awaits discovery.

Anselm's infamous letter to Gunhilda unintentionally revealed that the marriage between Count Alan and the daughter of Harold was long and happy, but the far more important facts about the nature and composition of Alan's tenures, how acquired and through whom, can only be revealed by probing the text of Domesday Book.[122] Of the three principal components, the first of them was essentially a high-status collection of family lands belonging to Eadgifu, enhanced by what had been given to her by Earl Harold. The second and third components were both strategic in nature, especially in Yorkshire, and both were associated with the military and administrative authority of earls and their men. Alan's primary *antecessores* here were (Earl) Ralph the staller in Lincolnshire, and in Yorkshire Earl Edwin and a number of important thegns who had probably been clients of Edwin's predecessor Earl Tostig as well as himself. There is no doubt whatever that antecession underpinned all the estates that made up the honour, despite its diverse make-up, and whatever the date of the grant of Richmondshire. This was not only an important means of ensuring the legality of the new tenurial landscape, it ensured that it remained recognizably located in the past, because estates were by and large retained intact, supporting many of the pre-Conquest social structures. Richmondshire had a distinctive composition, but it was largely a pre-Conquest English creation for defensive purposes adapted in post-Conquest circumstances for the same purpose. Throughout the honour the chief demesne manors in the principal centres have been shown to have been the sites of early castles and hence of estate management.

Because of the clarity of the antecession principle in the lands derived from Eadgifu, as well as those deriving from the former earls of East Anglia, it has been possible to make identifications among the English named in Domesday Book, a still relatively under-studied group, and several more could have been added if space allowed. A more or less complete prosopography of Domesday Book is possible if we accept that some individuals may never be more than names attached to a specific tenurial context, that clumping several name records together under one heading is an onomastic not a prosopographic exercise, and that a prosopography of Domesday will not and cannot read like an Almanach de Gotha. Prosopography is not an exercise in family reconstruction, though that will be part of it. It is about understanding social dynamics from the nature of the connexions between members of a group at all social levels. If we learn to decode Domesday formulae, to study

---

[122] Sharpe, 'King Harold', 6–14.

them systematically, we will have much of what we need to understand the social structures underpinning the pre-Conquest estates and their honorial successors thereafter.

As was true of all tenants-in-chief, Alan's authority and wealth derived from English *antecessores* and was embedded in local society, without which it could not have been sustained. Domesday shows that Alan frequently retained English tenants on their lands, and could rely on them to plead his cause when legal challenges were mounted to his right. A number of plausible identifications of the English, often with common names, in his honour can be made by tracing links between what they held or had held in the honour to other parts of the same manors. This not only reveals the names of many king's thegns that might otherwise be lost, it also shows these men – and women – holding in multiple ways with multiple roles. The glue that bound together the tenancies-in-chief of the top-level tenurial revolution was the legal principle of sokeright. The complex and diverse relationships between thegns and their men that Domesday occasionally allows us to glimpse ensured the success of the transition from one tenurial elite to another without the trauma of revolution. In the case of the honour of Richmond we can see this with unusual clarity because the English retained at least modest holdings in each of the main constituent parts of the honour throughout the period from c. 1068x69 to 1086 and beyond.

8

The Episcopal Returns in Domesday

Pamela Taylor

THIS PAPER IS a preliminary exploration of the Domesday returns for bishops with English sees in the light of current debates around written returns. The bishops held estates in every Domesday county except Rutland and some of their endowments, unlike the recent assemblages of the bishops of Norman sees, provide examples of associated private hundreds.[1] They were also routinely involved in local government (far more so than even the best-placed abbots) and therefore well placed to negotiate the whole inquest process with maximum efficiency. Two examples of effectively unaltered returns, those of Bishop Wulfstan of Worcester for Oswaldslow and Abbot Baldwin of Bury within Suffolk, include some highly tendentious claims, but it is unhelpful to conflate two distinct issues.[2] Embedded returns, contrary to knee-jerk assumption, need not reflect manipulation, and in challenging this assumption the paper also contributes to the wider debates around forgery.[3] Instead of focussing yet again on Oswaldslow, 'some of the most blood-stained acres in English medieval historiography', it examines other

---

[1] Durham and Lincoln had estates in Witchley, a hundred that was later transferred from Northants to Rutland: *Domesday Book:* Rutland, ed. Frank Thorn, Chichester 1980, Notes (unpaginated).
[2] Registering the Oswaldslow return's exceptionality goes back at least to F. W. Maitland, *Domesday Book and Beyond*, Cambridge 1897, reprinted in differently paginated editions but indexed; for major recent comment, Patrick Wormald, 'Oswaldslow: an "Immunity"?', in *St Oswald of Worcester: Life and Influence*, ed. N. P. Brooks and C. Cubitt, Leicester 1996, 117–28; Stephen Baxter, 'The Representation of Lordship and Land Tenure in Domesday Book', in *Domesday Book*, ed. Elizabeth Hallam and David Bates, Stroud 2001, 73–102; Ann Williams, 'The Spoliation of Worcester', *ANS* 19, 1996, 388–408. On Bury, Baxter, 'Representation of Lordship', 93; John Palmer, this volume; Lucy Marten, personal communication; *Bury St Edmunds and the Norman Conquest*, ed. Tom Licence, Woodbridge 2014.
[3] For the need for care both in deploying the term forgery and in avoiding anachronistic reliance on formal documentary typologies, see David Bates, 'The Abbey and the Norman Conquest: An Unusual Case?', in *Bury*, ed. Licence, 5–21.

exceptional episcopal returns and their local administrative context.[4] The results suggest very few unaltered returns and no necessary relationship between any that exist and manipulation. On manipulation the paper ends by examining Archbishop Lanfranc's silence around TRE tenures.

That written returns were submitted to the Domesday inquests is uncontroversial.[5] Oral testimony remained supremely important but given the requirements for detail and the known deployment of written geld rolls it would be remarkable if those tenants-in-chief who were routinely using written documentation had not done so here.[6] The degree of writing probably varied between bishoprics but Worcester was certainly not alone.[7] The bishops, recruits from Normandy and Conquest survivors alike, were also keyed into general administration. The standard route to a see was via a spell in the royal household, in some cases as chancellor; nor was this a post-Conquest phenomenon, as the career of Giso of Wells (1061–88) amply demonstrates.[8] All immediately found themselves at least in theory presiding with the sheriffs in the shire courts and receiving the attendant writs, which presumably means that they were automatically involved in the first, county-based stages of the inquest.[9] The later teams deliberately sent to localities away from their own

---

[4] The phrase is Wormald's, 'Oswaldslow: an "Immunity"?', 117.

[5] V. H. Galbraith, *The Making of Domesday Book*, Oxford 1961, 65; David Roffe, *Decoding Domesday*, Woodbridge 2007, 87; Baxter, 'Representation of Lordship'; Sally Harvey, *Domesday. Book of Judgement*, Oxford 2014, 58–63; Palmer, this volume. David Roffe's severance in *Domesday: the Inquest and the Book* (hereafter *DIB*), Oxford 2000, and subsequently of the initial link between the inquests and Domesday Book is not considered here.

[6] On the geld rolls, see especially Sally Harvey, 'Domesday Book and its Predecessors', *EHR* 86, 1971, 753–73; Harvey, *Domesday*; Ann Williams, *VCH Dorset*, III, 1968.

[7] See below plus, for Durham and Exeter, A. J. Robertson, *Anglo-Saxon Charters*, Cambridge 1956, App. I. For the potentially comparable Carolingian commitment to the written word 'for communication, administration and record' see Rosamond McKitterick, *The Carolingians and the Written Word*, Cambridge 1989, especially 23–36. Patrick Wormald, 'Charters, Law and the Settlement of Dispute in Anglo-Saxon England', in *The Settlement of Disputes in Early Medieval Europe*, ed. Wendy Davies and Paul Fouracre, Cambridge 1986, 149–68, refers to 'England's Carolingian prelates' (p. 157) and stresses the role of the shire courts and the importance placed on written documents in recording and resolving disputes. Bates, 'The Abbey and the Norman Conquest', locates the process of making the Domesday texts 'within the documentary culture of the medieval West', drawing particular attention to the Carolingian polyptych as one such aspect.

[8] Galbraith, *Making of Domesday Book*, 50; H. R. Loyn, 'William's Bishops: Some Further Thoughts', *ANS* 10, 1987, 223–35; Simon Keynes, 'Giso Bishop of Wells (1066–88)', *ANS* 19, 1996, 203–71.

[9] Loyn, 'William's Bishops', 224–5, stresses their shire involvement but discounts regular presiding in person; C. P. Lewis, 'The Early Earls of Norman England', *ANS* 13, 1990, 207–23 at 209–10, notes the benefits and relative ease of the twice yearly attendance TRE. Robin Fleming, *Domesday Book and the Law: Society and Legal Custom in Early Medieval England*, Cambridge 1998, 15, calls abbots and bishops 'the most practiced litigators in the kingdom'.

each seem to have included a bishop, probably Durham in circuit II, Salisbury in III, Lincoln in V.[10]

The interesting question is not whether written returns existed but whether or why a few survived unscathed into the Domesday texts. Against Galbraith's conviction that all were re-formed beyond recognition during the Domesday processes, the quest for survivors has continued and is now being encouraged by computer-powered analysis of vocabularies and formulae.[11] It has to be said, though, that while this analysis has confirmed the exceptionality of Oswaldslow and Bury and the likelihood of underlying layers of documentation, it has not thrown up other similar candidates.[12] Some proposals for written sources are also questionable. Historians with experience limited to literate societies easily underestimate the far greater range and detail of oral memory in widely illiterate cultures, and at the purely practical as well as the socially-constructed level.[13] Perhaps because of time spent in South Asia I am not, for instance, persuaded that knowledge that Histon in Cambridgeshire was one of 'the twelve demesne manors of the bishopric' of Lincoln, even though these were spread across six counties, bespeaks underlying documentation.[14]

To shade the picture and the linguistic analysis, partial survival often seems plausible. Subdivisions between demesne lands and those of the bishop's monks or knights have been taken to reflect written originals but regularly exist within otherwise standardized accounts. Special cases such as the bishop of Thetford's market in Hoxne or the bishop of Winchester's rights in Taunton (see below) might perhaps achieve partial incorporation. In Yorkshire the ordering of wapentakes and ridings and the formulae for ploughlands are inconsistent between fiefs, a pointer to unmodified returns, but those of the archbishop of York and bishop of Durham are otherwise obeying the common formulae.[15] Archbishop Thomas (1070–1100)

---

[10] Loyn, 'William's Bishops', 228–30; Roffe, *Decoding Domesday*, 70–1; Baxter, 'Representation of Lordship', 81–2. The division of labour between the two stages remains controversial.

[11] Galbraith, *Making of Domesday Book*, 64–6, 81–4, although previously in 'The Making of Domesday Book', *EHR* 57, 1942, 161–77 at 175, he said: 'Traces of such written returns remain, perhaps, in the Domesday accounts of the lands of the bishop of Hereford and of the church of Worcester'; Palmer, this volume.

[12] Baxter, 'Representation of Lordship', describes techniques but states (p. 79) that only 'in a very few instances' can traces of seigneurial returns 'be inferred'. Roffe, *Decoding Domesday*, 212, calls divergences such as Worcester 'conspicuous by their rarity'.

[13] On the latter see particularly James Fentress and Chris Wickham, *Social Memory*, Oxford 1992.

[14] GDB, 190: CAM 3,3. The suggestion is in John Blair, 'Estate Memoranda of *c.*1070 from the See of Dorchester-on-Thames', *EHR* 116, 2001, 114–23 at 121. For further notes of caution, Graham Loud, 'An Introduction to the Somerset Domesday', in *The Somerset Domesday*, ed. Ann Williams and R. W. H. Erskine, London 1989, 1–31 at 1–2.

[15] D. M. Palliser, 'An Introduction to the Yorkshire Domesday', in *The Yorkshire Domesday*, ed. Ann Williams and G. H. Martin, London 1992, 1–38. Pierre Chaplais, 'William of St

had his extensive privileges within York attested by local jurors, probably some years before the Domesday process, but the text is too different to be a forerunner and in Domesday his rights appear only in the general city section.[16]

One possible approach to the transmission of unaltered returns is via survivals from earlier stages.[17] A single scribe was responsible for effectively all of GDB, but the less-edited texts in Exon Domesday (covering most of the five south-western counties and superseded by GDB) and LDB (Essex, Norfolk and Suffolk and probably also intended for supercession) were produced by teams of scribes and have significant links to ecclesiastical scriptoria. We now know that Exon Domesday, in the incomplete form in which it survives, was produced either in whole or very substantial part at Salisbury by some of the canons and/or *familia* who were also copying numerous books for Bishop Osmund (1078–99).[18] It is especially interesting that Osmund was a former royal chancellor and that all the Salisbury productions reflect a general, often hastily written, group effort, the work of otherwise busy men, and it is unfortunate that the missing sections include the heartland estates at Sherborne. Nevertheless comparison between the Exon and Exchequer Domesdays shows removal of surplus detail on stock and tenants' names but nothing more structural.[19]

LDB is complete for the three counties that it covers. Here a number of centres, and scribes, seem to have been involved and it has been mooted that Bury's unusual return may have been written up in the abbey's own scriptorium.[20] That said, LDB contains no Bury-trained scribal hand (although the abbey may of course have included scribes whose training had been elsewhere) and LDB's lines are ruled consistently throughout.[21] It has also been suggested that the high registration of disputes in Essex could be connected with 'the possible role of St Paul's, another house with a recent "Chancellor" as presiding bishop' in drafting what became

---

Calais and the Domesday Survey', in *Domesday Studies*, ed. J. Holt, Woodbridge 1987, 65–78, suggested William, bishop of Durham (1081–96) as the mastermind behind Domesday, but the evidence is insecure, cf. Frank and Caroline Thorn, 'The Writing of GDB', in *Domesday Book*, ed. Hallam and Bates, 37–72 at 71. William had Domesday estates across many counties but most were TRW acquisitions.

[16] GDB, 302v–304v: YKS landholders 2–3; Palliser, 'Introduction', 4, 14.

[17] For a summary and historiography, Roffe, *Decoding Domesday*, ch. 2.

[18] Teresa Webber, 'Salisbury and the Exon Domesday: Some Observations Concerning the Origin of Exeter Cathedral MS 3500', in *English Manuscript Studies* 1, ed. P. Beal and J. Griffiths, Oxford 1989, 1–18; Teresa Webber, *Scribes and Scholars at Salisbury Cathedral c.1075–c.1125*, Oxford 1992. The see had been moved from Sherborne by Osmund.

[19] For the texts' relationship, see Williams, *VCH Dorset*, III, 2–6.

[20] A. R. Rumble, 'The Domesday Manuscripts: Scribes and Scriptoria', in *Domesday Studies*, ed. Holt, 79–99; for Bury, Baxter, 'Representation of Lordship', 93; Palmer, this volume; Lucy Marten, personal communication.

[21] Points made by Teresa Webber and Richard Sharpe in discussion about a paper at the 2012 Bury conference that was not included in the eventual book: *Bury*, ed. Licence.

LDB.²² This is, however, part of a general argument about Domesday and dispute settlement, with no implication that either St Paul's (involved in only one of the twenty-six disputes recorded for Essex) or Salisbury was favouring its own entries. Since the hundred order is well maintained through all the chapters in Essex and Norfolk, though less so in Suffolk, the freedom of the scriptoria was obviously restricted.²³ The estates of the bishops of London (in Essex) and Thetford (in Norfolk and Suffolk) were also spread across various hundreds, a limiting factor for the control of any written input.

Both bishops' returns nevertheless include subdivisions. Maurice (1085–1107) has a sub-section headed *Feudum episcopi Londoniensis*, basically the military sub-tenures created on newly acquired estates, and it could be significant that in Essex these are treated as a separate group while in tightly controlled Hertfordshire there are only scattered references across the chapter.²⁴ If there was a written return, it was presumably differently ordered.

Bishop William of Thetford (1085–91), another royal clerk, was promoted to a see whose previous incumbent (Herfast, 1070–84) had been chancellor.²⁵ In both Suffolk and Norfolk his entries are specifically divided between the TRE endowment and the *feudum*, in this case straightforwardly the TRW accessions.²⁶ In Suffolk the two parts are given separate rubricated numbers, 18 and 19, to tie to the later-added index, while in Norfolk the whole is within number 10, but this is simply the choice (or slip) of the rubricator. The Norfolk chapter also contains a third section, headed *de invasionibus eiusdem feudi*, many of whose forty-five or so entries make it crystal clear that the annexations were by, not against, the fee.²⁷ The section cannot therefore be reflecting either the bishop's interest or his own return, and there are also a couple of examples of disputes, and thus of inquest procedures, in the first two sections.²⁸

In Suffolk, in contrast, the entry for Hoxne, the head of Bishop's hundred and 'the episcopal seat of Suffolk TRE', contains an aggrieved account of the decline

---

²² Patrick Wormald, 'Domesday Lawsuits: a Provisional List', in *England in the Eleventh Century*, ed. Carola Hicks, Stamford 1992, 61–102 at 72.
²³ Galbraith, *Making of Domesday Book*, 161; on Norfolk, Roffe, *Decoding Domesday*, 47–8.
²⁴ LDB, 11–11v: ESS 4; GDB, 133v–134v: HRT 4. On Maurice's *feudum*, Pamela Taylor, 'The Endowment and Military Obligations of the See of London: A Reassessment of Three Sources', *ANS* 14, 1991, 287–312 at 305–9, and references there cited.
²⁵ Herfast moved the see from Elmham to Thetford; William's successor, Herbert Losinga, moved it on to Norwich in the 1090s. *John Le Neve, Fasti Ecclesiae Anglicanae 1066–1300. II Monastic Cathedrals*, ed. Diana E. Greenway, London 1971, 55.
²⁶ LDB, 19v, 379v: NFK 10,20; SFK 19; on the endowment and fee, Barbara Dodwell, 'The Honour of the Bishop of Thetford/Norwich', *Norfolk History* 33, 1963, 185–99.
²⁷ LDB, 197v–201v: NFK 10,48–93.
²⁸ LDB, 193, 194, 197: NFK 10,19;21;43.

of the market since William Malet established one at Eye which reads like an in-house production, the more so because it comes within the body of the entry rather than at the end where inquest-inspired additions, here as in GDB, appear.[29] Even Bishop's hundred, by 1274 renamed Hoxne, may not by 1086 have been under current episcopal control; the bishop's only substantial estate was at Hoxne and his rivals included the Malets, Bury and Ely.[30] Suffolk's other former episcopal centre, (South) Elmham, was within Wangford hundred, and detail concerning the bishop's limited rights occurs at the end of an entry as, in part or whole, an inquest addition.[31] The bishop, we learn, had soke and sake over the ferting of Elmham (a quarter of the hundred) though not over Stigand's men, while the hundred testified that the abbot of Bury had a writ from King Edward saying he should have soke and sake over St Edmund's lands and men.[32] So even if the detail concerning Hoxne reflects an embedded return, that for Elmham does not.

It remains a stimulating possibility that the ex-royal household bishops and their clerks were disproportionately involved in the production of the earlier recensions, although Bury serves as a warning against over-generalization and monastic cathedral communities such as Worcester and Canterbury would doubtless have been equally adept. Without earlier recensions we do not know if either was involved.[33] We do know, though, that if, in rapidly descending orders of certainty, Osmund, Maurice or William and their clerks were involved, nothing untoward resulted. The bishops' general efficiency could as well have been deployed for purely straightforward ends as for manipulation.

The GDB scribe was not in a position to do more than order and abbreviate his material and, for all the marvel of his achievement, his level of standardization and reduction was variable. It has been said, perhaps in excuse, that the diplomatic of the royal and church entries of the first shire in each circuit tends to be chaotic but is then 'quickly resolved into a common form'; but the scribe cannot have taken long enough breaks to induce amnesia and even if this pattern applies in the north it does not fit circuit I, where Kent was the first shire but, for example, Hampshire retains detail normally removed elsewhere.[34] There is reasonable evidence of the

---

[29] LDB, 379: SFK 18,1.
[30] For the name change, Beatrice A. Lees, 'Introduction to Domesday', in *VCH Suffolk*, I, 1911, 357–411 at 358. Dodwell, 'Honour of the Bishop of Thetford/Norwich', 185, gives some earlier history and says without providing evidence that in 1066 the bishop possessed the hundred; collating the hundred map and list in SFK suggests the bishop had at most nine of the hundred's twenty-seven place-names.
[31] LDB, 397: SFK 18,4.
[32] On the ferting, Lees, 'Introduction to Domesday', 358.
[33] On Canterbury, see below.
[34] David Roffe, 'Domesday Book and Northern Society: a Reassessment', *EHR* 105, 1990, 310–36 at 321 n; Roffe covers all areas conscientiously in *DIB* and *Domesday Decoded*, but his heartlands are the East Midlands and the North. On circuit I, see below.

royal material being separately collected and entered.[35] For the bishops, though, the pattern is less obvious, not least because the fairly consistent GDB order is independent of the size of holding in the given county. In Oxfordshire, for example, the unexceptional returns for the few estates of the archbishop of Canterbury and of the bishops of Winchester, Salisbury, and Exeter are all ahead of the truly distinctive one for the bishop of Lincoln.[36] Relatedly, even bishops who generated an unusual return did not normally achieve similar results in other counties or circuits. Wulfstan in Gloucestershire is silent about his hundredal possessions; Remigius' Lincolnshire return breaks the hundred order by starting with the chief manor but otherwise conforms; Canterbury's TRE tenures are only given outside circuit I.[37] A literate administration might perhaps proffer written returns everywhere but, if so, most failed to survive the county process.

The reasons for the rare survivals, then, are to be found neither in a particular bishop's personality nor the putative scriptorium of an earlier recension but in the structure of the county and, to a lesser extent, the circuit to which the bishop (or anyone else) was responding. The commissioners for circuit III can take credit for exemplary returns but strong shrieval control in the constituent counties must have helped.[38] The scarcity of private hundreds in these (and other) counties around London is surely a related factor: in Middlesex, the most extreme example, the crown had virtually no land by 1066 but all the hundreds were royal and apparently configured specifically to prevent the substantial estates of the bishop of London and the archbishop of Canterbury from becoming private hundreds.[39]

That private hundreds might have been helpful is hardly news: Wulfstan's Worcestershire chapter begins with the statement that his cathedral church 'has one hundred which is called Oswaldslow in which lie 300 hides', and hundredal control has since Maitland been fingered as a significant factor.[40] In terms of possible manipulation of the actual inquest, the advantage of having one's own men provide the hundred verdicts has been noted.[41] Nevertheless the episcopal returns absolutely

---

[35] Roffe, *Decoding Domesday*, 75.
[36] GDB, 155–155v: OXF landowners 2–6; see below.
[37] F. R. Thorn, 'Hundreds and Wapentakes', in *The Gloucestershire Domesday*, ed. Ann Williams and R. W. H. Erskine, London 1989, 40–9, esp. 44; for the Lincolnshire hundred order, Roffe, *DIB*, 142; on Remigius in Oxfordshire and on Canterbury, see below.
[38] For praise of circuit III, Sally Harvey, 'Taxation and the Economy', in *Domesday Studies*, ed. Holt, 249–64 at 260–1 (although she then thought it the first circuit transcribed into GDB); Stephen Baxter, 'Lordship and Justice in Late Anglo-Saxon England: the Judicial Functions of Soke and Commendation Revisited', in *Early Medieval Studies in Memory of Patrick Wormald*, ed. Stephen Baxter and others, Farnham 2009, 383–419.
[39] Taylor, 'The Endowment and Military Obligations', 300–2; see also Pamela Taylor, '*Eadulfingtun*, Edmonton, and their Contexts', in *The English and their Legacy, 900–1200: Essays in Honour of Ann Williams*, ed. David Roffe, Woodbridge 2012, 95–114.
[40] GDB, 172v: WOR 2,1; as footnote 2 above.
[41] Fleming, *Domesday Book and the Law*; for county variation in reporting and jurors'

fail to show any general correlation between hundredal control and distortion of the process or record. There are blameless returns for ecclesiastical hundreds as well as counties where hundredal control seems immaterial.

It is particularly interesting that Oswaldslow was assessed in 1086 at 300 hides, since at the start of the century this seems to have been a recognized figure for a see's endowment and for a ship soke through which the bishops fulfilled their military obligations directly rather than within the shires.[42] In cases such as London, where the modest endowment was spread across several shires, the concomitant ship soke cannot have had much other administrative impact.[43] Where the ship soke was simultaneously a (triple) hundred within a single county, though, the dual role may have helped reinforce a degree of independence from the county structure. Although the military system, and in some cases the hundred structures, had changed by 1086, it is worth keeping the 300-hide dimension in mind.

After Oswaldslow the clearest example of an embedded episcopal return comes from Remigius of Lincoln in Oxfordshire. (The see had only been moved from Dorchester-on Thames in the 1070s, hence the core endowment here.) A surviving list of estate memoranda datable to 1067x1072 shows the prior use of writing and both the ordering of the Domesday account and some of the formulae are highly distinctive.[44] No sub-headings are used but after detailing five demesne estates followed by three held from the bishop by the abbot of Eynsham, the chapter moves on to tenanted land within each of the first five, and then some other tenancies.[45] This highly exceptional double listing and the use of the rare *in firma* rather than *in dominio* probably follow a written original. Oxfordshire has the worst hundred rubrication outside the south-west and although the bishop's chapter starts with one of the few, for Dorchester hundred, it contains no others; but whether the later hundreds of Dorchester, Thame, and Banbury were being accounted as one or as three scarcely matters, since either way they represent another clear ecclesiastical

---

attempts to avoid perjury, Alan Cooper, 'Protestations of Ignorance in Domesday Book', in *The Experience of Power in Medieval Europe, 950–1350*, ed. R. Berkhofer, A. Cooper, and A. Kosto, Aldershot 2005, 169–81; Baxter, 'Representation of Lordship', 81–2, notes the inbuilt checks.

[42] For the origins of Oswaldslow, Ann Williams, 'An Introduction to the Worcestershire Domesday', in *The Worcestershire Domesday*, ed. Ann Williams and R. W. H. Erskine, London 1988, 1–39; Steven Bassett, 'The Administrative Landscape of the Diocese of Worcester in the Tenth Century', in *St Oswald of Worcester*, 147–73. On ship sokes, Taylor, 'The Endowment and Military Obligations', 299–300.

[43] Taylor, 'The Endowment and Military Obligations', 293–303; *Charters of St Paul's, London*, ed. S. E. Kelly, Anglo-Saxon Charters 10, Oxford 2004, no. 25.

[44] GDB, 155–155v: OXF 6; Blair, 'Estate Memoranda', 122–3, details the likelihood of a written return (not, despite his footnote, pursued by Baxter in 'Representation of Lordship').

[45] On Eynsham, F. M. Stenton, 'Introduction to the Domesday Survey', in *VCH Oxon*, I, 1939, 373–95 at 379. The Domesday text makes unlikely Blair's assumption, 'Estate Memoranda', 122, that the demesne tenants were all knights.

triple hundred whose hidage too is close to 300.⁴⁶ Here as at Oswaldslow possession of the triple hundred may have aided transmission of the unaltered return, but the argument can also be tentatively broadened. By 1086 the continuing existence of a strong triple hundred denotes relatively weak shrieval control, and the weakness may have translated into a less controlled Domesday account.

Urse d'Abitot's complaint about his lack of revenue from Worcestershire is well known, and his situation truly was abnormal: private hundreds were less general than is often assumed, but Domesday Worcestershire was riddled with them.⁴⁷ Besides Oswaldslow, Pershore abbey held 100 hides and Westminster abbey 200 which, until transferred by Edward the Confessor, had also belonged to Pershore, so a disbanded triple, while Evesham abbey too had a private hundred.⁴⁸ It has been claimed that 'in Worcestershire Domesday there is a consistent hundredal order in almost all the fiefs except the Church of Worcester's', but all the private hundreds were basically self-contained and outside the sequence: excluding sub-tenancies, no one other than Pershore and Westminster had estates in Pershore and no one other than Evesham in Fishborough, while Evesham's lands at Hampton and Bengeworth were the only intrusions into Worcester's monopoly of Oswaldslow.⁴⁹ Letting through an unaltered return is more readily understandable within such a structure, although even Wulfstan's did not go entirely unchecked: at Hampton, where Worcester had only held the hundred geld contribution TRE, the other obligations were being fully discharged by Evesham 'as the county says'.⁵⁰

The sheriff of Oxford was spared Urse's precise problem but Oxfordshire contained seven royal manors with responsibility for groups ranging from two to four and a half hundreds apiece – and with a preponderance of triples.⁵¹ Without at all denying the coherent extractive power of the state, the severe limits on private hundredal justice, or the sheriff's overall obligation to account for the shire, it is

---

⁴⁶ Stenton, 'Introduction to the Domesday Survey', 374–9; John Blair, 'An Introduction to the Oxfordshire Domesday', in *The Oxfordshire Domesday*, ed. Ann Williams and R. W. H. Erskine, London 1990, 1–19, and F. R. Thorn, 'Hundreds and Wapentakes', in ibid., 20–9; *VCH Oxon*, VII, 1962, 2–3.
⁴⁷ GDB, 172: WOR C3; Williams, 'Introduction'. Helen Cam's carefully limited lists of private hundreds and their distribution have sometimes been over-generalized: Taylor, '*Eadulfingtun*'.
⁴⁸ *Domesday Book: Worcestershire*, ed. Frank Thorn and Caroline Thorn, Chichester 1982, App. I; Williams, 'Introduction', 13–17.
⁴⁹ P. H. Sawyer, 'The "Original Returns" and Domesday Book', *EHR* 70, 1955, 177–97 at 183. GDB, 172v–175v: WOR landholders 2, 8–10, esp. 2,74–5. GDB, 174: WOR 2,75 also records that Urse holds 6 hides in Bengeworth; this was perhaps a sub-tenancy since it does not appear in Urse's chapter. On the disputes over Hampton and Bengeworth, Williams, 'Introduction', 8; Wormald, 'Oswaldslow: an "Immunity"?', 124.
⁵⁰ GDB, 174: WOR 2,74.
⁵¹ Blair, 'Introduction', 21; Thorn, 'Hundreds and Wapentakes', 21–3.

arguable that the sheriff's activities were curtailed by those of the royal reeves.[52] Certainly only the similarly structured south-western shires match the dearth of hundred headings. Oxfordshire has long been blamed for providing one of the least informative Domesday accounts, but it is also notably inconsistent. TRE information is absent throughout the bishop of Lincoln's return but is given at the top of each entry in those of the four other bishops of English sees, holding between them five estates in four different hundreds within the county, and in the demesne estates of St Denis and St Frideswide.[53] Elsewhere (including on a tenanted St Frideswide estate) if it occurs it is always at the end, and Odo of Bayeux's return provides it for each of the four demesne estates but none of the sixty-odd tenanted ones.[54] Overall, and even allowing for the particularities of circuit IV, this surely indicates a weak process in which information was not extracted consistently; and, faced with this, the GDB scribe did not attempt consistency either. Even if the bishop of Lincoln was presented with an unusually open goal, though, he refrained from scoring. Perhaps his silence on liberties explains historians' failure until recently to notice the oddities.[55]

In Herefordshire Bishop Robert's chapter concludes: 'In total there are 300 hides in the bishopric although the bishop's men have given no account of 33'; but the figures as usual fail to tally and the hidages total 297.5.[56] Robert also had estates in the three neighbouring and historically related counties, but since those that had been held TRE or restored TRW add another 103.5 hides they cannot have been included.[57] The 300 Herefordshire hides may well at some stage have formed a ship soke, but at least by 1086 they were spread across eleven different hundreds and only entirely non-episcopal and recently disbanded Leominster shows the signs

---

[52] On the coherent power, see James Campbell *passim* and, most recently, George Molyneaux, 'Why Were Some Tenth-Century English Kings Presented as Rulers of Britain?', *TRHS*, 6th series 21, 2011, 59–91. See also N. D. Hurnard, 'The Anglo-Norman Franchises', *EHR* 64, 1949, 289–33, 433–60; Patrick Wormald, 'Maitland and Anglo-Saxon Law: Beyond Domesday Book', in *The History of English Law*, ed. John Hudson, Oxford 1996, 1–20; Wormald, 'Oswaldslow: an "Immunity"?'. Round's demolition of Eyton over the sheriff's accounting obligations is cruel but fair: J. H. Round, 'Introduction to Somerset Domesday', in *VCH Somerset*, I, 383–432 at 395–6.

[53] GDB, 155, 157: OXF landholders 2–5,13,14.

[54] GDB, 157: OXF 14,2 and landholder 7. Baxter, 'Representation of Lordship', 77, notes that while circuits IV and V often fail to identify the TRE holder the identification in Oxfordshire 'is particularly patchy'.

[55] Until Blair, 'Estate Memoranda'.

[56] GDB, 181v–182v: HEF 2,1;58; the statement is above 2,58, an estate with a separate origin.

[57] Worcs: Kyre 2h, Inkberrow 15.5h (GDB, 174: WOR 3,2–3); Glouc: Prestbury 30h (GDB, 165: GLS 4,1), on which as probable ancient endowment, J. H. Round, 'Domesday Introduction', in *VCH Hereford*, I, 1908, 263–307 at 282; Salop: Lydbury 53h, Onibury 3h (GDB, 252: SHR 2,1–2).

of a former ecclesiastical hundred.⁵⁸ This tighter county control is mirrored in the form of the record. Written returns have been thought to underlie aspects of Herefordshire Domesday, specifically the way that chief residences head some of the lay chapters and the inclusion of unusual pieces of information.⁵⁹ Neither example is unassailable in that chief residences were similarly moved between the Exon and Exchequer Domesday accounts, which suggests county or scribal process, and one cited example of unusual information, that of the bishop's men and the 300 hides, could equally reflect the inquest stage.⁶⁰ Either way, though, all the chapters have been highly standardized and the formulae for the bishop's return vary at best slightly.⁶¹ The names of single-tenant *milites* or *clerici* are, for instance, omitted. There is an early subheading, that 'the lands written below pertain to the canons of Hereford', but it seems only to cover the rest of the estates in that particular hundred.⁶²

Other ship sokes and putative triple hundreds had also by 1086 been overtaken by events. In exact coincidence with the Herefordshire figures, Bishop Æthelric of Sherborne had complained in 1001x1012 that he was no longer receiving ship-scot from 33 hides which had been part of the 'the three hundred hides which other bishops had for their scyre'.⁶³ By shire he meant his see's total endowment which, since the division in 909 to create the three county-based sees of Sherborne, Crediton, and Wells, had been restricted to Dorset.⁶⁴ Neither the addition in 1058 of Ramsbury nor the move to Old Sarum in 1075 (and consequent separation from Sherborne abbey) should, thinking of Dorchester/Lincoln, have obscured any continuing triple hundred. That Sherborne itself, once held by Bishop Æthelric, was held by Queen Edith TRE looks like an expression of disintegration.⁶⁵ The Domesday hundreds are obscure but Sherborne's estates were probably, then as later, spread across several, with only Sherborne hundred a possible candidate for

---

⁵⁸ C. P. Lewis, 'An Introduction to the Herefordshire Domesday', in *The Herefordshire Domesday*, ed. Ann Williams and R. W. H. Erskine, London 1988, 1–22 at 7–8, and F. R. Thorn, 'Hundreds and Wapentakes', in ibid., 23–30.
⁵⁹ V. H. Galbraith, 'The Making of Domesday Book', *EHR* 57, 1942, 161–77 at 175 (but without detail); Lewis, 'Introduction', 3–4.
⁶⁰ SOM, App. I. Galbraith, *Making of Domesday Book*, 79, thought the latter reflected the bishop's tenants supplying details out of court to the commissioners' staff.
⁶¹ Lewis, 'Introduction', 3–4.
⁶² *Contra* Lewis, 'Introduction', 19.
⁶³ Taylor, 'The Endowment and Military Obligations', 300, and sources there cited.
⁶⁴ Ann Williams, *Æthelred the Unready: The Ill-Counselled King*, London 2003, 80–2 and personal communication, argues that Æthelric controlled the three hundreds of Sherborne, Yetminster and Beaminster as a ship soke but not necessarily as 300 hides of endowment; Wessex hundreds seldom contained 100 hides and the bishop could anyway be responsible for the ship scot without holding the land.
⁶⁵ GDB, 77: DOR 2,6. For comments on the weakness and variability for different purposes of the Dorset and Somerset hundreds, see the appendices to DOR and SOM.

continuing episcopal control.[66] The Domesday text bears none of the signs of an embedded seigneurial return: the formulae are standard, Sherborne itself does not head the chapter, and the title for the section on the Sherborne monks' lands is at the end rather than the beginning.

In Somerset, whose administrative structure had been the classic West Saxon one of royal manors with attached hundreds, the bishop of Winchester's Taunton was one such, first alienated to the see *c.* 904, back in royal hands in the 950s and 960s, and only finally re-transferred by King Edgar.[67] Similarities between Domesday Taunton, where the bishop had hundredal jurisdiction and military powers, and Oswaldslow, have long been noted.[68] Comparing the Domesday and Exon versions of the 'customary rights (*consuetudines*) pertaining to Taunton' with a pre-Domesday, slightly differently focussed account of 'the dues which pertained to Taunton on the day when King Edward died' shows that if the bishop's Domesday submission was written it did not copy the pre-existing account.[69] If it was written, which seems plausible but because of the exceptionality unprovable, it contains nothing suspicious and, unlike Oswaldslow, nothing on excluding the sheriff. It must also have been modified since the estate descriptions exactly follow the county form. The unique note that the king had acknowledged his grant of additions into Taunton at Salisbury in the hearing of the bishop of Durham whom he had ordered to write it in the records (*in brevibus*) occurs at the end of the whole Winchester chapter in Exon Domesday, as one might expect for a late amendment, but within the appropriate entry in GDB.[70]

Taunton might have seemed a prime candidate for an embedded return both because of its own hundredal strength and because shrieval control in Somerset looks relatively weak. There were still royal manors with attached hundreds and Bishop Giso of Wells was successfully withdrawing his scattered estates into his own hundred.[71] Giso, another former royal clerk, was doubtless adept at writing but it now seems likely that some or all of his supposed *Historiola*, until recently taken as his own account and covering losses and recoveries, was actually a later product of the cathedral chapter.[72] It therefore becomes another example of an important pattern, a slightly later source deliberately written to assert the bishop's eager, in

---

[66] See the hundred maps and lists in *Domesday Book: Dorset*, ed. C. Thorn and F. Thorn, Chichester 1983.

[67] Loud, 'Introduction', 12, who also gives the hundred structure around the county's royal manors.

[68] GDB, 87v: SOM 2,2; Maitland, *Domesday Book and Beyond*; Eric John, *Land Tenure in Early England*, Leicester 1964, 134–6; Wormald, 'Oswaldslow: an "Immunity"?', 118.

[69] Robertson, *Anglo-Saxon Charters*, nos. XLV, App. I no. IV and commentaries; Loud, 'Introduction', 13; Round, 'Introduction to the Somerset Domesday', 400–4.

[70] GDB, 87v: SOM 2,9; Loud, 'Introduction', 6.

[71] SOM App. I.

[72] Keynes, 'Giso', esp. 213–26; on some of the estates, Loud, 'Introduction', 15–16.

this case anachronistic, separation of the chapter estates.[73] Giso's Domesday return perhaps displays a hint of a written one: the two final entries for TRW losses could be inquest-stage additions but could equally be original, not least because no claim is being stated for now-royal Milverton; but the lavish survival of tenants' names, scarcely pruned from their Exon level, is general across the county and therefore reflects nothing more than the GDB scribe's variability.[74] Overall too, here as in much of Taunton, the county formulae stand impenetrably firm.

The hundredally organized tax return preserved with Exon Domesday places all Giso's Somerset estates, the *Terra Gisonis*, in a single group or hundred while the similarly preserved Exon list II places them in several very small hundreds; either way they were Giso's recent withdrawals and were later (barring a few adjustments) accounted as a single, and in the sixteenth century as a triple, hundred.[75] If the bishopric had, as Æthelric of Sherborne's complaint implies, earlier possessed a 300-hide endowment, though, this had sunk without trace.[76] It has been suggested that Giso's new hundred initially existed only for tax purposes, and that other West Country hundreds too may have been 'temporary, artificial creations for the needs of a particular survey'.[77] This non-integration of the hundreds' various roles is presumably connected with the continuing importance of organization from (unhidated) royal manors and explains the lack of hundred ordering and rubrication in the Exon and Exchequer Domesdays.[78] But whatever the integrative mechanism, the returns for all the circuit II counties suggest well-controlled county structures. As a result Walkelin at Taunton, Giso in Somerset, even Osbern of Exeter in Devon, another likely candidate, offer few traces of embedded returns.[79]

The general importance of the hundred for the geld processes is beyond question but its other roles also seem restricted wherever there were other intermediate units. In much of the old Anglo-Danish area 'wapentake' was synonymous with the southern 'hundred' but Yorkshire's East Riding had eighteen small hundreds which were probably already subdivisions of the six wapentakes that they later became.[80] In Sussex the rapes may have had a tenth-century defensive origin but their importance surged under the Conqueror and it is unlikely that hundredal autonomy remained unscathed; the archbishop of Canterbury's long-held manor of Malling, 80 hides TRE and its own hundred, was also within the rape of Pevensey whose lord, the

---

[73] Keynes, 'Giso', esp. 223–5; for comparable activities in Kent, see below.
[74] GDB, 89v: SOM 6,18–19.
[75] SOM App. I.
[76] See above, at footnote 63. The TRE endowment in Somerset totalled *c.* 221 hides including some major eleventh-century acquisitions: cf Loud, 'Introduction', 15.
[77] SOM App. I; DOR Appendix: The Dorset Hundreds, second page.
[78] For comparison with Oxfordshire, see above.
[79] For Exeter, GDB landholder 2 in both Devon and Cornwall, see DEV General Notes.
[80] Palliser, 'Introduction to Yorkshire Domesday', 5–6, citing a personal communication from David Roffe.

count of Mortain, had withdrawn 5 hides from the hundred TRW.[81] Domesday Kent is fairly consistently ordered and rubricated by lathe, then within that by hundred, and it was the men of the four East Kent lathes who agreed Domesday's list of the royal laws.[82]

Kent is particularly significant to any discussion because of the Domesday-related texts surviving in Canterbury cathedral's Domesday Monachorum. The two summary lists of manors with their geld assessments (one covering the estates of the sees of Canterbury and Rochester, the other the rest) are not at issue here.[83] The text which provides fuller descriptions of the Canterbury and Rochester estates, and was probably written in Domesday Monachorum in the late 1090s, DM B, is, however, central.[84] It has been accepted so far that this and related texts in manuscripts from Rochester and St Augustine's are extractions from documents generated at an early stage in the Domesday inquiry, whether (pre-Galbraith) from the 'original returns' sent to Winchester or (Galbraith) 'from a draft of the Inquest proceedings, which lacked the manorial details still preserved in part of Domesday Book'.[85] Colin Flight, following Galbraith, titles his chapter 'The archbishop's response to the commissioners' questionnaire'. The differences between the DM B text and Domesday, notably the estate order and absence of any information on stock, ploughs and peasants in DM B, are thus ascribed to this derivation from an earlier stage.[86] Flight notes that the DM B was produced when the monks' desire to separate their endowment had been freshly sharpened by William II's exploitation of the archiepiscopal vacancy after Lanfranc's death, but nevertheless thinks that '[b]y some means the monks had got hold of the records of Lanfranc's administration'.[87]

Despite this unanimity, two other differences make it extremely hard to credit the DM B text as a forerunner, or as primarily a product of the archbishop rather than the monks. First, the archbishop was, like all bishops, answerable for the whole

---

[81] GDB, 16: SSX 2,1; the notes (unpaginated), start with the rapes.

[82] R. Eales, 'An Introduction to the Kent Domesday', in *The Kent Domesday*, ed. Ann Williams and G. H. Martin, London 1992, 1–49 at 9, 11–13, and F. R. Thorn, 'Hundreds and Wapentakes', in ibid., 50–72, which cite the seminal older literature; Galbraith, *Making of Domesday Book*, 152. GDB, 1–1v: KEN D11, covering D12–23.

[83] Cf especially R. S. Hoyt, 'A Pre-Domesday Kentish Assessment List', in *A Medieval Miscellany for D. M. Stenton*, ed. P. M. Barnes and C. F. Slade, Pipe Roll Society 36, 1962, 189–202; Harvey, 'Domesday Book and its Predecessors', 754–60; Frederic F. Kreisler, 'Domesday Book and the Anglo-Norman Synthesis', in *Order and Innovation in the Middle Ages: Essays in Honour of Joseph R. Strayer*, ed. W. C. Jordan and others, Princeton 1976, 3–16, 411–16; Eales, 'Introduction', 5–6.

[84] DM B, 80–98; Douglas also gives the Domesday entries in parallel. Also edited in Colin Flight, *The Survey of Kent: Documents Relating to the Survey of the County Conducted in 1086*, BAR British Series 506, 2010, ch. 2, available online.

[85] Galbraith *Making of Domesday Book*, ch. 10, esp. 148.

[86] Galbraith, *Making of Domesday Book*, 148.

[87] Flight, *Survey of Kent*, 39.

of his see's endowment, and this is obvious throughout the Domesday entries. In Kent the main heading, *Terra Archiepiscopi Cantuariensis*, covers the demesne estates and then come two sub-sections headed respectively *Terra Militum eius* and *Terra Monachorum Archiepiscopi*. Although this last is given a separate rubricated number, 3, to tie to the index, this was, as in Norfolk, the choice of the rubricator not a reflection of a separate return. The entries in 3 all begin 'The same archbishop holds' and the index is in fact differently divided, putting the archbishop as 2 'and his monks and men' as 3. The tripartite division may well reflect a written return and, whatever the re-ordering into the standard county sequence, is presumably likely to have been in place *ab initio*.[88]

The DM B text, in contrast, divides the Canterbury estates into only two sections, *De Maneriis Archiepiscopatus*, which also includes most of Domesday's *Terra Militum*, and then *Incipiunt* (Here begin) *Maneria Monachorum*. From here on Domesday's 'The same archbishop holds x' is uniformly 'X is a manor of the monks' and the archbishop is only mentioned when he or one of his knights is holding land which the monks classify as theirs; such claims are not reflected in Domesday Book, where the estates appear without comment in the archbishop's land or that of his knights.[89] It has long been noted that the DM B entry for Sandwich contains a post-Domesday update of the town's renders but this different division indicates that at the very least the monks had done a major reworking of their source, whatever its date. If this is so it becomes just as likely that they chose to omit the estate detail as that it was absent from their exemplar. All such alteration would be entirely in keeping with what we know of their other activities at this period.[90]

The second difference is much more significant: DM B contains notably more information on TRE tenures and recoveries than Domesday. For the Canterbury estates Domesday gives only the statement that Sandwich was not in the revenue

---

[88] GDB, 2; 3–5: KEN list of landholders; landholders 2–3.

[89] The *maneria monachorum* section is in Douglas, DM B, 88–96; examples of manors differently assigned in GDB include Mersham (GDB, 3v–4: KEN 2,22), Newenden (GDB, 4: KEN 2,27), Lenham (GDB, 4v: KEN 2,36), Berwick (GDB, 4v: KEN 2,42).

[90] *Charters of Christ Church Canterbury Part 1*, ed. N. P. Brooks and S. E. Kelly, British Academy Anglo-Saxon Charters 17, Oxford 2013, 58–72, following Robin Fleming, 'Christ Church Canterbury's Anglo-Norman Cartulary', in *Anglo-Norman Political Culture in the Twelfth Century Renaissance: Proceedings of the Borchard Conference on Anglo-Norman History 1995*, ed. C. Warren Hollister, Woodbridge 1997, 83–155, (her accusation at 86 of 'willfull' [sic] cooking of Christ Church's landbooks predates Baxter's application of the phrase to Worcester, 'Representation of Lordship', 74); David Bates, 'The Land Pleas of William I's Reign: Penenden Heath Revisited', *Bulletin of the Institute of Historical Research* 51, 1978, 1–19; Alan Cooper, 'Extraordinary Privilege: The Trial of Penenden Heath and the Domesday Inquest', *EHR* 116, 2001, 1167–92; Eales, 'Introduction', 6. Rochester and St Augustine's were similarly engaged.

TRE and the names of two previous archiepiscopal tenants in the *Terra Militum*.[91] Only for Stoke, a Penenden recovery for Rochester, are we told at the end of the entry, possibly as an inquest addition, that Earl Godwine had bought the manor from tenants without the bishop's knowledge and that Lanfranc had proved his claim to it against Odo of Bayeux.[92] On Stoke DM B gives only the bare fact of Lanfranc's recovery against Odo, but the monks were not very interested in Rochester.[93] For Canterbury it gives a little extra detail on Sandwich and a few more TRE tenants' names that on a bad day the GDB scribe might, perhaps, have omitted.[94] But, crucially, DM B also notes the recoveries of five estates, of which one within Orpington had been held by a free man TRE (*quidam liber homo*) and the other four: Sundridge, Statenborough, Langport, and Saltwood, by Earl Godwine.[95] If answers to one of the most important questions of the Domesday inquiry had been supplied initially, it is highly unlikely that they would then have fallen from the record.

Many contemporaries will have been well aware that Lanfranc's recovery of Kentish estates from Odo had started at the shire meeting held at Penenden *c.* 1072, when four estates and some pasture were recovered for Canterbury and two estates for Rochester, and continued thereafter.[96] The still-surviving neutral memorandum probably produced by a royal official in 1078/9 gives the outcomes since Penenden for twenty-two named places or lands that Lanfranc had claimed, not always successfully (only one name, Preston, coincides with the Penenden list), plus a statement that other claims were still to be adjudicated by the hundreds.[97] Two later Canterbury sources list twenty-six and twenty-seven estates as Lanfranc recoveries, nine or ten respectively outside Kent.[98] There is of course no exact correspondence between the sources. DM B mentions Stoke but not the other specifically Penenden

---

[91] GDB, 3–4: KEN 2,31–2. DM B's additional information on some of the TRW *Terra Militum* tenants is irrelevant here.
[92] GDB, 5v: KEN 4,16.
[93] DM B, 98; the lack of interest might help explain the greater similarity of the DM B and Domesday ordering of the Rochester estates.
[94] DM B, 89, 92–3: Sandwich (GDB, 3: KEN 2,2), Berwick (GDB, 4v: KEN 2,42), Newenden (GDB, 4: KEN 2,27), Leaveland (GDB, 4: KEN 2,34).
[95] DM B, 89, 92–4: Orpington GDB, 4, 4v: KEN 2,30, 3,1; Sundridge GDB, 3: KEN 2,5; Statenborough GDB, 4v: KEN 2,39; Langport GDB, 4v: KEN 2,43; Saltwood GDB, 4v: KEN 2,41.
[96] Bates, 'The Land Pleas', which overtook, among others, David Douglas, 'Odo, Lanfranc and the Domesday Survey', in *Historical Essays in Honour of James Tait*, ed. G. Edwards and others, Manchester 1933, 47–57; Cooper, 'Extraordinary Privilege'. F. R. H. Du Boulay, *The Lordship of Canterbury*, London 1966, 36–46, includes a footnoted table of Domesday estates and recoveries giving the additional DM B detail. See also Eales, 'Introduction', 45–7.
[97] Translation in Du Boulay, *Lordship of Canterbury*, 38–9.
[98] John Le Patourel, 'The Reports of the Trial on Penenden Heath', in *Studies in Medieval History Presented to F. M. Powicke*, ed. R. W. Hunt and others, Oxford 1948, 15–26 at 25–6;

recoveries; the 1078/9 memorandum states that Statenborough had been lost TRW and puts Newenden, said in DM B to have been held TRE of the archbishop by Leofric, among the losses to Earl Godwine. Nevertheless there is more than enough convergence between the neutral 1078/9 memorandum and DM B to confirm the latter's basic veracity and both records show that although the recoveries were from Odo many of the losses had been to Earl Godwine (d. 1053).

Although the recoveries are well known, Domesday's silence has escaped attention, even though *quis tenuit eam TRE* (who held it TRE) is considered one of the most basic questions of the enquiry and its importance for ecclesiastical tenures has also been widely recognized.[99] Lanfranc's non-compliance has probably slipped notice because of the general assumption that stating *in dominio* or giving the TRE and current hidage meant no change.[100] This may sometimes be true, although obviously not here, but as well as providing that information many, probably most, episcopal returns also specifically tick the *quis tenuit* box. In two other circuit I counties, for example, *in dominio de episcopatu suo* is reiterated throughout the chapters for the bishops of Winchester, Salisbury, and Exeter in Berkshire, and in Hampshire the bishop of Winchester's return constantly repeats *fuit semper, semper tenuit* (was always, always held) and so on.[101]

Apart from simple compliance, why would Lanfranc not detail his recoveries as title assurance and a projection of power – which is presumably what the monks were doing in DM B? And, except perhaps at Stoke, why were the lacunae not filled by the shire, where the recoveries must have been common knowledge, or by circuit commissioners unlikely to have been ignorant of the clashes between Lanfranc and Odo and their outcomes? In a study of the archbishop's manor of Mortlake (Surrey) and thence by extension the Canterbury recoveries in all counties other than Kent,

---

on the non-Kentish estates, Pamela Taylor, 'Domesday Mortlake', *ANS* 32, 2009, 203–29 at 222–7.

[99] Adolphus Ballard, *The Domesday Inquest*, 2nd edn, London 1923, 85, terms TRE tenures 'the next most important questions' behind assessment area and value, but looks at neither royal nor ecclesiastical returns. Baxter, 'Representation of Lordship', 90, claims it was 'The commissioners' preoccupation with reconstructing the tenurial landscape' TRE that gave Wulfstan his opportunity 'to construct his own version'. Paul Hyams, '"No Register of Title": the Domesday Inquest and Land Adjudication', *ANS* 10, 1986, 127–41, and J. C. Holt, '1086', in *Domesday Studies*, ed. Holt, 41–64 at 57, particularly stress the importance to the church of Domesday's confirmation of its titles. The contrary points about disputed titles, cf. Cooper, 'Protestations of Ignorance', esp. 176–7, are irrelevant here.

[100] Galbraith, *Making of Domesday Book*, 147, discussing DM B and the related St Augustine's *Excerpta,* claims that 'where the ownership has changed since 1066 the name of the owner TRE is generally included'. Flight, *Survey of Kent*, 152, contends that in Domesday 'in the first few chapters, nearly always, it could be taken for granted that the manor was held TRE by the current tenant's predecessor'.

[101] GDB, 58, 58v: BKS landholders 2–3, 5; landholder 4, the bishop of Durham, had a single TRW acquisition in the county (GDB, 40–41v: HAM 2).

I suggested elsewhere that Lanfranc ignored the *quis tenuit* question wherever he could, and looking in detail at Kent has done nothing to undermine the suggested reasons: that this was part of his strategy of *damnatio memoriae*, airbrushing his predecessor Stigand into oblivion, and that he could claim particular support for it in the county containing both his own and Odo's heartland.[102]

All this adds another dimension to the question of the relationship between local administrative structures and manipulation. In the three other circuits where Canterbury had lands, the TRE tenure is always given.[103] This suggests that the other circuits and/or their counties were strong enough, as certainly in III and possibly in VII, to insist on the information, or that Lanfranc exercised less control over his returns from distant estates. It is surprising to see that Newington in circuit IV Oxfordshire, supposedly a Lanfranc recovery, *de aecclesia fuit et est* (was and is the church's; it could, charitably, have been one of the TRW losses), but although Oxfordshire seems loosely controlled the identical formula appears in its Winchester and Salisbury chapters.[104] Lanfranc's only other alleged recovery outside Kent, but this time in circuit I, was at Mortlake, where the Domesday evidence comes solely from the hundred; elsewhere in Surrey, apart from noting that Walworth, now held by Bainard from the archbishop, had been for the monks' clothing (exactly the sort of information one would expect in the Domesday Monachorum account if it had gone beyond Kent), Lanfranc omits the TRE tenures while the other two bishops, Winchester and Exeter, two of whose three estates were without change, supply them.[105] In Sussex, the only other circuit I county with Canterbury estates, there is, like Surrey, an undivided return; here we learn that two estates had been transferred from the monks to Lanfranc and one had been held by the clergy from the archbishop TRE but otherwise the TRE tenures are again omitted, and again Exeter (and all five abbeys) provides them, although Chichester, the only other bishop, does not.[106]

The archbishop's omissions in Kent were not achieved via an unaltered return or hundredal control. The return has obviously gone through the county mill and obeys the standard ordering.[107] Before detailing the ordinary estates it starts with two urban exceptions. First comes a bare note of the holdings in Canterbury, with claims concerning fines and customs only to be found in the general (i.e., royal) city section.[108] Next is Sandwich, probably, judging from a cross-reference, removed

---

[102] Taylor, 'Domesday Mortlake', 222–6.
[103] Taylor, 'Domesday Mortlake', 222–4.
[104] GDB, 155: OXF 2,1;3,2;4,1; see above.
[105] GDB, 30v–31: SUR landholders 2–4.
[106] GDB, 16–17v: SSX landholders 2–8. The bishop of Chichester is silent on eight estates held *in dominio* while stating that the ninth *semper fuit in monasterio*: GDB, 16v–17: SSX 3,1–9.
[107] Sawyer, 'Original Returns', 192–4.
[108] GDB, 2, 3: KEN C2;7–8.2,1; see also Cooper, 'Extraordinary Privilege'.

from its original position within the monks' holdings; it is immediately said to lie in its own hundred, but the dominant voice is that of the men of Sandwich and they are obviously singing from their own hymn sheet.[109] For the rest of the entries (in the Phillimore numbering 2,3–40 and 3,1–23), work with the hundred maps suggests that the archbishop controlled one hundred in west Kent out of eighteen and in east Kent four or five out of forty-five.[110] To make these from Canterbury's view disappointing figures worse, the hundreds were distributed across five different lathes, none of which they had the remotest chance of dominating.

Lanfranc's silences are not the only oddities. Circuit I's existence is defined by distinctively shared formulae but the returns of its five constituent counties are notably unhomogenized, with Kent 'the most aberrant'.[111] This partly reflects unusual differences – Sussex's rapes, Kent's lathes and sulungs – but the variations go much further in terms of both process (Berkshire seems exceptionally well managed) and transcription – unnecessary tenants' names survive in Hampshire. Such variations, like the unusual layout at the start of Kent, seemed more readily explicable when the county and circuit were thought to be the GDB scribe's earliest enrolments, but we now know that his learning curve was elsewhere.[112]

The royal TRE tenures are provided in the other four counties but not in Kent. On their vanishingly rare occurrences in the immediately following Kent chapters, those of the archbishop and the bishop of Rochester, they are at the end of the entry. The next chapter, Odo's, omits them for the first three estates then begins regularly to supply the information (perhaps the GDB scribe had suddenly remembered this was normal), still at the end of the entry for the first 220 or so but then at the start for the final five. After another hiatus through the returns of Battle abbey and St Augustine's, the TRE detail stays at the start for the rest of the county.[113] Such a shift in placement part way through a chapter and county is unusual, and whatever the underlying documentation the GDB scribe was clearly somewhat disengaged.[114]

---

[109] GDB, 3: KEN 2,2, with a cross reference back at GDB, 5v: KEN 3,23; for ongoing disputes over Sandwich, see Nicholas Brooks, *The Early History of the Church of Canterbury*, Leicester 1984, 292–4; Eales, 'Introduction', 32, 41.

[110] Codsheath (GDB, 3: KEN 2,4–5); Sandwich (GDB, 3: KEN 2,2); Petham (GDB, 3v: KEN 2,15 and note); Westgate (GDB, 3v–4: KEN 2,16;24); Wingham (GDB, 3v: KEN 2,21); Selbrittenden (GDB, 4: KEN 2,27). The half sulung in Sheppey is the only entry for Teynham hundred (GDB, 4v: KEN 2,37) but looks inadequate.

[111] Eales, 'Introduction', 3–4.

[112] The recognized start has moved from I (Galbraith, *Making of Domesday Book*, 40 and, implicitly, Eales, 'Introduction') through III (*Domesday Re-Bound*, London 1954) to VI: Roffe, 'Domesday Book and Northern Society'; Thorn and Thorn, 'The Making of GDB', esp. 42–3. Wormald, 'Domesday Lawsuits', 67, stresses county variation within circuits.

[113] Flight, *Survey of Kent*, 153, suggests the scribe's remembrance of normality.

[114] Baxter, 'Representation of Lordship', gives a breakdown of formulae and their positioning.

A possible reason for this cluster of anomalies lies in the several ways in which the king and archbishop were uniquely bound together. Stigand's unwise appointment as archbishop by Edward in 1052, his retention of Winchester in illegal plurality and his continuance in office until 1070, all reflected badly on William himself and on Edward, his preferred predecessor.[115] Given that Lanfranc had apparently taught William to use *damnatio memoriae* against Harold, it is at least interesting that both avoided naming their predecessors in Kent.[116]

Leofwine, not Harold, had been Odo's predecessor as earl but on top of William's sensitivity around all the Godwinesons, on Odo too king and archbishop were intertwined. Earl Godwine had doubtless been predatory but he was also earl of Kent and a statement in the 1078/9 memorandum that King Edward had transferred the county's third penny from Archbishop Eadsige (1038–44) to Godwine suggests that the earldom had been transferred; with it presumably went comital lands to which Canterbury nursed an ongoing, and in the event partially rewarded, sense of entitlement.[117] Odo, the successor earl whose Kentish estates look similar to a castelry, cannot have been happy.[118] Lanfranc and Odo had known and apparently respected each other for years in Normandy and then initially in England, but while the technicolour Canterbury version of Lanfranc's routing of his villainous rival at Penenden is a post-Lanfranc confection, their growing enmity was real.[119] Clashing over estates in Kent cannot have helped (and Lanfranc was probably unamused that Odo succeeded to Stigand's private estates in Norfolk) but hatred may also have sprung from rivalry for the king's attention and/or affection.[120] It was probably Lanfranc's assurance that it was legitimate to judge Odo solely in his role as a secular earl that allowed William in 1082 to throw the man who was both his half-brother and bishop of Bayeux into gaol.[121] William had good reason to be supportive of a

---

[115] On Stigand, Brooks, *Early History*, 304–13; on Lanfranc's rejection of his predecessor, H. E. J. Cowdrey, *Lanfranc. Scholar, Monk and Archbishop*, Oxford 2003, 81–4; on William's piety, David Bates, *William the Conqueror*, London 1989, 148–51.

[116] George Garnett, 'Coronation and Propaganda: Implications of the Norman Claim to the Throne of England in 1066', *TRHS*, 5th series 36, 1986, 91–116; repeated in George Garnett, *Conquered England: Kingship, Succession, and Tenure, 1066–1166*, Oxford 2007, ch.1.

[117] See especially Du Boulay, *Lordship of Canterbury*, 38–9; Nicholas Brooks, *The Early History of the Church of Canterbury*, Leicester 1984, 300–1; Bates, 'The Land Pleas', 16; Eales, 'Introduction', 39–42; Robin Fleming, 'Domesday Estates of the King and the Godwines: A Study in Late Saxon Politics', *Speculum* 58, 1983, 987–1007.

[118] See Eales, 'Introduction', 44–5; Lewis, 'The Early Earls of Norman England', 216–18; Roffe, *Decoding Domesday*, 166–7.

[119] David Bates, 'The Character and Career of Odo, Bishop of Bayeux (1049/50–1097)', *Speculum* 50, 1975, 1–20; Bates, 'Land Pleas', followed in Cowdrey, *Lanfranc*, 109–15.

[120] Odo was landholder 2 in Norfolk; the TRE tenures are given.

[121] The assurance is only mentioned by William of Malmesbury: Bates, 'Character and Career of Odo', 16.

respected archbishop who, having experienced political insecurity, was at least as eager to serve his king as his God, and Lanfranc had achieved some extremely beneficial drops in hidation (i.e., taxation) in Kent.[122]

Lanfranc's animosity, and indeed duplicity, in other disputes is well recorded, and carrying Stigand's *damnatio memoriae* into Domesday not simply by using another available phrase but by avoiding the subject altogether seems entirely in character.[123] There was clearly no general commandment against mentioning Stigand, who is regularly and honourably named, notably in the returns of his successor at Winchester and in East Anglia. Harold, a more important embarrassment, is also frequently named but the whole concept of TRE and the associated fudging shows the successful *damnatio* of the memory of his kingship.[124] It is unlikely that the handling of this had to be spelt out: sheriffs, bishops, commissioners, and scribes had internalized the need for circumspection. Lanfranc's unchallenged silence and the remarkably light touch across circuit I, perhaps even the GDB clerk's lapses of concentration, become explicable if a similar health warning was perceived around Kent.

Lanfranc's achievement was probably unique. Normally the county process rendered the survival of intact returns and the possibility of manipulation equally rare. Many episcopal chapters doubtless show traces of written returns but analysis so far suggests that only Dorchester and Oswaldslow survived effectively intact, and it is unlikely to be coincidence that both were old-fashioned triple hundreds. Finally, Dorchester and Lanfranc demonstrate that there was no necessary correlation between intact returns and manipulation, and that silence can speak as loudly as words.

---

[122] See Cowdrey, *Lanfranc*; David Knowles, *The Monastic Order in England*, Cambridge 1940, esp. 109–10, 142. Frank Barlow, 'A View of Archbishop Lanfranc', *Journal of Ecclesiastical History* 16, 1965, 163–77. Kent's hidation dropped in general but Canterbury's in particular, cf. Harvey, 'Domesday Book and its Predecessors', 764; Harvey, 'Taxation and the Economy', 257–9; Eales, 'Introduction', 19.

[123] For Lanfranc's overstatement of the degree of document loss in the 1067 fire so as to justify the production of purported papal letters and privileges supporting his see's primatial authority, see *Charters of Christ Church Canterbury Part 1*, 58; for his behaviour towards Berengar of Tours, Toivo J. Holopainen, 'Lanfranc of Bec and Berengar of Tours', *ANS* 34, 2011, 105–21 and similarly (post-Domesday) to William, bishop of Durham, Cowdrey, *Lanfranc*, 219–24.

[124] Garnett, 'Coronation and Propaganda'.

9

Geospatial Technologies and the Geography of Domesday England in the Twenty-First Century

Andrew G. Lowerre

SCHOLARS HAVE MADE maps based on the information recorded in Domesday Book for more than a century, H. C. Darby's *Domesday Geography* series being the most famous and comprehensive body of Domesday maps to date.[1] It is now, however, more than thirty years since the publication of the final volume in Darby's series. The decades since have seen dramatic changes in our understanding of Domesday Book and how it was made, as well as in the capabilities and ubiquity of computers and digital mapping. Indeed, three different web-based systems allowing geographical interrogation and mapping of Domesday materials appeared in 2010. In this chapter, I examine how various geospatial technologies and digital datasets based on Domesday Book make it possible to query, map and analyse Domesday material, investigating the geography of Domesday Book and of Domesday England, in new ways.

I begin by defining the kinds of geospatial technologies to which I will refer. The first and most fundamental, of course, is the traditional map – whether drawn, printed or projected on paper or a computer screen. A map is a selective, two-dimensional, graphic representation of information about phenomena (physical, environmental, social, cultural or any combination thereof) in which the information

---

[1] H. C. Darby, *Domesday England*, 1986 revised paperback ed., Cambridge 1977; H. C. Darby, *The Domesday Geography of Eastern England*, 3rd edn, Cambridge 1977; H. C. Darby and E. M. J. Campbell, *The Domesday Geography of South East England*, Cambridge 1962; H. C. Darby and R. W. Finn, *The Domesday Geography of South West England*, Cambridge 1967; H. C. Darby and I. S. Maxwell, *The Domesday Geography of Northern England*, Cambridge 1962; H. C. Darby and I. B. Terrett, *The Domesday Geography of Midland England*, Cambridge 1954; H. C. Darby and G. R. Versey, *Domesday Gazetteer*, Cambridge 1975.

is explicitly tied to the spatial location of the phenomena as measured in reference to the surface of the Earth.[2] By traditional map, I mean a map in which the informational content and scale are fixed.

Next is web mapping which, as the name implies, comprises systems whereby maps are made available via the World Wide Web and are viewed in Internet browsing software. Google Maps™ and Microsoft's Bing Maps™ are two well-known examples.[3] Current web mapping systems allow a far greater degree of interactivity than do traditional maps: users can pan around to focus on different areas, zoom in and out to a variety of different scales, and often it is possible to click on a feature shown on the map to see more information about it. Similar to these are so-called virtual globe or geobrowser systems, such as Google Earth™ or NASA World Wind.[4] Such software enables users to view a wide variety of satellite and aerial photographic imagery, as well as other types of spatially located data, using a quasi-three-dimensional perspective.

The third main geospatial technology to which I will refer is Geographic Information Systems or GIS. There are many definitions of GIS, but one of the most widely quoted states that GIS is '[a] system for capturing, storing, checking, integrating, manipulating, analysing and displaying data which are spatially referenced to the Earth.'[5] Web mapping systems and virtual globes are similar in many ways to GIS, in that all three deal with spatially-referenced data, but web mapping systems and virtual globes lack the tools to manipulate and, most importantly, analyse the data. GIS software also tends to provide far more extensive options for querying and displaying data than do web mapping systems or virtual globes. Of course, the greater sophistication and complexity of GIS software compared with, say, Google Maps™, means that learning to use it requires a greater investment of time and effort. As both GIS and web technologies and infrastructure have developed, the boundaries between the different types of systems have blurred.[6] Here,

---

[2] This is to contrast with other kinds of 'mapping' or 'spatialization' of information where the information is not explicitly linked to a location on the surface of the Earth. Examples include the well-known map of the London Underground system, which shows the topological connections between individual lines and stations along those lines, but not their actual spatial locations, and the 'concept maps' discussed in D. J. Staley, *Computers, Visualization, and History: How New Technology Will Transform Our Understanding of the Past*, Armonk NY 2003, 125–140.
[3] Google Inc., *Google Maps UK*, http://maps.google.co.uk, accessed 02/10/2014; Microsoft, *Bing Maps*, http://www.bing.com/maps/, accessed 02/10/2014.
[4] Google, *Google Earth*, http://www.google.com/earth/index.html, accessed 02/10/2014; National Aeronautics and Space Administration (NASA), *World Wind*, http://worldwind.arc.nasa.gov/index.html, accessed 02/10/2014; goworldwind.org, *Get Started*, http://goworldwind.org/getting-started/, accessed 02/10/2014.
[5] Department of the Environment, *Handling Geographic Information: Report of the Committee of Enquiry chaired by Lord Chorley*, London 1987, 132.
[6] For discussion of the blurring of technological boundaries and the recent explosion of

however, I will use the term GIS to refer to combinations of dedicated software and spatially-referenced data used on a single computer or a local network, not over the Internet in a web browser.

One type of geospatial technology which I will not consider here is satellite-based navigation systems, the most common of which is the Global Positioning System or GPS network. It would, in theory, be possible to create a GPS-based application based on information in Domesday Book. For example, a car's sat-nav could read out the text of the relevant Domesday entries for the places one passes while driving across the country, pausing only to instruct you to take the second exit from the roundabout and then turn right in 100 yards. The market for such an application would, however, probably be limited, which perhaps explains why one does not yet exist.

I must also address a basic question: why put information recorded in Domesday Book on maps at all? My intention in posing the question is not to deny the usefulness of maps of Domesday's contents, but to pause and think about the purposes behind making them. The easiest answer to the question is the same as the argument for climbing Mount Everest. And F. W. Maitland famously predicted that the 'villages and hundreds which the Norman clerks tore to shreds [would be] reconstituted and pictured in maps',[7] a prediction which has, of course, come true. But 'it's there and we can' or 'Maitland told me to' are insufficient to justify the effort needed to construct Domesday maps, whether digital or otherwise. Darby's purpose in creating the *Domesday Geography* series was to attempt a reconstruction of a past geography,[8] while recognizing how incomplete that reconstruction would inevitably be.[9]

My own answer to that question encompasses three points. First, location, space

---

spatially aware web-based applications useful for humanities research, see L. J. Rouse, S. J. Bergeron and T. M. Harris, 'Participating in the Geospatial Web: Collaborative Mapping, Social Networks and Participatory GIS', in *The Geospatial Web: How Geobrowsers, Social Software and the Web 2.0 are Shaping the Network Society*, ed. A. Scharl and K. Tochtermann, London 2007, 153–8; T. M. Harris, L. J. Rouse and S. Bergeron, 'The Geospatial Semantic Web, Pareto GIS and the Humanities', in *The Spatial Humanities: GIS and the Future of Humanities Scholarship*, ed. D. J. Bodenhamer, J. Corrigan, and T. M. Harris, Bloomington & Indianapolis 2010, 124–42; I. N. Gregory and A. Geddes, 'Conclusions: From Historical GIS to Spatial Humanities: Challenges and Opportunities' in *Toward Spatial Humanities: Historical GIS and Spatial History*, ed. I. N. Gregory and A. Geddes, Bloomington and Indianapolis 2014, 172–85.

[7] F. W. Maitland, *Domesday Book and Beyond: Three Essays in the Early History of England*, 1987 reprint edn, Cambridge 1897, 520.

[8] See H. C. Darby, 'Domesday Woodland in East Anglia', *Antiquity* 8, 1934, 211–15 at 212; H. C. Darby, 'On the Relations of Geography and History', *Transactions and Papers (Institute of British Geographers)* 19, 1953, 1–11.

[9] Darby, *Domesday England*, 13–14; H. C. Darby, 'Domesday Book and the Geographer', in *Domesday Studies: Papers Read at the Novocentenary Conference of the Royal Historical*

and place – which are not precisely synonymous terms – matter, both to understanding Domesday Book itself and to understanding the world in which Domesday was created and which it so tantalizingly but imperfectly reflects. Using any of the geospatial technologies I discuss should allow and encourage students of Domesday to, in the words of Ian Gregory, 'think closely about how individuals and places interact over space, how different places behave in different ways, and that space is not a static concept but is something that changes and reinvents itself.'[10]

The second point follows closely on the first, in that maps are one of the best means available to record, visualize and explore the relationships and interactions between people, places and things in space. Visualization of Domesday materials, like a wide range of spatially-attributable humanities data, is doubtless a good thing.[11] There can, however, be problems with uninformed or uncritical visualization. Poorly conceived and drawn maps can confuse or even deceive their readers – whether deliberately or not.[12] Maps and map-makers are, by their nature, subjective, limited and selective in what they represent.[13] The apparently natural human tendency to perceive patterns in what we see – whether or not those patterns are actually there – highlights the considerable potential for misunderstanding and misinterpretation of Domesday maps. Nevertheless, maps, together with some of the tools available in some geospatial software, can enhance the investigation and understanding of the past in ways no other media or methods can.[14]

The third point is that Domesday Book does record real information about real-world phenomena or conditions, or what people in the late eleventh century thought was real enough to be worth recording, and that is it possible to link the vast majority of that information to existing real-world places we can identify. There is, of course, considerable debate about how Domesday Book came to be recorded in its present form, how comprehensive, representative, or reliable its contents might be, and what much of that content actually means. But these debates do not

---

Society and the Institute of British Geographers: Winchester, 1986, ed. J. C. Holt, Woodbridge 1987, 101–19.

[10] I. Gregory, 'Using Geographical Information Systems to Explore Space and Time in the Humanities', in *The Virtual Representation of the Past*, ed. M. Greengrass and L. Hughes, Farnham 2008, 135–46.

[11] M. Jessop, *The Domesday Book: Visualization Tools to Explore Identity at the Start of the Second Millennium*, http://www.bcs.org/upload/pdf/ewic_ev09_s2paper1.pdf, accessed 02/10/2014.

[12] M. S. Monmonier, *How to Lie with Maps*, 2nd edn, Chicago 1996.

[13] J. B. Harley, 'Historical Geography and the Cartographic Illusion', *Journal of Historical Geography* 15, 1989, 80–91.

[14] Staley, *Computers, Visualization, and History*, 35–57, 74–9. For a discussion of how and why GIS-based spatial statistics are useful and can improve on simple visualization of data on maps, see I. N. Gregory, '"A Map Is Just a Bad Graph": Why Spatial Statistics are Important in Historical GIS', in *Placing History: How Maps, Spatial Data, and GIS Are Changing Historical Scholarship*, ed. A. K. Knowles, Redlands CA 2008, 123–49.

preclude making maps of the information Domesday holds, and exploring the geography of some elements of Domesday's contents may contribute to those debates.

Ultimately, the importance of the application of any geospatial technology to Domesday Book lies not in the technology in and of itself, but in the provision of tools which allow students of Domesday and Domesday England to ask and answer questions about Domesday Book and its contents, hopefully faster and better than before. So, what kinds of geographic questions can or might be asked of Domesday and its contents, and how well do applications of different geospatial technologies help to provide answers?[15]

The most fundamental geographic question anyone might ask is, 'Where is this place that is mentioned in Domesday Book?' Closely related is the question, 'Does Domesday Book mention any place near "here"?' (wherever 'here' happens to be). The National Archives Labs Domesday on a Map web mapping system is one place to start answering these basic questions.[16] The web page provides a map of Domesday places, overlaid on modern background mapping, and the ability to search for places, using a modern place name, postcode, or a Domesday place name.

At the time of the conference (September 2011), a so-called 'heat' map, depicting the density of Domesday places across the country, was the first type of map displayed.[17] As one zoomed in, 'estimated place boundaries' appeared – purely geometric outlines derived from the points representing Domesday places which do not reflect late-eleventh-century estate or administrative boundaries.[18] At the time of writing (October 2014), neither the 'heat map' nor the 'estimated place boundaries' display on the map. After further zooming, Domesday places are indicated as

---

[15] I do not discuss John Palmer's *Domesday Explorer* CD-ROM, launched at the Domesday conference in 2000: see J. Palmer, M. Palmer and G. Slater, *Domesday Explorer CD-ROM version 1.0: Professional Edition* [CD-ROM], Chichester 2000; J. J. N. Palmer, 'Great Domesday on CD-ROM', in *Domesday Book*, ed. E. Hallam and D. Bates, Stroud 2001, 141–50. For a review of this resource, including discussion of the mapping system included in it, see R. Fleming and A. Lowerre, 'MacDomesday Book. Review Article', *Past & Present* 184, 2004, 209–32, especially 219–20.

[16] The National Archives, *Domesday on a Map*, http://labs.nationalarchives.gov.uk/domesday/, accessed 02/10/2014.

[17] The 'heat' map is not clipped to fit the coastline, so the map (if taken literally) suggests that there were a good number of Domesday places off the northern coast of Norfolk or adrift in the Wash.

[18] Known as Thiessen polygons, Voronoi diagrams or Dirilecht domains, the polygons are constructed from a set of points such that the boundary separating any two points is equidistant between those points: A. Okabe, B. Boots, K. Sugihara and S. N. Chiu, *Spatial Tessellations: Concepts and Applications of Voronoi Diagrams*, 2nd edn, Chichester 2000. Thiessen polygons have long been used as a means of assigning areas to locations represented as points, but their geometric simplicity frequently does not effectively model past territories: see I. Gregory and P. S. Ell, *Historical GIS: Technologies, Methodologies and Scholarship*, Cambridge Studies in Historical Geography 39, Cambridge 2007, 68–70; J. Conolly and M. Lake, *Geographical Information Systems in Archaeology*, Cambridge 2006, 211–13.

unlabelled orange teardrops. Clicking on a place marker displays a pop-up window, which shows the modern place-name and its Domesday variants, as well the folios on which the place is described.[19] Rather than reusing the coordinates included in any other existing editions or datasets,[20] TNA Labs determined the mapped locations of Domesday places using an automated process.[21] They admit that the results are not perfect and estimate that roughly 5 per cent of their locations for Domesday places are incorrect.[22]

The Open Domesday web site developed by Anna Powell-Smith, using the AHRC-funded Domesday dataset developed by John Palmer and his team, can also provide quick and easy answers to the 'where is my place?' question.[23] Open Domesday shows points for Domesday places in three different sizes, depending on the total recorded population of the place, overlaid on modern background mapping provided by Google Maps™. The search function works well for modern place names or postcodes, but does not allow searching for the Domesday variants of place names.[24] It is also possible to find all the places in a given hundred, wapentake or county by locating at least one place in the area of interest, and then clicking on the

---

[19] The list of variants is indicated as 'Historic names for (place) and the time at which time [sic] were in use.' The pop-up window also includes a function to save the unique web address (Uniform Resource Locator or URL) for each place depicted, to use as a reference or to link to or from another web page.

[20] For example, the Alecto facsimile: Alecto Historical Editions, *The Digital Domesday Book* [CD-ROM], Alecto Historical Editions, London 2002; *Great Domesday*, ed. R. W. H. Erskine and A. Williams, Library ed., London 1986–1992; *Little Domesday Book: Essex*, ed. A. Williams, London 2000; *Little Domesday Book: Norfolk*, ed. A. Williams, London 2000; *Little Domesday Book: Suffolk*, ed. A. Williams, London 2000. John Palmer's AHRC-funded dataset could also have been used: J. Palmer, F. Thorn, C. Thorn and N. Hodgson, *Electronic Edition of Domesday Book: Translation, Databases and Scholarly Commentary, 1086*, computer file, UK Data Archive, 2007. A partially updated version of this dataset is available from the University of Hull's Digital Repository: https://hydra.hull.ac.uk/resources/hull:domesdayDisplaySet, accessed 14/03/2012.

[21] The National Archives, *Launching 'Domesday on a Map'*, http://labs.nationalarchives.gov.uk/wordpress/index.php/2010/10/launching-domesday-on-a-map/#more-397, accessed 02/10/2014.

[22] The National Archives, *The National Archives Labs Blog: Domesday on a Map*, http://labs.nationalarchives.gov.uk/wordpress/index.php/2010/10/domesday-on-a-map/, accessed 14/02/2011. At the time of writing (October 2014), this web page is no longer available. The estimate of 5 per cent was given in a TNA Labs reply to a user post made on 22 October 2010 at 2:37 pm. Searching for a location outside Great Britain returns a result of 'Nothing found', but the system will happily find locations outside England, e.g., Swansea or Edinburgh, and zoom to them.

[23] A. Powell-Smith, *Open Domesday: The First Online Copy of Domesday Book of 1086*, http://www.domesdaymap.co.uk/, accessed 02/10/2014; Palmer, Thorn, Thorn and Hodgson, *Electronic Edition of Domesday Book*.

[24] Like the background mapping, the location search function seems to be provided by Google Maps™, so it is possible to enter such places as Tokyo or Johannesburg in the search

hyperlink for the hundred, wapentake or county in which the place lay. Doing so brings up a list of all the places in the administrative district in question (along with figures for their tax assessments and population), and shows only the relevant places as markers on the background map.[25]

One can also search the Prosopography of Anglo-Saxon England's 'Domesday Online'[26] system, but only using the modern English names of places that appear in Domesday. It is not possible to search using UK postcodes, county, hundred or wapentake names, or the names of places not mentioned in Domesday. The limitations of the locational search are perhaps not surprising, given the system's prosopographical rather than more generally geographical focus. If one's query is essentially place- rather than person-based, Domesday on a Map or Open Domesday may provide more useful results than PASE Domesday Online.

Following the question, 'Where is it?', the next question one is likely to ask about a place is, 'What does Domesday say about it?'. TNA Labs Domesday on a Map does not directly provide answers to this or any other further questions, because here the content of the Domesday text sits behind a pay wall. The folio references for each Domesday place are links to TNA's 'Documents Online' order system, from which digital copies of the relevant extracts from the Alecto facsimile and translation can be purchased at the price of £3.30 each (at the time of writing). Obtaining information on more than a handful of places via this system would rapidly become expensive and difficult to manage.

Open Domesday offers a summary of information about each Domesday place. Given that the system is very much a work in progress, any description of its contents may potentially soon be out of date. At the time of writing, however, Open Domesday lists the county and hundred (wapentakes are not distinguished as such), the total population and 'tax paid', enumerates the values, people, ploughlands, ploughteams and other resources, and records the lord of the holding in 1066 and in 1086, as well as the tenant-in-chief in 1086. For places covered by Little or Exon Domesday, numbers of livestock both TRE and TRW are given, but – like Palmer's AHRC dataset – the web pages present only the TRW population figures. Where a given place is described in more than one Domesday entry, the page summarizes each individual entry separately. A thumbnail image of the relevant passage scanned from the nineteenth-century Ordnance Survey facsimile edition accompanies each

---

box. The map jumps to those locations, and, of course, there are no Domesday places to be seen.

[25] The listing of places in their respective hundreds is not without its flaws: for example, the system does not differentiate between Gartree wapentake in Leicestershire and Gartree wapentake in Lincolnshire, treating places in the two counties as belonging to the same 'hundred' (http://www.domesdaymap.co.uk/hundred/gartree/, accessed 02/10/2014).

[26] Prosopography of Anglo-Saxon England (PASE), *PASE Domesday*, http://domesday.pase.ac.uk/, accessed 02/10/2014.

entry.[27] To examine the facsimile more closely, one can click on the thumbnail to open the image in a larger pop-up window, or one can view an image of the whole of the relevant folio on a separate web page. Each Domesday place has its own unique web page, which can be linked to or cited. The Phillimore reference for each entry is recorded, but the folio number is not.[28]

The site supplies an approximation of the Domesday text, based on the values given in the statistical databases created by Palmer and his team, but the manner in which the information is presented is sometimes idiosyncratic. For example, tax assessments are recorded as so many 'geld units', making no distinction between hides, carucates, sulungs or East Anglian carucates and acres. Only the briefest of explanations are given for technical terms, though there is a link to the online help file for Palmer's *Domesday Explorer*.[29] The potential for misunderstanding the terms and values given is considerable, and reference to other editions of Domesday Book and to the documentation for Palmer et al.'s *Electronic Edition* is often necessary when trying to make sense of sometimes opaque formulations. Users who do not have much experience with Domesday Book may find the summary information in Open Domesday sufficient to their needs; those who are already experts probably will not.[30]

Assuming one has found one's place of interest, PASE Domesday Online does provide selected pieces of information in tabular form. For each holding in the place, the table lists the shire in which the place lies, the Phillimore reference for the entry, the TRE and TRW holders and their overlords, if any, a 'fiscal value' (i.e., geld assessment) and TRE and TRW values recorded in decimal pounds.

Moving from a focus on individual places to finding a range of places sharing some similar feature, a likely question is, 'Where are all the places in which some person of interest held land?'. This query underlies the concept of a 'feudal' or tenurial geography of Domesday, something that has been on many scholars' wish-lists for decades.[31] Open Domesday provides a straightforward means of answering this

---

[27] Ordnance Survey and W. B. Sanders, *Domesday Book, or the Great Survey of William the Conqueror (Facsimiles of the Parts Relating to the Various Counties)*, 2 vols. and also 33 pts. in 35 vols., Southampton 1861–1864.

[28] The scanned images from the nineteenth-century facsimile are arranged by county and 'page' number, e.g. 'Cornwall, page 4' (http://www.domesdaymap.co.uk/book/cornwall/04/, accessed 02/10/2014). Folio numbers for the images are not given.

[29] Given on the 'About' page: http://www.domesdaymap.co.uk/about/, accessed 02/10/2014.

[30] Powell-Smith and Palmer hope the web site will be a platform from which to create a 'crowd-sourced' transcription and translation of the Latin text, but at the time of writing, neither are available. Given the web site's status as a work in progress, it is hoped that these lacunae will be addressed in due course.

[31] S. P. J. Harvey, 'Review: Recent Domesday Studies', *EHR* 95, 1980, 121–33, 133; J. J. N. Palmer, 'Computerizing Domesday Book', *Transactions of the Institute of British Geographers* 11, 1986, 279–89, 288; Palmer, 'Great Domesday on CD-ROM', 147.

question. The 'Names' section of the web site presents the user with an alphabetical list of all TRE and TRW landholders, beginning with 'A.' (probably Æthelwig of Thetford, *antecessor* of Roger Bigod)[32] and ending with 'York St Peter, canons of, Institution, English canon'. Most landholders' names are hyperlinks, and clicking on a link brings up a list of all the places in which that landholder held land and a map indicating their locations. The list of places gives the hundred or wapentake and county in which each place lay,[33] but no statistics for geld assessment or values. The map of places works well enough if a landholder held in a relatively small number of locations not widely distributed. But for lords such as Earl Morcar or Geoffrey, bishop of Coutances, the on-screen map is not large enough to depict in one view all the places in which those men held land.

The key to the hyperlinked landholders' names in Open Domesday is John Palmer's identifications – building on the work of a range of other scholars[34] – of sometimes disparate instances of personal names in the Domesday text as one or more individuals. The problems of identifying both TRE and TRW landholders are well known, and Palmer's identifications are doubtless among the best and most comprehensive currently available. There is, however, no allowance for uncertainty in the way Open Domesday sets out the material. The system gives the impression that all the identifications are straightforward and uncontroversial, which is not always the case.

PASE Domesday Online approaches the question from a different angle. Rather than present the user with all the identifications already determined, PASE Domesday Online is intended as a tool 'to enable users to assemble the information they need to make prosopographical judgments about pre-Conquest landholders',[35] or, to use Chris Lewis's phrase, 'join the dots.'[36] The system is, naturally, focused on pre-Conquest individuals, but one can look for post-Conquest lords as well. It

---

[32] LDB, 141–141v: NFK 1,239 n.
[33] Curiously arranged in alphabetical order by hundred/wapentake name.
[34] Including P. A. Clarke, *The English Nobility under Edward the Confessor*, Oxford 1994; A. Williams, *The English and the Norman Conquest*, Woodbridge 1995; L. C. Loyd, *The Origins of Some Anglo–Norman Families*, ed. C. T. Clay and D. C. Douglas, Publications of the Harleian Society 103, Leeds 1951; I. J. Sanders, *English Baronies: A Study of their Origin and Descent, 1086–1327*, Oxford 1960; K. S. B. Keats-Rohan, *Domesday People: A Prosopography of Person Occurring in English Documents 1066–1166. I. Domesday Book*, Woodbridge 1999; K. S. B. Keats-Rohan, *Continental Origins of English Landholders 1086–1166: A Prosopography of post-Conquest England Compiled from the Sources*, CDROM, version 2.0, Coel Enterprises, 2009.
[35] Prosopography of Anglo-Saxon England (PASE), *About PASE > Research Methodology > Domesday Book*, http://www.pase.ac.uk/about/methodology/domesday.html, accessed 02/10/2014.
[36] C. P. Lewis, 'Joining the Dots: a Methodology for Identifying the English in the Domesday Book', in *Family Trees and the Roots of Politics: the Prosopography of Britain and France from the Tenth to the Twelfth Century*, ed. K. S. B. Keats-Rohan, Woodbridge 1997, 69–87.

is possible to search simply for names like 'Swein' or 'Aubrey', for by-names such as 'Cild' or 'de Ferrers', for 'descriptors' such as 'thegn' or 'sheriff', for names of religious institutions, for example the abbey of Holy Trinity at Fécamp, or any combination thereof. It is also possible to limit one's search just to TRE holders, their overlords, TRW tenants-in-chief or their tenants. The results of a search are presented as a table and on a map, though it must be noted that, at the time of writing (October 2014), the mapping elements of the system no longer function.[37] The following discussion describes the mapping available at the time of the conference (September 2011). The size and default scale of the map are such that all the places found will appear. The points representing places can be colour-coded based on the TRE holder, TRE overlord, TRW tenant-in-chief or TRW subtenant. For example, one can search for the name 'Morcar' as a TRE landholder,[38] with the places grouped by TRW tenant-in-chief, producing a map that depicts where lands ascribed to Morcar passed to King William, Drogo de la Beuvriere, Earl Roger, Count Alan and an assortment of other post-Conquest lords.

One serious problem with PASE Domesday Online is that the mapping software has difficulty displaying points that lie close to the Prime Meridian, leading to some bizarre cartographic outcomes when interrogating the data. To give just one example, a search for the TRW lord Hardwin de Scales produces a map which, at a national scale, seems to show the distribution of Hardwin's lands reasonably enough.[39] But when zoomed in, the map displays the points for many places in clearly erroneous locations. The PASE team were made aware of the problem and investigated how to fix it.[40]

A significant limitation of both Open Domesday and PASE Domesday Online is that neither is capable of showing the lands of more than one person at a time. Users can, of course, have the sites open in multiple browser tabs or windows and flip back and forth between them, but seeing all the estates of, say, Eskil of Ware together with those of Wulfmær of Eaton *on the same map* is impossible. To do so, it is necessary to use something like the offline version of PASE Domesday.

The key element of PASE Domesday Offline is a file containing the dataset that lies behind PASE Domesday Online.[41] This file stores both spatial data representing the Domesday place named in each holding and the data on landholders, fiscal

---

[37] The PASE technical director has been informed of this issue, as well as other broken web links on the PASE Domesday pages: J. Bradley, pers. com., 30 September 2014.
[38] That is, excluding cases where someone named Morcar was TRE overlord of a holding.
[39] The following parameters were used in the search: 'Name Type;' = Normalised Name; 'Name;' = Hardwin; 'Description type:' = By-name; 'Description:' = de Scales. All other parameters were left blank.
[40] S. Baxter, pers. com., 30 June 2011.
[41] Prosopography of Anglo-Saxon England (PASE), *Download the PASE Domesday Dataset*, http://domesday.pase.ac.uk/offline/data.html, 2010 version, accessed 31/08/2011. At the time of writing (October 2014), the downloadable file is no longer available.

assessments and annual values. The offline PASE Domesday dataset includes a slightly more detailed version of the data than is deployed in the online system. For example, the offline dataset records geld assessments in hides and virgates, carucates and bovates, acres and sulungs, maintaining the variety used in the Domesday text itself, while the online version conflates all the different assessments into a single field. Similarly, the offline dataset has separate fields to record pounds, shillings and pence for TRE and TRW annual values, as well as calculated fields recording the values in decimal pounds; the online version has only the fields for decimal pounds.[42] Utilizing the downloaded data requires GIS software, and the PASE team provide a link to a 'lightweight' GIS application that was freely available in 2011,[43] but this is only one of a wide range of such programmes. Regardless of what GIS software one might deploy, the downloadable PASE Domesday dataset can be interrogated to find, identify and plot the holdings of anyone recorded in Domesday Book, and map more than one landholder at a time, as shown in Figure 1.[44]

Having found all the places where one's person of interest held land, a natural follow-on question is, 'Where did my person hold *how much* land?'. Open Domesday does list all the places where a particular lord held land, but it provides no statistics regarding how much land in each location. To find out, a user must click on and examine the details for each place in turn.

PASE Domesday Online can readily produce a map using dots of increasing size to represent how much land a given lord held, based either on fiscal assessments or TRE or TRW annual values. The same effect can be achieved using the PASE Domesday dataset offline in a GIS. The main limitation is that the PASE Domesday dataset only records the fiscal assessments and fairly simplified versions of the annual values for each holding. Mapping the lands of, for example, Ilbert de Lacy based on the ploughlands or population of his holdings is not possible.

It is worth digressing briefly to discuss the cartographic content and quality of the maps produced by the different resources discussed here. One point of basic cartographic critique of the maps in Domesday on a Map and Open Domesday is that they lack any indication of scale or legends explaining the features depicted in the

---

[42] For a detailed list and explanation of the data fields contained in the downloadable dataset, see S. Baxter and M. Jessop, *PASE Domesday GIS User Guide*, http://pase.cchcdn.net/domesday/gis_offline_help.pdf, accessed 27/06/2011. At the time of writing (October 2014), the User Guide is no longer available.

[43] Prosopography of Anglo-Saxon England (PASE), *Download Software*, http://domesday.pase.ac.uk/offline/software.html, accessed 31/08/2011. The user guide provides extensive instructions on how to use the software to investigate the PASE Domesday dataset: Baxter and Jessop, *PASE Domesday GIS User Guide*. At the time of writing (October 2014), the software application specified on the PASE website is no longer available, but other, comparable applications are.

[44] The problem which PASE Domesday Online has displaying places lying near the Prime Meridian does not appear to affect the downloaded dataset.

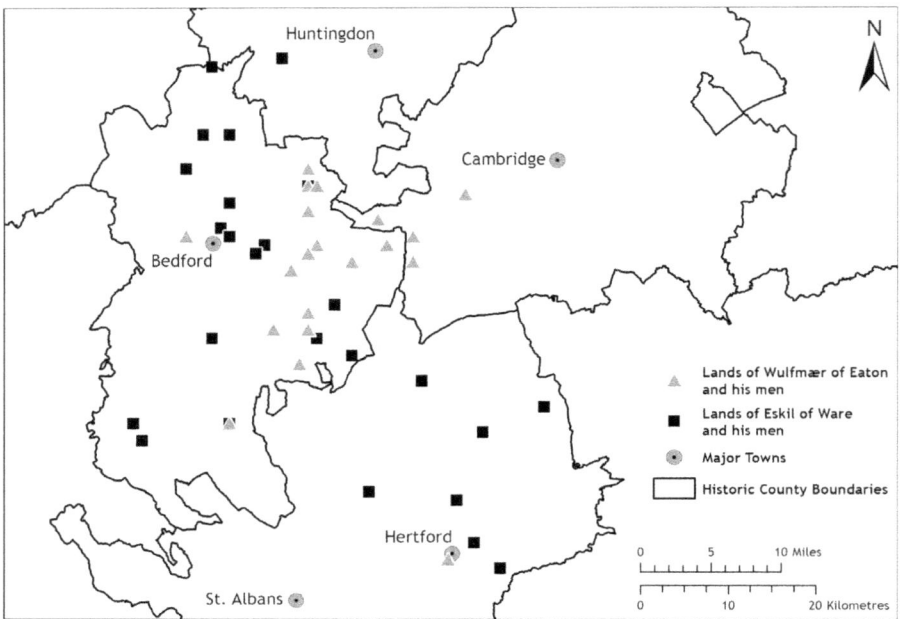

Figure 1: Lands of Wulfmær of Eaton and Eskil of Ware and their men, created using downloadable PASE Domesday dataset in GIS. County boundaries provided by the Historic County Borders Project (http://www.county-borders.co.uk/hcbp_4.htm)

background mapping. PASE Domesday Online includes both, and such map furniture can readily be added to a map created using any GIS package. Domesday on a Map and Open Domesday both use background mapping depicting a wide range of modern features, while PASE Domesday Online shows only county boundaries and major rivers. The usefulness and appropriateness of different, and different amounts, of non-Domesday information in the maps will depend on the audience. The key question one should ask here is not, 'Is that a nice-looking map?' but rather, 'Does that map help me answer my question?'. The ends to which one wishes to put maps of Domesday's contents must influence strongly the degree of complexity and sophistication needed in one's maps. One might ask a straightforward question but need a map drawn to professional cartographic standards to go into a peer-reviewed journal published by a university press. It is also possible, though perhaps less likely, that one might have asked and answered a quite complex question, but be satisfied with a fairly basic map depicting that answer.

Increasing the complexity of the questions, one might query how much of any of the myriad resources Domesday records were distributed across a region, county or the whole of Domesday England, and, more intriguingly, who held them? Much of this sort of information is mapped in Darby's *Domesday Geographies*, except, of course, for the matter of 'who held it'. Neither Open Domesday nor PASE Domesday – whether online or off – allows the creation of maps of these assets. To map all the cottars in Cambridgeshire or woodland in Warwickshire, one must look elsewhere.

At the moment, the only place one can turn is to the *Electronic Edition* of Domesday created by John Palmer and his team, the same dataset used to create Open Domesday. The searchable text and extensive notes in Palmer's electronic edition are immensely useful, and the fact that it can be downloaded at no cost is a tremendous boon. The various statistical databases do not, however, lend themselves to incorporation into a rigorous GIS. The dataset includes National Grid References for all the identifiable places, but the coordinates are given only to the nearest kilometre.[45] This leads to a somewhat artificial appearance when plotted on a map. And in a number of instances, the same NGR is given for more than one distinct place. Of course, these issues could be relatively easily overcome by refining the grid references. More problematic is the structure of the statistical data. The main statistics database follows the Phillimore reference system, so each entry in the text gets a record in the database. This approach makes it easy to refer to individual entries, but single Domesday entries sometimes describe more than one place. As a result, statistics for geographically disparate locations are lumped together in single database records.

Also, in seeking to make the data accessible and to keep the database simple, the flexibility and detail of the statistics have been heavily curtailed. To give just one example: the dataset records meadow using two fields, one for the amount of meadow, the other for the units. So, if there were 93 acres of meadow, the first field would record '93' and the second 'acres'. The problem is that the 'amounts' field stores textual rather than numeric data, to accommodate cases where Domesday gives amounts such as 'meadow 2 leagues and 5 furlongs in length and 4 furlongs in width'. This means that the numeric values recorded in this field cannot easily be tabulated. The same difficulty arises with the recording of pasture and woodland. So, some elements of the *Electronic Edition* of Domesday Book are extremely valuable, but the limitations imposed by the data structure make the statistical data rather less useful from a geographic perspective than might have been hoped.

In an attempt to develop a digital Domesday resource explicitly designed to take advantage of the tools provided by GIS software, I have been working with

---

[45] In cartographic terms this means that the point representing a Domesday place is located at the south-western corner of a 1x1 km square. And while the *Electronic Edition* dataset does include alphanumeric National Grid References (NGRs) for places, it does not provide the kind of *x,y*-coordinates required by GIS software to map the places (see Fleming and Lowerre, 'MacDomesday Book', 230 n.29). Users must convert the NGRs to coordinate pairs themselves. The PASE Domesday dataset employs the NGRs included in the *Electronic Edition* dataset: see Prosopography of Anglo-Saxon England (PASE), *About PASE > Research Methodology > Domesday Book*.

another Domesday database, that created in the 1980s by a team led by Robin Fleming.⁴⁶ I have used data from four counties – Bedfordshire, Cambridgeshire, Huntingdonshire and Northamptonshire – in a pilot project to investigate migrating the data to a more up-to-date format and then 'spatially enabling' them using GIS.⁴⁷

Rather than compressing into a small number of variables the sometimes bewildering variety of ways different types of information are recorded in Domesday, Fleming created her data in a highly atomized fashion, reflecting the complexity of the text.⁴⁸ This does mean that the database has a very large number of fields, which can be challenging to manage. The advantage of this approach is that data that have been finely split can subsequently be lumped together again if the need arises – the reverse is far more difficult. I took the 1980s-vintage data for the four pilot counties and painstakingly converted, reformatted and reorganized them into a relational database, so they are now in the 'rows-and-columns' format suitable for most modern database, spreadsheet and GIS software. Fleming's data used Darby and Versey's *Domesday Gazetteer* as the source for identifications of Domesday places, and part of the migration process included updating those identifications to reflect the most current knowledge.⁴⁹ I also carefully restructured the data so that statistics from disparate locations are not inadvertently lumped together.

In my GIS, I have represented Domesday places not only as points, but as areas or polygons as well. The coordinates for the points are taken from the indices and maps that accompany the Alecto facsimile. The polygons are based on early nineteenth-century parish boundaries.⁵⁰ Of course, Domesday places and parish boundaries do not match one-to-one, so I modified the parish boundaries,

---

⁴⁶ R. Fleming, 'A Report on the Domesday Book Database Project', *Medieval Prosopography* 7, 1986, 55–61. Fleming's dataset covers only the counties of GDB.

⁴⁷ A. Lowerre, 'Mapping Domesday Book using GIS', *Research News* 8, 2008, 3–7. The pilot project used Microsoft Access 2002 and Esri ArcGIS 9.2. I am currently working on migrating the rest of Fleming's data for the remaining counties. I hope to capture comparable data from LDB in due course.

⁴⁸ By way of comparison, Palmer's databases use about 150 fields for all of Great and Little Domesday; my pilot database for just four counties contains about 400 different variables, which is less than a quarter of the total number in Fleming's full dataset, which, as previously noted, does not include data from Little Domesday.

⁴⁹ Using the identifications in the Alecto facsimile edition and in Palmer et al.'s *Electronic Edition*.

⁵⁰ The parish boundaries used here were originally mapped by Roger Kain and Richard Oliver at the University of Exeter, and a GIS dataset of these boundaries was developed by Nick Burton and others at the University of Portsmouth: R. J. P. Kain and R. R. Oliver, *Historic Parishes of England and Wales: An Electronic Map of Boundaries before 1850 with a Gazetteer and Metadata*, computer file, AHDS History, UK Data Archive, 2001; N. Burton, J. Westwood and P. Carter, *GIS of the Ancient Parishes of England and Wales, 1500–1850*, computer file, AHDS History, UK Data Archive, 2004.

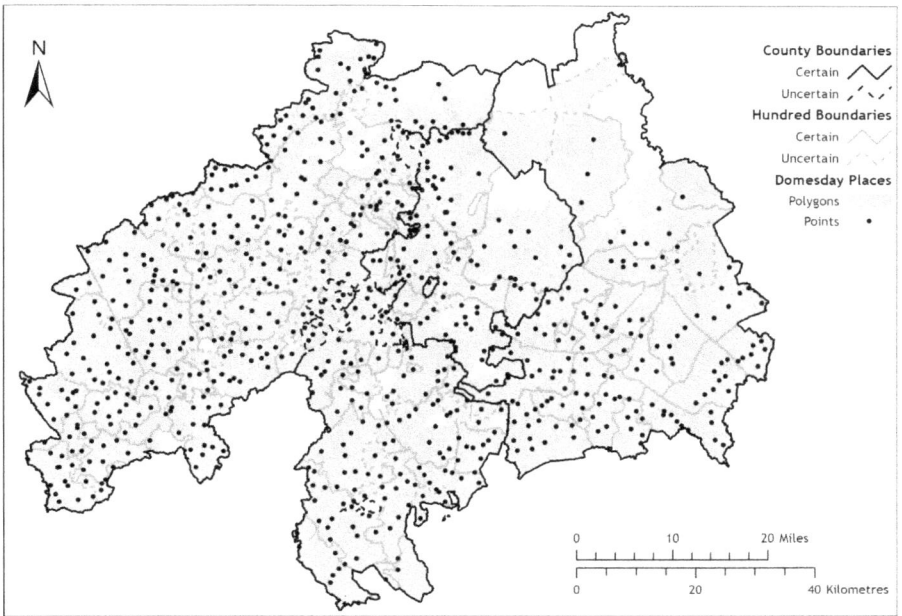

Figure 2: Domesday places in the four-county pilot study area shown as points and polygons, along with hundred and county boundaries

where appropriate, to model as closely as possible the administrative land units of late eleventh-century England.[51] Using the parish polygons, it is also possible to reconstruct the boundaries of the various administrative districts recorded in Domesday, such as hundreds and counties.[52] Figure 2 shows the point and polygon representations of Domesday places in the pilot area, as well as hundred and county boundaries.

So, with the database linked to the points and polygons in the GIS, all the tedious calculation and mapping that took Darby and his team years can be done in minutes or hours. For example, after adding up the total non-servile population (i.e., all those not recorded as slaves) for each point, the GIS can calculate or interpolate the population density per square kilometre over the whole four-county area. The general picture of population density in the region is familiar, but the results

[51] A more detailed description of the method used (applied to a different dataset based on the same four Domesday counties) is given in A. Lowerre, *Placing Castles in the Conquest: Landscape, Lordship and Local Politics in the South-Eastern Midlands, 1066–1100*, British Archaeological Reports, British Series 385, Oxford 2005, 204, 206–208.

[52] Cf ibid., 209–10. It would also be possible to reconstruct boundaries for wapentakes, Kentish lathes, Sussex rapes and Yorkshire and Lincolnshire ridings using the same method.

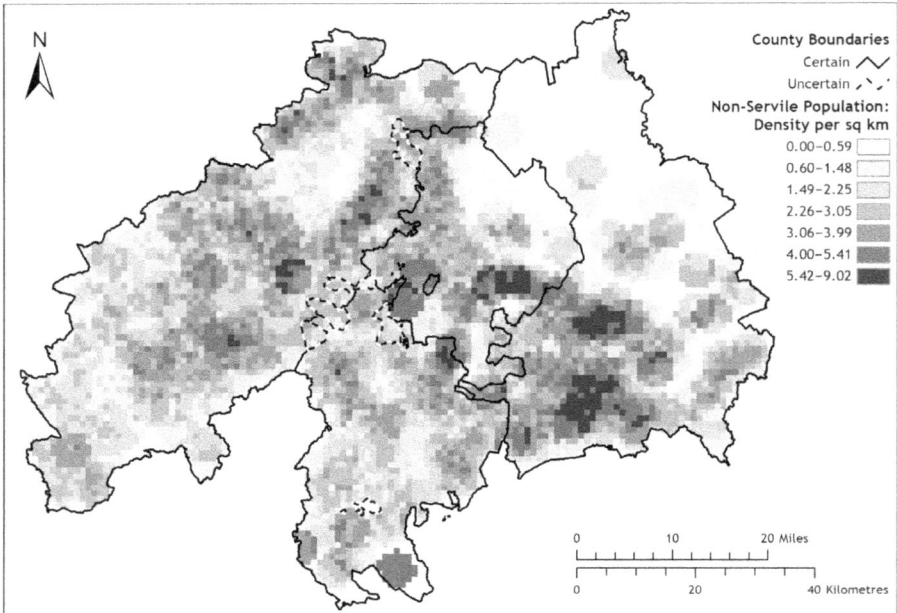

Figure 3: Density per square kilometre of non-servile population recorded in Domesday Book

presented in Figure 3 provide a far more fine-grained estimation of Domesday population density than any of Darby's maps.

As is well known, Domesday Book describes woodland in multifarious ways. In the four counties discussed here, amounts of woodland were most commonly recorded in one of four ways: in acres; in leagues, furlongs and perches in length and breadth; in terms of the number of pigs that could be fed in the woodland; and, in a much smaller number of cases, monetary values or renders. Converting all these measures to a single common denominator is impossible – how many pigs'-worth of woodland in a square league? – so depicting all the woodland statistics on a single map is challenging.[53] One approach, which is fast and easy with the computerized numeric data, is to calculate the standard deviations for woodland values in each category. Mapping the standard deviations, which indicate how much each instance varies from the average, shows which vills had unusually low, middling or unusually high amounts of recorded woodland, as shown in Figure 4. Of course, some Domesday formulae, such as 'there is wood for fences and houses', do not lend themselves to such calculation and are most effectively mapped as points. Figure 4 depicts the locations for these woodland references, together with woodland recorded as being 'for iron for ploughshares' or 'bearing mast', as well as

[53] Darby, *Domesday England*, 191.

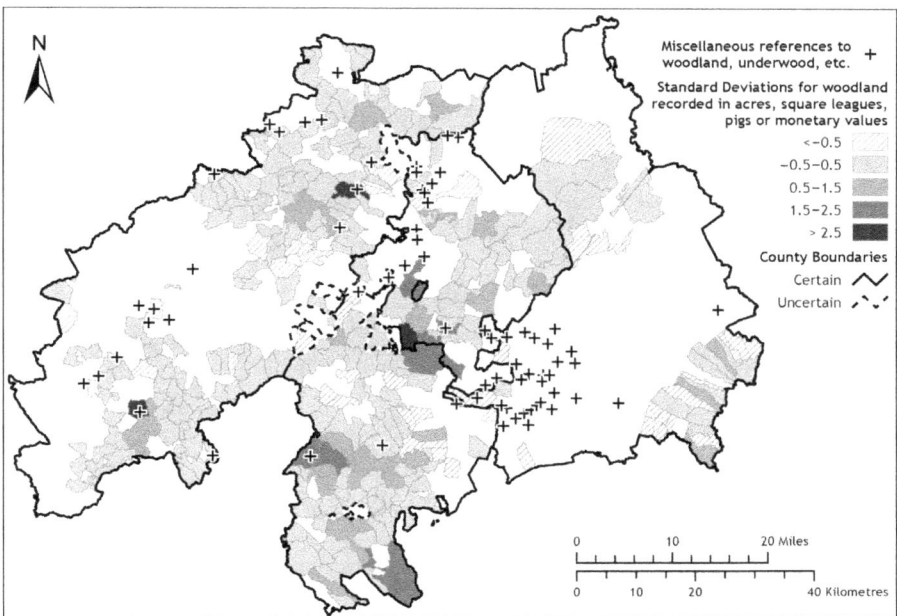

Figure 4: Variation from the average amount (standard deviation) of woodland per vill using the four main woodland measures, combined with miscellaneous references to woodland, underwood, scrubland, ash groves and spinney

mentions of underwood (*nemus*), scrubland (*silva minutia*), ash groves (*fraxinetum*) and spinney (*spinetum*).

The next examples illustrate answers to the question posed earlier, i.e., 'Who held how much, and where?'. The GIS can readily calculate the total number of ploughlands in each vill polygon, and then compare those sums to the total number of ploughlands belonging to different types of tenants-in-chief.[54] Mapping these proportions, as in Figure 5 (A–C), helps illuminate the distribution of resources available to different lords. In 1086, King William's manors were scattered across the four counties, while those of religious houses – especially the great Fenland abbeys of Ely, Peterborough and Ramsey – lay predominantly to the north and east of the area, leaving the rest of the land in the hands of other lords. Similarly, it is possible to investigate the extent to which lands were held in demesne or distributed to tenants in 1086. Mapping the percentage of the total TRW value of estates held in demesne (see Figure 5D) gives an indication of how different approaches to

---

[54] Values for demesne ploughlands described as 'besides' or 'apart from' the hidated land in a holding, e.g., in Huntingdonshire (GDB 204, 204v, 205, 206v: HUN 4,1–3.6,1–2;4–7.6,8–9;11;13;19.8,2.20,3) and TRW '*inland* for X ploughs', recorded in Northamptonshire (GDB 219v: NTH 1,8–9) are not included in the ploughland totals.

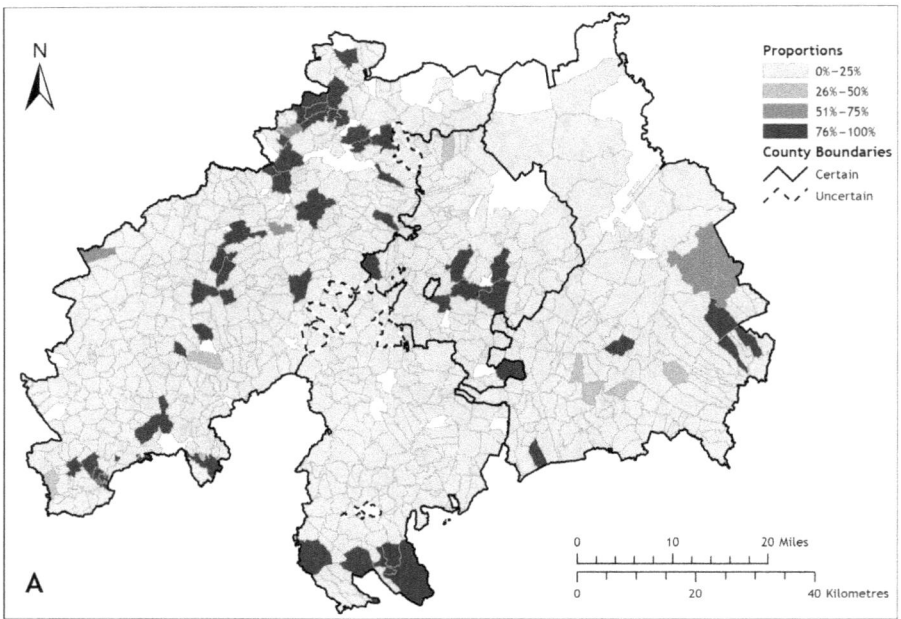

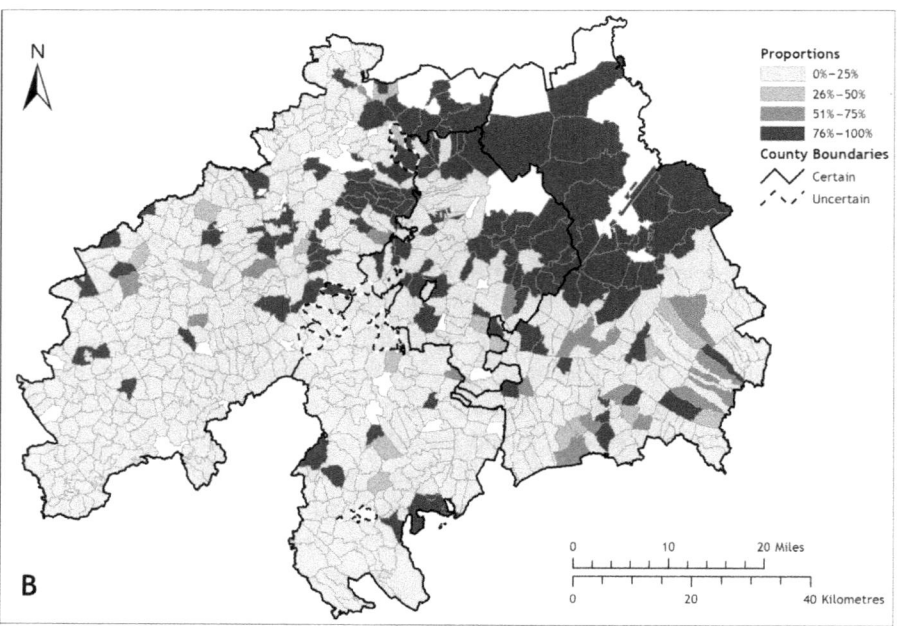

Figure 5: Proportions per vill of: A) ploughlands held by King William; B) ploughlands held by religious houses; C) ploughlands held by all other tenants-in-chief; D) total simplified TRW value held in demesne

GEOSPATIAL TECHNOLOGIES

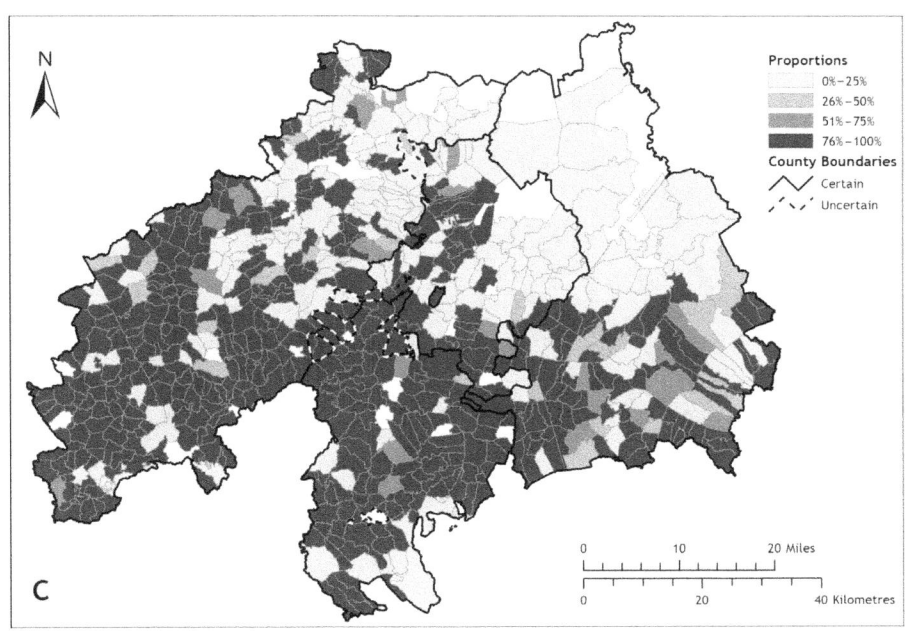

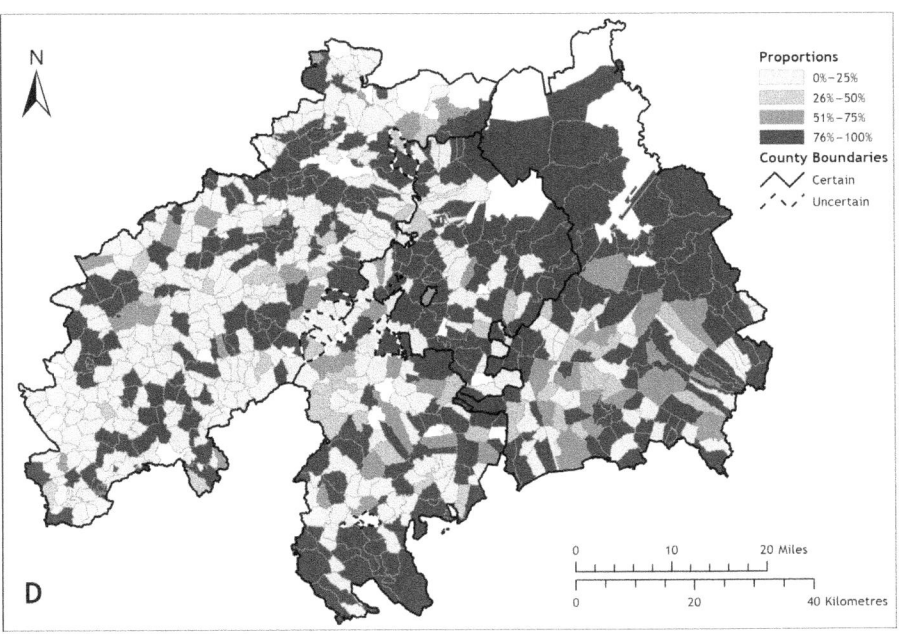

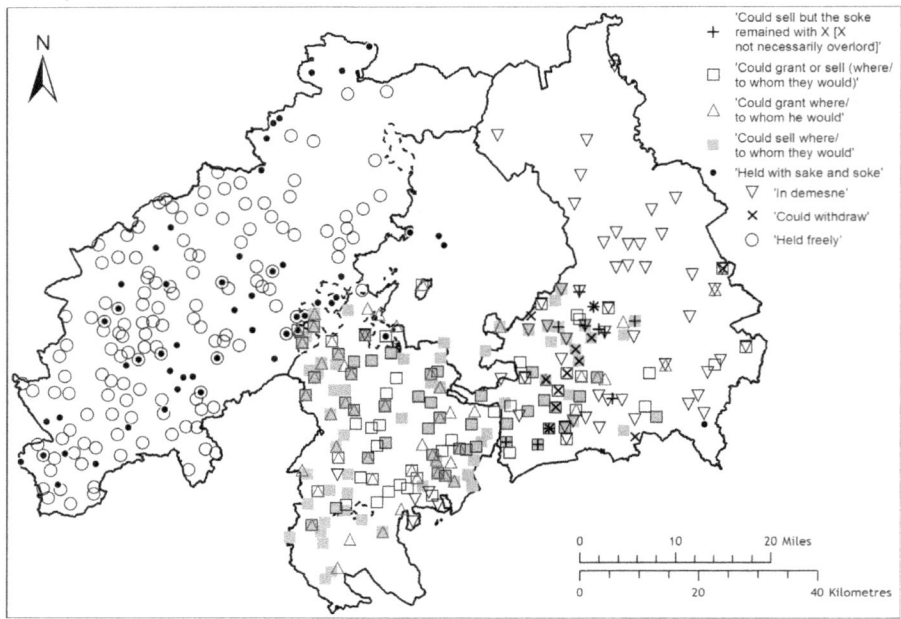

Figure 6: Distribution of the eight most commonly recorded forms of tenure for TRE landholders

landholding varied across the four counties.[55] Lands in north-east Huntingdonshire and northern Cambridgeshire were largely kept in demesne, as was the case in southern Bedfordshire. Tenants held much of Northamptonshire, and the rest of the area was mixed. Comparison of the four maps in Figure 5 suggests patterns that would otherwise be difficult to recognize. For example, in areas where either the king or religious houses held the bulk of the land, other tenants-in-chief tended to keep estates in neighbouring vills in demesne.

It is also possible to investigate *how* land was held in different places. Fleming's dataset includes roughly 330 codes recording the various formulae used to describe different forms of tenure, both TRE and TRW. The kind of analysis Stephen Baxter undertook county by county can be undertaken at much higher spatial resolution.[56] Figure 6 depicts the distribution of the eight most commonly-recorded formulae

---

[55] Totals for each polygon are sums of values recorded using all different formulae for TRW monetary values or renders (e.g. 'is worth', 'renders', 'value by weight at 20d to the *ora*', and 'renders in blanch coin'), as well as for 'is and was', 'always', and 'is and always was' values.

[56] S. Baxter, 'The Representation of Lordship and Land Tenure in Domesday Book', in *Domesday Book*, ed. E. Hallam and D. Bates, Stroud 2001, 73–102. The offline PASE Domesday dataset allows this kind of analysis, but only in a very basic fashion and only for TRE landholders. The PASE GIS dataset includes a 'yes/no' field indicating whether or not the TRE landholder had 'power of alienation' over his or her property.

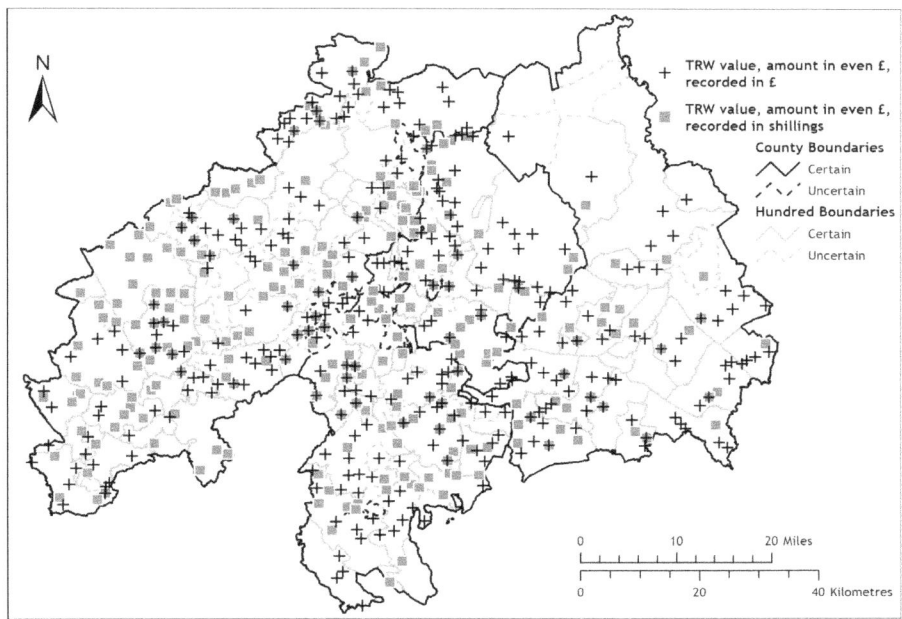

Figure 7: Distribution of different methods of recording TRW values in whole pounds

used for TRE holders' tenure in the four counties. The breaks between circuits are obvious – Bedfordshire and Cambridgeshire in Circuit III, Northamptonshire in Circuit IV, and Huntingdonshire in Circuit VI – but some curious details also come to light. The entry stating that Wulfwine, a thegn of King Edward, held land TRE in Horseheath with sake and soke is the only one of its kind in Cambridgeshire.[57] Some formulae ('in demesne' and variations on 'could grant/sell') are used in both circuit III counties, but others ('could withdraw' and 'could sell but the soke remained with X [X not necessarily overlord]') are not. At the moment, I can only note that these patterns exist; further work will be required to explain them.

As noted earlier, the data on monetary values are highly atomized, and so it is possible to examine potential spatial patterns in subjects as obscure as Domesday's accounting practices. Why does the text record in one instance that an estate was worth £3 TRW, while in another instance it says another estate was worth 60 shillings, sums which are, in the end, the same amount of money? One as-yet-unexplored avenue of investigation is whether there is any spatial pattern to the ways in which values were recorded. Figure 7 contrasts all the places where the simple TRW value – using the '*valet*' formula – of a holding was in whole pounds and

---

[57] GDB 199v: CAM 29,8. TRW, Gerard held the sake and soke of 1½ virgates from Count Alan at Whittlesford: GBD 194 (CAM 14,18).

the text records the amount in pounds with those places where the TRW value was in whole pounds, but the text records the amount in shillings. Generally, the two different bookkeeping methods were not used in the same locations, but there are places where they were. There do not appear to be patterns based on circuit, county, or hundred boundaries. One accounting method or the other may have been preferred by different lords. The point here is not to delve into the geography of late eleventh-century accountancy for its own sake, but to demonstrate how the data might be used to investigate what David Roffe has called the 'metastructures' of Domesday: the patterns of textual formulae and methods of recording information that can help illuminate how the data were originally collected and then compiled into the form known today.[58]

I will finish with a brief investigation of how GIS-based analysis can contribute to the debate regarding the nature of Domesday's statistics. It has long been recognized that Domesday Book's record of places, people and manorial appurtenances is neither comprehensive nor exhaustive. Nevertheless, most scholars would likely accept Darby's statement that 'it is probably safe to assume that a picture of England based on Domesday Book, while neither complete nor accurate in all its details, does reflect the main features of the geography of the eleventh century'.[59] David Roffe, however, has argued that, in general, the statistical data in Domesday refer only to land and other resources that were 'geldable'.[60] He contrasts the *warland*, which Domesday describes, with the *inland*, which Domesday does not, and states that '[t]he extent of inland is essentially unquantifiable'.[61] This interpretation calls into serious doubt even Darby's qualified position. So much may have been left out of the text that any map based on what Domesday Book does record is so flawed as to be meaningless. Roffe's argument, as I understand it, that 'Domesday statistics are finite data cast adrift in an uncharted sea',[62] is predicated on the idea that there were many places with huge inlands and tiny warlands. There is no way to know exactly how much was left out, but it is possible to examine how likely it is that there are vast quantities of land missing from the Domesday account and perhaps even suggest where such places might be.

Using the GIS I have developed, I have explored how Domesday measures of land relate to the areas of the polygons representing late eleventh-century vills. I have limited my analysis here only to Bedfordshire because Domesday's records for ploughlands, woodland and meadow are, generally, the most straightforward of the four counties for which I have the necessary data. The representations of the

---

[58] D. Roffe, *Decoding Domesday*, Woodbridge 2007, 291–304.
[59] Darby, *Domesday England*, 14.
[60] Roffe, *Decoding Domesday*, 198–203.
[61] Ibid., 313.
[62] Ibid., 315.

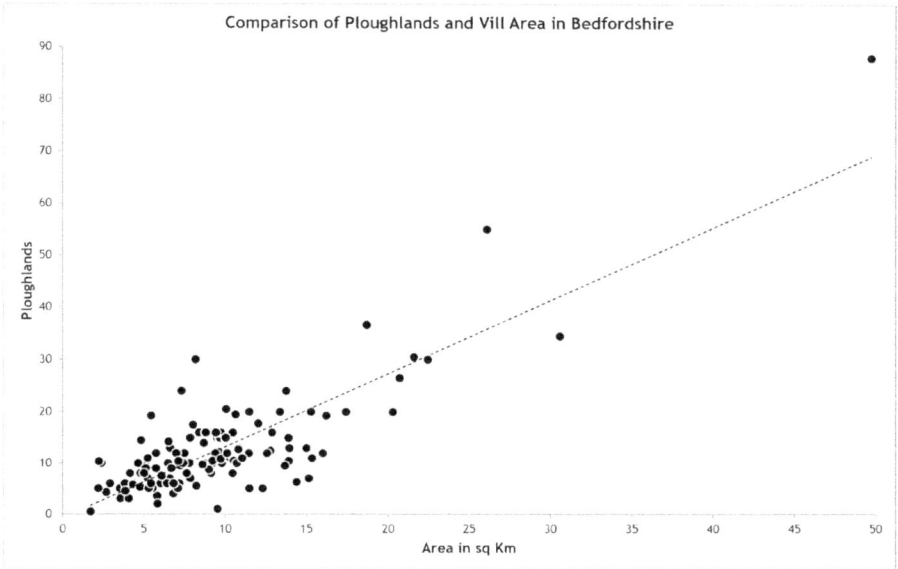

Figure 8: Scatterplot comparing ploughland values to vill areas in Bedfordshire. The dotted line shows the linear trend in the data

county's vills in the GIS are also uncomplicated by the extent of the Fenland.[63] The basic approach is most clearly illustrated with the ploughland values. Roffe contends that ploughlands were 'a non-fiscal measure of fiscal land',[64] i.e., a measure of real land, but only that land subject to the geld. If there were many instances where there was much ungelded inland and little geldable *warland* in a vill, then a scatter plot comparing ploughlands against the areas of the vill polygons would have many wildly spread data points. What Figure 8 actually shows is a marked trend that, as ploughlands increase, so does the area of the vill. The correlation is far from perfect, but the relationship is clear. Whether one assumes Roffe's interpretation of ploughland values is correct or not, Figure 8 suggests that in Bedfordshire, ploughlands do largely correspond to the areas of the vills in which they were recorded.

Using Ordinary Least Squares (OLS) regression analysis allows the relationships between some of Domesday's measures of land and the areas of the vill polygons to be investigated in greater depth.[65] The method seeks to predict values for one variable

---

[63] Lowerre, *Placing Castles in the Conquest*, 204–6.
[64] Roffe, *Decoding Domesday*, 207.
[65] For discussions of how Ordinary Least Squares regression works and the application of the method to geographical problems, see C. D. Lloyd, *Spatial Data Analysis: An Introduction for GIS Users*, Oxford 2009, 31–9; A. Mitchell, *The ESRI Guide to GIS Analysis Volume 2: Spatial Measurements & Statistics*, Redlands, CA, 2005, 210–19.

Table 1: Dependent Variable: area of vill polygon (in square km) > Number of observations: 127

Explanatory Variables	Coefficient	Standard Error	t-Statistic[a]	Probability[a]	Variance Inflation Factor (VIF)[b]
Intercept (constant)	3.302831	0.456369	7.237198	0.000000**	-----
Ploughlands	0.351564	0.040387	8.704803	0.000000**	2.270341
Woodland (in pigs)	0.008025	0.001496	5.363207	0.000001**	1.702679
Meadow (in ploughs)	0.105172	0.056176	1.872192	0.063556*	1.506947

Multiple R^2	0.748047		
Adjusted R^2	0.741902		
Akaike's Information Criterion (AICc)	650.107547		
Joint F-Statistic[c]	121.728863	Probability	0.000000**
Koenker (BP) Statistic[d]	2.317384	Probability	0.509199
Jarque-Bera Statistic[e]	12.124879	Probability	0.002329**

* Statistically significant at the 0.10 level ** Statistically significant at greater than 0.01 level

[a] The t-statistic and associated probability value assess whether an explanatory variable is statistically significant

[b] Measures redundancy among explanatory variables; generally, VIF values greater than 7.5 indicate redundancy

[c] The Joint-F statistic and associated probability value assess the statistical significance of the model as a whole

[d] The Koenker (BP) statistic and associated probability value asses whether there is statistically significant nonstationarity or heteroscedasticity in the model.

e The Jarque-Bera statistic and associated probability value assess whether there is statistically significant bias in the model.

(known as the dependent or response variable) based on the values of one or more other variables (known as independent or explanatory variables). I used the totalled values for ploughlands, woodland (in pigs) and meadow (in ploughteams) for each vill polygon as explanatory variables on the basis that they would account for the types of land-use that would cover the largest surface area of the vills. The response variable was the area of each vill polygon.[66] Table 1 presents the results of the regression analysis, together with the results of diagnostic tests assessing the validity of the regression model. As would be expected, the correlation between the explanatory and response variables is positive: as the amounts of ploughland, woodland, and

---

[66] Ploughland, woodland and meadow values for all places that could be linked to polygons were included in the analysis except the land held by Herbert the king's reeve in Eversholt, Woburn, and Potsgrove (GDB 218v: BDF 57,1) and that held by Hugh the butler in Shirdon (GDB 216: BDF 35,2). Ploughland values are absent from these entries, and so in the GIS, the polygons for Shirdon and Eversholt, Woburn and Potsgrove (taken together) have ploughland values of zero. It seems more likely that ploughland values for these holdings were left out in error by the Domesday scribe than that the holdings had no ploughland at all. As such, these lands have been omitted from the OLS analysis.

meadow recorded in each vill increase, so does the area of each vill polygon. The adjusted R^2 value of 0.74 indicates that the explanatory variables account for 74% of the variation in the response variable. In other words, taken together, the values for ploughlands, woodland, and meadow explain nearly three-quarters of the variation in the area of the polygons representing the Domesday vills.

Figure 9 maps the standard deviations for the regression residuals – the differences between the values for the area of the vill polygons predicted by the analysis and the actual recorded values – and illustrates where the regression has accurately or over- or under-predicted the areas of the vill polygons based on the ploughland, woodland, and meadow values. Large positive residuals indicate an underestimate of the area of the vill and large negative residuals an overestimate. Those polygons where the regression markedly underestimated the area may indicate places where Roffe's 'phantom' lands are most likely to lie. It is worth noting, however, that there are some vills where the regression noticeably overestimated the area. Large under- and over-predictions may be the results of factors other than, or in addition to, the existence of 'phantom' resources. The parish boundary polygons used to represent the vills may, in some instances, be poor representations of the eleventh-century extents of those vills. Topographic differences, e.g., in elevation, soils or distance to rivers, both between and within the vills, could account for some of the unexplained variation. There may also be relevant variables that Domesday Book does record, e.g., references to pasture[67] or carucates of land held in demesne,[68] which I have not included in the regression model.

These results are very much preliminary, and a great deal more research is required to explore the problem. I should note that Roffe takes 'overstocking' – where more ploughs than ploughlands were recorded on an estate – as the most reliable indicator of 'phantom' resources,[69] and Bedfordshire is not a county where overstocking is common. Expanding my analysis to include other counties – particularly those where overstocking is frequent – is clearly necessary. Nevertheless, this work does suggest that Domesday statistical data, and maps drawn using them, may not be quite so adrift as Roffe intimates. He may well be correct that many, perhaps most, of Domesday's statistics refer only to 'geldable' land and other resources. It seems unlikely, however, that values for ploughlands, woodland, and meadow could explain 74% of the variation in the areas of the vill polygons if there were vast quantities of unrecorded resources present in the vills. It is also clear that approaching the question from this angle would be difficult, if not impossible, without using GIS as a tool, or with the Domesday datasets created by the PASE project or Palmer and his team.

There are, of course, a vast number of other geographically-focused approaches to investigating Domesday Book and its contents, of which I will mention only

[67] GDB 212, 214v215v, 217, 217v: BDF 26,6.24,29.32,13.53,5.53.20.
[68] GDB 211, 212, 216, 216v: BDF 10,1.19,1.20,1.36,1.49,1.
[69] Roffe, *Decoding Domesday*, 203, 209.

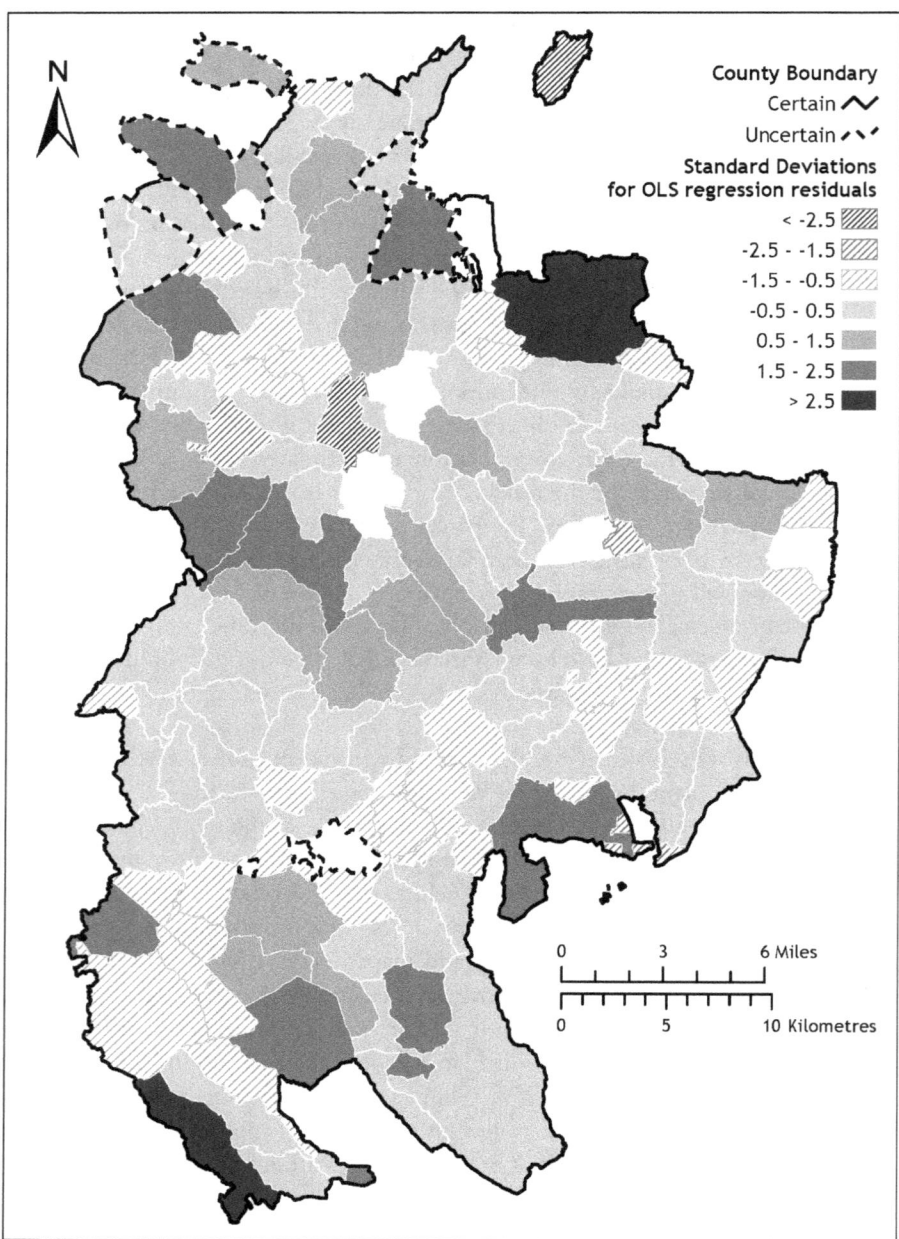

Figure 9: Standard deviations of OLS regression analysis residuals for each vill polygon

two more. There are new possibilities for statistical and econometric analysis of Domesday materials, explicitly taking into consideration geographic aspects of the data. Andrew Wareham has addressed many of the shortcomings of McDonald and Snooks's work, but neither they nor he considered location in their calculations.[70] Moving beyond the relatively simple OLS regression used above, spatially-aware techniques such as Geographically Weighted Regression can model the extent to which statistical relationships may differ from place to place, rather than assuming that relationships between variables were constant across the whole area studied.[71] And where any data from Domesday are referenced to the OS National Grid, they can easily be combined with any other relevant, GIS-ready data, e.g., from other documents, about soils, field systems, archaeology or, indeed, anything else that might be of interest. The possibilities, while not limitless, are still considerable and remain largely unexplored.[72]

To conclude, the main point I derive from this discussion of geospatial technology and Domesday geography is perhaps predictable: the complexity of the geographically-oriented questions one poses of Domesday (and any related materials) and the complexity of the maps one might create to answer those questions are a good indication of the complexity of the geospatial tools and data one will need to employ. The ability of geospatial technologies to help advance knowledge of Domesday geography was noted at the 2000 Domesday conference and even earlier at Domesday's novocentenary,[73] but their full potential is still yet to be realized. There have been considerable advances in making Domesday maps since the turn of the millennium. What both Open Domesday and PASE Domesday (online and off)

---

[70] A. Wareham, 'The "Feudal Revolution" in Eleventh-Century East Anglia', *ANS* 22, 2000, 293–321; A. Wareham and X. Wei, 'Taxation and the Economy in Late Eleventh-Century England: Reviving the Domesday Regression Debate', *ANS* 29, 2006, 214–27; J. McDonald and G. D. Snooks, *Domesday Economy: A New Approach to Anglo-Norman History*, Oxford 1986.

[71] A. S. Fotheringham, C. Brunsdon and M. Charlton, *Geographically Weighted Regression: The Analysis of Spatially Varying Relationships*, Chichester 2002; A. S. Fotheringham, 'Geographically Weighted Regression', in *The SAGE Handbook of Spatial Analysis*, ed. A. S. Fotheringham and P. A. Rogerson, London 2009, 243–53. For some examples of Geographically Weighted Regression (GWR) applied to historical data, see Gregory and Ell, *Historical GIS*, 173–5. For a review of spatially-aware regression techniques other than GWR, see L. Anselin, 'Spatial Regression', in *The SAGE Handbook of Spatial Analysis*, ed. Fotheringham and Rogerson, 254–75. I intend to apply GWR to the question of the relationship between Domesday's measures of land and vill areas in a future publication.

[72] For examples of how Domesday GIS data can be combined with other data, see Fleming and Lowerre, 'MacDomesday Book', 223–9; Lowerre, *Placing Castles in the Conquest*, chapter 6.

[73] Palmer, 'Great Domesday on CD-ROM', 147–9; Palmer, 'Computerizing Domesday Book', 288; J. D. Hamshere, 'Domesday Book: Estate Structures in the West Midlands', in *Domesday Studies: Papers Read at the Novocentenary Conference of the Royal Historical Society and the Institute of British Geographers: Winchester, 1986*, ed. Holt, 155–82.

demonstrate are the possibilities for using interactive maps to explore the contents of Domesday Book and for developing and quickly testing hypotheses. Unfortunately, the issues currently (October 2014) affecting TNA Labs's Domesday on a Map and PASE Domesday also highlight the fragility of such systems. It must be recognized, however, that none of these systems, nor the Domesday GIS I am developing, nor any other geospatial technology provides a 'magic bullet' for the study of Domesday geography. A computer will not do the most difficult tasks – asking questions or explaining possible answers – by itself: 'Technology empowers. But thinking enables.'[74] Nevertheless, with the kinds of tools discussed here and enough creativity in their use, it is possible to transform understanding of the geography of Domesday Book and of Domesday England.

[74] D. S. Moore, 'Statistics among the Liberal Arts', *Journal of the American Statistical Association* 93, 1998, 1253–9 at 1258.

10

Condensing and Abbreviating the Data: Evesham C, Evesham M, and the Breviate

Howard B. Clarke

As long ago as 1832 Sir Francis Palgrave thought it 'not improbable' that the two volumes of Domesday Book represent different stages in the condensation of the inquest material and that volumes similar to Little Domesday once existed for other parts of the country.[1] Whatever view we may take about the nature of the processes involved and their timing before or after the Conqueror's death, we all recognize that Great Domesday Book (GDB) is the result of a massive and indeed impressive exercise in condensing a much larger body of already redacted material into a single volume. The question to be considered here is whether, subsequently, this process was taken even further and, if so, when and why was this done. In other words, when was the document that appears to lie behind the breviate itself created as an abbreviation of the original condensation? In order to suggest some answers to these important questions, I propose to examine two of the early surveys preserved in the first cartulary of Evesham abbey, Worcestershire.

The breviate of Domesday has been discussed by previous scholars, especially V. H. Galbraith and in much greater detail by Elizabeth Hallam(-Smith) in her marvellous *Domesday Book through Nine Centuries*, but it can be argued that its real significance has been underestimated. This may partly be owing to the fact that the three surviving copies date from much later than GDB, the first being the Exchequer *Abbreviatio* belonging to the early 1240s.[2] Back in 1974 Galbraith devoted a short chapter of *Domesday Book: Its Place in Administrative History* to the

---

[1] F. Palgrave, *The Rise and Progress of the English Commonwealth*, 2 vols, London 1832, II, ccccxlvi n.6.
[2] TNA E36/284. Of this there are two copies: TNA E164/1, fols 19–232 and BL, Arundel MS 153.

breviate. He pointed out that the abbreviation was carried out mechanically, boiling down the entries to the name of the tenant, sometimes the name of the hundred, the name of the vill and the number of taxation units (carucates, hides or sulungs). Attention was drawn to similarities between the breviate and a survey preserved in Hemming's cartulary of the lands of the church of Worcester, now known as Worcester B, on the one hand, and the much later Herefordshire Domesday on the other. Rannulf Flambard and Bishop Samson are brought into play and there is a brief mention of 'a rather muddled story' by Orderic Vitalis about a new Domesday survey. Galbraith foresaw that 'further research may show that the text of the breviate was in more common use locally in the twelfth century than that of Domesday Book'.[3] If this really was the case, the origin of the breviate demands closer scrutiny and in particular the date when a further abbreviation of the inquest materials may have been undertaken.

The two Evesham surveys that may shed light on this have been labelled Evesham C and Evesham M. The cartulary in which they are preserved (BL, Cotton MS Vespasian B xxiv) is arranged conventionally on a topographical basis. Most of the monks' lands lay in Worcestershire and in Gloucestershire. Surveys A to J (there is no survey 'I' lest it be confused with the Roman numeral for 'one') relate to the county in which the abbey itself was situated, while surveys K to M are concerned with Gloucestershire. Otherwise the two documents are of a similar, if not quite identical, character and belong to a category that can be classified as county hidage schedules arranged by fiefs. Each will now be examined in some detail, beginning with the less useful of the two.

Evesham C

A few extracts from this document were printed by William Tindal as early as 1794,[4] but for long afterwards nothing was said until it was included in my doctoral thesis in the 1970s.[5] There its identity as an abstract of the Worcestershire section of GDB was established and followed subsequently by Frank Thorn and the late Caroline Thorn in their Phillimore edition.[6] Although this text is basically an abstract of

---

[3] V. H. Galbraith, *The Making of Domesday Book*, Oxford 1961, 214.
[4] W. Tindal, *The History and Antiquities of the Abbey and Borough of Evesham*, Evesham 1794, 74 n*.
[5] H. B. Clarke, 'The Early Surveys of Evesham Abbey: An Investigation into the Problem of Continuity in Anglo-Norman England', unpublished PhD thesis, University of Birmingham 1977, 213–18.
[6] WOR appendix IV (unpaginated). In order to maximize the potential for comparison with GDB and the *Abbreviatio*, the numeration of both surveys has been brought into line with the entry numbers in the Phillimore editions. This means that there are some discrepancies with the numeration in my doctoral thesis (1977) and in the appendices of the two Phillimore volumes.

Domesday, it is not without some points of interest, not least its date. Like other such documents, it raises the question of what possible use to contemporaries were these jejune lists of taxation units and their holders? Evesham C consists of an abbreviated version of fiefs II to VIII of Worcestershire Domesday, starting with that of the church of Worcester and ending with that of the abbot of Westminster (Appendix A). The survey is not in its present form an account of ecclesiastical fiefs in the county, for it omits numbers IX–XIII, including that of the abbot of Evesham himself. Nor is the apparent incompleteness of Evesham C due to the loss of folios from the cartulary, for the next though very different survey, Evesham D datable to *c.* 1108 (the latest possible date for Evesham C), commences in the middle of folio 10v. Whilst it is conceivable that the royal demesne (*terra regis*) was commonly treated as a separate entity, it is hard to imagine such a survey detached from the remainder of the county. This cartulary copy seems to have been written in three different hands of the late twelfth century, each more hurried or slovenly than its predecessor. The entering of such material into a cartulary must have been regarded as an exacting chore and it is possible that the scribes decided not to continue with a document of considerable length and little contemporary relevance. Another possibility is that the immediate exemplar of this late twelfth-century copy was itself a mere fragment, for otherwise we should expect the copyists to have progressed at least as far as the Evesham fief (number X). Whatever the explanation, Evesham C is probably a fragment of an abbreviation of the entire Worcestershire Domesday, with the exception of the royal demesne.[7]

The text proceeds with the seven fiefs and all of the individual items in the same order as in GDB. Evesham C generally records the name of the manor and its 1086 holder, the name of the hundred (though not invariably), together with the number of hides and virgates and a statement as to whether or not they paid geld. In other words the manorial details have been ruthlessly discarded from most entries. Even so, the ultimate exemplar of Evesham C was clearly much more detailed, as is proved by the Laugherne entry that reproduces the manorial data found in GDB.[8] Throughout Evesham C the phraseology is very close to that of GDB, which may or may not have been the cartulary exemplar's direct source. The few factual differences can mostly be ascribed to errors in the transmission of Evesham C, for the Domesday readings are supported by other documents, such as the comparable abbreviation in Hemming's cartulary (Worcester B).[9] In one instance a difference in nomenclature was probably intentional: in Evesham C 42 *Stephanus filius Wlwi*

---

[7] The *Inquisitio Comitatus Cantabrigiensis*, which survives only in a twelfth-century Ely manuscript, also omits the royal demesne, as does the more exact parallel, Evesham M.
[8] Evesham C 13; GDB, 172v: WOR 2,11;13.
[9] Hemming, *Hemingi Chartularium Ecclesiae Wigorniensis*, ed. T. Hearne, 2 vols, Oxford 1723, I, 298–313. For example, Evesham C 49 records 26 hides instead of 25 (ibid., 304, where the footnote is incorrect; GDB, 173v: WOR 2,48).

represents GDB's *Stefanus filius Fulchered*, as it does in the following survey in the same cartulary.[10]

As has already been indicated, Evesham C is not altogether a mechanical abbreviation of the Domesday material: an element of selectivity can be detected. This is particularly apparent in two items where greater detail was extracted about places of interest to the Evesham monks: Daylesford and Evenlode in the Cotswold region and Little Hampton in the Avon valley.[11] Besides these there are a few instances where Evesham C supplies information not found in GDB. A marginal addition refers to Sheriff Urse's 5-hide holding at Dorn, part of the bishop of Worcester's capital manor of Blockley.[12] In Evesham C 53 part of the text has been crossed out. The scribe first recorded, as in GDB,[13] that Urse held 1¾ hides in Warndon and White Ladies Aston, which belonged to the capital manor of Northwick. But in the margin this was altered to 2 hides in Warndon and Trotshill, together with half a hide in White Ladies Aston. It is possible that Urse's tenure of Dorn was omitted by mistake from GDB,[14] but the changes at Warndon and White Ladies Aston occurred presumably after 1086. Since these changes are expressed in the present tense, Evesham C is probably reproducing its immediate source, which must predate the death of Urse in 1108. Thus 1086 x 1108 become the dating limits of Evesham C, depending partly on the dating of the condensation known as GDB. In two other cases this survey provides useful topographical evidence. Evesham C 79 places Urse's half-hide subtenancy in the manor of Hanbury at Astwood (*Estwde*), which is equivalent to the *Estona Ricardi* of Evesham B 1.[15] Secondly Evesham C 102 locates King William's 5¾ hides of land in the great Westminster manor of Longdon at Eldersfield.[16] Local knowledge was clearly being used to identify certain manors more precisely.

By way of experiment the contents of Evesham C have been compared with those of the *Abbreviatio* for the biggest fief, that of the church of Worcester. Out of the eighty-four entries, forty-three (51.2%) contain the same information, with variations in phraseology and the spelling of the names of people and places of a character that one might expect of a process of medieval abstraction from an earlier source and/or a later copy. Twenty-seven entries (32.1%) have less information

---

[10] GDB, 173; BL Cotton MS Vespasian B xxiv, fol. 11 (Evesham D 7). On this personal name, see *DB* GLS, appendix n.EvC 41.
[11] Evesham C 44, 74. The case of Peopleton (Evesham C 123) is harder to explain.
[12] Evesham C 45.
[13] GDB, 173v: WOR 2,53.
[14] It may correspond to the unnamed 5-hide holding of a man called Hereward in Evesham A 120 ('Evesham A, a Domesday Text', ed. P. H. Sawyer, in *Miscellany I*, Worcestershire Historical Society 1960, 31 and n.2).
[15] BL, Cotton MS Vespasian B xxiv, fol. 8, datable to 1136; cf. GDB, 174: WOR 2,79.
[16] Cf. GDB, 174v: WOR 8,9c. This item corresponds to Evesham A 54 and 57 ('Evesham A', ed. Sawyer, 27).

and thirteen (16.7%) have more. Clearly the process of abbreviation was originally conducted independently, though quite possibly more or less simultaneously. The *Abbreviatio*'s additional details are varied in nature and not consistent: circumstances in the time of King Edward, statements that the land was for the support of the monks or alternatively that it was waste, the name of the hundred, and subtenures. Two exceptionally long entries, equivalent to Evesham C 1 and 79, are complete in the *Abbreviatio*.

Of more interest, perhaps, are those entries where the reverse is true. Again the differences are varied and apparently inconsistent: the name of a subtenant and the demesne hidage are the commonest. For the two entries relating to Laugherne, north-west of Worcester, Evesham C 11 and 13 add the Domesday valuations in both cases and manorial details as well in the latter. These entries demonstrate clearly that Evesham C was derived ultimately from a text very close to GDB, if not GDB itself. The same goes for a further two entries that are omitted entirely from the *Abbreviatio*, both relating to houses in Worcester.[17] With regard to the additional information there appears to be no geographical logic, in the sense that one might expect further details relating to places near to the abbey itself. Nearest to Evesham are Bredon to the south-west, Rous Lench to the north and Blockley (now in Gloucestershire) to the south-east. If there is any consistency about these entries in Evesham C, it lies in the interest taken in over half of them in the position of Sheriff Urse, with whom the churches of this county had had unfortunate experiences. In the case of one of these the Evesham monks were festering, amongst other things, over the sheriff's appropriation of 1 hide of land at Bengeworth, directly across the River Avon from the abbey.[18]

The fief of the church of Worcester was chosen here for comparative purposes not only because of its size but also because of the existence of the parallel abbreviation in Hemming's cartulary, Worcester B. How do the Evesham and Worcester texts compare? The answer is obvious: in most entries the information provided by Hemming is fuller; only fifteen (17.9%) are essentially the same in both versions. In addition Urse's 5-hide holding at Dorn is a marginal insertion in both manuscripts.[19] In one instance Evesham C's manorial details do not occur in Hemming's text, possibly an error on the part of the former's original abbreviator.[20] On the other hand Evesham

---

[17] Evesham C 50, 51. Compared with GDB, the former omits the statement about work in the bishop's court and the latter the annual render. Both Evesham C and the *Abbreviatio* omit the entry (GDB, 173v: WOR 2,50) concerning three houses in Droitwich.

[18] GDB, 174, 175v: WOR 2,75.10,12. The double entry reflects the fierce controversy between the two churches over possession of Bengeworth and Hampton.

[19] Evesham C 45; BL, Cotton MS Tiberius A xiii, fol. 139; Hemming, *Chartularium*, ed. Hearne, I, 304.

[20] Evesham C 13. Here the Evesham scribe has replaced the more classical and literary *quercus* of GDB with *cainas*, 'oaks' (WOR appendix IV). Hemming omits the manorial details systematically.

C 53 looks like a case of marginal updating, accounting for holdings at Warndon and White Ladies Aston by Sheriff Urse of 2½ hides rather than the 1¾ of the other three texts. Finally Evesham C 74, dealing with controversial Hampton, is omitted altogether from Worcester B. Thus the inescapable conclusion seems to be that Evesham C and Worcester B are independent abbreviations of GDB's account of Worcestershire, made not long after the original condensation of the circuit reports at a time when the tenurial and subtenurial details were still mainly relevant. At the very least, they represent a breviate in the making.

Evesham M

The closest parallel to Evesham C is Evesham M, an abbreviated version of Gloucestershire Domesday giving similar basic information (Appendix B). The text follows immediately upon that of Evesham K, which was arguably a genuine Domesday satellite representing an early stage in the production of GDB.[21] The hand of Evesham M is similar to, and perhaps identical with, the smaller, interlinear hand of Evesham K. The text as we have it ends abruptly on account of the loss of one folio.

Evesham M is a much reduced schedule of the Gloucestershire fiefs of Domesday tenants-in-chief. For each fief is recorded the name of the tenant-in-chief, a list of his (and in one case her) manors and their tax assessments, together with references to exemption from payment. The name of the hundred is stated only occasionally. The surviving portion of the text relates to the first forty-nine fiefs in Gloucestershire Domesday and there is every reason to believe that the remaining fiefs were treated likewise on the lost folio. As in Evesham C, the royal demesne is missing completely and the material is arranged in basically the same order as that in GDB. To this statement there are two exceptions. First, the fiefs of the church of Cirencester and of Reinbald the dean are in reverse order in Evesham M, a minor difference that may be connected with the misplacing of these fiefs in GDB where they are directed to their proper places by caract-marks.[22] Secondly, the fief of Archbishop Thomas of York comes last instead of first in the ecclesiastical division. Evesham M is generally different from Evesham K in its neglect of the hundred to which each manor belonged.[23] One of the few exceptions, Evesham M 210, is a longer item that demonstrates the very close relationship between this Evesham document and GDB. This and other items suggest that Evesham M's ultimate exemplar was abstracted from a fuller text that included the names of the hundreds. As in the case

---

[21] Clarke, 'Early Surveys', 246–70, 553–68; idem, 'The Domesday Satellites', in *Domesday Book: a Reassessment*, ed. P. Sawyer, London 1985, 50–70 at 62–5.
[22] GDB, 166v.
[23] Excepting Evesham M 2, 112, 210.

of Evesham C the most likely candidates as the common source are GDB itself or an already abbreviated version for circuit V.[24]

While this close relationship can hardly be in doubt, some qualifications must be made. Occasionally there are semantic differences, as in Evesham M 43 where *boscum* is equivalent to GDB's *siluam*. Such differences are extremely common as between Exon Domesday and GDB. In three instances the tax assessments are not identical.[25] All are minor discrepancies that arose probably from mistakes in the transcription of Evesham M, for the Domesday figures are supported by those in Evesham K. The summary nature of Evesham M is emphasized by an arithmetical addition of the tax assessments at the end of the longer fiefs, preceded by the word *summa*. Shorter fiefs have no *summae* presumably because the totals could be calculated more or less at a glance. *Summae* are not a normal feature of GDB, though the Evesham fief in Gloucestershire does refer to the abbey's 56 hides in the ferding of Winchcombe without the use of the word *summa*.[26] Exon Domesday contains more elaborate summaries for fiefs held by a number of tenants-in-chief in south-western England.[27] For the fiefs of the bishop of Worcester and William d'Eu the *summae* in Evesham M are considerably at variance with the details given against each manor.[28] All this suggests that *summae* were incorporated in the immediate exemplar and that the cause of the discrepancies was either mathematical error or failure to bring *summae* into line with changes in the composition of fiefs.

Evesham M 1 is written in the larger hand of Evesham K and acts as a heading to this second hidage schedule of Gloucestershire. The Domesday satellite deals with the disputed manors of Northleach, Oddington and Standish differently from GDB, attributing them to Gloucester abbey and Walter fitzPons rather than to Archbishop Thomas. Evesham M lists these manors three times. First, the 1086 position is given broadly but not identically as described in GDB, with Archbishop Thomas as the holder of 34 out of a total of 50 hides and the claimant of the remaining 16 from Walter fitzPons, Sheriff Durand and Earl Hugh of Chester.[29]

---

[24] In the language of one recent reconstruction of the Domesday process the 'C text', a collection of county booklets, would be another possibility (C. Flight, *The Survey of Kent: Documents Relating to the Survey of the County Conducted in 1086*, British Archaeological Reports, British Series 506, Oxford 2010, 14). A much more detailed analysis of this concept is to be found in C. Flight, *The Survey of the Whole of England: Studies of the Documentation Resulting from the Survey conducted in 1086*, British Archaeological Reports, British Series 405, Oxford 2006, 38–80.

[25] Evesham M 14, 51, 100.

[26] GDB, 166: GLS 12,10, where the reference is to TRE. The Yorkshire summary at the end of GDB is arranged geographically (GDB, 379–82: YKS S) and was probably included in the regional draft (Galbraith, *Making of Domesday Book*, 177). See also Clarke, 'Domesday Satellites', 67 and n.93.

[27] Exon, fols 528rv, 530v–531. The term *summa* is not used.

[28] Evesham M 15, 131, the latter probably a copying error.

[29] Evesham M 2–4. Evesham M 2 omits to state that Archbishop Thomas holds Oddington

Secondly, the 1066 position is given, also as described in GDB in the past tense, with Archbishop Ealdred as the holder.[30] Thirdly, in the complete version of the archbishop's fief, the 1066 position is repeated in exactly the same words as before.[31] Despite the threefold treatment of these manors, nothing new is revealed about them. Nevertheless their tenurial position must have been of interest to local churchmen, while pressure was clearly being exerted on Archbishop Thomas to hand back this substantial portion of the endowment of Gloucester abbey. Eventually, on Palm Sunday 1095 (18 March) according to this abbey's *Historia et cartularium*, they were restored.[32] Of this there is no hint in Evesham M, which originated presumably before 1095.

Apart from the provision of *summae*, the omission of the royal demesne and the special attention paid to Northleach, Oddington, and Standish, Evesham M is not far removed from GDB. In all probability it belongs to the same category as Evesham C, a post-Domesday summary of information likely to be of lasting value: the names of landholders and manors and the number of taxable units. The authority most interested in possessing a ready guide to the distribution of hides and their analogues elsewhere in England was the crown, either in the person of the local sheriff or in the body of the king's treasury. This would account for the absence from these documents of the royal demesne, for it was administered separately from the rest of the county. Both Evesham C and Evesham M appear to reflect ways in which, to quote the edition of Herefordshire Domesday, Domesday Book 'lived on as a final test of the number of hides for which each separate manor had to answer'.[33] It is true that there are no *summae* in the extant text of Evesham C, but the only fiefs

---

and Evesham M 4 omits the single hide at Standish held by the abbot of Gloucester (GDB, 164v: GLS 2,4;10). On the other hand GDB does not state that the archbishop was claiming in the interests of Gloucester abbey or that Durand was holding wrongfully.

[30] Evesham M 5–7. Evesham M 6 omits the 1 hide at Coberley (GDB, 164v: GLS 2,8), with the result that only 49 hides are accounted for. The reference to Durand in Evesham M 7 seems to be misplaced.

[31] Evesham M 95, 99, 101. The last Anglo-Saxon abbot of Evesham, Æthelwig, had been consecrated by Ealdred at the Gloucester court session in 1058 (Thomas of Marlborough, *History of the Abbey of Evesham*, ed. and trans. J. Sayers and L. Watkins, Oxford 2003, 100–1) and it is possible that a memory of the late archbishop persisted at Evesham in the early 1090s.

[32] *Historia et Cartularium Monasterii Sancti Petri Gloucestriae*, ed. W. H. Hart, 3 vols, RS 33, 1863–7, I, 11–12. Here Abbots Barton is also connected with the restoration. This manor formed the nucleus of the abbey's endowment, with a tax assessment of 21¾ hides, yet neither GDB, nor Evesham K, nor Evesham M indicates that it had been appropriated by the archbishop. The charter declares that the abbey had been deprived of these manors for thirty-nine years, which refers back to 1056, two years before the beginning of the abbacy of Wulfstan, who permitted Ealdred to receive the manorial income.

[33] *Herefordshire Domesday, c. 1160–1170*, ed. V. H. Galbraith and J. Tait, Pipe Roll Society 63, 1950, xxviii.

of any size are those of the bishop of Worcester and the abbot of Westminster, both of whom held complete hundreds whose hidage is stated.[34]

The opinion just quoted was formulated on the basis of a much later document, a list of Herefordshire fiefs with their constitutent manors assessed in hides, all in close agreement with GDB.[35] Some fiefs end with a *summa* that does not always conform mathematically with the individual particulars, while the last item is a *summa denegeldi*, according to which just over 900 hides were due to pay £103 15s. 6d. as this county's contribution to the tax. Herefordshire Domesday dates from the 1160s, about the time of the abandonment of danegeld. Thus for Herefordshire there exists a direct connection between a feudally arranged summary of hides and a statement of danegeld. And the first Evesham cartulary provides similar evidence for Gloucestershire and Worcestershire, also in circuit V, and from a period near to the Domesday inquest itself.

As in the case of the Worcestershire document Evesham C, Evesham M can be compared with the Gloucestershire portion of Hemming's abbreviation of the Domesday survey of his church's lands (Worcester B).[36] Again Hemming gives more details and again it is likely that Evesham M and Hemming's text are independent abstracts from a common source, either GDB itself or possibly a revised version of the report for circuit V. The scope of Evesham M is almost identical to that of the official breviate of GDB, as preserved in the three thirteenth-century copies. This is important because the dating evidence for Evesham M, such as it is, brings the prospect of an official abbreviation to within a few years of the making of Domesday Book itself.

Why were two hidage schedules of Gloucestershire preserved by the Evesham monks? Their lands comprised 56 hides, with a claim to 1 hide at Childswickham (or Wickhamford) near Evesham,[37] more than in any other county apart from Worcestershire. The dispute over Northleach, Oddington, and Standish was presumably of greater concern to the monks of Gloucester than to those of Evesham, but an interest in the affairs of neighbouring churches had been expressed by the last Anglo-Saxon abbot, Æthelwig. According to the domestic chronicle part of Thomas of Marlborough's *Historia*, Æthelwig gave and lent money to Bishop Wulfstan of Worcester in order to preserve the see from the ambitious archbishop of York. The same abbot is said to have assisted Abbot Serlo of Gloucester on a number

---

[34] Evesham C 1, 92.
[35] *Herefordshire Domesday*, ed. Galbraith and Tait, 1–74.
[36] Hemming, *Chartularium*, ed. Hearne, I, 309–11.
[37] Though recorded in GDB, Evesham F and Evesham K, this hide is not mentioned in Evesham M (GDB, 166: GLS 12,6; BL, Cotton MS Vespasian B xxiv, fols 11, 59v). The claim is probably associated with one of the abbey's many forged Anglo-Saxon charters (S. 1174). The entry in the Phillimore edition (GLS 12,6 and corresponding note) favours Wickhamford rather than Childswickham. On the confusion surrounding the early forms of these place-names, see also Clarke, 'Early Surveys', 421–2. The villages are about 4 km apart.

of occasions.[38] No details are reported, but Æthelwig may have been requested to intervene on behalf of impoverished Gloucester with a view to recovering the manors acquired by Ealdred. There was a topographical interest, too, for Oddington was surrounded on three sides by the Evesham manors of Adlestrop, Broadwell, and Maugersbury. No doubt the course of this dispute was carefully monitored by the Evesham monks, who were keenly aware of their seigneurial neighbours. And whatever the motive for the preservation of these Gloucestershire schedules, the existence of two of them implies that they came from different sources. The hypothesis that one stems from the Domesday inquest and the other from a process of post-Domesday abbreviation best accords with the duplicate nature of their contents, as it does with the many variations in their spelling of place-names.

County hidage schedules arranged by fiefs

To summarize, the Evesham monks came to acquire and to preserve two post-Domesday hidage schedules arranged basically in the same order as GDB. There are hints in both cases that more detailed information was available and that a few alterations and additions were made in the process. Both documents omit the royal demesne. On the basis of slender internal evidence a date of 1086 x 1108 is proposed for Evesham C and 1086 x 1095 for Evesham M. While conclusive proof is lacking, it is highly probable that both schedules go back to the same period of time and to the same body of source material. This in turn suggests that GDB had itself been abbreviated, either locally or centrally or both, within nine years of the inquest of 1086. By 1095 many of the manorial statistics must have become out of date, whereas the fiscal and tenurial information may not have changed all that much. To judge by the *summae* in Evesham M, the chief purpose of such documents was to record the individual and total fiscal liability of the manors held by each tenant-in-chief, though the *summae* are not invariably accurate. Beyond this there is little to indicate the uses to which these county-based hidage schedules were put in the Norman period.[39]

Versions of these, detailing the holdings of subtenants and drawn up locally, could also have been produced. One early survivor is the Worcester relief of 1095, preserved by Hemming and rediscovered by J. H. Round.[40] The death of Bishop Wulfstan II in January of that year had presented Sheriff Urse, and no doubt in the background Rannulf Flambard, with the opportunity to levy a feudal relief on the

---

[38] Thomas of Marlborough, *History*, 164–5.
[39] This type of survey is to be distinguished from hidage summaries arranged by fiefs (my Type 3) on the one hand and from county hidage schedules arranged by hundreds (my Type 8) on the other hand (Clarke, 'Early Surveys', 317–19, 340–3).
[40] Hemming, *Chartularium*, ed. Hearne, I, 79–80; J. H. Round, *Feudal England: Historical Studies on the Eleventh and Twelfth Centuries*, London 1895, reset 1964, 241–2.

church's subtenants. The total came to £250. The individual sums look arbitrary in relation to Domesday hidage totals, but other factors may have been taken into account at this social level. Apart from Wulfstan's steward (*dapifer*) Orderic, the biggest contributor was the abbot of Evesham[41] – a church towards which Urse probably harboured hard feelings. The abbey's holdings as a subtenant of the diocesan amounted to a mere 9 hides, located at Hampton and Bengeworth, as Evesham C confirms.[42]

There is another document with *summae* that bears some resemblance to both of the Evesham surveys; this is a Kentish record that has been named ε (for 'epitome') by its recent editor.[43] Earlier writers classified this as a pre-Domesday assessment list,[44] whereas Colin Flight argues that it is in fact a breviate. Like the Evesham texts it aimed to answer three questions: who are the barons holding land in this county, which manors does each of them hold, and for how many taxation units (sulings in Kent) is each of these manors assessed? Most of the text, though not quite all, is written out more or less in a continuous stream, with occasional blank lines. Small pieces of information are not to be found in GDB. Most notably of all, a *summa* is provided at intervals, as a subtotal integrated into the main text.[45] On the other hand, the author was not concerned to preserve the order of GDB if it did not suit him to do so and a certain amount of editorial reorganization was undertaken to cater for the 'transformation of the feudal landscape of Kent which followed from the failed rebellion of 1088'.[46] Flight does not venture to date this text, except to suggest that it belongs to the twelfth century and, by implication, early in that century.

A connection with danegeld assessment has been alleged in the case of a hidage schedule of tenants-in-chief in the county of Hereford. This document is an appendage to the main text of the twelfth-century Herefordshire Domesday.[47] It is similar to Evesham C and Evesham M in its feudal arrangement and in its concentration on the tax assessments of manors listed after the name of each landholder. It differs in its provision of a contemporary list of landholders, with dating limits of 1137 x 1139.[48] In its present form this Herefordshire schedule seems to be incomplete but, in the opinion of its editors, the intention was to facilitate the levying of danegeld

---

[41] Round, *Feudal England*, 244.
[42] Evesham C 74–5.
[43] Flight, *Survey of Kent*, 208–11. I am grateful to David Roffe and Pamela Taylor for drawing my attention to this text and its analysis.
[44] Ibid., 201 n.1.
[45] Ibid., 201, 204–5.
[46] Ibid., 204, 206.
[47] Printed with facsimile in *Herefordshire Domesday*, ed. Galbraith and Tait, 78–9.
[48] W. E. Wightman, *The Lacy Family in England and Normandy, 1066–1194*, Oxford 1966, 181.

and feudal aids.[49] Thus, although the two Evesham schedules had an earlier origin, the uses to which all three were put could have been similar.

The main text of Herefordshire Domesday is also a list of fiefs and manors derived directly or indirectly from GDB. In this respect it resembles Evesham C and Evesham M. But it is much more detailed, giving the Domesday figures for ploughs, peasants and valuations. For about one-third of the entries the name of the current holder has been written in the margin by another scribe, which the editors depict as a unique attempt to bring Domesday Book tenurially up to date, a personal experiment 'designed to straighten out the tangle of hidage and of danegeld'.[50] The total amount of danegeld due from the county is stated in an account of the sheriff's farm that follows on immediately,[51] which suggests that such a document was still considered relevant to the assessment of this tax, and possibly even to its collection on some sort of 'feudal' basis. More important by the 1160s, however, was the assessment of scutages, *auxilia*, and *dona*, and herein may lie the chief value of the twelfth-century Herefordshire Domesday.[52] Whereas the two Evesham documents represent the immediate post-Domesday usage of county hidage schedules arranged by fiefs, the main text of Herefordshire Domesday dates from the time when, at long last, the ancient levy of danegeld was abandoned by stages and the knight's fee was recognized as the prime unit of taxation. This recognition is exemplified in the *cartae baronum* of 1166.[53]

Also belonging to the second half of the twelfth century is an abbreviation of Kent Domesday.[54] This document was initially drawn up in the form of a roll, though it has since been rearranged as the leaves of a book. Unlike Herefordshire Domesday this abbreviation shows no signs of having been brought up to date. It does, however, demonstrate the fact that the task of abbreviating GDB had been undertaken as an official, curial exercise within a century of the 1086 inquest.[55] Thus the importance of Evesham C and Evesham M is that they advance the date of this official undertaking to within a few years of the making of GDB itself. They are in effect precursors of the thirteenth-century breviate texts and, while GDB was not a tax book, it could be argued that the breviate was exactly that or, more practically, a booklet in the hands of every sheriff. And from the chronology of these two hidage schedules arranged by fiefs, it may be inferred that the need to revise lists of rural landholders in the West Midland counties was not felt before the death of Sheriff Urse in 1108.

[49] *Herefordshire Domesday*, ed. Galbraith and Tait, 127.
[50] Ibid., xxii, xxiv.
[51] Printed with facsimile in *Herefordshire Domesday*, ed. Galbraith and Tait, 75. The editors stress the point that this is an integral part of the book (ibid., xxxi).
[52] Ibid., xxxi.
[53] Cf. J. A. Green, 'The Last Century of Danegeld', *EHR* 96, 1981, 241–58 at 258.
[54] BL, Cotton MS Vitellius C viii, fols 143–156.
[55] *Herefordshire Domesday*, ed. Galbraith and Tait, xxix.

Flambard's Domesday?

If Evesham C and Evesham M are in effect precursors of the thirteenth-century breviate texts, and if their exemplar(s) date(s) from (say) the early 1090s, can we identify who may have been responsible for this very practical administrative tool? To quote the current American president, 'Yes, we can!' We even know something of his personal appearance – rather handsome, 1.75 m (5 feet 9 inches) tall, short-headed with a sloping forehead and a strong jawline. He normally dressed well and spoke with a ready tongue. He has been mentioned already and he was, of course, Rannulf Flambard, who has been linked in the past with the compilation of GDB itself – by Sally Harvey and by David Roffe.[56]

Irrespective of whether we think that GDB was compiled as an integral part of the inquest of 1086 during the last months of the Conqueror's reign, or as a kind of bureaucratic afterthought early in the reign of his successor, there would have been an immediate and widespread demand for an abbreviated version, or abbreviated versions, of the original condensation. These came into existence both for individual fiefs across several counties and for whole counties as regular administrative entities. Moreover those early references to *breves*, etc., so often interpreted as GDB itself, are equally likely to have been to these useful summaries containing the basic data – who held what, where it was, and for how many taxable units. Taxes could be levied geographically as danegeld or tenurially as charges on fiefs. It was the breviate rather than GDB itself that was ideally suited, with its summaries, to function as a feodary, serving shire by shire the administration of feudal incidents.[57] But it could also have functioned as a means of making tenants-in-chief responsible for the collection and payment of geld. Under constant pressure to produce funds for royal policy, administrative efficiency throughout the land of England was what mattered.

There would have been endless talk in Rufus's administrative circle during the late 1080s and early 1090s, some of it picked up eventually in a fairly remote corner of Normandy by Orderic Vitalis. Book VIII of the *Ecclesiastical History* contains a passing reference to an alleged remeasurement, with the consent of the king (William Rufus), of 'all the ploughlands, which in English are called hides, with a rope, and made a record of them'.[58] It may be that this passage has not always been understood correctly by modern scholars. For one thing, it is not an allusion to the Domesday survey of 1086,[59] to which there is an unexceptionable reference in Book

---

[56] D. Roffe, *Domesday: the Inquest and the Book*, Oxford 2000, 113 (summarizing Harvey), 246–7; idem, *Decoding Domesday*, Woodbridge 2007, 105–8; Sally Harvey, *Domesday: Book of Judgement*, Oxford 2014, 115–32 for the fullest statement of the argument.

[57] Contrast Roffe, *Domesday: the Inquest and the Book*, 243.

[58] Orderic, IV, 172–3: *Annuente rege omnes carrucatas quas Anglice hidas uocant funiculo mensus est et descripsit* .... The suggestion that this is 'a reference to the compilation of Domesday Book' (Roffe, *Decoding Domesday*, 106) is unconvincing, to say the least.

[59] Contrast S. P. J. Harvey, 'Domesday Book and Anglo-Norman Governance', *TRHS*, 5th

IV: 'King William [the Conqueror] carefully surveyed his whole kingdom, and had an exact description (*ueraciter describi fecit*) made of all the dues owed in the time of King Edward (*tempore regis Eduardi*)'.[60] The Domesday survey was mooted late in the year 1085, soon after Orderic was sent by his father to Saint-Evroult at the age of ten.[61] Some sort of memory of the great survey of his homeland may have lived on. In Book VIII, written probably in 1133–5, he is referring to something quite different.

It is important to consider Orderic's sources of information as a general rule. According to his modern editor, he relied very little on written sources for the period with which we are concerned, 1083–95. His sources were almost exclusively oral and he was dependent on the accuracy of his reporters. Events might be distorted both by Orderic and by his reporters, if only unintentionally. Moreover he tended to conflate different sources.[62] In part these circumstances account for Orderic's vagueness on chronology; events were either being reported in retrospect or the author failed to make a record of dates.[63] It is true that Orderic was probably on a visit to England c. 1114, calling in at Crowland and Worcester, but he appears to have expressed no interest in a proposed resurveying of the country.[64] Furthermore, account must be taken of the fact that the latter is placed in the middle of a sustained and fierce diatribe against Rannulf Flambard. It may be the case that what was mooted by Flambard and his associates was treated by Orderic, accidentally or intentionally, as historical actuality.

In any case, had not England already been resurveyed in the form of Domesday ploughlands? Unfortunately the latter have proved to be endlessly controversial. Partly this is because there are so many variations in the formula that was used – variations by circuit, by county and by fief – suggestive, at least in part, of variations in levels of understanding of what was required. By way of illustration H. C. Darby produced appendices relating to three counties: Shropshire in circuit V, Leicestershire in circuit IV and Yorkshire in circuit VI. Although the latter had two formulae, the two other counties each had four, apart from the lack of mention in all three cases.[65]

---

series 25, 1975, 175–93 at 188–9, 192; Sally P. J. Harvey, 'Taxation and the Ploughland in Domesday Book', in *Domesday Book: a Reassessment*, ed. P. Sawyer, London 1985, 86–103 at 100; Harvey, *Domesday: Book of Judgement*, 128–9.

[60] Orderic, II, 266–7. A brief reference in Book VII links the survey with the military crisis of 1085 and the 'finding' of 60,000 knights to defend the country (Orderic, IV, 52–3). By a striking coincidence the number of knights is the same as a modern scholar's estimate of the number of Domesday ploughlands (Harvey, 'Taxation and the Ploughland', 99).

[61] Orderic, I, 5.

[62] Ibid., 51.

[63] Orderic, IV, xx–xxiv.

[64] Orderic, I, 25, 32. As it happened, Evesham abbey was a member of Saint-Evroult's prayer union (M. Chibnall, *The World of Orderic Vitalis*, Oxford 1984, map II).

[65] H. C. Darby, *Domesday England*, Cambridge 1977, 347–51.

Ultimately, it was concluded, 'we cannot use the ploughland figures to provide a consistent picture of the available arable land throughout all England in 1086'.[66] Although similar variations were cited, Sally Harvey argued strongly for a single, fiscal explanation of the phenomenon.[67] She pointed out that, whereas the hidage or carucage figures are expressed in the past tense in some counties, the ploughland data are almost always stated in the present tense.[68] Yet this radical fiscal reassessment attempted through the Domesday inquiry was never 'fully' implemented according to the same author.[69] The question, it seems to me, is whether the Domesday ploughland reassessment, if that is what it was, was ever implemented at all, for we are also told that 'danegeld seems to have been levied annually at the normal rate of 2s. a hide in Henry I's reign'. Quite so! All the signs are that the hide and its analogues remained the basis for taxation down to the 1160s.[70]

Orderic's phraseology is important. He claims that Flambard incited 'him [William Rufus] to revise the survey of all England ... and should make a new division of the land of England'.[71] In other words, one survey – the Domesday one – had already been conducted and a new one was being contemplated. In the end, the land of England was not remeasured *funicolo*, 'with a rope';[72] rather the resource that was already to hand was boiled down to its essentials. In the words of a recent appraiser of Flambard's career, he 'may have made some experiments, but it is probable that he used the Domesday survey to enforce the collection of the geld in full, not to reform the system'.[73] Amongst other things it would have been a cheaper and more immediately achievable option. 'Full of ideas and imaginative schemes', as Frank Barlow wrote of him, Flambard's Domesday was almost certainly not GDB, but it could have been the ancestor of the breviate of Domesday. Evesham C

---

[66] Ibid., 120.
[67] Harvey, 'Taxation and the Ploughland'.
[68] Ibid., 92.
[69] Harvey, 'Domesday Book and Anglo-Norman Governance', 186 and n.58; S. P. J. Harvey, 'Taxation and the Economy', in *Domesday Studies: Papers read at the Novocentenary Conference of the Royal Historical Society and the Institute of British Geographers, Winchester, 1986*, ed. J. C. Holt, Woodbridge 1987, 249–64 at 249; Harvey, *Domesday: Book of Judgement*, 210–38 for a general restatement on taxation.
[70] Cf. Green, 'Last Century of Danegeld', 243, 248–9, the latter being a table of carucate assessments for Alstoe and Martinsley wapentakes and hidage assessments for Witchley hundred.
[71] Orderic, IV, 172–3: *incitans ut totius Angliae reuiseret descriptionem, Anglicaeque telluris comprobans iteraret particionem ....*
[72] Domesday ploughlands may simply have been estimates, perhaps supplied by the commissioners where precise data were not available (Roffe, *Domesday*, 159), hence the artificial nature of many of them.
[73] J. O. Prestwich, 'The Career of Ranulf Flambard', in *Anglo-Norman Durham 1093–1193*, ed. D. Rollason, M. Harvey and M. Prestwich, Woodbridge 1994, 299–310 at 309. Cf. Green, 'Last Century of Danegeld', 245.

and Evesham M stand as witnesses to that possibility, as well as to the fact that 'the individual shire ... [was] the primary geographical arena of the Domesday survey'.[74]

Acknowledgement

I wish to thank Dr Chris Lewis for a number of incisive comments that have been taken into account here.

---

[74] Clarke, 'Domesday Satellites', 64, corresponding to Flight's 'B text'. This was also the source of the early survey entitled '*Excerpta de compoto solingorum comitatus Cancie secundum cartam regis ... in regis Domesday*', which is concerned mainly but not entirely with the lands of St Augustine's abbey (Excerpta; Flight, *Survey of Kent*, 13–14, 74).

APPENDIX A

A numbered edition of Evesham C, cross-referenced to the Phillimore entry numbers for Worcestershire.

BL, Cotton MS Vespasian B xxiv, fols 8v–10v.
Date   1086 x 1108

fol. 8v]
1: 2,1]   ¶ Ecclesia Sancte Marje Wirecestrie habet unum hundredum quod uocatur Oswaldeslawe, in quo iacent ccc[1] hide, de quibus episcopus ipsius ecclesie a constitutione antiquorum habet omnes redditiones soccorum et omnes consuetudines inibi pertinentes ad dominicum uictum et regis seruicium et suum, ita ut nullus uicecomes ullam ibi possit habere querelam.
2: 2,2]   In ipso hundredo tenet episcopus Cameseiam. Ibi xxiiii hide geldantes. De hiis v hide sunt uaste.
3: 2,3]   De quo tenemento[2] tenet Vrso vicecomes iii berwicas. Ibi vii hide. Mukehulla, Stoltona, Wlfrintona.
4: 2,4]   De ipso tenemento tenet Rogerus de Laci ii hidas in Wlfrintona et Aulfus de eo. Tempore regis E[dwardi] erant in dominico.
5: 2,5]   De eodem tenemento tenet Walterus Poer ii hidas in Witintona.
6: 2,6]   ¶ In eodem hundredo tenet episcopus Wirecestrie Wicam. Ibi xv hide geldantes. In dominio sunt iiii^{or} hide vna uirgata minus.
7: 2,7]   De hoc manerio tenet Vrso v hidas in Holt.
8: 2,8]   Idem Vrso tenet i hidam in Witlega.
9: 2,9]   Idem Vrso tenet i hidam in Kekinwiche et Walterus de eo.
10: 2,10]   Idem Vrso tenet i hidam in Cloptona.
11: 2,11]   Idem tenet iii uirgatas in Lawerne. Ibidem habet Urso dimidiam hidam[3] de dominio episcopi et ualet vi solidos.
12: 2,12]   Idem Vrso tenet i hidam in Grimhelle.
13: 2,13]   De eodem manerio tenet Robertus dispensator dimidiam hidam in Lawerne et ibi habet i carrucam cum i bordario et i molendino de v^{que} solidis et vi acras de prato et xij cainas. Kÿnewardus tenet et ualet xx solidos.
14: 2,14]   De ipso manerio tenet Osbertus filius Ricardi i hidam in Codderegge.
15: 2,15]   ¶ In eodem hundredo tenet episcopus Fladebÿrÿam. Ibi sunt xl hide geldantes.
16: 2,16]   De hoc manerio tenet episcopus de Hereford v hidas in Inteberga.

---

[1] A blank space after *ccc*.
[2] For GDB's *manerio* in this and the following two entries. Chris Lewis informs me that *tenementum* is entirely absent from GD B; it was presumably a later copyist's choice.
[3] GDB, 172v has 1 virgate, as has Worcester B.

17: 2,17]   In ipso manerio tenet Vrso v hidas ad Hebbelench.
18: 2,18]   Idem Vrso tenet vii hidas in Bissoppeslench et Aluredus de eo. Ibi sunt in dominio iii caruce et dimidia.
19: 2,19]   De eodem manerio tenet Robertus dispensator v hidas in Pideletmore.
20: 2,20]   De ipso manerio tenet Ailricus archidiaconus i hidam in Bradelega.
21: 2,21]   De eodem manerio tenet Rogerus de Laci x hidas in Bissamtona.
22: 2,22]   ¶ In eodem hundredo tenet episcopus Bredonam. Ibi xxxv hide geldantes. In dominio sunt x hide.
23: 2,23]   Ad hoc manerium iacent iii hide ad Tedintonam et i hida ad Muttonam.
24: 2,24]   De hoc manerio tenet Ailricus archidiaconus ii hidas ad Codestun'.
25: 2,25]   De hoc manerio tenet Vrso vii hidas ad Rudmerlege et Willelmus de eo ii hidas de istis.
26: 2,26]   Idem Vrso tenet ii hidas ad Penedoc.
27: 2,27]   Idem tenet iii hidas ad Wasseburnam.
fol. 9]
28: 2,28]   Idem tenet iiii hidas ad Westmanecote.
29: 2,29]   De eodem manerio tenet Durandus ii hidas in Norton'.
30: 2,30]   De ipso manerio tenet[4] Brichtricus filius Algari i hidam in Bisselega.
31: 2,31]   ¶ In predicto hundredo tenet episcopus Rippel cum uno membro Vpentona. Ibi xxv hide geldantes.
32: 2,32]   De hoc tenet Ordrich i hidam in Cromba.
33: 2,33]   Ibidem tenet Siward v hidas in Cromba.
34: 2,34]   De eodem tenet Rogerus de Laci iii hidas in Hulcromba.
35: 2,35]   De eodem tenet Urso i hidam in Oleuest.
36: 2,36]   De eodem manerio tenet Radulfus de Bernai i hidam in Cuinhulla.
37: 2,37]   De eodem ten' Brichtrich i hidam in Burlege.
38: 2,38]   ¶ Item in eodem hundredo tenet episcopus Blockelai. Ibi xxxviii hide geld'. In dominio xxv hide et dimidia.
39: 2,39]   De hoc manerio tenet Ricardus ii hidas in Dichford.
40: 2,40]   Anesgotus i hidam et dimidiam.
41: 2,41]   Ad supradictum manerium pertinet j hida Lacumbe ad uictum monachorum.
42: 2,42]   ¶ Stephanus filius Wlwi iii hidas in Dailesford.
43: 2,43]   Herewardus v hidas in Eunelade.
44: 2,44]   Has duas terras Dailesford et Eunelade tenuit abbas de Euesha' de episcopo Wirec' quousque episcopus Baiocensis de abbatia accepit et ipse terre fuerunt de uictu monachorum.
45]   (De hoc manerio tenet Vrso v hidas in Dorna.)[5]

[4] GDB, 173 has *tenuit*.
[5] Evesham C 45 in the right-hand margin in a different hand and with transposition signs.

46: 2,45]   ¶ Item in eodem hundredo tenet episcopus Tredintonam cum uno membro Tidelminton'. Ibi xxiii hide geld'.

47: 2,46]   In Blakewell' ii hide.

48: 2,47]   De eodem manerio Gilebertus filius Turoldi iiii hidas.

49: 2,48]   In eodem hundredo tenet episcopus Norwic' cum uno membro Tibertonie. Ibi xxvi hide geld'.[6] De iis sunt iii et dimidia in dominio.

50: 2,49]   Ad ipsum manerium pertinent Wirecestrie quater xx[ti] et x domus. De his habet episcopus xlv et Vrso xxiiii. Ex hiis Osbertus filius Ricardi viii, Walterius Poer xi, Robertus dispensator i. ¶ De burgo Wirec' habuit episcopus in tempore regis E[dwardi] iii[um] denarium et modo habet cum rege et comite.[7] Tunc vi libras, modo viii.

51: 2,51]   ¶ In foro Wirec' tenet Vrso de episcopo xxv domos.

52: 2,52]   De eodem tenet Vrso v hidas in Hindelep et Alcrintone.

53: 2,53]   (Idem tenet ii hidas in Warmendona et Trotteswella. Item Vrso tenet in Estona dimidiam hidam.)[8]

54: 2,54]   Idem i hidam in Cudeleie.

55: 2,55]   De ipso manerio tenet Ordrich iii hidas et i uirgatam in Estona.

56: 2,56]   Ordrich tenet i hidam in Odungeleie.

57: 2,57]   Ailricus archidiaconus i hidam in Hudintune.

58: 2,58]   Walterus Poer i hidam et dimidiam in Hudintone et in Radleie.

59: 2,59]   Idem iii hidas in Chirchulle.

60: 2,60]   Idem iii hidas in Bradicote.

61: 2,61]   Herlebaldus i hidam in P(i)rẏa.

62: 2,62]   ¶ Item ecclesia tenet Ouerberiam cum Penedoc. Ibi vi hide.

63: 2,63]   Item eadem tenet Segesbergam. iiii hide geld'.

64: 2,64]   Ipsa ecclesia tenet [fol. 9v] Scepwaston'. ii hide.

65: 2,65]   Item eadem tenet Heruertonam cum Wiburgestoke. iii hide.

66: 2,66]   Item eadem Grimeleiam. iii hide.

67: 2,67]   Vnam ex hiis tribus tenet Rodbertus dispensator in Kekinwiche.[9]

68: 2,68]   Item eadem Hallage cum Bradewas. vii hide geld'.

69: 2,69]   De hoc manerio tenet Walterius de Burch dimidiam hidam in Heresbẏrẏa.

70: 2,70]   De eodem Rogerus de Lacẏ iii hidas et dimidiam in Spechleie et Humeltun'.

71: 2,71]   Item de eodem Hugo de Grentemeinil dimidiam hidam in Lappewrth', que reddebat per annum viii denarios de chirichet ecclesie Wigornie.

---

[6] GDB, 173v has 25 hides, as has Worcester B.
[7] Altered from *comitatu*.
[8] Evesham C 53 in the right-hand margin in a different hand and substituted for *Idem tenet i hidam et iii uirgatas in Warmendona et Estona*, which is crossed out.
[9] *Kekinwiche* (Kenswick) apparently in error for GDB's *Cnihtewic* (Knightwick).

72: 2,72]   ¶ Item eadem Croppetornam cum Nudertona. Ibi l hide.[10]
73: 2,73]   De hoc manerio tenet Robertus dispensator xi hidas.
74: 2,74]   et abbas de Euesha' v hidas in Hamtona, de quibus episcopus Wirecestr' tempore regis E[dwardi] tantummodo geldum habuit. De cetero tota quieta est.
75: 2,75]   De eodem manerio tenet abbas de Euesha' (iiii hidas) in Benningwrth' et Vrso vi hidas in eodem.
76: 2,76]   Item eadem tenet Cliuam cum Lench. Ibi x hide et dimidia.
77: 2,77]   Item eadem Sepsintun'. vi hide. Una earum non geldat. Walterus Poer tenet eam.
78: 2,78]   Ad hoc manerium pertinet i berwica. Ibi v hide. Rogerus de Laci tenet eas.
79: 2,79]   Item episcopus tenet[11] Hambẏrẏ. xiiii hide. Vrso tenet de hac dimidiam hidam in Estwde.
80: 2,81]   Ipsa ecclesia tenet Stokes cum Estona, et Bedindonam. Ibi x hide.
81: 2,82]   Item eadem Hurtleberi. Ibi xx hide.
82: 2,83]   Item eadem Wlfwardele. v hide.
83: 2,84]   Item eadem tenet Aluithecrirche in Camel hundredo. Ibi xiii hide. Ibi iiii^{or} berwiches: Costune, Warestel, Tonge, Ouerestun'.
84: 2,85]   Item eadem tenet Eardeluestun' et Kintitun'. xv hide.
85: 3,1]   ¶ Episcopus Hereford' in Dudintre hundredo Bockinton'. viii hide
86: 3,2]   et in Cura ii hide. Vrso tenet de episcopo duas earum.
87: 3,4]   Idem episcopus tenet Inteberge. xv hide et dimidia. Ex hiis x geld'.
88: 4,1]   In Clent hundredo. ¶ Ecclesia Sancti Dionisii i hidam.
89: 5,1]   ¶ Ecclesia Couintr' i hidam in parco Salawarpe.
90: 6,1]   ¶ Ecclesia Cormell' i hidam[12] in Tametebẏri in Dudintr' hundredo.
91: 7,1]   ¶ Ecclesia Sancti Petri de Gloecestr' tenet dimidiam hidam in Wich et est in eadem consuetudine qua est dimidia (hida) regis que est ibi.
92: 8,1]   ¶ Ecclesia Sancti Petri de Westmustier tenet Persor'.[13] Rex Edwardus tenuit hoc manerium et eidem ecclesie dedit quietum sicut ipse eum in suo dominio tenebat. Ibi cc hide. De hiis sunt in Persor' ii hide, que nunquam geldebant [sic] tempore regis E[dwardi].
93: 8,2]   In Wica sunt de istis vi hide (et dimidia).[14] De hiis vi hidis tenet Vrso i hidam. Gilebertus dimidiam hidam.
94: 8,3]   In Pennesham ii hide.

---

[10] Nota in the left-hand margin in a different hand.
[11] After tenet the name Hertleberie is crossed out.
[12] GDB, 174 has ½ hide.
[13] A cross-shaped caract-mark in the left-hand margin.
[14] GDB, 174v has 6 hides.

95: 8,4]   In Burlingeham iii hide et i uirgata. De istis tenet Vrso ii hidas et i uirgatam.
96: 8,5]   ⁊ In Brichthelmetona x hide.
97: 8,6]   In Depeford x hide. De hac terra habent due Francigene ii hidas. De ista terra tempore regis E[dwardi] [fol. 10] tenuit Alcot monachus i hidam.
98: 8,7]   In Hekinton' xvi hide. De hiis sunt in dominio ix hide. De hac terra tenet Vrso iiii hidas una uirgata minus. De hac terra tenet Turstanus filius Roci iii hidas.
99: 8,8]   ⁊ In Bezford x hide. De hac terra tenet Vrso v hidas. De eadem terra Walterus Poer i hidam que nunquam geldabat.
100: 8,9a]   ⁊ In Langedone xxx hide. Ex hiis in dominio xi hide.
101: 8,9b]   Tempore regis E[dwardi] ix liberi (homines) tenuerunt xviii hidas.
102: 8,9c]   De hac terra tenuit rex Willelmus v hidas et iii uirgatas (Eadresfeld).[15] Reinbaldus et Aluricus tenent.
103: 8,9d]   De eadem terra tenet Draco filius Ponci i hidam.
104: 8,9e]   De eadem terra tenet Vrso v hidas.[16]
105: 8,9f]   De hac terra tenet Willelmus filius Baderonis ii hidas et dimidiam.
106: 8,9g]   De eadem terra Rogerus de Lacẏ v hidas.[17]
107: 8,10a]   ⁊ In Poiwica iii hide.
108: 8,10b]   Vrso tenet terras quas tenuerunt Ailward et Sewlf et Brichtmer et Ailwine et ibi habet vii carucas.
109: 8,10c]   Gilebertus filius Turoldi tenet quod tenuit [sic] Alwi et Ketelbertus et ibi sunt in dominio ii caruce et i caruca vii bordariorum.
110: 8,10d]   Walterus Poer tenet quod tenuit Godricus et ibi habet dimidiam carucam et bordarii ii carucas.
111: 8,10e]   Quidam Francigena (Artur) tenet quod tenuit Edwardus.
112: 8,11]   ⁊ Snodesbirẏ sunt xi hide. De hiis in dominio vii et una uirgata et ex hiis (i hida) nunquam geld'. De hac tenet Urso iiii hidas i uirgata minus. Alwardus tenet.[18]
113: 8,12]   In Husintr' vi hide.
114: 8,13]   ⁊ In Wich i hida que nunquam geld'. De Wich de decima regis viii libras habet Sanctus Petrus.
115: 8,14]   ⁊ Willelmus filius Corbeceon tenet in Dormestun' v hidas. De Willelmo tenet Albertus ii hidas.
116: 8,15]   Vrso tenet Pidelet. Ibi v hide.
117: 8,16]   Idem Vrso tenet Neuenton'. Ibi x hide. De his x hidis tenet

---

[15] Eadresfeld in the left-hand margin in a different hand and with transposition signs.
[16] On this entry, see *DB* GLS, appendix n.EvA 55.
[17] On this entry, see *DB* GLS, appendix n.EvA 53.
[18] As the sense demands, GDB, 174v has *tenuit*.

Herebrand*us* de Vrsone iii hidas et i uirgatam. Qui has terras tenent seruiebant sicut alii liberi homines.

118: 8,17]   Idem Urso tenet Grafton'. Ibi ii hide una uirgata minus. Qui hanc tenet in prato uno die falcabat et alia seruitia faciebat.

119: 8,18]   Idem tenet Pidelet. Ibi iiii^or hide. Ex his una nunquam geld'.

120: 8,19]   ⁋ Walt*erus* Poer tenet Piritune. Ibi vi hide.

121: 8,20]   Idem Walt*erus* tenet Grafton'. Ibi vii hide.

122: 8,21]   In Piplintona iiii hide et dimidia in dominio. Vnus rodman tenet iii uirgatas.

123: 8,22]   In eadem berwicha tenet Godric*us* iii hidas et dimidiam que nunquam geld'. Halewi tenet i hidam et i uirgatam. Hec uirgata nunquam geld'. Alter Alewi tenet i hidam et Wlfrich tenet iii uirgatas. Una ex hiis non geldabat tempore regis E[dwardi] et ipsi seruiebant ut alii liberi homines. Nunc Walt*erus* Poer tenet terram Godrich et Alewi et ibi i caruca. Vrso vicecomes tenet hidam quam alter Alwi tenebat. Nichil est ibi [fol. 10v] nisi duas acras prati et tamen reddit c denarios. Quod Walt*erus* tenet ualet l solidos.

124: 8,23]   Gileb*ertus* filius Turoldi tenet Cumbrintun'. Ibi ix hide. Ibi vnus Francigena tenet i hidam. Huic pertinet i berwich x hidarum. Wlf et Angod*us* tenuerunt. Modo tenet has predictus Gileb*ertus*.

125: 8,24]   Vicecomes tenet Broctun' et Aulfus de eo. Brichtmer ten(uit).[19] Ibi sunt iii hide.

126: 8,25]   ⁋ In Wirecestresire tenet Rob*ertus* Parler de Gileb*er*to filio Turoldi vnum frustum terre et uocatur Nafford. Hec terra non geldat nec pergit ad hundredum.

127: 8,26a]   Aluredus de M*er*leberge tenet Stokes. Ibi xv hide. Idem ipse tenet xij hidas et i uirgatam tempore regis E[dwardi]. Duo uero rodmanni tenebant iii hidas una uirgata minus, Alward et Wlfrich. Modo totum tenet Aluredus.

128: 8,26b]   De hac terra tenent duo rodmanni i hidam.

129: 8,26c]   De eadem terra Will*elmus* et Boselin ii hidas et iii uirgatas.

130: 8,27]   Vrso tenet Cumbrinton'. Ibi ii hide. Artur tenuit.

131: 8,28]   Omnes he supradicte terre iacuerunt et iacent ad P*er*soram. Hoc manerium tempore regis E[dwardi] reddebat quater xx^ti et iii libras et l sextaria mellis cum omnibus placitis francorum hominum.

---

[19] Altered from *tenet* and followed by a change of hand.

APPENDIX B

A numbered edition of Evesham M, cross-referenced to the Phillimore entry numbers for Gloucestershire

BL, Cotton MS Vespasian B xxiv, fols 62–63v.
Date   1086 x 1095

fol. 62]

1]   De Otintune,[1] Lecche et Stanedis.[2]

2: 2,4]   Otintune cum berewic Condicote x hide. Hec terra numquam geld'. Sanctus Petrus de Gloecestr' habuit in dominio donec rex Willelmus uenit in Angliam et est in Salamanesberie hundredo.

3: 2,8]   ¶ Lecche et Cumberlege xiii hide. Thomas tenet. Preter has xiii hidas habet Walterus filius Poinz xii hidas ibi, quas Thomas archiepiscopus calumpniatur ad opus Sancti Petri.

4: 2,10]   ¶ Stanedis xv hide. Thomas tenet. De Stanedis tenet Hugo comes i hidam iniuste et Durandus vice[fol. 62v]comes iii hidas iniuste, quas Thomas archiepiscopus calumpniatur ad opus Sancti Petri.

5: 2,4]   ¶ Eldredus archiepiscopus tenuit in Otintona et Cundicota x hidas quietas.

6: 2,8]   ¶ Aldredus archiepiscopus tenuit in Leccha xxiiii hidas.

7: 2,10]   ¶ Aldredus archiepiscopus tenuit in Stanedis xv hidas. Ex his tenet Durandus vicecomes iii hidas.[3]

8: 3,1]   In Westberia Sancte Marie de Wirecestr' sunt l hide.

9: 3,2]   Eadem ecclesia tenet Colesburnam pro viii hidis.

10: 3,3]   Eadem Haicotam pro i hida.

11: 3,4]   Becgeburiam xxi hidis.

12: 3,5]   Widiedonam xxx hidis. Ex his sunt iii quiete.

13: 3,7]   Cliuam pro xxx hidis.

14: 3,6]   Cundicotam pro iii hidis.

15]   Summa centum et xxix hide.[4]

16: 4,1]   Episcopus Herefordie tenet in Presteberia xxx hidas.

17: 5,1]   ¶ Episcopus Exonie tenet Aldelandam pro ii hidis. Ex hiis est una quieta.

18: 5,2]   In Tidrintona v hidas.

19: 6,1]   ¶ Episcopus de Sancto Laudo tenet in Actona ii hidas et dimidiam.

---

[1] *Otintune* in capital letters.
[2] Followed by one blank line.
[3] Followed by one blank line.
[4] Followed by one blank line.

20: 6,2]   In Ambroc ii hidas.
21: 6,3]   Idem episcopus tenet manerium de i hida de lxiiii acris terre, quam Goisiner*us* de illo tenet.
22: 6,4]   In Estoc ii hidas. Ex hiis est una quieta.
23: 6,5]   In Didintona v hidas.
24: 6,6]   In Wapeleie i hidam.
25: 6,7]   In Leiga i hidam.
26: 6,8]   In Mardicote ii hidas.
27: 6,9]   In Dodintune i hida et dimidia et tercia pars dimidie hide.
28]   Summa xviii hide et tercia pars dimidie hide.
29: 7,1]   ¶ Sanctus Petr*us* de Bada tenet Aluestona*m* pro v hidis. Ex hiis sunt ii hide quiete.[5]
30: 7,2]   Egestona*m* pro v hidis. Ex hiis sunt quiete ii.
31: 8,1]   ¶ Ecclesia Glastonie tenet in Puliceirca xx hidas.
32: 9,1]   ¶ Ecclesia Malmesb*er*ie tenuit[6] in Letletona v hidas. Ex hiis sunt ii quiete et dimidia.
33: 10,1]   ¶ Ecclesia Sancti Pet*ri* de Gloec' tenet in Bertona xxii hidas vna virgata minus quietas.
34: 10,2]   Eadem in Froecestra v hidas.
35: 10,3]   In Boxewelle v hidas.
36: 10,4]   In Culna iiii hidas.
37: 10,5]   In Aldeswarda xi hidas.
38: 10,6]   In Bochelanda x hidas.
39: 10,7]   In Hinnetona xv hidas.
40: 10,8]   In Hamma vii hidas.
41: 10,9]   In Prestona ii hidas.
42: 10,10]   In Ledena iiii hidas.
43: 10,11]   Mortune v hidas inter boscum et planum.
44: 10,12]   In Hamnell' ii hidas.
45: 10,13]   In Duntesburne v hidas.
46]   Summa quater xx^{ti} et xvi hide et iii virgate.
47: 11,1]   ¶ Ecclesia Wincelc' tenet in Scireburn' xxx hidas. Ex hiis sunt x quiete.
48: 11,2]   In Blandintona vii hidas.
49: 11,3]   Theninga iii hidas.
50: 11,4]   In Fralintona i hidam.
51: 11,5]   In Aldrtona ii hidas.
52: 11,6]   In Niwetona iii hidas et dimidiam.
53: 11,7]   In Stantona iii hidas.

---

[5] Evesham M 29 and 30 are equivalent to Bath B 16, which is a combined entry in this hidage schedule for an individual fief extracted from GDB (*DB Somerset*, appendix II).
[6] Possibly in error for *tenet* (GDB, 165).

54: 11,8]   In Cherletona ii hidas liberas[7] et quietas.
55: 11,9]   In Stawella[8] vii hidas.
56: 11,10]   In Huniburna x hidas.
57: 11,11]   In Almeltona iii hidas et dimidiam.
58: 11,12]   In Hidecota ii hidas liberas.[9]
59: 11,14]   In Wenric iii hidas et dimidiam.
60]   Summa lxxvii hide et dimidia.
61: 12,1]   ¶ Ecclesia de Euesha' tenet in Medgaresburi viii hidas et nona hida pertinet ecclesie de Ædwardestowe quieta.
62: 12,2]   In Tadestrop vii hidas.
63: 12,3]   In Burtona x hidas.
64: 12,4]   In Bradewella x hidas.
65: 12,5]   In Swella iii hidas.
66: 12,6]   In Wilderesheia viii hidas.[10]
67: 12,7]   In Westona iii hidas et una libera.
68: 12,8]   In Stocha [fol. 63] ii hidas.
69: 12,9]   In Hedicota iii hidas.
70: 12,10]   Summa lvi hide.
71: 13,1]   ¶ Ecclesia Abendone in Dumeltona tenet vii hidas et dimidiam.
72: 14,1]   ¶ Ecclesia de Persora tenet jn Culega v hidas.
73: 14,2]   In Hauochesberia xvii hidas.
74]   Summa xxii hide.
75: 15,1]   ¶ Ecclesia de Couentreu tenet in Mersetona x hidas.
76: 16,1]   ¶ Ecclesia de Cormeliis tenet in Nuwent vi hidas liberas.
77: 17,1]   ¶ Ecclesia de Lira tenet in Duntesborna i hidam et i virgatam.
78: 18,1]   ¶ Ecclesia de Eglesham tenet in Mudestona xiiii hidas.
79: 19,1, 2] ¶ Ecclesia de Westmustier tenet lxx hidas. Ex hiis habet Gerardus camerarius xi quietas.[11]
80: 20,1]   ¶ Ecclesia Sancti Dionisii tenet lx hidas.
81: 21,1]   ¶ Ecclesia de Lanheie tenet in Estona iiii hidas.
82: 22,1]   ¶ Ecclesia Sancti Ebrulfi tenet in Rawelle x hidas quietas.
83: 23,1]   ¶ Ecclesia de Cadomo tenet in Pendeberia iii hidas.
84: 23,2]   In Hantona viii hidas.
85: 24,1]   ¶ Ecclesia Trowaz tenet in Horseleia x hidas.
86: 26,1]   ¶ Reinbaldus tenet in Hamenell' iiii hidas et i virgatam.

---

[7] The accusative case is given in full.
[8] *Stawella* (Stowell) apparently in error for GDB's *Snawesille* (Snowshill).
[9] The accusative case is given in full.
[10] On this entry, see GLS appendix n.EvK 133–5.
[11] Evesham M 79 treats Gerard's subtenure as additional to the overall assessment of the complex manor of Deerhurst at 59 hides (GDB, 166).

87: 26,2]   In Drifeld' vii hidas.
88: 26,3]   In Norcoto i hidam.
89: 26,4]   In Prestetona viii hidas preter dominium.
90]   Summa xx hide et i virgata.
91: 25,1]   ¶ Ecclesia de Cirecestr' tenet ii hidas quietas.
92: 2,1]   ¶ Stigandus archiepiscopus tenuit in Cherchesdona xv hidas et dimidiam.
93: 2,2]   In Vchelicota iiii hidas.
94: 2,3]   In Nortuna v hidas et dimidiam.
95: 2,4]   ¶ Eldredus archiepiscopus tenuit in Otintona et Condicota x hidas quietas.
96: 2,5]   Stigand*us* archiepiscopus tenet[12] in Swindona iii hidas.
97: 2,6]   In Scippetona i hidam.
98: 2,7]   In Hacgpen i hidam.
99: 2,8]   Eldred*us* archiepiscopus tenuit in Lecche xxiiii hidas.[13]
100: 2,9]   Stigandus archiepiscopus tenet[14] in Cumtona x hidas.[15]
101: 2,10]   Eldredus archiepiscopus tenuit in Stanedis xv hidas. Ex his tenet Durand*us* vicecomes iii hidas.
102: 2,11]   Sanctus Oswaldus de Gloec' tenet in Wideford ii hidas.
103: 2,12]   Idem in Cernai iiii hidas.
104: 2,13]   In Lessedona ii hidas.
105]   Summa quater xx[ti] et xvi hide.
106: 27,1]   ¶ Rog*erus* comes tenet in Ha*m*tona v hidas.
107: 28,1]   ¶ Hug*o* comes tenet in Biselega viii hidas.
108: 28,5]   In Westona iii hidas.
109: 28,2]   In Troham i hidam.
110: 28,3]   Idem tenet in Hecgesworda dimidiam hidam geldantem, quam Rog*er*us de Laceio calumpniatur.
111: 28,4]   Idem in Campedena xv hidas.
112: 28,7]   Idem tenet in Langetreu hundredo iiii hidas et duo homines, Elnot et Elwine, tenuerunt de illo.[16]
113]   Summa xxxi hide et dimidia.
114: 29,1]   ¶ Comes de Morit' tenet in Langeb*er*ge ii hidas.
115: 30,1]   ¶ Episcopus Lexoniensis tenet in Redmertona ii hidas.
116: 30,2]   In Leseb*er*ga v hidas.
117: 30,3]   In Sopesb*er*ia v hidas.

---

[12] GDB, 164v has *tenuit*.
[13] Evesham M 99 omits a further hide at Coberley (GDB, 164v).
[14] GDB, 164v has *tenuit*.
[15] GDB, 164v states 9 hides.
[16] On this entry, see GLS appendix n.EvM 108, 112.

118]	Summa xii hide.
119: 31,1]	⁋ Will*elmu*s de Ow tenet in Stanhus vii hidas.
120: 31,2]	In Aluredestona iii hidas.
121: 31,3]	Ibidem ii hidas, quas Vlnot tenuit.
122: 31,4]	In Wigeweita vi hidas geldantes.
123: 31,5]	In Wullauestona ii hidas.
124: 31,6]	In Tideham i[17] virgatam et dimidiam.
125: 31,7]	In Dundesborna v hidas et dimidiam.
126: 31,8]	In Tortuna i hidam.
127: 31,9]	In Sciptona ii hidas.
128: 31,10]	In Culcortona iii virgatas et v acras.
129: 31,11]	In Becgewrda viii hidas.
130: 31,12]	In Suella iii hidas.
131]	Summa xxxv hide et dimidia et dimidia virgata.
132: 32,1]	⁋ Will*elmu*s filius Baderon tenet in Cirec' ii hidas.
133: 32,2]	In Dudesborna iii hidas et dimidiam.
134: 32,3]	In Serdedona i hidam.
135: 32,4]	In Westona iii hidas.
136: 32,5]	In Thebristona v hidas.
137: 32,6]	In Hunteleia ii hidas.
138: 32,7]	In Oppa v hidas.
139: 32,8]	In Staura i hidam liberam.[18]
140: 32,9]	Idem ii virgatas et dimidiam de firma Westberie.[19]
141: 32,10]	(⁋ In Neuha' i hidam liberam.)[20]
fol. 63v]	
142: 32,11]	⁋ Lidenai vi hidas.
143: 32,12]	In Hiwoldestune iii hidas.
144: 32,13]	In Hacgepen v hidas.
145]	Summa xxxviii hide et dimidia virgata.
146: 33,1]	⁋ Will*elmu*s camerarius in Winecote iii hidas.
147: 34,1]	⁋ Will*elmu*s Guizenbod tenet in Penbewrtha vi hidas et i virgatam.
148: 34,2]	In Wenintona v hidas.
149: 34,3]	In Clostuna x hidas.
150: 34,4]	In Ebrictona x hidas.
151: 34,5]	In Caldicote iii hidas.
152: 34,6]	In Eilewrd' i hidam.
153: 34,7]	In Fernecote iii hidas.

---

[17] Altered from *ii*.
[18] The accusative case is given in full.
[19] An erasure after *Westberie*.
[20] Evesham M 141 in the lower margin. The accusative case is given in full.

154: 34,8] In Getinge x hidas et i est quieta.
155: 34,9] In Cadesleda ii hidas.
156: 34,10] In Theointuna vi hidas.
157: 34,11] In Bernitone ii hidas.
158: 34,13] In Dubentone i hidam.
159] Summa lix hide et i virgata.
160: 35,1] Will*elmu*s filius Widonis tenet in Derham vii hidas.
161: 35,2] Idem tenet iii hidas unde ecclesia de P*er*sore fuit saisiata per Dur*andum* vicecomitem.
162: 36,1] ⁋ Will*elmus* Frusseleu tenet in Wlletona ii hidas.
163: 36,2] In Connicote dimidiam hidam.
164: 36,3] In Litletona i hidam.
165: 37,1] ⁋ Will*elmu*s filius Normanni tenet in Morcote i hidam.
166: 37,2] In Bichonofre dimidiam hidam.
167: 37,3] In Dena ii hidas et ii virgatas et dimidiam quietas.
168: 37,5] Idem i hidam et dimidiam virgatam.
169: 38,1] ⁋ Will*elmu*s Leowriz tenet in Lainchantuna iii hidas.
170: 38,2] Idem in Heilles xi hidas.
171: 38,3] In Witetona iii hidas.
172: 38,4] In Siptona iii hidas i virgata minus.
173: 38,5] ⁋ In Turkedene v hidas et i virgatam (et dimidiam).[21]
174: 39,1] ⁋ Rog*erus* de Lacei tenet in Chenepelai iii hidas.
175: 39,2] In Oxehell' iii hidas.
176: 39,3] In Chersewella i hidam et i virgatam.
177: 39,4] In Hicumba ii hidas.
178: 39,5] In Risedona viii hidas.
179: 39,6] In Gitinga x hidas geldantes preter dominium.
180: 39,7] In Duntesborna ii hidas.
181: 39,8] In Wica i hidam.
182: 39,9] In Egeswrtha i hidam et dimidiam.
183: 39,10] In Modieta dimidiam hidam.
184: 39,11] In Tedeham dimidiam hidam.
185: 39,12] In Quenintone viii hidas.
186: 39,13] In Lecche v hidas.
187: 39,14] In Etrop ii hidas.
188: 39,15] In Wenriz ii hidas.
189: 39,16] Idem tenet ibidem i hidam et i virgatam.
190: 39,17] In Stratona v hidas.
191: 39,18] In Suintona vi hidas.

---

[21] *et dimidiam* in the right-hand margin.

192: 39,19]   In Acla i hidam et dimidiam.
193: 39,20]   Idem in Sloptra iii hidas.
194: 39,21]   In Wrmintona v hidas.
195]   Summa lxxi hide et dimidia.
196: 40,1]   ⁊ Rogerus de Bealmont in Dorsintune x hidas.
197: 41,1]   Rogerus de Juri in Hamtone x hidas, vnde due sunt quiete.
198: 41,2]   In Tetteberia xxiii hidas.
199: 41,3]   In Uptune ii hidas et i virgatam.
200: 41,4]   In Culcurtune i hidam et dimidiam.
201: 41,5]   In Heseldena iii hidas et iii virgatas.
202]   Summa xl hide et dimidia.
203: 42,1]   Rogerus de Bercalai tenet in Cuthberlege x hidas.
204: 42,2]   In Dodintune iii hidas et ii partes dimidie hide.
205: 42,3]   In Sistone v hidas.
206]   Summa xviii hide et ii partes dimidie hide.
207: 43,1]   ⁊ Radulfus de Berchalai tenet in Wapeleie i hidam.
208: 43,2]   In Stanlege iiii hidas et dimidiam.
209: 44,1]   Radulfus Painell' tenet in Torelton' iiii hidas et dimidiam
210: 44,2)   et[22] in Langetreu hundredo tenet Rogerus de Iuri de Radulfo Painel i virgatam et dimidiam, quam utrique dereliquerunt.
211: 45,1]   ⁊ Radulfus de Toeni tenet in Cheuringewrd' x hidas.
212: 45,2]   In Hicumbe x hidas.
213: 45,3]   In Brumeberga v hidas.
214: 45,4]   In Hareulle v hidas.
215: 45,5]   In Hamenei et Cernei iiii hidas.
216: 45,6]   In Swella vii hidas.
217]   Summa xli hide.
218: 46,1]   ⁊ Robertus de Toenei in Risedona[23] xiii hidas.
219: 46,2]   In Horeduna x hidas.
220: 46,3]   In Salpertona et Frantona x hidas.
221]   Summa xxxiii hide.
222: 47,1]   ⁊ Robertus dispensator in Wichewene x hidas.
223: 48,1]   ⁊ Robertus de Oilli in Risedona x hidas.
224: 48,2]   In Turchedene v hidas et ii virgatas et dimidiam.
225: 48,3]   In Niwentone v hidas.
226]   Summa xx hide et dimidia et dimidia virgata.
227: 49,1]   ⁊ Ricardus legatus in Tormentone viii hidas.
228: 50,1]   ⁊ Osbernus Giffardus in Rochamtona iii hidas …[24]

---

[22] *et* above an erasure.
[23] Altered from *Risedono*.
[24] The text breaks off at the foot of fol. 63v.

11

'A Deed without a Name'

Sally Harvey

Part of the mystique of the two volumes of Domesday lies in the name: although neither book was given a title, an author, or an attribution, the name by which it came to be known rings of the Apocalypse and still resonates. Yet, we cannot date or document the long-surviving epithet given by the 'native English' with any certainty before *c.* 1179 when it was then explained, or rather explained away, as 'metaphorical', *per metaphoram*, by Richard fitzNigel in his treatise on the workings of the Exchequer.[1]

In the text itself, Domesday is called a *descriptio*. But if someone had asked a friendly traveller to describe England in the eleventh century and been greeted with a reading of Domesday, he would not have been amused; the written work is so encyclopaedic as to elevate the Book into a class of its own. Yet it is because of the plenitude of data that Domesday Book contains – almost all of it eluding precise, undisputed, interpretation (providing all the fun of being a detective without the danger) – that many of us, under its spell, have entered William's service and, as Maitland predicted, 'become that man's man'.[2] But therein lies a danger; it was a very partial document.

Descriptio was, of course, a technical word in medieval usage. Literally 'a writing down', the term was adopted by the text itself for the occasion and process of recording information, and most notably in the colophon at the end of Little Domesday;[3] it covered all the labour of compiling, ordering, and re-writing. The acts of recent conquerors, verbal opinions, and the returns from present holders of lands with vested interests thereby became a matter of record. The term echoed Carolingian records of revenues from royal lands and fiscal rights that, once written,

---

[1] *Dialogus de Scaccario*, ed. C. Johnson, London 1950, xx–xxii, 64.
[2] F. W. Maitland, *Domesday Book and Beyond*, 2nd edn, Cambridge 1987, 520.
[3] GDB, 3, 164, 252, 269: KEN 2,2; GLS 1,63; SHR C12; CHS FT2,19; LDB, 450.

were difficult to gainsay, 'descriptions' serving to define, maintain, and defend rights to property and wealth.[4]

In earlier usage, *descriptio* might mean description, delineation, or a proper disposition, order, or arrangement. The term was variously associated with *mansi*, with customary dues, with rents, with tribute, and with heavy new impositions. A *descriptio causarum* was glossed as 'an index or book in which judicial cases were arranged in order'.[5] In England, the next quoted usage of *descriptio* after Domesday is for a tax or levy, and to describe dues.[6] Its meaning and use became fused with *discriptio*: which was used for a 'division', 'distribution', or 'apportionment', and a *discriptor* in Frankish texts was one who recorded men by position and by hundred.[7] All such usages are relevant to both the Domesday inquest and the Book. Richard fitzNigel, too, took up the concept of apportionment – the survey was conducted so that 'everyone may be constrained within his own rights and not encroach on those of others without punishment'.[8] Each of these older usages corresponds with particular aspects of Domesday Book: many familiar to bishops and royal clerks educated in continental practices.

But *descriptio* was not a name: it was its function. In official contemporary sources, Domesday was known by other functional names, one being 'the king's book'.[9] The king's lands have, of course, prime place in each county and for the rest the text records the lands that he had granted or, in the case of ecclesiastical lands, those, but not all, that he had confirmed. It was, above all, both the king's rent book and – in a more complicated way – the king's tax book.[10] These roles were reflected in another of its contemporary official and functional titles, that which occurs in the later pages of Domesday itself, where Domesday refers to an addition to its pages 'after the Book of Winchester was made', probably between 1114 and 1124.[11] Winchester, indeed, being already long known as the location of the chief royal treasury – although other royal treasuries might also have existed.

One area that has not been discussed much, as far as I am aware, in the many

---

[4] R. McKitterick, *The Carolingians and the Written Word*, Cambridge 1989, esp. 163.
[5] *Index seu libellus in quo causae iudicandae ex ordine recensentur*, C. Du Fresne, Dom. Du Cange, *Glossarium Mediae et Infimae Latinitatis cum Supplementis Integris Monachorum Ordinis S. Benedicti*, 7 vols, Paris 1840–50, II, 815–16.
[6] R. E. Latham, *Medieval Latin Word List*, British Academy 1975, 141; see also *The Chronicle of Jocelin of Brakelond*, ed. H. E. Butler, London 1962, 29.
[7] C. T. Lewis and C. Short, *A Latin Dictionary*, Oxford 1966, 555, 589; Du Cange, *Glossarium*, 815–16.
[8] *Dialogus de Scaccario*, ed. Johnson, 63.
[9] E.g. *liber regius*, V. H. Galbraith, 'Royal Charters to Winchester', *EHR* 35, 1920, 383–400 at no.12, 1096 x 1100.
[10] See chapters 7 and 8 in my recent book, *Domesday: Book of Judgement*, Oxford 2014.
[11] G. Fellows Jensen, 'The Domesday Account of the Bruce Fief', *Journal of the English Place-Name Society* 2, 1969–70, 8–17; *The Great Roll of the Pipe for the Thirty First Year of the Reign of Henry I, Michaelmas, 1130*, ed. J. Green, PRS, new series 57, 2012, xxii.

Domesday studies of the last thirty years, has been its name. I always used to assume that it referred straightforwardly to those courts held all across the country: 'doom' being the Anglo-Saxon word for a law or judgment, plus the word for 'day', *daeg*; so the name referred to the results of the unique Law Day or Days, held in counties across the country, with many of the population 'witnessing' in both the literal legal and in the metaphorical sense. Numbers that have been suggested for those who swore evidence to the proceedings range from 7,000 people upwards.[12] From the Domesday mention of some 6,500 vills, with eight representatives from each vill, plus twelve men from each hundred, plus some 3,000 landholders named in the text, David Roffe proposes that 'in all, over 60,000 witnesses were probably heard in the court of the Domesday inquest'.[13] Yet perhaps not all the small and scattered vills in the west and north would have been so represented, so maybe my guesstimate would place it somewhere around 40,000 plus. Certainly, many people would also have gathered to watch the proceedings and they too were probably expected to murmur a general assent to the oaths sworn and the conclusions reached.[14] For one educated contemporary from eastern England, the survey was made 'according to the sworn evidence ... by almost all the inhabitants of the land, whereby each one gave a true verdict when questioned about his own land and substance, and about the land and substance of his neighbours'.[15]

But even now, despite the swing of the pendulum in recent years towards emphasizing the word 'conquest', rather than the word 'Norman', in the study of the Norman Conquest, despite careful and vivid portrayals of hundred and shire and sheriff in action from Christopher Lewis, Robin Fleming, and Richard Abels,[16] we perhaps have not fully appreciated the trauma as well as the drama of these court

---

[12] Fleming originally suggested that 'as many as 7 or 8,000 people attended the inquests', but has since emphasized the range of meetings and courts that may have taken place and how easily the witnesses and magnates' own followers snowballed. R. Fleming, 'Oral Testimony and the Domesday Inquest', *ANS* 17, 1994, 101–22 at 105, cf. R. Fleming, *Domesday Book and the Law: Society and Legal Custom in Early Medieval England*, Cambridge 1998, 15–17.

[13] D. Roffe, *Domesday: The Inquest and the Book*, Oxford 2000, 123.

[14] A later tenth-century record of a land grant, made in the presence of men of East and West Kent, asserted that a 'good thousand men gave the oath', and that further shires took cognizance of the decision – although the numbers should not necessarily be taken literally (S. 1458). 'To these things the great multitude agreed', the account of the Sandwich plea of 1127 (D. M. Stenton, *English Justice between the Norman Conquest and the Great Charter 1066–1215*, London 1965, 116–23 at 121).

[15] *Feudal Documents from the Abbey of Bury St. Edmunds*, ed. D. C. Douglas, British Academy, Records of Social and Economic History 8, 1932, 3; cf *Hemingi Chartularium Ecclesiae Wigorniensis*, ed. T. Hearne, 2 vols, Oxford 1723, I, 49, 72.

[16] C. P. Lewis, 'The Domesday Jurors', *Haskins Society Journal* 5, 1993, 17–44; R. Fleming, *Kings and Lords in Conquest England*, Cambridge 1991, and R. Fleming, *Domesday Book and the Law*; R. Abels, 'Sheriffs, Lord-Seeking and the Norman Settlement', *ANS* 19, 1997, 19–50; G. Garnett, *Conquered England*, Oxford 2007.

occasions, twenty years after the conquest: with the new elite with their back to the wall and their whole profitable future in jeopardy. (In 1085–6 the Danish fleet, supported by a further large fleet provided from the Danish king's ally, the count of Flanders, was threatening William's hold on his conquests, rendering the king, rightly, extremely apprehensive.[17]) And perhaps the context provided by Robert Bartlett's study of the ordeal over the centuries deserves wider attention in the context of Domesday.[18]

In the Domesday courts, the hundred jurors were not simply presenting facts as jurors of recognition. Nor did 'the Domesday inquest attest a king working with his barons and the community of the shire to a common end, albeit with an eye to striking as hard a bargain as he could'.[19] Whether the majority of those assembled attended with the intention of serving a common end is highly questionable. There was coercion at all levels. One of several vivid vignettes of Norman rule from the Abingdon archives shows a senior royal clerk, probably the future bishop of Lichfield/Chester, appearing at a judicial dispute that he had initiated accompanied by his armed and mounted retinue, complete with spears.[20] Further, the apparently straightforward Domesday questions were not merely straightforward but, in fact, also clever. It is to be hoped that few readers have had the unpleasant experience, as I have had on three occasions, of giving witness for the police in a court of law. The unlimited personal aggression permitted by the opposition's lawyers apart, the fact that, after waiting for long hours, a witness is permitted only to answer questions put, but not to make public relevant but unsought material is, at the least, infuriatingly frustrating. We remind ourselves that the men of the locality and the Domesday hundred jurors – even if half of the latter were permitted to be Englishmen – were asked simply: 'Who held the land in King Edward's time?' and 'Who holds it now?' They were not permitted to say who *should* hold it now, or point out that it had been theirs, or their fathers' land, and that none of their family had rebelled against anyone. Largely, they were only allowed to say, or to be recorded as saying, whether they had witnessed the king's seal or official messenger who had authorized the change;[21] or whether the 1086 holder had indeed his proper and authorized predecessor, or *antecessor*.[22]

---

[17] ASC E, 1085, 1086, ed. D. Whitelock, London 1961; *rex timore percitus*, William of Malmesbury, *Saints' Lives*, ed. M. Winterbottom and R. M. Thomson, Oxford 2002, 144–6; 'the only person who shook his [William's] royal state was Cnut, king of the Danes', Malmesbury, *Gesta Regum*, I, 478–9; J. R. Maddicott, 'Responses to the Threat of Invasion, 1085', *EHR* 122, 2007, 986–97.
[18] R. Bartlett, *Trial by Fire and Water: the Medieval Judicial Ordeal*, Oxford 1986.
[19] Roffe, 'Preface', *Domesday: The Inquest and the Book*, x.
[20] *Historia Abbendoniensis: History of the Church of Abingdon*, ed. and trans. J. Hudson, 2 vols, Oxford 2007 and 2002, I, 372–5.
[21] E.g. GDB, 35v; LDB, 195: SUR 21,3; NFK 10,28.
[22] E.g. GDB, 32v, 40: SUR 8,18; HAM 2,1.

A priest was indispensable in the taking of oaths and in the conduct of ordeals. Both 'invoked God. Both brought the supernatural into the courtroom.'[23] Both oaths and ordeals were within the Church's jurisdiction. The priest's presence was mandatory throughout the Domesday inquiry: the 'terms of reference', as surviving in the Inquest of Ely, *Inquisitio Eliensis*, specifically demanded the presence of the priest as well as the reeve and the men of the vill, as well as the representatives of the hundred. Perjury was a serious crime: the very livelihoods of those who perjured themselves were clearly at stake.[24] Probably every stage of the inquiry required the swearing of oaths, even on mere money matters: as we know from an earlier case, quoted in Domesday, of Bruman the reeve who had absconded with the customs-duties paid by foreign merchants.[25] And if some of the great men — commissioners and sheriffs rather than witnesses — did not swear in the Domesday courts, they certainly had to swear, along with their leading followers and tenants, to the king in person at Salisbury on 1 August 1086.[26]

In England, before the Norman Conquest, ordeals were normally of water or hot iron: an iron was heated and carried or a stone was put into boiling water and extracted. Detailed contemporary instructions survive and dictate careful ceremonies with numerous prayers and invocations, amongst them: 'The iron used in the ordeal was first exorcised and then God's blessing invoked. The priest concluded, "May the blessing of God the Father, the Son and the Holy Spirit descend on this iron, to discern the true judgement of God".'[27] Similar blessings were uttered over the water employed in the ordeal of cold water, as over the shield and staff used in the ordeal by battle.

Appraisal of the results placed power in the hands of churchmen.[28] In ordeals, it was the priest who unwrapped the bandaged hands of those who had undergone the ordeal of hot iron and pronounced the *iudicium dei*. He determined whether the water in a forced immersion had received an innocent person or rejected a guilty one. Ordeals in late Anglo-Saxon England took place on occasion within the church building, linking the main church of the hundred to the administration of hundredal justice.[29] The priest's presence and adjudication presumably brought in revenues (later, the Pipe Rolls record payment to a priest for officiating at two ordeals in 1168).[30] In Domesday, the bishop of Winchester showed himself anxious to retain his jurisdiction at a suitable central place: on his Somerset estates, the Domesday

---

[23] R. Bartlett, *England under the Norman and Angevin Kings 1075–1225*, Oxford 2000, 180.
[24] E.g. Robertson, VI, Æthelred, 36; VIII Æthelred, 27; II Cnut, 6 and 36.
[25] GDB, 2: KEN C8.
[26] ASC E, 1086.
[27] *The Pontifical of Magdalen College*, ed. H. A. Wilson, Henry Bradshaw Society 39, 1910, 179–85, 207–9; translation, Bartlett, *England under the Norman and Angevin Kings*, 181.
[28] Bartlett, *Ordeal*, 90–1.
[29] J. Blair, *The Church in Anglo-Saxon Society*, Oxford 2006, 448.
[30] *Pipe Roll, 14 Henry II*, Pipe Roll Society 12, 1890, 48.

detail insists that 'those who have to swear an oath or undergo an ordeal', *sacramentum vel iudicium*, were to come to his borough of Taunton.[31] Probably men of the hundreds and vills gathered in the same way for the Domesday inquiry.

Under Anglo-Saxon law, resort to the ordeal was required for serious crimes such as plotting against the king and false coining. Furthermore (as also in Charlemagne's empire), the ordeal was specified for men of ill-repute, or for the servile class in criminal cases, especially theft. For free men of good and unquestioned repute, on the other hand, oaths and the oaths of compurgators normally sufficed.[32] This past principle may well explain the handling of witnesses and their attitudes in the undecided and intriguing case added to Great Domesday at the last minute, in a leaf inserted into Hampshire's quires. Picot the Cambridgeshire sheriff, in challenging the appearance of 2½ virgates amongst the lands of the Hampshire sheriff, Hugh de Port, enlisted the support of 'villeins and low people, *de villanis et vili plebe*, and reeves' – all of whom were likely to be English – who were, seemingly, 'willing to maintain by oath or by the judgement of God', that he who had held the contested land before 1066 had been a free man and could decide the affiliation of his land as he wished (probably with the post-Conquest consequence that the land might be appropriated for the king's use). The Hampshire sheriff and his tenant, on the other hand, had the support of the 'better and old men of the whole county and of the hundred', who, significantly, 'refused to accept any law except the law of King Edward, until it be determined by the king'.[33] This stipulation would make consequential sense if these mature men were thereby refusing to submit to the ordeal to uphold their side of the story, maintaining that, as men of standing, 'better and old men', their oath alone should suffice, as the law used to operate under King Edward. They certainly were not going to offer to undergo the ordeal as if they were criminals or servile or of doubtful reputation – not unless the king's court and the king in person coerced them to do so.

Since ordeals were employed in Anglo-Saxon England for criminal cases, not for civil cases or those concerning property, drawing on the ordeal to substantiate witness in the Domesday inquiry was all the more shocking. Albeit, cases in western Europe show that the process of threatening the ordeal was sometimes employed simply as a bargaining tool or to bring a case to a conclusion, since some tenurial disputes were quite capable of running for generations (as indeed they were in England).[34] But, as used by conquerors in seeking the assent of the conquered to changes in tenure, there seems no doubt of the ordeal's explicit threat.

---

[31] GDB, 87v: SOM 2,4.
[32] E.g. Robertson, II Cnut, 22. As under the Carolingians, Bartlett, *Ordeal*, 32.
[33] *Nolunt accipere legem nisi regis Edwardi usque dum diffiniatur per regem*, GDB, 44v: HAM 23,3.
[34] S. D. White, 'Proposing the Ordeal and Avoiding It', in *Cultures and Power: Lordship, Status and Process in Twelfth-Century Europe*, ed. T. N. Bisson, Philadelphia 1995, 90–125.

Perhaps there were echoes here of the influential Archbishop Lanfranc's experience of Pavia, where, in a debate concerning tenure (in which he was supposed to have participated), Lanfranc supported Otto I's ruling that there should be recourse to trial by battle when pleas of land depended on the authenticity of documents and oath-helpers, since 'those who do not fear God and are not afraid to perjure themselves, made acquisitions by oaths with all the appearance of legality'.[35] Nor were the ordeals of fire and water in evidence after William's reign for property cases. Indeed, most of the deviations from this tradition in England are recorded in Domesday or in the other land pleas of his reign.[36]

But recourse to the Norman custom of trial by battle or duel became established, and continued. Battle, however, was a less sacral ordeal than other forms of trial, and the presence of clergy was not indispensable.[37] Domesday adheres to this distinction. Whereas it mentions trial by battle seven times, and on six occasions it was offered as an alternative to the *iudicium*, battle itself was never in Domesday termed a *iudicium* or judgement of God.[38] Although much-used amongst Germanic peoples in Europe, trial by battle was not employed in England before its introduction under the Normans, who continued to draw on it to decide cases of theft or homicide, as well as to decide land disputes (rightly only those concerning land valued at 10s. at the least).[39]

The ordeal was proposed as a means of investigating unresolved problems of tenure on up to twenty occasions in Great and Little Domesday, as a further means of maintaining a case; yet even these few entries betray hints of the pressures on the existing communities.[40] Once 'an Englishman' and several times men with English names are volunteered to stand the ordeal on a future occasion to support an incomer's claim to tenure.[41] In the Lincolnshire 'Claims' the two champions produced by the respective claimants were Algar and Ælfstan of Frampton respectively.[42] The requirement for the men of the hundred to give evidence in the Domesday inquest placed locals anxious or desperate to be taken into the service of powerful sheriffs or lords into conflict with their less well-placed neighbours: 'A certain Englishman', a follower of Hermer de Ferrers, offers to undergo the ordeal to uphold the case

---

[35] M. Gibson, *Lanfranc of Bec*, Oxford 1978, 7–8.
[36] Bartlett, *Ordeal*, 63.
[37] Bartlett, *Ordeal*, 63, 121.
[38] Seven references in DB; six times as an alternative to the ordeal, GDB, 377v; LDB, 146v, 176, 189v–90, 213, 277v: LIN CK66; NFK 4,25.9,42;219;227.15,2.66,81. Once, GDB records the ordeal as commuted for a yearly payment of gold or hawks to the king (GDB, 36v: SUR 36,1).
[39] E.g. *Leges Henrici Primi*, ed. L. J. Downer, Oxford 1972, 186–9, nos. 59,15–16a.
[40] Fleming, *Domesday Book and the Law*, 18–19.
[41] LDB, 190, 310v–311, 332: NFK 9,227; SFK 6,79.7,13. Also GDB, 44v: HAM 23,3, above.
[42] *per iudicium aut per bellum*, GDB, 377v: LIN CK66.

that Hermer's predecessor was, in King Edward's day, in possession of one free man now claimed by Hermer. But 'this the whole hundred disputes either by battle or ordeal'; and the Englishman has had to give a pledge.[43] (Hermer was probably already among the circle of royal officials, since he shortly became sheriff of Norfolk, to be restrained from interfering with the lands and the men of the abbey of Bury St Edmunds.[44]) Those Englishmen in the service of Normans were certainly put into conflict with their neighbours, and on a second occasion 'the hundred' offers the ordeal to counter the offer of an ordeal by Hermer's champion.[45] In addition to these two examples, an ordeal, or battle, is offered *against* the witness of the hundred three more times. In one instance a king's man offers the ordeal or battle against the hundred to claim the land for the king, whilst a man of Count Alan of Brittany offers ordeal or battle to support the claims of the hundred – and his lord – for 16 acres; another king's man offers to bear the ordeal for 10 acres against the hundred – although here we are not told whether the hundred replied in kind.[46] A third case names the man offering battle or the ordeal on Hermer's behalf – Ulfkil.[47] Only once is a person with a Norman name, one Ralph, a man of Godric the reeve, offered up for ordeal or battle;[48] the subjects are otherwise anonymous, or have English names. The social turmoil thereby generated locally can only be imagined, whilst the threatened processes of battle or ordeal in local courts give us a glimpse of the inquiry's insidious effects. It has been astutely pointed out that even those occasions when the hundred say that 'they do not know', or 'have not seen', a writ or messenger probably signalled how hazardous it was to be put into the position of being asked to verify one claim or another: when 'caught between a rock and a hard place, struggling to navigate their way between two enormously powerful Normans', as Alan Cooper put it.[49] (He also sees some such entries as signs of 'resistance', as well as of 'simple ignorance' and fear.) It was, too, a question of whether to ingratiate oneself with the new establishment, or whether to try to stand up for the erstwhile holdings of one's fellows and their heirs, or of the Church, and defend them from the king's clutches.[50]

Other cases could be heart-rending if visualized. One woman, probably in hopes

---

[43] *vel bello vel iudicio*, LDB, 189v–190: NFK 9,219,227.
[44] *Regesta Regum Anglo-Normannorum I, 1066–1100*, ed. H. W. C. Davis, Oxford 1913, no. 291, 1087 x 1091; R. Sharpe, 'The Use of Writs in the Eleventh Century', *Anglo-Saxon England* 32, 2004, 247–91 at 275–77.
[45] LDB, 208a: NFK 13,19.
[46] LDB, 146v, 166: NFK 4,25.8,71.
[47] LDB, 213: NFK 15,2.
[48] LDB, 176: NFK 9,42.
[49] A. Cooper, 'Protestations of Ignorance in Domesday Book' in *The Experience of Power in Medieval Europe, 950–1350*, ed. R. F. Berkhofer, A. Cooper, and A. J. Kosto, Aldershot 2005, 169–81 at 179. E.g. GDB, 60c: BRK 21,13.
[50] E.g. GDB, 40, 42, 50: HAM 2,1.4,1.69,15.

of getting the land back, offers the ordeal in order to verify the evidence of the hundred on her former 16 acres of land; another woman, similarly, offers the ordeal to affirm that her former land – 7 acres of woodland and a further acre – did not carry a mortgage.[51] (Almost the only women's voices in Domesday!) In these and several other cases, it is made clear that it was the former holder of the land that was prepared to offer the ordeal, presumably in the hope of returning as a tenant.[52] An unnamed member of the king's household is expected to undergo the judicial ordeal merely in order to maintain the crown's claim upon a ¼ acre of land and a customary due on pasture.[53] Once we are told of a 'judgement', a *iudicium*, of another hundred, but not its mode.[54] The possible use of the ordeal to verify landholding put the men of the locality, and all who swore, in danger of being treated in the Domesday courts as if they were of criminal repute or servile status.

There is no mention in Domesday, however, of ordeals having already taken place. But, as seventeen of the twenty-one references to the ordeal survive in the unabbreviated Little Domesday, with thirteen recorded in the county of Norfolk alone, it must remain an open matter whether resort to the ordeal was as rare as its mention implies, or whether it went unrecorded or abbreviated out in most counties.[55] Furthermore, it is at least possible that many of Domesday's tenurial decisions had already witnessed, or threatened, an ordeal. Outside the Domesday inquiry, a Rochester source informs us of two trials that took place around 1080 to decide the tenure of land at Isleham, Cambridgeshire. At first, the county's decision favoured the sheriff Picot, representing the king; but Odo of Bayeux, supportive of the bishopric of Rochester's claim, was suspicious of the partiality of the men of the county court, through their fear of the notorious sheriff Picot, *timore vicecomitis*, and, after receiving trusted information of perjury, Odo summoned the first representatives of the county court, and a second jury, to a re-trial in London before 'the better barons', at which all the jurors were found guilty of perjury and the case was given to Rochester. One set of jurors having contested what the other set had sworn, their allegations were tested by the prospect of an ordeal of hot iron. Whilst it was not spelt out whether that jury actually went to the ordeal and failed, or whether their courage failed first, the twenty-four jurors were all sent back to their county with the swingeing fine of £300 (a sum worthy of a baronial income).[56] Perhaps significantly, the contentious decision was only referred to in Domesday as

---

[51] LDB, 277v, 137: NFK 66,80.1,213.
[52] E.g. also, LDB, 332a: SFK 7,13.
[53] LDB, 110v: NFK 1,10.
[54] GDB, 165v: GLS 11,14.
[55] GDB contains the Taunton reference, GDB, 87v: SOM 2,4; also GDB, 44v, 336, 377v: HAM 23,3.LIN C4;CK66.
[56] *Quod quia se facturos promiserunt, et facere non potuerunt*, Regesta: Bates, 712–14, no. 225, 1077 x 1082/3, possibly 1077 x 1080. The case was far from clear-cut anyway; the background is explained in Fleming, *Domesday and the Law*, 18–20.

a judgement of Lanfranc and the king's order.[57] In the dispute over the rights of the bishop of Worcester, one side offered trial by battle and the other the ordeal. 'The settlement was witnessed by knights of the church of Worcester and of the bishop, who were ready to affirm it on oath and by battle if the abbot wished to deny it against Rannulf, brother of Abbot Walter, as well as by priests, holy men, and deacons who were ready to confirm it by the ordeal' (literally *iuditio dei*, or judgement of God).[58] For clergy, however, less physically-taxing ordeals were normally offered, such as taking communion bread without choking, or repeating prayers without stumbling. In fact, God's judgement had become more than a metaphor in the disposition of land and the settlement of disputes. Under Norman rule, and in the Domesday inquiry, it meant recourse to the ordeal in 'civil' cases, and, for those proven perjured, severe punishment.

Pressure not to question the changes in land tenure over the last two decades was undeniable. Jurors, and others, swore on the Gospels or on relics and, if queried, they might be subject to the ordeal. The 'better men of the shire' found themselves obliged to be present during these proceedings; they could not absent themselves – in Kent, the fine for non-appearance at the shire moot was £5, a sum representing perhaps the annual profit from a fertile 600-acre estate or the sale of a one-hide estate.[59] They too might be required to give witness. The prospect of an ordeal of hot iron (which, with sepsis, could lead to death) certainly entailed the inability to function for a period, with the possibility – ever-present in the court proceedings – of a near-unpayable fine, and consequent loss of land.

The pressures put on the men of the shire, the hundred, or the vill, show that the inquiry was more than a simple fact-finding exercise: what might be termed an inquiry of recognition or presentment. It was the resident community galvanized into acknowledging formally the loss of their lands. Robert Bartlett sees the ordeal as a device not of weak but of strong kingship: 'it could be enforced in an exercise of power, yet it represented submission to that power as submission to the deity'.[60] The choice set before men of the hundred and the county was between swearing on the Gospels to a distribution of land that was contrary to their or their neighbours' interest, or refusing to do so and facing what we would today term a form of torture, itself labelled as God's judgement, *iudicium dei*. Weighing these choices in the balance was certainly dreadful enough to be accorded the name Domesday.

Whilst a priest was required to bless the instruments of the ordeal, to supervise its carrying out, and to make the decision as to the results, leading ecclesiastics were educated men, the backbone of the king's administration, and its lawyers, who, for the most part, endeavoured to mitigate the worst effects of a military society. Some

---

[57] LDB, 381: SFK 20,1.
[58] *Regesta*, Bates, no. 349.
[59] GDB, 1: KEN D23.
[60] Bartlett, *Ordeal*, 36.

thinking churchmen had long reflected on ordeals and challenged them. Although the Carolingians employed the ordeal as a tool, the contemporary Archbishop Agobard of Lyons had argued against its use: 'The faithful should not believe that Almighty God wishes to reveal men's secrets in the present life through hot water or iron.' He was similarly against trial by battle. 'Can it really be that the Highest requires spears and swords to judge cases? We often see a rightful tenant or claimant, fighting in battle, overcome by the superior strength or some underhand trick of the unjust party.' 'We do not deny that God's providence sometimes clears the innocent and condemns the guilty, but it is in no wise ordained by God that this should happen ..., except at the Last Judgement.' His conclusion was that 'wise judgement, testimony and the oath are sufficient for reaching judicial verdicts'.[61]

Closer in date to the Domesday decades, the 1063 edict of the reforming Pope Alexander II denounced 'by apostolic authority that popular proof which has no canonical sanction, namely hot water, cold water, hot iron or any other popular invention, since these are the fabrications of malice'; they were not to be employed in the judgement of a priest.[62] Nevertheless, following a visit from a Norman delegation, the same pope granted Duke William a banner for the attack on England, together with his blessing.[63] Whether William's convenient interpretation of these, that his trial by battle – *iure belli* as his encomiast William of Poitiers calls it – put the acquisition of England onto a sound legal foundation was well founded is, however, another question, particularly given the penances that the papal legate imposed on the invaders for the slaughter perpetrated during their conquest.[64]

Throughout the twelfth century, thinking churchmen were increasingly opposed to the practice of ordeals, as was the laity. (Twelfth-century burgesses sought the privilege of exemption from the duel in their borough charters.) Some churchmen developed the thesis that to seek His direct intervention in this way was to try to 'tempt God'. Discussion finally ended when the 1215 Lateran Council forbade the clergy to take any part in ordeals.[65]

In considering the import of the name 'Domesday', we must remember that the contemporary Latin term for the ordeal was 'the Judgement of God' (*iudicium dei*).[66] I suggest, however, that thinking churchmen – the mainstay of the Norman 'civil service' – drew the line at referring to the formative text, in Latin, as anything

---

[61] Bartlett, *Ordeal*, 111.
[62] *Patrologiae Cursus Completus, Series Latina*, ed. J-P. Migne, Paris 1844, 146, no. cxxii; Bartlett, *Ordeal*, 82.
[63] Poitiers, 104–5; Orderic identifies Gilbert of Lisieux as the man who returned with the banner, *Orderic*, II, 142–3.
[64] Poitiers, 151–4; cf. *EHD*, II, no. 81.
[65] *English Historical Documents, 1189–1327*, ed. H. Rothwell, London 1975, cap.18, 654.
[66] See also the Domesday entry for Charford, GDB, 44v: HAM 23,3, where the text has been interpreted as either 'judgement of God' (Fleming, *Domesday Book and the Law*, 154, F.622) or 'a judgement day'. Either implied an ordeal.

other than a royal charter or treasury document: some persons, or deeds, could be so terrible as to be beyond naming. The names of Bede's 'perfidious kings' are unknown, because he deleted them with deliberation from the regnal lists;[67] the great historian did not even permit them to become notorious. It was not until almost a century after Domesday, and the tenurial take-over was irreversible, that Richard fitzNigel, born to a family with the highest episcopal and Exchequer traditions and expertise and himself brought up in the historical tradition of Ely, took the bull by the horns.[68] Having an English mother, he perhaps felt compelled to try to excuse the dreadfulness of the processes used to obtain its official standing and the Book's consequent English name as simply metaphorical:

> This book is metaphorically called by the native English 'Domesday', that is 'the Day of Judgement'. For, as the sentence of that strict and terrible last account cannot be evaded by any skilful subterfuge, so when this book is appealed to on those matters which it contains, its sentence cannot be quashed or set aside with impunity. That is why we have called the book 'the Book of Judgement', not because it contains decisions on various difficult points, but because its decisions, like those of the Last Judgement, are unalterable.[69]

Such was the official position of the establishment and Exchequer on the tenurial record, which set out to legitimate the conquest of the Norman duke. But we might better explain the name that its English contemporaries first gave the survey in terms of the dreadful choice that men of the vills, hundreds, and shires were forced to make in 1086 in court: a choice between either swearing on the Gospels to untruth on rightful tenure, to the ruin of their fellow countrymen, or, challenging the newly-imposed tenures, with the prospect of facing a physical ordeal and unknown further consequences.[70]

---

[67] *Bede's Ecclesiastical History of the English People*, ed. B. Colgrave and R. A. B. Mynors, Oxford 1972, 214–15
[68] On Richard's family see, *Dialogus de Scaccario*, ed. Johnson, xiv–xvi.
[69] *Dialogus de Scaccario*, ed. Johnson, 64.
[70] One of several reasons why my recent book on the great survey is entitled *Domesday: Book of Judgement*.

12

Talking to Others and Talking to Itself: Government and the Changing Role of the Records of the Domesday Inquest[1]

David Roffe

DOMESDAY BOOK IS the earliest of the English public records and one of the most famous documents in the western world. Its two volumes, Great Domesday (GDB) and Little Domesday (LDB), contain an account of lordship and land in England in 1086. The description of the manor of Copnor in Hampshire serves as a more or less typical extract. It reads as follows:

> Robert [son of Gerold] holds Copnor and Heldred from him. Tovi held it from Earl Godwin [in 1066] and he could not go to another. Then and now it was taxed for 3 hides. There is land for 3 ploughs. In demesne 1 plough, and there are 5 villagers, 2 smallholders, and 2 slaves with 2 ploughs. There is 1 salthouse worth 8d. Value in the time of King Edward [1066] and now 60s; when acquired 30s.[2]

Arranged by county and fee, there are over 29,000 entries of this kind. Some contain more detail, others less, but together they make up a survey of a realm that was unprecedented. Comprehensive government records, of course, were not unknown at the time. Some three hundred years earlier Charlemagne seems to have contemplated a comprehensive account of his empire, but it did not proceed much beyond

---

[1] This paper is based on a lecture delivered at a symposium on English and Japanese medieval documents at Kumamoto University, Japan, in 2001, and has previously been published in Japanese translation. I am grateful to the British Academy for providing a generous Overseas Travel Grant that allowed me to contribute.
[2] GDB, 46v: HAM 28,2.

surveys of the imperial demesnes and church lands.³ Closer to home, Anglo-Saxon England had produced extensive taxation records.⁴ Christian Europe, however, had never before seen anything on the scale of Domesday Book.⁵

It was an extraordinary achievement, and it was appreciated as such from an early period. Already by the early twelfth century Domesday Book was apparently a prized possession that was carefully preserved in the Treasury,⁶ and some sixty or so years later it had impinged itself on the popular imagination to such an extent that all-but-uniquely it was accorded its folk name.⁷ Richard fitzNigel, writing c. 1179 in the 'Dialogue of the Exchequer', explained that the survey was commonly known by the native English as Domesday, that is, the Day of Judgement:

> for as the sentence of that strict and terrible last account cannot be evaded by any skilful subterfuge, so when this book is appealed to on those matters which it contains, its sentence cannot be quashed or set aside with impunity. That is why we have called the book 'the Book of Judgement', not because it contains decisions on various difficult points, but because its decisions, like those of the Last Judgement, are unalterable.⁸

Domesday Book had assumed a unique place in English consciousness which it has retained to the present day.

Now, of course, like much else in post-industrial England, it has been hitched to 'heritage'. Many communities celebrated the new Millennium by producing what they called 'Domesdays for the Twenty-First Century'. They are largely a celebration of the past. In the Middle Ages, by contrast, Domesday Book had a potent

---

³ J. Percival, 'The Precursors of Domesday: Roman and Carolingian Land Registers', in *Domesday Book: a Reassessment*, ed. P. H. Sawyer, London 1985, 5–27; R. H. C. Davis, 'Domesday Book: Continental Parallels', in *Domesday Studies*, ed. J. C. Holt, Woodbridge 1987, 15–39.
⁴ According to later medieval tradition preserved in the *Historia Croylandensis* of Crowland abbey, King Alfred undertook a survey of the whole of England (*Rerum Anglicarum Scriptores Veteres*, I, ed. W. Fulman, Oxford 1684, 80). The extract that is given, however, is clearly drawn from records of the Domesday inquest (D. R. Roffe, 'The Historia Croylandensis: a Plea for Reassessment', *EHR* 110, 1995, 93–108).
⁵ For Islamic surveys in Sicily, see D. Clementi, 'Notes on Norman Sicilian Surveys', in V. H. Galbraith, *The Making of Domesday Book*, Oxford 1961, 55–58.
⁶ *EHD*, II, 853.
⁷ It was only the Ragman rolls that achieved a comparable fame (H. M. Cam, *The Hundred and the Hundred Rolls*, London 1930). They were named from the seal tags that stuck out of the rolls. That this characteristic should impinge itself on the popular mind attests not only the widespread use of the rolls in successive general eyres, but also the importance that was put on the proceedings that produced them.
⁸ *Dialogus de Scaccario, the Course of the Exchequer, and Constitutio Domus Regis, the King's Household*, ed. C. Johnson, London 1950, 64.

reality in the present.⁹ For landed families its significance was almost palpable, for it documented origins and validated title. Compiled within twenty years or so of the Norman Conquest, Domesday Book was a tangible representation of the tenurial revolution that had seen the all-but-complete eclipse of the Old English aristocracy by the companions of William the Conqueror. Domesday stood at the beginning of family history. Likewise, it marked, if not always the origins, then a supremely decisive stage in the history of religious institutions. From at least the late twelfth century no archive was complete without a copy of the Domesday entries for the estate. There could be no more powerful an argument for a claim on land or service than that it appeared in Domesday Book.

Beyond the upper ranks of society, its attraction was less concrete but the more compelling for that. The subject matter of Domesday Book is exclusively the land of the tenants-in-chief and the honorial barony. Its effectiveness in legal terms for the man in the furrow was largely confined to proof of tenure in ancient demesne. However, as Richard fitzNigel hints, the fact did not diminish expectation. Throughout the Middle Ages and beyond all manner of men saw in it the remedy for their ills. Time and again appeal was made to Domesday Book in the forlorn hope of demonstrating freedom in the face of seigneurial oppression where it could never have been of help.¹⁰ It was a fount of authority despite its limited application.

This, the triumph of expectation over experience, was due in large measure to the perception of the power of the book as a form of record. To the medieval mind the codex was immediately associated with authority with a force that is difficult to appreciate today. In England administrative and business records took the form of rolls throughout the Middle Ages. The book was reserved for very special texts, most notably the Gospels.¹¹ The eschatological referents of the name Domesday Book, then, were no mere whimsy. It was an object of authority because it was a *book*, and the fact that it was an old one only added to its mystique. Here, in the popular mind, was embodied the customs and practice of 'the good old days', an ever moving but deep-seated trait of the English character if we can talk of such. Domesday Book was tangible evidence of a golden age with which the evils of the moment could be pointedly compared. It figured in current political debate into the early modern period.¹²

---

⁹ For the best account of the social and political history of Domesday Book, see E. M. Hallam, *Domesday Book Through Nine Centuries*, London 1986.
¹⁰ For a list of known exemplifications, see ibid., 199–214.
¹¹ M. T. Clanchy, *From Memory to Written Record*, London 1979, 102–5.
¹² A parallel tradition saw Domesday Book as the embodiment of 'the Norman yoke'. Writing in the mid thirteenth century, Matthew Paris opined that here 'the manifest oppression of England began' (*Matthei Parisiensis, Monachi Sancti Albani, Historia Anglorum*, ed. F. Madden, 3 vols, RS 44. 1866–8, III, 172). By the seventeenth century the sentiment informed popular political debate, and it is a view that remains alive today. 'The [BSE]

In short Domesday Book was an icon of a political order. Like scripture its use was hedged about with all sorts of restrictions. Nevertheless, at a time when the royal archives were still considered to be the private preserve of the king's administration, Domesday Book was in a real sense 'a public record'. There are indications that in the twelfth and early thirteenth centuries, some individuals were allowed to browse. Sources like the Basset Cartulary and the Crowland Domesday hint at extensive searching of the text for the use of a family or religious institution.[13] Thereafter, exemplification of entries was undertaken by an Exchequer clerk and a fee was levied. Right up until the early nineteenth century such copies were made in an eleventh-century script to reproduce the forms of the text as closely as possible.[14]

As a type of document, then, Domesday Book is paralleled only by texts such as Magna Carta, the Bill of Rights, and the Declaration of Independence. But what was the reality behind the icon? What was in the mind of its originator? For Professor Sir James Holt it was consciously created as a symbol. He has argued that Domesday Book was compiled for William the Conqueror to recognize and complete the changes that the Conquest had seen.[15] In an age of spin, this is a view that has found wide favour.[16] However, it must be doubted that consciousness can be manipulated in quite such a cynical way. In the 1990s 'the Citizens' Charter', heralded as a new Magna Carta, was created for Britain, but it did not even survive the government that so ill-advisedly introduced it. An older, and still current, view maintains that Domesday Book was compiled for administrative purposes.[17]

What has not been in doubt is that Domesday Book was produced to be authoritative. It contains decisions. This is an understanding that has in its turn coloured

---

inquiry joins a long English tradition of detailed government-commissioned reports compiled with state-of-the-art technology. The *Domesday Book* was the first and BSE might be thought of as a tardy riposte to that Norman intrusion – the disease, after all, has crossed the Channel in the opposite direction.' (Hugh Pennington, review of *The BSE Inquiry: Vols I–XVI*, in *The London Review of Books*, 14 December 2000).

[13] Northampton, Northampton Record Office, ZB347; *Rerum Anglicarum Scriptores Veteres*, I, 80–2. The scribe of the Bassett cartulary copied from a number of GDB Nottinghamshire *breves* and, in the process, managed to confuse Colston Bassett with Car Colston. The compiler of the Crowland Domesday copied widely from GDB and also from a series of contemporary 'hundred rolls'.

[14] Hallam, *Domesday Book Through Nine Centuries*, 54.

[15] J. C. Holt, '1086', in *Domesday Studies*, ed. Holt, 41–64.

[16] See, for example, G. Garnett, *The Norman Conquest: a Very Short Introduction*, Oxford 2009; idem, *Conquered England: Kingship, Succession, and Tenure, 1066–1166*, Oxford 2007, 1–44; idem, 'What the Norman Conquest can teach us about "Regime Change"', http://www.historyextra.com/oup/what-norman-conquest-can-teach-us-about-regime-change, accessed 08/07/2012; S. Baxter, *Domesday*, DVD, BBC, 2010; Harvey, *Domesday: Book of Judgement*, chapter 1 and passim.

[17] Galbraith, *Making of Domesday Book*, 18–19; R. Fleming, 'Domesday Book and the Tenurial Revolution', *ANS* 9, 1986, 87–102.

the perception of the nature of the sources on which it drew and of the mechanisms that produced them. The process is recorded in a famous passage in the Anglo-Saxon Chronicle. In 1085 William the Conqueror spent Christmas at Gloucester and there he had much thought and deep discussion with his council about England:

> how it was occupied or with what sort of people. Then he sent his men over all England into every shire and had them find out how many hundred hides there were in the shire, or what land and cattle the king himself had in the country, or what dues he ought to have in twelve months from the shire. Also he had a record made of how much land his archbishops had, and his bishops and his abbots and his earls – and though I relate it at too great a length – what or how much everyone had who was occupying land in England, in land or cattle, and how much money it was worth. So very narrowly did he have it investigated, that there was no single hide nor virgate of land, nor indeed (it is a shame to relate but it seemed no shame for him to do) one ox nor one cow nor one pig which was there left out, and not put down in his record; and all these records were brought to him afterwards.[18]

Given that William left England for the last time in August 1086, it has been thought unlikely that these records were Domesday Book itself. Nevertheless, it has not been doubted that the work was compiled shortly after as a direct product of a process of more or less judicial determination.

In *Domesday: the Inquest and the Book*, I have argued that this is a misconception.[19] The production of Domesday Book was not, and could never have been, the aim of the process described in the Anglo-Saxon Chronicle. What William set in motion in 1086 was what near contemporary records describe as a *descriptio*, 'a writing down', and what from the twelfth century was called an *inquisitio*, 'an inquisition' or 'inquest'. Here was no exercise in decision making. It was rather an investigation and was preliminary to negotiation. The records from which Domesday Book was compiled were the product of a process of consultation.

The Inquest as investigation

By their nature interpersonal relations are rarely captured in business documentation. We all too regularly endorse minutes as an accurate record of a meeting knowing full well that they are a travesty of what actually happened: the blood on the carpet is never recorded. And yet, in the face of everyday experience, historians have been mesmerized by Domesday Book. To say that it stands in glorious isolation would be misleading, but it is a fact that there are relatively few survivals from the Domesday inquest. Two, the *Liber Exoniensis* (Exon) and the *Inquisitio Comitatus*

---

[18] *ASC*, 161–2.
[19] D. R. Roffe, *Domesday: the Inquest and the Book*. Oxford 2000, hereafter *DIB*.

Cantabrigiensis (ICC), are extensive sources covering a county or series of counties. Several others, notably Bath A, the Crowland Domesday, and the *Inquisitio Eliensis* (IE),[20] contain accounts of individual fees, but the remainder are summary texts which usually amount to little more than a list of place-names and assessments to taxation. None of the inquest texts can compare in breadth and accomplishment with either volume of Domesday Book, and so it has been assumed that they must be preparatory to its production. Along with LDB itself, they have all been characterized as 'satellites', and the task of the Domesday historian in the last thirty years has been to identify these sources and put them into some sort of order.[21] The problem is, however, that, beyond a belief in the integrity of the Domesday process, there is no intrinsic evidence for the resulting taxonomies. Exon and ICC were anterior to GDB and Bath A to Exon. Otherwise there are no overt relationships between the texts of the Domesday inquest, and no explicit statement of a programme to produce Domesday Book from them.[22]

It cannot be assumed that the business of the inquest is necessarily embodied in Domesday Book. However, in distinguishing the documentation of the one from the other we can begin to appreciate the inquest records for what they are. Consultation is no more explicit than in Domesday Book, but the nature of the activity that produced them can be reconstructed from the evidence they provide. The essence of the inquest was the production of verdicts under oath. From the prologue to IE, it is known that a jury of eight men, four English and four French, were called from each hundred and a further six villagers and the priest from every vill in the East Midland counties of Cambridgeshire and Hertfordshire.[23] That this was common practice is attested by numerous references to 'men of the hundred' and 'men of the vill' throughout Domesday Book. Jurors, however, did not provide all of the information. From their recorded verdicts it is clear that their evidence was largely confined to four main items, namely assessment to the geld (the national system of taxation on land), value, tenurial status, and title. It would seem that the

---

[20] *Two Chartularies of the Priory of St Peter at Bath*, ed. W. Hunt, Somerset Record Society 7, 1893, 67–8; *Rerum Anglicarum Scriptores Veteres*, I, 80–2; IE.

[21] For the most influential account, see H. B. Clarke, 'The Domesday Satellites', in *Domesday Book: a Reassessment*, ed. P. H. Sawyer, London 1985, 50–70. Several texts have been added to the corpus since then, for which see D. R. Roffe, *Decoding Domesday*, Woodbridge 2007, chapter 2.

[22] The so-called articles of inquiry preserved in the prologue to IE have often been cited as an indication that the production of a DB-like account of fees was intended from the start of the inquest. It should be noted, however, that the document contains no notice of the honour, and its questions could have as easily informed the production of the geographically arranged ICC as Exon or DB. My own analysis has indicated that it was drawn up after the compilation of LDB and was probably designed as a guide to the abbreviation of GDB (*DIB*, 114–17). For an alternative view, see Frank Thorn, above pp.111–2.

[23] ICC, 97.

sheriff, the king's representative in the shire, presided over the proceedings.[24] In parallel he also seems to have overseen a survey of the king's demesne estates and other sources of royal income.[25]

By contrast, commissioners were appointed to ascertain the resources of other estates. Schedules were drawn up from the verdicts of the hundred juries and each tenant-in-chief was invited to make an account of each of his estates under certain heads. The minutiae of estate management were essentially unverifiable. Beyond the salient details of tax assessment and probably value recorded in the schedules, then, much of the data was thus provided by private survey. Bath A is probably an example of the sort of document that was produced. A time and place was provided for the lord and his men to present their findings under oath, and then all the details were written down by the commissioners' clerks.[26]

In the south west this seems to have been the end of the process. The accounts of fees in Exon are perhaps best understood as examples of this process of what I have called 'inbreviation': they formed the immediate source of the corresponding passages in Domesday Book and there is no evidence that the data were ever organized in any other way.[27] In Cambridgeshire, by contrast, the inbreviated records were recast into an account of the shire that was arranged geographically by vill and hundred, and this compound document (the exemplar of the extant ICC) was attested by the various hundred juries.[28] There are signs that this procedure was adopted in at least a further twenty shires, including two out of the three of LDB.[29]

Both simple and compound verdicts like Exon and ICC are found in later medieval inquest records. The former, however, are less common and it can sometimes be shown that they were only returned through a lack of time to process the records or through oversight.[30] It was the norm to consolidate the presentments of the parties to the inquest into a single verdict which the hundred formally presented. In form this is a procedure that is found in many routine administrative and legal processes in the later Middle Ages. The sworn verdict underpinned much of the

---

[24] *DIB*, 117–28. Robert of Hereford, writing shortly after the event, asserts that men were sent to counties where they were unknown to check the findings of the inquest, thereby implying that the initial task was undertaken by locals (W. H. Stevenson, 'A Contemporary Description of the Domesday Survey', *EHR* 22, 1907, 72–84).

[25] *DIB*, 128–40.

[26] *DIB*, 140–6.

[27] *DIB*, 172–3. A hundredal order may be present in the various fees, but the diplomatic of the entries, both in Exon and GDB, does not suggest an ICC-like recension: otherwise we might expect entries in the form 'In X, y hides…', as in Cambridgeshire. See J. Palmer, 'The Domesday Manor', in *Domesday Studies*, ed. Holt, 139–54 at 143–4.

[28] *DIB*, 173–4. The GDB diplomatic is derived from the forms of ICC (Palmer, 'Domesday Manor', 143–4).

[29] *DIB*, 174–6.

[30] *DIB*, 170.

workings of the common law and became central to dispute resolution. Historians have therefore tended to see the Domesday verdicts as recognitions of right, in effect judgements, of a similar kind.[31]

That there are verdicts of this kind in Domesday Book is clear. Appended to the accounts of Huntingdonshire, Yorkshire, and Lincolnshire there are three series of *clamores*, that is disputes, and in some cases it is made clear that the verdicts that followed the pleadings were intended to resolve them.[32] Like the later proceedings the verdicts come at the end of a long process of indictment and pleading. The fact, however, serves to show that the verdicts in the body of the text, by far the majority, were of a different order. They emanate from the beginning of the Domesday process,[33] and recent study of the whole corpus has shown that they were signally ineffective. Undisputed verdicts not unnaturally caused few problems: the land to which they refer is found in the chapter of the plaintiff. The majority, however, were contested and the land is almost always found in the chapter of the tenant.[34] Attempts have been made to explain the apparent anomaly in terms of the intricacies of eleventh-century dispute resolution.[35] But the simple conclusion is that these verdicts were not intended to be determinations.

This was characteristic of all the major investigatory inquests of the twelfth and thirteenth centuries. There an uncontested verdict might assume the force of a judgement in the course of time. But otherwise, verdicts regularly heralded protracted legal processes in the years that followed.[36] As far as our evidence goes, this had always been the case. One of the earliest records of the procedure comes from the late tenth century. Some time in the reign of King Edgar the sons of Boga

---

[31] D. R. Roffe, 'The Hundred Rolls and their Antecedents: Some Thoughts on the Inquisition in Thirteenth-Century England', *Haskins Society Journal* 7, 1996, 179–87.

[32] GDB, 208, 208v, 373–377v: LIN CS.CN.CW.CK. In the Lincolnshire series the rubric for the South Riding of Lindsey reads 'Claims which are in the South Riding of Lincoln [sic] and their resolution through the men who have sworn (*clamores que sunt in Sudtreding Lincoliae et concordia eorum per homines qui juraverunt*)'. In reality, not all the claims were resolved (*DIB*, 184). The *Terre Occupate* of Exon and the *Invasiones* of LDB also list disputed lands, but there is no indication that proceedings had progressed much further than the statement of a claim (*DIB*, 184). For the continuation of legal action after the Domesday inquest, see D. Bates, 'Two Ramsey Writs and the Domesday Survey', *Historical Research* 63, 1990, 337–9.

[33] For a discussion of the relationship between the two types of presentment, see *DIB*, 83–4.

[34] P. Wormald, 'Domesday Lawsuits: a Provisional List and Preliminary Comments', in *England in the Eleventh Century*, Harlaxton Medieval Studies 2, ed. C. Hicks, Stamford 1992, 61–102; D. Roffe, 'A Profession of Ignorance: an Insight into Domesday Procedure in an Early Reference to the Inquest', in *Rulership and Rebellion in the Anglo-Norman World, c.1066–c.1216: Essays in Honour of Professor Edmund King*, ed. P. Dalton and D. Luscombe, Farnham 2015, 45–60.

[35] See, for example, R. Fleming, *Domesday Book and the Law*, Cambridge 1999, 11–17.

[36] Roffe, 'The Hundred Rolls and their Antecedents', 179–87.

of Hemingford claimed land from Ely abbey. Their plea turned on the timing of Edward the Elder's movements in 917 in his conquest of the Danelaw, and what was effectively a jury of old men was called to declare the facts. Their evidence favoured the abbey's interpretation, but, what is interesting for the present purposes, this verdict did not determine the matter. Ely only subsequently made good its title, after extensive pleadings in the hundred, by enlisting a host of oath helpers.[37]

The Domesday verdicts, then, anticipated decisions rather than embodied them. This explains a lot. The Domesday enterprise has been repeatedly criticized on the ground that it failed to accomplish what it set out to do.[38] This has seemed no more apparent than in one of its predominant concerns: tax capacity, that is the ability of the land to pay the tax assessed upon it. On the whole in 1086 most estates were capable of paying more than they did. Reduction of the burden of taxation on localities or favoured estates had been a well-established characteristic of Old English society, and since the Conquest much of the lord's demesne had been further exempted. Overall capacity was therefore to be measured in the inquest by the calculation or estimation of ploughlands, the number of ploughs that could be employed on the land in question. Thus, in almost every entry the tax assessment of each estate is followed by the statement that 'there is land for so many ploughs'.[39] It has seemed that here was a reassessment of liability, and the fact that it was never introduced has been cited as a measure of the failure of the Domesday process.[40]

In fact we can perceive that the data did find their mark. The way in which it did so is illuminating. Exemption was a proper concern when tax revenues were falling and its extent could only be reviewed by a full survey. Nevertheless, circumstances had to be considered. Non-payment was as likely to be sanctioned as illicit: the principle of acquitting land by personal service was well established and was to be restated in Henry I's coronation charter of 1101.[41] Tax allowances were as much a reality in the eleventh century as today. In the event a balance was struck. Government did not demand that land should render tax to its full capacity in return for a re-imposition of the geld on the lord's demesne.[42] The ploughland figures were clearly intended to inform rather than determine future action. The records of the Domesday inquest were less a statement of intent than a common ground of more or less unalloyed (or at least communally agreed) fact on which negotiation could be based.

---

[37] *Liber Eliensis*, ed. E. O. Blake, Camden Society, 3rd series 92, 1962, 98–9.
[38] See for example, H. G. Richardson and G. O. Sayles, *The Governance of Medieval England*, Edinburgh 1963, 28–9: 'an inestimable boon to a learned posterity, but a vast administrative mistake'.
[39] *DIB*, 149–65.
[40] L. Warren, 'The Myth of Norman Administrative Efficiency', *Transactions of the Royal Historical Society* 34, 1984, 113–32.
[41] *Select Charters*, ed. W. Stubbs, 9th edn revised by H. W. C. Davis, Oxford 1913, 119.
[42] J. A. Green, 'The Last Century of Danegeld', *EHR* 96, 1981, 241–58; *DIB*, 234–42.

Of those negotiations we know little. They probably took place in August 1086 in Salisbury where William the Conqueror sought the homage of all those who held freely in England.[43] Otherwise, we have no record of the proceedings. Nevertheless, there are indications that geld was not the only subject of debate. Personal service was also at issue and was probably the most important matter to be decided. Hitherto it has not figured at all in discussions of the purpose of the inquest since it is largely unnoticed in the Domesday corpus. Had it not seemed so self-evidently true, the omission might have caused more perplexity than it has. How can a major survey of land exclude one of the king's main interests in it? In fact, it is now apparent that if service were a central concern it might not be explicitly noticed in a process designed to establish 'fact'. Rather an unambiguous 'given' might be expected and one can indeed be identified. The manor, however defined, seems to have been a common denominator on which all were agreed or could agree.[44] Thus, from numerous references it is clear that there was considered to be an appropriate size for the entity and that set numbers had been granted to lords after the Conquest. All this hints at a measure of service. The total held by each tenant-in-chief was carefully recorded in the inquest and the common language employed to do so (in marked contrast to all other Domesday records) indicates that the government requested the information.[45] Personal service, it would seem, was very much a concern in 1086.

Orderic Vitalis, writing some forty years later in what is the first extant account of the purpose of the Domesday inquest, maintained that it was indeed from this time that the *servitium debitum*, the quota of knights owed by each tenant-in-chief, was established.[46] The silence of the contemporary sources highlights a central paradox of the inquest as a procedure: its records neither say what they mean nor mean what they say. Without context we cannot easily interpret them. This was the case throughout the Middle Ages. In 1279, for example, Edward I initiated the most comprehensive survey ever undertaken by any king, Domesday notwithstanding. The surviving rolls detail every holder of land from king to the humblest peasant. And yet there are just two passing notices of it in contemporary sources. As a result, no one has been able to come up with a convincing reason for the inquest.[47] The same might have held true for the Ragman inquest of 1275 had not more intensive sources survived. There the audit of the royal fisc and the review of the activities of royal and seigneurial bailiffs can be put in the context of a period of civil war,

---

[43] *ASC*, 162; Holt, '1086', 41–64.
[44] In GDB the manor was a moving feast, but a common point of reference seems to have been that it was a nexus of tribute (*DIB*, 211–20).
[45] *DIB*, 240–1.
[46] Orderic, II, 267.
[47] S. Raban, 'The Making of the 1279–80 Hundred Rolls', *EHR* 70, 1997, 123–45; S. Raban, *A Second Domesday? The Hundred Rolls of 1279–80*, Oxford 2004, 45–6.

popular pressure for reform, the dismissal of sheriffs, appropriate legislation to right the wrongs identified, and enforcement of the new measures.[48]

A similar pattern can be fleetingly perceived in all the major surveys of the twelfth and thirteenth centuries. The inquest, and its records, can only be understood as an element in a dialectic of investigation, negotiation, and action in the face of social and political uncertainty. So must be understood the Domesday inquest. None of the contemporary sources explicitly notice a context, but it is not difficult to see why William might want to audit his resources in land and taxes and think about service in 1085. Earlier in the same annal in which the inquest is recorded, there is an account of a threat of invasion:

> In this year people said and declared for a fact, that Cnut, king of Denmark, son of King Swein, was setting out in this direction and meant to conquer this country with the help of Robert, count of Flanders, because Cnut was married to Robert's daughter. When William, king of England, who was then in Normandy – for he was in possession of both England and Normandy – found out about this, he went to England with a larger force of mounted men and infantry from France and Brittany than had ever come to this country, so that people wondered how this country could maintain all that army. And the king had all the army dispersed all over the country among his vassals, and they provisioned the army each in proportion to his land. And people had much oppression that year, and the king had the land near the sea laid waste, so that if his enemies landed, they should have nothing to seize on so quickly. But when the king found out for a fact that his enemies had been hindered and could not carry out their expedition – then he let some of the army go to their own country, and some he kept in this country over winter.[49]

Cnut's claim to the throne was as good as William's and there can be little doubt that this was a crisis of the first order. A review of resources would seem to be directly related to the expenses incurred. But a consideration of knight service might hint at a more general concern for the defence of the realm. The king cannot have relished the need to resort to hired troops in a time of emergency and equally the tenants-in-chief must have been loath to billet them. Do we not see in the Domesday process a forging of a new social contract? The homage made to William at Salisbury in August 1086 was presumably in return for lands held on new terms of service. Thereafter the king could never entirely dispense with mercenaries, but he could always call on his tenants-in-chief for assistance.

We can see at last that the inquest was a mechanism of consultation. Through it

---

[48] J. R. Maddicott, 'Edward I and the Lessons of Baronial Reform: Local Government 1258–93', in *Thirteenth Century England I: Proceedings of the Newcastle upon Tyne Conference*, ed. P. R. Coss and S. D. Lloyd, Woodbridge 1986, 1–30.
[49] *ASC*, 161.

government could talk to its subjects. It now becomes apparent why the tenant-in-chief and his men participated in the process. They were not cowed into submission to the will of a king intent on demonstrating his executive power. Rather they accepted the responsibility to meet a threat to the commonweal. It was a defining moment. As reconstructed here, the outcome was an increased burden of taxation and service, but there was a return. The definition of duty also defined right: the tenant-in-chief and his men were confirmed in their title.

Equally, there was a return for the free communities of the shire. The attestation of the hundred validated the whole process, and in pre-Conquest England the interests that they represented must have participated in the negotiations that followed. There is, however, no sign that they were present at Salisbury, and it would be anachronistic to expect them to be so.[50] Custom demanded the jurors' attendance at the Domesday inquest. Nevertheless, their interests were probably served beyond the avoidance of penalties for non-attendance in the processes of the inquest itself. In 1086 freedom and the right to land were still defined by the payment of geld, and what the hundred juries seem to have been involved in in the first stage of the Domesday inquest was an *inquisitio geldi*, a review of the geld.[51] Here again the statement of duty defined title. The imperative for the free man to register liability was tangible. Equally important, however, was that to reveal privilege. Exemption profited the lord not by his own non-payment but by diverting the geld of the peasantry to himself. The danger to the free man was obvious and it was therefore in his interest to establish that the land was exempt rather than unassessed lest his freedom become compromised.

Recording the Inquest

The Domesday inquest was clearly communal business of the highest importance and it is therefore not surprising that those who participated wanted a record of it. Significantly, all the extant inquest records are preserved in private archives. Many of the schedules were probably acquired as a matter of course: private survey was, after all, guided by official records of this kind. But Exon, ICC, and IE cannot have found their way into Exeter and Ely's archives in this way. Conscious attempts must have been made to acquire or copy documents that represented the wider community of the shire and beyond.[52] The inquest records were preserved for themselves as evidence of the business they informed.

---

[50] F. M. Stenton, *The First Century of English Feudalism 1066–1166*, Oxford 1932, 111–13.
[51] *DIB*, 133–40.
[52] It is possible that official involvement of some foundations brought documents into their archives, but unlikely. According to Bishop Robert of Hereford, commissioners were not drawn from the regions that they oversaw (Stevenson, 'A Contemporary Description of the Domesday Survey', 72–84).

Government probably had a somewhat different attitude to them. The documentation from the initial stage of the inquest survived in the Treasury as 'hundred rolls' for some time. A document known as Abingdon A and part of the Crowland Domesday were copied from them,[53] and it would seem likely that they were also used in the compilation of the Lindsey, Leicestershire, and Northamptonshire Surveys of the early twelfth century.[54] Other documents from the Domesday inquest, however, are conspicuous by their seeming absence from the king's archives. That sources like Exon and ICC must have come into the hands of royal officials is obvious, and their preservation in private archives may therefore be purely fortuitous. But it is probably significant that Domesday verdicts were not the only ones which are unrepresented in the public records. Survivals from the many thousands that must have been produced in the Middle Ages are comparatively rare.[55] It is not difficult to see why. With the resolution of the matters in hand, inquest records lost the purpose that had brought them into being. There was no longer any need for the formal declarations. The data themselves, however, remained of interest, and throughout the medieval period abbreviations were made to facilitate reference and use. What was preserved largely depended on what was considered to be of permanent value, and thus it is that matters central to the inquest, such as the articles of inquiry and the careful record of witnesses and jurors, were omitted as ephemeral. The aftermath of the inquest saw a change from an interest in the information as a means to an end to an end in itself. We must conclude that, once abbreviated, original verdicts were either not carefully kept or were simply thrown away.[56]

So, the records of the inquest tended to be superseded by abbreviations. The replacement of the one with the other determined the use to which the data could then be put. There is no substitute for the real thing. A note on the flysheet of the Book of Fees, apparently written when the work was compiled from a series of thirteenth-century inquest records in 1302, warns the reader:

> Remember that this book was composed and compiled from several official inquests ... and therefore the contents of this book are to be used for evidence here in the Exchequer and not for the record.[57]

---

[53] D. C. Douglas, 'Some Early Surveys from the Abbey of Abingdon', *EHR* 44, 1929, 618–25 at 623; Roffe, 'Historia Croylandensis', 93–101.
[54] *The Lincolnshire Domesday and Lindsey Survey*, ed. C. W. Foster and T. Longley, Lincoln Record Society 19, 1921, 237–60; *The Leicestershire Survey, c. A.D. 1130*, ed. C. F. Slade, Department of English Local History, University of Leicester, Occasional Papers 7, Leicester 1956; *VCH Northants*, II, 357–92.
[55] D. Crook, *Records of the General Eyre*, London 1982, 34–7.
[56] Presentments made by jurors other than the hundred were usually not even returned to government. They were either immediately disposed of after they had been engrossed in more official records or were kept by justices or commissioners.
[57] *The Book of Fees*, Public Record Office, 2 vols in 3, London 1920–31, i, xx.

From the thirteenth century abbreviations had no legal standing and were intended simply for reference.

This is surely how we must see Domesday Book, at least at the time when it was compiled, if not subsequently.[58] It is undoubtedly an abbreviation. A novel programme was brought to bear on the work.[59] LDB was compiled first, and from the beginning a new presentation was adopted. The geographical arrangement of the verdicts in the shires in which that form was found and the fee-based accounts elsewhere were jettisoned. Both were replaced by the hybrid county and fee arrangement. LDB was the work of seven scribes. GDB was largely the work of one and he was responsible for further refinements in the account. The record of demesne livestock was suppressed and subsequently interest in the manor was phased out. Throughout the names of jurors were omitted, some data discarded and much reformulated. By the time he got to the end of his work in the Leicestershire folios, the account had been pared down to an economical form that would not have been recognized by the jurors who had validated its source. Domesday Book could never have embodied the business of the Domesday inquest. Its compilation suggests that the interests of government had moved on.

I have argued elsewhere that its new concern was probably the administrative problems that the settlement of the revolt against William Rufus of 1088 presented.[60] Such dating evidence as there is indicates that work was underway in the reign of the Conqueror's son. A note, the colophon, at the end of LDB states:

> This survey (*Ista descriptio*) was made in the year 1086 from the Incarnation of the Lord and the twentieth of the reign of William, not only through these three counties but also through the others.[61]

But the use of the word *ista*, 'this there', indicates that the survey referred to was not the volume but the inquest itself.[62] In GDB there is firmer evidence and that points to a later date. In the Huntingdonshire folios, some hundred folios into the work as the scribe wrote it, William de Warenne is styled 'earl', a title he only received when he was created earl of Surrey by William Rufus sometime between late 1087 and mid 1088.[63] No other anomalies of this kind have been identified. However,

---

[58] In the eleventh and twelfth centuries the written word commanded an intrinsic authority that it did not later. Nevertheless, even then the act of writing itself clearly did not transform evidence into judgement; only time could do that.
[59] For a full account for the making of Domesday Book, see *DIB*, 186–223.
[60] *DIB*, 242–8.
[61] LDB, 450a: SFK 77,4.
[62] For the use of *descriptio* as the survey, as opposed to its records, see F. R. Thorn and C. Thorn, 'The Writing of Great Domesday', *Domesday*, ed. E. Hallam and D. Bates, Stroud 2001, 37–73 at 69 and note 109.
[63] C. P. Lewis, 'The Earldom of Surrey and the Date of Domesday Book', *Historical Research* 63, 1990, 327–36. Lewis notes Orderic Vitalis' somewhat confused references to William

the apparently well-informed Orderic Vitalis notes for the year 1089 that Rannulf Flambard, William Rufus's chief minister, 'revised' the survey of England.[64] Do we not see here a reference to the transformation of the inquest records – the referent of his earlier notice of the Domesday process (cf. Clarke, above pp.259–62) – into a register?

Conclusion

Government had talked to others. Now it talked to itself. The earliest references to Domesday Book do not suggest that it was a communal document. It is first noticed in a charter dating between 1099 and 1101 in which it is called 'the king's book', and thereafter it is known variously as 'the book of the treasury', 'the book of the Exchequer', and 'the register'.[65] Of the handful of surviving cartularies compiled between 1086 and 1150, only one, that of Worcester, contains an extract from the record and then in special circumstances. Domesday Book was a private document compiled for the king's use. How it came into the public gaze thereafter is unrecorded. But with the development of its reputation and authority in the course of time, the story comes full-circle. Like the records from which it was compiled, it talked to a wider audience. However, what it talked of was other things. Society had moved on. And so had government. Information is power and so the production of Domesday Book had a very different focus from the processes that had generated its data. By a subtle alchemy the abbreviation of the records transformed them from a basis for negotiation to a hard political fact. Domesday Book is thus a poor guide to the business of 1086 and the more so is its subsequent use.

---

de Warenne's elevation to the earldom, but bases his dating of the event on the early twelfth-century Hyde Chronicle which he convincingly argues was well informed since written at Lewes. It is too easy to claim that the scribe was confused when he wrote the Huntingdonshire entry (Thorn and Thorn, 'The Writing of Great Domesday Book', 69–72). Anyone versed in the intricacies of tenure in Circuit VI will know that soke relationships between tenants-in-chief were common. Outside Domesday Book, however, they are rarely noticed. The reference to the earl in the Sussex folios (in Circuit I, the third to be abbreviated) is unequivocal (GDB 26: SSX 12,9).

[64] Orderic, IV, 172.
[65] V. H. Galbraith, *Domesday Book: Its Place in Administrative History*, Oxford 1974, 100–4.

Caroline Thorn: an Appreciation

Frank Thorn

Caroline Maureen Jane THORN née Parker
Born in London on 25 June 1949
Died of lymphatic cancer in the Royal United Hospital in Bath on 6 July 2011
Aged 62

Caroline Thorn made a quiet but significant contribution to the elucidation of Domesday Book for over thirty-five years and she became one of that small group of scholars who had worked on every line of the Book and of its many 'satellites'.

She was born in London and educated in Godalming and Guildford in Surrey, but spent her holidays on the loughs and mountains of Northern Ireland, before studying Latin and Ancient Greek in the then innovative and thriving department of Classics at Southampton University, where she met her future husband Frank who was researching for a doctoral thesis on the Roman poet Vergil. She obtained a first-class degree in 1970 followed by an MA in Medieval History (1971) during which she studied historiography, the renaissance of the twelfth century and a number of texts in medieval Latin, being tutored in palaeography by Dr Paul Harvey. Her dissertation was on the life of St Oswald.

Caroline settled in Bath, Somerset, and continued to study various medieval texts with a view to editing and publishing, but her scholarship found a sharper focus when in 1975 she replied to a televisual solicitation by Dr John Morris of University College London, who, on a programme called 'Look Stranger', was calling for help from 'married women with Latin'. The Phillimore edition of Domesday, begun in that year and promised at twelve counties a year over three years, was already behind schedule; Caroline joined the editorial team and worked on every county in the series as a sub-editor and proof-reader but was also engaged to translate (the whole of Wiltshire and Somerset and most of Devon), and to insert additional information from the Exon Domesday into the translations of the Great Domesday text. This last introduced her to the Exon manuscript which she visited frequently and on which she became an expert.

Caroline Thorn at the highest point of the Inca Trail, in Peru in 2009

John Morris died suddenly in 1977 and Caroline with others, under the benevolent direction of John McNeal Dodgson, also of University College London, was promoted to county editor. She worked as a research assistant to John Dodgson for several years and in all she completed twelve volumes for the series, mostly with her husband. The accuracy and comprehensive annotation of their volumes were widely regarded as setting a new standard. In terms of bulk, if not of quality, statistics show the difference. The ratio of pages of text to those of notes in John Morris's first three volumes (Huntingdonshire, Middlesex and Surrey) was 64 to 3, 54 to 3 and 98 to 4 respectively; the ratios of Caroline's last contributions to the series with her husband in 1985–86 were Devon (390 to 299) and Shropshire (156 to 143). 'This series was fine until the scholars got hold of it' as Philip Harris, the then chairman of Phillimore, observed.

When, in 1986, Alecto Historical Editions in association with the Public Record Office began publishing their facsimile edition, in various permutations involving texts, translations, introductions and maps, it was inevitable that Caroline would be drawn into it. With the calligrapher Michael Gullick she had just published an article entitled 'The Scribes of Great Domesday Book: a Preliminary Account' and was invited to contribute a palaeographical article to the Alecto *Domesday Studies* general volume. This became the important 'Marginal Notes and Signs in Domesday Book'. As part of the Alecto editorial team, she was responsible for editing the translations and introductions and for checking the original manuscript in order to add the marginal boxes to the translations; also for examining whether the facsimile accurately reproduced the manuscript (each volume has her lists of where the photographic process might lead to a misreading) and proof-reading each county edition. Her contributions to the translations (based on those of varying quality in the volumes of the Victoria County History) were many and important especially in improving the lucidity of the borough entries. Furthermore, because the VCH volume for Devon had been translated from the Exon Domesday, she provided a completely new translation of the Great Domesday version.

During this period, Michael Gullick and Caroline began a collaboration on a book provisionally called 'The Scribal History of Great Domesday Book'. Its core consists of a list of all entries added to the manuscript by its scribes after the initial 'campaigns', an identification of all the major additions made by the main scribe and a complete list of the material added by scribe B. Caroline's part was virtually complete by 2000 when a substantial lecture, subsequently published as 'The Writing of Great Domesday Book', was delivered at the Public Record Office for her by her husband.

The Alecto project finished in 1992 and between 1994 and 2002 Caroline continued with her book and also tutored in medieval Latin as part of an MA course in local history for Bristol University, initially for the Department for Continuing Education, latterly for the Department of Archaeology. The course was ambitious in aiming to teach students enough Latin to enable them to read administrative documents with confidence and it was hard work for all, but Caroline greatly enjoyed the preparation of the course materials (from scratch), the contact with some highly intelligent and motivated students and even the weekly marking of 'homework'.

Between 2004 and 2007 Caroline was a research associate of the University of Hull working under Professor John Palmer on an AHRC-funded project, her part of which was to 'tidy up' the translation and notes for an electronic version of the Phillimore edition. This was far from only being some mechanical process of conversion and the ensuring of consistency, since she suggested many corrections to the translations and made many additions to the notes. In particular she produced new and ampler versions of the notes for eight counties and began a revision of the ways in which the many spellings of Domesday personal names could be allocated to single standardized forms. The project achieved the highest rating ('outstanding') and for Caroline, although there were many frustrations, she was fulfilled by the scholarship it entailed.

After the deposit of that project in 2007 (in the Hull and Essex electronic archives) Caroline continued to work on revisions, including of personal names, and at her death there were only three counties left before a new deposit would have become possible. She also left 'The Scribal History of Great Domesday Book' awaiting the contribution of her collaborator, a half-completed book on Exon and enough material for further county annotations and for a definitive translation (or a revision of a translation) of Great and Little Domesday. Her husband intends to publish her two books and continue her detailed commentaries on Domesday counties.

As a scholar, Caroline was a self-effacing 'backroom girl'. She was not aware of any acclamation of her work nor motivated by the expectation of it. She was driven by a classicist's desire to understand the detail of this gigantic text and to interpret it to the best of her ability. She had passion, determination and the highest standards. She was meticulous in all she did and usually dissatisfied with it: the arrival of a newly published volume was not provocative of celebration but of dread. She never lectured publicly (her husband did it for her), but she was brilliant in seminars and discussions, and her opinions were increasingly sought by other scholars. She became an expert palaeographer and probably handled the two manuscripts of Domesday more than anyone except their keepers. She was also a consultant for the proposed digitization of the Exon manuscript.

If the above portrait suggests only the dry, the academic and the cerebral, it does not do Caroline justice. She invested in friends, maintaining many from school and university days. She built her own dinghy, climbed many mountains, including in the Alps and Pyrenees, and had a taste for travel: the list would have been longer but already comprised Namibia, Cape Town, Egypt, Australia, New Zealand, and Peru. Her love of France led eventually to the purchase of a house there, and she lived to see its almost complete renovation, largely self-done. She gardened, she cooked to cordon bleu standards, she entertained and she brought up two children of whom she was so proud: Katie read Classics at Manchester and is in publishing. Peter read History at Oxford and is a lawyer in Sydney. Her first grandchild, Freddie, delighted her.

In January 2011 Caroline did some arduous backpacking in New Zealand, apparently in perfect health, although with some dorsal pain of longstanding. It was only at Easter that she visibly deteriorated. She was diagnosed with a stage-four lymphatic cancer in mid May and died, sedated, during a promising treatment in early July.

Caroline Thorn: List of Publications

The Letters Patent of King Edward the Sixth Establishing a Free Grammar School at Bath, King Edward's School, Bath 1972. With F. R. Thorn.

The Phillimore printed edition of *Domesday Book*, text, translation, commentary and annotations, indices of persons and places, maps, appendices, Chichester 1975–1992:

Volume 6	*Wiltshire* (1979)
Volume 10	*Cornwall* (1979)
Volume 21	*Northamptonshire* (1979)
Volume 8	*Somerset* (1980)
Volume 16	*Worcestershire* (1982)
Volume 17	*Herefordshire* (1983)
Volume 7	*Dorset* (1983)
Volume 9	*Devon* (2 vols.) (1985)
Volume 25	*Shropshire* (1986)
Volume 31	*Lincolnshire* (1986)

All volumes were jointly edited with F. R. Thorn, except Lincolnshire (with Philip Morgan). She is also credited for sub-editing volume 15, *Gloucestershire* (1982), edited by J. S. Moore.

'The Scribes of Great Domesday Book: a Preliminary Account', *Journal of the Society of Archivists* 8, 1986, 78–80. With Michael Gullick.

'Marginal Notes and Signs in Domesday Book', in *Domesday Book Studies*, ed. A. Williams and R. W. H. Erskine, London 1987, 113–35. The book was republished as R. W. H. Erskine and A. Williams, *The Story of Domesday Book*, Chichester 2003, with revised pagination: the chapter is now pp.174–203.

The Alecto County Edition of *Domesday Book*, London 1987–1992:
    Volume 22   *The Devonshire Domesday* (1991), translation.

'The Writing of Great Domesday Book' in *Domesday Book*, ed. D. Bates and E. Hallam Smith, Stroud 2001, 37–72, 200–3. With F. R. Thorn.

'King Edward's "Charter": the Founding of King Edward's School at Bath', in *450 Years: King Edward's School, Bath, 1552–2002*, ed. John Wroughton, Bath 2002, 108–30.

The AHRC Domesday Project 2004–2007, the Electronic Phillimore:
New editions of the following counties with revised and expanded annotation: Cornwall, Derbyshire, Huntingdonshire, Leicestershire, Nottinghamshire, Rutland, Staffordshire, Shropshire. With F. R. Thorn.

The Scribal History of Great Domesday Book, incomplete at the time of her death. With F. R. Thorn and Michael Gullick.

Exeter Domesday Book, incomplete at the time of her death. With F. R. Thorn.

Index

Aanor, daughter of Judhael of Totnes 189 and n.97
abbas 126
Abbreviatio, Exchequer 250, 24, 251, 303
abbreviation 110, 111, 138, 140–1, 146, 152, 247–62, 285, 301–3
Abels, Richard 49, 279
Abingdon, church of 271
 archives 280
Abingdon A 301
Abington Pigotts (Cambs) 3, 89, 155–67
Absalom 188
accountancy 48, 240
Acla, *see* Coates (Gloucs)
acra 132
 East Anglian 226
Acton, Iron (Gloucs) 269, 270
Actona, *see* Acton, Iron (Gloucs)
Adelaide of Aumale, mother of Countess Judith 187 n.88
Adelulf, man of Hardwin de Scales 164, 165
Adelund 186
Adlestrop (Gloucs) 256, 271
Admington (Warks) 271
adulterium 131 n.121
advowson 56
æceres 132
Ædwardestowe, *see* Stow-on-the-Wold (Gloucs)
Ælfgar, *see* Beorhtric, son of
Ælfgar, earl of Mercia, 88, 157, 158, 159, 160, 162, 163, 164, 165, 166, 182, 183, 184
 men of, *see* Alwi, Alwine, Goda, Gotman, Winterled
 free woman of, *see* Modgifu
Ælfgifu, daughter of Leofwine 172
Ælfric 186, 267
Ælfric the priest 177
Ælfric son of Rolf, burgess of Ipswich 177 n.29
Ælfric Wanz` 177 n.29
Ælfric of Wenhou 178
Ælfstan of Frampton 283
Ælnod, sokeman of King Edward 160
aeria 115
Æthelmaer, bishop of Elmham 181, 184
Æthelred II, king of England 182
Æthelric the archdeacon 264, 265
Æthelric, bishop of Sherborne 207 and n.64, 209
Æthelweard 267
Æthelwig, abbot of Evesham 254 n.31, 255–6
Æthelwig, bishop of Thetford 227
ager, agri 114, 132. *See also hundredum*
Agobard, archbishop of Lyon 287
Ahitophel 188
aids, feudal 258
Ailmer, *see* Warin, grandson of
Ailnoth of Canterbury 147
Ailric, *see* Æthelric 264
Ailsi, a man of Eadgifu 187
 son, *see* Godwin
Aiulf 263, 268
Aki 86
Alan, count, of Brittany, Alan Rufus 4, 86. 88, 169–96, 228, 239 n.57, 284
 brother, *see* Brien, Stephen
 brother-in-law, *see* Enisan
 father, *see* Eudo
 half-brothers, *see* Bardulf, Bodin, Ribald
 wife, *see* Gunhilda
Alan, son of Ralph de Gael 189
Albert 267

albus 127–8
Alcrintone, *see* Offerton (Worcs)
Aldelandam, *see* Oldland (Gloucs)
alder-grove, *see alnetum*
Alderton (Gloucs) 270
Aldeswarda, *see* Aldsworth (Gloucs)
Aldrtona, *see* Alderton (Gloucs)
Aldsworth (Gloucs) 270
Alecto facsimile and translation of Domesday Book 7, 9, 10, 11, 12, 54, 69, 107, 224 n.20, 225, 232, 307
Alestan 181 n.50
Alexander II, pope 287
Alfred, son Judhael of Totnes 189 and n.97
Alfred, king of Wessex 290 n.4
Algar 174 n.11, 283
Algar of Kettleburgh 180 n.46
Algar, man of Archbishop Stigand 164, 165
Algot the monk 267
allographs 72–5
Almaer, brother of Ansgot 180
Almaer of Bourn 176
Almaer, man of Earl Waltheof 187 n.88
Almanach de Gotha 195
Almar, man of Eadgifu 160
Almeltona, *see* Admington (Warks)
alms, free 38
alnetum 115
Alnoth 103, 272
Alsi 186
Alsi, thegn of King Edward 185, 186
Alsi, nephew of Ralph the staller 185 and n.71, 186
Alstoe wapentake (Rutl) 261 n.70
Aluestonam, *see* Olveston (Gloucs)
Aluithecrirche, *see* Alvechurch (Worcs)
Aluredestona, *see* Alverston [in Woolaston] (Gloucs)
Alvechurch (Worcs) 266
Alvred 264
Alvred, man of Hardwin de Scales 160, 163, 164, 165
Alvred of Marlborough 268
Alverston [in Woolaston] (Gloucs) 273
Alward 176
Alward, sokeman of King Edward 160
Alweard 267, 268
Alwi, man of Earl Ælfgar 164, 165
Alwig 103, 267, 268
Alwine 267

Alwine, man of Earl Ælgar 160
Alwine, man of Eadgifu 178
Alwine *hamelecoc*, king's beadle 157, 158, 164 165, 166
Ambroc Actona, *see* Acton, Iron (Gloucs) 270
Ambroc, *see* Hambrook (Gloucs)
Amoundeness 192
Ampney [in Driffield] (Gloucs) 275
Ampney St Mary (Gloucs) 27, 271
Anand 174 n.11
ancient demesne, tenure in 291
Angers, abbey of Saints Serge and Bacchus of 179
Anglo-Saxon Chronicle 51, 111, 142, 144, 147, 173, 187, 188, 293
annexations 201. *See also Clamores*, Ely C, Ely D, *Invasiones*, *Terrae Occupatae*
annona 133. *See also bled annonae*
Anselm, archbishop of Canterbury 195
Ansgot 264
Ansgot, brother of Almaer 180
Ansquetil de Furnellis 179 n.39
Ansquetil de Rots 176
antecession 4, 38–9, 155–68, 169–96
antecessor 4, 39, 103, 131, 169, 173, 174 n.13, 178, 180, 186, 187, 191, 193, 194, 195, 196, 227, 280
arabilis 117
arare 117
aratrum, aratura 117
archiepiscopus, archipresbiter, archipresul, 126
Armingford hundred (Cambs) 3, 88, 90, 155–67, 176
Arnketil 103, 192
Arnketil, son of, *see* Gospatric
Arnold (Notts) 84
arpent, arpenz 130
Arthur 268
Arthur the Frenchman 267
articles of inquiry 2, 16, 19, 20, 91, 109–15, 134, 141, 280–1, 294, 301
Asgot 268
ash grove, *see fraxinetum* 235
Ashton, Cold (Gloucs) 270
Aske Hall (Yorks) 192
assart, *see assartum*
assartum, essartum, essarz, esserz, exsartum, exserta 115, 130
Aston Fields (Worcs) 266
Aston Subedge (Gloucs) 271

Aston, White Ladies (Worcs) 93, 250, 252, 265 and n.7
Astwood (Worcs) 250, 266
Athelney (Soms) 43
Aubrey, count, 170
aula, *haula* 132, 133. *See also* hall
Aumale, countess of 178
auxilia 258
Aycote (Gloucs) 269
Aylworth (Gloucs) 273

Baddington (Worcs) 266
Baderon, son of, *see* William
Badgeworth (Gloucs) 273
Bailey, Keith 56
Bailey, Mark 42
Bainard 214
Baldwin, abbot of Bury St Edmunds 4, 70, 71, 72, 197
Bamburgh (Northumberland) 187
Bampton double hundred (Oxon) 57
Banbury hundred (Oxon) 204
Bardulf, half-brother of Count Alan 179, 193
Barham (Cambs) 179 n.39
Barkston (Lincs) 104
Barley (Worcs) 93, 264
Barlow, Frank 261
Barlow, George 53
barones 114
barony, tenure by 39
Barrington, Little (Gloucs) 274
Barrow on Humber (Lincs) 57
Bartlett, Robert 280, 286
Barton [in Gloucester] (Gloucs) 270
Barton, Abbots (Gloucs) 254 n.32
Barton-Upon-Humber (Lincs), St Peter's church of 57
Basildon, Lower (Berks) 101
basileus 126
basilica 126
Bassett cartulary 292
Bassingbourn (Cambs) 88, 89, 176
Bates, David 1
Bath (Soms), St Peter of 270
Bath A 111, 294, 295
Battle abbey 215
battle, trial by 283–4, 287. *See also* ordeal
Baxter, Stephen 8, 24, 25, 26, 36, 37, 57, 70, 72, 238
Bayeux, bishop of 22, 216, 264

Beaminster hundred (Dors) 207 n.64
Becgeburiam, *see* Bibury (Gloucs)
Becgewrda, *see* Badgeworth (Gloucs)
Bedale, fee of 191
Bede 288
Bedfordshire 49, 232, 238, 240, 241, 243
Bedindonam, *see* Baddington (Worcs)
bee-hive, *see rusca*, *uas*
Beffcote (Staffs) 93
Belton (Lincs) 104
Bengeworth (Worcs) 93, 205, 251, 257, 266
Benhall (Suff) 174 n.11
Bennington, Long (Lincs) 183
Benningwrth', *see* Bengeworth (Worcs)
Bentley (Suff) 182 n.53
Beorhtmær 267, 268
Beorhtric son of Ælfgar 264
Berengar of Tours 217 n.123
berewick 82, 84, 88, 268, 269
bergensis 129
Bergholt, East (Suff) 177 and n.26, 178
Beria (Suff) 177 n.28
Berkeley (Gloucs), *see* Ralph of
Berkshire 56, 215
Bernitone, *see* Barrington, Little (Gloucs)
Bertona, *see* Barton [in Gloucester] (Gloucs)
Berwick (Kent) 211 n.89, 212 n.94
Besford (Worcs) 267
Bezford, *see* Besford (Worcs)
biberium 121
Bibury (Gloucs) 269
Bichonofre, *see* Bicknor, English (Gloucs)
Bicknor, English (Gloucs) 274
Bilborough (Notts) 84
Bill of Rights 292
billeting 28, 29, 142–5, 147, 299
Bing Maps 220
Birlingham (Worcs) 267
Biscot (Beds) 55 n.23
Biselega, *see* Bisley (Gloucs)
Bishampton (Worcs) 93, 264
Bishop's hundred (Suff) 201, 202. *See also* Hoxne hundred
Bishop's Stortford (Herts) 178
Bisley (Gloucs) 272
Bissamtona, *see* Bishampton (Worcs)
Bisselega, *see* Bushley (Worcs)
Bissoppeslench, *see* Lench, Rous (Worcs)
Blackwell (Warks) 93, 265
Blair, John 57

Blakenham (Suff) 186
Blakewell, see Blackwell (Warks)
blancus 127–8
Blandintona, see Bledington (Gloucs)
blank lines 102–3, 105, 107
blatum 133
bled annonae 133
Bledington (Gloucs) 270
Blockelai, see Blockley (Gloucs)
Blockley (Gloucs) 93, 250, 251, 252, 264
Bloxwich (Staffs) 93 n.50
Bochelanda, see Buckland (Gloucs)
Bockinton', see Bockleton (Worcs)
Bockleton (Worcs) 266
Bodin, half-brother of Count Alan 179, 191, 192, 193
Boga of Hemingford 296
bohtei 120. See also *hida*
book as record type 291. See also *codex*
Book of Fees 301
bookland 37, 38, 41, 57, 185
bordarii 119, 124–5
borough 15, 16, 26, 30–3, 57, 67 n.17, 100, 106, 107, 135, 140, 152, 157
   borough work 100. See also *burgherist*
   customary tenements 31, 100
   sokes in 31
boscum, boscus 124, 136, 253
Boselin 268
botl 120. See also *hida*
Bourn (Cambs) 176.
   See Almaer of
Bourton-on-the-Water (Gloucs) 271
bovate 229
Box and Cox analysis 50
Boxewelle, see Boxwell (Gloucs)
Boxwell (Gloucs) 270
Boxworth (Cambs) 88, 89
Boynton (Suff) 177
Braceby (Lincs) 104
Bradelega, see Bradley Green (Worcs)
Bradewas, see Broadwas (Worcs)
Bradewella, see Broadwell (Gloucs)
Bradicote, see Bredicot (Worcs)
Bradley Green (Worcs) 93, 264
Bramcote (Notts) 84
Bramfield (Suff) 177 n.26, 180
Brantham (Suff) 177 and n.26, 178
breach of the peace, see *gribrige*
Bredicot (Worcs) 93, 265

Bredon (Worcs) 93, 251, 264
Bredonam, see Bredon (Worcs)
Breteuil 127 n.91
Bretons 149, 172, 173, 179, 182, 189, 190
breve 20, 259
breviate 5, 20, 22, 29, 247–8, 252, 255, 257, 258, 259, 261
Brichthelmetona, see Bricklehampton (Worcs)
Brichtricus filius Algari, see Beorhtric son of Ælfgar
Bricklehampton (Worcs) 267
Bridbury, A. R. 44, 50, 51
Brien, count, brother of Count Alan 173, 174
Briggs, Keith 42
Bristol Channel 147
Brittany 173, 189, 190, 194
Broadwas (Worcs) 93, 265
Broadwell (Gloucs) 256, 271
Broctun', see Broughton Hackett (Worcs)
brocus, broca 115
Brompton, Patrick (Yorks) 192
Bromsberrow (Gloucs) 275
Brooks, Nicholas 37, 39
Broughton (Yorks) 191
Broughton, Brant (Lincs) 183
Broughton Hackett (Worcs) 268
Broxtow (Notts) 84
bruaria 115
Bruisyard (Suff) 180
Bruman the reeve 281
Brumeberga, see Bromsberrow (Gloucs)
Brundall (Norf) 185
Brundon (Essex) 186
BSE inquiry 291 n.12
Buckinghamshire 56
Buckland (Gloucs) 270
bures, buri 131
burgensis 129, 135
Burghal Hidage 56
burgherist 131
Burgric, a man of Ralph the staller 178
burgus 128
Burlege, see Barley (Worcs)
Burlingeham, see Birlingham (Worcs)
Burnham Thorpe (Norf) 185
Burrough Green (Cambs) 88
Burton abbey 52
Burton Lazars (Leics) 93

Burtona, *see* Bourton-on-the-Water (Gloucs)
Bury St Edmunds abbey 15, 70, 71, 91, 151, 175, 182, 185, 194, 199, 200, 202
    abbot of 186, 202. *See also* Baldwin, Leofric, Leofstan,
    liberty of 182 n.55
    return of 200
    scriptorium of 15, 200
Bushley (Worcs) 93, 264
Bylaugh (Suff) 187 n.89

caballus 135–6
Cadesleda, *see* Castlett (Gloucs)
Caen, nuns of 271
cainas 128
Caldecote (Cambs) 176
Caldicote [in Hawling] (Gloucs) 273
calfskin 12
callis 134
Cam, Helen 55
cambio 129
Cambridgeshire 2, 3, 12, 15, 18, 19, 39, 57, 232, 238
    sheriff of, *see* Picot
Came hundred (Worcs) 266
Camel, *see* Came (Worcs)
Cameseia, *see* Kempsey (Worcs)
Campbell, James 55
Campden, Chipping (Gloucs) 272
Campedena, *see* Campden, Chipping (Gloucs)
candidus 127–8
Canterbury (Kent) 214. *See* Ailnoth of
    archbishop of 23, 37, 39, 176, 203, 209, 212, 215, 216. *See also* Anselm, Eadsige, Lanfranc, Stigand
    Christ Church 21, 202, 203, 209–16
    St Augustine's 21, 22, 67, 210, 215
    see of 210
Canterbury Cathedral, Register K 21
Cantley (Yorks) 186
capitale manerium 95, 250
capitula, *see* articles
*car*o 76
*car*1 76
caruca, carruca 114–18
Carlton (Suff) 177 n.29
Carswalls (Gloucs) 274
Cartae Baronum 145 n.44, 258

cartage 176 n.20, 179 n.39
carucata, carrucata 43, 117, 226, 229
carucate, *see carucata*
carucation 55
cas(s)atus 119
castellaria, castellatus 133–4. *See also* castlery
castellum, castrum 133
castlery 39, 148, 174, 190, 191, 193, 216. *See also castellaria*
castle-guard 176 n.23, 177 n.29
Castlett (Gloucs) 274
Catterick (Yorks) 190, 191
Caxton (Cambs) 88, 89
census 51, 114
ceorl 114, 117
cereal crop, *see frumentum*
Cernai, *see* Cerney, North (Gloucs)
Cernei, *see* Cerney Wick (Gloucs)
Cerney, North (Gloucs) 272
Cerney Wick (Gloucs) 275
Charford (Hants) 287 n.66
Charingworth (Gloucs) 275
Charlemagne 289
Charlton Abbots (Gloucs) 271
Chenepelai, *see* Kempley (Gloucs)
Cherchesdona, *see* Churchdown (Gloucs)
Cherletona, *see* Charlton Abbots (Gloucs)
Chersewella, *see* Carswalls (Gloucs)
Cheshire 39, 53, 170
Chester (Ches) 32, 135
    bishop of 96, 280
    St Werburgh of 96
Cheuringewrd', *see* Charingworth (Gloucs)
Chichester (Sussex), bishop of 214
Childswickham (Gloucs) 275, 255
Chirchulle, *see* Churchill (Worcs)
Churchdown (Gloucs) 272
churches, survey of 100, 101
Churchill (Worcs) 93, 265
churchscot 265
Cinque Ports 148
circuits 24
    returns 2, 3, 14–15, 22–3, 59, 65–6, 99, 100, 110, 111, 125, 128, 132, 138–9, 141, 152, 153
Cirec', *see* Cirencester (Gloucs)
Cirencester (Gloucs) 273
    church of 252, 272, 273, 292
claims 20. *See* Ely C. Ely D
Clamarhoc, *see* Eudo son of

Clamores 38, 106, 129, 182, 129, 283, 296 and n.32. *See also* annexations, Ely C, Ely D, *Invasiones*, *Terrae Occupatae*
Clareia (Norf) 174 n.11
Clarke, Howard 5, 22, 29
Cleeve (Gloucs) 269
Cleeve Prior (Worcs) 266
Clent hundred (Worcs) 266
clerici 126
Clifton (Yorks) 194
Cliuam, *see* Cleeve (Gloucs)
Clopton (Cambs) 89, 161 n.10
Clopton (Worcs) 93, 263
Clopton, Lower (Warks) 273
Cloptona, *see* Clopton (Worcs)
Clostuna, *see* Clopton, Lower (Warks)
Clothall (Herts) 176
Cnut IV, king of Denmark 3, 141–3, 147, 182, 150, 280, 299
  Life of 150
Cnut, king of England 182
Coates (Gloucs) 275
Coberley (Gloucs) 254 n.30, 272 n.12, 275
Coberley, Upper (Gloucs) 269
cob-horses, *see runcini*
coceti 118
Codestun', *see* Cutsdean (Gloucs)
codex 291. *See also* book
Codsheath (Kent) 215 n.110
COEL database 33–4, 171, 172
Cofton Hackett (Worcs) 266
coinage 127–8
Colchester (Essex) 15, 150 n.82
Coleby (Lincs) 183
Colesbourne (Gloucs) 269
Colesburnam, *see* Colesbourne (Gloucs)
coliberti 125, 131 n.119
Colmworth (Beds) 86
Coln St Aldwyns (Gloucs) 270
colophon 146
Colston Bassett (Notts) 292 n.13
Colston, Car (Notts) 292 n.13
Colswein 176. *See also* Warin
Comberton (Worcs) 268
Combs (Suff) 173 n.11
comes 126
comital estates 38, 57
commendation 37, 38, 41, 49, 86 n.18, 90, 164, 167, 175, 177, 180, 186

commissioners 21, 41, 100, 167 n.22, 203, 213, 281
Compton Abdale (Gloucs) 272
compurgators 282
computatur 128
Conan, earl, chamberlain of, *see* Ralph son of Meldred
Condicota, *see* Condicote (Gloucs)
Condicote (Gloucs) 269, 272, 274
Congreve (Staffs) 93
Conington (Cambs) 88 n.27, 89
Connicote, *see* Condicote (Gloucs)
consuetudo, consuetudines 37, 48, 91, 114, 115, 159, 161, 167, 208, 278
consul, consulatus 126
consultation 28–30, 293–4, 299–300
conversion tables 14
Cookley (Suff) 186
Cooper, Alan 25, 284
Copnor (Hants) 289
Corbett, William 34
Corbucion, son of, *see* William
Cormeilles, Sainte-Marie of 266, 271
corn, *see frumentum*
Cornwall 13, 39
Cosby (Leics) 167
coscet, coscez, coscets, cozets 118, See also *cotarii*, *cotmanni*
Costessey (Norf) 181, 182, 187 n.89
Costune, *see* Cofton Hackett (Worcs)
cotarii, cothcetli, coteri,114–6 118–9, 124–5. See also *coscet, cotmanni*
Cotheridge (Worcs) 93, 263
cotman(n)i, cotsaeta, cotsets, cotsetla 114, 118. See also *coset, cotarii, cotmanni*
cottagers, cottars 112, 114, 118, 231
Coulson, Charles 58
County Hidage 68 n.31
Cove, South (Suff) 181
Coventry, church of 266, 271
Cowley (Gloucs) 271
Cowley (Staffs) 93
Cowlinge (Suff) 177 n.26, 180
cows 114
Craven 192
Crediton, see of 207,
Creeting St Olave (Suff) 173 n.11
Creeting St Peter (Suff) 173 n.11
Crick, Julia 18 n.49
Crofton (Hants) 179

Cromba, *see* Croome, Earl's (Worcs)
Croome, Earl's (Worcs) 93, 264
Croome, Hill (Worcs) 93, 264
Croppetornam, *see* Cropthorne (Worcs)
Cropthorne (Worcs) 93, 266
crowd-sourcing 75, 76
Crowland abbey 43, 150, 151, 260, 290 n.4
   abbots of, *see* Ingulf, Wulfketel
   chronicle, *see* Historia Croylandensis
   liturgy of 151
Crowland Domesday 290 n.4, 292 and n.13, 294, 301
Croydon (Cambs) 88, 89, 161 n.10
cuo 76
Cudeleie, *see* Cudleigh (Worcs)
Cudleigh (Worcs) 93, 265
Cuinhulla, *see* Queenhill (Worcs)
Culcortona, Culcurtune, *see* Culkerton (Gloucs)
Culega, *see* Cowley (Gloucs)
Culkerton (Gloucs) 273, 275
Culna, *see* Coln St Aldwyns (Gloucs)
Cumberlege, *see* Coberley, Upper (Gloucs)
Cumbrinton', Cumbrintun, *see* Comberton (Worcs)
Cumtona, *see* Compton Abdale (Gloucs)
Cundicota, Cundicotam, *see* Condicote (Gloucs)
Cura, *see* Kyre (Worcs)
curia 132
curiales 26
Cuthberlege, *see* Coberley (Gloucs)
Cutsdean (Gloucs) 93, 264

Daglingworth, *see* Duntisbourne (Gloucs)
Dailesford, *see* Daylesford (Gloucs)
dairies, dairy-farms, *see hardwica, wica, uaccaria*
Dalling, Field (Norf) 185
Dalton (Yorks) 191
dam, *see exclusa*
danegeld 255, 257, 258, 261
Danelaw 49, 85, 91, 148, 297
   northern 39, 54, 55
Danes 30, 148–9
Darby, H. C. 4, 119, 219, 221, 230, 232, 233, 234, 240, 260
dare 70
Darenth (Kent) 67
David, king of Scots 188

Daylesford (Gloucs) 93, 250, 264
Debach (Suff) 178
Declaration of Independence 292
deer park 58
Deerhurst (Gloucs) 166 n.21, 271 n.10
defdo, defendere, defendit, 66–9
Defford (Worcs) 267
demesne 47, 48, 50, 52, 57, 116–17, 235, 243, 297
dena, den 130
Dena, *see* Mitcheldean (Gloucs)
Denmark 8, 12, 142, 150
Dennington (Suff) 180 n.46
Denton (Lincs) 104
Depeford, *see* Defford (Worcs)
depression in status 49
Derby, West (Lancs) 95
Derby, West, hundred (Lancs) 99
Derbyshire 13, 38
Derham, *see* Dyrham (Gloucs)
descriptio 114, 146, 147, 277–8, 293, 302 and n.109
Descriptio Terrarum of Peterborough abbey 99
Dialogue of the Exchequer 1, 277–8, 288, 290
Dichford, *see* Ditchford (Gloucs)
Didintona, *see* Doynton (Gloucs)
Didlington (Norf) 186
Digital Domesday 1.1 10, 54
Digital Farley 11, 61–3, 72, 75, 76
Dirilecht domains 223 n.18
Dispenser, *see* Robert the bursar
disputes 15, 144, 200, 201. *See also* annexations, *Clamores*, Ely C, Ely D, *Invasiones, Terrae Occupatae*
Ditchford (Gloucs) 93, 264
Dives-sur-Mer 143
DM A 21
DM B 21, 22, 23, 111, 210–13
DM E 22, 23, 111
dnoio 76
Doddingtree hundred (Worcs) 266
Dodgson, John McNeal 75, 306
Dodington (Gloucs) 270, 275
Dodintune, *see* Dodington (Gloucs)
Dodnash (Suff) 178
Dol (Brittany) 189
Domesday Book, *see also* GDB, LDB
   CDROM *see Digital Domesday, Domesday Explorer*

Domesday Book (*cont.*)
    datasets 10, 46–7, 223–32, 243. *See* COEL, *Electronic Edition of Domesday*, PASE Online, PASE Offline
    date 28–9, 51 n.87, 257–60, 299–300
    edition, *see* Farley
    entry formation 42–3. 94
    facsimiles, *see* Alecto, Ordnance Survey
    multiple manor entry 94
    name 277–88, 290, 303. *See also descriptio*, Winchester, Book of
    statistics, nature of 47–8, 240–3
    translations, *see* Alecto, Phillimore, VCH
Domesday Explorer 9 n.5, 10, 226
Domesday Extracts 11
Domesday Gazetteer 232
Domesday Latin dictionary 75–6
Domesday Monachorum 21–3, 67, 210–13, 214
Domesday on a Map 223, 225, 229, 230, 246
Domesday People 171
Domesday Texts Project 107
dominium, dominicum, dominicatus 116
domus 114, 116
dona 258
Dorchester hundred (Oxon) 204, 217
Dorchester-on-Thames (Oxon) 204
    bishopric of 207, 217
Dormestun', *see* Dormston (Worcs)
Dormston (Worcs) 267
Dorn (Worcs) 250, 251, 264
Dorna, *see* Dorn (Gloucs)
Dorsington (Warks) 275
Dorsintune, *see* Dorsington (Warks)
Douglas, D. C. 8 n.4, 22, 23
Dover (Kent) 147
    St Martin's 32
Doynton (Gloucs) 270
drag-net, *see sagena*
Drayton (Lincs) 182 n.53, 183
Drayton (Staffs) 93
Drayton, Dry (Cambs) 179 n.37
Drayton, Fen (Cambs) 89
Drifeld', *see* Driffield (Gloucs)
Driffield (Gloucs) 272
Drogo de la Beuvrière 184, 228
Drogo son of Pons 267
Droitwich (Worcs) 33, 92 n.47, 93, 251 n.17, 266, 267

Dubentone, *see* Dumbleton (Gloucs)
Dudesborna, Dundesborna, *see* Duntisbourne (Gloucs)
Dudintr', Dudintre, *see* Doddingtree hundred (Worcs)
Dumbleton (Gloucs) 271, 274
Dumeltona, *see* Dumbleton (Gloucs)
Dunsthorpe (Lincs) 104
Dunston (Staffs) 93
Duntesborna, Duntesburne, *see* Duntisbourne. Duntisbourne Abbots, Duntisbourne Leer (Gloucs)
Duntisbourne (Gloucs) 273
Duntisbourne Abbots (Gloucs) 270, 274
Duntisbourne Leer (Gloucs) 271
Durand 264
Durand the sheriff 253, 254 n.30, 269, 272, 274
Durham, bishop of 198 n.7, 199, 208, 213 n.101. *See* William
    scriptorium of 12
Dyrham (Gloucs) 274

Eadgifu Pulchra, the Fair 86, 87, 88, 161 n.14, 174–9, 180, 181, 184, 187, 191, 193, 195
    daughter, *see* Gunhilda
    husband, *see* Harold, earl and king
    men of, *see* Ailsi, Almar, Alwine, Goda, Godwin, Osgot, Saevia, Turbern
Eadresfeld, *see* Eldersfield (Worcs)
Eadric Grim 178, 180
Eadric of Laxfield 180, 181 and n.46
    man of, *see* Godwin
Eadsige, archbishop of Canterbury 216
Ealdgyth, daughter of Wigod of Wallingford 172
Ealdræd, archbishop of York 254 and n.31, 256, 269, 272
Eardeluestun', *see* Eardiston (Worcs)
Eardiston (Worcs) 266
Earthcott, Gaunt's (Gloucs) 270
East Anglia 3, 16, 30, 46, 47, 54, 55, 147–53, 170, 182, 217
    earldom of 175, 182, 195
East Midlands 46
Eastbury (Worcs) 93, 265
Eastleach Turville (Gloucs) 274
Eastwell (Leics) 93
Eaton Socon (Beds), *see* Wulfmær of

Ebrictona, *see* Ebrington (Gloucs)
Ebrington (Gloucs) 273
Ebury (Middlesex) 90
ecclesia 126
Eckington (Worcs) 267
Edenham (Lincs) 85
Edgar Ætheling 193
Edgar, king of England 208, 296
Edgeworth (Gloucs) 272, 274
Edith, queen 94, 104, 106, 163 n.14, 180, 184, 207
    man of, *see* Godwin
Edmund, king and martyr 151
Edward 267
Edward I, king of England 143 n.36, 298
Edward of Salisbury 133
Edward the Confessor, king of England 52 n.219, 88, 94, 167, 168, 173 n.11, 178, 180, 182, 185, 205, 216, 266
    sokemen of, *see* Ælnod, Alward
    thegn of, *see* Alsi, Wulfric, Wulfwine
Edward the Elder, king of England 297
Edwin, earl of Mercia 184, 190, 191, 193, 195.
    men of, *see* Goda
Egestonam, *see* Ashton, Cold (Gloucs)
Egeswrtha, *see* Edgeworth (Gloucs)
Eight and Half Hundreds (Suff) 182 n.55
Eilewrd', *see* Aylworth (Gloucs)
Eldersfield (Worcs) 250, 267 and n.13
Electronic Edition of Domesday Book 10, 46–7, 226, 231, 232 n.49
Elmham, North (Norf) 201 n.25,
    bishop of, *see* Æthelmaer
    ferding of 202
Elmham, South (Suff) 202
Elsworth (Cambs) 89
Ely abbey 18, 19, 20, 68, 88, 149, 166, 177 n.29, 178, 180, 181, 202, 235, 288, 297
    abbot of, *see* Symeon
Ely A 20
Ely B 20
Ely C 20
Ely D 20
Emma, queen, brother of, *see* Richard II of Normandy
Engelric 36
Enisan, brother-in-law of Count Alan 191, 192, 194

episcopus 126
eques, equus, equites 114, 132 and n.128
Esbern 167
escangio, escangium 129
escort 176 n.20
Esger the staller 160
Eskil of Ware 86, 90, 103, 228
Essex 15, 19, 20, 64, 72, 148, 150, 153
Estoc, *see* Stoke, Harry (Gloucs)
Estona, *see* Aston Fields (Worcs), Aston Subedge (Gloucs), Aston, While Ladies (Worcs)
Estwde, *see* Astwood (Worcs)
Etrop, *see* Williamstrip (Gloucs)
Eudo son of Clamarhoc 189
Eudo, count of Brittany 179. *See* Count Alan
Eunelade, *see* Evenlode (Gloucs)
Eustace II of Boulogne 146 n.53, 148
Euston (Suff) 186
Evenlode (Gloucs) 93, 250, 264
Eversholt (Beds) 242 n.66
Everson, Paul 43
Evesham (Worcs) 251
    abbey 5, 205, 249, 256, 260 n.64, 271
    abbot of 204, 249, 257, 264, 266. *See* Æthelwig, Walter
    cartulary of 247
    monks of 250, 251, 255, 256
    surveys 248
Evesham A 11, 111
Evesham C 22, 111, 128, 246–50, 261–6
Evesham D 249
Evesham K 14, 111, 252, 254 n.32
Evesham M 22, 111, 250–4, 267–73
Evesham Q 111
excambio, excambitio, excambium 129
Excerpta 21, 22, 111, 130, 134
Exchequer 8, 247, 288, 292, 303. *See also* Abbreviatio
exclusa 115
Exeter, bishop of 198 n.7, 203, 213, 214, 269. *See* Osbern
exlex 135
Exning (Suff) 175, 187
Exon 3, 9, 11, 14, 15, 17–18, 20, 23, 65–6, 105, 138, 293, 305
    digitization of 308
    source of GDB 17–18, 139
exul 135

Eye (Suff) 202
  market 202
Eynsham, church of 271
  abbot of 204
eyries, nests, *see aeria, nidus*

fabrica plumbi 115
Faith, Rosamond 43
Fakenham, Little (Suff) 70
Farley, Abraham, 11 61
  edition of Domesday Book 9, 10, 62, 63, 72, 73, 74, 76, 77 n.59, 79, 107
farm of one night 55
Farmcote (Gloucs) 273
farms 102
Fawdon [in Whaddon] (Cambs) 188
Fawley, Little (Berks) 94
Fécamp, abbey of Holy Trinity of 228
fen, peat, silt 57
feodary 24, 141, 259
feortþing, ferding, ferting 131. See also Elmham, Winchcombe
Fernecote, *see* Farmcote (Gloucs)
ferraria, fabrica ferri 115, 127
Fersfield (Norf) 186
firma 204
First Crusade 189
Fishborough hundred (Worcs) 205
fisheries 48, 50, 51, 112, 115, 131
fisherman 125
fishing-net, *see sagena*
Five Boroughs 55
Fladbury (Worcs) 93, 263
Fladebÿrÿam, *see* Fladbury (Worcs)
Flanders 148. *See also* Robert, count of
Fleet (Lincs) 183
Fleming, Robin 25, 38, 39, 170, 232, 238, 279 and n.12
Flexmore (Herts) 86
Flight, Colin 15 n.33, 17, 18, 20 n.60, 21, 22, 23, 24, 41, 139, 210, 257
Folcard of St Bertin 148
folkland 38
food rents 37, 85
Fordley (Suff) 181 n.47
forest 58
forge, *see forgia*
forgery 197
forgia 115, 127
Forthampton (Here) 75

forum 115
fossa lapidum 115
Foulsham (Norf) 186
Fralintona, *see* Frampton Court (Gloucs)
Frampton (Lincs), *see* Ælfstan of
Frampton Court (Gloucs) 270
Frampton Mansell (Gloucs) 275
France 12
Frantona, *see* Frampton Mansell (Gloucs)
fraxinetum 235
free men 48–9, 51, 85, 86–92, 112, 113, 175, 176, 178, 185, 212, 267, 268, 282. See also *liber homo*
  the manor and 40, 48–9, 82–91
Freeby (Leics) 93
freedman, *see coliberti*
Frenchman 78, 267–8
Frocester (Gloucs) 270
Froecestra, *see* Frocester (Gloucs)
Frolesworth (Leics) 167
frumentum 133
Fulbeck (Lincs) 183
Fulbourn (Cambs) 175
Fulchered, *see* Stephen son of
fumagium 131 n.121
Funtley (Hants) 179

Gaël, seigneurie of 189
Galbraith, V. H. 7, 8, 14, 17, 18, 20, 21, 22, 23, 58, 138, 139, 141, 145, 199, 210, 247, 248
gallows sign, *see* paragraphos
Gamlingay (Cambs) 89
gardinum 115
Garnett, George 24, 39, 41
garrison theory 30–1
Gartree wapentake (Leics) 225 n.25
Gartree wapentake (Lincs) 225 n.25
GDB, *see also* Domesday Book, *Digital Domesday, Domesday Explorer*
  date 27–29, 51 n.87, 257–60, 299–300
  layout 81–108, 109
  order of writing 12–13, 140
  scribe 5, 12, 14, 15, 16, 24, 64, 66, 71, 75, 76, 81–108, 116, 125, 126, 129, 153, 212
  scribe B 14, 81 n.2, 307
GDP 50
gebur 114, 130
Gedney (Lincs) 183

geld 39, 48, 53, 130, 144, 145, 152 n.91, 209, 229, 297, 298
　accounts 111, 144, 198
　quotas 45
　vocabulary of 64
*geld*o 64–5
geldare 130
geldum, gield 64–5, 114, 129
Gelston (Lincs) 42
Gelston hundred (Lincs) 42
geneat 114
Geoffrey de Burgh 179 n.39
Geoffrey, bishop of Coutances 18, 227
Geoffrey de la Guerche 93, 172
Geoffrey de Mandeville 90. 160
Geographic Information Systems, *see* GIS
Geographically Weighted Regression 245
Gerard 239 n.57
Gerard the chamberlain 271
gerefa 134
Gerold, son of, *see* Robert
Getinge, *see* Guiting Power (Gloucs)
Getmapping 11
Gilbert 266
Gilbert Arbalaster 185, 186
Gilbert of Lisieux 287 n.63
Gilbert son of Turold 265, 267, 268
Gillepatric 192
Gilling (Yorks) 190, 191
　earl's hall at 190
Gilling wapentake (Yorks) 190
GIS 219–46
Gislingham (Suff) 186
Giso, bishop of Wells 198, 208, 209
　Historiola of 208
Gitinga, *see* Guiting, Temple (Gloucs)
Glastonbury abbey 43, 94–5, 125, 270
Glemham, Great, (Suff) 177 n.26
Global Positioning System, *see* GPS
globes, virtual 220
Gloucester (Gloucs) 2, 33, 110, 113 and n.15, 143, 293
　St Oswald of 272
　St Peter, abbey of 253, 254, 255, 256, 266, 269, 270
　　abbot of, 253 n.29. See Serlo
　　Historia and cartulary 254
　　monks of 255
Gloucestershire 13, 22, 75, 203, 248, 252
Goadby (Leics) 93

goats 114
Goda 164
Goda, Gode, 'man' of Earl Ælfgar 88, 157, 158, 159, 160, 161 and n.14, 162, 163, 166, 167, 176, 177 n.29
Goda, wife of Earl Siward of Northumbria 183
Goding 178
Godric 103, 181 n.50, 267, 268
Godric the reeve, man of, *see* Ralph
Godric the steward 175, 178 and n.32, 185, 186
　wife, *see* Ingreda
　son, *see* Ralph
Godwin the thegn 185
Godwin son of Ailsi, thegn of Queen Edith 177–8
Godwin, a man of Eadgifu 176, 177
Godwin *cild, scild*, man of Eadgifu and Earl Waltheof 176, 187 n.88
Godwin, man of Eadric of Laxfield 181 n.46
Godwin, brother of Ralph the staller 182, 185 and n.71, 186
Godwin, man of Archbishop Stigand 159 n.9, 160
Godwin, earl of Wessex 212, 213, 216
　tenant of, *see* Tovi
Godwinesons 216
Goismer 270
Golde 161 n.14
　son of, *see* Wulfric
Gonerby (Lincs) 104, 106
Google Earth 220
Google Maps 220, 224
gort, gurges 115
Gosberton (Lincs) 182 n.53, 183
Gospatric son of Arnketil 191, 192 and n.116
Gotman, man of Earl Ælgar 160
GPS 221
Grafton Flyford (Worcs) 268
Grafton', *see* Grafton Flyford (Worcs)
grain ordinance 1296, 143 n.36
granary, *see granagia, horreum*
granary-keeper, *see granetarius*
granetarius 127 n.88
grangia 127
Grantham (Lincs) 33, 104–7, 151, 184
　church of St Wulfram 104
　Mowbeck in 104
Grassi, John 52 n.219

graua 123
Gravesend (Essex) 146 n.53
grazing lands 112
grazing rights, grass render, *see herbagium*
Greenhill (Worcs) 93, 263
Gregory, Ian 222
gribrige 131
Grimeleiam, *see* Grimley (Worcs)
Grimhelle, *see* Greenhill (Worcs)
Grimley (Worcs) 93, 265
Guiting Power (Gloucs) 274
Guiting, Temple (Gloucs) 274
Gullick, Michael 13 n.25, 15, 307
Gunhilda, daughter of King Harold and Eadgifu 172, 195
   daughter, *see* Matilda
   husband, *see* Count Alan
Gunter of Le Mans 148
Gusford (Suff) 178
Guy, son of, *see* William
Gyrth, earl 88, 181, 182 and n.53, 177, 182, 185, 187 n.89

habere 112
Hacgepen, Hacgpen, *see* Hampen (Gloucs)
Haconby (Lincs) 84
Haicotam, *see* Aycote (Gloucs)
Hailes (Gloucs) 274
Haimo de Valeines 177 and n.29, 180, 181
Halewi, *see* Alwig 268
hall, halla, heall 40, 50, 84, 132–3, 190, 191, 192. *See also aula, haula*
Hallage, *see* Hallow (Worcs)
Hallam-Smith, Elizabeth 247
Halldorr 192
Hallikeld wapentake (Yorks) 190
Hallow (Worcs) 92 and n.47, 93, 265
Hambrook (Gloucs) 270
Hambÿrÿ, *see* Hanbury (Worcs)
Hamenei, *see* Ampney [in Driffield] (Gloucs)
Hamenell', *see* Ampney St Mary (Gloucs)
Hamma, *see* Highnam (Gloucs)
Hamnell', *see* Ampney St Peter (Gloucs)
Hamo de Doll, Hamo de Valenis 177 n.29
Hampen (Gloucs) 273
Hampnett (Gloucs) 275
Hampshire 202, 215
   sheriff of, *see* Hugh de Port
Hampton (Worcs) 93, 205, 251 n.18, 250, 252, 257, 266

Hampton, Meysey (Gloucs) 272
Hamtona, *see* Hampton (Worcs), Hampton, Meysey (Gloucs)
Hamtone, *see* Hampnett (Gloucs)
Hanbury (Worcs) 250, 266
Hang wapentake (Yorks) 190
Hantona, *see* Minchinhampton (Gloucs)
Happisburgh (Norf) 181 n.46
   soke of 181 n.46
hardwica 115
Hardwin de Scales 157, 158, 160, 161, 162, 163, 164, 165, 166, 228
   men of, *see* Adelulf, Alvred, Ralph, Robert
Hardwin, son of Ralph the staller 185–6
Hareulle, *see* Harnhill (Gloucs)
Harkstead (Suff) 178
Harlaxton (Lincs) 104
Harmby (Yorks) 192
Harnhill (Gloucs) 275
Harold, earl and king of England 24, 147, 174 n.11, 173, 175, 177, 181 and n.50, 182, 187, 195, 216, 217
   brother, *see* Gyrth
   daughter, *see* Gunhilda
Harold, son of Earl Ralph of Hereford 90
Harris, Philip 307
Harrowby (Lincs) 104
Harrying of the North 52, 193
Hartlebury (Worcs) 266 and n.11
Harvey, Paul 305
Harvey, Sally 5, 24, 25, 26, 29, 44, 47, 49, 51, 152 n.91, 259, 261
Harvington (Worcs) 93, 265
Haslingfield (Cambs) 88, 176
Hassingham (Norf) 186 n.80
Hastings, battle of 175, 182, 188
Hatley (Cambs) 89, 161 n.10
haula, see aula
Hauochesberia, *see* Hawkesbury (Gloucs)
Hawcombe (Dors) 124 n.68
Hawkesbury (Gloucs) 271
Haythby (Lincs) 99
Hazelton [in Rodmarton] (Gloucs) 275
heafod botl 40, 120. *See also* manor
Healfdene and his two brothers 103
hearth-tax, *see herdigelt*
heat map 223
Heather (Leics) 167 and n.23
heathland, *see bruaria*

Hebbelench, *see* Lench, Ab (Worcs)
Hebden (Yorks) 192
Hecgesworda, *see* Edgeworth (Gloucs)
Hedicota, *see* Hidcote Bartrim (Gloucs)
Heilles, *see* Hailes (Gloucs)
heinfara 131
Hekinton', *see* Eckington (Worcs)
Helmingham (Suff) 173 n.11
Hemblington (Norf) 90 n.34
Hemingford (Hunts), *see* Boga of
Hemming 85, 103
Hemming's cartulary 114 n.18, 248, 249, 251, 255, 256, 303. *See also* Worcester B
Henry de Ferrers 167
Henry I, king of England 8, 27, 141
 coronation charter of 297
 wife, *see* Matilda
Henry of Huntingdon 114 n.16
herbagium, herbacio, herbatio, herbatia, herbatura 115, 131
Herbert Losinga 201 n.25
Herbert, king's reeve 242 n.66
Herbrand 268
herdigelt 131
Hereford (Here), customs of 127, 133
 bishop of 96, 99, 207, 263, 266, 269. *See* Robert of Losinga
 canons of 96, 99, 207
Herefordshire 75
Herefordshire Domesday 29, 248, 254, 255, 257, 258
Heresbÿrÿa, *see* Eastbury (Worcs)
Hereward 103, 250 n.14, 264
Herfast, bishop of Thetford 201
heriet, heriete, herigete 134
heriot, *see heriet*
Herlebald 265
Hermer de Ferrers 283, 284
Hertfordshire 12, 19, 49, 68
Hertleberie, *see* Hartlebury (Worcs)
Heruertonam, *see* Harvington (Worcs)
Heseldena, *see* Hazelton [in Rodmarton] (Gloucs)
Hesse, Mary 42
Hesselton (Yorks) 192
Hethersett (Norf) 180
Hewelsfield (Gloucs) 273
Hickling (Notts) 85
Hicumba, Hicumbe, *see* Icomb Place (Gloucs)

hida, hid, hidda, hidra, hidria 114–20. *See also bohtei, botl*
hidage, hidation 45, 55, 68, 217, 248, 257, 258
hidagium 91
Hidcote Bartrim (Gloucs) 271
Hidcote Boyce (Gloucs) 271
hide 43, 44, 45, 112, 118, 131, 132, 144, 226, 229
Hidecota, *see* Hidcote Boyce (Gloucs)
Higham, Nicholas 42, 44, 143–4
Highnam (Gloucs) 270
Hill (Worcs) 93
Himbleton (Worcs) 93, 265
Hindelep, *see* Hindlip (Worcs)
Hindlip (Worcs) 93, 265
Hindrelaghe, *see* Richmond (Yorks)
Hinnetona, *see* Hinton on the Green (Worcs)
Hintlesham (Suff) 177 n.27
Hinton on the Green (Worcs) 270
Histon (Cambs) 199
Historia Croylandensis 145, 147, 151, 290 n.4
Hitchin (Herts) 86
Hiwoldestune, *see* Hewelsfield (Gloucs)
hlaford 37
Holbeach (Lincs) 183
Holdfast (Worcs) 93, 264
Holt (Worcs) 93, 263
Holt, J. C. 14, 41, 82, 139, 145, 292
Holt, Richard 31, 49
homage 170, 298, 299. *See also commendatio, homagium*
homagium, hominatio 134
homo, homines 115, 117
Honeybourne, Cow (Gloucs) 271
honorial barony 96, 171, 191, 291
Horeduna, *see* Horton (Gloucs)
horreum 127
horse, *see equus, caballus*
Horseheath (Cambs) 239
Horseleia, *see* Horsley (Gloucs)
Horsley (Gloucs) 271
Horton (Gloucs) 275
hortus 115
Hough-on-the-Hill (Lincs) 183 and n.59
Houghton (Lincs) 106
house-breaking, *see heinfara*
houses 113
Hoxne (Suff) 201, 202
 market 199, 202

Hoxne hundred (Suff) 202. *See also* Bishop's hundred
Hoyt, R. S. 22
Hubert de Montcanisy 178
Hucclecote (Gloucs) 272
Huddington (Worcs) 93, 265
Hudintone, Hudintune, *see* Huddington (Worcs)
Hugh de Beauchamp 90
Hugh de Boscherbert 124 n.69
Hugh the butler, pincerna 158, 242 n.66
Hugh, earl of Chester 96, 178, 190, 252, 269, 272
Hugh de Grandmesnil 265
Hugh the Great 142 n.27
Hugh de Montfort 180
Hugh d'Orivalle 150 n.82
Hugh de Port, sheriff of Hampshire 282
Hulcromba, *see* Croome, Hill (Worcs)
Hull, university of 62
Humber estuary 57
Humeltun', *see* Himbleton (Worcs)
hundred 54–7, 131, 209
  grant of 170, 174
  sequence of 17, 20, 21, 90, 103, 205, 211
  twelve-carucate 54, 183
  yield of 32
Hundred Ordinance 55
hundred rolls 298, 301
hundredum 114
Huniburna, *see* Honeybourne, Cow (Gloucs)
Hunteleia, *see* Huntley (Gloucs)
Huntingdonshire 19, 45, 187, 232, 238
Huntley (Gloucs) 273
Hurtleberi, *see* Hartlebury (Worcs)
Husintr', *see* Hussingtree, Martin (Worcs)
Hussingtree, Martin (Worcs) 267
huts 113
Hyde abbey 188
  chronicle 188, 303 n.63
Hykeham, North (Lincs) 184

ICC 9. 11, 14, 15, 17, 18–19, 22, 23, 27, 31, 59, 68, 70, 111, 138, 146, 157–67, 294 and n.22, 295, 300
Icomb Place (Gloucs) 274, 275
Icomb, Church (Gloucs) 93, 264
Idmiston (Wilts) 94
Ids database 36, 172 n.6, 227
IE 9. 11, 16, 18–20, 68, 111, 281, 294

Ilbert de Lacy 229
inbreviation 14, 17, 295
incressandum 77
Ingoldsby (Lincs), *see* Osbert of
  family of 184
Ingreda, wife of Godric the steward
Ingulf, abbot of Crowland 148, 151
inheritance 194
initial letter forms 84–107
  change of 84, 93, 104
Inkberrow (Worcs) 93, 206, 263
inland 43–6, 48, 60, 235 n.54, 240–3
inquest of sheriffs 26
Inquisitio Comitatus Cantabrigiensis, *see* ICC
Inquisitio Eliensis, *see* IE
inquisitio geldi 21, 27, 144, 300
Inteberga, Inteberge, *see* Inkberrow (Worcs)
intercommoning 54, 56
interlocking patterns of tenure 56–7, 88, 240
intermarriage 34, 169, 170, 172–3, 194–5
invasiones 140, 201, 296 n.32. *See also* annexations, *Clamores*, Ely C, Ely D, *Terrae Occupatae*
Ipswich, (Suff) 177 n.26
  burgess of, *see* Ælfric son of Rolf
Isaac, a man of Ralph de Gael 185
Isabella de Warenne, wife of William 188 n.90
Isle of Wight 58
Isleham (Cambs) 179 and n.39, 285

Jarvis, Daniel 11
Jeulin, P. 175
Jocelyn Brito 178
John of Worcester 187
Jones, Robert 58
Judhael of Totnes 189 and n.97
  daughter, *see* Aanor
  son, *see* Alfred
Judith, countess 167, 172, 187 and n.88
  husband, *see* Waltheof, earl,
  mother, *see* Adelaide of Aumale
jugum 129
jurors, juries 19, 23, 25, 26, 27, 92, 103, 124, 171, 181, 200, 278–88, 294, 295, 300, 301, 302. *See also* verdicts
Jutland 143

Kapelle, W. E. 58
Keats-Rohan, K. S. B. 3, 33, 34, 39, 78
Kekinwiche, *see* Kenswick (Worcs)

Kempley (Gloucs) 274
Kempsey (Worcs) 92, 93, 263
Kenswick (Worcs) 93, 263, 265 and n.9
Kent 22, 38, 39, 46, 49, 147, 210, 212, 215
   East and West 279 n.14
   lathes of 21, 210, 215
   sheriff of 22
Kentford (Suff) 18
Kentish Assessment List 22, 257
Ketelbern, free man 181 n.50
Ketilbiorn 267
Kettleburgh (Suff) 180 and n.46. *See* Algar of
Kettleby (Leics) 93
Keynsham (Soms) 180
Killerby [in Catterick](Yorks) 190
king's thegns 38–41, 170
Kington Langley (Wilts) 94
Kinoulton (Notts) 85
Kintitun', *see* Knighton on Teme (Worcs)
Kirby (Leics) 93
Kirkby Fleetham (Yorks) 190
knight service 8, 28, 29 and n.106, 37, 39,
   144, 145, 260 n.60, 298
Knighton on Teme (Worcs) 266
Knightwick (Worcs) 93, 265 n.9
Kolgrimr 107, 184
Kÿnewardus *see* Cyneweard
Kyre (Worcs) 206, 266

Lacock (Wilts) 113 n.15
Lacumbe, *see* Icomb, Church (Gloucs)
lacus 115
lænland, laenage 37, 38, 57, 159, 173 n.11,
   175, 176, 178 n.32, 184, 186
Lainchantuna, *see* Leckhampton (Gloucs)
lake, *see lacus*
Lambeth, church of 271
Lambourn (Berks) 94
Landbeach (Cambs) 86 n,23, 179 n.37
landhlaford 37
Landric 183
landrica 37
Lanfranc, archbishop of Canterbury 18, 29,
   143, 149, 186, 188, 189, 190, 198,
   210, 212–17, 283, 286
Langeberge, *see* Longborough (Gloucs)
Langedone, *see* Longdon (Worcs)
Langetreu. *see* Longtree hundred (Gloucs)
Langford (Wilts) 94
Langley (Wilts) 94

Langport (Kent) 212
Lappewrth', *see* Leopard (Worcs)
Lasborough (Gloucs) 272
Lassington (Gloucs) 272
Lateran Council 1215 287
Laugherne (Worcs) 93, 249, 251, 263
Lavelle, Ryan 55
Lawerne, *see* Laugherne (Worcs)
Laxfield (Suff) 177 n.29. *See* Eadric of
LDB 3, 5, 12, 14–16, 18. 19. 20, 23, 24, 25,
   27, 111, 137–54. *See also*, Domesday
   Book, GDB
   datasets 10, 46
   facsimile 9
   scribes 14, 24
lead works, lead mine, *see fabrica plumbi*,
   plumbaria
Leadenham (Lincs) 183
Leaveland (Kent) 212 n.94
Leccha, Lecche, *see* Northleach (Gloucs)
Lecche, *see* Eastleach Turville (Gloucs)
Leckhampton (Gloucs) 274
Ledena, *see* Upleadon (Gloucs)
Lee (Gloucs) 270
leet 54, 146
legrewita 131 and n.131
Leicester (Leics) 135
Leicestershire 13, 45, 172
Leicestershire Survey 301
Leiga, *see* Lee (Gloucs)
Leintwardine' (Salop) 135
Lench, Ab (Worcs) 93, 264
Lench, Atch (Worcs) 266
Lench, Rous (Worcs) 93, 251, 264
Lenham (Kent) 211 n.89
Lenton (Notts) 84
Leofnoth 94
Leofric 167, 213
Leofric *cilt* 172 and n.8
   father, *see* Leofwine
   sister, *see* Ælfgifu
Leofstan, abbot of Bury St Edmunds 177
   n.29
Leofwine 272
Leofwine, earl 107, 216
Leofwine, father of Leofric *cilt* 172 n.8
   daughter, *see* Ælfgifu
Leominster (Here) 206
Leopard (Worcs) 265
Leseberga, *see* Lasborough (Gloucs)

Lessedona, *see* Lassington (Gloucs)
Lessingham (Norf) 185
Letletona, *see* Littleton-on-Severn (Gloucs)
*leu, lev, leu*0, *leu*1, *lev*0, *lev*1, *lew*1, *leuga, lewa* 73–5
Leviet 176
Lewes (Sussex) 135, 303 n.63
Lewis, Christopher 19, 28, 35, 40, 53, 187, 192, 227, 263 n.2, 279
Ley Green (Herts) 86
Liber Exoniensis, *see* Exon
liber homo 40, 49, 114, 115, 116
Lichfield/Chester, bishop of 280.
Lidenai, *see* Lydney, Little (Gloucs)
Limfjord (Denmark) 142
Limpenhoe (Norf) 186
Lincoln (Lincs) 107
  bishop of 199, 203, 206, 207. *See* Remigius
  return of 206
Lincolnshire 38, 45, 54, 57, 72, 172
Lindsey Survey 301
Linton (Cambs) 179 and n.39
Linton priory 179
Lisieux, bishop of 272
Litla 70. *See also* Little Livermere, Little Fakenham
Litletona, *see* Littleton [in Dumbleton] (Gloucs)
Litlington (Cambs) 89, 157, 158, 159, 160, 164, 165, 166
Littleton [in Dumbleton] (Gloucs) 274
Littleton-on-Severn (Gloucs) 270
Livermere, Little (Suff) 70
livestock 15, 16, 19, 138, 140, 141, 144, 146, 200, 210, 302
loanland, *see lænland*
London 33, 135, 150 and n.82, 203, 204, 285
  bishop of 89, 150, 178, 201, 203. *See* Maurice
  St Martin le Grand 36
  St Paul's 175, 200, 201
  Underground 220 n.2
Londonthorpe (Lincs) 104
long 's' 72–3
Longborough (Gloucs) 272
Longdon (Worcs) 93, 250, 267
Longhope (Gloucs) 273
Longstanton (Cambs) 88 n.27
Longstowe (Cambs) 176
Longtree hundred (Gloucs) 272, 275

lordship and land 36–8
Loveden wapentake (Lincs) 183
Lowerre, Andrew 4, 45, 53
Loyn, Henry 7, 82
lucus 123
Ludham (Norf) 181 n.46
Lulham (Here) 96
Lydbury (Salop) 206
Lydney, Little (Gloucs) 273
Lyon, archbishop of, *see* Agobard
Lyppard (Worcs) 93
Lyre, Sainte-Marie of 271

MacDonald, John 47, 245
Maddicott, John 29, 30, 148
Madgetts (Gloucs) 274
Magna Carta 292
Maine, county of 188, 189
Maitland, F. W. 30–2, 39, 54, 203, 221, 277
Malcolm, king of Scots 193
  court of 193
Malet, Robert 174 n.11, 177n.29, 178, 180 and n.46, 181
Malet family 202
Malling (Sussex) 209
Malmesbury, church of 270
manerium, maneir, maner, manens, mansio 40, 84, 91, 95, 114, 119–21. *See also* manor, *capitale manerium*
manerium cum hundredo 55
manipulation 4, 8, 25–6, 197–218
Manni Swart 177 n.26, 180
  son, *see* Ulf
Mannington (Norf) 185
manor 16, 18, 39–41, 47, 50, 82–95, 112, 114, 115, 116, 119–21, 132, 135, 145–6, 152, 159, 161, 278, 302. *See also manerium*
  contributory 30–1
  free men and 40, 48–9, 82–91
  service and 144–5, 152, 298
manorialization 40, 49, 85–91
Mardicote, *see* Earthcott, Gaunt's (Gloucs)
maresc, maresch, mariscus 130
Margaret, queen of Scots 193, daughter of, *see* Matilda
marginal M, B, and S 82–91, 104–7, 146
market, *see mercatum*, Hoxne
marriage strategies, *see* intermarriage
Marston, Long (Warks) 271

Marten, Lucy 15, 36, 53, 55, 150, 180, 189
Martinsley wapentake (Rutl) 261 n.70
mast 234
Matilda, daughter of Gunhilda and Count Alan 172
　husband, see Walter d'Aincourt
Matilda, wife of Henry I 193, mother of, see Margaret
Matilda, wife of William I 142, 170, 179
Matthews, Stephen 53
Maugersbury (Gloucs) 256, 271
Maurice, bishop of London 148, 201, 202
Mayhew, Nicholas 50
McLuhan, Marshall 107
meadow 48, 112, 231, 240, 242, 243
Medgaresburi, see Maugersbury (Gloucs)
Melbourn (Cambs) 89, 161
Meldred, son of, see Ralph
Meldreth (Cambs) 89, 161, 176
Melton, Great (Suff) 178 n.32
Melton, Little (Suff) 178 n.32
Melton Mowbray (Leics) 93
Mentmore (Bucks) 178
mercatum 115
mercenaries 28, 29, 30, 142–5, 147, 299
Mercia 49
mere, mara 115
Merewine, son of, see Northman
Mersetona, see Marston, Long (Warks)
Mersham (Kent) 211 n.89
Merwin 176
Mew, Karen 58
Mickleton (Gloucs) 271
Middleham (Yorks) 192
　castle of 192
　fee of 192
　William's Hill in 192
Middlesex 2, 55, 203
Middleton (Yorks), see Ralph son of Meldred of
miles, milites 131–2
military service 32, 37, 144
Miller, Edward 18
mills 48–51, 112. See also *molinum*
millstone quarry, see *molaria*
millstone, see *mola*
Milverton (Soms) 209
Minchinhampton (Gloucs) 271
mines, see *mineria*
minieria 115
minsters, *parochiae* of 56

Mitcheldean (Gloucs) 274
Mitton (Gloucs) 264
Modgifu, a free woman of Earl Ælfgar 181 n.50
Modieta, see Madgetts (Gloucs)
Mohaut family 192
mola, molaria 115, 121
molinum, molendinum 115, 116, 121–2
Molyneaux, George 56
monasterium 126
monetarization 52
Monmouth priory 190
Moor (Worcs) 93, 264
moor, fen, see *mora*
Moorcote (Gloucs) 274
Moore, John 44
mora 115
Morcar, earl 107, 194, 227, 228
Morcote, see Moorcote (Gloucs)
Morden, Guilden (Cambs) 89, 157, 158, 159, 160, 161, 162, 163, 164, 165, 166, 167
Morden, Steeple (Cambs) 89, 157, 158, 159, 160, 161, 162, 167
Morris, John 305, 306, 307
Mortlake (Surrey) 213–14
Morton [in Churcham] (Gloucs) 270
Mortune, see Morton [in Churcham] (Gloucs)
motte 58
Mucknell (Worcs) 93, 263
Mudestona, see Mickleton (Gloucs)
Mukehulla, see Mucknell (Worcs)
multicolinearity 47
multiple estate 104
Munby, Julian 33
Muttonam, see Mitton (Gloucs)

Nafford (Worcs) 268
NASA World Wind 220
National Grid 231, 245
nauigo, nauigerium 121
Naunton [in Toddington] (Gloucs) 270
Naunton Beauchamp (Worcs) 267
negotiation 5–6, 8, 28, 44, 144–5, 152, 293, 297–300, 303
nemus, nemusculus, nemus ad sepes 123, 235
Netherton (Worcs) 93, 266
Neuenton', see Naunton Beauchamp (Worcs)
Neuha', see Newnham (Gloucs)
New Forest 58

Newenden (Kent) 211 n.89, 212 n.94, 213
Newent (Gloucs) 271
Newington (Oxon) 214
Newnham (Gloucs) 273
Newsham (Yorks) 191
Newton, Old (Suff) 186
nidus 115
Niwentone, *see* Naunton (Gloucs) 275
Niwetona, *see* Naunton [in Toddington] (Gloucs)
Nomina Villarum 20
Nongtone (Lincs) 104
Norcote (Gloucs) 272
Norcoto, *see* Norcote (Gloucs)
Norfolk 15, 20, 57, 181, 216
Norman yoke 24, 48, 150, 291 n,12
Norman, son of, *see* William
Normandy 29, 116, 142, 152, 178, 179, 189, 216
Northallerton (Yorks) 191
Northamptonshire 68, 187, 232, 238
  geld of 68–9
Northamptonshire Geld Roll 68 n.31
Northamptonshire Survey 301
Northleach (Gloucs) 253, 254, 255, 269, 272
Northman son of Merewine 106
Northumbria 147, 187
  earls of 183, 187, 190. *See* Siward, Tostig
Northwick (Worcs) 93, 265, 250
Norton (Suff) 175
Norton, Bishop's (Gloucs) 272
Norton, Bredons (Worcs) 93, 264
Norton', *see* Norton, Bredons (Worcs)
Nortuna, *see* Norton, Bishop's (Gloucs)
Norwic', *see* Northwick (Worcs)
Norwich (Norf) 33, 187, 201 n.25
  castle 189
Nottinghamshire 13, 38, 45, 172
Nudertona, *see* Netherton (Worcs)
Nuwent, *see* Newent (Gloucs)

Oadby (Leics) 167 and n.23
Oakham (Rutl) 94
OCR 76
Oddingley (Worcs) 93, 265
Oddington (Gloucs) 253, 254, 255, 256, 269, 272
Odo, bishop of Bayeux, earl of Kent 23, 142, 148, 170, 206, 212, 213, 214, 215, 216, 285

Odo the chamberlain 179
Odungeleie, *see* Oddingley (Worcs)
Offerton (Worcs) 93, 265
Olaf, king of Denmark 142
Oldland (Gloucs) 269
Oleuest, *see* Holdfast (Worcs)
olim formula 14
ollaria 115
OLS regression 241, 245
Olveston (Gloucs) 270
Onibury (Salop) 206
Open Domesday 61 n.1, 224, 225, 226, 227, 228, 229, 230, 231, 245
Oppa, *see* Longhope (Gloucs)
Optical Character Recognition, *see* OCR
orchard, *see* *uirgultum*, *pomerium*,
ordeal 278–88
Orderic Vitalis 145, 150, 188, 248, 259–62, 264–5, 303
Orderic, steward of Bishop Wulfstan of Worcester 257
Ordinary Least Squares regression, *see* OLS
Ordnance Survey facsimile 11, 61, 62, 225, 226 n.28
Orm 192
Orpington (Kent) 212
Orsett (Essex) 146 n.53
Orwell (Cambs) 176
Osbern, bishop of Exeter 209
Osbern Giffard 275
Osbert of Ingoldsby 184
Osbert son of Richard 263, 265
Osbert of Wiechesham 180 n.46
Osgot, man of Eadgifu 176
Osgot, man of Archbishop Stigand 157, 158, 159, 160, 161, 162, 166, 167
Osmund, bishop of Salisbury 104, 200, 203
Oswaldeslawe, *see* Oswaldslow 263
Oswaldslow hundred (Worcs) 4, 92, 197, 199, 203, 204, 205, 208, 217
Otintona, Otintune, *see* Oddington (Gloucs)
Otto I 283
Otto the goldsmith 164, 165
Ouerberiam, *see* Overbury (Worcs)
Ouerestun' (Worcs) 266
outlawry 134
Over (Cambs) 89
Overbury (Worcs) 93, 265
overstocking 42, 45, 46, 243
Oxehell', *see* Oxenhall (Gloucs)

Oxenhall (Gloucs) 274
Oxford (Oxon) 33, 100
  sheriff of 205
  university of 76
Oxfordshire 13, 56, 203, 204, 206

packhorse load, *see summa caballi*
pack-horses, *see runcini*
Page, Mark 58
Painswick (Gloucs) 274
Palgrave, Sir Francis 247
Palling (Norf) 181 n.46, 185
Palmer, John 2, 10, 11, 14, 18, 34, 35, 36, 46, 50, 52, 171, 224, 225, 227, 308
Palmer, Matthew 75 n.54
pannage 53
Papworth (Cambs) 88, 89, 161 n.14, 176, 177 n.29, 179 n.37
Papworth hundred (Cambs) 88
paragraphos, gallows sign 32, 70, 100
Parham (Suff) 177 and n.29
Paris, Matthew 24, 291 n.12
parish boundaries 54, 232, 243
parochial structure 56
pars, particula terrae, telluris or *ruris* 120
pascua, pascuum, pastura 72, 73, 115, 116, 122, 132
PASE 36, 172 n. 6, 225, 228, 229
  Offline dataset 228–9, 238 n.56, 243, 245, 246
  Online dataset 225–31, 238 nn.44 and 56, 343, 245, 246
pasture 48, 122, 132, 231, 243
pati 76
patronage 56, 57
Pavia (Italy) 283
Peatling (Leics) 167
Pebworth (Worcs) 273
pecunia, pecus, pectoris 129 and n.106
Penbewrtha, *see* Pebworth (Worcs)
Pendeberia, *see* Pinbury (Gloucs)
Pendock (Worcs) 93, 264, 265
Penenden Heath (Kent), pleas at 212, 216
Penkridge (Staffs) 93
Pennesham, *see* Pensham (Worcs)
Pensham (Worcs) 266
Peopleton (Worcs) 250 n.11, 268
Perry (Worcs) 93, 265
Pershore (Worcs) 205, 266, 268
  abbey 166 n.21, 205, 271, 274

Pershore hundred (Worcs) 205
Persor', Persoram, *see* Pershore (Worcs)
Peterborough abbey 99, 103, 149, 184, 235. *See also Descriptio Terrarum* of
Pevensey, rape of (Sussex) 209
Phepson (Worcs) 266
Phillimore edition of Domesday Book 9, 10, 17, 61, 63, 69, 107, 226, 231, 248, 305, 308. *See also Electronic Edition of Domesday Book*
Pickhill (Yorks), castle of 191
Picot of Lascelles 192
Picot, sheriff of Cambridgeshire 157, 158, 160, 161 and n.10, 162, 166, 167 and n.22, 282, 285
Piddle, Hill (Worcs) 264
Piddle, North (Worcs) 267, 268
Piddle, Wyre (Worcs) 93, 264
Pidelet, *see* Piddle, North (Worcs)
Pideletmore, *see* Piddle, Moor, Wyre (Worcs)
pig-pasture, *see dena*
pigs 53, 114
Pinbury (Gloucs) 271
Pipe Rolls 34
Piplintona, *see* Peopleton (Worcs)
Pirehill hundred (Staffs) 99
Piritune, *see* Pirton (Worcs)
Pirton (Worcs) 268
Pirÿa, *see* Perry (Worcs)
piscina, piscaria, piscarius, pescaria, piscatoria 115–16, 122–3. *See also* fisheries
ploughs 42, 45, 46, 65, 112, 113, 117, 210, 225, 243, 258, 297
  service with 44, 50
  wheeled 114 n.19
ploughland 15, 16, 20, 28, 42, 44–6, 53, 55 n.232, 59, 65. 69, 99, 141, 144, 199, 225, 235 and n.54, 240–3, 259, 260 and n.60, 261, 262 n.72, 297
ploughshares, iron for 234
plumbaria 115
Plumstead (Norf) 186
Poer, *see* Ponther 263
Poiwica, *see* Powick (Worcs)
pomerium 115
Pons, *see* Drogo son of
Ponton, Great (Lincs) 104–6
population 225, 229
potaria 115

Potsgrove (Beds) 242 n.66
potteries, *see ollaria, potaria*
Powell-Smith, Anna 11, 75, 224
Powick (Worcs) 267
Pratt, David 29, 39 n.155, 40, 45
pratum 115–17
predecessor, *see antecessor*
prefectus, prepositus 134
presbiteri 126
Prestbury (Gloucs) 206 n.57, 269
Presteberia, *see* Prestbury (Gloucs)
Prestetona, *see* Preston [near Cirencester] (Gloucs)
Preston (Kent) 212
Preston [near Cirencester] (Gloucs) 272
Preston [in Dymock] (Gloucs) 270
Prestona, *see* Preston [in Dymock] (Gloucs)
Prestwich, J. O. 29
proceres 114
profits of justice 85
prosopography 3, 4, 60, 169–74, 195, 225, 227
prouincia 114
Public Record Office 7, 307. *See also* TNA
publica uia regis 134
Pucklechurch (Gloucs) 270
Puliceirca, *see* Pucklechurch (Gloucs)
Pyrford (Surrey) 28
  charter 29

quadraria 115
quarries, *see quadraria*
quartermaster's manual 144
Queenhill (Worcs) 93, 264
Quenington (Gloucs) 274
Quenintone, *see* Quenington (Gloucs)
quercus 128
querelae 26
Quidenham (Norf) 185
quotarii 118

Radfield hundred (Cambs) 88
Radleie, *see* Radley (Worcs)
Radley (Worcs) 93, 265
radman, radcniht 119, 131, 268
Ragman inquest, rolls 290 n.7, 298
Ralph 94, 158, 165. *See also* Warin
Ralph *anglicus, see* Ralph de Gael, Ralph the staller
Ralph of Berkeley 275

Ralph de Bernay 264
Ralph de Gael, earl 148, 149, 150, 153, 170, 174, 175, 177, 178, 180 and n.46, 181, 182, 184–90
  brother, *see* Hardwin
  cousin, *see* Alsi
  father, *see* Ralph the staller
  man of, *see* Isaac
  son, *see* Alan
  uncle, *see* Godwin
Ralph, a man of Godric the reeve 284
Ralph, son of Godric the steward, *see* Ingreda, wife of
Ralph, earl of Hereford, *see* Harold, son of
Ralph, man of Hardwin 166
Ralph de Limesy 186
Ralph son of Meldred of Middleton, chamberlain of Count Conan 193, 194
Ralph Paynel 135, 275
Ralph de Tosny 275
Ralph the staller 90 n.34, 149, 174, 177, 181–4, 185, 286, 187 n.89, 195
  brother, *see* Godwin
  man, *see* Burgric
  nephew, *see* Alsi
  sons, *see* Hardwin, Ralph de Gael
Ramsay, abbey of 43 and n.177, 85, 184, 235
Ramsbury (Wilts) 207
Rannulf Flambard 248, 256, 259–62, 303
Rannulf, brother of abbot Walter 286
Ravensworth (Yorks) 190
  fee of 191
Rawelle, *see* Roel (Gloucs)
*recep*o, *recepit* 69, 70
recognition 280, 286, 293, 296–7
Record Type 11, 107
Rectitudines Singularum Personarum 114
redditus 115
Redmarley d'Abitot (Worcs) 93, 264
Redmertona, *see* Ridmarton (Gloucs)
Reed (Herts) 176
reeve, *see gerefa*
regalia, audit of 27
Regenbald the priest 271
register 303
Reinbald 267
Reinbald the dean 252
Reinbaldus, *see* Regenbald

releuatio, releuamen, releuamentum 134
Remigius, bishop of Lincoln 203, 204
Repps (Norf) 186
returns 2, 4, 8, 24, 71, 197, 277
    circuit 3, 14, 20, 22, 59, 65, 99–100, 138–41, 152–3
    geld 209
    original 138, 210
    seigneurial 22, 23, 25, 32, 63, 70, 71, 92, 97, 197–217
rex 126
Ribald 179, 192
Ribald, half-brother of Count Alan 193
Richard 160, 264. *See* Osbert son of
Richard II, duke of Normandy 182
Richard fitzGilbert of Clare 177 n.29, 188
Richard the legate 275
Richard fitzNigel 1, 6, 24, 25, 277, 278, 288, 290, 291
Richmond (Yorks) 190, 191
    castle of 184, 190
    castle-guard at 176 n.23
    castlery 39, 174
Richmond, honour of 3, 169–96
    chamberlain's fee 191, 193. *See* Ralph son of Meldred
    steward's fee 192, 193
Richmondshire 190, 191, 195
Ridmarton (Gloucs) 272
Rippel, *see* Ripple (Worcs)
Ripple (Worcs) 93, 264
Risedona, *see* Rissington, Great, Little, or Wyck (Gloucs)
rispalia 123 n.63
Rissington, Great (Gloucs) 275
Rissington, Little (Gloucs) 275
Rissington, Wyck (Gloucs) 274
Roald fitzHarscoit 191
Robert 158, 165
Robert the bursar 263, 264, 265, 266, 275
Robert Curthose 141, 152
Robert, count of Flanders 141, 142, 299
Robert Gernon 88
Robert son of Gerold 289
Robert, man of Hardwin 166
Robert of Losinga, bishop of Hereford 26, 51, 97, 113, 114, 206, 295 n.24, 300 n.52
Robert, count of Mortain 142, 173 n.11, 190, 210, 272
Robert d'Oilly 172, 194, 275

Robert Parler 268
Robert of Rhuddlan 178
Robert de Tosny 180, 275
Robert de Verly 185, 186
Robert fitzWymarc 149
Rochamtona, *see* Rockhampton (Gloucs)
Rochester (Kent) 21, 22, 23, 210, 212, 215
    bishop of 21, 215
    bishopric of 210, 212, 285
Roci, *see* Turstin son of
Rockhampton (Gloucs) 275
Roel (Gloucs) 271
Roffe, David 1, 2, 5, 76 n.55, 110 and n.3, 140, 141, 143, 144, 171, 172, 175, 183, 184, 195, 240, 241, 243, 259, 279
Roger 94
Roger de Beaumont 275
Roger of Berkeley 275
Roger Bigod, sheriff of Norfolk and Suffolk 153, 227
Roger of Hereford 149, 186, 187, 188
Roger d'Ivry 275
Roger de Lacy 263, 264, 265, 266, 267, 272, 274
Roger, earl, of Montgomery 96, 157, 158, 159, 160, 161, 162, 163, 164, 166, 172, 189, 228
Roger of Poitou 180 and n.46, 192
Rolf 103. *See* Ælfric son of
Rookwith (Yorks) 177 n.29
Roughton (Norf) 174 n.11
Round, John Horace 16, 18, 19, 20, 23, 45, 58, 138, 141, 256
rubrication 13, 14, 81 n,2, 98 n.66, 100, 105, 107, 109, 110, 153, 201, 209, 211
Rudmerlege, *see* Redmarley d'Abitot (Worcs)
rulings 13, 105
Rumble, A. R. 15
Rumburgh priory 180 n.46, 187 n.89
runcini 114
running heads 140
rusca 115, 127
rusticus 126
Rutland 72, 106

S1 63, 64, 70
saca et soca 38–9, 85, 90, 92 n.45, 103, 182, 184, 191, 202, 239
sacerdotes 126

Saevia, tenant of Eadgifu 188
Sæwulf 267
sagena 128
St Benet of Holme, abbey of 178 n.32, 180 n.46
  cell of, *see* Rumburgh
St Briavels, *see* Lydney, Little
St Etheldreda, soke of 177
St Etheldritha 151
St Frideswide 206
St Guthlac 151
St Wulfram 151. *See also* Grantham
Saint-Denis, church of 166 n.21, 206, 266, 271
Saint-Evroul, church of 260 and n.64, 271
Saint-Jacut, church of 179
Saint-Lo, bishop of 269, 270
Saint-Ouen de Rouen 175
Saint-Wandrille, church of 151
sake and soke, *see saca et soca*
Salamanesberie, *see* Salmonsbury hundred (Gloucs)
Salawarpe, *see* Salwarpe (Worcs)
salictum 115
salinae 115
Salisbury (Wilts) 28, 110, 145, 150 n.82, 200, 208, 298, 299, 300
  bishop of 199, 201, 203, 213. *See* Osmund
  church of 214
  oath of 26, 41, 91, 95, 141, 281
  scriptorium of 17, 200
Sall (Norf) 185, 186
Salmonsbury hundred (Gloucs) 269
Salpertona, *see* Sapperton [near Cirencester] (Gloucs)
salt 135
Saltwood (Kent) 212
saltwork, *see salina*
Salwarpe (Worcs) 266
  park of 266
Sampford, Great (Essex) 175, 178
Samson, bishop of Worcester 248
Sandwich (Kent) 211, 212 and n.94, 214, 215, 279 n.14
Sapperton [near Cirencester] (Gloucs) 275
Sapperton (Lincs) 104
sargina 128
sartum 130
Sarum, Old (Wilts) 207
satellites, use of term 11 and n.21

Sawyer, Peter 20, 24
Saxmundham (Suff) 174 n.11
Saxthorpe (Norf) 185
Sbern, man of Earl Waltheof 187 n.88
scoo 70
Scepwaston', *see* Shipston on Stour (Warks)
schedules 14, 15, 20–1, 32, 53, 96–103, 106, 248–58, 270, 295, 300
Scippetona, *see* Shipton Solers (Gloucs)
Sciptona, *see* Shipton Moyne (Gloucs)
Scireburn', *see* Sherborne (Gloucs)
Scotland 193
scotum 115
scrubland, *see silva minutia*
scutage 258
Sedgeberrow (Worcs) 92 n.47, 93, 265
Segesbergam, *see* Sedgeberrow (Worcs)
Sepsintun', *see* Phepson (Worcs)
Serdedona, *see* Siddington (Gloucs)
Serlo, abbot of Gloucester 255
serui 114, 124. *See also* slave
seruitium 114
service 8, 20, 28, 37, 41, 44, 48, 51, 52, 53, 59, 85, 144, 145–6, 152, 153, 298, 299, 300. *See also* knight service
servitia debita 145, 298
Sewell (Beds) 55 n.23
Sharnford (Leics) 167
Sharpe, Richard 172–3
sheepskin 12
Sheppey (Kent) 215 n.110
Sherborne (Dors) 97 n.65, 200 and n.18, 207
  bishop of, *see* Æthelric
  church of 207, 208
  see of 207
Sherborne (Gloucs) 270
Sherborne hundred (Dors) 207 and n.64
Shingay (Cambs) 89, 157, 158, 159, 160, 161, 163, 164, 166
ship soke 204, 206, 207 and n.64
shipscot 207
Shipston (Worcs) 93
Shipston on Stour (Warks) 265
Shipton Moyne (Gloucs) 273
Shipton Oliffe (Gloucs) 274
Shipton Solers (Gloucs) 272
Shirdon (Beds) 242 n.66
shire 55, 56, 58
  court 27, 111
  farm and pleas 32, 152

shiring 56
Shrewsbury (Salop) 135
Shropshire 96
Siddington (Gloucs) 273, 274
Sigeræd 90
silua, silua ad sepes, silua minuta, silua pascualis 72, 115, 116, 123, 124, 235, 253
Siptona, *see* Shipton Oliffe (Gloucs)
Siston (Gloucs) 275
Sistone, *see* Siston (Gloucs)
Siward 103, 183, 264
Siward, earl of Northumbria 107, 183
    wife, *see* Goda
Siward, free man of Stigand 177 n.27
Skillington (Lincs) 104, 106
Slaughter, Upper (Gloucs) 275
slaves 20, 112, 113, 124, 233, 289
Sloptra, *see* Slaughter, Upper (Gloucs)
small-holding, *see hortus, gardinum* 115
smithy, *see ferraria, forgia*
Snodesbirÿ, *see* Snodsbury, Upper (Worcs)
Snodsbury, Upper (Worcs) 267
Snooks, Graeme 47, 50, 245
Snowshill (Gloucs) 271
soc, soca, socha 2, 37–41, 48, 49, 52, 85, 86 n.18, 90, 104, 106, 119, 159, 161, 167, 169, 174 n.13, 175, 176, 177, 178, 183, 196, 303 n. 63. *See also* manor, *saca et soca*, ship soke sokeland
    manor and soke 40–1, 85–92
    title and soke 37–41
    urban 31
    value and soke 50–2, 90. *See also hidagium*
sochemani 40, 46, 48, 49, 51, 85, 86, 87, 90, 91, 95, 106, 112, 114, 115, 116–19, 157, 158, 159, 160, 161, 162, 164, 165, 166
    depression in status 49
Sodbury, Little (Gloucs) 272
Soham, Earl (Suff) 177 n.26
sokage tenure 176
soke, *see soc*
sokeland 37, 43 and n.177, 56, 82, 84–5, 88, 90–1, 104–6, 159, 177, 183
sokemen, *see sochamanni*
Solberge (Yorks) 192
solidus 72
Somerby (Lincs) 104

Somerset 208, 209
Sopesberia, *see* Sodbury, Little (Gloucs)
Soulbury (Bucks) 178
Southampton (Hants) 58
Southwell (Notts) 123 n.61
Spechleie, *see* Spetchley (Worcs)
Spetchley (Worcs) 93, 265
spinetum 115, 235
spinney, *see spinetum*
Sporle (Norf) 185
Sprottr 191
stabilitio, stabilitura 133
Stafford (Staffs) 33
Stafford, Pauline 55
Staffordshire 72
Stainfield (Lincs) 84
staller 182, 185. *See also* Esger, Ralph, Wigod
Stamford (Lincs) 107
standard deviation 234, 243
Standish (Gloucs) 253, 254, 255, 269, 272
Stane Street 150 n.82
Stanedis, *see* Standish (Gloucs)
Stanhus, *see* Stonehouse (Gloucs)
Stanlege, *see* Stanley, Leonard (Gloucs)
Stanley, Leonard (Gloucs) 275
Stanton (Gloucs) 270
Stanton, Fen (Hunts) 88 and n.27, 89
Stantona, *see* Stanton (Gloucs)
Statenborough (Kent) 212, 213
Staura, *see* Stears (Gloucs)
Staveley (Yorks) 192
Stawella, *see* Snowshill (Gloucs)
Stears (Gloucs) 273
Stenton, F. M. 143
Stephen, count 180 n.46, 187 n.89
Stephen, king of England 188 n.90. *See* William, son of
Stephen son of Fulchered 250
Stephen, abbot of St Mary, York 194 n.121
Stephen de Turre 176 n.23
Stephen son of Wulfwy 249, 264
Stepney (Middlesex) 90
Stigand, archbishop of Canterbury 149, 157, 158, 159, 160, 162, 164, 166, 181, 187, 202, 214, 216, 217, 272
    men of, *see* Algar, Godwin, Osgot, Siward, William
Stocha, *see* Stoke, Lark (Gloucs)
Stocker, David 43

Stoke (Kent) 212, 213
Stoke, Harry (Gloucs) 270
Stoke, Lark (Gloucs) 271
Stoke, North (Lincs) 184
Stoke Prior (Worcs) 266
Stoke, Severn (Worcs) 268
Stoke, South (Lincs) 104, 184
Stokes, *see* Stoke Prior (Worcs), Stoke, Severn (Worcs)
Stokesby (Norf) 186
Stoltona, *see* Stoulton (Worcs)
Stonehouse (Gloucs) 273
stone-pit, *see fossa lapidum*
Stort, river 150 n.82
Stortford, Bishop's (Herts), castle of 150 n.82
Stoulton (Worcs) 93, 263
Stow hundred (Suff) 173 n.11
Stow-on-the-Wold (Gloucs) 271
  church of St Edward of 271
Stratona, *see* Stratton (Gloucs)
Stratton (Gloucs) 274
Stric, man of Earl Waltheof 187 n.88
Strumpshaw (Norf) 90 n.34
Stutton (Suff) 178
Suella, *see* Swell, Lower (Gloucs)
Suffolk 20, 42, 49, 53, 63
Suintona, *see* Siddington (Gloucs)
sulung 43, 129, 131, 226, 255, 257
summa 248–61, 269, 270, 271, 272, 273, 274, 275
summa caballi 135
summa danegeldi 255
summaries in Exon, IE, and GDB 4, 18, 20, 27–8, 41, 127, 141, 144–5, 295
sumpsit 73
Sundridge (Kent) 212
sunt 72–3
surety, *see* tithing, warranty
Surrey 46, 55, 214
Sussex 46, 194, 209, 215
  castleries of 148
  rapes 39, 170, 209
Swaffham (Norf) 182, 185, 187 n.89
Swale, river 191
Swavesey (Cambs) 88, 89, 176, 179 and n.37
  priory 177 n.29, 179
Swell, Lower (Gloucs) 271, 273
Swell, Upper (Gloucs) 271
Swella, *see* Swell, Upper or Lower (Gloucs)
Swepstone (Leics) 167 and n.23

Swindon (Gloucs) 272
Swindona, *see* Swindon (Gloucs)
Symeon, abbot of Ely 18
Sysonby (Leics) 93

t1 ra 76
Tadestrop, *see* Adlestrop (Gloucs)
Tadlow (Cambs) 161 n.10
taignus, tanus, tegnus, teignus, teinus, þegen 117, 130
taini regis 35
Tait, James 30 n.110
Tametebÿri, *see* Tenbury Wells (Worcs)
Tarlton (Gloucs) 273, 275
Taunton (Soms) 94, 199, 208, 209, 285 n.55
  borough of 282
Taunton hundred (Soms) 208
taxation 5, 20, 28–9, 43–6, 59, 64–9, 144–7, 152, 170, 226, 297, 300. *See also defendit,*
Taylor, Ian 3, 16, 30, 59
Taylor, Pamela 4, 15, 21, 25, 36, 55
Taynton (Gloucs) 274
Teddington (Worcs) 93
Tedeham, *see* Tidenham (Gloucs) 274
Tedintonam, *see* Teddington (Gloucs) 264
Tenbury Wells (Worcs) 266
tenementum 121 n.56, 263 n.2
tenuit formula 38, 167, 175
terra 37, 70, 85, 86, 90, 159, 161, 167
terra arabilis 115
Terrae Occupatae 120, 296 n.32, *See also* annexations, *Clamores, Invasiones*
terra regis 27, 39, 32, 44, 55, 93, 96, 98–9, 101–33, 157, 164, 178, 249
Tetbury (Gloucs) 275
Tetteberia, *see* Tetbury (Gloucs)
Tewksbury (Gloucs) 56, 94
  church of 98 n.65
Thacker, Alan 24
Thame hundred (Oxon) 204
Thame, river 31
Thames, river 31, 57
Thatcher government 62
Thebristona, *see* Tibberton (Gloucs)
thegn 87, 90, 95, 106, 169. *See taignus*
  king's 37–41, 170, 177, 180, 191, 196
  median 37, 39, 169
thegnland 94 and n.54
Thelveton (Suff) 185

Theninga, *see* Twyning (Gloucs)
Theointuna, *see* Taynton (Gloucs)
Thetford (Norf) 148, 201n.25
    bishop of 150, 199, 201. *See* Æthelwig, Herfast, William
Thiessen polygons 223 n.18
thol et theim 131
Thomas of Marlborough, *Historia* of 255
Thomas, Hugh 35
Thomas, archbishop of York 199, 252, 253, 253 n.29, 254, 269
Thorbern 176
Thoresby (Yorks) 192
Thorfinnr, Torfinnr 191, 192
Thorfinnr son of Thore 192 n.116
Thorgot 91 n.34
Thorir 103
Thorn, Caroline 8, 12 n.24, 13 n.25, 14 and n.33, 17, 24, 42, 107 n.92, 109 n.1, 139, 248, 305–10
Thorn, Frank 2, 8, 12, 14 and n.33, 16, 17, 19, 24, 54, 107 n.92, 139, 248
Thorney abbey 148, 150
    Liber Vitae of 150, 189 n.46
Thorr 191, 192
Threo wapentake (Lincs) 104
Througham (Gloucs) 272
Thurleston (Suff) 177 and n.29
Thurstan 177
Thurston (Suff) 177 n.29
Tibberton (Gloucs) 273
Tibberton (Worcs) 93, 265
Tibertonie, *see* Tibberton (Worcs)
Tideham, *see* Tidenham (Gloucs) 273
Tidelminton, *see* Tidmington (Warks)
Tidmington (Warks) 93, 265
Tidrintona, *see* Tytherington (Gloucs)
tithing 49, 91 n.35. *See also* warranty
TNA 1, 7, 11, 12, 70. *See also* Public Record Office
    Labs 224. *See also* Domesday on a Map
Toft (Cambs) 88, 179 n.37
Tonge (Worcs) 266
Torelton', *see* Tarlton (Gloucs)
Tormarton (Gloucs) 275
Tormentone, *see* Tormarton (Gloucs)
Tortuna, *see* Tarlton (Gloucs)
Tostig, earl 107, 192, 195
Totmonslow hundred (Staffs) 99
Tovi, tenant of Earl Godwin 289

Treasury 278, 287, 290, 301, 303
Tredington (Warks) 93, 265
Tredintonam, *see* Tredington (Warks)
Troarn, church of 271
Troham, *see* Througham (Gloucs)
Trotshill (Worcs) 250, 265
Trotteswella, *see* Trotshill (Worcs)
Trysull (Staffs) 91 n.34
Tuffa, man of Earl Waltheof 187 n.88
tunesman 49
Turbern, man of Eadgifu 176
Turkdean (Gloucs) 274
Turkedene, *see* Turkdean (Gloucs)
Turold, son of, *see* Gilbert
Turstin 181 n.50
Turstin son of Roci 267
Twyning (Gloucs) 270
Tytherington (Gloucs) 269

uaccaria 115
ualeo 74
uas 115, 127
uenatio 133
uendo, uendere 70
uestura, uestitus 132
uillani, uillici 48–9, 74, 114, 115, 117, 124
uilla 74, 117, 120. *See also* vill
uinea 115, 130
uirgata, uirga 74
uirgultum 115
Ulf 268
Ulf Fenman 85, 88
Ulf son of Manni 177 n.26, 180
Ulfketill 191
Ulfkil 284
Ullington (Worcs) 273
underwood, *see nemus*
Upleadon (Gloucs) 270
Upton upon Severn (Worcs) 93, 264
Upton, Tetbury (Gloucs) 275
Uptune, *see* Upton, Tetbury (Gloucs)
urbanization 31
Urse 94
Urse d'Abitot, sheriff of Worcestershire 167 n.22, 205, 250, 251, 252, 256, 257, 258, 263, 264, 265, 266, 267, 268
utlagaria, utlagh, utlago, utlagus 134–5

Vale of York 192
Valeines fee 177 n.29

valuation clause 101–2
value 28, 35–6, 40, 47, 50–2, 59, 65, 85, 91, 101–2, 103, 113, 114, 115, 144, 225, 226, 229, 235–40, 251, 258
VCH 307
Vchelicota, *see* Hucclecote (Gloucs)
verdicts 5, 295, 296, 301–2. *See also* jurors
Versey, G. R. 232's
vill 54, 55, 156, 157
  dimensions of 15, 54, 140
village plan analysis 43
villan, villein, *see uillani*
vineyard, *see uinea*
Voronoi diagrams 223 n.18
Vpentona, *see* Upton on Severn (Worcs)

Wain (Herts) 86
Walcot by Threekingham (Lincs) 99
Walcot on Trent (Lincs) 99
Wales 12, 32, 133 n.145
Walkelin, bishop of Winchester 18, 157, 209
Walker, James 50
Wallingford (Berks) 31, 33. *See* Wigod of
Wallop, Nether (Hants) 101
Walter 263
Walter d'Aincourt 85, 102, 172
  wife, *see* Matilda
Walter de Burgh 265
Walter, abbot of Evesham, brother of, *see* Rannulf
Walter fitzPons 253, 269
Walter Ponther 263, 265, 266, 267, 268
Waltham (Lincs) 56, 183
Walthamstow (Essex) 187 n.88
Waltheof, earl 149, 151, 167, 172, 187, 188, 190, 194
  men of, *see* Almaer, Godwin *scild*, Sbern, Stric, Tuffa, Wulfric
  wife, *see* Countess Judith
Walworth (Surrey) 214
Wangford hundred (Suff) 202
Wantisden (Suff) 177 n.26, 178
Wapeleie, *see* Wapley (Gloucs)
Wapley (Gloucs) 270, 275
Wardon (Worcs) 265 and n.7
Ware (Herts), *see* Eskil of
Wareham, Andrew 36, 47, 51, 245
Warenne Chronicle, *see* Hyde
Warestel, *see* Wast Hills (Worcs)

Warin son of Ralph son of Ailmer son of Colswein 176 n.23
warland 44–6, 48, 240–1
Warmendona, *see* Wardon (Worcs)
Warndon (Worcs) 93, 250, 252
warranty 49, 91 n.35. *See also* surety, tithing
Warwick (Warks) 33
Warwickshire 172
Washbourne, Little (Gloucs) 93, 264
Washingborough (Lincs) 183
Wast Hills (Worcs) 266
waste, wasting 52–3, 99, 147, 193
water-meadow, *see brocus*
Watton (Herts) 176
web mapping 220
Webber, Teresa 17
Wei, X. 47
weir, *see gort*
Welby (Leics) 93
Welldon Finn, Rex 17, 20, 139
Wells, see of 207
Welsh marches 13, 39
Welton (Lincs) 104
Welton family 183
Welwyn (Herts) 161 n.14
Wendy (Cambs) 89
Wenhou (Suff), *see* Ælfric of
Wenintona, *see* Ullington (Worcs)
Wenric, Wenriz, *see* Windrush (Gloucs)
Wessex 48
Westberia, *see* Westbury on Trym (Gloucs)
Westberie, *see* Westbury-on-Severn (Gloucs)
Westbury on Trym (Gloucs) 269
Westbury-on-Severn (Gloucs) 273
Westmancote (Worcs) 93, 264
Westmanecote, *see* Westmancote (Worcs)
Westminster (Middlesex), St Peter's 166 n.21, 176, 205, 249, 250, 255, 266, 271
Weston (Suff) 186
Weston Colville (Cambs) 176 n.22
Weston, Market (Suff) 186
Westona, *see* Westonbirt (Gloucs), Weston-on-Avon (Warks)
Westonbirt (Gloucs) 272, 273
Weston-on-Avon (Warks) 271
Weston-on-Trent (Notts) 123 n.61
Whaddon (Cambs) 89, 176
Whaplode (Lincs) 183
wheat, *see frumentum*
Whitley (Worcs) 93

Whittington (Gloucs) 274
Whittington (Worcs) 93, 263
Whittlesford (Cambs) 88, 239 n.57
Whittlewood Forest 58
Wiburgestoke (Worcs) 265
wica 115
Wica, *see* Painswick (Gloucs), Wick (Worcs)
Wicam, *see* Wick Episcopi (Worcs)
Wich, *see* Droitwich (Worcs)
Wichewene, *see* Childswickham (Gloucs)
Wick (Worcs) 266
Wick Episcopi (Worcs) 93, 263
Wickham, West (Cambs) 179 n.39
Wickhamford (Gloucs) 255 and n.37
Wicklaw, liberty of (Cambs) 182 n.55
Wideford, *see* Widford (Oxon)
Widford (Oxon) 272
Widiedonam, *see* Withington (Gloucs)
Wigeweita, *see* Wyegate (Gloucs)
Wigod of Wallingford 194. *See* Ealdgyth, daughter
Wihenoc 189
Wihomarc 179, 187, 192
Wikimedia Foundation 75
Wilderesheia, *see* Willersey (Gloucs)
Willersey (Gloucs) 271
William 264
William I, king of England, Conqueror, the Conqueror 8, 29, 34, 41, 46, 110, ,112, 113, 114, 139, 141, 142, 143, 145, 147–50, 153, 155, 166, 167, 173, 182, 188, 189, 190, 192, 193, 194, 216, 228, 235, 250, 267, 277, 287, 289, 291, 292, 293, 298, 299
William II, king of England, Rufus 8, 141, 152, 190, 194, 210, 259, 261, 302
William son of Baderon 267, 273
William the chamberlain 164, 165, 273
William son of Corbucion 267
William, bishop of Durham 200 n.15
William d'Eu 253, 273
William de Ecouis 186
William Froisseloup 274
William Guizenboded 273
William son of Guy 274
William Leofric 274
William Malet 149, 202
William of Malmesbury 142 and n.27, 143
  Life of St Wulfstan 29

William son of Norman 274
William fitzOsbern 58, 75, 170, 187
William of Poitiers 287
William, son of King Stephen 188 n.90
William, man of Archbishop Stigand 159 n.9, 160
William, bishop of Thetford 148, 201, 202
William Tindal 248
William de Warenne 28, 176 n.20, 302 and n.63
  wife, *see* Isabella
Williams, Ann 3, 35, 36, 39, 49, 90, 171, 172, 195
Williamstrip (Gloucs) 274
Willingham (Cambs) 89
Willington (Beds) 86
Willoughby Waterless (Leics) 167
willow-bed, *see salictum*,
Wiltshire 2, 13
Wimpole (Cambs) 179 n.37
Winchcombe (Gloucs) 253, 270
  church of 270
  ferding of 253
Winchester (Hants) 5, 22, 23, 33, 113 n.15, 210, 278
  bishop of 144, 157, 158, 159, 161, 162, 166, 199, 203, 208, 213, 214, 216, 217, 253, 255, 158, 162, 281, 286. *See* Walkelin
  St Peter's 157, 161. 214
Winchester, book of 5, 278. *See also* Domesday Book
Wincot (Warks) 273
Windrush (Gloucs) 271, 274
Winecote, *see* Wincot (Warks)
Winnibriggs wapentake (LIncs) 104
Winterled, man of Earl Ælfgar 160, 164, 165
Wirec', Wirecestrie, *see* Worcester (Worcs)
Wissett (Suff) 177 n.26
Witchingham (Norf) 186. *See* Osbern of
Witchley hundred (Rutl) 261 n70
Witetona, *see* Whittington (Gloucs)
Witham, river 104
Withington (Gloucs) 269
Witintona, *see* Whittington (Worcs)
Witlega, *see* Witley, Little (Worcs)
Witley, Little (Worcs) 263
Wlf, *see* Ulf
Wlfrich, *see* Wulfric 268
Wlfrintona, *see* Wolverton (Worcs)

Wlfwardele, *see* Wolverley (Worcs)
Wlletona, *see* Wotton [in Gloucester] (Gloucs)
Wlwi, *see* Wulfwy 264
Woburn (Beds) 242 n.66
Wolgarston (Staffs) 93
Wollaton (Notts) 84
Wolverley (Worcs) 266
Wolverton (Worcs) 93, 263
wood, woodland for fences, *see nemus*
woodland 5, 48, 77 n.59, 112, 115, 123–4, 132, 231, 234–5, 240, 242, 243
Woolaston (Gloucs) 273
Woolley (Hunts) 161 n.14
Worcester (Worcs) 31, 32, 33, 93, 147, 251, 260, 263, 264, 265
  bishop of 92, 144, 167 n. 22, 198, 250, 253, 255, 263, 264, 265, 266, 286. See Samson, Wulfstan
  borough of 32, 265
  chronicler 152 n.91
  church of 25, 92, 202, 203, 205, 248, 249, 250, 251, 263, 265, 269, 286
  relief of 1095, 256
  surveys 5
Worcester B 248, 249, 251, 252, 255
Worcestershire 2, 22, 205, 248, 252, 268
  sheriff of, *see* Urse
World Wide Web 220
Wormington (Gloucs) 275
Wotton [in Gloucester] (Gloucs) 274
Wright, Arthur 43 n.175
writs 126, 129, 130, 131, 133, 170, 194, 298, 202
Wrmintona, *see* Wormington (Gloucs)

Wulfketel, abbot of Crowland 106, 148, 151
Wulfmær of Eaton 228
Wulfmaer, free man 180 n.46
Wulfnoth 173 n.11, 273
Wulfric 268
Wulfric, thegn of King Edward 178
Wulfric, son of Golde 161 n.14
Wulfric, man of Earl Waltheof 187 n.88
Wulfstan, a free man of Eadgifu 177
Wulfstan, bishop of Worcester 4, 70, 71, 177 n.27, 197, 203, 213 n.99, 254 n.32, 255, 256.
  steward of, *see* Orderic
Wulfweard, Wulfweard White 179, 180
Wulfwine, thegn of King Edward 239
Wulfwy, *see* Stephen son of
Wullauestona, *see* Woolaston (Gloucs)
Wyegate (Gloucs) 273
Wyfordby (Leics) 93

x-ray diffraction analysis 12

Yardley (Bucks) 178
Yetminster hundred (Dors) 207 n.64
York 187, 193, 200
  archbishop of 199, 255. See Ealdræd, Thomas
  St Mary's 194, abbot of, *see* Stephen
  St Olave's 194
  St Peter's 227
  vills relating to 99
Yorkshire 4, 13, 15, 38, 57, 172
  wapentakes and hundreds of 209
Yorkshire Summary 14, 27, 99, 253 n.26

www.ingramcontent.com/pod-product-compliance
Lightning Source LLC
Chambersburg PA
CBHW051557230426
43668CB00013B/1882